AF726562

CODIFICATION, TRANSPLANTS AND HISTORY

Law Reform in Louisiana (1808) *and Quebec* (1866)

CODIFICATION, TRANSPLANTS AND HISTORY

Law Reform in Louisiana (1808) *and Quebec* (1866)

JOHN W. CAIRNS

TALBOT
PUBLISHING
Clark, New Jersey

Copyright © 2015 John W. Cairns

ISBN 978-1-61619-509-0

All rights reserved. No part of this publication may be reproduced, stored in a retrieval system, or transmitted, in any form or by any means, electronic, mechanical, photocopying or otherwise, except for the inclusion of brief quotations in a review, without prior permission in writing from the publishers.

TALBOT PUBLISHING

AN IMPRINT OF

THE LAWBOOK EXCHANGE, LTD.

33 Terminal Avenue
Clark, New Jersey 07066-1321

Please see our website for a selection of our other publications and fine facsimile reprints of classic works of legal history: www.lawbookexchange.com

Library of Congress Cataloging-in-Publication Data

Cairns, John W. author.
Codification, transplants and history : law reform in Louisiana (1808) and Quebec (1866) / John W. Cairns.
pages cm
Based on author's dissertation (doctoral - University of Edinburgh, 1980), issued under title: The 1808 Digest of Orleans and 1866 Civil Code of Lower Canada : an historical study of legal change.
Includes bibliographical references and index.
ISBN 978-1-61619-509-0 (hardcover : alk. paper)
1. Civil law--Québec (Province)--History--19th century. 2. Law reform--Québec (Province)--History--19th century. 3. Civil law--Louisiana--History--19th century. 4. Law reform--Louisiana--History--19th century. I. Title.
KDZ127.C35 2015
340.5'609714--dc23 2015009790

Printed in the United States of America on acid-free paper

For Alan and Camilla Watson

CONTENTS

PREFACE

The Ph.D. thesis on which this book is based was written at the University of Edinburgh between 1977 and 1980 under the supervision of Professor Alan Watson and Dr R.A.A. McCall Smith. The then Scottish Education Department awarded me a major Scottish Studentship to carry out the research, for which I remain very thankful. I continue to be especially grateful to both Alan and Sandy, not only for their encouraging and kind supervision, but also for many years of further warm friendship and support. Even in those more generous days of funding for students, my late parents, Donald and Helen Cairns, helped with the odd handout of cash. They knew how much their continued encouragement meant to me. The thesis was written by fountain pen (these were the days before word processors) and was then typed up by mother, who kindly offered to do this, to save me the cost of a typist. She typed much of it in an eccentric greenhouse in the garden of the home in Stirlingshire in which I had been brought up, using an old mechanical Remington, thereby giving the original version a wonderful, textured appearance that word-processing can never achieve.

I had the good fortune, due to the endeavours of Alan Watson and the kindness of the late Professor Saúl Litvinoff, to spend the summer of 1981 in the Center of Civil Law Studies at the Louisiana State University in Baton Rouge, with the aim of working towards a publication. But my return to my then post at the Queen's University of Belfast, and the difficulty of continuing the work on the other side of the Atlantic in the days before the internet and cheap air travel, led to my dropping it. I moved on to other topics. Revisiting it, however, has made me realize how much it has shaped my subsequent academic interests.

I would hesitate to say that the thesis initially fell upon stony ground; but despite there being copies available in North America, it attracted relatively little attention. Richard Kilbourne cited it in his study of the development of Louisiana codification.[1] It was listed in a bibliography on the legal history of Quebec and part of a chapter was revised and published in 1987 in a special issue of the *McGill Law Review* devoted to legal history.[2] Brian Young made use of it in his study of the politics lying behind codification in Quebec.[3] It was only as the new millennium dawned that I became aware that scholars were once again becoming interested in it, as I received requests from U.S. Law Librarians to make copies of it for the research

---

[1] R.H. Kilbourne, *A History of the Louisiana Civil Code: The Formative Years, 1803-1839*, Baton Rouge, Paul M. Hebert Law Centre Publications, 1987, p. 1 n. 2.

[2] G.B. Baker, K.E. Fisher, V. Masciotra and B. Young, *Sources in the Law Library of McGill University for a Reconstruction of the Legal Culture of Quebec, 1760-1890*, Montreal, McGill University, 1987, p. 51 n. 60; J.W. Cairns, "Employment in the Civil Code of Lower Canada: Tradition and Political Economy in Legal Classification and Reform", 32 *McGill Law Journal* (1987), pp. 673–709.

[3] B. Young, *The Politics of Codification: The Lower Canadian Civil Code of 1866*, Montreal and Kingston, Osgoode Society for Canadian Legal History and McGill-Queen's University Press, 1994, pp. 235 and 244.

of Faculty members. The revival of interest in mixed legal systems may have had something to do with this, and Professor Vernon Palmer of Tulane Law School referred to it in generous terms in some of his publications.[4]

This renewal of interest led to an invitation to speak at a conference held at Tulane Law School in 2008 to mark the bicentenary of the promulgation of the Digest of the Civil Laws Now in Force in the Territory of Orleans. At that conference I was to share a platform with the late and much missed Professor George Dargo. I was looking forward to meeting him. I had read his seminal study, *Jefferson's Louisiana*, and made considerable use of it in my doctoral research.[5] I knew he had read my thesis, as I had received a request from the Law Librarian of his University to make a copy, and had deduced (rightly) that this was for him for his preparation of his conference paper. I wondered what he would make of it; though much influenced by his work, I had also been critical. Not all scholars relish criticism. But Professor Dargo was warm and generous, and, not sparing my blushes, publicly praised my thesis and stressed its importance as an unpublished work. In 2009, the Lawbook Exchange Ltd. published a revised edition of *Jefferson's Louisiana*;[6] there was a book signing and lunch in New Orleans in January 2010 and George (as I think of him) suggested to his publishers that they publish my thesis.

The Lawbook Exchange then approached me, suggesting that they would like to consider publication of my work. I was of course very flattered. I thought hard about it, but accepted the suggestion to send a copy for Greg Talbot and Valerie Horowitz to examine. The decision was for publication, despite its length! The typescript then had to be copied and scanned, and the scanning checked – a huge labour for many people. In this I benefited considerably from the help of Dr Karen Baston in checking some of the chapters. The Law School of Edinburgh helped in making this possible, as well as in other ways with occasional small grants. Valerie Horowitz has been unstintingly helpful and patient with an individual who also found himself very busy with other projects, while the vicissitudes of life meant that he sometimes could not devote the immediate attention to it that he would have wished. I do wonder whether we would have embarked on it, if we had all realized the time it would take and the sheer labour involved. But I am really very grateful to Greg Talbot for his faith in the project and his support, as well as to Valerie for all her

---

[4] V.V. Palmer, "The French Connection and the Spanish Perception: Historical Debates and Contemporary Evaluation of French Influence on Louisiana Civil Law", 63 *Louisiana Law Review* (2003), pp. 1067–1126 at pp. 1073 n. 13 and 1078 n. 31; V.V. Palmer, "The Recent Discovery of Moreau Lislet's System of Omissions and its Importance to the Debate over the Sources of the Digest of 1808", 49 *Loyola Law Review* (2003), pp. 301–337 at pp. 302–305, 306–307. See also V.V. Palmer, *The Civilian Experience: Critiques of Codification in a Mixed Jurisdiction*, Durham N.C., Carolina Academic Press, 2005, pp. 23 n. 15, 25–26, 35, 55 n. 9.

[5] G. Dargo, *Jefferson's Louisiana: Politics and the Clash of Legal Traditions*, Cambridge MA, Harvard University Press, 1975.

[6] G. Dargo, *Jefferson's Louisiana: Politics and the Clash of Legal Traditions*, revised edition, Clark N.J., Lawbook Exchange, 2009.

help. It is a huge pleasure as well as honour to see it appear in revised form under the imprint of Talbot Publishing.

My visit to New Orleans in 2008 had revived my interest in the legal history of Louisiana. I was able either to renew or to make for the first time the acquaintance of many of Louisiana's friendly group of legal historians or those interested in legal history, such as Richard H. Kilbourne, Jr., Vernon Palmer, Shael Herman, Agustín Parise, Seán Donlan, John H. Lovett, and Louis V. de la Vergne. I also met for the first time Georgia Chadwick, Director of the Law Library of Louisiana, who has been generous with time and help in many ways, and whose enthusiasm has done so much to promote the legal history of Louisiana. The legal historians of Louisiana owe her a great deal. My interest in Quebec also started to revive. An excellent Russian doctoral student, Asya Ostroukh, came to work with me, writing a thesis on the influence of French law in Louisiana, Quebec and Switzerland. Though I have never developed the links with Quebec scholars that I have with those of Louisiana, I subsequently met Professor Michel Morin of the Université de Montréal, one of Quebec's leading legal historians, now a friend, while I was also aware of the work of Professor Silvio Normand of Université Laval, as well as other notable scholars such as Donald Fyson and indeed Brian Young. With nearly double the population of Louisiana, and many more universities, legal history in Quebec has been admirably active and varied as a discipline. Professor Morin has very kindly helped me recover the more recent bibliography of Quebec legal history.

Work on this field introduced me to many other scholars to whom I have become indebted, such Mike Hoeflich, now of the University of Kansas. One further I must single out. That is Professor Joseph W. McKnight of the S.M.U. Law School in Dallas, Texas. I first met Joe in Baton Rouge in 1981, at a party in the Common Room of the Law Center. He was kind, and the next evening invited me for dinner with his wife Mimi. Over many years Joe offered guidance and advice, while he and Mimi offered generous and kind hospitality in both Dallas and Oxford, England. More recently, my colleagues Paul du Plessis and Guido Rossi have kept my interest in Louisiana and Quebec alive and provided much needed support. We make a good team.

As an eighteenth-century scholar, I am very aware of the pleasures of melancholy. One melancholy pleasure in the work was to discover (what I had either forgotten or never realized) that I had cited in my thesis work carried out by a close friend, Elizabeth Kingdom, from before I knew her. As a start was made on this project in 2010, she became gravely ill, and my partner Don and I spent much of that year looking after her and organizing her care. Don was able to ensure that she could go home for her final weeks. Liz lived close to us, and I had the privilege one night of sitting with her, keeping watch, as she died. She would have been pleased with this volume and amused at the citation of her early publication: as her own students had remarked, in a description of her printed on a tee-shirt they presented to her to mark her receipt of a teaching award, she "liked a laugh". Needless to say, I also owe a lot to Don.

Finally, in our modern distrusting world, we are subject in British Universities to constant monitoring, with requirements to defend our actions through processes of accounting and detailed record keeping. In a recent review of our teaching and research supervision in the Law School in Edinburgh, I was part of a panel of supervisors of doctoral research called to account for and explain our procedures. At the end we were afterwards asked if we had any comments. I stated that I found supervision of Ph.D. students one of the most satisfactory and rewarding aspects of my job. Afterwards I reflected that there was more to it than this, and that my relationship with my own supervisor has become one of the most important and indeed defining relationships of my life. I therefore dedicate this volume with love and gratitude to Alan and Camilla.

INTRODUCTION

The core research at the heart of this book has never been superseded. It remains the only attempt at a systematic exploration of the detailed choices made by the two sets of codifiers in drawing up their respective civil codes. Of course, it cannot cover every article of each code: many volumes would be needed to achieve that. Instead, it focuses on family relationships and the closely linked topic of servants, what we would now think of as employment. As well as examining the sources of individual articles, it explores the essential organizing concepts used, such as paternal authority and marital authority. Both codifications are placed in their general economic and social contexts. Enough of each code is examined to allow the drawing of general conclusions.

The work was originally undertaken as an exercise in exploring legal transplants, drawing on the arguments and theses propounded by Alan Watson in his then recently published book, *Legal Transplants: An Approach to Comparative Law*.[1] The aim was to explore the interrelationship of legal and social change through a study of the transplanting of law from Europe to Louisiana and Quebec (at the time of their first codifications called respectively the Territory of Orleans and Lower Canada).

There were two main reasons underlying the choice of Louisiana and Quebec. First, both had a complicated legal history reflecting a complex political history of colonization involving competition between European powers. Louisiana had started as a French colony; it had next become a Spanish colony, with its law changed to Spanish colonial law; France regained Louisiana, but then sold it to the United States, which was starting to embark on its own great colonial adventure that eventually led it to expand to the Pacific. This raised interesting questions about the law in force, and indeed of access to its sources. In much of what had been the huge French territory, common law was soon introduced;[2] the small Territory of Orleans, which, with the addition of some further parishes from what was then West Florida, and adjustments of the border with Texas, later became the State of

---

[1] A. Watson, *Legal Transplants: An Approach to Comparative Law*, Edinburgh, Scottish Academic Press, 1974; 2nd ed., Athens Ga., University of Georgia Press, 1993.

[2] M.S. Arnold, *Unequal laws Unto a Savage Race: European legal Traditions in Arkansas, 1686–1836*, Fayetteville, University of Arkansas Press, 1985; S. Banner, *Legal systems in Conflict: Property and Sovereignty in Missouri, 1750–1860*, Norman, University of Oklahoma Press, 2000; P.J. Kastor, *The Nation's Crucible: The Louisiana Purchase and the Creation of America*, New Haven, Yale University Press, 2004.

Louisiana, retained its older law with some reforms.[3] Quebec had been a French colony; it was acquired by Britain by military conquest, possession confirmed by the subsequent peace treaty. Its boundaries have also had a complex history. But, after a failed attempt to introduce English law, and as French Canada was divided administratively by Great Britain, French law was restricted to what became Quebec or Lower Canada. But following the period of confusion and conflict after the Conquest, problems of access to the laws also arose, especially after codification in France meant that the sources of French *ancien droit* still in force in Quebec and the relevant commentaries became potentially less accessible. Both jurisdictions thus had been colonies of what one might call civil-law polities acquired by common-law polities. Both jurisdictions responded to the legal complexities of their situation by codifying their private laws. In both jurisdictions, English or Anglo-American criminal law was swiftly introduced, as well as English-style courts and procedures.[4]

Second, as well as this fascinating legal-historical complexity, it was possible either to know precisely or to infer with a fair degree of confidence the sources examined by each set of codifiers. Though there were constraints on their choice of sources to consider in drafting the articles for their codes, both certainly showed a certain degree of freedom in their attitudes. With a measure of reflection it became possible to hypothesize why they made the choices they did, relating them to legal tradition, economic requirements, economic ideologies and the like. This indicated the kind of factors that are likely to influence codifiers more generally, with implications for our understanding of how they work. The thesis thus had certain theoretical

---

[3] G. Dargo, "The Digest of 1808: Historical Perspectives", 24 *Tulane European and Civil Law Forum* (2009), pp. 1–30 at p. 11; V.V. Palmer, "Two Worlds in One: The Genesis of Louisiana's Mixed legal System, 1803–1812", in V.V. Palmer, *Louisiana: Microcosm of a Mixed Jurisdiction*, Durham NC, Carolina Academic Press, 1999, pp. 23–39; S.P. Donlan, "Entangled in Red, White and Blue: Spanish West Florida and the American Territory of Orleans, 1803–1810", in T. Duve (ed.), *Entanglements in Legal History: Conceptual Approaches*, Frankfurt am Main, Max Planck Institute for European Legal History, 2014, pp. 213–251.

[4] W.M. Billings, "The Origins of the Criminal Law in Louisiana", 32 *Louisiana History* (1991), pp. 63–76; W.M. Billings, "A Neglected Treatise: Lewis Kerr's *Exposition* and the Making of Criminal Law in Louisiana", 38 *Louisiana History* (1997), pp. 261–286; M.F. Fernandez, "Local Justice in the Territory of Orleans: W. C. C. Claiborne's Courts, Judges, and Justices of the Peace", in W.M. Billings and M.F. Fernandez (eds.), *A Law Unto Itself?: Essays in the New Louisiana Legal History*, Baton Rouge, Louisiana State University Press, 2001, pp. 79–98; M.F. Fernandez, *From Chaos to Continuity: The Evolution of Louisiana's Judicial System, 1712–1862*, Baton Rouge, Louisiana State University Press, 2001, pp. 16–39; D. Fyson, *Magistrates, Police, and People: Everyday Criminal Justice in Quebec and Lower Canada, 1764–1837*, Toronto, Published for the Osgoode Society for Canadian Legal History by University of Toronto Press, 2006.

concerns about legal change and reform that were developed in the context of British thinking about jurisprudence in the later 1970s.

The primary theoretical approach derived from Watson's theory of transplants. His views were much criticized at the time;[5] but in recent years the idea of legal transplants has attracted considerable favourable (as well as otherwise) attention, being viewed not only as providing an important methodology for comparative law, but also as analytically useful in current global and post-colonial approaches to law.[6] The research on transplants in this book is indeed still found useful in this context.[7]

When the work was originally carried out, Louisiana legal historians were embroiled in a heated debate over the sources of the first Louisiana Civil Code of 1808—A Digest of the Civil Laws Now in Force in the Territory of Orleans, With Alterations and Amendments Adapted to its Present System of Government—and some even questioned whether it was a "true code". Given that Spanish colonial law had been in force when the U.S.A. acquired the vast territory out of which the later state of Louisiana was to be created, it was notable that the code was based on French law. The discovery, however, of a copy of the Digest interleaved with references to Spanish law—known as the de la Vergne volume—led to a claim, most forcibly expressed by Professor Robert Pascal of Louisiana State University, that, though the Digest might be expressed in French, often using articles drawn from the *Code civil des français* or its *projet* of 1800, it was in fact intended to express the Spanish law in theory in force, and to do so, not as a "code", but as a mere "digest".[8] The de la Vergne volume had references to other sources as well, but none to the French Code. Shortly after Professor Pascal had expressed this strong view, Professor Rodolfo Batiza of the Tulane Law School had engaged in detailed research to demonstrate the actual sources of the specific articles of the Digest of 1808. His studies showed that these were overwhelmingly French in origin—above all the *Code civil* and its *projet*, but also the works of R.J. Pothier. Of course, Batiza identified other sources. The codifiers had also consulted Jean Domat, some

---

[5] See J.W. Cairns, "Watson, Walton, and the History of Legal Transplants", 41 *Georgia Journal of International and Comparative Law* (2013), pp. 637–696 at pp. 640–672.

[6] *Ibid.*, pp. 672–686; J.L. Halpérin, "Transplants of European Normativity in India and in Japan: A Historical Comparison", 22 *Rechtsgeschichte* (2014), pp. 150–157. See also, e.g., G.R. Bandeira Galindo, "Legal Transplants Between Time and Space", in Duve (ed.), *supra* note 3, pp. 129–148. Many other essays in this collection discuss legal transplants; even if they disagree with Watson's approach, they demonstrate the continuing power of the idea.

[7] A. Parise, "Libraries of Civil Codes as Mirrors of Normative Transfers from Europe to the Americas: The Experiences of Lorimier in Quebec (1871–1890) and Varela in Argentina (1873–1875)", in Duve (ed.), *supra* note 3, pp. 315–384 *passim*.

[8] R.A. Pascal, "A Recent Discovery: A Copy of the "Digest of the Civil Laws" of 1808 with Marginal Source References in Moreau Lislet's Hand", 26 *Louisiana Law Review* (1965), pp. 25–27 at p. 26.

Spanish sources, local statutes, and even the English author William Blackstone, as well as texts of Roman law; but Batiza demonstrated that the articles were mainly drawn from the French codification.[9] Of course, this did not defeat the clever idea that it might be Spanish law in French dress; but it did make it much less plausible. Professor Pascal responded vehemently, again arguing that the Digest, "though written largely in words copied from, adapted from, or suggested by French language texts, was intended to, and does for the most part, reflect the substance of the Spanish law in force in Louisiana in 1808".[10]

Professor Batiza challenged Professor Pascal to demonstrate his case through making an appropriate detailed study of the Digest;[11] but he has not done so, though he and others have continued to assert the view that the Digest essentially consists of Spanish law expressed in French terms. The emphasis here should be on the word "assert": no detailed study has been carried out to support the claim. The claim in fact rests primarily on a simple syllogism: the redactors were instructed to base the Digest on the law in force; the law in force was Spanish; therefore the Digest is a redaction of "Spanish" law.

In 1972, Dean Sweeney of the Tulane Law School described the debate between Batiza and Pascal as a "tournament of scholars".[12] In 1983, Professor Yiannopoulos of Tulane attempted to sum up the position and mediate between the protagonists, though pointing out the conclusive nature of Batiza's research.[13] He described the dust as having now settled; but it has been repeatedly kicked up again. In the intervening years Professor Pascal himself boldly restated his thesis in the Foreword he provided in 1987 for Richard Kilbourne's excellent and subtle study of the history of the Louisiana Code.[14]

---

[9] R. Batiza, "The Louisiana Civil Code of 1808: Its Actual Sources and Present Relevance", 46 *Tulane Law Review* (1971), pp. 4–165. Further on the use of Blackstone, see J.W. Cairns, "Blackstone in the Bayous: Inscribing Slavery in the Louisiana Digest of 1808", in W. Prest (ed.), *Re-Interpreting Blackstone's Commentaries: A Seminal Text in National and International Contexts*, Oxford, Hart Publishing, 2014, pp. 73–94; *infra*, pp. 208–210, 214, 216, 338, 359–360, 378, 386–388, 396,421–422, 438, 456, 460, 462, 474, 489, 495, 498–499, 511.

[10] R. Pascal, "Sources of the Digest of 1808: A Reply to Professor Batiza", 46 *Tulane Law Review* (1972), pp. 603–627 at p. 604.

[11] R. Batiza, "Sources of the Louisiana Civil Code of 1808, Facts and Speculation, A Rejoinder", 46 *Tulane Law Review* (1972), pp. 628–652 at pp. 651–652.

[12] J.M. Sweeney, "Tournament of Scholars over the Sources of the Civil Code of 1808", 46 *Tulane Law Review* (1972), pp. 585–602.

[13] A.N. Yiannopoulos, "The Early Sources of Louisiana Law: Critical Appraisal of a Controversy", in E.F. Haas (ed.), *Louisiana's Legal Heritage*, Pensacola, Fl.: Perdido Bay Press for the Louisiana State Museum, 1983, pp. 87–106.

[14] R.A. Pascal, "Foreword", in R.H. Kilbourne, *A History of the Louisiana Civil Code: The Formative Years, 1803–1839*, Baton Rouge, Paul M. Hebert Law Centre Publications Institute, 1987, pp. vii–viii.

Alain Levasseur of Louisiana State University has repeated Pascal's view in his invaluable and richly documented biographical study of Louis Moreau Lislet, one of the redactors of the Digest of 1808; but Levasseur merely repeats the examples selected by Professor Pascal, and relies on his sense of the nature of Moreau Lislet as a man.[15] Professor Moréteau, also of Louisiana State University, has repeated it as recently as 2012; he asserts that the redactors could use the French law to express the Spanish law in force, because it and the Spanish law were much the same and that when they differed, the "substance of the Digest differs", presumably from the French law.[16]

This book contains the only systematic research that has addressed this issue in any kind of thorough fashion; its detailed study of the articles chosen, examined against the social and economic context, and against the Spanish and French laws, demonstrates that, however the redactors understood the instructions they were given, they were most certainly not enacting Spanish law in French words. It is true, of course, that there was influence from Spanish law in some areas of law; but what is much more interesting is that the redactors were being creative, though undoubtedly most influenced by the French Code and its *projet*. In other words, they were not constrained by a narrow positivist view of the sources they could employ with the specific aim of enacting the Spanish law supposed to be in force. They drew heavily on the French Code, not because they thought it encapsulated Spanish law, but because they chose to do so, following an intuitive sense of what was needed.

The de la Vergne volume has already been mentioned. The proponents of the Pascal thesis have seen it as supporting the "Spanish" origin of the articles of the code. For this to be so, they have to accept that, in the annotations on the interleaves, the sources of the articles are being revealed. The view also relies on a contentious interpretation of an ambiguous preface. Again, the references are manifestly not to the sources of the Digest's articles. They do have an origin in the work of Moreau Lislet.[17] Professor Palmer of Tulane has also ingeniously used the absence of references in the de la Vergne volume to demonstrate "that a large-scale reception of French substantive law took place in 1808".[18] I have shown elsewhere that Moreau

---

[15] A.A. Levasseur, "Grandeur and Mockery", 42 *Loyola Law Review* (1997), pp. 647–725; A.A. Levasseur, *Louis Casimir Elisabeth Moreau-Lislet: Foster Father of Louisiana Civil Law*, Baton Rouge, Louisiana State University Law Center Publications Institute, 1996, repr. Baton Rouge, Claitor's Publishing Division, 2008, pp. 167–280.

[16] O. Moréteau, "*De Revolutionibus*: The Place of the Civil Code in Louisiana and in the Legal Universe", 5 *Journal of Civil Law Studies* (2012), pp. 31–66 at pp. 36–38; O. Moréteau and A. Parise, "Recodification in Louisiana and Latin America", 83 *Tulane Law Review* (2009), pp. 1103–1162 at pp. 1112–1121.

[17] Pascal, *op. cit. supra* note 8.

[18] V.V. Palmer, "The Recent Discovery of Moreau Lislet's System of Omissions and its Importance to the Debate Over the Sources of the Digest of 1808", 49 *Loyola Law Review*

initially drew these notes from a Spanish collection of the 1790s, and that he was evidently compiling cross-references to equivalent Spanish sources *ex post facto*—he was not indicating the "origins" of individual articles of the Digest in Spanish sources.[19]

Proponents of what one might call the Pascal view have also tended to deny that the Digest was intended to be a "true" code. Of course, "what is a true code?" is in many ways as meaningful a question as "what length is a piece of string?"; but the proponents of the Pascal view start from a stance well explained by the late George Dargo, who relied for this on an explanation given to him by Professor Pascal. He wrote:

> A digest is a summary or compilation of pre-existing law designed to make that law known and available. Prior law remains authoritative. A code, on the other hand, replaces prior law and itself becomes the definitive and final statement of the law for purposes of adjudication.

The issue is discussed in much fuller detail below.[20] It is important to realize, however, that for Professor Pascal and his supporters it is important to downplay the significance of the Digest as a code; in their eyes, to accept that the Digest is a code is to undermine the claim that its sources are necessarily Spanish. If it is a Digest it must be a compilation of pre-existing law, and since the pre-existing law was Spanish, *ergo*, the sources of the Digest are Spanish. It is also important to realize that the definition is drawn in such a way as to prove what is wanted to be proved. This is no doubt why Professor Moréteau has chosen instead to describe the Digest as not a code "in the French sense".[21]

These claims have been based on three main observations: first, it is called a Digest and not a Code; second, the law enacting it did not abolish all prior law, only law inconsistent with the Digest; and third, the courts did not treat it as a code.

I think the issue of the name need not be considered too deeply. We are dealing with the early nineteenth century; the analytical and terminological distinctions hardened by later comparative-law studies did not exist. True, it was an issue raised almost immediately. W.C.C. Claiborne, Governor of the Territory of Orleans, approved the Digest; he later justified himself to the Secretary of State, James Madison, writing: "The 'Civil Code' alluded to in my last letter, is nothing more than a 'Digest of the Civil Laws now in force

(2003), pp. 301–337 at p. 316 (V.V. Palmer, *The Louisiana Civilian Experience: Critiques of Codification in a Mixed Jurisdiction*, Durham N.C., Carolina Academic Press, 2005, p. 36).

[19] J.W. Cairns, "The de la Vergne Volume and the Digest of 1808", 24 *Tulane European and Civil Law Forum* (2009), pp. 31–81.

[20] See *infra*, pp. 61–73.

[21] Moréteau, *op. cit. supra* note 16, p. 37.

in this Territory'."[22] But Claiborne has seized on a name to try to justify an action of which he thought the central U.S government—to which he was indebted for patronage and from which he no doubt hoped for more—would disapprove: he was deliberately downplaying the significance of what had happened. In fact, the act of the Territorial Legislature that named the two redactors, James Brown and Louis Moreau Lislet, to draft what became the Digest, appointed them to draft "a Civil Code for the use of this territory". They were instructed to "make the civil law by which this territory is now governed, the ground work of said code".[23] The Digest refers to itself as a "code" in a number of its articles.[24] In most of these the usage has not simply been the result of following the wording of the French *Code civil*; the redactors have *chosen* the term. The manuscript notes of the de la Vergne volume also refer to the Digest as a "code".[25] The legislature likewise could continue to refer to it as a "code", and in the same act as "the digest of the civil laws".[26] The word "digest" was also used in varied ways. On 25 January 1816, a Resolution of the Louisiana Senate and House of Representatives provided for the appointment of a "person learned in law" to prepare "a general Digest of all the governor's ordinances issued during the first degree of government of this State and the acts of the Legislative Council, and of the several Legislatures of this State, that are now in force".[27] A year later, the

---

[22] W.C.C. Claiborne to J. Madison, 5 Apr. 1808, in *The Official Letterbooks of W.C.C. Claiborne, 1801–1816*, ed. by D. Rowland, Jackson, State Department of Archives and History, 1917, repr. New York, AMS Press, 1972, vol. 4, pp. 168–169. On Claiborne's character and the issue of patronage, see the subtle analysis in Kastor, *op. cit. supra* note 2, pp. 93–101.

[23] Resolutions [Résolution relative à la formation d'un Code Civil], in *Acts Passed at the First Session of the First Legislature of the Territory of Orleans, Begun and Held in the City of New-Orleans, on the 25th Day of January, in the Year of Our Lord, One Thousand Eight Hundred and Six and of the Independence of the United States of America the Thirtieth*, Published by Authority, New-Orleans, Printed by Bradford and Anderson, Printers to the Territory, 1807, pp. 214–219.

[24] *A Digest of the Civil Laws Now in Force in the Territory of Orleans, With Alterations and Amendments Adapted to its Present System of Government*, By Authority, New-Orleans, Printed by Bradford and Anderson, Printers to the Territory, 1808, pp. 182–183 (art. 153), 184–185 (art. 154), 324–325 (arts. 3–4), 334–335 (art. 53), 420–421 (art. 1), 456–457 (art. 26).

[25] Cairns, *op. cit. supra* note 19, pp. 45–47 for numerous examples.

[26] "An Act to alter and amend the 21st and 37th articles, chapter 2, title 1, book 3, of the civil code, concerning successions", c. 12, in *Acts Passed at the Second Session of the Third Legislature of the Territory of Orleans, Begun and Held in the City of New-Orleans, on Monday the Twenty-Third Day of January, in the Year of Our Lord One Thousand Eight Hundred and Eleven, and of the Independence of the United States of America the Thirty-Fifth*, By Authority, New-Orleans, Printed by Thierry, Printer of the Territorial Laws, 1811, pp. 42–45.

[27] *Acts Passed at the Second Session of the Second Legislature of the State of Louisiana. Begun and Held at the City of New-Orleans, on the Third Day of January, in the Year of Our Lord One Thousand Eight Hundred and Sixteen*, By Authority, New-Orleans, Printed by Peter K. Wagner, Printer to the State, 1816, pp. [2]–[3].

same bodies clarified that this should "not be so construed as to include in that digest the civil code".[28] In 1822, when it was proposed to revise the Digest, the Resolution of the Senate and House of Representatives described it as revision of the "civil code".[29] All of this means that use of the term "Digest" should not have too much weight placed on it.

Turning to the second observation used to ground the claim, we may note that the preamble to the law enacting the Digest referred to the "confused state in which the civil laws of this territory were plunged, by the effect of the changes which happened in its government", with the consequent necessity of making known "the laws which have been preserved after the abrogation of those which were contrary to the constitution of the United States, or irreconcilable with its principles", so that it was necessary to "collect them in a single work, which might serve as a guide for the decision of the courts and juries, without recurring to a multiplicity of books, which, being for the most part written in foreign languages, offer in their interpretation inexhaustible sources of litigation". This does not say the aim was wholesale reform; but it does show that the obvious intention was to avoid the need for reference to the older laws. This suggests that the intention was to progress from the past. The statute further stated: "That whatever in the ancient civil laws of this territory, or in the territorial statute, is contrary to the dispositions contained in the said digest, or irreconcilable with them, is hereby abrogated." Given the wording, it is very difficult to believe other than, at some level, the Digest was intended to be a "new start".[30] The contrast is usually drawn with the promulgation of the *Code civil*, and its apparently complete abrogation of earlier laws: "From the day when these laws become effective, the Roman laws, the ordinances, the general and local customs, the charters and the regulations all cease to have the force either of general or special law concerning the subjects covered by the present

---

[28] Resolution, 22 Feb. 1817, in *Acts Passed at the First Session of the Third Legislature of the State of Louisiana. Begun and Held in the City of New-Orleans, on Monday the Eighteenth Day of November, in the Year of Our Lord One Thousand Eight Hundred and Sixteen, and of the Independence of the United States of America the Fortieth*, By Authority, New-Orleans, Printed by J. C. de St. Romes, State Printer, 1817, pp. 212–213.

[29] Resolution of 14 Mar. 1822, in *Acts Passed at the Second Session of the Fifth Legislature of the State of Louisiana. Begun and Held in the City of New-Orleans, on Monday the Seventh Day of January, in the Year of Our Lord, One Thousand Eight Hundred & Twenty-Two, and of the Independence of the United States of America the Forty-Sixth*, New-Orleans, Printed by J. C. de St. Romes, State Printer, 1822, pp. 108–109.

[30] "An Act Providing for the promulgation of the Digest of Civil Laws now in force in the territory of Orleans", c. 29, s. 2, in *Acts Passed at the First Session of the Second Legislature of the Territory of Orleans, Begun and Held in the City of New-Orleans, on Monday, the Eighteenth Day of January, in the Year of Our Lord, One Thousand Eight Hundred and Eight, and of the Independence of the United States of America, the Thirty-Second*, Published by Authority, New-Orleans, Bradford and Anderson, Printers, 1808, pp. 120–129 at p. 126.

Code."[31] But matters are not quite so simple: codes vary in the extent of their repeal of the earlier law. For example, the Civil Code of Lower Canada, by its articles 2613 and 2615, allows reference to earlier law, and J.E.C Brierley has described the Lower Canadian Civil Code as presuming "the continuance of the prior law save when it is otherwise provided".[32] It certainly is a code "in the French sense". Further, in France, the *ancien droit* was repealed completely; but the *droit intermédiare* was not formally repealed at all.[33] Also, in matters not covered by the new *Code civil*, the old law remained in force. The terms of the abrogation in the territorial statute enacting the Digest are being invested with far too much significance: it was a practical provision with an obvious meaning—the Digest was to govern in the matters with which it dealt.[34]

Third, that the Louisiana courts did not treat the Digest as if it were a code in the sense discussed is irrelevant. Examination of the decisions of the Louisiana courts suggests that there was a revival of the Spanish law with the use of that law to avoid the application of clear statements in certain instances found in the Digest.[35] That the courts later chose, in Kilbourne's terms, "to de-emphasize" the Digest provides no argument as to what was intended in 1808;[36] nor does it provide any evidence that the Digest originated in Spanish law. Indeed, it perhaps suggests recognition of the opposite. But, as I have argued here and elsewhere, it is this revival of Spanish law that explains the production of the de la Vergne volume.[37] Finally, it is worth noting that, after enactment of the Civil Code of Lower Canada, the judges in Quebec tended to act as if their law were still based on custom, preferring to base decisions on doctrinal writing rather than the legislation embodied in the Code. According to André Morel, it was only after 1885 that the wording of the Code took priority as central to interpretation of the law.[38] Indeed, all

---

[31] Found quoted in Moréteau, *op. cit. supra* note 16, p. 38.

[32] J.E.C. Brierley, "Quebec's Civil Law Codification", 14 *McGill Law Journal* (1968), pp. 521–589 at pp. 556–558; the quotation is from J.E.C. Brierley, "Quebec's Common Laws (*droits communs*): How Many Are There?", in E. Caparros (ed.), *Mélanges Philippe Pigeon*, Montreal, Wilson and Lafleur, 1989, pp. 109–128 at p. 118 (found quoted in B. Young, *The Politics of Codification: The Lower Canadian Civil Code of 1866*, Montreal and Kingston, Osgoode Society for Canadian Legal History and McGill-Queen's University Press, 1994, p. 178).

[33] G. Marty and P. Raynaud, *Droit Civil: Vol. 1: Introduction générale à l'étude du droit*, Paris, Sirey, 1972, p. 129 n. 2.

[34] See further *infra*, pp. 15–16, 61–73.

[35] Kilbourne, *op. cit. supra* note 14, pp. 61–77.

[36] *Ibid.*, p. 62; *infra*, pp. 463–472.

[37] Cairns, *op. cit. supra* note 19, pp. 79–81; *infra*, pp. 444–461. The courts also continued to cite Blackstone, see S.M. Sheppard, "Legal Jambalaya", in Prest (ed.), *op. cit. supra* note 9, pp. 95–104.

[38] S. Normand, "An Introduction to Quebec Civil Law", in A. Grenon and L. Bélanger-Hardy, *Elements of Quebec Civil Law: A Comparison with the Common Law of Canada*, Toronto, Thomson-Carswell, 2008, pp. 25–97 at p. 36; A. Morel, "L'émergence du nouvel ordre

codes have a complex relationship with the prior law, which is typically used to interpret them.[39]

If, contrary to the optimistic view of Yianopoulos in 1983, the dust has not settled on the Batiza-Pascal debate, the substantive chapters in this book show that, whatever the two redactors of the Digest of 1808 may have thought they were doing, as a simple matter of fact they were not producing articles embodying Spanish law in French dress. Professor Palmer stated in 2003 that what was needed was a "side-by-side comparison of the substantive differences between Castilian law and the borrowed provisions in the Digest".[40] This book is the closest attempt at such a comparison.

More recently, Professors Warren Billings and Mark Fernandez have argued for the development of a "New Louisiana Legal History".[41] Professor Billings was apparently the first to use this term in print in his arguably rather ungenerous review of Richard Kilbourne's *History of the Louisiana Civil Code*.[42] The New Legal Historians see themselves as providing a necessary corrective to the (presumably) traditional legal historians' supposed obsession with the notion that Louisiana is exceptional in the context of the United States, and their supposed, almost exclusive, narrow focus on rules, and thus on the internal history of Louisiana law. Billings and Fernandez also argue that it is now necessary to reorient the legal history of Louisiana away from "exceptionalism", and to understand it in the context of U.S. legal history more generally, especially that of the South. This, they think, would provide a better interpretative framework, one which would also raise new questions, such as those about the position of women, blacks, and slavery, as well as raising broader issues of social, economic, and political history. Though acknowledging the importance of Dargo's monograph, they reject the significance of the "clash of cultures" approach they see embedded in his work; instead, with an emphasis on a history of assimilation, they stress that it is important to realize that the law of Louisiana has a continuous history as a "mixed system".[43]

---

juridique instauré par le Code civil du Bas-Canada (1866–1890)", in *Le nouveau Code civil: interprétation et application: Les journées Maximilien Caron 1992*, Montreal, Les éditions Thémis, 1993, pp. 49–63.

[39] J.W. Cairns, "Comparative Law, Unification, and Scholarly Creation of a New *Ius Commune*, 32 *Northern Ireland Legal Quarterly* (1981), pp. 272–283 at pp. 277–280.

[40] V.V. Palmer, "The French Connection and the Spanish Perception: Historical Debates and Contemporary Evaluation of French Influence on Louisiana Law", 63 *Louisiana Law Review* (2003), pp. 1067–1126 at p. 1081 (Palmer, *Louisiana Civilian Experience supra* note 18, p. 60).

[41] For an excellent account that provides a crucial critique, see S.P. Donlan, "Clashes and Continuities: Brief Reflections on the 'New Louisiana History'", 5 *Journal of Civil Law Studies* (2012), pp. 67–79.

[42] *Ibid.*, p. 69; W.M. Billings, Book Review, 30 *Louisiana History* (1989), pp. 324–326 at p. 324.

[43] See, e.g., M.F. Fernandez, "Introduction", in Billings and Fernandez (eds.), *op. cit. supra* note 4, pp. 1–22.

Of course, the New Louisiana Legal History has perhaps exaggerated both its novelty and its difference from earlier research. For example, the New Louisiana Legal Historians' discovery of Louisiana as a "mixed system" is hardly novel, as Seán Donlan has clearly pointed out.[44] But fair enough—many of their aims are important and laudable. No one can doubt the importance of a broader view of legal history than one that simply involves the examination of the development of rules. Under their banner interesting and important work has been carried out. One can point to Fernandez's monograph on the development of the judicial system;[45] the essays in *A Law Unto Itself?*, edited by both Billings and Fernandez;[46] and the extensive and fundamentally important writings of the late Professor Judith Schafer on slavery, which are claimed by the New Legal Historians.[47]

The New Louisiana Legal History has provided both a critical history of older Louisiana legal history and its own history of itself, as well as producing a number of programmatic statements on which the above account of its aims has been based. Its own history starts with a meeting between Professor Billings and the late Judge Albert Tate in 1976. Judge Tate showed Professor Billings the archives of the Supreme Court of Louisiana, which needed a home, and Professor Billings, agreeing with Judge Tate about their significance, managed to ensure that they were deposited in the University of New Orleans, now designated as the Court's official depository. As an archivist sorted out the confused collection, Professor Billings encouraged his students to explore them in their work. This proved fruitful. In 1982, he became the Court's official historian. Professor Billings has also pointed to the significance of the organization by E.F. Haas of a symposium that led to publication of an influential collection of essays. This took place as Richard Kilbourne and Judith Schafer were embarked on the work that was to make them well known, and helped crystalize the aims of the new movement in Louisiana Legal History.[48]

Professor Billings' essay in the volume edited by Haas provided the first programme for the New Louisiana Legal History. It is in part a traditional

---

[44] Donlan, *op. cit. supra* note 41, pp. 75–76.
[45] Fernandez, *From Chaos to Continuity supra* note 4.
[46] Billings and Fernandez (eds.), *op. cit. supra* note 4.
[47] See, e.g., J.K. Schafer, *Slavery, the Civil Law, and the Supreme Court of Louisiana*, Baton Rouge, Louisiana State University Press, 1994; J.K. Schafer, *Becoming Free, Remaining Free: Manumission and Enslavement in New Orleans, 1846–1862*, Baton Rouge, Louisiana State University Press, 2003. Professor Schafer was also a prolific publisher of insightful and informative articles and chapters on slavery.
[48] W.M. Billings, "Confessions of a Court Historian", *Louisiana History* (1994), pp. 261–270 at pp. 262–266 (repr. as "Preface", in J.K. Schafer and W.M. Billings (eds.), *An Uncommon Experience: Law and Judicial Institutions in Louisiana 1803–2003*, Lafayette, Centre for Louisiana Studies, University of Southwestern Louisiana, 1997, pp. 3–10 at pp. 3–6); W.M. Billings, "Preface", in Billings and Fernandez (eds.), *op. cit. supra* note 4, pp. [ix]–xii.

call for a return *ad fontes* (always worthwhile), with a discussion of the available records and some of the problems with them; but he also said that Louisiana legal historians are always asking the same questions:

> Is Louisiana a civilian or common law jurisdiction, or is it a mixture of both? If wholly civilian, which tradition, the Spanish or the French predominated? Parenthetically, those who debate that proposition, really never indicate the importance of that distinction to the growth of law or culture. What were the sources of Louisiana law? When was the law first codified? Was James Brown's and Louis Moreau Lislet's handiwork of 1808 a code or Digest? After 1803, how were the conflicts between Louisiana and American legal customs resolved? What is the role of our judges? ... Apart from these queries there is a fascination for demonstrating the uniqueness of Louisiana law that borders on the obsessive, just as there is a frequent preoccupation with comparative analyses.
>
> To be sure these are vital questions: had they not been asked, there would be no Louisiana legal history and we would not now be pondering that heritage. Still, constantly asking them yields basically the same results, even as they lead scholars to the same types of sources.[49]

He then provided a first version of the aims already described. He repeated this programme in his presidential address at the meeting of the Louisiana Historical Association in 1994, listing much the same questions, perhaps put more strongly, while once more critically commenting that "[e]xceptionalism ... became the organizing principle of Louisiana legal history".[50] He repeated this again in his "Introduction" to the selected essays on Louisiana legal history that he and Judith Schafer edited as one of the volumes of the Louisiana Purchase Bicentennial Series in Louisiana History, once more setting out his programme for a more cultural approach to law.[51] It is obvious that Professor Billings was in part very understandably reacting against the heat of the Batiza-Pascal debate, which one suspects he saw as being as significant as a debate over how many angels could dance on the head of a pin.

It is interesting in this respect to reflect on the reviews of Professor Schafer's study of slavery cases before the Louisiana Supreme Court published in 1994. All acknowledge the excellent qualities of the volume. It is best to start with the review by Thomas D. Morris printed in 1997.[52] Morris himself had just published *Southern Slavery and the Law, 1619–1860*

---

[49] W.M. Billings, "Louisiana Legal History and its Sources: Needs, Opportunities and Approaches, in Haas (ed.), *op. cit. supra* note 13, pp. 189–202 at p. 195.
[50] Billings, "Confessions" *supra* note 48, p. 266.
[51] [W.M. Billings], "Introduction", in Schafer and Billings (eds.), *op. cit. supra* note 48, pp. 11–19 at p. 16.
[52] T.D. Morris, Book Review, 15 *Law and History Review* (1997), pp. 188–190.

in 1996.[53] Thus, the very issue that the New Louisiana History emphasized—assimilation of the legal history of Louisiana to that of the South generally—was potentially relevant to his assessment. He picked up the theme of "Americanization" in Schafer's book, which he interprets as meaning that "Louisiana's legal system came more and more to resemble the common law of the other slave states". He finds the mechanism of this change obscure.[54] But, much more interestingly, Professor Morris identifies a "countertheme … that runs throughout the book that suggests that Louisiana's slave law was often unique and 'Americanization' did not occur".[55] He goes on to argue that the "whole problem of the relationships between the common law slave states and Louisiana was more intricate than Schafer suggests" and that she was "surely correct that in many ways Louisiana was unique".[56] Another reviewer, in assessing the book, commented that "there is no doubt that slave law in the Bayou state was characterized by a number of unique features".[57] Yet another simply stated that the book showed that "[i]n many instances, Louisiana's law was simply different".[58]

The reviews of Schafer's excellent book reveal a problem in one of the core claims of the New Louisiana Legal History. To ignore the impact or consequences coming from the actual rules—or to downplay their importance—is to deny some of the interest and significance of the legal history of Louisiana in a way that potentially misrepresents it. In reality, of course, Schafer was far too good a historian to do so; hence the tensions and "counterthemes" noted by reviewers of her book. But this raises important questions about the agenda of the New Louisiana Legal History, as does the remark of a perceptive reviewer of Fernandez's *From Chaos to Continuity*, who commented that Fernandez had overstated his case, adding that "[i]f Louisiana is to be gathered into the common law herd, it should be accepted as one of the black sheep and not passed off as a clone".[59]

Billings may have been understandably frustrated by the Pascal-Batiza debate; but ignoring it, or failing to engage with it, has had unfortunate consequences. First, it becomes possible to give a highly misleading account of the actual sources.[60] Further, perhaps because of the emphasis on the significance of the work of the Louisiana Supreme Court that derived from

---

[53] T.D. Morris, *Southern Slavery and the Law, 1619–1860*, Chapel Hill, University of North Carolina Press, 1996.
[54] Morris, *op. cit. supra* note 52, p. 188.
[55] *Ibid.*, p. 189.
[56] *Ibid.*
[57] W.K. Scarborough, Book Review, 41 *Civil War History* (1995), pp. 341–342 at p. 342.
[58] M.S. Mayer, Book Review, 24:2 *History: Reviews of New Books* (1996), p. 56.
[59] R.F. Karachuk, Book Review, 44 *Louisiana History* (2003), pp. 116–118 at p. 118.
[60] M. Fernandez, "Edward Livingston, America, and France", in P.J. Kastor and F. Weil (eds.), *Empires of the Imagination: Transatlantic Histories of the Louisiana Purchase*, Charlottesville, University of Virginia Press, 2009, pp. 268–298 at p. 280.

focus on its archive, the New Louisiana Legal History has tended easily to assume that the Digest should be understood as not a "true code", because of the work of the Louisiana courts.[61] In itself this would not be significant, but Billings has claimed that Richard Kilbourne "has resolved the origins question by convincingly demonstrating the dominance of Spanish law in the making of the code".[62] This is a major claim. And it is misleading. Kilbourne does not state this. He has certainly shown the significance of the Spanish law in his *History of the Louisiana Civil Code*. He has demonstrated its influence on practice in the territorial and early state periods.[63] Kilbourne is a careful historian who never writes that Spanish law is the dominant *source* of the actual articles of the Digest of 1808, and indeed he does not need to do so, the point being irrelevant for his carefully nuanced book; it is Professor Pascal who states this in his Foreword.[64] The research that is the foundation of Kilbourne's book does not venture into this territory.

One suspects that the New Louisiana Legal Historians have set up the presumably "Old Louisiana Legal Historians" as some kind of straw man to be knocked down. No one can quarrel with much of their agenda—legal history has to go beyond doctrinal and "internal" legal history and also embrace social, economic, intellectual, and indeed cultural history more generally; in fact, in the context of most contemporary legal history, aspects of the New Louisiana Legal History do not seem startlingly novel, and Donlan has even argued that its focus on the Supreme Court is rather old-fashioned.[65] What is curious is Billings' claim that, in the 1980s, legal history in Louisiana was "still very much in the mould of the lawyers-turned-historians who pioneered it at the beginning of the twentieth century".[66] He presumably sees them as still akin to the "lawyer-annalists".[67]

Of course, if one is arguing for something new or different, it is always useful to provoke a reaction to gain attention. And Billings' instinct that there was something rather odd about the Pascal-Batiza debate was undoubtedly correct. Batiza's work may have contained errors—how could it not, given its scope?—but it was a solid achievement; it was never met with a corresponding matching refutation, only rhetoric. One may even ponder whether the heat of the debate discouraged further investigation of its issues. There can be little doubt, however, that the emphases of the New Louisiana Legal Historians have been beneficial, whether or not it was Professor Billings who woke the Louisiana lawyers from their supposed dogmatic slumbers. The

---

[61] Fernandez, *From Chaos to Continuity supra* note 4, pp. 57–73.
[62] [Billings], *op. cit. supra* note 51, p. 17. See also, Billings, "Confessions" *supra* note 48, p. 268.
[63] Kilbourne, *op.cit. supra* note 14, pp. 44–95.
[64] Pascal, *op. cit. supra* note 14.
[65] Donlan, *op. cit. supra* note 41, pp. 71–72.
[66] Billings, "Confessions" *supra* note 48, p. 266.
[67] [Billings], *op. cit. supra* note 51, p. 12.

interpretative framework for which he and Professor Fernandez have argued may be questioned, and insistence on particular interpretative frameworks can stifle and distort as well as assist; but the argument for a serious widening of the material considered with a consequently more rounded, richer understanding of legal history was correct, and indeed reflected contemporary developments in legal history more generally. One can see this very clearly in the rich collection edited by Vernon Palmer to mark the bicentenary of the Digest of 1808.[68] In the Foreword, Professor Palmer made some important comments:

> [T]he Digest's rightful place in history remains in many respects ambiguous and unfathomed. There remain many more questions than answers.... Furthermore, the sources and aims of the Digest, and even whether it should be properly called a Digest rather than a Code, are questions that have never been definitively answered.[69]

This book provides answers to some of these questions; whether the answers are definitive is for others to judge.

Similar tensions to those identified in the legal historiography of Louisiana may be found, of course, in that of most jurisdictions. It is possible—if one wishes—to identify them in Quebec. Thus, the late Jean-Marie Fecteau argued eloquently for the need to bridge the gap between the work of historians and that of lawyers to create a richer scholarship.[70] Fecteau recognized four types of legal-historical scholarship as current in Quebec, one of which was traditional legal history, which he noted was remarkably resilient.[71] Likewise, Brian Young, in his study of codification in Lower Canada, commented that his aim "was to provide an entry for the generalist into the study of nineteenth-century Quebec legal history, thus breaking down the insularity of that discipline".[72] He accordingly identified a division between general historians and legal historians, the latter focusing more on technical matters—a division not too dissimilar, perhaps, to that within the legal historians of Louisiana. In Quebec, however, in contrast to Louisiana, the development of broader approaches has not been so specifically elaborated into a stark dispute between a supposed "new" Quebec legal history created in opposition to an "old" one. Furthermore, though Quebec's legal historians have been apt to decry "the very poor state of legal history in

---

68 See "The Bicentennial of the Digest of 1808—Collected Papers", 24 *Tulane European and Civil Law Forum* (2009).

69 V.V. Palmer, "Foreword", 24 *Tulane European and Civil Law Forum* (2009), pp. i–ii at p. i.

70 J.-M. Fecteau, "Savoir historique et mutations normatives: les defis d'une nécessaire convergence entre droit et histoire", in P. Noreau (ed.), *Dans le regard de l'autre – In the Eye of the Beholder*, Montreal, Les éditions Thémis, 2007, pp. 35–56.

71 *Ibid.*, pp. 42–44.

72 Young, *op. cit. supra* note 32, p. xiii.

Quebec" and its "insularity", to an outsider—given the size of the jurisdiction—it seems flourishing.[73] Indeed, G. Blaine Baker's recent and invaluable historiographical survey shows that much has been achieved since the *tour d'horizon* provided by Vince Masciotra in 1987.[74] Without minimizing problems, it is also worth noting that tensions over how to approach and understand legal history may be creative and stimulating. However that may be, it is certainly impressive to see how much has been written on legal history in recent years by scholars in Quebec, whether located in history departments or in law schools.

Quebec scholars have never questioned that there was interpretative value to be gained in understanding their legal history by reflecting on whether or not there was a conflict or competition between legal systems after the British Conquest of New France; they have generally also seen this period as having had a fundamental impact on the development of their laws. But the situation is complicated. It is helpful to set out briefly some of the facts. In 1759, the British defeated the French army just outside the city of Quebec. In 1760, Montreal capitulated. The Treaty of Paris confirmed Britain's possession of Canada in 1763. A Royal Proclamation of 7 October 1763 dealt with Britain's new acquisitions in the Americas, and seemingly introduced English common law to Quebec in both criminal and civil matters.[75] The following year an ordinance created courts on the English model, again with phrasing suggesting that English laws were to be applied, except before the new Court of Common Pleas in cases arising before 1 October 1764.[76] The exact impact of all of this has been much debated. For example, in 1960, André Morel argued that the French Canadians boycotted the new legal institutions, relying instead on arbitration.[77] Subsequent research has questioned this; in particular, Jean-Philippe Garneau argued in 2000 that there was continuity in French-Canadian practices in this respect before and after the Conquest.[78] Exploration of this issue led to an extensive archival study by Arnaud Decroix, David Gilles, and Michel Morin that

---

[73] J.-M. Fecteau, Book Review, 15 *Law and History Review* (1997), pp. 384–387 at p. 384; see also S. Normand, Book Review, 35 *Les cahiers de droit* (1994), pp. 961–964 at p. 961: "L'histoire du droit québécois souffre de sous-développement…."

[74] G.B. Baker, "Quebec and the Canadas: A Legal Historiography, 1760–1867", in G.B. Baker and D. Fyson (eds.), *Essays in the History of Canadian Law: Quebec and the Canadas*, Toronto, University of Toronto Press, 2013, pp. 3–95; V. Masciotra, "Quebec Legal Historiography", 32 *McGill Law Journal* (1987), pp. 712–732.

[75] See *infra*, pp. 88–89.

[76] Public Archives of Canada, *Documents Relating to the History of Canada, 1759–1791*, ed. by A. Shortt and A.G. Doughty, 2nd ed., Ottawa, J. L. de Taché, 1918, pp. 205–210.

[77] A. Morel, "La réaction des Canadiens devant l'administration de justice de 1764 à 1774: une forme de résistance passive", 20 *Revue du Barreau* (1960), pp. 53–63.

[78] J.-P. Garneau, "Droit et 'affaires de famille' sur la Côte-de-Beaupré: histoire d'une rencontre en amont et en aval de la Conquête britannique", 34 *Revue juridique Thémis* (2000), pp. 515–561.

essentially supported Garneau's view, concluding that the French-Canadian use of arbitration in certain areas was not a rejection of the new institutions, but rather continuation of an older practice, one, indeed, that came to involve the new judges. The three authors further showed that, whatever may have been stated in the Proclamation and Ordinance, use of the Custom of Paris continued in many respects, with juries in the Court of Common Pleas (used by both communities) in many ways acting like arbitrators.[79] In other words, the situation in Quebec after 1763 was complicated, fluid, and perhaps even confused; individuals and officials were pragmatic and collaborative in their approach, and the new institutions encouraged such pragmatism.[80] The existing inhabitants did not boycott the new courts. They may have protested about innovations, but they made use of the new institutions when it suited them, even embracing an understanding of British constitutionalism.[81] Under the Quebec Act of 1774, the "laws and Customs of Canada" were reintroduced.[82] But, as Arnaud Decroix has shown, even after it came into force, English law was sometimes still invoked by litigants, just as the Custom of Paris had been before the new enactment: the population remained opportunistic and pragmatic in its approach to the law, a practice encouraged by the fluidity of the situation.[83] In response to the new Act, François-Joseph Cugnet, a French-Canadian who flourished under the British regime, published a number of short works setting out a "Canadian law" based on the French customary law to suit the new situation;[84] but at much the same time, Blackstone's *Commentaries* became an important resource in the colony.[85]

Thus, after the Conquest, whatever may have been the intention of the British colonial administration, modern research has shown that the relationships between the laws, colonists and colonial administrators were complex and variable, a situation continuing to some extent after the Act of

---

[79] A. Decroix, D. Gilles and M. Morin, *Les tribunaux et l'arbitrage en Nouvelle-France et au Québec de 1740 à 1784*, Montreal, Les éditions Thémis, 2012.

[80] D. Gilles, "L'arbitrage notarié, instrument idoine de conciliation des traditions juridiques après la Conquête britannique? (1760–1784)", 57 *McGill Law Journal* (2011), pp. 135–185.

[81] M. Morin, "Les revendications des nouveaux sujets, francophones et catholiques, de la Province de Québec, 1764–1774", in Baker and Fyson (eds.), *op. cit. supra* note 74, pp. 131–186 at pp. 154–161; M. Morin, "The Discovery and Assimilation of British Constitutional Law Principles in Quebec, 1764–1774", 36 *Dalhousie Law Journal* (2013), pp. 581–616.

[82] J.E.C. Brierley and R.A. Macdonald (eds.), *Quebec Civil Law: An Introduction to Quebec Private Law*, Toronto, Emond Montgomery Publications Ltd., 1993, pp. 14–17; Normand, *op. cit. supra* note 38, pp. 28–31.

[83] A. Decroix, "La controverse sur la nature du droit applicable après la Conquête", 56 *McGill Law Journal* (2011), pp. 489–542.

[84] S. Normand, "François-Joseph Cugnet et la reconstitution du droit de la Nouvelle-France", 1 *Cahiers Aixois d'histoire des droits de l'outre mer français* (2002), pp. 127–145.

[85] M. Morin, "Blackstone and the Birth of Quebec's Distinct Legal Culture", in Prest (ed.), *op. cit. supra* note 9, pp. 105–124.

1774.[86] Moreover, there was considerable continuity from the French colonial period, of which the seigneurial system of land tenure, the subject of some recent important studies by Benoît Grenier, provides an obvious example.[87] Historians have accordingly paid considerable attention to the further development of the law in the British colonial period to 1840.[88] Among issues examined have been the further development of a Canadian legal literature and the early appearance of the legal profession.[89] Given the preservation of English procedure and English criminal law, the legal culture became "mixed" in nature.

From around 1840, after the Rebellions of 1837–1838, Quebec's legal historians generally acknowledge that there was an era of rapid change in the law of Lower Canada, most notably with the abolition of the *seigneurial* system of land tenure. It was out of this era of political reform, social change, and economic development that the project of codification developed in Quebec.[90] It was also during this period of change that law schools were created, while the bar was incorporated and acquired a charter for its library.[91] The middle years of the century also saw the appearance of the first legal periodicals, as well as of regular law reports.[92] Quebec jurists were perfectly familiar with the latest European thinking about law, even if they continued to prefer Pothier to Savigny.[93] Study of the activities of the

---

[86] See D. Gilles, "Les acteurs de la norme coloniale face au droit métropolitain: de l'adaption à l'appropriation (Canada XVIIe–XVIIIe siècles)", 4 *Clio@Thémis* (2011); Decroix, *op. cit. supra* note 83, pp. 520–534.

[87] B. Grenier, *Brève histoire du régime seigneuriale*, Montreal, Les éditions du Boréal, 2012; B. Grenier, *Seigneurs campagnards de la nouvelle France: présence seigneuriale et sociabilité rurale dans la vallée du saint Laurent à l'époque préindustrielle*, Rennes, Les presses universitaires de Rennes, 2007.

[88] E. Kolish, *Nationalismes et conflits de droit: le débat de droit privé au Québec, 1760–1840*, Montreal, Hurtubise HMH, 1994.

[89] S. Normand, "Les débuts de la littérature juridique québécoise, 1767–1840", in Baker and Fyson (eds.), *op. cit. supra* note 74, pp. 96–130; J.-P. Garneau, "Appartenance ethnique, culture juridique et représentation devant la justice civile de Québec à la fin du XVIIIe siècle", in C. Dolan (ed.), *Entre justice et justiciables: les auxiliaires de la justice du môyen age au XXe siècle*, [Quebec], Les presses de l'université Laval, 2005, pp. 405–424.

[90] Brierley and Macdonald (eds.), *op. cit. supra* note 82, pp. 19–23.

[91] S. Normand, "La transformation de la profession d'avocat au Québec, 1840–1900", in Dolan (ed.), *op. cit. supra* note 89, pp. 425–439; G. Gallichan, "La Bibliothèque du Barreau de Québec: l'émergence d'une institution", 34 *Les cahiers de droit* (1993), pp. 125–152 at pp. 136–137; L. Lortie, "The Early Teaching of Law in French Canada", 2 *Dalhousie Law Journal* (1975), pp. 521–532.

[92] S. Normand, "Profil des périodiques juridiques québécois au XIXe siècle", 34 *Les cahiers de droit* (1993), pp. 153–182; Morel, *op. cit. supra* note 38, p. 54.

[93] E.H. Reiter, "Imported Books, Imported Ideas: Reading European Jurisprudence in Mid-Nineteenth-Century Quebec", 22 *Law and History Review* (2004), pp. 445–492.

courts shows an ability to cope with the mixed system.[94] If there was a significant development of Quebec's mixed legal culture, there was nonetheless considerable continuity.[95] Thus, André Morel has shown that, in the first half of the nineteenth century, Quebec lawyers relied for their law on the new commentaries on the Napoleonic Code as well as on the writers of the *ancien droit*. They continued to do so after codification, in Morel's view only coming to treat their law as now founded on legislation in the middle years of the 1880s.[96]

David Howes has provided a somewhat different perspective on the legal history of Quebec in the period with which we are concerned. Noting the problems of access to sources, he has argued that Quebec's legal culture prior to codification was essentially oral, focused on rhetoric and polemical argument.[97] He has also argued that, after codification, the judges retained a "polyjural" and "nomadic" (his terms) tradition, interpreting the Code according to the requirements of a "universal" law.[98] He further suggested that this same attitude of "residual orality" can be found in the work of Maximilien Bibaud, one of the first law teachers in the Province, who saw Roman law as the repository of universal principles.[99] Some comments are necessary. It can be argued that Quebec's lawyers clearly lived in a culture of law books, which even shaped their oral discourse;[100] lawyers were certainly interested in the printed text.[101] Indeed, study of the paratextual material associated with legal texts could also be seen as emphasizing this.[102] Finally, Michel Morin has queried Howes' views, first, by questioning the premises

---

[94] M. Morin, "La perception de l'ancien droit et du nouveau droit français au Bas-Canada, 1774–1866", in H.P. Glenn (ed.), *Droit québécois et droit français: communauté, autonomie, concordance*, Cowansville, Les éditions Yvon Blais, 1993, pp. 1–41 at pp. 13–25.

[95] S. Normand, "Une culture en redéfinition: la culture juridique québécoise durant la seconde moitié du XIXe siècle", in B. Melkevik (ed.), *Transformation de la culture juridique québécoise*, [Sainte-Foy QC], Les presses de l'université Laval, 1998, pp. 221–235.

[96] Morel, *op. cit. supra* note 38, pp. 60–62.

[97] D. Howes, "La domestication de la pensée juridique québécoise", 13 *Anthropologie et sociétés* (1989), pp. 103–125 at pp. 104–107.

[98] *Ibid.*, pp. 107–115; D. Howes, "From Polyjurality to Monojurality: The Transformation of Quebec Law, 1875, 1929", 32 *McGill Law Journal* (1987), pp. 523–558.

[99] D. Howes, "The Origin and Demise of Legal Education in Quebec (or Hercules Bound)", 38 *University of New Brunswick Law Journal* (1989), pp. 127–149. For a different view, see S. Normand and M. Dumais, "Le droit romain dans le droit coutumier du Bas Canada selon François-Maximilien Bibaud", in E. Hermon (ed.), *La question agraire à Rome: droit romain et société*, Como, Edizioni New Press, 1999, pp. 165–173.

[100] See, e.g., Reiter, *op. cit. supra* note 93, pp. 448–449.

[101] C. Veilleux, "Le livre à Québec, 1760–1867: les gens de justice et leurs œuvres", 34 *Les cahiers de droit* (1993), pp. 93–124.

[102] S. Normand, "La périphérie du texte dans les ouvrages juridiques québécois", 39 *Les cahiers de droit* (1998), pp. 75–133.

on which his arguments are based, and second, through a very detailed analysis of the actual work of the courts.[103]

The above provides the background to current research on the Civil Code of Lower Canada. But the starting point for research into it in many ways still remains John Brierley's classic article from 1968.[104] In Baker's important historiographical survey, the author commented that the work of Brian Young and Brierley resulted in much being known about "the personalities, politics and processes of those reforms in Canada East [Quebec] by the union legislature".[105] As well as Brierley's article, Baker here cited Young's study, *The Politics of Codification: The Lower Canadian Civil Code of 1866.*[106] Brierley explored the circumstances, both political and juristic, that led to codification and the actual way the codifiers set about their task. The account of codification in this book relies very heavily on Brierley's path-breaking research, which is set out in an article that is much richer than this brief description would suggest.

Young's monograph is a powerful complement to Brierley's article. It does not focus on legal technicalities. Instead, Young first explores the political and economic backgrounds that led to codification, which he sees as a political act that was the result of collaboration between the Anglophone and Francophone élites. He also views it as the result of compromise, not only between competing ideals and constituencies, but also between varying laws. He also considers that the growing industrialization of Lower Canada, along with reforms already rationalizing and liberalizing the laws, constituted a necessary background to the decision to codify. Young provides a valuable account of the codifiers and the politics of establishing the Codification Commission, while also exploring the way the Commission worked. Finally, he explores the attitude of the codifiers by examining, first, their treatment of women as traders, which he sees as exemplifying the continuing strength of custom in the Code, and second, their attitude to obligations, which he considers as central to the Code and as emphasizing a belief in freedom of contract.

Both the overall thrust of Young's book and its specific content are generally compatible with and complementary to the study published here, which touches on similar topics, including even the treatment of women as traders and the codifiers' belief in contractual liberty.[107] Commenting on Young's and Brierley's work, Baker remarked: "Less is understood about the content of the legal change wrought by the Civil Code of Lower Canada or

---

[103] M. Morin, "Des juristes sédentaires? L'influence du droit anglais et du droit français sur l'interprétation du code civil du Bas Canada", 60 *Revue du Barreau* (2000), pp. 247–386.
[104] Brierley, "Quebec's Civil Law Codification", *supra* note 32.
[105] Baker, *op. cit. supra* note 74, p. 12.
[106] Young, *op. cit. supra* note 32.
[107] See *infra*, pp. 266–269, 344, 356, 402, 421–423, 478, 481–482, 494–496.

the motives for those substantive changes."[108] In his notes, however, he did refer to a small number of works that have considered these, including the thesis on which this book is founded.[109] In addition to the thesis, Baker cited three other chapter-length, if substantial, studies: first, he referred to an article by Brisson and Kasirer that explored the development of the law relating to married women from 1866 to 1991;[110] second, he cited Greenwood's argument that the Commission inscribed in the Code a tension between a backward-looking attitude to family and a forward-looking one to economic freedom, which he described as ambivalent and even "Janus-like";[111] and third, he cited Morel's important study of what the author saw as the creation of a new legal order between 1866 and 1890, inaugurated by the codification of private law in 1866.[112] The important review of Young's book by Jean-Marie Fecteau cited the works of Morel, Brierley, and Cairns as those in which the code had been examined, if, in contrast to Young, all focusing on "the legal dimension".[113] And indeed, Young himself cited the thesis on which this book is based for specialist article-by-article detailed examination of the Code.[114]

None of the articles cited by Baker or Fecteau carries analysis exactly equivalent to the sustained and detailed examination of the technical work of the codifiers provided here. Nor do other significant papers focusing on the Civil Code of Lower Canada.[115] The closest that comes to it may be Normand and Fyson's important study of Roman law as a source;[116] Gilles' study of the study of the role of Domat is also relevant.[117]

If one were to identify one major tendency in the general scholarship on the Civil Code of Lower Canada, it would be to understand the Code as involving ether a compromise or a tension between the principles of the older *droit coutumier* and economic liberalism. This emphasizes the need for the work now presented in this book and the extent of its continuing relevance.

---

[108] Baker, *op. cit. supra* note 74, p. 12.

[109] *Ibid.*, pp. 55–56 n. 65.

[110] J.-M. Brisson and N. Kasirer, "The Married Woman in Ascendance, the Mother Country in Retreat: From Legal Colonialism to Legal Nationalism in Quebec: Matrimonial Law Reform, 1866–1991", 23 *Manitoba Law Journal* (1995), pp. 406–449.

[111] M. Greenwood, "Lower Canada (Quebec): Transformation of Civil Law, from Higher Morality to Autonomous Will", 23 *Manitoba Law Journal* (1995), pp. 132–182.

[112] Morel, *op. cit. supra* note 38.

[113] Fecteau, *op. cit. supra* note 73, p. 384.

[114] Young, *op. cit. supra* note 32, pp. 121, 217 n. 3.

[115] S. Normand, "La codification de 1866: contexte et impact", in Glenn (ed.), *op. cit. supra* note 94, pp. 43–62.

[116] S. Normand and D. Fyson, "Le droit romain comme source du *Code civil du Bas Canada*", 103 *Revue du notariat* (2001), pp. 87–113.

[117] D. Gilles, "Les *Lois civiles* de Jean Domat, prémices des codifications? Du Code Napoléon au *Code civil du Bas Canada*", 43 *Revue juridique Thémis* (2009), pp. 1–49.

A lively area of discussion in recent years has been the changing impact of the Civil Code in the years after its promulgation. Indeed, many of the studies considered above on the legal history of Quebec also deal with this. Sylvio Normand has set out an important programme for the study of legal publication in this period.[118] One can also point to Kasirer's fascinating study of the physical form of the editions of the Code.[119] Likewise one should note Normand and Saint-Hilaire's study of the *Bibliothèque du Code civil* of Lorimier and Vilbon, which shows that the authors located the *Code* in a past literary tradition, but nonetheless produced a book that suited contemporary transformations in legal practice.[120] In this connection it is also worth mentioning Normand's study of Mignault.[121]

Much of the legal history of Louisiana and Quebec has not been touched on here, partly because of the focus on the historiography of the two codes, and partly because of gaps in the literature. It is evident, for example, that more work could be done on the legal history of colonial Louisiana in particular. This is not to say that the excellent archival resources for study of colonial Louisiana have been neglected. But, other than the important work of Hans Baade in the 1970s, in recent years it has mainly been historians, such as Gilbert Din, who have worked on them.[122] There has been a significant focus, for example, on slavery and free blacks.[123] Colonial legal history has not in itself been particularly explored. Though Mark Fernandez's book on the history of Louisiana's courts has a chapter on the French and Spanish eras, the New Louisiana Legal History, with its focus on assimilation to the rest of the U.S.A., has largely ignored the colonial period.[124] This means that the collection on the legal history of Louisiana edited by Billings and Schafer

---

[118] S. Normand, "L'histoire de l'imprimé juridique: un champs de recherche inexploré", 38 *McGill Law Journal* (1993), pp. 130–146.

[119] N. Kasirer, "Si la Joconde se trouve au Louvre, où trouve-t-on le *Code civil du Bas Canada*", 46 *Les cahiers de droit* (2005), pp. 481–518.

[120] S. Normand and M. Saint-Hilaire, "*La Bibliothèque du Code civil* : un ouvrage au confluent de la tradition et de la modernité", 32 *Revue générale de droit* (2002), pp. 305–334.

[121] S. Normand, "Le droit civil canadien de Pierre-Basile Mignault ou la fabrication d'un palimpseste", in N. Kasirer (ed.), *Le faux en droit privé*, [Montreal], *Les éditions Thémis*, 2000, pp. 133–154.

[122] H. Baade, "Marriage Contracts in French and Spanish Louisiana: A Study in 'Notarial' Jurisprudence", 53 *Tulane Law Review* (1979), pp. 1–92; H. Baade, "The Law of Slavery in Spanish Luisiana, 1769–1803, in Haas (ed.), *op. cit. supra* note 13, pp. 43–86; G.C. Din and J.E. Harkins, *The New Orleans Cabildo: Colonial Louisiana's First City Government, 1769–1803*, Baton Rouge, Louisiana State University Press, 1996.

[123] G.C. Din, *Spaniards, Planters, Slaves: The Spanish Regulation of Slavery in Louisiana, 1763–1803*, College Station TX, Texas A. and M. University Press, 1999; T.N. Ingersoll, *Mamon and Manon in Early New Orleans: The First Slave Society in the Deep South, 1718–1819*, Knoxville, University of Tennessee Press, 1999; K.S. Hanger, *Bounded Lives, Bounded Places: Free Black Society in Colonial New Orleans, 1769–1803*, Durham NC, Duke University Press, 1997.

[124] Fernandez, *From Chaos to Continuity supra* note 4, pp. 1–15.

has very little on the colonial era, other than on slavery. It is interesting to compare this with Quebec, where legal historians (however defined) have fruitfully paid attention in recent years to the French colonial era, drawing on significant archival resources. The work of David Gilles has shown what can be done with this material.[125] Louis Lavallée pointed out in the 1970s the wonderful resource that is the notarial archives.[126] He himself put this resource to good use.[127] The important studies of Grenier on the *seigneuries* have already been cited.[128] Some scholars have examined the seigneurial system as a whole, while others have advanced knowledge through detailed studies of specific *seigneuries*.[129] John A. Dickinson, a leading historian of New France, published a study of civil procedure before the *Prévôté de Québec* in 1982;[130] with an interest in administration, social control and regulation, Dickinson saw the law and institutions of New France as authoritarian and paternalistic.[131] There has been significant interest in the role of women, family and law.[132] While some attention has been paid to the first nations in discussion of colonial Louisiana, consideration of them has

---

[125] D. Gilles, "Aux sources de l'herméneutique du droit québécoise: enquête d'un discours sur le droit avant la Conquête", 44:3 *Revue juridique Thémis* (2010), pp. 49–120.

[126] L. Lavallée, "Les archives notariales et l'histoire sociale de la Nouvelle-France", 28 *Revue d'histoire de l'Amérique française* (1974), pp. 385–403.

[127] L. Lavallée, "La vie et la pratique d'un notaire rural sous le régime français: le cas de Guillaume Barette, notaire à La Prairie entre 1709–1744 ", 47 *Revue d'histoire de l'Amérique française* (1994), pp. 499–519.

[128] See *supra* note 87.

[129] A. Laberge and B. Grenier (eds.), *Le régime seigneurial au Québec: 150 ans après. Bilans et perspectives de recherche à l'occasion de la commémoration de l'abolition du régime seigneurial*, Quebec, Centre interunivesitaire d'études québécoises, 2009; J.-F. Niort, "Aspects juridiques du régime seigneurial en Nouvelle-France", 32 *Revue générale de droit* (2002), pp. 443–526; S. Dépatie, M. Lalancette, and C. Dessureault, *Contributions à l'étude du régime seigneurial Canadien*, Montreal, Hurtubise HMH, 1987.

[130] J.A. Dickinson, *Justice et justiciables: la procédure civile à la Prévôté de Québec, 1667–1759*, Quebec, Les presses de l'université Laval, 1982.

[131] J.A. Dickinson, "Réflexions sur la police en Nouvelle-France", 32 *McGill Law Journal* (1987), pp. 496–522; J.A. Dickinson, "New France: Law, Courts, and the Coutume de Paris, 1608–1760", 23 *Manitoba Law Journal* (1995), pp. 32–54; J.A. Dickinson, "La justice seigneuriale en Nouvelle-France: le cas de Notre-Dames des Anges", 28 *Revue d'histoire de l'Amérique française* (1974), pp. 323–346. But see also, J.-P. Garneau, "Rendre justice en Nouvelle-France: les voies et les limites de l'obéissance", 18 *Bulletin d'histoire politique* (2009), pp. 87–102.

[132] F. Parent and G. Postolec, "Quant Thémis rencontre Clio: les femmes et le droit en Nouvelle-France", 36 *Cahiers de droit* (1995), pp. 293–318; J.M. Augustin, "Les premiers contrats de marriage à Montréal de 1668 à 1684, et la coutume de Paris", 30 *Revue juridique Thémis* (1996), pp. 1–20; B. Grenier, "Réflexion sur le pouvoir féminin au Canada sous le régime français: le cas de la 'seigneuresse' Marie-Catherine Peuvret (1667–1739)", 42 *Histoire sociale / Social History* (2009), pp. 297–324; B. Grenier and C. Ferland, "'Quelque longue que soit l'absence': procurations et pouvoir féminin à Québec au XVIIIe siècle", 37 *Clio: femmes, genre, histoire* (2013), pp. 197–225.

become rather more integrated into discussions of the colonial legal history of Quebec, a development in which the work of Michel Morin has recently been particularly important, with broad implications.[133] David Gilles has discussed the troubled topic of Amerindian slavery.[134]

Some might class some of the work mentioned above as social rather than legal history; but I am firmly of the view that in the house of legal history there are many mansions.

The aim of this introduction is to provide a context for the book that follows. I think it is clear that its fundamental research continues to be relevant and important for the further development of our understanding of the legal histories of Louisiana and Quebec. It also demonstrates that study of each illuminates knowledge of the other. Appropriate comparison in legal history is important and fruitful; it is necessary to reflect on transnational impacts and potential legal transplants and explore them for their significance.

More broadly, the research published here, by analyzing the work of the codifiers, demonstrates that both sets of codifiers must have worked in similar ways, even if only those of Quebec produced records in an attempt to document their work. But even their *Reports* do not tell the full story; perhaps, they even create one. Thus, a supposedly conservative code, such as that of Lower Canada, still involves choice and innovation. Both sets of codifiers operated with an intuitive sense of what they thought was needed. They did not found their decisions about the law on any kind of detailed and profound study of the history of their respective legal systems in the style of Savigny, nor on any type of social-science research. Instead they operated, without much public scrutiny, as legal technocrats, confident of their own mandarin or patrician views, inscribing into their codes what they saw as

---

[133] G.C. Din and A.P. Nasatir, *The Imperial Osages: Spanish-Indian Diplomacy in the Mississippi Valley*, Norman, University of Oklahoma, Press, 1983; C. Vidal, "From Incorporation to Exclusion: Indians, Europeans, and Americans in the Mississippi Valley from 1699 to 1830", in Kastor and Weil (eds.), *op. cit. supra* note 60, pp. 62–92; S. Normand, "Les droits des amérindiens sur le territoire sous le régime français", in A. Lajoie, J.-M. Brisson, S. Normand and A. Bisonette (eds.), *Le statut juridique des peuples autochtones au Québec et le pluralism*, Cowansville, Les éditions Yvon Blais, 1996, pp. 107–141; M. Morin, "La dimension juridique des relations entre Samuel de Champlain et les autochtones de la Nouvelle-France", 38 *Revue juridique Thémis* (2004), pp. 389–426; M. Morin, "Propriétés et territoires autochtones en Nouvelle-France. I – Contrôle territorial et reconnaissance de territoires nationaux", 43 *Recherches amérindiennes au Québec* (2013), pp. 59–75; M. Morin, "Propriétés et territoires autochtones en Nouvelle-France. II – La gestion des districts de chasse", 44 *Recherches amérindiennes au Québec* (2014), pp. 129–136; M. Morin, "Fraternité, souveraineté et autonomie des autochtones en Nouvelle-France", 43 *Revue générale de droit* (2013), pp. 531–598.

[134] D. Gilles, "La norme esclavagiste, entre pratique coutumière et norme étatique: les esclaves panis et leur statut juridique au Canada", 40 *Ottawa Law Review* (2009), pp. 73–116.

necessary and appropriate.[135] Of course, all were lawyers with experience of practice; all must have used what they probably considered a common-sense approach to what was needed in their codes. They were pragmatic. They drew on what was to hand and what they considered valuable and permitted by their legislative instructions and the current practice in their legal system. But in choosing potential sources for individual articles of their codes, both sets of redactors acted in a relatively free way, unconstrained, in varying degrees, by what was understood to be the existing law. This led them to develop codes that were a compromise based on their own intuitive sense of the needs of their respective societies, selecting from sources considered authoritative and legitimate to use. They thus created codes that were truly original, if located within an arguably French tradition. This book shows the process they used to achieve this and attempts to reconstruct their thinking and motivation.

---

[135] This argument has been made strongly for Quebec; but it obviously also applies to Louisiana: see, e.g., Young, *op. cit. supra* note 32, pp. 3–5, 107–108, 121–140; Brierley and Macdonald, *op. cit. supra* note 82, pp. 24–32. On the development of the Quebec patriciate and its attitudes, see B. Young, *Patrician Families and the Making of Quebec: The Taschereaus and McCords*, Montreal and Kingston, Queen's University Press, 2014.

Abbreviations

Ancien Denisart	J. B. Denisart, *Collection de décisions nouvelles et de notions relatives à la jurisprudence actuelle*, 7th ed., Paris, veuve Desaint, 1771
Asso y Manuel	Jordan de Asso y del Rio and D. Miguel de Manuel y Rodriguez, *Instituciones del derecho civil de Castilla*, 7th ed. by Joaquin María Palacios, Madrid, Tomás Alban, 1806
Baade, "Marriage Contracts":	H. Baade, "Marriage Contracts in French and Spanish Colonial Louisiana", 53 *Tul. L. Rev.* (1978), pp. 1–92
—, "Form":	"The Form of Marriage in Spanish North America", 61 *Cornell Law Review* (1975), pp. 1–89
Batiza, "Sources":	R. Batiza, "The Louisiana Civil Code of 1808: Its Actual Sources and Present Relevance", 46 *Tul. L. Rev.* (1971), pp. 4–165
—, "Rejoinder":	"Sources of the Civil Code of 1808, Facts and Speculation: a Rejoinder", 46 *Tul. L. Rev.* (1972), pp. 628–652
—, "Textual Evidence":	"The Actual Sources of the Marriage Contract Provisions of the Louisiana Civil Code of 1808: the Textual Evidence", 54 *Tul. L. Rev.* (1979), pp. 77–116
Boston Univ. L. Rev.	*Boston University Law Review*
Brierley, "Codification":	J. Brierley, "Quebec's Civil Law Codification", 14 *McGill Law Journal* (1968), pp. 521–589

Brissaud, *History*:	J.B. Brissaud, *History of French Private Law*, trans. by R. Howell, Continental Legal History Series, vol. 3, London, John Murray, 1912
Buckland, *Textbook*:	W.W. Buckland, *A Textbook of Roman Law*, 3rd ed. by P.G. Stein, Cambridge, University Press, 1963
C. or Cod:	*Codex Justinianus*: vol. 2 of C.I.C.
C.I.C.:	*Corpus iuris civilis*, ed. T. Mommsen, P. Krüger, and R. Schoell, Berlin, Weidmann, various dates. (Where necessary texts have been checked against the earlier editions available to the redactors.)
C.L.:	*Civil Code of Louisiana*, 1825
C.N.:	*Code civil des français*, 1804 (Code Napoléon)
C. Q.:	*Civil Code of Lower Canada* or *Code civil du Bas Canada*, (Quebec Code)
C.S.L.C.	*Consolidated Statutes for Lower Canada*, Quebec, S. Derbishire and G. Desbarats, 1861
Can. Bar Rev.	*Canadian Bar Review*
Can. Hist. Rev.:	*Canadian Historical Review*.
D.:	*Justiniani Digesta*: vol. 1 of C.I.C.
D.L.V.:	de la Vergne manuscript: *A Reprint of Moreau-Lislet's Copy of A Digest of the Civil Laws now in force in the Territory of Orleans (1808) Containing Manuscript References to its Sources and Other Civil Laws on the Same Subjects*, Baton Rouge, Claitor's Publishing Division, 1971

D.O.: *A Digest of the Civil Laws Now in Force in the Territory of Orleans with Alterations and Amendments Adapted to its Present System of Government*, New Orleans, Published by Authority, printed by Bradford and Anderson, 1808

Dargo, *Jefferson's Louisiana*: G. Dargo, *Jefferson's Louisiana: Politics and the Clash of Legal Traditions*, Cambridge MA, Harvard University Press, 1975

Domat, *Droit public* J Domat, *Les loix civiles dans leur ordre naturel; le droit public, et legum delectus*, new ed., Paris, veuve Cavelier, 1766

Domat, *Loix civiles* J. Domat, *Les loix civiles dans leur ordre naturel; le droit public, et legum delectus*, new ed., Paris, Michel Brunet, 1735

Febrero, *Contratos* J. Febrero, *Librería de escribanos, é instrucción juridíca theórico práctica de principiantes. Parte Primera divida en tres tomos. Trata de testamentos, y contratos*, Madrid, Impr. de P. Marin, 1789

Febrero, *Juicios* J. Febrero, *Librería de escribanos, é instrucción juridíca theórico práctica de principiantes. Parte Segunda divida en tres tomos. Trata de los juicios de inventario, y partición de bienes de difunto, ordinario, executive, y de concurso, y prelación de acreedores*, Madrid, Impr. de P. Marin, 1790

Ferrière, *Corps et Comp.*: C. de Ferrière, *Corps et compilation de tous les commentateurs anciens et modernes sur la coutume de Paris*, 2nd ed., Paris, Henri Charpentier, 1714

Franklin, "Eighteenth Brumaire": M. Franklin, "The Eighteenth 'Brumaire' in Louisiana: Talleyrand and the Spanish

	Medieval Legal System of 1806", 16 *Tul. L. Rev.* (1942) pp. 514–561
—, "Existential Force":	"Some Considerations on the Existential Force of Roman Law in the Early History of the United States", 22 *Buffalo Law Review* (1972), pp. 69–105
—, "Expulsion":	"The Place of Thomas Jefferson in the Expulsion of Spanish Medieval Law from Louisiana", 16 *Tul. L. Rev.* (1942), pp. 319–338
Fuero real:	*Fuero real de España: diligentemente hecho por el noble Rey Don Alonso IX*, glossed by A.D. de Montalvo, Medina del Campo, printed by Pedro de Castro for Guillermo de Miles, 1544
Gaius, *Inst.*:	*Gai Institutiones*: edn. de Zulueta, Oxford, 1946.
Inst.:	*Iustiniani Institutiones*: vol. 1 of C.I.C.
La.	Louisiana Reports, 1830–1841
La. Bar. Assoc. Repts.	*Louisiana Bar Association Reports*
La. Bar J.	*Louisiana Bar Journal*
La. Hist.	*Louisiana History*
La. Hist. Quar.:	*Louisiana Historical Quarterly.*
La. L. Rev.:	*Louisiana Law Review.*
La. Leg. Arch.:	*Louisiana Legal Archives*, 3 vols., New Orleans, Baton Rouge, T.J. Moran's Sons, State of Louisiana, 1937–1942
Maleville, *Analyse*	J. de Maleville, *Analyse raisonnée de la discussion du Code civil au Conseil d'État: contenant le texte des lois: le précis des observations faites sur chaque*

	article, et les motifs de la décision du Conseil: l'indication de la conformité et de l'opposition de ces articles aux lois anciennes: les arrêts rendus par la Cour de cassation, pour en fixer le sens: et les observations particulières de l'auteur, 2nd. ed., Paris, Garnery, 1807
Mart.:	*Martin's Reports of Cases Argued and Determined in the Superior Court of Orleans and in the Supreme Court of the State of Louisiana*, reissue, New Orleans, S.M. Stewart, 1846–1853
McCord, Preface:	Preface to *The Civil Code of Lower Canada*, ed. T. McCord, Montreal, Dawson Bros., 1867
—, Synopsis:	Synopsis of the Changes in the Law effected by the Civil Code of Lower Canada, *The Civil Code of Lower Canada*, ed. T. McCord, Montreal, Dawson Bros., 1867, pp. I–XXX
Merlin, *Répertoire* (4)	P.A. Merlin, *Répertoire universel et raisonné de jurisprudence*, 4th ed., Paris, Garnery, 1812–1815
Merlin, *Répertoire* (5)	P.A. Merlin, *Répertoire universel et raisonné de jurisprudence*, 5th ed., Paris, Garnery, 1827–1828
Mich. L. Rev.:	*Michigan Law Review*
Miss. Vall. Hist. Rev.:	*Mississippi Valley Historical Review*
Nouveau Denisart	J. B. Denisart, *Collection de décisions nouvelles et de notions relatives à la jurisprudence actuelle*, 8th ed., Paris, veuve Desaint, 1783–1807. This edition by J.B.F. Bayard and A.G. Camus was interrupted by the Revolution and then continued post-codification with volumes by L. Calenge published chez Lamy. These later

volumes will be identified by date in the footnotes.

Nov.: *Novellae constitutiones*: vol. 3 of C.I.C.

Nov. Rec. Cast.: *Novísima recopilación de las leyes de España*, Madrid, n.p., 1805–1807.

Olivier-Martin, *Histoire*: Fr. Olivier-Martin, *Histoire du droit français des origines à la Révolution*, Paris, Domat Montchrestien, 1948

Pan. fran.: [J.B. Delaporte and P.N. Riffé-Caubray], *Les pandectes françaises: ou, Recueil complet de toutes les lois en vigueur, contenant les codes civil, criminel, de commerce, militaire, de marine, judiciaire, et les dispositions des autres lois, soit romaines, soit coutumières, soit édits, ordonnances ou déclarations, soit décrets, que ces codes laissent subsister, avec des observations formant un traité substantiel et succinct de chaque matière*, Paris, Perlet, 1803–1806

Part.: *Las Siete Partidas del rey Don Alfonso el sabio, cotejadas con varios codices antiguos por la Real Academia de la Historia*, Madrid, Atlas, 1972 [repr. of ed., Madrid, Imprenta Real, 1807]

Pascal, "Reply": R. Pascal, "Sources of the Digest of 1808: a Reply to Professor Batiza," 46 *Tul. L. Rev.* (1972), pp. 603–627.

Partidas: *Las siete partidas del rey don Alfonso el sabio: cotejados con varios códices antiguos*, Madrid, Real Academia de la Historia, 1807; *Las siete partidas de las leyes del sabio rey Don Alfonso el nono, glosadas ... por Gregorio López*, Madrid, s.n., 1843–1844

Pothier, *Œuvres*	R.J. Pothier, *Œuvres de Pothier, annotées et mises en correlation avec le Code civil et la législation actuelle*, ed. by M. Bugnet, Paris, Cosse et Marchal, Henri Plon, 1861
	Individual works cited thus:
Pothier, *C. d'Orl.*:	*Coutume d'Orléans*, vol. 1 of *Œuvres*
—, *T. Comm.*:	*Traité de la communauté*, vol. 7 of *Œuvres*
—, *T.C.L.*:	*Traité du contrat de louage*, vol. 4 of *Œuvres*
—, *T.C.M.*:	*Traité du contrat de mariage*, vol. 6 of *Œuvres*
—, *T.D.P.*:	*Traité du Domaine de Propriété*, vol. 9 of *Œuvres*
—, *T.D.T.*:	*Traité des donations testamentaires*, vol. 8 of *Œuvres*
—, *T.V.*:	*Traité du contrat de vente*, vol. 3 of *Œuvres*
—, *T.G.N.B.*:	*Traité de la garde noble et bourgeoise*, vol. 6 of *Œuvres*
—, *T.O.*:	*Traité des obligations*, vol. 2 of *Œuvres*
—, *T.P.C.*:	*Traité des personnes et des choses*, vol. 9 of *Œuvres*
—, *T.P.M.*:	*Traité de la puissance du mari*, vol. 7 of *Œuvres*
—, *T.S.*:	*Traité des successions*, vol. 8 of *Œuvres*
Preliminary Report	*Preliminary Report of the Code Commissioners*, 13 Feb. 1823, in *La. Leg. Arch.*, vol. 1, pp. LXXXV–XCV

Proj. An VIII:	*Projet de Code civil, présenté par la commission nommée par le gouvernement le 24 thermidor, an VIII*, Paris, Chez Emery, 1801
1823 Projet:	*Additions and Amendments to the Civil Code of the State of Louisiana*, in *La. Leg. Arch.*, vol. 1
Rec. Cast.:	[*Nueva*] *recopilación de las leyes destos reynos, hecha por mandad del Rey Don Felipe Segundo*, Madrid, C. de Barrio y Angulo y D. Diaz de la Carrera, 1640–1641
Rec. Ind.:	*Recopliación de leyes de los reynos de las Indias*, 4th Impresion, Madrid, viuda de D. Joaquin Ibarra, 1791
Reports (*First* to *Seventh*, and *Supplementary*):	*Reports of the Commissioners Appointed to Codify the Laws of Lower Canada in Civil Matters*, 2nd ed., 3 vols., G. Desbarats, 1865: *First Report*; *Second Report*; etc.
R.duB.:	*La revue du barreau de la province de Quebec*
R.H.A.F.:	*Revue d'histoire de l'Amerique française*
R.H.D.F.E.:	*Revue historique du droit français et étranger*
R.I.D.C.:	*Revue internationale de droit comparé*
Sweeney, "Tournament":	J.M. Sweeney, "Tournament of Scholars over the Sources of the Civil Code of 1808", 46 *Tul. L. Rev.* (1972), pp. 585–602
T.D.C.Q.	G. Trudel et al., *Traité de droit civil du Québec*, Montreal, Wilson and Lafleur, 1942–1958
Toro	*Leyes de Toro*

Tul. L. Rev.:	*Tulane Law Review*
Watson, *Society*:	Alan Watson, *Society and Legal Change*, Edinburgh, Scottish Academic Press, 1977
—, *Transplants*:	*Legal Transplants: An Approach to Comparative Law*, Edinburgh, Scottish Academic Press, 1974

James Brown (1766-1835),
Matthew Harris Jouett, photograph of oil portrait, ca. 1820.
(*Courtesy of Liberty Hall Historic Site Collections*)

Part I

1

THE REASONS FOR SUCH A STUDY, AND ITS METHOD AND SUBJECTS

NEED FOR THIS STUDY

At present, the nature of the relationship between law and the wider social structure within which it operates is problematic. No one now would regard law as an autonomous body of knowledge and practice distinct from the society within which it exists. Indeed, it is the society wherein the law is found which gives it its meaning.[1] Opinions vary greatly, however, as to the nature of the relationship between any law and the society within which it orders certain social relationships.[2]

To demonstrate the variance of views over the nature of this relationship, it is convenient to quote various authors and briefly to discuss their views. It should be noted here that we are mainly interested in the effect of social change on law.

Professor Lawrence Friedman states:

> . . . rules flow from the social setting. They change as it changes. They rise and fall with these forces, like a tide, obeying the pull of a power that cannot be seen.[3]

Again he remarks:

---

[1] Cf. J.R. Lucas, "The Phenomenon of Law", in P.M.S. Hacker and J. Raz (eds.), *Law Morality and Society: Essays in Honour of H.L.A. Hart*, Oxford, Clarendon Press, 1977, pp. 85–98 at p. 85: "We should, . . . see law as a social phenomena, but intelligible only in a social context, and not—as lawyers are too ready to suppose—an autonomous discipline which can be explained and understood entirely in its own terms."

[2] Here it may appear that a false distinction is being posed between law and society as two discrete entities; it is clear, however, that law is a part of society and is an institution of regulation of society along with, for example, morality. The terms are being used here loosely for the sake of convenience; but definitions will be given at the end of this section.

[3] L. Friedman, *The Legal System: A Social Science Perspective*, New York, Russell Sage Foundation, 1975, p. 309. Professor Friedman's account of the interaction of social and legal change is, of course, rather more sophisticated than this quotation might suggest. Nevertheless, the quotation does present what are substantially his views. See *ibid.*, pp. 269–309, for further discussion.

> The problem of legal change is a little like Zeno's paradox, the race between the tortoise and the hare. Any given state of law is a kind of equilibrium. Everybody's interest is reflected in proportion to his power. How then is it possible to change? The simplest explanation is that the outside context changes. . . . Wars, acts of God, new technology, or development or decay of the economy alter social relations, and legal change follows rapidly, obediently, thereafter.[4]

Friedman's conception is one of a close and necessary connection between social change and legal change: the latter necessarily follows on the former, in an unspecified mechanistic fashion. He does, however, admit of other factors bringing about legal change: hence he admits a reform may meet even a purely "aesthetic" need.[5] What is important to note is that Friedman regards social change as the prime cause of legal change, the latter flowing inevitably from the former, without adequately specifying what exactly is the mechanism bringing about such legal change.

The now discredited views of the historical school of law are too well known to merit more than a brief mention here. In 1927, Walton gave an adequate short statement of their position: "The law of a people, like their language, has an organic connection with their peculiar being and character."[6] Curiously enough, this view has had a great appeal and still has adherents[7]—perhaps because individual legal systems are unique. A necessary connection, however, between an individual people and its laws cannot be demonstrated.

The attitude taken by Marxism to law is the subject of controversy. Marx himself never directly discussed the role of law in capitalist societies, although there exists a large number of texts in which law is discussed in relation to another topic.[8] With the recent attention among Marxist thinkers paid to the role of ideology, law has been more thoroughly considered from a Marxist perspective.[9] This said, it should be pointed out that classic (perhaps naive or "vulgar") Marxist doctrine has posited a direct relationship between society and law, based on certain texts, notably the famous 1859 *Preface to a Contribution to the Critique of Political Economy.*

Classic or vulgar Marxism argues that the mode of production of any society determines all non-economic phenomena. Law is class law working for the benefit of those who own the means of production: "your jurisprudence is but

---

[4] *Ibid.*, p. 307.
[5] *Ibid.*, pp. 269–274.
[6] F.P. Walton, "The Historical School of Jurisprudence and Transplantation of Law", 7 (3rd ser.) *Journal of Comparative Legislation* (1927), pp. 183–192 at p. 184; see also R. Pound, *Interpretations of Legal History*, Cambridge, Cambridge University Press, 1923, ch.1 and pp. 67–68.
[7] See Watson, *Society*, pp. 1–2; Watson, *Transplants*, pp. 21–22.
[8] For an idea of the range of texts dealing with law produced by Marx and Engels, see M. Cain and A. Hunt, *Marx and Engels on Law*, 1979, London, Academic Press, 1979.
[9] See, e.g. Cain and Hunt, *ibid.*; C. Sumner, *Reading Ideologies: An Investigation into the Marxist Theory of Ideology and Law*, London, Academic Press, 1979; P. Hirst, *On Law and Ideology*, London, MacMillan, 1979; and B. Edelman, *Ownership of the Image*, trans. E. Kingdom, London, Routledge & Kegan Paul, 1979.

the will of your class made into a law for all".[10] The economy provides the "base" while all other social phenomena—including law—form part of the "superstructure". Changes in the "base" result inevitably in changes in the "superstructure". As the 1859 *Preface* put it:

> In the social production which men carry on they enter into definite relations that are indispensable and independent of their will; these relations of production correspond to a definite stage in the development of their material powers of production. The totality of these relations of production constitutes the economic structure of society—the real foundation, on which legal and political superstructures arise and to which definite forms of social consciousness correspond. The mode of production of material life determines the general character of the social, political and spiritual processes of life. . . . With the changes of the economic foundation the entire immense superstructure is more or less rapidly transformed.[11]

Thus, in classic Marxist theory, changes in the economic structure transform the system of law; although it is conceded by Engels that changes in the superstructure may affect the base,[12] and that law seeks a coherent statement, thus conceivably delaying the effect of changes in the economic base.[13] Engels later denied strict "vulgar" economic determinism, and in 1890 claimed that the concept of the economic base had been given such a prominent position in order to emphasize a new mode of analysis of society.[14]

As pointed out above, the contemporary re-evaluation of the role of ideology among Marxist thinkers has provided a re-assessed view of law.[15] The structuralist reading of Marx provided by the influential French philosopher Louis Althusser has profoundly influenced many of these thinkers.[16] Althusser

---

[10] K. Marx and F. Engels, *Manifesto of the Communist Party* (1848), Peking, Foreign Languages Press, 1972, p. 52.

[11] K. Marx, "Preface to Contribution to Critique of Political Economy" (1859), which can be found translated in slightly different versions (there are no material differences) in K. Marx, *Economy, Class and Social Revolution*, ed. Z.A. Jordan, London, Nelson, 1972, p. 198; K. Marx, *Early Writings*, London, Penguin, 1975, pp. 425–426; or Lord Lloyd, *Introduction to Jurisprudence*, 3rd ed., London, Stevens, 1972, p. 655. Here I have quoted Lloyd's version.

[12] Lloyd, *op. cit. supra* note 11, p. 632 n. 8.

[13] See letter F. Engels to C. Schmidt, 27 Oct., 1890, found quoted in Cain and Hunt, *op. cit. supra* note 8, pp. 56–58 at p. 57: "In a modern state, law must not only correspond to the general economic condition and be its expression, but must also be an *internally coherent* expression which does not, owing to internal conflicts, contradict itself. And in order to achieve this, the faithful reflection of economic conditions suffers increasingly."

[14] Letter F. Engels to J. Bloch, 21st–22nd Sept., 1890: "Marx and I are partly to blame for the fact that the younger people sometimes lay more stress on the economic side than is due to it. We had to emphasise the main principle vis-à-vis our adversaries, who denied it, and we had not always the time, the place or the opportunity to allow the other elements in the interaction [i.e. elements of the superstructure] to come into their rights". This can be found quoted in Marx, *Economy, Class, supra* note 11, p. 38. On these later letters of Engels, see Cain and Hunt, *op. cit. supra* note 8, pp. 48–51.

[15] See references, *supra* note 9.

[16] Althusser always rejected the name of structuralist; but there are clearly identifiable elements of structuralism in his work. See R. Keat, and J. Urry, *Social Theory as Science*, London, Routledge

rejected the base-superstructure distinction and exclusive concern with the economy, in an influential 1971 essay,[17] though he maintained that the economic structural level was still the primary determinant of the social totality. Edelman, for example, applied Althusserian Marxism in a fascinating study of French copyright law.[18] In 1977, Barry Hindess and Paul Hirst, two British Marxists, abandoned economism completely,[19] and, building on this, Hirst went on to argue that Marxism had consistently failed to understand modern aspects of property law (corporations and joint stock companies) due to certain theoretical inadequacies.[20] Hirst goes on to argue that law and legislation should be understood as processes, subject to many varied determinations, and that legislation is not a mere expression of the influences acting upon it, but a translation of these influences into something different: these influences are not merely reflected in the law, but are synthesized into something new.[21]It is obvious that Hirst's sophisticated analysis of law is far removed from vulgar Marxism.

I have stressed the varying Marxist approaches to the origins of legal change because the subtlety and sophistication of some of these approaches are often not appreciated, and "vulgar" Marxism is frequently taken as the norm.[22]

All the above views, though they differ one from the other, posit a close, necessary relationship between law and other social phenomena, arguing that changes in the wider society inevitably result in legal change. Traditional legal text books have tended to treat law as an autonomous body of knowledge which develops through an inherent logic of its own. This view is such that it merits no consideration.[23] Recently, one author has argued that law and society are frequently out of phase. Professor Alan Watson has argued:

& Kegan Paul, 1975, p. 132; M. Poster *Existential Marxism in Post War France*, Princeton, Princeton University Press, 1975, p. 147 n. 91.

[17] See Poster, *op. cit. supra* note 16, p. 347. An approachable account of Althusser's essay can be found in the introduction by P. Hirst to the translation of Edelman, *op. cit. supra*, note 9, pp. 4–6. A critique of Althusser's position will be found in, e.g., Sumner, *op. cit. supra* note 9, pp. 25–50.

[18] Edelman, *op. cit. supra* note 9.

[19] See B. Hindess and P. Hirst, *Mode of Production and Social Formation*, London, Macmillan, 1977, esp. the following significant remarks, p. 57: "Neither the persisting nor the suppression of the economic, political or cultural/ideological forms can be deduced from the concept of the social formation in which they appear. In particular, the social formation cannot be resolved into the classical Marxist formula of economic base and its political-legal and ideological-cultural superstructures. Legal and political apparatuses and cultural or ideological forms provide the forms in which the conditions of existence of determinate relations of production are secured, but they are not organised into definite structural levels which merely reflect the structure of an underlying economic base. This means that political forces and ideological forms cannot be reduced to the expressions of 'interests' determined at the level of economic class relations."

[20] Hirst, *op. cit. supra* note 9, ch. 5, pp. 96–144.

[21] *Ibid.*, pp. 113–114. The review by Kelvin Jones of Hirst's book, to be found in 8 *International Journal of the Sociology of Law* (1980), pp. 83–90, is useful.

[22] Cf. the remarks of Sumner, *op. cit. supra* note 9, p. 253.

[23] See *supra*, note 1.

> [T]hough there is a historical reason for every legal development, yet to a considerable extent law in most places at most times does not progress in a rational or responsive way, and that the divergence between law and the needs and wishes of the people involved or the will of the leaders of the people is marked. . . .[24]

> Society and ruling classes are, in practice, able to tolerate a great deal of private law which serves neither the interests of society at large or its ruling class nor the interests of anyone else.[25]

> Theories of law and society, and of legal development, tend to focus on important innovations. This leads to the impression of a very close inherent relationship between law and the society within which it operates. . . . The dynamic casual relationship between legal rules at any one time and the society within which they operate...should be given less stress and the elements of inaction, above all the force of inertia, should be upgraded.[26]

Watson's notion of what makes a law "rational" for any particular society is perhaps a difficult one; it is clear, however, that he is arguing that legal change is not necessarily the result of social change, and that social change does not inevitably result in legal change.

We may conlcude that the relationship of law to non-legal social phenomena is both uncertain and the object of many different approaches and theories. Simple mechanistic and functionalist explanations of legal change seem to be *ex facie* inadequate. This study will, it is hoped, add to our knowledge of the origins of legal change through the investigation of two societies' codifications. Roscoe Pound has stated that "Physical environment may not be ignored by jurist or legal historian".[27] Although we will not be directly discussing geography,[28] it should be remembered that both Louisiana and Quebec took their laws from European countries which had a different geography, and that such changes in geographical surroundings could make certain changes in the law desirable: for example changes in the law on water rights.

This study aims to elucidate the relationship between social and legal change by examining the choice of laws on codification, and the nature of the reforms undertaken. No attempt will be made to draw up general "laws" of legal development in the sense that Maine did.[29]

The notion of "laws" operating within society is one developed by nineteenth-century positivistic social science on analogy with the natural sciences.

---

[24] Watson, *Society*, p. 5.

[25] *Ibid.*, p. 6.

[26] *Ibid.*, p. 8, where he also states what he means by the "elements of inaction". See also A. Watson, "Comparative Law and Legal Change", 37 *Cambridge Law Journal* (1978), pp. 313–336.

[27] Pound, *op. cit. supra* note 6, p. 117.

[28] But see some of the remarks in the final part of this book on the Quebec codification, and shoreline in Louisiana.

[29] Cf. H.S. Maine's famous remark in *Ancient Law*, London, J. Murray, 1930 (first published 1861), p. 170: "the movement of the progressive societies has hitherto been a movement from Status to Contract".

Since then, the philosophers of natural science have themselves rejected the simple notion of physical phenomena being governed by objectively valid and inevitably correct laws.[30] The idea of 'hypothesis" has replaced that of "law". Hypotheses are regarded as organizing data in such a way as to make sense of them, and to provide a tool for further research, which further research could refine the hypotheses or lead to their overthrow. Thus, hypotheses and empirical research are in a relationship of mutual dependency. Theory and practice interact and change one another. If this is applied to the task on hand, we can see that the conclusions to be drawn from our study of Quebec and Louisiana should not be regarded as "laws" of legal development, but rather as hypotheses that are amenable to change in the light of further research along the lines indicated by them.[31]

Further, the particular subjects of study might be such as to render the formulation of "laws" implausible. Both Louisiana and Quebec are being studied on codification of their laws, and it might be argued that the results might be peculiar to codified systems of law,[32] or indeed might be specific to the two legal systems studied.

It is maintained, however, that some extent of generalization from the circumstances of Louisiana and Quebec is possible and valid. First, what is being sought here is not a universal theory of legal development, but the isolation and understanding of those factors influencing legal change or stasis. Second, both Louisiana and Quebec formed part of the continental civilian tradition, and the historical circumstances resulting in legal change or stasis in their particular case would seem likely to apply in other civilian codifications, if due allowance is made for particular local circumstances. Third, although codification might well provide an unparalleled opportunity for reform and rationalization of the law,[33] and although other legal systems may progress more slowly, it would seem reasonable to suppose that the factors influencing or preventing legal change, on abstraction from the particular to the more general, might well be the same in the legal systems of developed western societies.

The terms "law" and "society" have been used so far rather imprecisely; and now it is necessary to define them in a way which does not purport to be

---

[30] One thinks of the seminal work of Henri Poincarré. For one theory of scientific method, see T.S. Kuhn, *The Structure of Scientific Revolutions*, Chicago, University of Chicago Press, 1962; P. Feyerabend, *Against Method: Outline of An Anarchist Theory of Knowledge*, London, Verso,1978, may be found stimulating.

[31] On the inadequacies of "laws" of legal development, see further, e.g., Watson, *Transplants*, pp. 12–15; B.S. Jackson, *Essays in Jewish and Comparative Legal History*, Leiden, Brill, 1975, pp. 8–11. Dr. Jackson argues cogently (*ibid*, pp. 11–12) for a common pattern of growth of sophistication in legal science, as "the literary presentation is independent of the norms it describes, and would seem to provide the most promising area of law in which the search for universals may be conducted".

[32] On this, and its implications for this study, see *infra*, section "On the Suitability of Louisiana and Quebec as Objects of Study".

[33] On this, and on law reform in uncodified systems, see *infra,* section "On the Suitability of Louisiana and Quebec as Objects of Study".

comprehensive, but which is sufficient for the purposes of this study. "Law" is being used here in the limited sense of positive law: law as is to be found in the statutes, ordinances and juristic writings. Since what is being studied is the positive law applied in both jurisdictions, no questions will arise as to the nature of law as a system of norms. Law will be treated as a given, a datum of investigation. "Society" will be used to refer to those areas of human life potentially regulated by law. That is, it will refer to the interrelated and mutually dependent structures of economy, family system, land ownership, relations of employment, and general ideology that form a totality such as one could describe as "Louisiana society". This is not, perhaps, the most elegant or adequate description of society, but it provides a suitable model for investigation. As pointed out above, law is one other aspect of social life: it also is part of that totality called "society". That is, the legal provisions on a certain area of human activity may well influence human activity in that area: law also is a determining factor in society. To make this study feasible, we have to conceive of law as isolated from other social phenomena, and, given that we are concerned here with the effect upon law of other social phenomena, and that we are looking at such effect at one instant, namely of codification, such separation of law from the other aspects of society is inevitable and valid for the grounding of empirical research.

METHOD OF STUDY

A basic assumption being made here is that all legal change or legal stasis has an identifiable historical cause, and that such historical cause is rational, in the sense that it is not the result of a mere arbitrary whim on the part of legislator or jurist.

This study relies on the fact that it is possible—with some fair degree of certainty—to identify the provisions considered for inclusion in the codes of Louisiana and Quebec. Further, it is also possible to build up a picture of the pre-codification law in both societies. Hence, one can compare the reformed law (the code) with the pre-code law, and with the range of options considered by the redactors for inclusion in the code. Thus, trends and patterns in the reform of the law may be identified, and related to the wider society; and the factors influencing the redactors—the efficient causes of legal change—may be identified. The Quebec redactors themselves left useful indications of motives in some cases of changes or stasis.

In Quebec, the redactors left indications of the sources considered,[34] while for Louisiana, we can be fairly certain that the redactors considered those references found in the de la Vergne volume,[35] the Code Napoléon and its *projet*, and the provisions traced by Batiza (whether or not they are sources).[36] We can be certain of this because the 1808 Digest is demonstrably composed of a mélange of these materials: Castilian law, French customary law, and French codified law.

In the next chapter, there will be a description of Quebec and Louisiana societies. In the third chapter, the juridical culture of both societies will be described, paying close attention to the circumstances surrounding codification, and the legal history of both societies. The second part of the work will be devoted to an analysis of the codes' provisions on family and employment, relating these provisions to the pre-codification law and the wider society, explaining the circumstances which have resulted in legal change or legal stasis, and the reasons behind the selection and rejection of provisions. The third part of the work will be devoted to explaining in more general terms the interrelation of law and other social phenomena in Quebec and Louisiana, paying attention to its wider and more general implications, and to dealing with incidental problems relating to the history of codification in both countries, the nature of codification itself and the role of lawmakers.

THE SUITABILITY OF LOUISIANA AND QUEBEC AS SUBJECTS OF STUDY

Rich Juridical Culture

As Chapter 3 will make more apparent, the juridical culture of both Louisiana and Quebec was particularly rich. Both formed part of the learned European continental civilian tradition, while being, at the time of their respective codifications, open to influence from Anglo-American common law. This background meant that on codification, the codifiers would have been able to draw on wide and varied sources for inspiration, and for selecting rules. Indeed, as pointed out above, it is clear that in both codifications, there was a great deal of conscious

---

[34] See the *Reports of the Commissioners Appointed to Codify the Laws of Lower Canada in Civil Matters*. I have used the 2nd edition by Desbarats, Quebec, 1865, published in 3 volumes: volume I contains the first, second and third Reports, volume II, the fourth and fifth, and volume III, the sixth, seventh and supplementary. As explained in the list of abbreviations, they will be cited by report and page, e.g.: *Second Report*, p. 33. For the Commissioners' citations of sources consulted, I will use the versions in McCord's 1867 edition of the Code, as they are more accurate than those in the 2nd ed. of the *Reports*: see McCord, Preface, pp. iii–iv.

[35] On the nature of this volume see *infra*, chaps. 3 and 6.

[36] See Batiza, *Sources*, Appendices A, B and C. On the significance of Batiza's work, see *infra*, chaps. 3 and 6.

"transplantation" of rules:[37] that is, both sets of redactors always had the provisions of other jurisdictions in mind and deliberately accepted or rejected them.

Societies in Transition

Quebec's law was codified in 1866; that of Louisiana in 1808. As will be shown in chapter two, at the period of their respective codifications, both societies were in the process of a transformation. Both societies were radically different from those of the period and countries from where they drew their laws. There had been material and ideological changes in the structure of the economy and the family. Both societies were developing along the model of laissez-faire liberalism. Quebec and Louisiana are thus very suitable subjects of study, since their laws were transplanted from different societies and conditions and since their own societies were in a period of transition. These changes ought to emphasize the relationship between legal change and other social change and help point out the nature of that relationship and the factors promoting and preventing legal change.

The Validity of Generalizations from Quebec and Louisiana

We have already touched on the question of whether or not the results of our investigation of change and stasis in the codifications of Louisiana and Quebec could form the basis of valid generalizations about factors influencing legal change or whether the results would be too specific to the two societies.[38] From what has been said above, it must be accepted that generalization from the two codifications would be valid for other early to mid-nineteenth-century codifications, and probably law reform of that period generally.

There are, however, two separate problems. First, there is the possible problem that the period since the promulgation of the Quebec code has seen a burgeoning of law dealing with welfare, labour and tax.[39] Much of the law in these areas could be argued to be of a different nature from that studied here, such law being, in interventionist states, the result of conscious and deliberate governmental planning on the basis of carefully formulated social and economic policies. In the two codifications we are studying, to reform or not to reform the law, to decide what the law already was, and to select suitable provisions, was largely left to the discretion of the two sets of redactors. Such an argument, therefore, could have considerable force. Two points fail to be made. As regards those forms of law outlined above considered as typical of the interventionist state, one can say that because such laws are planned by governments, and are

---

[37] On this notion of "legal transplant", see Watson, *Transplants*, generally, and especially, pp. 6–9; 19–20; 21–30; 95–101; 102–106.

[38] See *supra*, text at notes 31–33.

[39] R. David in "The Civil Code in France Today", 34 *La. L. Rev.* (1974–1975), pp. 907–919 at pp. 913–919 acknowledges the growth of other areas of the law in a similar fashion.

the result of policy decisions, their origins and causes are more readily ascertainable than those of reforms in the traditional private law fields. This said, I would not argue that the results, as regards the influences on legal development, obtained from this study, should be applied to modern welfare-type law. In this study, however, we are dealing with traditional private law, which is still the paradigm for law in general,[40] and hence generalizations from this study could still be valid for traditional private law, as will be argued next.

Second, it could be argued that, with the growth of the modern interventionist state, reform in even the traditional areas of private law has become a matter of conscious governmental planning, and that this means that the 1808 and 1866 Louisianan and Quebec experiences can tell us nothing relevant about modern law. Again, this is an argument with some force. This argument loses some of its cogency, however, if the following points are considered. First, although the two sets of redactors appear to have been given considerable latitude in their work, it should be recalled that their codes had to be approved by their legislatures. This means that there was an opportunity for executive or legislative opposition to provisions.[41] The complex nature of a civil code would make it a very difficult piece of legislation to scrutinize; but the Quebec redactors, in their comprehensive *Reports*, indicated major changes in the substantive law. Further, any provision of a radically unacceptable nature in either of the two codes undoubtedly would have led to their rejection: hence, although the actions of the redactors were generally uncontrolled, the fact that the codes would have to be passed would cause the redactors to modify their work to be acceptable, had they the desire to change the law drastically in an unacceptable way (which is unlikely given the structure of the society within which the redactors operated and their own place within that society).[42] The position is similar in modern reform of uncontroversial areas of the law: reform is a task handed to specialists, such as the Law Commissions in England and Scotland. Such specialist bodies, as well as considering "modernization", are concerned with general principle, over-all coherence, tradition, and those considerations which Professor Friedman has called "aesthetic".[43] Although even scholarly law reformers are concerned with modernizing the law, as were the Quebec and Louisiana

---

[40] B. Audit in "Recent Revisions of the French Civil Code", 38 *La. L. Rev.* (1978–1979) pp. 747–804, remarks at p. 748: "Certainly in a liberal society this branch of the law is the fundamental one, and this accounts for the symbolic and practical importance of the code which states its rules". He goes on to remark that "the evolution of social and economic conditions in those same societies since the enactment of the codes has caused in each of them a decline in the relative importance of civil law and hence of the civil code". The same argument as used above applies here. He later (*ibid.*, p. 749) reasserts, however, that "one could state rightly that the civil law contained in the code constituted the essential part of private law".

[41] For example, some trifling reforms the C.Q. redactors introduced as to who should be able to convoke family councils were rejected.

[42] See *infra*, chaps. 3, 6–8.

[43] Friedman, *op. cit. supra* note 3, p. 271.

redactors, modern law reform is not always guided by social purposes and practical functions.[44]

It would then be acceptable to generalize from the experience of Louisiana and Quebec, at least as regards traditional private law. It should be borne in mind, however, as pointed out above, that we are not seeking to establish universal rules of legal development: what we are concerned with is exploring the reasoning behind stasis and reform in the two codifications to investigate the nature of the relationship between social change and legal change. Hence, the reasons behind the choice of law on codification in Louisiana and Quebec, while indicating the factors influential on legal change, are important in demonstrating the multiplicity of influences on law reform, and the importance of lawmakers as the mediators between law and the wider social structure. What should be clear is that, in selecting Louisiana and Quebec for investigation, we are not choosing two jurisdictions likely to be in any relevant way exceptional.

Advantages of Studying a Codified System

Before discussing the advantages of studying a codified system, it is necessary to define "code" and "codification". Here certain key attributes common to codes will be pointed out,[45] drawing on knowledge of several civilian codes and abstracting from them important common features. The definition of code is also important because there is at present a dispute over the exact nature of the 1808 Digest of the Territory of Orleans (the Louisiana Code of 1808). From the definition given here, it will be possible later to assess the arguments of those who reject the 1808 Digest as not being a true "code".[46]

The term "code" has never had an exact and specific meaning—its meaning has varied in time and place. The term, or one of its variants, has been utilized to refer to compilations of law from Roman times onwards; but the nature, content and form of the compilations has varied.[47] From the early nineteenth century, however, the term "code" has had a particular meaning in civil law countries. This particular meaning originates in the Code Napoléon,[48] the promulgation of

---

[44] On the Law Commissions, see further Watson, *Transplants*, pp. 91–92; Watson, *Society*, pp. 102–104. Friedman, *op. cit. supra* note 3, remarks at p. 270: "As a general rule, revisers of law do not pay much attention to impact. They more or less assume that 'better' laws will have serious results in the world of behavior."

[45] The literature on codification is vast, and there will be no attempt here to review it or refer to it *en masse*.

[46] On this, see *infra*, chap. 3, section "The 1808 Redaction: 'Digest' or 'Code'?", and chap. 6.

[47] See generally J. Vanderlinden, *Le concept de code en Europe occidentale du XIIe au XIXe siècle: essai de définition*, Brussels, Éditions de l'Institut de sociologie de l'Université Libre de Bruxelles, 1967, who argues that a common concept can be shown for the period to be studied. Nevertheless there was great variance in both form and substance between the codes he examined. See *ibid.*, pp. 22–46, for an account of different examples of codes.

[48] When promulgated in 1804, it was of course called the *Code civil des français*. Nevertheless, for convenience, I will generally refer to it as the Code Napoléon, following contemporary usage in France where the term Code Napoléon is used to refer to the original code before revision.

which provided a new paradigm for a code. The coining of the neologisms "codification", "codify", and "codifier" by Jeremy Bentham gave linguistic expression to the paradigm set by the French code and those that followed it.[49]

Certain features of this new model of code can be picked out to demonstrate what was meant by it. Firstly, codes are legislative enactments—positive law *par excellence*. Secondly they cover a specific area of the law. Thirdly, they aim to cover that area as comprehensively as possible, though, of course, this aim is impossible to fulfill, codifiers being neither clairvoyant nor infallible. Codes may approach perfection; they never achieve it. Fourthly, codes are arranged according to some logical system. Fifthly, they approach lucid, coherent expression as far as possible. Some have been inclined to emphasize that codes provide "a fresh start"; and, of course, they do in so far as they provide a reform and restatement of the law designed, through legislation, to replace the old law. Codes, however, are largely built out of old material, which is, of course, reformed in the process of codification. Thus, the German code would have been impossible without the work of the Pandectists, while the Code Napoléon was constructed out of the old law, and that of the revolutionary period and the Directorate. It clearly can be seen that codes attempt rationalization of the law. They are the ultimate in rationality in a Weberian sense, in that they provide a logical system of rules that stand out with the legal process, and on which the actors in the legal process can rely for decisions.[50]

Having given a working definition by selecting the key elements of a code, it is appropriate to refine it further by discovering the functions that can be served by codification. It may be used: 1) to unify the law; 2) to rejuvenate the law by removing illogicalities and inconsistencies and by introducing new solutions if thought necessary. These two functions can be called unification and modernization, and both arise out of a tendency towards rationalization.[51] From

---

[49] See J. Vanderlinden, "Code et codification dans la pensée de Jeremy Bentham", 32 *Tijdschrift voor Rechtsgeschiedenis* (1964), pp. 45–78, esp. at p. 46. Bentham himself wrote, "For characterising an object which not only is new, but is designed to be presented as such, a word as plainly new as the object itself is meant to be represented as being is much more convenient than any old word taken from the old-established stock of words belonging to the language". See G. Wallas, "Notes on Jeremy Bentham's attitude to word Creation", in L. Pearsall Smith et al., *Needed Words etc.*, Society for Pure English, Tract no. XXXI, Oxford, Clarendon Press, 1928, pp. 333–334.

[50] Weber was not, of course, primarily concerned with the *substance* of the law as we are here. He was concerned with the legal process. Yet, it is clear that he regarded codification as part of the tendency towards rationalization of the law in its social operation. He also identified this tendency towards rationalization with the growth of European capitalism. This gave him problems when he considered unmodified English law—the law of a highly developed capitalist state. See on this, D.W. Trubek, "Max Weber and the Rise of Capitalism", 3 *Wisconsin Law Review* (1972), pp. 720–753 at p. 747. On Weber's concept of rationality, see R. Bendix, *Max Weber: An Intellectual Portrait*, London, Methuen, 1966, ch. 12.

[51] On what I have called functions, see further, R. Pound, "Codification in Anglo-American Law", in B. Schwarz (ed.), *The Code Napoleon and the Common Law World*, New York, New York University Press, 1966, pp. 267–297 at p. 278; and H.R. Hahlo, "Here lies the Common Law: Rest in Peace", 30 *Modern Law Review* (1967), pp. 241–259 at pp. 243–244. Doubtless other functions could be identified; these two seem the most important. Hahlo mentions protection of a legal

these two functions, one can deduce that the process of codification involves a review of the substance of the law as well as its formal rearrangement. This review allows a re-appraisal of the law when faced with changing circumstances. This re-appraisal of the law combined with the modernization function means that, in the process of codification, choices are constantly being made between competing provisions—whether of differing jurisdictions in unifying the law, or of doctrinal views in settling doubtful points, or of competing sources if foreign law or juristic writings have been referred to in order to modernize. Ferdinand Stone stated it thus:

> Codification as a method demands that stock be taken of existing legal materials and so forces an examination not only of those ideas existing in the State that is engaged in codification but also in all other civilized States.[52]

Other writers have also stressed the importance of examining foreign laws in codifying with a view to a transplant.[53]

From all this, one can see that the fact that Louisiana and Quebec have civil codes is very useful for this study, since codification allows re-assessment of the law, its reform and free transplantation of law. Thus, the historical causes of legal change ought to be more easily identifiable, since wholesale legal reform would be undertaken, of necessity, with codification. The process of reform has been speeded up, and made to cover a substantial area of law, while the codifiers had to make rational choices between possible provisions.

The positivistic attitude in which a code is drawn up aids this study in so far as codifiers thought it possible to formulate definitive rules to guide and reflect social life. They did not conceive of rules functioning in an unintended way. Here we are concerned with the views of the codifiers and the factors which would influence them in their redaction of their respective civil codes, in order to discover the historical causes of legal change or stasis. The codifiers' belief in positive law and the possibility of their reform of the law in line with the influence on them enables us to avoid three problems in assessing the relationship between written law and other social phenomena. First, as Karl Renner points out,[54] a rule of law can remain the same in formulation, but, due to changes (or differences in the case of a transplant) in the social and economic

---

system against the invasion of foreign rules, and cites, as an instance of this, Quebec, on this see *infra*, chap. 3, "Quebec".

[52] F. Stone, "A Primer on Codification", 29 *Tul. L. Rev.* (1954–1955), pp. 303–310 at p. 307.

[53] See Audit, *op. cit. supra* note 40, pp. 781–783; Léon Julliot de la Morandière, "Preliminary Report of the Civil Code Reform Commission of France", 16 *La. L. Rev.* (1955–1956), pp. 1–56 at p. 55; C.J. Morrow "An Approach to the Revision of the Louisiana Civil Code", 10 *La. L. Rev.* (1949–1950), pp. 59–72 at pp. 64 and 66. None of these writers, of course, uses the term "transplant".

[54] See K. Renner, *Institutions of Private Law*, trans. A. Schwarzschild, London, Routledge & Kegan Paul, 1949, generally and esp. pp. 74–77. Note *ibid.*, p. 75: "A legal institution is a composite of norms. If in the change of economic systems it has remained constant but its functions have either increased or diminished, changed or disappeared, then we speak of a change in the functions."

structure, operate in a totally different way. This obviously poses problems in deciding whether for example, a rule from fourteenth-century Castile, derived from Castilian social life is apt for nineteenth-century Louisiana. In this study, however, we can avoid this problem because we are concerned with the choice made by the codifiers, not with how the rules functioned after codification, but why the codifiers in 1808 or 1866 chose any particular rule.[55] Second, no written rule is ever comprehensive. New fact-situations constantly arise which stretch the interpretation of a verbally formulated rule, Furthermore, since rules are stated in general terms, they inevitably have a penumbra of vagueness, or, in Hartian terms, an inherently "open texture".[56] Together, the penumbra of vagueness and the development of new fact situations allow for the development of the law away from its original positive statement.[57] This means that it would be difficult to relate the authoritative statement (article of a code) to social reality, because the rule as applied would be rather different. Since, however, we are here studying law at codification, and its relationship to fact situations at that time and before further development, we can avoid this problem. Third, studying codification enables us to avoid the problem of legal interpretation. Interpretation of an original rule by subsequent jurists, judges and the like can cause the rule to come to mean something totally different from its original formulation.[58] Similarly, Professor Sacco has pointed out that what is basically the same provision can be interpreted differently in different countries.[59] This problem of interpretation of an article of a code away from its obvious meaning does not affect us in this study, because we are examining the provisions at the time of codification, before interpretation could take place, and we can safely assume that the codifiers meant the provisions they chose to bear their obvious meaning.

All the above indicates why law at the time of codification is particularly appropriate for this study. The study itself will produce some further understanding of the *process* of codification. Certain points relating to the nature of codes will be raised later in chapter three.

---

[55] Cf. Watson, *Transplants*, pp. 19–20.

[56] H.L.A. Hart, *The Concept of Law*, Oxford, Clarendon Press, 1961, p. 120 and pp. 122–124.

[57] See H.L.A. Hart, "Positivism and the Separation of Law and Morals", 71 *Harvard Law Review* (1958), pp. 606–612 at p. 612.

[58] One thinks especially of rabbinical interpretation of, for example, the *lex talionis* of Exodus 21.24 to mean damages. For an amusing but profound example of such interpretation by Rabbi Jose ben Taddai, see D. Daube, *Civil Disobedience in Antiquity*, Edinburgh, Edinburgh University Press, 1972, p. ix.

[59] R. Sacco, "Definitions savantes et droit appliqué dans les systèmes Roman-istes", 17 *R.I.D.C.* (1965), pp. 827–837 *passim*.

2

INTRODUCTION TO LOUISIANA AND QUEBEC

> When you meet people who tell you that climate has no influence on the character of peoples, assure them that they are mistaken. We have seen the French of Canada: they are a tranquil, moral, religious people. We are leaving in Louisiana other Frenchmen: restless, dissolute, lax in all things. Between them are fifteen degrees of latitude, which we truly think the best reason that can be given for the difference.[1]

Thus wrote Alexis de Tocqueville in 1832, reflecting a traditional view of the influence of climate on behaviour.[2] In this chapter we will examine economic and social life in Louisiana and Quebec at their periods of codification. The nature of the family in history and the master servant relationship will be examined more rigorously in chapters four and five: this chapter is more of an impressionistic survey.

LOUISIANA

The Mississippi river system dominated Louisiana. It provided the main commercial artery and means of transport.[3] The river was central to the economy as it carried trade from the western states and territories of the U.S.A., and was the route of all Louisiana's exports and imports. Further, all settlement was

---

[1] Letter A. de Tocqueville to E. de Chabrol, 16 Jan. 1832, found quoted in G.W. Pierson, *Tocqueville and Beaumont in America*, New York, Oxford University Press, 1938, p. 632.

[2] See C. de Montesquieu, *The Spirit of the Laws*, trans. by T. Nugent, New York, Hafner, 1949, ch. XIV: "Of Laws in Relation to the Nature of the Climate". For a discussion of Montesquieu's views on climate, see *The Spirit of the Laws: A Compendium*, ed. by D.W. Carrithers, Berkeley, University of California Press, 1977, Introduction, pp. 44–51. See also *ibid.*, pp. 417–418.

[3] Travelling upriver was by no means as easy as travelling down: far more boats came downstream to New Orleans than ever travelled back up. East-west traffic was a problem, as the river-system flowed north to south. On the problems of transport and the flow of streams, see F.B. Kniffen, *Louisiana: Its Land and People*, Baton Rouge, Louisiana State University Press, 1968, p. 142. On the smaller number of boats sailing upstream, see A.P. Whitaker, *The Mississippi Question, 1795–1803: A Study in Trade, Politics and Diplomacy*, American Historical Association, New York, D. Appleton-Century Co., 1934, p. 141.

along the banks of the river, the farms being protected from inundation by the augmentation of the natural levees by artificial ones.[4]

Towards the end of the period of Spanish rule in Louisiana, two changes of major importance took place in the economic system of the colony:[5] the first was the development of New Orleans as the natural entrepôt of the American west, and the second, the development of the cotton and sugar industries in Louisiana.

The westward spread of U.S. citizens into Kentucky, Tennessee and Ohio (the area then called the Northwest Territory)[6] stimulated the growth of New Orleans as an entrepôt during Spanish rule. The settlers in these areas were mainly farmers, who, if they wished to rise above the level of subsistence farming, had to get their goods quickly to market: however, the spread west meant that the markets and ports in the east were farther away.[7] Before the railways, the simplest mode of transport was by water; there was, however, no eastwards river system these farmers could utilise, and to transport goods to market overland would have been prohibitively expensive. The water system of the Mississippi penetrated the whole area, however, and the obvious solution to the problem facing the farmers was to transport their goods to market through New Orleans.[8] Berquin-Duvallon in 1802 described New Orleans as:

> destined by nature to become one of the principal cities of North America, and perhaps the most important place of commerce in the new world, if it can only maintain the incalculable advantage of being the sole *entrepôt* and central point of a country almost flat, immense in its extent, of which the Mississippi is the great receptacle of its produce, and where the soil is fertile, the climate generally salubrious, and the population increasing beyond all former example.[9]

For various reasons, mainly the result of the war in Europe during the 1790s, the Spanish authorities tolerated the U.S. to New Orleans trade.[10] In the 1790s, Spain wished peace with France, while also by placating the United

---

[4] Spanish regulations required the building of levees: see article 3 of the regulations of Intendant Morales, 1799, quoted in F.P. Burns, "The Spanish Land Laws of Louisiana", 11 *La. Hist. Quar.* (1928), pp. 557–558 at p. 570. On the levees generally see, Kniffen, *op. cit. supra* note 3, pp. 45–46, p. 128.

[5] See J. G. Clark, *New Orleans 1718–1812: An Economic History*, Baton Rouge, Louisiana State University Press, 1970, relevant chapters for an account of the early economy.

[6] See Whitaker, *op. cit. supra* note 3, pp. 3–15.

[7] A glance at any map of the area will reveal the nature of the problem. The map in Whitaker, *op. cit. supra* note 3, facing p. 3 may be consulted conveniently.

[8] Clark, *op. cit. supra* note 5, p. 212, concludes: "Farmers east of Pittsburgh found it cheaper to ship their produce to market via New Orleans than to forward it to Philadelphia."

[9] See [P. L.Berquin-Duvallon], *Travels in Louisiana and the Floridas in the year 1802, Giving a Correct Picture of those Countries*, trans by J. Davis, New York, I. Riley, 1806, pp. 35–36. Berquin-Duvallon was from St. Domingue, and came to Louisiana fleeing the uprisings. One needs only to read his work to realise he is a notable "Louisianaphobe", and his judgments on the inhabitants unreliable.

[10] See C.R. Arena, "Philadelphia-Spanish New Orleans Trade in the 1790s", 2 *La. Hist.* (1961), pp. 429–445.

States, wanting to prevent an Anglo-American attack on Louisiana: this was achieved in 1795 by the Treaty of San Lorenzo (Pinckney's Treaty), which granted to the Americans free navigation of the Mississippi, and the privilege of depositing goods at New Orleans and re-exporting them without payment of duty. This Treaty basically granted legality to a trade that had been carried on for a number of years.[11] Thus, from the last decade of the eighteenth century, up to 1803, there was a large volume of American trade through New Orleans.

> The productions of Louisiana are—sugar, cotton, indigo, rice, furs and peltry, lumber, tar, pitch, lead, flour, horses and cattle. Population alone is wanting to multiply them to an astonishing degree.[12]

Thus said an 1803 United States' pamphlet. During the 1790s, there was a shift in the staple crops produced in Louisiana. Up to this period, indigo had been an important staple, but in the 1790s, a series of crop failures so set back its production, that Berquin-Duvallon could remark in 1802 that "[i]ndigo, within 20 years, has been generally abandoned in Louisiana".[13] Sugar and cotton became the important staples. The climate of Louisiana suited cotton production, and the invention in this period of the cotton gin made large scale commercial production feasible.[14] It was, however, sugar production to which plantation owners changed after the failure of the indigo crops. For the first time sugar cane production was successful in Louisiana. The war and revolution in the West Indies, by disrupting production there, left open the lucrative European market for Louisiana sugar. This strife also raised the price of sugar, and caused many experienced sugar planters to emigrate from the West Indies to Louisiana.[15]

During this same period, Americans came to dominate economic life in Louisiana. Louisiana had always been underpopulated, and the Spanish government encouraged Americans to settle.[16] The influence of these anglophone subjects of Spain was increased by the constant presence of U.S. citizens in Louisiana on business.[17] The war in Europe again was effective in bringing Louisiana within the U.S. sphere of economic interest.[18] In 1796 Spain went to war against Britain. At sea, Spain was not successful, and, to prevent her colonies collapsing, she

---

[11] See Clark, *op. cit. supra* note 5, pp. 205–212, and for an excellent, clear account, see Whitaker, *op. cit. supra* note 3, pp. 79–97.
[12] *An Account of Louisiana, Being an Abstract of Documents, in the Offices of the Departments of State, and of the Treasury*, Philadelphia, William Duane, 1803, p. 39.
[13] Berquin-Duvallon, *op. cit. supra* note 9, p. 131. On the failure of the indigo crops see Clark, *op. cit. supra* note 5, pp. 187–188.
[14] For an account of this industry's growth, see Clark, *op. cit. supra* note 5, p. 217.
[15] See Berquin-Duvallon, *op. cit. supra* note 9, pp. 128–131. See also, Clark, *op. cit. supra* note 5, pp. 217–218 and Whitaker, *op. cit. supra* note 3, pp. 131–132.
[16] See Clark, *op. cit. supra* note 5, p. 207, and C.R. Arena, "Landholding and Political Power in Spanish Louisiana", 38 *La. Hist. Quar.* (1955), pp. 23–39 at pp. 24–25.
[17] Whitaker, *op. cit. supra* note 3, pp. 141–142 also points out that during this period many of the men on the flat boats bringing produce down from the west stayed behind in New Orleans on the completion of the journey.
[18] See *supra*, text at notes 6–11.

authorised neutral vessels to carry virtually all goods to Spanish-American ports, and to load all goods bar specie. The U.S.A. was in fact the only neutral country capable of acting on this authorisation. Clark points out that:

> Implementation of the territorial and commercial clauses of Pinckney's treaty and the exigencies of war tightened the dependence of New Orleans upon the United States. Settlers on the east bank of the Mississippi and north of the 31st parallel, largely Anglo-Saxon, were now American citizens. American ships were admitted legally to the river and could dispose of goods and obtain cargoes at the deposit without the payment of any duties; or they could trade directly with merchants in New Orleans as a result of the neutral shipping regulations with duties assessed under prior regulations. Far more than 50 per cent of the vessels entering the port of New Orleans carried the American flag while other vessels, under Spanish registry, were owned by Americans.[19]

The U.S. control of Louisiana's trade continued until its acquisition of the territory in 1803, despite Spanish attempts in 1799 and 1800 to reduce the privileges granted,[20] and the suspension of the right of deposit in October, 1802.[21] By the time of the transfer of Louisiana to the United States, American control of Louisiana's trade was complete. Berquin-Duvallon remarked in 1802:

> Relative to what concerns the commerce of the colony, I shall observe, . . . that, from the beginning of the maritime war, which has lately terminated, that is, about nine years, this commerce has been entirely in the hands of the Americans, who have shared the profits with the English, to whom they are factors or agents.[22]

As Clark points out, the Purchase merely gave political legitimacy to economic fact.[23]

During the period 1803 to 1808, the economic foundation of Louisianian society remained the same, sugar and cotton, produced by slave labour, still being the staple crops of the territory. The farmers in the western lands of the United States produced crops, especially grain, which were exported through New Orleans and which, by their importation into the territory, supported Louisiana's plantation economy.[24] There were two main influences on the territory's economic life in this period. First, the new century was to be dominated by the ideals of liberal capitalism: "The new century, in New Orleans as

---

[19] Clark, *op. cit. supra* note 5, p. 242.
[20] *Ibid.*
[21] Whitaker, *op. cit. supra* note 3, pp. 189–199; Clark, *op. cit. supra* note 5, p. 246.
[22] Berquin-Duvallon, *op. cit. supra* note 9, p. 142.
[23] Clark, *op. cit. supra* note 5, p. 248: "the great number of American vessels . . . in New Orleans adequately symbolised that the city functioned within the American economic sphere of influence and that the Louisiana Purchase, in a sense, merely added political legitimacy to economic facts operative for over a decade."
[24] For an account of the grain trade at this period, see W.F. Galpin, "The Grain Trade of New Orleans, 1814–1814", 14 *Miss. Vall. Hist. Rev.* (1928), pp. 496–507.

well New York and Liverpool, was the century of the bourgeoisie."[25] Second, with United States' control of the territory, and with economic affairs being mainly in the hands of Americans, their notions of how the economy ought to be run were implemented.

The Americans seem to have had a more entrepreneurial attitude than the Creoles; or, at least, their government did not discourage such an attitude. An obvious example of this is found in land speculation. Both the Spanish and French administrations did their utmost to prevent land speculation, the latter going so far as to annul and concessions made to those who speculated in land.[26] After the Louisiana Purchase, however, there was widespread speculation in land, many Americans taking advantage of the confusion over the status of Spanish land grants in order to make substantial profits.[27] It is clear that, while the Spanish government carefully regulated the market,[28] in the first decade of American sovereignty, principles of free enterprise were applied.[29] The total change wrought in the mechanisms of the Louisianian economy is conveyed by the following two quotations from Clark's standard work on Louisianian economic history. During the colonial period in New Orleans the Cabildo (city council) regulated the market:

> . . . through the application of methods derived from the medieval city. Such concepts as fair price, reasonable profit, consumer access to the market place, purity in products, accuracy and standardization of weights and measures, and prohibitions against engrossment or forestalling were all applied in the name of public welfare. Climaxing during the Spanish period, the role of the city government in these matters then declined in the face of contradictory concepts of the market place introduced by the Americans and current in other cities throughout the United States.[30]

Clark also remarks that:

> While the Spanish had acted leniently toward Louisiana in formulating economic policy, the regulation of economic and political affairs in New Orleans was a fact of life. . . . Relative to the past, American sovereignty meant a free economy in New Orleans and the territory. . . .[31]

---

[25] Clark, *op. cit. supra* note 5, p. 271.
[26] C.R. Arena, "Land Settlement Policies and Practices in Spanish Louisiana", in J.F. McDermott (ed.), *The Spanish in the Mississippi Valley*, Urbana, University of Illinois Press, 1974, pp. 51–60 at p. 54.
[27] See H.L. Coles, "The Confirmation of Foreign Land Titles in Louisiana", 38 *La. Hist. Quar.* (1955), pp. 1–22 at pp. 11–12.
[28] Arena, *op. cit. supra* note 26, p. 59; J.G. Clark, "The Role of the City Government in the Economic Development of New Orleans: Cabildo and City Council, 1783–1812", in McDermott (ed.), *op. cit. supra* note 26, pp. 133–148 at p. 140.
[29] See Clark, *op. cit. supra* note 28, pp. 144–145.
[30] Clark, *op. cit. supra* note 5, p. 261.
[31] *Ibid.*, p. 281.

He then concludes that "the days of the fair price and regulated market place were numbered".[32]

It may be seen that through the period of the Louisiana purchase and onwards, with the ever-increasing United States' influence in Louisiana, the organisation of the market (and hence of economic affairs generally) altered from careful regulation based on notions of fair price and fair profit towards a free market and the maximisation of profits. Thus, one may say that there is a definite trend in the organisation of economic affairs towards the ideal of economic liberalism. It is perhaps not insignificant that copies of Adam Smith's *The Wealth of Nations* were in circulation in Louisiana in this period.[33]

In the early territorial period, manufacturing industry in Louisiana was negligible.[34] In 1802, Berquin-Duvallon stated that in the suburbs of New Orleans there were two cotton mills and a sugar bake-house.[35] The 1803 *Account of Louisiana* likewise mentions some manufacturing establishments; but it should be noted that much of the manufacturing was of necessities for consumption within the territory.[36] Clearly, industrialisation had not taken place; there was no production of goods in bulk for export for profit. It should be noted that those manufacturing establishments that there were tended to employ slave labour.[37] There was, therefore, little opportunity for the employment of a class of wage labourers.[38]

So far it has been argued that there was an identifiable trend in Louisiana from regulation of the market towards the ideals of liberal economics. The most important units of production in the territory, the plantations were dependent on slave labour. The mercantile houses conformed to the ideals of liberal capitalism. Some authors have been inclined to see a conflict between the slave-owning planters as New World "aristocrats", and the merchants as "bourgeois". Such a distinction between the planters and merchants is false, and based (one suspects)

---

[32] *Ibid.*, p. 283.

[33] See R.P. McCutcheon, "Books and Booksellers in New Orleans, 1730–1830", 20 *La. Hist. Quar.* (1937), pp. 606–618, esp. at pp. 612, 615, and 618. This article is useful for gaining an impression of the intellectual climate of Louisiana. See the same author's, "Libraries in New Orleans 1771–1833", 20 *La. Hist. Quar.* (1937), pp. 152–155. Moreau Lislet was involved in some of the library projects. Note that the influential reviews of the period were available. Recently, of course, there have been doubts thrown on Smith's role as the apostle of laissez-faire economics, and it has been alleged that Smith's *œuvre*, if looked at as a whole, belies the position attributed to him by nineteenth-century economic liberalism. See D. Winch, *Adam Smith's Politics. An Essay in Historiographic Revision*, Cambridge, University Press, 1978, pp. 13–14; 80–81 etc. for a discussion of this and for reference to other writers who have developed the new view of Smith's work. What is relevant, of course, as regards Smith's influence, is what *others* thought of his work. P. Stein, "Adam Smith's Jurisprudence-Between Morality and Economics", 64 *Cornell Law Review* (1979), pp. 621–638, may be found useful.

[34] See Clark, *op. cit. supra* note 5, p. 269.

[35] Berquin-Duvallon, *op. cit. supra* note 9, p. 32.

[36] See *Account of Louisiana*, *supra* note 12, pp. 41–42.

[37] Clark, *op. cit. supra* note 5, p. 269 states: "Slaves were . . . employed by their owners or as hired hands in the few manufacturing establishments located in or near the city."

[38] *Ibid.*: "Opportunities for employment in New Orleans for the unskilled or semi-skilled free worker were restricted by the lack of an industrial base and by the presence of slavery."

on the naive view that slavery is incompatible with liberal capitalism.[39] For the planters, as for the merchants, "their wealth was gained through the application of bourgeois-capitalist standards, ideals and methods of operation".[40] The merchants and planters were often the same people. Related to this are the arguments of Professor Mitchell Franklin, who posits an ideological conflict between the slave-owners supporting the "mediaeval Spanish law" and the liberals supporting the Code Napoléon. He appears to argue that slavery was the product of mediaeval feudalism (whatever he exactly means by this term) in Louisiana, the result of Talleyrand's "penchant hispanophile".[41] This is unconvincing, Clark and Dargo (who merely follows Clark) argue that slavery was an economic necessity in Louisiana, on the grounds that a primary cause of the economic failure of French Louisiana was the lack of slaves.[42] They may be correct that slavery was an economic necessity, but their argument on the basis of French colonial Louisiana is not convincing, as, by the early nineteenth century, material circumstances might well have changed. What is relevant, however, is that Louisianians regarded slavery as necessary for the economic survival of the territory.[43] Slaves were regarded by their owners as capital investments in bourgeois economic terms. The desire for the preservation of slavery was the result of supposed or actual economic necessity, and had nothing to do with the machinations of Talleyrand, as Franklin suggests but inadequately demonstrates.[44] Slavery and support for slavery do not indicate what Franklin would call a "feudal" mentality. Similarly, there may have been conflict between merchants and planters over specific issues; but this conflict was never on an ideological level.

The ideology of the plantation owners and business community was that of liberal capitalism, and, although there were few industrial enterprises, production being primarily agricultural, the territorial period saw the setting up of the

---

[39] For an argument on the relation between slavery and economic formation, see Orlando Patterson, "On Slavery and Slave Formations", 117 *New Left Review* (1979), pp. 31–67.

[40] Clark, *op. cit. supra* note 5, p. 270.

[41] See generally, Franklin, "Expulsion", "Eighteenth Brumaire", and "Existential Force".

[42] Clark, *op. cit. supra* note 5, pp. 128–129, 134–135 and 317–318; Dargo, *Jefferson's Louisiana*, p. 30 and p. 190 n. 33.

[43] E. Mazureau, a leading New Orleans attorney (see *infra* note 47), in reply to Tocqueville's question whether it would be possible for whites to cultivate the land without slaves, said that he did not think so. He stated that, like Tocqueville, he himself had come from Europe opposed to slavery, but had changed his mind, because he did not think that Europeans could work in the fields exposed to the Louisiana sun, and that to do so would risk death, or would permit so little work to be done as to be uneconomic: Pierson, *op. cit. supra*, note 1, p. 627; A. de Tocqueville, *Journey to America*, trans. by G. Lawrence, ed. by J.P. Mayer, London, Faber & Faber, 1959, p. 102. Mazureau's view would be typical. The same opinion was expressed in 1804 by an American, who thought the prohibition of the slave trade would result in economic disaster: see quotation and text in J.G. Taylor, "The Foreign Slave Trade in Louisiana after 1808", 1 *La. Hist.* (1960), pp. 36–43 at p. 37. The opposite view could be held, however. B*** D*** [L.N. Baudry des Lozières], *Voyage à la Louisiane, et sur le continent de l'Amerique septentrionale, fait dans les années 1794 à 1798*, Paris, Dentu, an XI–1802, p. 109 stated: "La Louisiane est peut-être la colonie qui pourrait le plus se passer d'esclaves, puisque son climat permet davantage aux européens de travailler eux mêmes." Most Louisianians would have disagreed with this.

[44] Franklin, "Eighteenth Brumaire".

first chartered corporations in Louisiana, the New Orleans business community being heavily involved in them.[45]

The economic strength of the anglophone presence in Louisiana has already been alluded to, as have class divisions within white society. Louisianian society was heterogeneous and culturally diverse, consisting of Anglo-Americans, native Louisianians of French, Spanish, French-Canadian, Acadian and German descent, and "free people of colour" and slaves.[46] Etienne Mazureau,[47] a leading attorney, remarked to Alexis de Tocqueville in 1832 that, "Not a country in America or Europe but has sent us some representatives. New Orleans is a patchwork of peoples."[48] At first sight, the ethnic diversity might seem to make it difficult to generalise as to the nature of family organisation in Louisiana; the diversity, however, was not really so great as might appear, as by the time of the Purchase, the German and Spanish descended inhabitants had largely been assimilated to the more numerous French Creole group.[49] Thus, among the white population, the only real social and cultural divide was between the francophones and the Anglophones. The great divide was, of course, that between the blacks and the whites.

Others have treated the cultural and political polarisation of the francophone and anglophone groups,[50] and we need not discuss it here in any detail. Although the Anglo-American group was substantial, and important in commercial life,[51] and although there was continuing immigration, the bulk of the population was francophone—the "ancient inhabitants" and many "foreign French"

---

[45] Clark, *op. cit. supra* note 5, pp. 330–359.

[46] J.G. Tregle, "Early New Orleans Society: A Re-appraisal", 18 *Journal of Southern History* (1952), pp. 20–36; L.W. Newton, "Creoles and Anglo-Americans in Old Louisiana—a Study in Cultural Conflicts", 14 *Southwestern Social Science Quarterly* (1933), pp. 31–48; R. Le Conte, "The Germans in Louisiana in the Eighteenth Century" (trans. and ed. by G. Conrad), 8 *La. Hist.* (1967), pp. 67–84; D.E. Everett, "Emigrés and Militiamen: Free Persons of Colour in New Orleans, 1803–1815", 38 *Journal of Negro History* (1953), pp. 377–402; A. Dunbar-Nelson, "People of Colour in Louisiana", 2 *Journal of Negro History* (1917), pp. 51–78; J.E. Winston, "The Free Negro in New Orleans, 1803–1860", 21 *La. Hist. Quar.* (1938), pp. 1075–1085. In 1807 there were 4,000 free blacks out of a total population—white, free black and black slave—of 53,000 in Louisiana: Dargo, *Jefferson's Louisiana*, p. 7. On the continued importation of black slaves after prohibition of the foreign slave trade, see Taylor, *op. cit. supra* note 43.

[47] Tregle, *op. cit., supra* note 46, p. 31 calls Mazureau "the brilliant lawyer and orator". He was one of the "foreign French" immigrants to Louisiana, arriving in 1804. He had left France on Napoleon's seizure of power. He became the partner of Edward Livingston.

[48] Pierson, *op. cit. supra* note 1, pp. 627–628; a slightly different translation will be found in Tocqueville, *op. cit. supra* note 43, p. 192.

[49] On the assimilation of the Germans, see Le Conte, *op. cit. supra* note 46, p. 83; Kniffen, *op. cit. supra* note 3, p. 124. Newton, *op. cit. supra* note 46, pp. 31 and 34, quotes the famous historian Charles Gayarré who said of the Germans that by 1803 they were "so Frenchified as to appear of Gallic parentage". On the assimilation of the Spaniards, see Kniffen, *op. cit. supra* note 3, p. 130. Kniffen thinks that by the end of the 18th century, there were only two cultural groups, French and Anglo-Saxon. On the early history of Germans in Louisiana, see R. Kondert, "Les Allemands en Louisiane", 33 *R.H.A.F.* (1979), pp. 51–65.

[50] See works cited under note 46 *supra*; Dargo, *Jefferson's Louisiana*, *passim*, and esp. pp. 6–19.

[51] See Clark, *op. cit. supra* note 5, pp. 330–359.

immigrants.[52] The French speakers shared a common cultural background, although the French immigrants, many from St Domingue, appear to have regarded the Louisianian French as boorish provincials.[53] The anglophones were diverse in origin (American, Scots, English, Irish). It has been estimated that at this period the anglophones were outnumbered seven to one.[54]

It is uncertain to what extent, if any, the fact of the francophones and anglophones forming two cultural groups, would be reflected in family organisations. In chapter 4, it will be shown that this period was a crucial one in the development of the modern family. Some general remarks may be made. The family tended to be "a much more potent force than elsewhere in the republic".[55] Tocqueville in 1832 touchingly described the venerable lawyer Mazureau on New Year's Day "receiving . . . the homage of his assembled posterity".[56] Family ties being close does not mean that some extended patriarchal-style family necessarily existed; on the contrary, a patriarchal extended family would not be likely in a developing frontier country, where intellectual life was conscious of the ideas of the Enlightenment and of notions of free will and individuality, and where it doubtless would be easy for sons to leave home and set up on their own account. Further, in a country where commerce and industry were starting to develop, the concentration in a few hands of control over property, presupposed by a patriarchal extended family, would hardly be appropriate. Family ties were close, but they were affective or associative rather than hierarchical.[57]

The above remarks apply to the white population, but not to the black, which was, at this period, more numerous than the white.[58] During the period of Spanish colonial government, it appears that the free people of colour had a relatively privileged position in comparison to that they held after the Louisiana Purchase,[59] although they were, of course, of low social status: this higher position did last for a while after the cession, before they were assimilated to the

---

[52] Many of the Francophone immigrants rose rapidly to prominence in Louisiana, often being better educated and more capable than the Creoles. Moreau Lislet, the redactor, from St Domingue, was one of them. See Tregle, *op. cit. supra* note 46, pp. 30–31.

[53] *Ibid.*

[54] Dargo, *Jefferson's Louisiana*, pp. 9–10.

[55] A.W. Calhoun, *A Social History of the American Family*, New York, Barnes and Noble, 1945, vol. 2, p. 334. Calhoun's remarks apply to the whole of the antebellum south, which does not make them less applicable to Louisiana. See also *ibid.*, vol.1, pp. 331–336 on the family in the French colonies in the west of North America: his account is, however, old-fashioned, first published in 1917–1919, and not very helpful.

[56] Pierson, *op. cit. supra* note 1, p. 626: "We saw there children, grandchildren, nephews, great-nephews, first cousins, distant cousins." See also Tocqueville, *op. cit. supra* note 43, pp. 171–172.

[57] Types of family and the historical changes in the family and the consequent legal implications will be discussed *supra*, chap. 4 introduction.

[58] In 1807 there were 26,000 whites, 4,000 free blacks and no less than 23,500 black slaves: Dargo, *Jefferson's Louisiana*, p. 7. Until 1840, New Orleans was a predominantly black city, see J. S. Kendall, "New Orleans' 'Peculiar Institution'", 23 *La. Hist. Quar.* (1940), pp. 864–886 at p. 869.

[59] See D.E. Everett, "Free Persons of Color in Colonial Louisiana", 8 *La. Hist.* (1966), pp. 21–50 at p. 49.

position of free blacks in the other slave states.[60] There were no restrictions on their contractual competence or powers of ownership, and they had full competence in litigation against whites and other blacks. Among the free blacks, however, family ties were negligible, often the only known relationship being that of mother and child. Among the slaves, in many cases no such institution as "family" could be said to exist, because of the effects of slavery and the total control over slaves exercised by masters.[61]

The discussion of slavery brings up a related point: the position of free labourers vis-à-vis the family. Again this will be discussed more thoroughly elsewhere,[62] but a few remarks are appropriate here. The Seventh *Partida*, book 33, *ley* 6, tells us that in mediaeval Castile a servant was regarded as one of the family, another person under the power of the patriarch. In general, by the early nineteenth century, this familial conception of the master-servant relationship had given way or was giving way to a contractual one. Further, the development of industrial, factory-style manufacture and the disappearance of the artisan, involved the development of a class of wage labourers far removed from any familial relationship with their master. In Louisiana, as already pointed out, industrialisation had not really begun, and the class of people who hired out their labour for wages, though it existed, was insignificant. Further, slavery would of course restrict the opportunities of employment for free labourers.[63] One can conclude, provisionally, that the status of free servant in Louisiana would appear to be one in the process of changing from a familial relationship to a contractual one: how far had gone the trend towards rendering the relationship to the master contractual must be left undecided.

We can conclude this survey by remarking that there was a definite trend towards individualism and liberalism in Louisianan society. The regulated market had been replaced with the free market, while the plantation economy based on the new staple crops of cotton and sugar was supported by the imports from the American west. The mercantile community was strong, and industrialisation was starting, although as yet negligible. Individualism and economic liberalism can also be traced in the affective or associative family, based on free individuals, and in the increasing contractualisation of the master to servant relationship.

At the top of Louisianan society were the planters, merchants and professional classes. There was no large class of wage labourers, but there were artisans working for themselves to supply the needs of the colony: most of the labour was carried out by slaves. The blacks, both the free and the enslaved, came at the bottom of the social pyramid. The fact of slavery does not affect the conception of Louisiana in the territorial period as a society enthusiastically adopting the precepts of nineteenth-century social and economic liberalism.

---

[60] See articles cited note 46 *supra*, and Dargo, *Jefferson's Louisiana*, p. 7.
[61] On the reasons for this, see Calhoun, *op. cit. supra* note 55, vol. 2, pp. 243–279, where he shows clearly how slavery affected family ties between blacks in the South.
[62] See *infra*, chap. 5, introduction.
[63] See *supra*, text at notes 34–38.

QUEBEC

As in Louisiana, the dominating feature of the geography of Quebec is a river—the St. Lawrence.[64] Settlement had originally taken place along the banks of the St. Lawrence; the farms tended to be small and narrow, due to subdivision on inheritance. The St. Lawrence River and canal system was vital for the trade and transport of the province. However, at the period of codification, the trade and transport of the province had been affected by the growth of the railways.

During French rule in Canada, the economy had two main bases: the fur trade with Europe, and agriculture.[65] These two bases provided separate focal points, as the fur trade was carried on according to the mercantilist principles of the day, while the produce of agriculture was mainly for consumption within the colony. There was virtually no industry.[66] The economy of New France was carefully regulated by the Crown officials and governing bodies. Thus, the Sovereign Council[67] regulated the Indian trade, trade between Canadians and French merchants and internal commerce generally.[68] The Council later lost some of these powers to Crown officials such as the Intendant. Thus, the Council and the Governor and Intendant regulated the profits of French merchants trading in Canada,[69] and made detailed regulations on how the market was to be conducted, fixing the price of bread, meat and liquors.[70]

No substantial class of merchant entrepreneurs developed in Canada during the French régime. External trade was in the hands of French merchants, while the wealthier colonists tended to spend their wealth in conspicuous consumption. It has been argued that the failure of such a class to arise was due to a contempt for trade, based on an aristocratic military cast being given to society by the presence of large bodies of soldiers in the province, and provincial demands for commissions (and indeed noble status). The officer class and the

---

[64] On the geography of Quebec, see generally R. Blanchard, *Le centre du Canada français "Province de Québec"*, Montreal, Beauchemin, 1947, *passim* and, on the river system, *ibid.*, pp. 52ff.; on the harshness of the winters and the abundance of summer rainfall, see P. Bieys, "Southern Quebec", in J. Warkentin (ed.), *Canada: A Geographical Interpretation*, Toronto, Methuen, 1970, pp. 281–333 at pp. 290–291.

[65] Here we will only highlight certain areas of the socioeconomic development of Quebec. For a full treatment of the economic history, see especially, J. Hamelin, *Économie et société en Nouvelle France*, Quebec, Presses universitaires Laval, 1960; F. Ouellet, *Histoire économique et sociale du Québec, 1760–1850: structures et conjoncture*, Montreal, Fides, 1966; J. Hamelin and Y. Roby, *Histoire économique du Québec, 1851–1896*, Montreal, Fides, 1971. On the French *régime*, see L. Dechêne, *Habitants et marchands de Montréal au XVII*[e] *siècle*, Paris, Plon, 1974, pp. 125–347.

[66] For a brief but useful outline, see Hamelin, *op. cit. supra* note 65, pp. 21–34; on the fur trade, *ibid.*, p. 47–57; and on corn, *ibid.*, pp. 58–71, On commerce and agriculture, see Dechêne, *op. cit. supra* note 65, pp. 125–347.

[67] On the Sovereign Council, see further chapter 3 *infra*.

[68] See on this R. du B. Cahall, *The Sovereign Council of New France: A Study in Canadian Constitutional History*, New York, Columbia University, P.S. King, 1915, pp. 196–199.

[69] *Ibid.*, pp. 226–230.

[70] *Ibid.*, p. 235.

seigneurs became intermingled.[71] From a rather different perspective, Hamelin comes to a similar conclusion: before 1760 there existed no *bourgeoisie canadienne-française* of any significance. He rejects as myth the thesis that the *grande bourgeoisie* either emigrated after 1760 or, cut off from trade, disappeared as a class.[72] He states that: "Le commerce avec la métropole, les grandes pêcheries et le monopole de la vente du castor étaient aux mains des métropolitains, le chantier de construction navale et les Forges St. Maurice dans celles du roi.[73] Thus, at the time of the conquest there was no form whatsoever of capitalist-style enterprise in French Canada.

In New France, land was held under the seigneurial system and hence was not easily treated as a marketable commodity, as the mutation fines payable to a feudal superior on transfer of property discouraged dealings in land.[74] There also could be problems in gaining a clear title to land due to the lack of registration of title deeds in any way easy to check. That land was not easily transferable or mortgageable in the French period was no great disadvantage, since the *habitants* were not capitalists: they farmed, passed their farms to their children on death without need to pay mutation fines and were apparently reasonably prosperous. The *seigneurs* do not appear to have made large profits from their *seigneuries*.[75] The value of land was low due to it being in plentiful supply while the population was small;[76] the lowness of profits discouraged *seigneurs* from attempting to improve their *seigneuries*.[77] Agriculture was not integrated into the commercial system of the colony, while the fur trade was more attractive and lucrative than farming.

Britain captured Canada in 1760, her possession confirmed by the 1763 Treaty of Paris.[78] Britain applied the principles of mercantilism to her trade with her new colony. This trade was mainly in the staples of fur, wood and corn, with the latter two becoming much more important than the former.[79] From the onset of British rule, the economy began to change: commerce expanded under the direction of British merchants, and the land was increasingly populated. The prosperity of Quebec became more and more dependent on the trading privileges she had with Britain under the old colonial system. *Seigneurs* adopted capitalist notions of ownership and tried to maximise their profits.[80] Generally,

---

[71] See W.J. Eccles, "The Social, Economic and Political Significance of the Military Establishment in New France", 52 *Can. Hist. Rev.* (1971), pp. l–22; W.J. Eccles, *France in America*, New York, Harper & Row, 1972, pp. 110–114; W.J. Eccles, *Canadian Society during the French Regime*, Montreal, Harvest House, 1968.

[72] Hamelin, *op. cit. supra* note 65, pp. 127–137.

[73] *Ibid.*, p. 137.

[74] See W.B. Munro, *The Seigniorial System in Canada: A Study of French Colonial Policy*, New York, Longmans, Green & Co., 1907, pp. 95–97.

[75] F. Ouellet, *Éléments d'histoire sociale du Bas-Canada*, Montreal, Hurtubise HMH, 1972, p. 94.

[76] See R.C. Harris, *The Seigneurial System in Early Canada: A Geographical Study*, Madison, University of Wisconsin Press, 1966, pp. 88–116.

[77] Ouellet, *op. cit. supra* note 75, pp. 95–96.

[78] See *infra*, chap. 3.

[79] See Ouellet, *op. cit supra* note 65, première partie, *passim*, esp. ch.7.

[80] *Ibid.*, pp. 352–353.

the English merchants regarded the seigneurial system as retarding the development of the province according to their notions of free enterprise.[81]

Great changes in the economy started to take place in the period leading up to codification. Although the majority of the population was still one of peasant farmers, an important mercantile class based in Montreal and reliant on trade for its livelihood had developed. While the export of staple crops was still the most important aspect of the economy, industrialisation was beginning.[82] Since the economy was dependent on preferential trade with Britain, there had been extensive canalisation of the St. Lawrence system to aid the Canadian trade and gain the trade of the American mid-west. It was intended that Montreal become the rival of New York as the entrepôt of both the Canadian and American west.[83]

While Canada was dependent on privileged trading with Britain, Britain itself was moving from protectionism to free trade.[84] The 1846 repeal of the Corn Laws and that subsequently of the Navigation Acts attracted commerce away from Montreal to New York and the other U.S. ports, because, although the route through the St. Lawrence to Britain was shorter, New York as an entrepôt had many advantages over Montreal.[85]

In the 1850s a new factor affected Canadian (and Quebec) economic development—the building of the railways. Montreal sought to use the railways to reinforce its metropolitan role.[86] The building of the railways had two major effects on the Canadian economy: first, it stimulated industrialization;[87] second, it re-oriented the economy of Upper and Lower Canada towards the United States. The railways did not reinforce the St. Lawrence canal system; rather they opposed it and directed Canadian traffic to the United States, with the result that the Canadian economy became even more inextricably bound up with the American. The Quebec economy now became reliant on trade with the U.S.A. In fact, a whole series of events acting together brought this about: as already mentioned, the end of the old colonial system, the technological development of the railways, the interplay of market forces as a result of the capitalist drive to maximise revenue from investment and minimise operating costs, and finally

---

[81] *Ibid.*, p. 403.

[82] A. Faucher, *Québec en Amérique au XIXe siècle: essai sur les caractères économiques de la Laurentie*, Montreal, Fides, 1973, pp. 26–27; S. Ryerson, *Unequal Union: Roots of the Crisis in the Canadas, 1815–1873*, 2nd ed., Toronto, Progress Books, 1973, pp. 267–268.

[83] On canalization, see G.N. Tucker, *The Canadian Commercial Revolution, 1845–1851*, ed. by H.G.J. Aitken, Toronto, McClelland and Stewart, 1964, pp. 19–32; Faucher, *op. cit. supra* note 82, pp. 20–23 and 39–41; Hamelin and Roby, *op. cit. supra* note 65, pp. 104–112. On Montreal-New York rivalry, see Tucker, *op. cit.*, pp. 33–45; Faucher, *op. cit. supra* note 82, pp. 39–41.

[84] See generally, R.L. Schuyler, *The Fall of the Old Colonial System: A Study in British Free Trade, 1770–1870*, London, Oxford University Press, 1945; Faucher, *op. cit. supra* note 82, pp. 35–39.

[85] Tucker, *op. cit. supra* note 83, pp. 40–43.

[86] Faucher, *op. cit. supra* note 82, p. 44. On the railways generally, see *ibid.*, pp. 43–68.

[87] For an interesting view on this, see Ryerson, *op. cit. supra* note 83, pp. 253–254.

the Treaty of Reciprocity of 1854 between Canada and the U.S.A.[88] After the end of British protectionism Canada had to trade to survive, and trade with America was easiest and most profitable.

Only merchants based primarily in Montreal, a small proportion of the population, took active part in this commerce, as the vast majority of the population still consisted of peasant farmers. How were the latter faring during these years? The abolition of the seigneurial system obviously affected them, but it is doubtful if it had any great *material* effect on them, since they neither gained nor lost land and had to pay a certain sum in lump or over a period of years to redeem their feudal obligations. The *habitants* were most affected during this period by overpopulation, as the land in the *seigneuries* was over-crowded and often subdivided into lots too narrow to be economically farmed. Since industry was not developing at a rate sufficient to keep up with rural overpopulation, the surplus tended to emigrate to the United States or to colonise new lands away from the *seigneuries*.[89] As well as subdivisions of land making farming no longer economically viable, the agriculture practised by the French Canadians was generally outmoded: "on persistait à conserver les techniques du XVIIIe siècle," remarks Faucher.[90] More progressive techniques in agriculture were practised near Montreal and in the Eastern Townships; both technique and profitability did improve, however, as the century wore on.[91]

At the time of codification, although industrialisation was commencing, [92] the mainstay of the Quebec economy was still the export of corn and timber. This commerce was, however, almost entirely in the hands of the anglophones, while the francophones, although important in the liberal professions, tended to farm or have menial occupations. Indeed, the bulk of the population was still peasant farmers; while rural overpopulation was causing many French Canadians to seek work in the industry of the United States.

The largely anglophone entrepreneurial class espoused the doctrines of liberal capitalism, and believed in unregulated freedom of the market. These views, originally prevalent only among the Montreal bourgeoisie, filtered down to other levels of society. In the early years of the nineteenth century, the liberal professions in the province had rejected commercial capitalism;[93] but by 1847, Louis-Joseph Papineau, the staunch paternalistic upholder of seigneurialism, could declare that he was: "Disciple dès ma première jeunesse de l'école d'Adam Smith et de tout temps ennemi de tout monopole et privilège"[94] Although Quebec was in many ways isolated and backward, it was still open to

---

[88] See generally, D.C. Masters, *The Reciprocity Treaty of 1854: Its History, Its Relation to British Colonial and Foreign Policy and to the Development of Canadian Fiscal Autonomy*, Toronto, McClelland and Stewart, 1963; Faucher, *op. cit. supra* note 82, pp. 56–57.

[89] See Faucher, *op. cit. supra* note 82, p. 189; Hamelin and Roby, *op. cit. supra* note 65, pp. 161ff.

[90] Faucher, *op. cit. supra* note 82, p. 190.

[91] *Ibid.*, pp. 191–192; Hamelin and Roby, *op. cit. supra* note 65, pp. 185–204.

[92] On the slowness of industrialization, see Hamelin and Roby, *op. cit. supra* note 65, pp. 261–289.

[93] See Ouellet, *op. cit. supra* note 65, pp. 204–212 and 229–234.

[94] Speech retorted in *La Revue Canadienne*, 21 Dec. 1847; see Tucker, *op. cit. supra* note 83, p. 79; see *supra*, note 33.

exterior influences from both Britain and the United States. The French, American and industrial revolutions all had an effect. Ouellet admirably sums it up thus:

> Après 1789, l'accélération de la croissance économique, la hausse des prix, la commercialisation accrue de l'agriculture donnent plus de relief aux défis anciens. Puis l'introduction du parlementarisme, la révolution française et la montée des classes moyennes inscrirent de nouvelles pressions en faveur d'une transformation des mentalités. Ces réalités, penseraiton-on, préparent l'éclosion d'une société bourgeoise de caractère capitaliste et individualiste. Tout, dans le monde de l'époque, incite à une semblable évolution.[95]

Several examples will usefully illustrate this growth of a liberal capitalist ideology. First, forest land, previously publicly owned and government administered,[96] was sold by the government for commercial exploitation. Second, the employer-employee relation was redefined. Thus, the business community of Quebec made the following declaration in 1867:

> Every individual has the right to settle for himself the rate of remuneration for his services; and it is not illegal for a number to agree upon a rate of wages. This is but the full exercise of freedom, and against it there can be no complaint. The employer is left with the choice of submitting or procuring other labour; and, he, too, is thus free.[97]

The process of industrialisation, slow though it was, was forming in Quebec an urban labour force. No longer were employees (servants) part of a family grouping, or employed by artisans or apprenticed to their trade; they were now in a contractual relationship with their employer,[98] as the above quotation shows. Workers no longer tended to be skilled artisans owning the tools of their trade; they were being turned into unskilled labourers.[99] This development of a class of wage labourers, and the contractualisation of the relationship between master and servant under the tenets of economic liberalism, along with the change in the nature of the family, will be discussed in more depth later.[100]

The third and most obvious example of the growth in Quebec of liberal capitalist notions of individualism is the controversy over seigneurial tenure of land. In many ways this tenure did appear to hinder industrialisation and the full enjoyment of private property.[101] (That those taking part in the controversy thought in terms of private property as absolute enjoyment is in itself signifi-

---

[95] Ouellet, *op. cit. supra* note 65, pp. 549–550.

[96] See on this Hamelin and Roby, *op. cit. supra* note 65, pp. 208–214.

[97] Reported in the *Morning Chronicle*, 6July 1867, p. 2, col. 3, found quoted in Hamelin and Roby, *op. cit. supra* note 65, p. 310.

[98] See Ryerson, *op. cit.*, pp. 170–191; Hamelin and Roby, *op. cit.*, pp. 305–324.

[99] Hamelin and Roby, *op. cit.*, p. 306; R. Tremblay, "La formation matérielle de la classe ouvrière à Montréal entre 1790 et 1830," 33 *R.H.A.F.* (1979), pp. 39–50.

[100] See *infra*, chap. 5, introduction.

[101] See Ouellet, *op. cit supra* note 65, pp. 463–464.

cant.) The abolition of seigneurial tenure was achieved just prior to codification, and it is unnecessary to discuss it here in any detail.[102] The views of J.C. Taché may be taken as representative of one side of the controversy, as he highlights a disadvantage keenly felt in the 1850s:

> L'inféodation ne lie pas seulement le Censitaire; mais elle lie la société toute entière.... Le crédit foncier, les entreprises publiques et privées, les droits des tiers: tout est soumis au Régime de cette Tenure. Je citerai un exemple, duquel je ferai ressortir un fait important dans la cause. La province en commun avec de puissantes compagnies est engagée dans la confection d'un réseau de voies ferrées; mais il faut traverser le sol Seigneurial et en asquérir une portion; or chaque parcelle du sol féodal, en vertu de l'indivisibilité du cens, est soumis au droit de Lods et Ventes,[103] qu'une transaction arrive equipolent à Vente, et il faudra payer aux Seigneurs la douzième partie de la valeur des chemins de fer. Dans ce cas, comme dans celui de la fondation ou de l'agrandissement des villes ou de l'établissement d'usines ou de manufactures, ce n'est pas le Censitaire actuel de la propriété rurale qui souffre le mal le plus grand;[104] mais l'industriel; mais le capitaliste, et par contre-coup la société entire, dont le progrès peuvent se trouver retardés, paralysés même.[105]

The seigneurial system was regarded as opposing economic growth, and opposition to it was articulated in terms of the needs of industry and capitalism: the retardation of industrial growth being recognised as detrimental for society as a whole. The opposition to feudal tenure was not merely on this material basis; opposition was also made on ideological grounds. Ouellet convincingly shows that the jurists and liberals of the period conceived of property as individual and absolute, and consequently found the seigneurial system contrary to the public interest as based on out-moded notions of dependency and aristocracy inimical to liberalism, both political and economic.[106]

---

[102] For a conventional, rather old fashioned account, see Munro, *op. cit. supra* note 74, pp. 224–251. See also Ouellet's article, "L'abolition du régime seigneurial et l'idée de propriété", 14 *Hermès* (1954), pp. 21–36 (also found in Ouellet, *op. cit. supra* note 75, pp. 297–315); M. Seguin, "Le régime seigneurial au pays de Québec, 1760–1854", 1 *R.H.A.F.* (1947–1948), pp. 382–402, 519–532.

[103] What have previously been called mutation fines: see *supra*, text at note 74.

[104] It appears that the *censitaires* also wished for the abolition of the seigneurial regime: see *Lord Durham's Report on the Affairs of British North America*, ed. by C.P. Lucas, Oxford, Clarendon Press, 1912, vol. 2, pp. 24–25. At this period the *censitaires* were generally in debt to their *seigneurs*, and were hard hit by their feudal burdens: see Ouellet, *op. cit. supra* note 65, pp. 353–354. Indeed, between 1840 and 1843, no less than 20% of actions in King's Bench were those of *seigneurs* suing their *censitaires* for debts: see "Report of the Commissioners appointed to inquire into the Seigniorial Tenure", found in W.B. Munro (ed.), *Documents Relating to the Seigniorial Tenure in Canada: With a Historical Introduction and Explanatory Notes*, Toronto, Champlain Society, 1908, p. 352.

[105] J.C. Taché, *De la tenure seigneuriale en Canada, et projet de commutation*, Quebec, Lovell & Lamoureux, 1854, pp. 5–6; also quoted in Ouellet, *op. cit. supra* note 102, p. 24.

[106] See Ouellet, *op. cit. supra* note 102, *passim*.

The above discussion of the economic history of Quebec shows that the economy was developing towards liberal capitalism. Initially, the movement towards this style of economic regulation came with the British capture of the province: under the French régime, there had been a close regulation of the market. Although the largely anglophone commercial classes were the first to espouse the doctrines of laissez-faire economics, by the mid-nineteenth century, these doctrines were widely supported throughout Quebec society, notably by the French Canadian professional classes. Although industrialisation had commenced, the economy was still largely based on trade in staple crops: this trade was now governed by the rules of economic liberalism, as evinced by the 1854 Reciprocity Treaty with the United States, and the end of privileged trade with Britain. The ideology of liberal capitalism was reflected in conditions of employment, while also structuring the debate over the abolition of the seigneurial system.

As we can identify a shift in the structure of the Quebec economy in the period leading from British capture to codification, so we identify a change in the nature of the family when taken from France to Canada. Garigue has argued that the French Canadian family of the eighteenth and nineteenth centuries was rather different from the French family of the same period and before colonization.[107] He gives as an example the prevalence of the *communauté taisible* among peasants of *ancien régime* France, which required a particular form of family organisation, and which was not taken to New France.[108] The *communauté taisible* was a device developed by serfs to prevent land reverting on death to the seigneur under the rules of *mortaille* or *mainmorte servile*: the land was owned jointly and indivisibly, so there was never a succession on a death, thus allowing the serfs to keep their land.[109] This device required that married sons stay with their mother and father and that family property be pooled and owned by the whole family group.[110] The family was thus one of close paternal and fraternal links. This form of family organisation outlived the institution of serfdom, but was nonetheless not taken by the colonists to New France for several reasons.[111] Plentiful land rendered paternal and fraternal links less strong, and marriage, rather than paternal or fraternal bonds, came to define the family. Women came to have an enhanced status, because, first, of their original shortage, and, second, of the frequent absence of their husbands, making them more independent and responsible.[112] Further, the parent-child relationship

---

[107] P. Garigue, *La vie familiale des Canadiens français: précédée d'une critique*, Montreal, Presses de l'université de Montréal, 1970, pp. 14–18.

[108] *Ibid.*, p. 15 with references there cited.

[109] See generally, Fr. Olivier-Martin, *Histoire du droit français des origines à la Révolution*, Paris, Domat Montchrestien, 1948, p. 635 (no. 475), p. 271 (no. 202).

[110] Garigue, *op. cit. supra* note 107, p. 15.

[111] See *ibid.*, pp. 15–16.

[112] *Ibid.*, p. 17, Garigue mentions that rules on periods of mourning, designed to prevent the remarriage of widows, were never enforced in New France. Garigue is labouring under a slight misapprehension here. Such periods of waiting before remarriage were found in Roman law, and

altered with the growth of New France. Society encouraged large families,[113] and, by 1709, one commentator was already remarking on the different status of children in New France: parents were reported as not having the same authority as French parents over their offspring, and children had much greater independence.[114] Garigue concludes that by the eighteenth century the French Canadian family was typically North American. Louise Dechêne, in her useful study, argues that the special pressures (as outlined above) of colonial life intensified the forces that, at this period, were bringing about the development of the modern family in Europe, resulting in the early development of the privatized affective family.[115]

If we need not concern ourselves with the usefulness of the categories of analysis developed by Garigue, the description given of the family in Quebec, however, is useful.[116] The family is based round marriage, rather than lineage or some collective extended grouping. Children are independent in comparison to those in France. Family ties and relationship undoubtedly were strong in mid-nineteenth century Quebec; but such ties were affective or associative rather than hierarchial. The Superior of the Seminary of St Sulpice remarked thus in 1831 to Tocqueville:

> [The Canadian Race] lacks that adventurous spirit and that scorn of the ties of birth and family that characterize the Americans. The Canadian removes only to the farthest extremity of his parish and [of the commune] of his parents, and he goes to establish himself as near as possible."[117]

This also suggests that French Canadian family ties were in general stronger than those of the anglophone North Americans. By the mid-nineteenth century, of course, the overpopulation of seigneurial land was forcing many *habitants* to leave; and this tendency would weaken family ties. The colonisation of

---

hence in the *droit écrit* of southern France and ultimately in the *Code Napoléon*, They never formed part of the *Coutume de Paris* applied to New France.

[113] The French Regime, Canadian Historical Documents Series vol. 1, ed. by Cameron Nish, Scarborough, Ont., Prentice-Hall of Canada, 1965, pp. 57–58, for government incentives to marry early and have large families.

[114] Garigue, *op. cit. supra* note 107, p. 17.

[115] See Dechêne, *op. cit. supra* note 65, p. 434. Dechêne, *ibid.*, pp. 141–449 gives an excellent account of the family in the 17th century. More account will be paid to what she says in chapter 4, where it will be more relevant. For Garigue's view that the French Canadian family was typically North American, see *op. cit. supra* note 107, p. 7. On the general movement in Europe, see *infra*.

[116] On categories and typology see *infra*, chap. 4, introduction.

[117] Pierson, *op. cit. supra* note 1, p. 316; Tocqueville, *op. cit. supra*, note 43, p. 39. The Superior points out, however, that the younger population is ever more mobile. At the beginning of the 19th century, Lord Selkirk (*Lord Selkirk's Diary, 1803–1804: A Journal of his Travels in British North America and the Northeastern United States*, ed. by P. White, Toronto, Champlain Society, 1958, p. 224) wrote: "All that are in a thriving way set out their children on new lots as they come up, giving them some money to stock them—they do not send them off as in New England to seek their land at hundreds of miles distant, but take up their land in the seine or adjoining *seigneurie*, the young men live at home for some years after going occasionally at suitable seasons to carry on their improvements".

New France, although it weakened the old extended patriarchal family, strengthened the relationships of the new-style family.[118] The French Canadians, surrounded by anglophones, attributed great importance to family life and the ties of family generally.

There were, of course, substantial numbers of people in Quebec, not of French descent, and who generally controlled economic organisation and the colonial administration. There is no reason to believe that the nature of the family relationships among the anglophone population was appreciably different from that among the francophone. Considering, however, the stress placed on the family in French Canada, and considering the emphasis placed on there being closer family ties among francophones than anglophones, it is fair to conclude that family ties among the anglophones were less close. The evidence of the Superior of the Seminary of St. Sulpice would tend to confirm this.[119]

Consonant with this development in Quebec of a new-style family based around marriage and with close parent-child ties, is the exclusion of the servant from the family, and his demotion to a purely contractual relationship, as pointed out above.[120]

Overall, it may be concluded that, in Quebec, in the mid-nineteenth century, there had been a move towards an individualist conception of man, in both the social and economic spheres. There had been a shift from the regulated market to free enterprise, and instead of hierarchical, extended family ties, there were close ties between the spouses and between the parents and children of an affective nature.

There had been a shift from protected trade with Britain in staple crops to free trade with the United States. Industrialisation and factory production had begun, stimulated by the growth of the railway system. There was, however, still insufficient industrial production to absorb the excess population on the land. Commerce and industry were largely in the hands of the anglophone population, while the francophones were strong in the liberal professions. Both the anglophone businessmen and francophone professionals adopted the ideology of liberal capitalism. The majority of the population was still peasant farmers, however; and although an urban labour force was developing, it was still numerically insignificant in comparison to the *habitants*.

---

[118] Garigue, *op. cit. supra* note 107, p. 94: "La colonisation du Canada produisait une vie familiale ayant des caractéristiques particulières mais dont un certain nombre sont communes aux families des groupes ethniques nord-américains. De plus, étant donné le 'vide' démographique du Canada, dès l'origine de la Nouvelle-France la famille fut l'instrument principal du peuplement. . . . Après la Conquête de 1760, l'importance sociologique de la famille fut assurée par deux phénomènes sociaux: a) Le développement d'une vie rurale qui conserve, jusqu'à un certain degré, plusieurs des caractéristiques sociales de la colonisation de la Nouvelle-France; et b) Le développement d'une 'compensation sociologique' entre les institutions, résultant en une intensification de l'importance attribuée par les Canadiens français à leur vie familiale."

[119] See *supra*, text at note 117.

[120] See *supra*, text at notes 96–100.

3

THE LEGAL BACKGROUND TO CODIFICATION IN LOUISIANA AND QUEBEC

LOUISIANA

French Colony

The original motive for French colonization of Louisiana would appear to have been the desire to protect the other French colonies in North America from British aggression. Tentative explorations of the Louisiana area had been made by Cavelier de la Salle in the late seventeenth century:[1] although these explorations produced no immediate result, the importance of Louisiana had been recognized.[2] Hence, over the period 1699–1702, under the direction of two Canadian brothers, Pierre le Moyne d'Iberville and Jean-Baptiste le Moyne de Bienville, the colony was gradually occupied for France.[3] At its greatest extent, French Louisiana consisted not only of the present state, but also of substantial parts of Alabama, Arkansas and Missouri.

From the legal historical point of view, the first events of major importance in Louisiana were the founding of the Conseil Supérieur in 1712,[4] and the grant of Louisiana by charter in the same year to the financier Antoine Crozat.[5] Crozat's charter provided that:

---

[1] M. Giraud, *Histoire de la Louisiane française*, Paris, Presses universitaires de France, 1953–1974, vol. 1, pp. 3–12.

[2] R.W. van Alstyne, "The Significance of the Mississippi Valley in American Diplomatic History, 1686–1810", 36 *Miss. Vall. Hist. Rev.* (1949), pp. 215–238, points out that the Mississippi and its tributaries gave access and control to the whole of North America. The significance is that which made New Orleans the natural entrepôt for the American West as pointed out *supra*, chap. 2.

[3] Giraud, *op. cit. supra* note 1, vol. 1, pp. 24–43 and 44–56. On the early history of Louisiana, Giraud's four-volume work is invaluable. See also M. Giraud, "France and Louisiana in the Early Eighteenth Century", 36 *Miss. Vall. Hist. Rev.* (1950), pp. 657–674.

[4] For the period before this, see Giraud, *op. cit. supra* note 1, vol. 1, *passim*; H.P. Dart, "Courts and Law in Colonial Louisiana", 22 *La. Bar Assoc. Repts.* (1921), pp. 17–63 at pp. 21–22; H.P. Dart, "Legal Institutions in Louisiana", 2 *La. Hist. Quar.* (1919) pp. 72–103 at pp. 72–73.

[5] J. G. Hardy, "The Superior Council in Colonial Louisiana", in J.F. McDermott (ed.), *Frenchmen and French Ways in the Mississippi Valley*, Urbana, University of Illinois Press, 1969, pp. 87–101 at pp. 87–88; Dart, "Courts and Law" *supra* note 4, pp. 22–25; Dart, "Legal Institutions" *supra* note 4, p. 74–81; Giraud, *op. cit. supra* note 1, vol. 1, pp. 279–280. A full translation of the Letters

> Nos Edits, Ordonnances Et Coutumes Et les usages de la Prevosté et Vicomté de Paris seront observés pour Loix et Coutumes dans le d. Pays de la Louisiane.[6]

The Superior Council acted as a law court, as well as carrying out general legal administration and registration of deeds. The Superior Council originally had been set up only provisionally, but it was made permanent in 1716.[7] In 1717, Crozat transferred his monopoly rights to the newly established *Compagnie d'Occident*.[8] The charter of this company empowered it to grant land in *franc alleu*,[9] thus preventing the introduction of feudal tenure, and stated that:

> Seront tous les juges Etablis en tous les d. Lieux tenus de juger suivant les Loix Et Ordonnances du Royaume Et se Conformer a la Coutume de la Prevosté Et Vicomté de Paris suivant laquelle les habitants pourront Contracter sans que Lon y puisse introduire aucune autre Coutume pour Eviter La diversité.[10]

Although the colony reverted, to the Crown in 1731, the administration of justice in Louisiana remained on the basis set out above until the end of the French regime.[11]

The law thus brought into force in Louisiana comprised the *Coutume de Paris*, royal legislation precedent to the charter, and, ultimately, the Superior Council's own enactments. The issue of the validity in Louisiana of royal legislation subsequent to 1717, if not registered by the Superior Council, will not be considered here.[12]

At this period, France was a country with a multiplicity of jurisdictions. First, there was the major division between the *pays du droit écrit* (the basically Roman law south) and the *pays du droit coutumier* (the customary law north).[13]

Patent establishing the Superior Council may be found in Dart, "Legal Institutions" *supra* note 4, pp. 76–78; see also H.W. Baade, "Marriage Contracts", pp. 7–8.

[6] Found quoted in Baade, "Marriage Contracts", p. 7. An English translation may be found in E.G. Brown, "Law and Government in the 'Louisiana Purchase': 1803–1804", 2 *Wayne Law Review* (1956), pp. 169–189 at p. 179.

[7] For the text of the Edict of 18th Sept., 1716, making the Council permanent, see Dart, "Legal Institutions" *supra* note 4, pp. 82–84.

[8] See Giraud, *op. cit. supra* note 1, vol. 2, pp. 67–69; Dart , "Legal Institutions" *supra* note 4, p. 85; and Baade, "Marriage Contracts", pp. 7–8.

[9] See Dart, "Legal Institutions" *supra* note 4, p. 85; Dart, "Courts and Law" *supra* note 4, p. 23.

[10] Found quoted Baade, "Marriage Contracts", p. 8. Brown, *op. cit. supra* note 6, p. 179 quotes the following translation: "The judges established in all the said places shall be held to adjudge according to the laws and ordinances of the kingdom, and the officers to follow and conform themselves to the customs of the Prevoté and vicomté of Paris, according to which the inhabitants may contract, without that any other custom may be introduced to avoid diversity."

[11] An edict of 1719 did, however, introduce some changes. For full text see Dart, "Legal Institutions" *supra* note 4, pp. 86–90. See also Baade, "Marriage Contracts", pp. 7–10.

[12] See Baade, "Marriage Contracts", pp. 8–9. He relies on Quebec authority. The matter was more important in Quebec: see *infra*.

[13] A useful map of the divisions in jurisdiction in France may be found in [various authors], *A General Survey of Events Sources Persons and Movements in Continental Legal History*, ed. by J.H. Wigmore, Continental Legal History Series, vol. 1, London, John Murray, 1912, opposite p. 201.

The *pays du droit coutumier* was itself divided into many jurisdictions in which there were differing bodies of customary law.[14] These *coutumes* had been "codified' in the fifteenth and sixteenth centuries.[15] (By "codified" is meant their reduction to writing in concise, systematic form.) It is this multiplicity of laws which necessitated the designation of one particular *coutume* as applicable in Louisiana.[16]

The exact scope of the *Coutume* is important. As indicated, many royal ordinances on various matters of importance were now in force in Louisiana.[17] The *Coutume* itself did not provide a complete system of law, being a very short system of rules couched in a terse, concise style, and by no means covering all areas of the law:[18] for example, it contained provisions on neither the general law of obligations nor the law of special contracts. The *Coutume de Paris* was not exceptional in this respect, and throughout the *pays du droit coutumier*, the law of obligations was based on that of Rome.

It is necessary to touch on the vast topic of the reception of Roman law in Europe, in order to understand the position of Roman law in the French coutumes.[19] In the medieval period, the received Roman law became regarded

---

[14] The area of *droit écrit* was also divided into various jurisdictions based around the four *Parlements* of Toulouse, Aix, Bordeaux and Grenoble. There was some diversity in the law applied in the South, under local customs. For some examples, see *infra*, chap. 4, introduction. See also *General Survey supra* note 13, pp. 206–207.

[15] See J.P. Dawson, "Codification of the French Customs", 38 *Michigan Law Review* (1940), pp. 765–800; *General Survey supra* note 13, pp. 259–263.

[16] There seems to have been confusion in Canada initially as to which coutume should be applied: see *infra*.

[17] On royal legislation, see *General Survey supra* note 13, pp. 263–265.

[18] It contained 362 articles, divided into 16 titles (edition used, that in Ferrière, *Corps et comp.*):

1. Des fiefs (1–72).
2. Des censives et droits seigneuriaux (73–87).
3. Quels biens sont meubles et quels immeubles (88–95).
4. De complainte en cas de sasine et de nouvelleté, et de simple sasine (96–98).
5. Des actions personnelles et d'hypothèque (99–112).
6. De prescription (113–128).
7. De retrait lignager (129–159).
8. Arrêts exécutions et gageries (160–183).
9. De servitudes et rapports de jurés (184–219).
10. Communauté de biens (220–246).
11. De douaires (247–264).
12. De garde noble et bourgeoise (265–271).
13. Des donations et dons mutuels (272–288).
14. Des testaments et exécutions d'iceux (289–298).
15. Des successions en ligne directe et collatérale (299–344).
16. Des criées (345–362).

[19] The literature on the reception of Roman law is voluminous. A useful general introduction (in English) is H.R. Hahlo and E. Kahn, *The South African Legal System and its Background*, Cape Town, Juta, 1968, pp. 484–523 ("The Reception of Roman Law"). See also P. Vinogradoff, *Roman Law in Mediaeval Europe*, 2nd ed., Oxford, Clarendon Press, 1929; E. Levy, "Vulgarisation of Roman Law in the Early Middle Ages", in E. Levy, *Gesammelte Schriften*, Cologne, Böhlau, 1963, vol. 1, pp. 220–247. On the humanist attitude to Roman law, see M.P. Gilmore, *Humanists and Jurists: Six Studies in the Renaissance*, Cambridge MA, Bellknap Press,

as the *ius commune* of most of Europe.[20] This acceptance of the Roman law as the *ius commune* had political implications because of the claims of the Holy Roman Emperor to be the successor of the Roman Emperors.[21] The French Crown resisted the reception of Roman law, because such a reception might imply that the King of France was subject to the Emperor.[22] The reception of Roman law in the south was, however, a *fait accompli.*[23] Lest the argument be put that this necessarily implied the sovereignty of the Emperor, a theory was developed to the effect that the *droit écrit* was applied in the Midi only as custom and only with the permission of the French kings:[24] *rex in regno suo est imperator.*[25]

Roman law, however, was taught in the universities in all of France:[26] and, indeed, until the modern period, the only laws taught in universities were the Roman and Canon.[27] In 1219, however, the public teaching of Roman law had been prohibited in Paris, in the heartland of the *droit coutumier.*[28] (This ban lasted until 1679, although an exception was made in favour of Cujas.)[29]

Thus, in the Midi, the Roman law was accepted as the custom in force, whereas, in the north, the *droit coutumier* was the law in force, and Roman law had, in theory, no place. The theory took no account of the tremendous attraction of the Roman law; an attraction enhanced by the fact that any university-trained lawyer would have studied Roman law.

As pointed out, the *coutumes* were not complete systems. In general, the Roman law was followed in the area of obligations, and met little opposition. To a considerable extent, the customs themselves were interpreted using the Roman

---

1963. Also useful is W. Kunkel, *An Introduction to Roman Legal and Constitutional History*, 2nd ed., trans. J.M. Kelly, Oxford, Clarendon Press, 1973, pp. 177–191 (with bibliography at *ibid.*, pp. 227–228). See also P. Koschaker, *L'Europa e il diritto romano*, trans. by A. Biscardi (of *Europa und das römische Recht*), Florence, Sansoni, 1962.

[20] This statement compresses a lot of history and begs many questions: see H. Coing, "The Roman Law as *Ius Commune* on the Continent", 89 *Law Quarterly Review* (1973), pp. 505–517.

[21] On the political implications, see W. Ullman, *Law and Politics in the Middle Ages: An Introduction to the Sources of Medieval Political Ideas*, London, Sources of History Ltd., 1975, pp. 51–116 esp. at p. 67.

[22] See, e.g., É. Chénon, "Le droit romain à la Curia Regis de Philippe-Auguste à Philippe-Le-Bel", pp. 195–212, in *Mélanges Fitting*, Aalen, Scientia, 1969, vol. 1, pp. 195–212; Koschaker, *op. cit. supra* note 19, pp. 134–139.

[23] See e.g. *General Survey supra* note 13, pp. 204 and 206–207; F. Calasso, *Introduzione al diritto comune*, Milan, Giuffrè, 1951, pp. 134–135, 311; F. Calasso, *Medio evo del diritto*, Milan, Giuffrè, 1954, pp. 611–613.

[24] See, especially Chénon, *op. cit. supra,* note 22, pp. 209–210, esp. quotation from the 1312 ordinance of Philippe le Bel.

[25] *Ibid.* pp. 210–212; Koschaker, *op. cit. supra* note 19, p. 137, and Ullman, *op. cit.* supra note 21, pp. 102–103.

[26] On the universities in France, see *General Survey supra* note 13, pp. 209–213.

[27] Not until 1679 was French law taught in Paris. It was only in the seventeenth and eighteenth centuries that in most countries the native law came to be taught in the universities.

[28] See W. Ullman, "The Prohibition of Roman Law in Paris", 60 *Juridical Review* (1948), pp. 177–186; Chénon, *op. cit. supra* note 22, pp. 198–201; *General Survey supra* note 13, pp. 211–212; Koschaker, *op. cit. supra* note 19, pp. 134–137; and Ullman, *op. cit. supra* note 21, p. 103.

[29] See *General Survey supra* note 13, p. 212.

law.[30] Brissaud states that the Roman law was used extensively in the *pays du droit coutumier*, and referred to constantly, even when irrelevant.[31] Given that the jurists would have their initial training in Roman law, this influence is hardly surprising. Thus, the law as applied in the *pays du droit coutumier* had overall a distinctly Roman cast. An example of the adoption of the Roman law in the north is provided by the fact that, until its abolition in 1606, the *Senatusconsultum Velleianum* was applied.[32] An example of the penetration of Roman law into the very *coutumes* is provided by the work of Philippe de Rémi de Beaumanoir, in whose *Coutumes de Beauvaisis* of 1283, although based on customary law, a great deal of Roman law influence may be traced, even though his book did not touch on those areas usually regulated by Roman law in the *pays du droit coutumier*.[33]

Although, as a matter of fact, we can posit a great deal of Roman law influence in the *droit coutumier*, sufficient to allow us to regard this law as part of the continental civil law tradition, it should be pointed out that there were two schools of thought as to the use of Roman law in supplementing the *coutumes*. One school rejected the authority of Roman law, arguing that the Roman law should only be used when there is nothing in royal legislation, the particular custom concerned, and the general customs of France: this is an argument that there is a general *droit commun coutumier* (frequently identified with the *Coutume de Paris*).[34] The other school of thought argued that the Roman law was the *droit commun* in the *pays des coutumes*.[35] Neither school of thought had defeated the other by the end of the *ancien régime*. It should be recalled that there was no dispute that the law of obligations was Roman (as indeed were some other areas).[36]

One can conclude that the law brought into force in Louisiana in 1712 was an amalgam of codified custom, royal legislation and Roman law (as received). Thus the law in Louisiana formed part of the civil law tradition. Dart has shown, using the records of the Superior Council, that it is clear that the *Procureur du Roi*, the leading lawyer of the colony, was well acquainted with the best and

---

[30] See *ibid.*, p. 207; E. Chénon, *Histoire générale du droit français public et privé: des originines á 1815*, Paris, Sirey, 1926, vol. 2. i, pp. 331–334; Olivier-Martin, *Histoire*, pp. 427–428.

[31] See *General Survey supra* note 13, p. 208.

[32] See *infra*, chap. 4, introduction.

[33] See P. van Wetter, "Le droit romain et Beaumanoir", in *Mélanges Fitting supra* note 22, vol. 2, pp. 533–582.

[34] See, e.g. *General Survey supra* note 13, p. 208; Calasso, *Medio Evo supra* note 23, p. 614: Calasso, *Diritto Comune supra* note 23, p. 312.

[35] See supra, references in note 34. I found useful the arguments put forward by B.J. Bretonnier in C. Henrys, *Oeuvres... contenant son recuëil d'arrêts, ses plaidoyers et harangues, et vingt-deau questions postumes*, Paris, Michel Brunet, 1708, vol. 1, preface.

[36] See *General Survey supra* note 13, p. 209. See also Van Wetter, *op. cit. supra* note 33, p. 535, where he mentions the topics Beaumanoir did not cover because they would be governed by Roman law.

most useful commentaries on the *Coutume de Paris*, and, indeed, to some extent, with the Roman law.[37]

Spanish Colony

France ceded Louisiana to Spain by the secret Treaty of Fontainebleau of November 1762; this did not come into force until after the Treaty of Paris of 1763 concluded the Seven Years War.[38] Spain did not attempt to enter into possession until 1766, when Don Antonio de Ulloa arrived at New Orleans to take up the office of governor.[39] He was expelled in October 1768 by an uprising of the Louisiana population.[40] Under authority of a royal *cédula* issued at Aranjuez on 16th April 1769, Don Alexandro O'Reilly was sent with a military force to receive formal possession of the colony under international law as part of the territory of the Spanish King: O'Reilly took formal possession of the colony on 18th August 1769.[41]

Under the system to be described below, the Castilian law, as adapted, was applied by Spain to her colonies in the Americas. Unlike most of the Spanish conquests, Louisiana already had a functioning legal system of some sophistication. When Ulloa was governor, it appears that the Spanish authorities did not intend a drastic change in the laws applicable, since a *cédula* of 27th March 1767, ordering the abolition of the Superior Council, provided:

> That civil and criminal law suits and proceedings instituted between natives of the country, or when a Spaniard or foreigner is involved, be commenced, continued and decided according to the laws and customs having a constant and uninterrupted force in the colony, and in situations which are either doubtful or have not been specifically contemplated, according to the Laws of the New Compilation of the Indies, but when the lawsuit be instituted between Spaniards, it shall be decided according to the said Laws of the Indies.[42]

---

[37] See H.P. Dart, "Law Library of a Louisiana Lawyer in the 18th Century", 25 *La. Bar Assoc. Repts*. (1924), pp. 12–29 at pp. 22–28.

[38] See A.S. Aiton, "The Diplomacy of the Louisiana Cession", 36 *American Historical Review* (1931), pp. 701–720; W.J. Eccles, *France in America*, New York, Harper Row, 1972, pp. 215–217; J.P. Moore, *Revolt in Louisiana: The Spanish Occupation, 1766–1770*, Baton Rouge, Louisiana State University Press, 1976, p. 56. See also Baade, "Marriage Contracts", pp. 30–31.

[39] Moore, *op. cit. supra* note 38, pp. 1–20 on Ulloa and the possession of Louisiana.

[40] See *ibid*., pp. 143–164. Moore gives a very detailed account of Ulloa's governorship and the events leading to his expulsion. See also the interesting essay by P.H. Boule, "French Reactions to the Louisiana Revolution of 1768", in J.F. McDermott (ed.), Frenchmen and French Ways in the Mississippi Valley, Urbana, University of Illinois Press, 1975, pp. 143–157.

[41] For text of *cédula*, see Batiza, "The Unity of Private Law in Louisiana under the Spanish Rule", 4 *Inter-American Law Review* (1962), pp. 139–156 at pp. 143–144. Ulloa had been unable to take formal possession due to lack of troops: see Moore, *op. cit. supra* note 38, p. 198; on restoration of Spanish rule, see *ibid*., pp. 185–215.

[42] For text of *cédula*, see Batiza, *op. cit. supra* note 41, pp. 144–146. The provision quoted is the sixth, *ibid*., p. 145. The first provision provides for the abolition of the Superior Council, *ibid*.

These provisions were not implemented.

When O'Reilly took possession, the circumstances were changed. Baade has recently and rightly drawn attention to the treason trials held by O'Reilly after the rebellion, and has pointed out that it was decided that the correct criminal and public law to be used in these was that of Spain.[43] He then points out that the conduct of these trials according to Spanish law pointed to what was to come, more especially since the French Louisiana legal "establishment" had been heavily involved in the 1768 revolt.[44]

The *cédula* of Aranjuez of 16th April 1769 had given O'Reilly more than sufficient authority to change the laws and legal system generally;[45] and this he proceeded to do. On 25th November 1769, he issued an ordinance that abolished the Superior Council, and established a *Cabildo* or city council in the style of local government in Spanish America. The ordinance also states that the administration of justice prescribed by the laws of Spain would be established, as throughout Spanish America.[46] The preamble of this ordinance further said that:

> And as the want of advocates in this country, and the little knowledge which his new subjects possess of the Spanish laws might render a strict observance of them difficult ... we have thought it useful and even necessary to form an abstract or regulation drawn from the said laws. . . .[47]

The promised abstract was also issued on the 25th November, and mainly contained rules of procedure, though certain substantive law rules were also included.[48] The rules in the ordinance establishing the *Cabildo* were drawn in the main from the *Recopilación de las Indias*, while those in the abstract were drawn mainly from the *Recopilación* of Castile and the *Siete Partidas*.[49] These two documents (usually collectively known as "O'Reilly's Code") were drafted by the two academically-trained lawyers who had accompanied O'Reilly to Louisiana.[50]

---

43 Baade, "Marriage Contracts", pp. 35–36.

44 *Ibid.*, p. 36.

45 See Batiza, *op. cit. supra* note 41, pp. 143–144.

46 The preamble will be found quoted in *ibid.*, pp. 140–141.

47 See *ibid.* p. 141. On the administration of justice in Spanish America, see L.G. Hahle, "The Spanish Colonial Judiciary", 32 *Southwestern Social Science Quarterly* (1951), pp. 26–37.

48 The abstract was entitled: "Instructions as to the manner of instituting suits, civil and criminal, and of pronouncing judgments in general, in conformity to the laws of the Nueva Recopilacion de Castilla, and the Recopilacion de las Indias, for the government of the judges and parties pleading, until a more general knowledge of the Spanish language, and more extensive information upon those laws may be acquired: digested and arranged by Doct. Don Manuel Joseph de Urrustia, and the counsellor Don Felix Rey, by order of his excellency Don Alexander O'Reilly, Governor and Captain General of this province, by special commission of His Majesty." Quoted from Batiza, *op. cit. supra* note 41, pp. 141–142 n. 5. On the contents, see Dart, "Courts and Law" *op. cit. supra* note 4, pp. 53–60.

49 See e.g. Baade, "Marriage Contracts", p. 37. On these books of law, see *infra*.

50 The best account of this period, and of O'Reilly's work, is to be found in Baade, "Marriage Contracts", pp. 30–40, and H. Baade, "The Formalities of Private Real Estate Transactions in Spanish North America", 38 *La. L. Rev.* (1978), pp. 655–745 at 682–686.

Early in the new year, O'Reilly issued sets of instructions to various local governors and commandants throughout the newly acquired territory. These instructions, drafted by the same lawyers as had been "O'Reilly's Code", were essentially an adaption of the abstract to the needs of communities and to circumstances outside New Orleans.[51] This division between New Orleans and the rest of Louisiana is, according to Baade, reflected in the history of the law applied from 1769 to 1803, in that the proper Castilian law was applied in New Orleans itself, but not in the outlying areas. Baade has argued that we can describe the situation as that of a "dual state".[52]

On 17th October 1769, O'Reilly had written to the Council of the Indies, stating his intention to introduce the same law as applied throughout Spanish America, and arguing why he thought it expedient to do so.[53] In a letter of 27th January 1770, O'Reilly was informed of royal approval of his actions.[54] Formal approval by royal *cédula* came on 17th August 1772, on the recommendation of the Council of the Indies.[55]

In the past there had been considerable uncertainty over two matters: first, over whether or not O'Reilly was empowered to introduce the laws as applied in Spanish America; and, second, over whether or not he actually had done so.[56] There can now be no doubt: the work of Batiza,[57] Baade[58] and Brown[59] has shown that O'Reilly was so empowered and had acted on the authority given him. The Laws of the Indies were introduced *de facto* and *de iure*. Baade has shown that, early in 1770, even in outlying areas of the territory, there was already an awareness that Spanish American law (the law of the Indies) had been introduced.[60]

It is necessary to specify that the law introduced was that of the Indies, as Spain itself did not have a unified system of law. The political unification of Spain under the *Reyes Católicos*, and the *Reconquista* had not brought about legal uniformity. There were many differing customs and laws, varying from district to district.[61] In 1493, a Papal Bull provided that the lands discovered in

---

[51] See Baade, "Marriage Contracts", pp. 37–39; Baade, *op. cit. supra* note 50, pp. 683–684.

[52] On his idea of "dual state", see Baade, *op. cit. supra* note 50, pp. 684–686; Baade, "Marriage Contracts", pp. 73–79.

[53] For text, see Batiza, *op. cit. supra* note 41, pp. 146–147.

[54] For text, see *ibid.*, pp. 147–148.

[55] See, e.g., Baade, *op. cit. supra* note 50, p. 682.

[56] For the doubts, see Batiza, *op. cit. supra* note 41, pp. 142–143, and Brown, *op. cit. supra* note 6, pp. 182–186. In 1812, Jefferson argued that the French law was the law in force, (quoted Brown, *ibid.*, pp. 183–184), but this opinion reverses his previous views, and was designed to support his position on the vexed Batture Question, (see Dargo, *Jefferson's Louisiana*, pp. 74–101 on Batture question).

[57] Batiza, *op. cit. supra* note 41, passim.

[58] Baade, "Marriage Contracts", pp. 30–40, 73–79.

[59] Brown, *op. cit. supra* note 6, pp. 182–186.

[60] Baade, "Marriage Contracts", p. 74.

[61] On the differing municipal *fueros*, see S. Minguijón, *Historia del derecho español*, Barcelona, Editorial Labor, 1927, vol. 1, pp. 71–73; on the differing medieval kingdoms, see E.N. van Kleffens, *Hispanic Law until the Middle Ages*, Edinburgh, Edinburgh University Press, 1968, pp.

the Americas were to be the conjugal property of Ferdinand and Isabella, whose marriage had united Aragon and Castile: on the death of either, however, the new lands were to form part of the dominions of the Crown of Castile, but not of those of the Crown or Aragon.[62] The Crown had a definite policy that so far as possible, the laws of the new lands should be the same as those of Castile.[63]

Although the laws of Castile would apply, there was a great mass of legislation specifically for the Indies.[64] The volume of legislation was such that, from the sixteenth century, moves were made to collect the separate laws.[65] This movement eventually resulted in 1680 in the *Recopilación de leyes de los reinos de las Indias*.[66] Few of the provisions of the *Recopilación* touched on matters of what would now be called private law, and so of paramount importance was the following *ley*:

> Ordenamos y mandamos, que en todos los casos, negocios y pleytos en que no estuviere decidido, ni declarado lo que se debe proveer por las leyes de esta Recopilacion, ó por Cédulas, Provisiones, ú Ordenanzas dadas, y no revocadas, para las Indias, y las que por nuestra órden se despacharen, se guarden las leyes de nuestro Reyno de Castilla, conforme á la de Toro, así en quanto á la substancia, resolucion y decision de los casos, negocios y pleytos, como á la forma y orden de substanciar.[67]

Up to 1614, Castilian legislation had been automatically valid in the Indies; but after that date, it was only effective if reenacted by the Council of the Indies.[68]

The *Leyes de Toro* as referred to, provided an order of precedence for sources of Castilian law:[69] first the laws of Toro themselves, second, the *Ordenamiento de Alcalá* and indeed other *ordenamientos* and *pragmaticas*, third, the *fueros municipales y reales*, and, last, the *Siete Partidas*. Hence, royal legislation in Castile was the primary source, then the *fueros*, especially the *Fuero real*, and last the *Partidas*.[70] The *Leyes de Toro*, dating from 1505, themselves contained important provisions on private law.[71] The *Ordenamiento* de *Alcalá* of 1348 contained a provision setting out an order of precedence of

---

237–250; J.T. Vance, *The Background of Hispanic-American Law*, New York, Central book Co., 1943, pp. 202–230. On the separate provinces, see Minguijón, *op. cit.*, vol. 2, pp. 7–120.

[62] See, e.g. Van Kleffens, *op. cit. supra* note 61, pp. 262–263 n. 2.

[63] See *ibid.*, p. 263 and n 3; A. MacKay, *Spain in the Middle Age, From Frontier to Empire, 1000–1500*, London, MacMillan, 1977, p. 212.

[64] On this, see Vance, *op. cit. supra* note 61, pp. 127–140, 153–165; Baade, *op. cit. supra* note 50, pp. 666–668.

[65] On the movement to collect the laws, see Vance, *op. cit. supra* note 61, pp. 155–165.

[66] I have used the ed. of 1791.

[67] *Rec. Ind.* 2.1.2 (Book 2, title 1, *ley* 2; this system of referencing will be used for the other *Recopilaciónes*.)

[68] *Rec. Ind.* 2.1.39–40 for royal Cédula of December, 1614.

[69] *Ley* 1.

[70] See Van Kleffens, *op. cit. supra* note 61, pp. 232–234.

[71] On the *Leys de Toro*, see: *ibid.*, pp. 232–236; Vance, *op. cit. supra* note 61, pp. 117–120; Minguijón, *op. cit. supra* note 61, vol. 2, pp. 121–122; *General Survey supra* note 13, pp. 632–634.

sources, similar to that of the *Leyes de Toro*.[72] The *fueros municipales* were local customs.[73] The *Fuero real* was a custom applied throughout Castile, and introduced by Alfonso X in 1255.[74] *Las Siete Partidas*, stated by the *ley* to be supplementary if there be no provision in any other source, were a compilation of laws made for Alfonso X, but not achieving the force of statute until the *Ordenamiento de Alcalá*, although much used previously as a work of doctrine. The *Partidas* provided a synthesis of the law, and were Romanizing in effect.[75] Although the *Partidas* were last in the order of precedence, they were of major importance, and were the main source of private law in Spanish North America.[76]

Some other collections of law were important in Louisiana, and deserve mention here. First, the *Nueva recopilación*, issued by order of Philip II in 1567, was a collection of Castilian legislation up to that period.[77] Thus, many of the *Leyes de Toro* were included in it. Second, the *Fuero viejo* was a collection of customs dating from the time of Alfonso VIII. Some have doubted its original legal authority, and it certainly appears to originate in a private compilation. However this may be, the author of the de la Vergne manuscript in Louisiana refers to it.[78] The *Leyes de Estilo*, probably of 1310, were a series of provisions of a doctrinal character clarifying the *Fuero real*:[79] many were included in the 1805 *Novísima recopilación*,[80] and references to them are found in the de la Vergne manuscript.

Although no more need be said on the formal sources of law introduced into Louisiana by O'Reilly, it is useful to consider the place of the Roman law in the

---

[72] On this *ordenamiento*, see, Van Kleffens, *op. cit. supra* note 61, pp. 218–228; Vance, *op. cit. supra* note 61, pp. 108–113, and Minguijón, *op. cit. supra* note 61, vol. 1, pp. 82–83.

[73] Minguijón *op. cit. supra* note 61, vol. l, pp. 71–73; Vance, *op. cit. supra* note 61, pp. 79–83.

[74] See Van Kleffens, *op. cit. supra* note 61, pp. 167–171; Vance, *op. cit. supra* note 61, pp. 89–91, Minguijón, *op. cit. supra* note 61, vol. 1, pp. 77–78.

[75] On the *Siete Partidas*, see Van Kleffens, *op. cit. supra* note 61, pp. 171–184; Vance, *op. cit. supra* note 61, pp. 93–107; Minguijón, *op. cit. supra* note 61, vol. 1, pp. 78–80; *General Survey*, *op. cit. supra* note 13, pp. 620–632. Having generally used the 1972 Madrid reprint of the 1807 Real Academia edition, I have compared all quotations made here with Grogorio López' glossed edition, as the redactors of the 1808 D.O. would presumably have used an edition based on that of López with annotations. See Vance, *op. cit. supra* note 61, pp. 93–107 on editions. On the various versions of the *Partidas*, and their elaboration, see A. García Gallo, *Manual de historia del derecho español*, 2nd ed., Madrid, Artes Gráficas y Ediciones, 1964, pp. 390–394 (nos. 737–743).

[76] See Batiza, *op. cit. supra* note 41, p. 151, and n. 19.

[77] On the [*Nueva*] *Recopilación de las leyes destos reynos*, see Vance, *op. cit. supra* note 61, pp. 121–124; Minguijón, *op. cit. supra* note 61, vol. 2, pp. 122–123. In references, for convenience, I shall abbreviate it as *Rec. Cast.* (*Castilla*), following the D.L.V. I used a standard edition, that of 1640–1641.

[78] On the *Fuero viejo*, see Minguijón, *op. cit. supra* note 61, vol. 1, p. 76; Vance, *op. cit. supra* note 61, pp. 83–85; Van Kleffens, *op. cit. supra* note 61, pp. 128–130. The *Fuero viejo* was first published, Madrid, J. Ibarra, 1771, edited by I.J. de Asso y del Rio and M. de Manuel y Rodriguez: this is the edition I used.

[79] On them, see Vance, *op. cit. supra* note 61, pp. 107–108; Minguijón, *op. cit. supra* note 61, vol. 1, p. 81; Van Kleffens, *op. cit. supra* note 61, pp. 215–216.

[80] See Vance, *op. cit. supra* note 61, pp. 124–127. I used the official edition issued in Madrid, 1805–1807; again following the D.L.V., I shall cite it as *Nov. Rec.*

system outlined; more especially so, since it has been pointed out that the *Partidas* were Romanizing in effect. To this end it is necessary to discuss Castilian legal history. There are two aspects to the "reception" of Roman law in Castile: First, the enactment of Roman rules in legislation, and, second, the use of Roman law as a supplement to legislation, custom and the like.

The Iberian peninsula had formed part of the Roman Empire, and, in 409 A.D., had been invaded by "barbarian" tribes.[81] Of these tribes, the most significant were the Visigoths. Visigothic rulers issued various "barbarian" codes, composed of Roman and German elements.[82] The two earliest of these codes were that of Euric of 475 or 476 and the *Breviarium Alarici* or *Lex romana Visigothorum* of 506.[83] Under the king Reckesvinth, there was a complete revision of the Visigothic law, resulting in the 654 promulgation of the *Liber judiciorum*. This redaction was revised several times, reaching its final form under Egica in 694.[84] This work became known as the *Fuero juzgo*.

The *Fuero juzgo,* written in Latin, was the last stage achieved by the Visigothic law, for shortly after its promulgation came the Islamic Umayyad invasion and conquest of Spain. This *Fuero* was a prime source of Castilian law. Its Roman-law aspects were taken from a revised version of the code of Euric: the *Breviarium* of Alaric had no influence.[85] The Roman-law influence was fairly marked, and one commentator has described the work as an "especie de transacción entre las fórmulas y el rigorismo del derecho romano y las costumbres propias del pueblo godo".[86] Reckesvinth had abrogated the Roman law itself, and allowed it to be used only in education.[87] García Gallo comments that:

> El derecho romano fué totalmente desconocido y sólo indirectamente, en cuanto recogido en el *Liber Iudiciorum* o en los formularios visigodos, encontró aplicación.[88]

The exact extent of the operation of the *Fuero Juzgo* in the Christian areas during the period of Muslim occupation before the *reconquista* is uncertain.[89] We need not discuss the extent of Moorish influence on the law of Spain.[90]

---

[81] On Iberia under Rome, see Van Kleffens, *op. cit. supra* note 61, pp. 35–44; Minguijón, *op. cit. supra* note 61, vol. 1, pp. 16–33; *General Survey supra* note 13, pp. 592–594.

[82] On the Visigoths and their law, see Van Kleffens, *op. cit. supra* note 61, pp. 45–82; Minguijón, *op. cit. supra* note 61, vol. l, pp. 38–68; *General Survey supra* note 13, pp. 594–601.

[83] On these two codes, see Van Kleffens, *op. cit. supra* note 61, pp. 60–70; Minguijón, *op. cit. supra* note 61, vol. l, pp. 38–9 and 40–41; *General Survey supra* note 13, pp. 596–601 and Vance, *op. cit. supra* note 61, pp. 35–43 and 43–46.

[84] See Van Kleffens, *op. cit. supra* note 61, pp. 75–76; Vance, *op. cit. supra* note 61, pp. 50–52; Minguijón, *op. cit. supra* note 61, pp. 41–42.

[85] See Van Kleffens, *op. cit.*, pp. 76–77, Vance, *op. cit.*, pp. 53–54.

[86] Minguijón, *op. cit. supra* note 61, vol. 1, p. 42, giving the opinion of Francisco de Cárdenas.

[87] See Van Kleffens, *op. cit. supra* note 61, pp. 66–67 and 76–77.

[88] García Gallo, *op. cit. supra* note 75, p. 73.

[89] See, e.g. *General Survey supra* note 13, pp. 603–604; Van Kleffens, *op. cit. supra* note 61, pp. 79–80; Vance, *op. cit. supra* note 61, p. 58.

So far, the Roman law known in the Iberian Peninsula would have been the ante-Justinianic law of the Western Empire.[91] Just as the era of the *Reconquista* began, the study of Roman law in its Justinianic form had started in Italy, especially at Bologna. Spanish lawyers were not unaffected by the revival of Roman law. Many Spaniards went to Bologna to study,[92] returning with many law books.[93] In the early thirteenth century came the founding of the Spanish universities,[94] where Roman and Canon Law were taught—Salamanca becoming a noted centre of legal studies.[95] Not until the modern period did the Spanish universities teach the autochthonous law.[96] Roman law thus became known in learned circles in the Peninsula. The different kingdoms reconquered from the Moors, and the various existing states, received Roman law in varying degrees: the reception in Catalonia, for example, was particularly extensive.[97]

The use of Roman law had certain political implications. Castile was never part of the Holy Roman Empire—the *ius commune* was never, even in theory, in force *ratione imperii*. The formula *rex in regno est imperator* has been referred to already:[98] it is echoed in the second *Partida*:

> Et tiene el Rey lugar de Dios para facer justicia et derecho en el Reyno en que es señor, bien asi como desuso deximos quo lo tiene el emperador en el imperio. . . .[99]

Although Roman law was not applied *ratione imperii*, the Castilian kings were happy to use Roman law to reinforce absolutism.[100]

---

[90] See, e.g., *Van Kleffens, op. cit. supra* note 61, pp. 94–113; *General Survey supra* note 13, p. 581.

[91] From 544 to 629, Byzantium controlled the area around Cartagena. It is possible that the recently completed Justinianic compilation was applied to this area: if so, it has left no trace, and may be discounted.

[92] See R. Altamira, "Les lacumes de l'histoire du droit romain en Espagne", in *Mélanges Fitting supra* note 22, vol. 1, pp. 59–84 at 65–68; Calasso, *Medio Evo supra* note 23, p. 615; Calasso, *Diritto Comune supra* note 23, p. 321; also Van Kleffens, *op. cit. supra* note 61, pp. 176–177.

[93] See Van Kleffens, *op. cit.* p. 177.

[94] See Calasso, *Medio Evo supra* note 23, pp. 615–616; Calasso, *Diritto Comune supra* note 23, pp. 320–321; Koschaker, *op. cit. supra* note 19, p. 131; García Gallo, *op. cit. supra* note 75, p. 84 (no. 173); Van Kleffens, *op. cit. supra* note 61, pp. 177–178.

[95] Van Kleffens, *op. cit. supra* note 61, p. 178.

[96] See R.L. Kagan, *Students and Society Early Modern Spain*, Baltimore, Johns Hopkins Press, 1974, pp. 162–163, 226–227 and 234–235 on the teaching of Spanish law as distinct from Roman. This work is useful on the position of law in the university curriculum.

[97] E. de Hinjosa, "La réception du droit romain en Catalogne", in *Mélanges Fitting supra* note 22, vol. 2, pp. 39–408.

[98] See *supra*, text at note 25.

[99] *Part.* 2.1.7 (second *Partida*, first title, seventh *ley*.) See also Koschaker, *op. cit. supra* note 19, pp. 137–138. The *leyes* of the first title of this second *Partida* carefully discuss the meaning of Emperor, King and their respective spheres of duty. Note that Alfonso X had ambitions to be Holy Roman Emperor: see Van Kleffens, *op. cit.*, pp. 150 and 212. See also *Part.* 2.1.5. for a similar sentiment that the King rules like the Emperor in his Empire.

[100] MacKay, *op. cit. supra* note 63, pp. 99–100, 133, 138–140. The Aragonese Kings made similar use of Roman law: *ibid.*, pp. 111–113. Minguijón, *op. cit. supra* note 61, vol. 1, p. 84, states: "El influjo creciente del derecho romano y la preponderancia de los jurisconsultos en él formados favorecen la tendencia a la centralizacion y al absolutismo."

The factors influential in the penetration of Roman law into customary law France would undoubtedly be influential in Castile. In the medieval period a substantial number of lawyers would be university-trained in Roman law. The Roman system would be attractive because of its apparent superiority over the native law. Some aspects of Roman law favoured the absolutist and centralizing tendencies of the Castilian monarchy. The application of Canon law, closely related to the Roman, would have created conditions receptive to Roman jurisprudence. The details of the reception of Roman law in Castile are still largely unresearched; but the above factors would result in the medieval period in the increasing influence of Roman jurisprudence in legal circles: certainly all scholarly lawyers would have a thorough grounding in Roman law.

From this, some conflict between the native law and that of Rome may be deduced. The *Fuero real*, for example, was largely of native origin, with some traceable Roman influences;[101] in the nearly contemporary *Siete Partidas*, Roman law was very influential: "sopra tutto del campo del diritto privato e del penale, l'influenza dei testi romani e degl' insegnamenti del più celebrati glossatori italiani, particolarmente Azzone e Accursio, e evidente."[102] The *Siete Partidas* were a major factor in Romanizing the Castilian law, and in many respects marked a dramatic change in the native law.[103] Although the *Partidas* were not officially in force until the *Ordenamiento de Alcalá*, it is clear that from the time of their redaction, they profoundly influenced Castilian legal thought.[104] Even the supplementary position of the *Partidas* in the *Ordenamiento*'s order of precedence did not prevent them from becoming the major source of Castilian law.[105]

That the Roman law was in itself widely used in Castile may be deduced from the fact that several Castilian kings tried to prevent its use. Thus in August 1258, in a letter to the *alcaldes* of Valladolid, we find Alfonso X himself prohibiting the observance of the Roman laws in Castile.[106] In 1427, John II prohibited the citation before the courts of any civilian or canonist more recent than Bartolus or Joannes Andreae.[107] In 1713, the Council issued a resolution complaining of the belief that in the courts more weight should be given to the Roman and Canon laws than to the laws of Spain.[108]

Certainly, these laws seem to have been generally ineffective. Until the middle of the eighteenth century, all university instruction in law was in the

---

[101] See, e.g. Van Kleffens, *op. cit. supra* note 61, p. 180; *General Survey supra* note 13, p. 628.
[102] Calasso, *Diritto Comune supra* note 23, p. 321.
[103] See, e.g., *General Survey supra* note 13, pp. 621–622, 628–632; García Gallo, *op. cit. supra* note 75, vol. 1, p. 90 (no. 188); Minguijón, *op. cit. supra* note 61, vol. 1, p. 71 remarks: "El código de las Siete Partidas contribuyó sobremanera a la preponderancia del Romanismo."
[104] *General Survey supra* note 13, pp. 622–623.
[105] *Ibid.*, p. 663.
[106] *Ibid.*, p. 622.
[107] Calasso, *Diritto Comune supra* note 23, pp. 321–322; Van Kleffens, *op. cit. supra* note 61, pp. 19–20 and 225–226; *General Survey supra* note 13, p. 632.
[108] See *General Survey supra* note 13, p. 663, pp. 676–677.

Roman and Canon law.[109] Indeed, the *Reyes Católicos* had enacted in 1493 that anyone seeking a royal judicial appointment should have studied canon or civil law for at least ten years in a Castilian or foreign university.[110] Although the *Leys de Toro* required that office holders be versed in the laws of the realm,[111] it is doubtful if many new appointees would have had the stipulated knowledge. Kagan reports repeated complaints of the universities' failure to train adequately future magistrates, who left university unable to understand the law in force: he suggests that one reason for this was the failure of the universities to teach any law other than the Roman or Canon.[112] Inevitably such lawyers would tend to view Castilian law from the perspective of the law within which they were trained.

Thus, although, in theory, the Roman law could only be used as *ratio scripta*,[113] except where introduced by legislation, there can be no doubt of its major influence in shaping Castilian law. Commentaries on the native law were endowed with massive civilian learning; the native law was interpreted using the Roman law.[114] Despite all efforts, the Castilian law became Romanized, and took its place in the European civilian world.[115]

This, then, was the system introduced by O'Reilly into Louisiana by applying the Laws of the Indies to the newly acquired territories. There can now be no doubt that this system was in force in Spanish *Luisiana* both in theory and in practice.[116] The Spanish judicial records confirm this, and two examples drawn from them serve as a useful illustration. In 1784, Juan Esteban Boré brought a court action to prove that husbands can appoint their wives tutrices to their children in their will, without calling a family meeting. Relying on the *Siete Partidas*, the court held this proved.[117] In a 1771 case, brought by a tutor, the court decided that the family meeting had no place in Spanish law, and hence none in Louisiana.[118]

---

[109] See *supra*, references in note 94.
[110] *Rec. Cast.*, 3.9.2.
[111] *Ley* 2.
[112] Kagan, *op. cit. supra* note 96, pp. 234–235. Kagan's study is invaluable in helping understand the position of the *letrados* in Castilian society.
[113] As the de la Vergne manuscript recognized in the Avant-Propos, p. 7: "A l'égard des dispositions du droit Romain, elles ne peuvent être citées comme Loix en Espagne, mais seulement comme raison écrite."
[114] See *infra*, chap. 4, on the provisions of the *Leyes de Toro*, relative to the legal incapacity of married women.
[115] A neat, concise discussion of the place of Roman law in Castile, and its introduction to the New World colonies, may be found in G.P. Margadant, "The Hallowing and the Hollowing of Roman Law", in *Festschrift für Pan. J. Zepos*, Cologne, Ch. Katsikalis Verlag, 1973, vol. 3, pp. 595–614 at pp. 595–601.
[116] See *supra*, references in notes 56–59 *supra*; above all, Baade, "Marriage Contracts", pp. 73–79.
[117] Case found in 24 *La. Hist. Quar.* (1941), 604, relying on *Part.* 6.16.4 and 9.
[118] Case found in 8 *La. Hist. Quar.* (1925), 183.

The Territorial Period

The Law Prior to the 1808 Digest

In October 1800, Spain retroceded Louisiana to France by the secret Treaty of San Ildefonso, on condition that Napoleon erect an Italian kingdom for the Duke of Parma, brother-in-law of Carlos IV of Spain, but with the proviso that France should not cede Louisiana to any third country.[119] Napoleon attempted to put this plan into operation, but, disliking the Duke of Parma, persuaded Carlos that the kingdom be given to Parma's son, Luis, Prince of Parma.[120] Although Napoleon had not fully carried out his side of the agreement,[121] he pressured the Spanish Crown into formally surrendering Louisiana to France in October 1802. For various reasons, including the likely reopening of hostilities in Europe,[122] Napoleon decided to sell Louisiana to the United States, and did so on 30th April 1803.[123] Spain protested, but in her weak state could do nothing; and, accordingly, the French government, in the person of Pierre Clement de Laussat, newly appointed Prefect of Louisiana, received Louisiana from Spain on 30th November 1803, and transferred the territory to the United States on 30th December 1803.[124] During his time as Prefect, Laussat made no significant attempt to alter the laws in force,[125] and, therefore, the United States took control of Louisiana with the laws enforced by Spain still applying.

The vast territory acquired by the United States was split up. Lower Louisiana, centered on New Orleans, was designated as the Territory of Orleans.[126] It is with this Territory, the future state of Louisiana, that we will be concerned, as it was only here that civil law was preserved: upper Louisiana, for example, the future state of Missouri, quickly adopted common law.[127]

A former governor of the Mississippi Territory, William C.C. Claiborne, was appointed Governor of the Territory of Orleans.[128] His first official action was to issue a proclamation that provided for the continuance of the laws already in force.[129] Thus, the Spanish Laws of the Indies remained in force,

---

[119] On the background to this, see A. DeConde, *This Affair of Louisiana*, New York, Scribner, 1976, pp. 91–96.

[120] *Ibid*., p. 96 (by the Convention of Aranjuez).

[121] *Ibid*., p. 104 for details.

[122] *Ibid*., pp. 157–158 and 162–166.

[123] On the negotiations, see *ibid*., pp. 167–175.

[124] *Ibid*., pp. 204–206. It had been intended that the two transfers take place on the same day so that American troops could be on hand to quell any demonstrations. The Americans were not ready on time, so that the transfers took place on different days: both, however, were peaceful.

[125] See Brown, *op. cit. supra* note 6, pp. 186–187; Dargo, *Jefferson's Louisiana*, p. 105.

[126] I will, for convenience, continue to refer generally to the Territory of Orleans as Louisiana.

[127] See K. Knaup, "The Transition from Spanish Civil Law to English Common Law in Missouri", 16 *St. Louis Uniersity Law Journal* (1971), pp. 218–231.

[128] On W.C.C. Claiborne, and his governorship, see Dargo, *Jefferson's Louisiana*, pp. 23–50.

[129] See Dargo, *Jefferson's Louisiana*, p. 105; Brown, *op. cit. supra* note 6, p. 176 and E.G. Brown "Legal Systems in Conflict: Orleans Territory 1804–1812", 1 *American Journal of Legal History* (1957), pp. 35–75 at p. 36.

although it was the earnest desire of President Jefferson to replace the existing laws with Anglo-American common law in order to aid absorption of Louisiana into the Union.

Various writers have discussed the conflict and confusion over the laws in force in Louisiana prior to the promulgation of the 1808 Digest.[130] This conflict was dominated by competition between the civil law and the Anglo-American common law, and has been most carefully investigated already,[131] so that it is unnecessary here to discuss it in any depth. There is a dispute over the sources of the 1808 Digest, a dispute directly relating to the history of Louisiana law prior to the redaction of the code.[132] Professor Pascal argues that, in his own term, "Spanish-Roman" law was in force in Louisiana prior to the Digest, the redactors were ordered to compile the Digest according to the law in force, and that the redactors carried out their orders, so that the Digest, despite its copying from the French code, is in fact a Digest of the "Spanish-Roman" law. (He also considers that the Digest is not a "true code": this view we will assess below.)[133] Professor Batiza, on the basis of painstaking comparison of the text of individual articles of the Digest with other legal materials, argues that the sources of the overwhelming majority of articles are to be found in the work of the French codifiers, and also of certain French doctrinal writers, although some articles are drawn from Castilian, Roman and English law.

This dispute focuses not only on the actual source of many articles, but also on the appropriate methods of research. In chapters four and five there will be a consideration of the two viewpoints as they relate to sections of the code and individual articles, and, in the concluding part of the thesis, both Batiza's and Pascal's work will be evaluated. However, some aspects of Pascal's views fall for consideration here. His view that the Digest is a guide to the "Spanish-Roman" sources, denies that there are innovations. From this two results flow. This view, first, denies there has been any borrowing from other systems, and, second, denies that the 1808 redaction is a "code". Were Pascal correct in these two contentions, much of this study would be invalidated, since it posits the redactors innovating and changing the law by selecting between competing sources.

Pascal's view relies on the redactors considering themselves free to examine only the sources as laid down in the *Recopilación de las Indias*:[134] this being, in Austinian terms, the positive law formally in force by legislative authority of the

---

[130] See, e.g. Brown, *op. cit. supra* note 129, *passim*; Dargo, *Jefferson's Louisiana*, pp. 105–153; A. Tate, "The Splendid Mystery of the Civil Code of Louisiana", 25 *La. Bar J.* (1977), pp. 29–39 at 32–35.

[131] See supra, references in note 130, especially Dargo *Jefferson's Louisiana*.

[132] See on this dispute: Sweeney, "Tournament"; Batiza, "Sources"; Batiza, "Rejoinder"; Pascal, "Reply"; Franklin, "Existential Force"; Baade, "Marriage Contracts", pp. 83–84; L.A. Darby and T.J. McDonald, "A Recent Discovery: Another Copy of Moreau Lislet's Annotations to the Code of 1808", 47 *Tul. L. Rev.* (1973), pp. 1210–1213; Dargo, *Jefferson's Louisiana*, pp. 156–164.

[133] See *infra*, "The 1808 Redaction: 'Digest' or 'Code'?"

[134] See *supra*, text at notes 61–80.

sovereign.[135] His view further relies on there being no use of or influence of French law in territorial Louisiana prior to 1808. These two points will now be considered in turn.

Louisiana as a Civilian Jurisdiction

The period of redaction of the Digest would tend to suggest that the redactors would be supporters of natural law theories: indeed, evidence from the Digest itself shows that this suggestion is correct.[136] That the redactors were supporters of natural law implies that they would not consider their actions hampered by a narrow conception of the positive law in force in Louisiana. Further, that the redactors should consider non-Castilian sources in drawing up the code is hardly surprising anyway, considering that codification is linked to evaluation of the law in comparison with other legal systems.[137] Indeed, the redactors of the 1825 Civil Code of Louisiana (one of whom had been an 1808 redactor), in their introduction to the 1823 Projet, specifically mentioned this process of evaluating the law in the light of other systems of law, stating that in their task of revising the civil code they would "keep a reverent eye" on the legal principles of the past. They described the *Siete Partidas*, the English law, and the "comprehensive" Codes of France as "rich mines from which we can draw treasures of Legislation"; but they further remarked that where these systems differ they would refer to Roman law, described as "eternal truth", "prophetic legislation", and as containing "maxims applicable to all nations, at all times and under every form of government".[138] There is no reason to suppose that in 1808 the redactors had thought differently.

The redactors' conception of the role of Roman law is significant: they clearly equate it with *ratio scripta*. As pointed out earlier, in the medieval period

---

[135] Pascal assumes that the *theoretical* approach of the redactors would be that of the positive theory of law as exemplified in the writings of John Austin; namely that the redactors would regard as law only that which has been posited or commanded by the sovereign. Therefore, the redactors would feel free to examine only those sources formally in force in Louisiana, as the "national" law: other sources would have no validity since they lacked the sanction of the sovereign. On Austin, see, e.g., G.W. Paton, *A Textbook of Jurisprudence*, 4th ed. Oxford, Clarendon Press, 1972, pp. 5–14. For consideration of Austin as an analytical philosopher, see A.R. White, "Austin as a Philosophical Analyst", 64 *Archiv für Rechts-und Sozialphilosophie* (1978), pp. 379–399; G. Maher, "Analytical Philosophy and Austin's Philosophy of Law", 64 *Archiv für Rechts-und Sozialphilosophie* (1978), pp. 401–416. W.L. Morison, "Some Myths about Positivism", 68 *Yale Law Journal* (1958), pp. 212–233, gives a sympathetic treatment of Austin. E. Ruben, "John Austin's Political Pamphlets, 1824–1859", in E. Attwool (ed.), *Perspectives in Jurisprudence*, Glasgow, 1977, pp. 20–41, argues that Austin's positivistic view of law is due to his role as defender of the middle class.

[136] See *infra*, chap. 6, "Natural Law Influence on the Digest".

[137] See *supra*, chap. 1, "The Suitability of Louisiana and Quebec as Subjects of Study". On whether the Digest of 1808 can truly be described as a code, see *infra*, "The 1808 Redaction: 'Digest' or 'Code'?"

[138] "Preliminary Report of the Code Commissioners, Dated February 13, 1823", in *La. Leg. Arch.*, vol. 1, pp. LXXXV–XCV at pp. LXXXIX–XC

the Roman or civil law came to be regarded as the *ius commune* of much of Europe.[139] As in Castile and France,[140] the Roman law supplemented and even superseded the local law in a substantial part of Europe.[141] This resulted in there being a fairly fundamental similarity between the laws of much of Europe; whatever their nationality, the jurists who used and wrote about the Roman law shared a common legal cultural background through their university training. Students would readily study abroad; teachers moved from country to country. Because of this common legal culture, and because most juristic works were written in Latin, legal ideas were readily passed from one country to another. It should be remembered that, before the development of the humanist approach to Roman law, the Roman law was studied as law immediately applicable. For example, Voet in his *Commentarius ad Pandectas*,[142] which dealt with both the Roman and the modern law, cited many foreign authors: to indicate that this was not a mere academic exercise, it may be pointed out that he infrequently cited humanist scholars, but cited many practice-oriented foreign writers.[143]

By the seventeenth and eighteenth centuries, however, the idea of Roman law as the *ius commune* of Europe was breaking down, and differing systems of national law developing.[144] It is clear, nonetheless, that the various civilian legal systems continued to influence one another, not only in juristic writing, but also in legal practice. Some examples drawn from the work of Coing neatly illustrate this. First, in the eighteenth century, the Hanoverian Court of Appeal used the works of Argentré, a sixteenth century French commentator on local custom. Second, a Portuguese judge is known to have used the writings of the German jurist Carpzow in his work. Third, the German bankruptcy law originates in the writings of a seventeenth-century Castilian judge.[145] This mutual influence of the civilian systems continued into the nineteenth century: the century when the Code Napoléon influenced the law of most civilian countries. Zajtay explains it thus:

> L'unité de la famille des droits romano-germaniques, fondée sur la réception du système scientifique du droit romain, s'est trouvée, de son côté, à la base de nombreux phénomènes intéressants, notamment des échanges et des influences réciproques qui ont eu lieu entre ces droits au cours de leur histoire. Rappelons

---

[139] See *supra*, references in notes 19, 20, 21 and 23.
[140] See *supra*, text at notes 13–36 and 81–115.
[141] See *supra*, references in notes 19, 20, 21 and 23.
[142] J. Voet, *Commentarius ad pandectas*, Leiden, Johannes Verbessel, 1698–1704.
[143] See R. Feenstra and C.J.D. Waal, *Seventeenth-century Leyden Law Professors and their Influence on the Development of the Civil Law: A Study of Bronchorst, Vinnius and Voet*, Amsterdam, North-Holland Publishing Co., 1975, p. 41.
[144] See K. Luig, "The Institutes of National Law in the Seventeenth and Eighteenth Centuries", 17 (N.S.) *Juridical Review* (1972), pp. 193–226. This is, of course, the period of the development of the nation state, and, as seen already, of the start to the teaching of national law in European Universities.
[145] Coing, *op. cit. supra* note 20, pp. 514–515.

> notamment que cette unité a permis au droit français de jouer au XIXe siècle le rôle d'un véritable droit commun des pays latins.[146]

Thus, one may say that, in civil law Europe, there was a free flow of legal ideas from one area to another—the various civilian systems borrowing from and influencing one another. The civil law was regarded as "supra-national", transcending national legal systems; whether it was conceived of as, in the early period, the *ius commune*, or, as later, *ratio scripta*.

There is evidence of this "supra-national" outlook in Louisiana prior to and after codification. During the period of conflict prior to the promulgation of the Digest, there was a clear tendency to oppose civil law to common law, regarding civil law as the Roman law in modern use. The civil law was identified as a whole system with minor national variations opposed to the Anglo-American law. Thus, after Governor Claiborne had vetoed the Act of 1806 which laid down the civilian sources to be consulted in Louisiana,[147] the New Orleans' newspaper, *Le Telegraphe*, in June 1806, published a "Manifesto" which stated:

> We certainly do not attempt to draw any parallel between the civil law and the common law; but, in short, the wisdom of the civil law is recognized by all Europe.[148]

In 1807, Edward Livingston proposed that an Anglo-French translation be made of the entire body of Roman and Byzantine law, including some ante-Justinianic Roman law. He declared that mastery of the Roman law was indispensable for the Louisiana legislators, and that since Roman law operated in the Spanish, Portuguese, and Dutch colonies, knowledge of it would aid the Louisianians.[149] Livingston declared himself to be a convert to the Roman law. The debate over the law was couched in terms of the civil law against the common law, not the Castilian law as provided by the Laws of the Indies against the common law.[150] If final proof were needed, it is sufficient to examine a statement of the 1825 redactors, who said it was their intention to free the:

> Courts in every instance from the necessity of examining into Spanish Statutes, ordinances and usages, Latin Commentaries, the work of French and Italian Jurists, and the heavy tomes of Dutch and Flemish annotations, before they could decide the law.[151]

---

[146] I. Zajtay, "La permanence des concepts du droit romain dans les systèmes juridiques continentaux", 18 *R.I.D.C.* (1966), pp. 353–363 at p. 359.
[147] The text of this Act may be found in Brown, *op. cit. supra* note 129, pp. 47–48, and Franklin, "Expulsion", p. 323.
[148] This document may be found quoted almost in full in Brown, *op. cit. supra* note 129, pp. 49–52. The quotation here is at *ibid.*, p. 51.
[149] See Franklin, "Expulsion", pp. 324–325 n. 2.
[150] See Dargo, *Jefferson's Louisiana*, pp. 105–153 *passim.*
[151] "Preliminary Report, 1823", *supra* note 138, p. XCII.

The sources listed are significant. Obviously the Spanish sources are given precedence; but a train of learned civilian sources—not of Spanish origin—follows them. This listing of sources relevant for reaching a decision would have been one familiar in any civilian country before codification.[152] That the redactors of the 1825 Code should stress *Spanish* law is also significant. In the period between 1808 and 1825, there had been a revival of Spanish (more properly Castilian) law, resulting in decisions such as *Cottin.*[153] It is important to note that, prior to 1808, the "civil law" was not clearly differentiated by all into its national variations.

The civilian legal systems borrowed freely from one another, the borrowing facilitated by their common Roman law background. Louisiana formed part of this tradition. Therefore, those who are surprised at the redactors of the Digest of 1808 copying extensively from the work of the French redactors,[154] or those who deny the possibility that it could have done so,[155] are mistaken. The 1808 Digest followed civilian tradition: indeed, many countries adopted versions of the French code far closer to the original than the Digest. Further, given the influence of French sources in Louisiana during the early territorial period, borrowing from the Code Napoléon is even less surprising.

French Law in Louisiana Prior to the 1808 Digest

The records of the Louisiana Superior Court in the Territorial period have disappeared;[156] and there was no system of court reporting until the start of *Martin's Reports*, in which the earliest reported cases come from 1809.[157] This makes it difficult to reconstruct what exactly was the attitude of the court, and the use it made of the various possible legal materials. Nonetheless, informal sources and accounts indicate that there was both knowledge and use of French law in territorial Louisiana. It is, however, difficult to evaluate these accounts, and to decide whether the reporters of the use of French law were simply mistaken, or if there was a residual use of such law tolerated outwith the courts, or, indeed, if the use of French law was the result of the confusion and uncertainty in the courts.[158] It is useful, accordingly, to examine a sample of such statements.

---

[152] It is useful to compare the remarks of the redactors with the range and hierarchy of sources used in the decisions of the *Rota Fiorentina* in the eighteenth century. See G. Gorla, "A Decision of the *Rota Fiorentina* of 1780 on Liability for Damages Caused by the 'Ball Game'", 49 *Tul. L. Rev.* (1975), pp. 346–357 at p. 348.

[153] 5 Mart. O.S. 93 (1817).

[154] Brown, *op. cit. supra* note 129, p. 58 states: "Why Brown and Moreau Lislet departed from their instructions and based the Code of 1808 upon the contemporary French codification is not known."

[155] Batiza, "Reply", pp. 607–609; Dargo, *Jefferson's Louisiana*, pp. 160–164.

[156] See on this and lack of court reporting, Dargo, *Jeffersons' Louisiana*, p. 225 n. 17 and p. 246.

[157] This series was started by F.X. Martin and continued by others.

[158] See Brown, *op. cit. supra* note 129, *passim*; Dargo, *Jefferson's Louisiana*, pp. 105–153 *passim*.

In his study of marriage contracts in colonial and territorial Louisiana, Hans Baade shows that, after the Purchase, there was a revival of French forms.[159] He has thus provided particularly important evidence of the everyday use of French laws. He does not think, however, that there had been before codification a "definitive reestablishment on a customary basis of French family property law".[160]

One statement of interest is that made by Daniel Clark, a prominent merchant of New Orleans,[161] in answer to a query of Jefferson, who sought information on Louisiana before the transfer in order to aid ratification of the treaty of transfer by Congress.[162] To the question: "Whence is their Code of Laws derived?", Clark replied: "The Code of laws is derived from the Recopilacion de Indias, and Leyes de Castilla & les uses & Coutumes de Paris for what respects usages and Customs. . . ."[163] Brown suggests that Clark:

> As a merchant . . . knew that the laws of Spain were the official laws in force. As an individual, he may have known of instances where the French residents . . . had been guided by French custom and law in private decisions and family relationships.[164]

Edward Livingston had taken up practice as an attorney in New Orleans, and was consequently in a position to know the problems of legal practice and the authorities cited and used in court. In May 1804, he wrote thus:

> The Governor conceives himself authorized to legislate and his ordinances in English mixed with those of his predecessors in Spanish and *French*, the laws of Castille [sic], the *Customs of Paris*, the Leyes de Partidas, *les edits du Roi*, the Statutes of the United States and the omnipresent Common Law of England make a confusion worse than that of babel . . . .[165]

James Brown, one of the redactors of the 1808 code, stated in 1805 that it was necessary to adopt a code to ease the confusion in the courts and to aid a reception of common law before the territorial legislature started to function, as:

> The members of the Council and House of Representatives will generally be attached to French Laws and will pass only acts resembling the Civil Laws and the Spanish Ordinances formerly in force here.[166]

---

[159] See Baade, "Marriage Contracts", pp. 54–57 and 79–82.
[160] *Ibid.*, p. 80.
[161] See J.G. Clark, *New Orleans, 1718–1812: An Economic History*, Baton Rouge, Louisiana State University Press, 1970, pp. 272, 336 and 251. At the time of the Purchase, Clark was acting as U.S. consul in New Orleans: *ibid.*, p. 215.
[162] See Jefferson to Claiborne, 17 July, 1803, found quoted in Brown, *op. cit. supra* note 6, pp. 170–171.
[163] Quoted *ibid.*, p. 172.
[164] *Ibid.*, p. 182. Cf. Baade, "Marriage Contracts", p. 80.
[165] Found quoted in Dargo, *Jefferson's Louisiana*, pp. 111–112 (emphasis mine).
[166] Found quoted in Brown, *op. cit. supra* note 129, pp. 40–41 at p. 41. Cf. Dargo, *Jefferson's Louisiana*, pp. 114–115.

Both Clark and Livingston are reliable and credible witnesses to the law applied in Louisiana, and, from their testimony, one must conclude that, at last to a limited extent, the French law was still applied in Louisiana. Both Livingston and Brown emphasize the confusion reigning in the courts: this is perhaps not surprising when one considers that the first judge appointed to the Louisiana bench was one John Prevost, a common lawyer. Indeed, the Louisiana Remonstrance of 1804,[167] stated that the judges were "uncertain of [by] what codes they are to decide, wavering between the civil and the common law, between the forms of French, Spanish and American jurisprudence . . .".[168] In an attempt to end this confusion, on the instigation of Prevost, a case was brought argued by the leading New Orleans attorneys, in which Prevost decided that the civil law was in force in Louisiana, including in the definition of "civil law", the Roman, French and Spanish laws.[169] The 1825 Code, in article 3521, states that the French law had been in force along with the Spanish and Roman, when Louisiana was acquired by the United States. This is valuable evidence of the use of French law.

From this brief survey, one may conclude that French law was both known and perhaps even applied in Louisiana before codification. If applied this may have been the result of, first, the uncertainty over the laws in force arising out of the transfer of sovereignty, second, the influx of American attorneys, ignorant of the exact nature of the law in force, and third, the only judge being common-law trained and uncertain as to the law to apply. Two important conclusions may be drawn. First, it would appear that some knowledge of French law must have been fairly widespread and access to French legal materials possible during the territorial period. This means that there would have been no difficulty for the 1808 redactors in drawing on pre-codification French sources had they so chosen. It is also evident that the redactors had access to the French code and its 1800 *projet*.[170] Second, there may have been some use of French law in the early territorial period. If so this would tend to suggest that the redactors would be inclined to utilize French law in drawing up their code, especially since French law had been given judicial authorization. Such an inclination would be supported by the civilian "supra-national" attitude in Louisiana outlined above.

Pascal's view, that the Digest of 1808 was composed of "Spanish Roman" law because "Spanish-Roman" law was the law in force, may be discounted, and for two reasons. First, the civilian tradition in Louisiana was not one that had a rigidly positive and nationalistic outlook on law. Second, to some extent, French law had been used in Louisiana, and had even been given judicial authority.

It is convenient, if not quite logical, to allude here to the Anglo-American common law. Some of the preceding quotations have referred both to its

---

[167] On which see Dargo *Jefferson's Louisiana*, p. 17.

[168] Found quoted in *ibid.*, p. 117.

[169] See Dargo, *Jefferson's Louisiana*, p. 132. On the need for this case, see Brown, *op. cit. supra* note 129, pp. 38–40.

[170] Batiza, "Sources", p. 11; Pascal, "Reply", p. 625.

influence in Louisiana and to the desire of many Americans for a reception of common law in Louisiana. Knowledge of common law was obviously widespread in Louisiana, many American attorneys having moved to New Orleans. All this, taken in conjunction with the fact that one of the redactors was by training a common lawyer, would have allowed the redactors, in their work of codification, to draw easily on common law.

The 1808 Redaction: "Digest" or "Code"?

There is a dispute over whether or not the 1808 Digest should be classed as a "digest" or a "code".[171] From the discussion in chapter one[172] of the distinguishing features of a code, it would seem correct to define the 1808 redaction, officially entitled, *A Digest of the Civil Laws now in Force in the Territory of Orleans*, as a code in the Romanistic civilian tradition. The dispute centres over the meaning to be attributed to "code" and "digest". Dargo gives a neat definition of both:

> A digest is a summary or compilation of pre-existing law designed to make that law known and available. Prior law remains authoritative. A code, on the other hand, replaces prior law and itself becomes the definitive and final statement of the law for purposes of adjudication.[173]

Dargo believes the 1808 redaction to be a "digest", and so does Professor Pascal. Pascal claims that the work is a "digest" in order to reinforce his argument on the sources: this is because, if the redaction is a "digest" or compilation of the laws previously in force, the sources of the redaction must be the existing "Spanish" law.[174] T.W. Tucker also argues that the Digest is a mere "Digest of the Spanish laws, which retained their subsidiary force".[175] Professor Batiza, taking the opposing view, remarks that: "The Code of 1808 . . . in scope, structure and drafting technique is an authentic civil code in the western tradition inaugurated by the *Code Civil des Français* in 1804, rather than a digest."[176] On the basis of the previous discussion, Professor Batiza's view must be taken as correct.

Although Pascal himself puts forward no arguments for the 1808 redaction to be considered a "digest", Dargo does argue for this stance, acknowledging indebtedness to Pascal for the arguments.[177] Tucker also argues for his view.[178]

---

[171] See *supra*, chap. 1, "On the Suitability of Louisiana and Quebec as Objects of Study"; and *supra*, text at notes 133–137.
[172] See *supra*, chap. 1, "On the Suitability of Louisiana and Quebec as Objects of Study".
[173] Dargo, *Jefferson's Louisiana*, p. 157.
[174] Pascal, "Reply", p. 604 n. 4.
[175] T.W. Tucker, "Interpretation of the Louisiana Civil Codes, 1808–1840: The Failure of the Preliminary Title", unpublished LL.M. thesis, University of Glasgow, 1972, p. 94.
[176] Batiza, "Rejoinder", p. 630.
[177] Dargo, *Jefferson's Louisiana*, p. 232 n. 11.
[178] Tucker, *op. cit supra* note 175, pp. 101–108.

With one exception, all these arguments relate to matters outwith the structure and contents of the actual code. This otherwise pointless dispute must be discussed as Dargo and Pascal use their "digest" theory as further proof that the sources of the 1808 redaction are Spanish. (They do not appear to appreciate the circularity of their argument: since only Spanish sources were used, the 1808 redaction is a "digest"; that it is a "digest" proves that only Spanish sources were used.) Were the code a "digest"—as they have defined it—this study would be, to some extent, pointless: the redactors would not have been selecting freely among competing provisions or consciously updating the law.

The arguments of Dargo and Tucker are the following. First, the word "Digest" was used to describe the redaction. Tucker quotes the full title[179] and declares that it "implies . . . that the work is but an outline, a resumé of a larger system, which is to remain in force".[180] Dargo does not explicitly argue on the basis of the title. Second, the preamble to the statute providing for the promulgation of the digest/code stated that: " . . . it had become indispensable to make known the laws . . . and to collect them in a single work, *which might serve as a guide* for the decision of the courts and juries without recurring to a multiplicity of books. . . ."[181] Dargo remarks that "a guide to sources was not a finished code".[182] Third, the Digest in article 3 (pp. 2–3) of its preliminary title apparently recognizes custom as a source of law. Dargo argues that: "Since modern civil codes are based on legislative positivism this provision contravened a fundamental principle of code law."[183] Fourth, s. 2 of the Act promulgating the Digest stated:

> *And be it further enacted*, That whatever in the ancient civil laws of this territory, or in the territorial statute, is contrary to the dispositions contained in the said digest, or irreconcilable with them, is hereby abrogated.[184]

Dargo deduces: "The obvious reference was inescapable: all other prior law not so abrogated remained in force."[185] Tucker reaches a similar conclusion.[186] Fifth, Dargo and Tucker both point to a series of decisions in which the Louisiana courts adopted the view that the 1808 compilation was merely a "digest" (in their definition).[187] Sixth, Dargo points to a letter from Claiborne to Secretary Madison, in which the Governor said: "The 'Civil Code' alluded to in my last letter is

---

[179] *A Digest of the Civil Laws Now in Force in the Territory of Orleans with Alterations and Amendments Adapted to its Present System of Government.*

[180] Tucker, *op. cit supra* note 175, p. 101.

[181] Dargo's emphasis (*Jefferson's Louisiana*, pp. 157–158)—the reason for giving it will be made obvious. For the actual text of the Act, see J.H. Tucker, "Source Books of Louisiana Law", in *La. Leg. Arch.*, vol. 1, pp. XV–LXXIV at pp. XIX–XX.

[182] Dargo, *Jefferson's Louisiana*, p. 158.

[183] *Ibid.*, p. 158.

[184] For text, see Tucker, *op. cit. supra* note 181, p. XIX.

[185] Dargo, *Jefferson's Louisiana*, p. 158.

[186] Tucker, *op. cit supra* note 175, p. 101.

[187] Dargo, *Jefferson's Louisiana*, p. 158; Tucker, *op. cit. supra* note 175, pp. 109–115.

nothing more, than a 'Digest of the Civil Laws in Force in this territory'."[188] Tucker, as contemporary evidence, quotes the writings of Martin, Moreau Lislet and Carleton, and Mazureau.[189] Seventh, Tucker argues for his "digest" view from the *purpose* of the redaction, stating that the Louisianians "did not codify to do away with the old laws; they codified so they could keep them".[190]

We will deal with these arguments in turn.

1. No significance should be ascribed to the use of the word "digest". It is obvious that at this period the two words "code" and "digest" could be used interchangeably. Similarly, "code" could be used to refer to any body of laws. Many examples could be given of these usages;[191] but to prove the point, only a few examples are necessary. The *Encyclopédie* had declared: "Code signifie en général *recueil de droit*; mais on donne ce nomme à plusieurs sortes de recueils fort différens les uns des autres."[192] There is ample evidence of this loose usage in Louisiana. In the introduction to their translation of the *Partidas*, Moreau Lislet and Carleton state:

> [T]he legislature of the territory of Orleans . . . ordered a digest of those laws to be made. . . . This code commonly known under the name of the Civil Code. . . .[193]

The Manifesto in *Le Telegraphe* said of the vetoed 1806 Act:[194] "By this measure one will not place the courts so to speak between the different codes…."[195] The civil law and the common law were the "codes" referred to. The Louisiana Remonstrance stated that the judges were "uncertain of [by] what codes they are to decide, wavering between the civil and the common law".[196] The whole corpus of Roman law could also be called a "code".[197] James Brown, one of the Digest redactors, wrote: "The Civil Law—the Spanish Ordinances—

---

188 Dargo, *Jefferson's Louisiana*, p. 157.

189 Tucker, *op. cit. supra* note 175, pp. 105–109. Martin was the law reporter and judge, see *supra*, note 157. Tucker is relying (1) on the two-volume *History of Louisiana from the Earliest Period*, by F.X. Martin first published in New Orleans in 1827–1829; (2) on the two-volume translation by L. Moreau Lislet and H. Carleton of selections from the *Siete Partidas*; and (3) on a eulogy of Judge Matthews in 1837 by Etienne Mazureau, the lawyer whom Tocqueville interviewed: see *supra*, chap. 2 at notes 43 and 47.

190 Tucker, *op. cit supra* note 175, pp. 102–105.

191 See *supra*, text at notes 161–168 for some examples; see also Dargo, *Jefferson's Louisiana*, pp. 105–153 *passim*.

192 *Encyclopédie, on dictionnaire raisonné des sciences et des arts et des métiers par une société de gens de lettres*, ed. by D. Diderot and F. d'Alembert, Paris & Neufchastel, Briasson et al. [imprint varies], 1751–1765, vol. 3, s.v. "Code".

193 Quoted Brown, *op. cit. supra* note 129, pp. 74–75.

194 See *supra*, notes 147 and 148 and related text.

195 Quoted in Brown, *op. cit. supra* note 129, pp. 74–75.

196 Quoted Dargo, *Jefferson's Louisiana*, p. 117.

197 See James Workman, found quoted *ibid.*, p. 124. It is obvious he does not refer merely to the *Codex Justinianus*.

the British Statute and Common Laws, and the codes of all the States are spread before us . . . ."[198]

"Code" and "digest" had very similar meanings in Louisiana at this period: both could be used to refer to any compilation of law, and "code" could refer to any whole system of laws.[199] Furthermore, "digest" as a term meaning systematic compilation of laws was familiar in any civilian jurisdiction because of the Justinianic compilation, and no significance should therefore be attached to its use. Therefore, the argument of Tucker on the basis of the title should be dismissed.

2. The preamble to the statute promulgating the Digest does not bear the interpretation put on it by Dargo. The preamble states that the Digest was intended to

> serve as a guide for the decision of the courts and juries, without recurring to a multiplicity of books, which, being for the most part written in foreign languages, offer in their interpretation inexhaustible sources of litigation.[200]

It is unclear how Dargo manages to make "a guide for the decision of the courts" come to mean "a guide to sources". The real meaning is obvious: the legislature intended the Digest to supplant the old sources, to make examination of them unnecessary. The preamble conceives of the Digest as something new replacing the old sources—exactly the opposite of the meaning Dargo attributes to it. Further, and most damningly for the Dargo-Pascal thesis, the notion that the Digest was a guide to the sources is contradicted by s. 5 of the same statute which states that, in the case of "obscurity or ambiguity, fault or omission", the courts should consult both the French and English texts which should "mutually serve to the interpretation of one and of the other".[201] Were the Digest articles merely a guide to sources, this provision would be unnecessary, as the courts could examine the original text. This section of the statute clearly envisages the Digest as being the ultimate authority. Therefore, the preamble of the Act promulgating the Digest, and the Act itself both conceive of the Digest as something new replacing the old sources. The preamble has a meaning exactly the opposite of that attributed to it by Dargo.

3. The argument based on the Digest's recognition of custom as a source of law is irrelevant. Such recognition is not necessarily inconsistent with the principles of codification.[202] The article defines what is custom recognizable in

---

[198] J. Brown to J. Breckinridge, 22 Jan. 1805, found quoted in Brown, *op. cit. supra* note 129, pp. 40–41.

[199] See also Franklin, "Existential Force", p. 83.

[200] See notes 181 and 184 *supra*.

[201] Tucker, *op. cit. supra* note 181, pp. XIX–XX.

[202] The Swiss Civil Code of 1907, art. 1, para. 2, recognizes customary law as a source supplementing the code: "A défaut d'une disposition légale applicable, le juge prononce selon le droit coutumier...."

law. It poses a distinction between *loi* and *coutume*, both of which come under the generic term *droit*. Dargo apparently thinks that defining custom as a source of law means that the Digest may be supplemented by custom, and accordingly is not a "true code". This does not follow. That custom is defined as a source of law (*droit*) in the abstract does not detract from the Digest as a code of *loi*. The article is merely didactic in intention, and was copied from article 5 of the preliminary book of the *Projet de 1'an VIII* (1800); this article was excluded from the finished Code Napoléon, not because the codifiers had changed their mind, but because it was considered that definitions could more appropriately be dealt with by doctrine.[203] The 1800 *Projet* was used as a source and model by the Louisiana redactors, and it is likely that this article was selected for the sake of logical completeness: since the aim of the Preliminary Title was to define *droit*, custom, as one aspect of *droit*, had to be defined.[204] This article, therefore, should not be understood as meaning that the 1808 Digest not being a "true code".

4. The statutory provision abrogating all laws contrary to the Digest provisions or irreconcilable with them did not inevitably mean that the pre-Digest law had to be consulted in order to discover what were the complete provisions of the law. This view originates in a series of court decisions starting in 1812, which will be examined below. As shown above (under 2) the avowed intention of the legislature was *to avoid* the necessity of consulting the old law. If s. 2 is read along with the preamble, it is apparent that the legislature intended to prevent any reference to the old laws: first, to avoid delay and expense in litigation, and second, to avoid attempts to overthrow the provisions of the Digest. Tucker argues as follows:

> It is not enough to argue that the Digest's enactment implicitly repealed the old laws. . . . It is hard to believe that anyone could grasp the significance of a self-contained statement of the law without realizing, not the utility, but the absolute necessity of repealing anterior laws.[205]

What is at issue here is the *intention* of the legislature. Tucker is arguing that because the legislature did not expressly repeal anterior laws, *it must have been intended* that they should still be used, and that the Digest of 1808 is consequently not a "true code". This argument must be dismissed. As shown, the intention of the legislature was clearly to avoid use of the old laws, and, contrary to Tucker's view, the legislature did not anticipate or intend a revival

---

[203] See J.E.M. Portalis, "Exposé des motifs", in P.A. Fenet, *Recueil complet des travaux préparatoires du Code civil*, Osnabrück, O. Zeller, 1968 (repr. of ed. of 1827), vol. 6, pp. 42–43; cf. A.J. Arnaud, *Essai d'analyse structurale du Code civil français*, Paris, Librairie générale de droit et de jurisprudence, 1973, pp. 43–45.

[204] A. Colin and H. Capitant, in *Traité de droit civil*, Paris, Dalloz, 1957, vol. 1, p. 171 (no. 295): "Malgré l'existence du code civil, malgré la prééminence affirmée de la loi, la coutume, sous diverses formes, continue à être une source de droit." See also F. Gény, *Méthode d'interprétation et sources en droit privé positif*, trans. J. Mayda, 2nd ed., [St Paul, West Pub. Co.], for the Louisiana State Law Institute, 1954 [1963], pp. 226–227 (no.112).

[205] Tucker, *op. cit. supra* note 175, p. 102.

of the old law to displace the Digest. The legislature intended the Digest to stand on its own.

A further point is that codification does not necessarily involve a complete abrogation of the old laws. Thus, the Quebec code of 1866 leaves open the possibility of appeal to the prior law.[206] The law of 30 *Ventose, an XII* (21st March 1804), promulgating the French code abrogated the *ancien droit* "dans les matières qui forment l'objet du Code". (Should any topics exist completely ignored by the Code, the old law would still apply.) This *loi* did not mention the *droit intermédiaire*, which leads Marty and Raynaud to conclude that:

> Le droit intermédiaire au contraire, non compris dans la formule d'abrogation, ne disparaissait que dans la mesure où il n'était pas compatible avec le droit nouveau.[207]

This is the same position as with the law promulgating the 1808 Digest. Presumably neither Dargo nor Tucker would argue that the 1804 Code Napoléon and 1866 Quebec code were not "true codes". This fourth argument, therefore, must be dismissed.

5. The next argument is founded on a series of Louisiana court decisions from 1812 onwards that restricted the application of the Digest. On this three points should be made. First, the Louisiana courts would appear to have wanted to restrict the operation of the Digest as much as possible, and to revive the Castilian law.[208] Second, this revival of Castilian law seems to have surprised at least some distinguished Louisiana civilians. Third, how the courts treated the Digest in the period 1812–25 does not have any impications for our understanding that legislature and redactors intended in 1808 that the Digest should be a complete code. To demonstrate these points, one of these cases will be discussed carefully, showing how the court treated the Digest. It should also be pointed out that the courts likewise tried to restrict the operation of the 1825 code and to continue their revival of the Castilian law. Unless Dargo and Tucker want to argue that the 1825 code was not a "true code", they must admit that the motives of the court in restricting the Digest and reviving Castilian law were other than belief that the Digest was not a "true code".

The obvious case to discuss is the most important, the watershed case of *Cottin* v. *Cottin*, decided in 1817.[209] The facts were these. The plaintiff's son died leaving a pregnant widow, who was delivered of a child who lived only a few hours. The point at issue was whether or not the child inherited. The Digest

---

[206] In arts. 2613 and 2615: see Brierley, "Codification", pp. 556–558.

[207] G. Marty and P. Raynaud, *Droit civil, tome 1: Introduction générale à l'étude du droit*, 2nd ed., Paris, Sirey, 1972, p. 129 n. 2.

[208] See *infra*, chap. 6, "Reaction of the Courts to the 1808 Digest", where the Louisiana courts' treatment of the Digest will be analysed carefully, and a conclusion reached as to how the Digest came to be restricted and Castilian law revived.

[209] *Cottin* v. *Cottin* 5 Mart. (O.S.) 93 (1817).

had two relevant provisions: D.O. 64 and 65 (p. 159).[210] These provided that anyone who is free may inherit, but a child *in utero* when the succession opens must be born capable of living (*viable*) in order to inherit. D.O. 6 (p. 9) stated that abortive children were "such as by an untimely birth are born dead or incapable of living". It might have been thought that articles 64 and 65 sufficiently provided for the case: the child, though it had died soon after birth, should inherit, were it to be judged to have been born capable of living. In his plea for a rehearing, defence counsel, Edward Livingston, strongly argued this view.[211] The court, however, took into account article 6 which stated that abortive children were those incapable of living because of untimely births. The court then turned to the *Nueva recopilación*, a provision of which declared that a child that did not live twenty-four hours was deemed abortive.[212] Although the Digest on its own apparently provided adequately for the solution of the problem, the court reasoned:

> There is . . . no doubt, that according to the Roman law, and to the laws of many modern nations, this child would be deemed capable of inheriting.
>
> In Spain, however, the laws of which were, and have continued to be, ours, where not repealed, there exists a particular disposition . . . .[213]

On any sensible construction of the Digest provisions, the old law had been repealed or superseded and new provisions made. For a determination of the dispute, the relevant matter for decision was whether or not the child was *viable*. The court, however, by making use of D.O. 6 (p. 9), managed to switch the point at issue to whether or not the child was abortive. Although the Digest provided an answer—an abortive child was one born dead or incapable of living because of untimely birth—the court referred to the *Nueva recopilación*'s provision on abortive children—an abortive child was one not living twenty-four hours. It then declared that the child, not living twenty-four hours, was abortive (ignoring the test of "untimely birth"), and therefore not viable. Consequently, the child could not inherit. The court would seem to have been seeking to outflank the Digest and reassert the Castilian law. D.O.6 (p. 9) was drawn from Domat, while D.O. 65 (p. 159) was copied from the French code.[214] Domat and the French code would have allowed the child to inherit. The redactors had changed the law, and the court in *Cottin* was seeking to reverse that change, using a loophole provided by s. 2 of the Act promulgating the Digest.

The court's treatment of the 1825 code indicates that the revival of Castilian law and downgrading of the Digest by *Cottin* were not the result of the nature of the Digest as not being a "true code". Article 3521 of the 1825 code states:

---

[210] There being only one edition, it is simplest to cite the articles of the Digest by number and page.

[211] *Cottin supra* note 209 pp. 97–104.

[212] *Rec. Cast.* 5.8.2. For court's argument, see *Cottin supra* note 209, pp. 93–94.

[213] *Cottin supra* note 209, p. 93.

[214] See Batiza, "Sources", appendix C, pp. 46 and 74. The de la Vergne manuscript, in relevant interleaf, refers to Domat and the *Rec. Cast.*

> From and after the promulgation of this code, the Spanish, Roman and French laws, which were in force in this state, when Louisiana was ceded to the United States, and the Acts of the Legislative Council, of the legislature of the State of Louisiana, be and are hereby repealed in every case, for which it has been especially provided in this code, and that they shall not be invoked as laws, even under the pretence that their provisions are not contrary or repugnant to those of this code.

Nothing could have been clearer. Despite this, in the 1827 case of *Flower* v. *Griffith*,[215] the Louisiana Supreme Court argued that where a provision of the 1808 Digest had been excluded from the 1825 Code, and where the legislature reveals no intention to suppress such provision, then it must be held to be still in force.[216] Although the point in the case related to the Digest, the fact that the court refused to give any force to article 3521 meant that the old Castilian law was still in force except where specifically abrogated by the new code. As a result of this case of 1827, the state legislature passed two Acts in 1828, one providing that "all the civil laws which were in force before the promulgation of the Civil Code lately promulgated, be and are hereby abrogated"; while the other specifically repealed all the articles of the 1808 Digest (with certain exceptions). The Louisiana courts now fought a rearguard action, subsequently deciding that these acts repealed only the positive, written or statute laws of Spain and did not abrogate those legal principles established or settled by the courts' decisions.[217]

---

[215] *Flower* v. *Griffith* 6 Mart. (U.S.) 89 (1827).

[216] The decision of the court turned on the method of promulgating the 1825 Code as a series of revisions and amendments of the Digest. The decision of Judge Porter is in fact logical if contrary to the intention of the 1825 redactors and legislature: see his judgment at pp. 90–92. Tucker, *op. cit. supra* note 175, pp. 139–141, gives a fair account.

[217] On the 1828 Act, see Tucker, *op. cit. supra* note 181, p. XXVII. The relevant case is *Reynolds* v. *Swain* 13 La. 193 (1839). On the acts and cases, see J.T. Hood, "The History and Development of the Louisiana Civil Code", 19 *La. L. Rev.* (1958), pp. 18–33 at p. 31. Tucker, *op. cit. supra* note 175, pp. 138–157 gives a good account of the treatment of the 1825 Code. There was, perhaps, rather more reason behind the courts' revival of the Castilian law after the 1828 Act. The 1825 C.L., art. 3251, stated that it was only in cases provided for by the Code that the Spanish laws were abrogated; the 1828 Act repealed *all* the Spanish laws. There is an important difference: under the 1825 Code, areas not covered by the code and genuine *lacunae* would be provided for by the Spanish law; the 1828 Act prevented this. An "eminent lawyer" complained to Alexis de Tocqueville, about the state legislature (found quoted in G.W. Pierson, *Tocqueville and Beaumont in America*, New York, Oxford University Press, 1938, p. 633):

> "They make, unmake, slice and cut up at random. Here's an instance: Since the cession to Spain, many points in our civil law have been regulated according to Spanish law. At the end of 1828, at the end of the session, a bill was passed unperceived which abrogated all these laws, in a body, without putting anything in their place. The next day, the bar and bench learned with stupefaction of the performance of the day before. But the deed had been done."

See A. de Tocqueville, *Journey to America*, trans. by G. Lawrence, ed. by J.P. Mayer, London, Faber & Faber, 1959, p. 106. Tocqueville had forgotten the name of the lawyer. Tucker, *op. cit. supra* note 175, p. 157 n. 307, suggests it was Mazureau.

If one admits that the 1825 Code is a "true code", and, Tucker, for example, does, relying on the intention of the legislators and redactors,[218] then one must accept that, considering the courts' treatment of the 1825 Code, one cannot argue from the decisions of the Louisiana courts as to the nature of the Digest. The Louisiana courts restricted the 1808 Digest and revived the Spanish law for reasons that had nothing to do with whether or not the Digest was a "true code". One could surmise that they preferred the Castilian law to the transplanted French code, or perhaps, influenced by the common law's restrictive attitude to statutes, they wished to restrict the role of the Digest and develop case law and principles.[219] Tucker himself states that the intention of the legislature and redactors in 1808 is irrelevant, and that what is relevant is the attitude of the courts to the Digest: "Regardless what the 1808 enactment was supposed to be, the cases tell us what it was."[220] To be consistent, should he not apply this to the 1825 Code, and decide that, no matter what is said in the *Preliminary Report*, the 1825 Code is a "mere digest"?

The attitude of some Louisiana lawyers shows that the reasoning of the Louisiana courts as exemplified by *Cottin* was both novel and unexpected.[221] In their introduction to their 1820 translation of the *Siete Partidas*, Moreau Lislet and Carleton wrote:

> It was . . . perceived that the Civil Code did not contain many and important provisions of the Spanish laws still in force, nor any rules of judicial proceedings; that the statutes regulating these proceedings had proved insufficient, and particularly as the case of *Cottin* vs. *Cottin* . . . determined that the Spanish laws 'must be considered as untouched, whenever the alterations and amendments introduced in the Digest do not reach them; and that such parts of those laws only are repealed as are either contrary to, or incompatible with the provisions of the code.' *It thus appeared that a much greater portion of the Spanish laws remained in force than had been at first supposed.*[222]

This is a clear statement of the novelty of the reasoning in *Cottin*. Before the relevant decisions no one considered that the Digest ought to be interpreted in this manner, and it was not drawn up along the lines *Cottin* indicated. (It ought to be remembered that Moreau Lislet was one of the 1808 redactors: his evidence is particularly important.) It is perhaps significant that the *1823 Projet* recommended the amendment of the articles dealt with in *Cottin*, so that, in

---

[218] See Tucker, *op. cit. supra* note 175, pp. 120–157.
[219] See *infra*, chap. 6, "Reaction of the Courts to the 1808 Digest".
[220] Tucker, *op. cit. supra* note 175, p. 109. See also *ibid.*, p. 95 and p. 101 n. 205: "The reader may answer for himself whether after the court had finished with the 1808 'enactment', it matters at all what the draftsmen 'intended'—code or digest."
[221] Cf. *ibid.*, pp. 114–115.
[222] Found quoted in Brown, *op. cit. supra* note 129, pp. 74–75 (emphasis added).

effect, the decision on the law in *Cottin* was reversed in the 1825 Code, and the French law substituted.[223] The redactors commented:

> There is a great difference between the conditions required by the Spanish laws and those required by our code, for the child born alive to inherit and transmit successions.
>
> By the Spanish law the child must have lived 24 hours at least, and have been baptised. (Recopilacion de Castille, book 5, tit.8. law 2.)
>
> The 65th article of this title of our code, in the part which we have retrenched, required that the child should be born capable of living, which, according to the interpretation we have given under the title of father and child, means that the child must be born alive after the sixth month of its conception.
>
> We have thought that in relation to right of succession granted to children born of the same marriage, there would be no inconvenience in permitting them to inherit from the instant they should be born alive, however few moments they may have lived.[224]

This is an obvious direct criticism of the position taken by the court in *Cottin*, tending to suggest that the 1825 redactors did not support the approach taken in *Cottin* to the Digest of 1808. Further, in their *Preliminary Report* of 1823, the redactors state that the Digest "took away on those subjects which are contained in its provisions, the necessity of a reference to the Spanish and Roman authorities...." This is surely contrary to *Cottin*. The redactors recognize the Digest as imperfect, but state that reference to old authorities was only necessary in cases not covered in the code.[225] Other evidence supports the contention that the redactors of the 1825 Code (Moreau Lislet, Livingston and Derbigny) believed the *Cottin* approach to be wrong. They proposed introducing a new article to abolish all grounds of nullity of marriage bar absolute impotence. They said:

> This amendment is necessary to remove all doubt relative to other causes of nullity which existed under the Spanish laws . . . . The general tenor of the code on this subject, induces the belief that it was not the intention of its framers to permit these causes of nullity to remain in our laws; but as they are not expressly abrogated, there must be an absolute disposition in order to prevent in future any resort to them.[226]

The new article and this comment are again a result of *Cottin*. The redactors here make clear their objection to the court's reasoning. The implication is that the 1808 redactors had not envisaged that the possibility of revival (such as in *Cottin*) existed: in other words, the 1808 redactors had considered the Digest as

---

[223] D.O. 6 (p. 9) was suppressed on the recommendation of the *1823 Projet*, p. 3; D.O. 65 (p. 159) was amended, and several new articles added: C.L. 947–951. See *1823 Projet*, pp. 117–118. On the French law substituted, see R. Batiza, "The Actual Sources of the Louisiana *Projet* of 1823: a General Analytical Survey", 47 *Tul. L. Rev.* (1972), pp. 1–115, appendix B, at p. 51.

[224] *1823 Projet*, p. 118.

[225] *Preliminary Report*, p. LXXXVII.

[226] *1823 Projet*, p. 10. The new article included in the 1825 Code is 116.

complete in itself. If Batiza is correct, and this section of the *Projet* was drafted by Moreau Lislet,[227] then we have strong evidence that the 1808 redactors had intended that the Digest revoke the prior laws, even where not contrary to them: in the areas the Digest covered, it was intended to replace the old laws.

The fifth argument for the Digest not being a "true code" may be dismissed. First, when one considers the reactions to *Cottin* shown by Moreau Lislet and Carleton in their preface to their translation of the *Partidas* and by the 1823 redactors in some of their comments on proposed amendments, reactions showing that the *Cottin* interpretation was novel, one must accept that to argue from *Cottin* (and other decisions of the period) as to the nature of the Digest, and the intentions of the 1808 redactors, is plainly unhistorical. Second, it is obvious that the Louisiana courts wished to revive the old law and restrict the Digest, and, hence, their opinions on the nature of the Digest are suspect. Thus, these decisions do not prove that the 1808 Digest was not a code in the civilian sense.

6. The sixth argument that the Digest is not a "true code" is based on contemporary evidence. Dargo points to the letter from Claiborne to Madison.[228] Claiborne's statement is of doubtful importance for two reasons. First, the letter is an example of special pleading by Claiborne intended to exculpate him from any possible blame for approving the Digest when the federal administration hoped for a reception of the common law. Second, Claiborne was not a civilian lawyer and not competent to state whether the Digest was a "code" or "digest", or whether it embodied the laws previously in force. Indeed, he seems merely to have seized on the name of the compilation (note that he quotes it almost exactly) as providing an escape route against complaints of his approval of the Digest.

Tucker cites Martin's *History of Louisiana* as evidence that the Digest was not a "true code", but a "digest".[229] Martin, *writing after the decision in Cottin*, states that the Digest would have been more useful had the legislature sanctioned it as a system complete in itself and repealed all former laws. This statement is unexceptional given the period in which Martin was writing, that is, after the decision in *Cottin* had been given: it is no evidence for the intention of the legislature and redactors in 1808. Tucker cites another passage from Martin's *History*, which states that: "In practice, the work was used as an incomplete digest of existing statutes."[230] The same comment may be made on this passage as on the previous one: Martin was accurately describing circumstances when he wrote, after the watershed decision in *Cottin*. This is not evidence of the intentions of the redactors and legislature. Tucker cites a

---

[227] Batiza, *op. cit. supra* note 223, p. 4.

[228] See *supra*, text at note 188 for quotation.

[229] Tucker, *op. cit. supra* note 175, p. 106. The relevant passage of Martin's *History* is found quoted in F. Stone, "The Civil Code of 1808 for the Territory of Orleans", 33 *Tul. L. Rev.* (1958), pp. 1–6 at p. 5.

[230] Found quoted in Batiza, "Sources", p. 30 n. 172. Tucker cites the passage at *op. cit. supra* note 175, p. 106.

passage from Moreau Lislet and Carleton's introduction to their translation of the *Partidas*.[231] Again this passage, even if it bears the interpretation put on it by Tucker, dates from after *Cottin*. The last author Tucker cites as contemporary evidence is Etienne Mazureau.[232] The passage from Mazureau dates from 1837. It is not a reliable guide to the intentions of the legislature and redactors in 1808. Finally, Tucker cites an anonymous writer in 1818.[233] What this writer says does not in fact support Tucker's argument. The writer states:

> In 1808, the civil code was adopted, which is principally a transcript of the code Napoleon, or civil code of France. Where that is silent, its omissions are supplied by a resort to principles derived from the Roman law, and the codes founded on it, including the laws of Spain, France and the commentaries upon them.[234]

The Digest of 1808 covered only the areas traditionally included in a civil code: this obviously meant areas of the law were excluded. For example, there were no provisions on commercial law. The 1818 writer is no doubt correct, but his evidence does not support Tucker's thesis.

This sixth argument on the basis of contemporary or near-contemporary evidence must be dismissed. The examples brought forward by Dargo and Tucker do not uphold their contentions as to the nature of the Digest.

7. The final argument is one made by Tucker, namely that the purpose of the redaction was to preserve the old laws, not to abolish them.[235] He claims:

> The various acts drawn up . . . from the 1804 Manifesto through the Act promulgating the Digest, and the rapidity of their succession, emphasizes the direction of their concern which is less toward the specification of a civil law system than toward the repulsion of the common law.[236]

This is indeed correct: it does not however support Tucker's view. The native Louisianians did indeed wish to preserve the civil law against the common law: this was one reason for the vetoed 1806 Act and the decision to compile the Digest. Another reason was to resolve the confusion over which were the authoritative formal sources of law. A further reason behind the Digest was to prevent the necessity of recourse "to a multiplicity of books, which, being for the most part written in foreign languages, offer in their interpretation inexhaustible sources of litigation".[237] The codification was indeed to keep the

---

[231] The passage may be found in Batiza, "Sources", p. 30 n. 173. It is from p. xxii of the introduction.

[232] Tucker, *op. cit. supra* note 175, p. 107. The passage from Mazureau may be found quoted in Stone, *op. cit. supra* note 229, p. 5.

[233] Tucker, *op. cit. supra* note 175, p. 108.

[234] Found quoted *ibid.*, pp. 108–109. Tucker cites as the source: "Note, 'On Louisiana Law'", 3 *Wheaton Reps*. 202 n.1 (1818) (not seen).

[235] Tucker, *op. cit. supra* note 175, pp. 102–105.

[236] *Ibid.*, p. 104.

[237] Act promulgating Digest, in Tucker, *op. cit. supra* note 181, p. XIX.

old laws, but reduced to a new form to render unnecessary consultation of the old sources. This seventh and final argument for the Digest not being a "true code" must therefore be dismissed.

The seven points intended to establish the Digest as not being a "code" must be dismissed as either wrong or irrelevant. Dargo and Tucker fail to prove their argument. The internal evidence of the Digest shows that it was intended as a code in the tradition of the Code Napoléon—a comprehensive restatement of the law. The Act promulgating the Digest shows that the legislature intended the Digest to be complete in itself, and to replace the old law on the topics with which it dealt.[238] That the courts, for reasons of their own, chose to ignore the intention of the legislature does not matter, as we are here concerned with the actions of the redactors.

As already pointed out, Dargo and Pascal wish to regard the Digest of 1808 as a "digest" (according to their own definition) in order to bolster their claim that the compilation was based on "Spanish" sources. It is inappropriate here to preempt discussion in the following chapters of the sources of the Digest; but it is safe to say that French sources were quite extensively used. Further, even were this not the ease, and the sole sources of the Digest of 1808 were Castilian, the Digest would still be an authentic civilian code. The Digest provided a new synthesis of the law: it rationalized and modernized. The legislature intended the Digest to supplant reference to the old sources of law on the topics that it governed, and only the later actions of the courts prevented this happening. Were the Digest to embody only "Spanish" sources, it would still be a code, for, as Brierley remarks: "Codification . . . is not in its essence a technique for bringing about a revolution in the content of the law."[239] Since the Digest of 1808 is a true code, it represented for the redactors a break with the past, providing an opportunity for revision of the law into a coherent system using the legal materials at hand.

Preliminary Observations on the 1808 Digest

The Instructions of the Legislature

On 7th June 1806, by a resolution of both houses of the Legislature of the Territory of Orleans, Louis Moreau Lislet and James Brown were appointed "to compile and prepare jointly a Civil Code for the use of this territory".[240] The resolution further stated that "the two jurisconsults shall make the civil law by which the territory is now governed, the ground work of said code".[241] Given the dispute between Pascal and Batiza, it is important to understand what the

---

[238] See *supra*, text at notes 200–201.
[239] Brierley, "Codification", p. 565.
[240] Tucker, *op. cit. supra* note 181, p. XVIII.
[241] *Ibid.*

legislature intended by these instructions, and how Brown and Moreau Lislet would be likely to interpret them.

Sweeney gives the phrase "civil law" a broad interpretation, as meaning the law applied in the modern Romanist systems.[242] Pascal interprets the instruction to mean that the redactors were instructed to use "Spanish-Roman" law.[243] It is necessary to examine the legislature's instruction in context. First, the civilian legal systems tended to have a "supra-national" attitude, and there is evidence of such an attitude in Louisiana.[244] Second, it appears that prior to the 1808 redaction, the Louisiana courts used a whole range of civilian learning, with Castilian law as the primary source.[245] Third, an 1805 court decision had recognized Spanish, Roman and French law as providing the law in force in Louisiana,.[246] Fourth, the whole thrust of the dispute over the law was one opposing civil law to common law, which tends to suggest that the legislature was not concerned with subtle differentiation among the national laws of civilian states, but with opposing common law.[247] Fifth, Moreau Lislet and Brown did in fact incorporate a substantial proportion of law other than (in Pascal's phrase) "Spanish-Roman" into the Digest, and, after promulgation of the Digest, no one complained about what had been done.[248] A few years later, of course, the courts do appear to have reasserted the primacy of the Castilian law;[249] but it is implausible to suggest that this was because they believed that Moreau Lislet and James Brown had disobeyed their instructions.[250] Indeed, in the case of *Hayes* v. *Berwick*,[251] one of the decisions often cited as indicating that the Digest was not a true code,[252] the court said: "What we call the Civil Code, is but a digest of the civil law, which regulated this country under the French and Spanish monarchs."[253] The court here recognized the Digest as being compiled out of the civil law in a broad sense, not out of the "Spanish-Roman" law.

From the background to the legislature's instructions, it is clear that by "the civil law" was intended civil law in a fairly broad sense: certainly broad enough to encompass French law, which had been used in Louisiana and given recent judicial sanction. Pascal's argument that what was meant was "Spanish-Roman"

---

[242] Sweeney, "Tournament", pp. 601–602.
[243] Pascal, "Reply", pp. 605–607.
[244] See *supra*, "Louisiana as a Civilian Jurisdiction".
[245] See *supra*, text at notes 151–152.
[246] See *supra*, text at note 169.
[247] See *supra*, text at notes 147–152.
[248] See Dargo, *Jeffersons' Louisana*, p. 164. There is on record one complaint (found quoted *ibid.*, p. 231 n. 80), from before promulgation of the Digest. Jeremiah Brown wrote: "It is a matter of public notoriety that our St Domingo Lycurgus is avowedly copying his new code from that of Bonaparte, to the infinite delight of the whole party by whom he is employed." What Brown is complaining of is that common law has not been adopted: he has no interest in differing national civil laws.
[249] See *supra*, text at notes 208–226.
[250] Indeed I would argue they had obeyed their instructions.
[251] *Hayes* v. *Berwick* 2 Mart. (O.S.) 138 (1812).
[252] See Dargo, *Jefferson's Louisiana*, p. 158.
[253] *Hayes supra* note 251, p. 140.

law is misguided. He takes too narrow a view of what amounted to the civil law in force in the territory, and of what the legislature intended. There is no evidence of any disapproval of the inclusion in the Digest of civil law from countries other than Spain. Since this is so, the redactors must be taken as having followed the instructions of the legislature.

The Redactors

Louis Casimir Elisabeth Moreau Lislet was born in 1767 at Cap Français, St Domingue. He received his education in France in languages and law.[254] It has been suggested that at some point he had been secretary to Toussaint l'Ouverture;[255] however this may be, he came to Louisiana to escape the excesses of the slave insurrection in St Domingue. He was thus one of the powerful group of "foreign French" who distinguished themselves in Louisiana.[256] Moreau Lislet was an obviously successful lawyer, learned and knowledgeable, possessing an extensive library of works on Spanish, French, Roman and common law in their original languages.[257]

The other "jurisconsult" appointed, James Brown, was born in Virginia in 1766, and had practised law in Kentucky. Soon after the Louisiana Purchase he moved to New Orleans, where he apparently established himself fairly quickly as a successful attorney.[258] The following excerpt from a letter written by Brown to Henry Clay is instructive as to the reasons for Brown's success:

> My success as a lawyer continues to be flattering and if the change in our government contemplated by Congress does not obscure my prospects, I hope to acquire the means of a genteel support in a few years independent of my profession. My knowledge of two or three of the modern languages has saved me from ruin, or what was as bad, a resort to Kentucky for the means of support. I stand at the head of my profession and am employed in every important case, whilst lawyers of respectability who cannot speak French or Spanish are left without the means of a decent support.[259]

---

[254] Most of this information is taken from the entry on Moreau in the *Dictionary of American Biography*, London, Oxford University Press, 1922–1958, which may be consulted if further information is required. Unfortunately, no biography of Moreau exists.

[255] By Franklin, see "Existential Force", p. 94; M. Franklin, "Libraries of Edward Livingston and Louis Moreau Lislet", 15 *Tul. L. Rev.* (1941), pp. 401–414 at p. 403 n. 10. Franklin bases this on the evidence of de Clouet, a Spanish agent in Louisiana in 1812.

[256] See J.G. Tregle, "Early New Orleans Society: A Reappraisal", 18 *Journal of Southern History* (1952), pp. 20–36 at p. 31.

[257] See Franklin, *op. cit. supra* note 255, pp. 405–409 for an inventory of Moreau's books at the time of his death in 1832.

[258] On Brown, see his entry in the *Dictionary of American Biography supra* note 254; J.A. Padgett (ed.), "Some Letters of James Brown of Louisiana to Presidents of the United States", 20 *La. Hist. Quar.* (1937), pp. 58–136 for the short biography at pp. 58–61.

[259] Letter, 12 Mar. 1805, found in J.A. Padgett (ed.), "Letters of James Brown to Henry Clay, 1804–1835", 24 *La. Hist. Quar.* (1941), pp. 921–1177 at pp. 923–924.

Perhaps Brown mildly exaggerates here; but his choice of his knowledge of languages as the reason for his forensic success in New Orleans is significant, showing he could consult the sources of Louisiana law in their original texts. Brown had arrived in New Orleans in late November 1804,[260] and had early diagnosed the problems of the legal system in Louisiana, which led to his recommending in January 1805, that a code he compiled from all the legal sources available.[261] He anticipated that a code could be adopted which "would meet the approbation of our Judges and American Lawyers".[262] This tends to suggest that he expected such a code to be based primarily on the common law. This is confirmed by his later letter of September 1805, where, in complaining of Claiborne, he said: "A firm Governor will protect us against the introduction of the civil law, the French administration of justice, and the French language."[263] It is thus clear that just nine months before Brown and Moreau Lislet were appointed to draw up "a Civil Code for the use of ... the territory", Brown had apparently been in favour of a reception of common law. He thus seems a rather curious choice for the legislature to have made: perhaps his views were generally unknown, or the legislature was swayed by his legal ability and facility in French and Spanish, and it was thought politic to appoint at least one American redactor.

On all this, several remarks can be made. Between them, the two redactors would have a wide knowledge of the French pre-codification and codified law,[264] Spanish law, Roman law both as found in the *Corpus iuris civilis* and as developed by the modern civilians, and English common law. Both had a knowledge of French, English, Spanish, and, presumably, Latin (Moreau Lislet's library contained a number of Latin texts).[265] Thus, as well as having a knowledge of the various systems of law, the redactors would be able to read them in their original language: a necessary accomplishment, since translations would not readily be available. Given Moreau's French background and Brown's background in common law, it is tempting to suggest that the former might have favoured French law, the latter common law: this, however, is far too speculative.

Method of Working

It is convenient to make some provisional remarks on the redactors' method of working. The Digest seems to have been completed in a remarkably short time. Moreau and Brown having been appointed on 7 June, 1806, already by 22

---

[260] Dargo, *Jefferson's Louisiana*, p. 115.

[261] J. Brown to J. Breckinridge, 22 Jan 1805, found quoted in Brown, *op. cit. supra* note 129, pp. 40–41.

[262] *Ibid.*; Dargo, *Jeffersons' Louisiana*, pp. 114–115.

[263] Found quoted in Dargo, *Jefferson's Louisiana*, pp. 131–132.

[264] See *supra*, note 170 on codified French law being known in Louisiana. On French law generally, see *supra*, text at notes 156–170.

[265] See Franklin, *op. cit. supra* note 255, pp. 405–409.

January 1807, Poydras, in his official reply to Claiborne's January message to the legislature, was able to say that the project of the code was "well advanced".[266] The Digest was adopted by the territorial legislature on 31 March, 1808, and it is fair to assume that it had been completed earlier. The 1823 *Preliminary Report* states that the 1808 Digest was "hastily compiled. Sufficient time was not given for an accurate examination of the existing Law in its various sources".[267]

The speed of completion of the Digest suggests the likely working method adopted in redaction. In its general style and structure, the Digest closely resembles the Code Napoléon of 1804 and the latter's *Projet* of 1800 (which the Digest resembles more is irrelevant). It is reasonable to suppose that either or both of the French compilations served as the basic model of style and structure for the 1808 redactors. They then will have proceeded by a methodical examination of the French code and *projet*, leaving articles of which they approved, replacing provisions not thought appropriate, and inserting articles of which the French redactions had no equivalent. Such a method of working would be fairly rapid, and would allow the codifiers to review the law and change it where considered appropriate. This is a plausible conjecture given the time taken to compile the Digest, and its general appearance. This does not imply that there was a slavish copying of the French provisions, nor that the redactors adopted French provisions because they thought them to be substantially the same as those of the "Spanish-Roman" law (to use Pascal's phrase).[268] On the contrary, Moreau Lislet, and probably Brown too, would be well aware of the differences between the French law, the Castilian law as applied in Louisiana, and the Roman law. This is readily demonstrated. First, provisions of Castilian law, and indeed of Roman law, were adopted in place of articles of the French code.[269] Second, Moreau, at least, was aware of differences between the French and Castilian law, since, in the famous Batture case,[270] he has been described as making "a wise tactical switch from French law to Spanish law as the basis of argument".[271] Indeed, the Batture case highlighted differences between the Castilian and French laws, and an able and learned lawyer such as Moreau Lislet would be well aware of them. Thus, where a particular provision was selected or rejected, this must be the result of choice, not of uncritical imitation.

Professor Batiza has concluded that Moreau Lislet *alone* compiled the 1808 Digest.[272] Tucker has suggested the same, but with greater caution.[273] Both

---

[266] See Dargo, *Jefferson's Louisiana*, pp. 154–155.

[267] *Preliminary Report*, p. XCIII.

[268] Pascal, "Reply", pp. 605–607.

[269] There is little point in referring to instances of this. Several may be noted in subsequent chapters.

[270] See on this case, Dargo, *Jefferson's Louisiana.*, pp. 74–101.

[271] *Ibid.* p. 82.

[272] He first suggested this, fairly tentatively, in Batiza, "Sources", p. 28 and n. 164. He stated it more firmly in Batiza, *op. cit. supra* note 223, p. 4.

deduce this from a statement made in the 1823 *Preliminary Report*, where the writers, after praising the Digest, state that the problems of construction of some of the Digest articles arise mainly from faulty translation and errors due to its quick compilation. They continue: "Sufficient time was not given for an examination of the existing Law in its various sources. No decisions had then been reported to throw light on their operation, and *the unaided exertions of one person* were not sufficient for the completion of the task."[274] The relevant sentence is, of course, ambiguous. The meaning depends on what is "the task" referred to. Batiza and Tucker obviously believe "the task" to be the redaction of the Digest. "The task" could also be the examination by one redactor of the courts' operation of the laws, or the examination by one redactor of the "various sources" of the "existing Law". Of the three possible meanings it is difficult to say which is correct. Batiza's and Tucker's interpretation would seem the least likely. First, the Digest was completed in a very short time, which suggests that both men worked on it. Second, if only one man had drawn up the Digest, it would surely be surprising if this enigmatic sentence were to be the only record of this remarkable feat. Third, both Moreau and Brown were paid for their work as redactors, and paid exactly the same amount:[275] this would have been unfair had only Moreau done the work, and indeed one cannot imagine the legislature so acting. Therefore, this suggestion of Batiza and Tucker must be rejected as being inherently improbable and inadequately supported by the evidence.[276]

Mitchell Franklin has suggested that Brown was helped in the work of redaction by Edward Livingston:

> It may be ventured that through Brown, Livingston also participated in preparing the civil code of 1808. Livingston is usually introduced to the history of Louisiana codification through his role in the codification movement ending in 1826. However, Brown wanted Livingston associated with him in preparing the code of 1808, but Claiborne prevented an official connection.[277]

There is absolutely no evidence to support Franklin's suggestion. He refers to a letter of 1805 from Brown to Breckinridge, where the former regrets that Claiborne's hostility will not allow the appointment of Livingston as Brown's assistant, Livingston being the only man whom the Council seemed willing to

---

[273] See Tucker, *op. cit. supra* note 175, p. 104 n. 211. Tucker reports a tradition that Brown left Louisiana immediately after compilation of the Digest. He wonders if Brown could have left before. He quotes the passage (see *infra*, text at note 274), and comments that if one person drew up the Digest it would have been likely to be Moreau: he points out that Moreau was the most popular choice for redactor of the 1825 Code.

[274] *Preliminary Report*, p. XCIII (emphasis added).

[275] See Hood, *op. cit. supra* note 217, pp. 25–26.

[276] The statement of Jeremiah Brown quoted *supra* in note 248 is not evidence for Batiza's or Tucker's view. Jeremiah Brown recognized James Brown as having a role in the redaction, although he characterized the role as that of "mask" behind which the law was codified on the Napoleonic model: see Dargo, *Jefferson's Louisiana*, pp. 151–152. It should be recalled that Jeremiah Brown blamed the reception of French law on the foreign French from St Domingue: *ibid.* p. 151.

[277] Franklin, "Eighteenth Brumaire", p. 554 n. 189.

appoint;[278] and to a letter from Prevost to Madison of 1804 in which it was also stated that Claiborne was opposed to the employment of Livingston and Brown in such an important task.[279] There is absolutely no hint anywhere of Livingston's possible collaboration with Brown. (Both these letters were written long before Brown was appointed as a redactor.) Furthermore, Brown does not say he wanted Livingston associated with him, only that Claiborne opposed Livingston, the only man the Council was likely to appoint. This claim of Franklin's should therefore be rejected.

The following conclusions may be drawn from the above discussion of the working method of the redactors. First, although there is virtually no evidence as to the method employed, it is likely that the redactors constructed their code around the French code of 1804 or it's *projet*.[280] Second, although the Digest was completed in a short time, it would be wrong to conclude that the redactors fudged the distinction between the French and the Castilian law. Third, it must be assumed that both Brown and Moreau Lislet, and only they, drew up the Digest. (It should be pointed out that either of them alone, and Livingston, too, probably had the knowledge and capacity to consult all the relevant sources.) Fourth, according to Moreau Lislet, the Digest was drawn up in French, and then translated into English.[281]

Conclusion on the Background to Codification in Louisiana

By the time of redaction of the 1808 Digest, Louisiana had passed through a complicated legal history. The original French colonization had brought the application of French customary law. The cession to Spain had resulted in the application of Castilian law by way of the laws of the Indies. Both the French customary law and Castilian law had been influenced considerably by the reception of Roman law. With the Louisiana Purchase, there came confusion over the laws actually in force—a confusion made worse by the Louisianian fear of an imposed reception of Anglo-American common law. To sort out the confusion, and to make the laws more readily accessible, the territorial legislature ordered the codification of the law. Codification was undertaken by

---

[278] J. Brown to J. Breckinridge, 22 Jan. 1805, found quoted in Dargo, *Jefferson's Louisiana*, p. 115.

[279] J.B. Prevost to J. Madison, 19 Dec. 1804, found quoted in Dargo, *Jefferson's Louisiana*, pp. 113–114.

[280] As will be seen *infra*, the Quebec redactors used a similar procedure.

[281] In the 1822 case of *Dufour* v. *Camfranc* 11 Mart. (O.S.) 675, Moreau said in court (at p. 701): "We have nothing to do with the imperfections of the translation of the Code—the French text, in which it is known that work was drawn up, leaves no doubt." See E. Dubuisson, "The Codes of Louisiana (Originals written in French; Errors of Translation)", 25 *La. Bar Assoc. Repts.* (1924), pp. 143–157 at p. 144. The territorial act of 14 Apr. 1807, ch. XXXI, s. 2, provided remuneration for the translators: see *ibid.* What of the close similarities between the English versions of some articles and Blackstone? Does this affect Moreau's declaration? Further, Moreau stated this as counsel. Some further points about this will arise *infra*.

Brown and Moreau Lislet, the code being entitled "Digest". This code was intended to replace the old laws, in the areas for which it made provision.

The complex and varied background to codification in Louisiana would have allowed the redactors access to many different sources of law. The legal system had a rich civilian heritage; and the civilian tradition allowed for the easy transmissibility of rules from one country to another, because of the common foundation in Roman law.

The multiplicity of possible sources of law for the code made inevitable a process of selection among competing potential provisions. The probable working method of the redactors, and the revival of French law after 1803, might suggest that there would be a prejudice in favour of the utilization of French law; a use of French law made more likely by the obvious superiority of the French *Code civil* to any other source available. There would be no barrier to such a "reception" of French law, as what was wanted was a code which would settle confusion and uphold civil law, and thus prevent a reception of common law.

QUEBEC

The background to the redaction of the 1866 Civil Code of Lower Canada is simple in comparison to that of the redaction of the Louisiana Digest. This part of the chapter is therefore shorter than the previous one, as much less of the background is controversial.

The French Period

Not until the early seventeenth century did France successfully establish a colony in Canada, although the land had been claimed for France in 1534 by Jacques Cartier.[282] The successful establishment of the colony came after the 1608 founding of Quebec by Samuel de Champlain.[283] Although in the early years of the colony it is likely there would have been little need for a developed system of law, some legal provisions would be necessary to provide for the granting of land for settlement and development. Land was granted under the seigneurial system of tenure, but it appears that there was confusion over which

---

[282] On Cartier's claim, see M. Trudel, *The Beginnings of New France, 1524–1663*, trans. by P. Claxton, Toronto, McClelland and Stewart, 1973, pp. 11–33; G. Lanctôt *A History of Canada*, trans. by J. Hambleton and M.M. Cameron, Cambridge MA, Harvard University Press, 1963–1965, vol. 1, pp. 52–63. In 1541 an attempt at settlement was made by Jean-François de la Roque de Roberval: see Trudel, *op. cit. supra*, pp. 34–53 and Lanctôt, *op. cit. supra*, vol. 1, pp. 64–75. Another attempt was made in 1598 by Mesgouez de la Roche: see Trudel, *op. cit. supra*, p. 56 and Lanctôt, *op. cit. supra*, vol. 1, p. 80.

[283] On Champlain and the founding of Quebec, see, e.g., Trudel, *op. cit. supra* note 282, pp. 93–98. The colony was captured by the English in 1629 (they had captured Acadia in 1627); but the French regained control in 1632: *ibid.*, pp. 172–180; Lanctôt, *op. cit. supra* note 282, vol. 1, pp. 131–137.

coutume should be applicable.[284] No provision had been made for the extension of any particular *coutume* to Canada, and, in the early years, parts of more than one seem to have been applied. The inhabitants of the colony came from differing French provinces, though mainly from those on the Atlantic coast, with the largest single group being Norman.[285] This variety in the provenance of the inhabitants has caused one writer to speculate that: "Il est probable que chacun y était régi par le droit coutumier de sa province d'origine";[286] while the high proportion of Normans has led some to consider that the *Coutume de Normandie* was probably frequently applied.[287] It does appear that the *Coutume de Paris* was often referred to in judicial proceedings in the colony, and often the inhabitants referred to it in their notarial documents as the law to be applied.[288] The necessity of invoking a particular *coutume* indicates the uncertainty over the law applicable.

Early seigneurial land grants show variation in the *coutumes* used. So far, the early history of seigneurialism in New France seems to have been misunderstood. Early grants of land *en fief et seigneurie* made by the *Compagnie des Cent Associés* (the company organized by Richelieu to be in charge of Canada) often included a clause specifying that, on each mutation of tenure, the revenue of one year from the land should be payable to the seigneur.[289] This payment was the incident of tenure called *relief* or *rachat*.[290] Such a payment was not exigible under the *Coutume de Paris* when the mutation was by inheritance in the direct line.[291] Thus, such seigneurial grants were not being made according to the *Coutume de Paris*. Some seigneurial grants did, however, specifically state that the *Coutume de Paris* governed the

---

[284] On the variety of customary laws in the north of France, see *supra*, text at notes 13–16.

[285] See M. Trudel, *La population du Canada en 1663*, Montreal, Fides, 1973, pp. 43–47, 150, on the preponderance of Normans among immigrants and those born in Canada.

[286] C.F.S. Langelier, *Cours de droit civil de la province de Québec*, Montreal, Wilson & Lafleur, 1905–1911, vol. 1, p. 51 found quoted in E. Deleury, M.Rivet, and J.M. Neault, "De la puissance paternelle à l'autorité parentelle: une institution en voie de trouver sa vraie finalité", 15 *Les Cahiers de Droit* (1974), pp. 779–870 at p. 815.

[287] R. Besnier, "Le régime des tenures en droit canadien-français", 14 (4th ser) *R.H.D.F.E.* (1935), pp. 734–747 at p. 734 remarks in discussing the large number of Normans: "De là vient qu'entre 1534 et 1664 la législation civile de la Nouvelle-France ait fait l'objet d'une lutte entre la coutume de Paris et la coutume de Normandie". See also Deleury et al., *op. cit. supra* note 286, p. 815.

[288] Olivier-Martin states: "Nous avons nombre de sentences de la prévôté de Québec et on y constate que très fréquemment cette prévôté, bien avant 1664, se réfère expressément à la Coutume de Paris. Quant aux gens du Canada, nous avons des preuves nettes que dans leurs arrangements familiaux, notamment dans les contrats de mariage, ils se réfèrent volontiers aux usages de la Coutume de la prévôté et vicomté de Paris." Taken from his article "Comment la Coutume de Paris s'est installé en Nouvelle-France", in *Le Devoir*, lundi, 24 Oct. 1938, p. 5, found quoted in Deleury et al., *op. cit. supra* note 286, p. 815.

[289] G. Doutre and E. Lareau, *Le droit civil canadien suivant l'ordre établi par les codes, précédé d'une histoire générale du droit canadien*, Montreal, A. Lareau, 1872, pp. 27–28 (only one volume ever published).

[290] See W.B. Munro, *The Seigniorial System in Canada: A Study of French Colonial Policy*, New York, Longmans, Green & Co., 1907, pp. 62–63.

[291] *Coutume de Paris*, art. 3.

grant, and even stated that the *Compagnie des Cent Associés* intended to apply this *Coutume* to the whole of New France.[292] In a land grant of 15th November, 1653, it was stated that *relief* should be payable on each mutation of tenure, and that this provision followed the *Coutume* of *Vexin-le-Français*.[293] This was the first document to mention this *coutume*.

On the basis of this 1653 statement, scholars have always assumed that in the earlier grants stipulating for relief, the law being followed was that of *Vexin français*, and that the grants were made according to this custom in order to allow the *seigneur* greater returns from his vassals.[294] This view, however, is surely wrong.

Vexin français was in the *Ile de France*, on the border with Normandy: directly across the border was *Vexin normand*. The two *Vexins* had originally been one, but had been separated by Charles the Simple, one half being allotted to the *Ile de France*, the other to Normandy.[295] According to Yver's analysis, the *Coutume du Vexin français* was of the Parisian type, though influenced by the *Coutume de Normandie*.[296] In the modern period, the *Coutume* was a *coutume locale*, not a *coutume générale*,[297] and had to be proved for each fief by the *seigneur*.[298] This provision on *relief* of the *Coutume du Vexin français* was unique in the *Ile de France*, and was described by Dumoulin as *valde odiosum et illiberale*.[299] The *Coutume de Paris* specifically referred to this provision of *Vexin français*.[300]

It might be thought that the traditional view of these early Canadian provisions on relief was the correct one; but the evidence can be interpreted in a more satisfactory way. The major problem for the traditional interpretation is to explain why a provision of a fairly unimportant local custom of a few fiefs in the west of the *Ile de France* was applied in Canada. The explanation that this was to allow *seigneurs* greater revenue is not convincing if we consider rather

---

[292] See, e.g. A. Gérin-Lajoie, "Introduction de la Coutume de Paris au Canada", 1 *R.duB.* (1941), pp. 61–65 at p. 62 and W.B. Munro, "The Custom of Paris in the New World", in F. Berolzheimer (ed.), *Rechtswissenschaftliche Beiträge: Juristische Festgabe des Auslandes zu Josef Kohlers 60. Geburstag 9. März 1909*, Stuttgart, F. Enke, 1909, pp. 132–148 at p. 137.

[293] Doutre and Lareau, *op. cit. supra* note 289, p. 40

[294] See Doutre and Lareau, *op. cit. supra* note 289, p. 28; Munro, *op. cit. supra* note 292, pp. 137–138; Gerin-Lajoie, *op. cit. supra* note 292, p. 63; R.Besnier, *op. cit. supra* note 287, p. 734 n. 1.

[295] See M.R. Généstal, "La formation et le développement de la Coutume de Normandie", in *Travaux de la Semaine d'histoire du droit tenue à Guernsey du 26 au 30 mai 1927*, Caën, A. Olivier, 1928, pp. 37–55 at p. 41; Ferrière, *Corps et comp.*, vol. 1, art. 3, 4th gloss, cols. 207–209, explanation by Chopin. J. Yver, *Égalité entre héritiers et exclusion des enfants dotés*, Paris, Sirey, 1966, p. 233 states that Vexin was "un pays que seule une frontière politique sépare en Vexin français et Vexin normand, et qui continue a faire partie de la province ecclésiastique de Rouen".

[296] Yver, *op. cit. supra* note 295, pp. 232–234: he notes that the *coutume* was excluded from Normandy and also from the *Usus et consuetudines Franciae*.

[297] On *coutume générale* and *coutume locale*, see Chénon, *op. cit. supra* note 30, vol. 1, pp. 500–502.

[298] See C.J. de Ferrière, *Dictionnaire de droit et de pratique*, 3rd ed., Paris, Theodore le Gras, 1749, vol.2, pp. 1073–1074, s.v. "*Vexin-le-François*".

[299] Quoted in Ferrière, *Corps et compilation*, vol. 1, art. 3, 4th gloss, no. 5, col. 210.

[300] The relevant provision (art. 3) is found *infra*, note 316.

more evidence than that considered by other writers.[301] The bulk of the colonists in Canada came from the west of France, especially Brittany and Normandy, the largest one group being Norman.[302] Until 1663, appeals from the *prévôté de Québec* went to the Parlement de Rouen.[303] The colony at the same time formed part of the Archdiocese of Rouen.[304] It should be noted that *not until 1653* was the custom of *Vexin français* mentioned in a grant. Since this is so, and given the strong Norman presence and influence in the colony, it may plausibly be suggested that the colonists, in inserting the clause providing for payment of relief on each mutation, were following the *Coutume de Normandie*: the *coutume* with which many would be most familiar. Article 163 of the reformed *Coutume* stated that: "Par mart ou mutation du vassal, relief est dû et hommage nouveau."[305] Relief was similarly payable under the old custom.[306] Henri Basnage, Seigneur du Franquesney, a noted commentator on the *Coutume de Normandie*, discussing article 163, remarked that the custom here differed from that of Paris, where only hommage was due on succession in the direct line, while only in the fiefs of *Vexin français* was *relief* due as in Normandy.[307] It is much more likely that, in the early seigneurial grants in New France which provided for payment of relief on each mutation of tenure, the Norman custom was being followed, rather than the obscure rule of *Vexin français*. The colonists did not need to be Norman for the rule on relief to be the one to which they were accustomed: for *Bretons* the rule was the same. In Brittany *rachat* was due on each mutation of tenure, under both the old[308] and the reformed *coutume*.[309]

---

301 Other writers have merely examined the statement in the 1653 land grant, accepted it and applied to the period before 1653, and examined Ferrière's commentary on article 3 of the *Coutume de Paris*, without pursuing the matter any further. There is also some confusion over the nature of the *Coutume du Vexin français*. Gerin-Lajoie, *op. cit. supra* note 292, p. 63 describes Vexin as part of Normandy with a distinct custom; Munro, *op. cit. supra* note 292, p. 137 n. 5, describes the custom as "a code of rules not forming part of the Custom of Paris, but in a way supplementing the latter." This is very vague. Trudel, *op. cit. supra* note 282, p. 246 describes the custom as the codified law of the *Coutume de Normandie*. Confusion obviously reigns.

302 See *supra*, text at note 285.

303 See, e.g. Besnier, *op. cit. supra* note 287, p. 735.

304 See Doutre and Lareau, *op. cit. supra* note 289, p. 43.

305 *Coutumes du pays et duché de Normandie*, Rouen, J.B. Besonge, 1732, art. 164, provided that: "Tous fiefs qui doivent relief, doivent aide de relief, avenant la mort du Seigneur immediat: et cet aide est dû aux hoirs des seigneurs par les vassaux pour leur aider à relever leurs fiefs vers les chefs-seigneurs." Article 165: "Les héritiers de celui qui a fait profession de religion, doivent relief et hommage au seigneur duquel le fief est tenu et leur est dû aide de relief par leurs Vassaux, laquelle aide est acquitée par demi relief."

306 See *Le grand coustumier du pays et duché de Normendie* [sic], Rouen, N. Le Roux pour F. Regnault ... J. Wallard ... & pour G. Anger, 1539, ch. xxxiiii on relief (glossed by Guillaume le Rouille Dalençon).

307 See *Œuvres de Maître Henri Basnage*, 4th ed., Rouen, Knapen, 1778, vol. 1, p. 257; or *La coutume reformée du pais et duché de Normandie, commentée par Me Henry Basnage [etc]*, 2nd ed., Rouen, veuve Maurry etc., 1694, vol. 1, p. 242.

308 Art. 76; text in B. d'Argentré, *Commentarii in patrias Britonum leges, seu consuetudines generales antiquiss. Ducatus Britanniae*, Brussels, F. Foppens, 1664.

309 Art. 67; text in B. d'Argentré, *Coustumes generales du pays et duché de Bretagne reformées en l'an mil cinq cents quatre-vingts*, Amsterdam, J. Stammius, 1664.

Commenting on article 76 of the old custom, although the comment would also apply to article 67 of the new, d'Argentré stated of this rule "sed diverso jure quam Franci ultimur, apud quos in linea directa relevium non debetur".[310]

The *Coutume de Bretagne* was of course related to the Norman, both being of the western group of customs which had many unique features, and were quite distinct from the *coutumes* of the Paris-Orleans type.[311] Indeed, the *Coutumes* of Normandy and Brittany were sufficiently different from other French customs that Loisel did not consider them in the composition of his *Institutes coutumières*.[312] Loisel did, however, mention the rule of *Vexin français* as an exception to the norm.[313]

In sum, it is contended here that the presence, in early seigneurial grants, of clauses providing for the payment of *relief* on every mutation of ownership should probably be ascribed to the following by the colonists of their accustomed rules relating to fiefs (that is, the rules of Normandy and Brittany) rather than to the adoption of the *Coutume* of *Vexin français*.[314]

If this argument is correct, it is still necessary to explain why a 1653 land grant stated that a clause for *relief* to be payable on each mutation was following the custom of *Vexin français*. This is readily accomplished. It will be recalled that some grants had stated that the company intended to introduce the *Coutume de Paris*.[315] There has obviously been a decision made to apply this custom as the uniform law in New France. However, once this *coutume* was examined, it must have been discovered that several land grants, made according to the traditions of the bulk of the colonists, were prohibited by article three. The same article, however, stated that the clause they were using was part of the custom of *Vexin français*.[316] Given that the *Compagnie des Cent Associés* wished to apply

---

310 D'Argentré, *op. cit. supra* note 308, col. 303, *nota* 3.

311 See J. Yver, "Les caractères originaux du groupe de coutumes de l'ouest de la France", 29 *R.H.D.F.E.* (1952), pp. 18–79. Unfortunately, Yver only discusses the law relating to family, and does not deal with the points we are considering here.

312 See M. Reulos, *Étude sur l'esprit, les sources et la méthode des Institutes coutumières d'Antoine Loisel*, Paris, Sirey, 1935, pp. 74–75. Talking of the use made of the various *coutumes* by Loisel, Reulos says: "La Bretagne et la Normandie surtout sont exclues à cause de leur particularisme trop accentué."

313 *Institutes coustumieres ou manuel de plusieurs et diverses reigles . . . du droit coustumier et plus ordinaire de la France*, ed. by M. Reulos, Paris, Sirey, 1935, based on 3rd ed. of 1611: Book IV tit. III, rule, XXII: "Es lieux où est deu relief en toute mutation, comme au Vuexin; quand quint est deu, n'est deu relief."

314 Gérin-Lajoie, *op. cit. supra* note 292, p. 63, states that some of the colonists were Norman, and took to Canada with them the *Coutume du Vexin*, Vexin being a part of Normandy with a distinct custom. There was, of course, a Norman *Vexin*, however, the custom referred to was that of French *Vexin*. Further, that there should be a significant number of colonists from either *Vexin* is improbable. It is much more likely that the relevant clauses were based on Norman or Breton practice. Gérin-Lajoie's hypothesis is riddled with errors and confusion; see *supra*, note 301.

315 See *supra*, note 292.

316 *Coutume de Paris*, art. 3: "Quand aucun Fief échet par succession de pere, mere, ayeul ou ayeule, il n'est dû au Seigneur féodal dudit Fief par les descendans en ligne directe, que la bouche et les mains, avec le serment de fidelité, quand les dits pere, mere, ayeul ou ayeule, on fait et payé les droits et devoirs en leurs temps: en ce non compris les Fiefs qui relevent et se gouvernent selon

the *Coutume de Paris*, to justify the past granting of fiefs with relief payable on each mutation of tenure, and to legitimize such a clause in the 1653 grant, the clause was stated to be following the custom of *Vexin français*: a custom included in article three of the reformed *Coutume de Paris*. This does not necessarily mean that the drafter of the relevant 1653 grant was deliberately concealing the origin of the clause in the earlier grants: he may simply have been ignorant of the *Coutumes* of Normandy and Brittany. It is surely of importance that this clause was stated to be following the customs of *Vexin français* only after the apparent decision to apply the *Coutume de Paris* to New France.

We may conclude that the early seigneurial grants providing for the payment of relief on each mutation of tenure were the result of the colonists following the established practices of their main provinces of origin. A later grant stated this provision followed the custom of *Vexin français*. This later statement may be attributed to the attempted introduction of the *Coutume de Paris*. Thus, the tradition that the early grants were following the *Coutume* of *Vexin français* must be discarded: they were following the *Coutume de Normandie* or *Coutume de Bretagne*, the customs with which the majority of the colonists would be familiar.

It would appear that the *Coutume de Normandie* was a stronger influence in New France than previously has been thought.[317] There is evidence of the application of the *Coutume de Paris*. The lack of a clear provision as to the laws applicable, as the colony developed, must have been likely to cause problems. The legal system was, however, finally settled in 1663 or 1664 by the explicit provision that the Custom of Paris was to regulate legal affairs. There is a dispute over which year is the correct one for the introduction of the *Coutume*. The answer to this problem depends on the interpretation of two charters. The first, that of 1663 setting up the Sovereign or Superior Council, provided thus:

> Nous [Louis par la grâce de Dieu, roi de France et de Navarre] . . . donnons et attribuons au conseil souverain le pouvoir connaître de toutes causes civiles et criminelles, pour juger souverainement et en dernier ressort selon les loix et ordonnances de notre royaume, et y procéder autant qu'il se pourra en la forme

---

la Coûtume du Vexin le François; esquels Fiefs, qui se gouvernent selon la Coutume dudit Vexin, eat dû relief a toutes mutations, et aussi ne sont dus quints."

[317] None of the writers to whom has been attributed the traditional view of the clause on relief appear to be aware that such was the normal provision under the *Coutume de Normandie*. If the argument outlined above is the correct interpretation of this early period (remembering that I am relying on others' descriptions of the relevant deeds), then it is obvious that a reappraisal of early Quebec legal history is necessary. This reappraisal would involve the analysis of the surviving legal documents of the period, with a view to their assessment according to legal practices under the various *coutumes*, especially, obviously, the *Coutume de Normandie*. As far as I am aware, there has been no attempt to carry out such a thorough analysis. Significant for what may probably be found, is the fact that in the first *seigneurie* granted, that of Beauport, as well as the clause for payment of relief on each mutation, there was a clause empowering the *seigneur* to grant land, not only *en censive*, but also *en fief*: Doutre and Lareau, *op. cit. supra* note 289, p. 27. This was not allowed under the custom of Paris, but was under that of Normandy.

> et manière qui se pratique et se garde dans le ressort de notre cour de Parlement de Paris. . . .[318]

The second charter, the *Édit d'établissement de la Compagnie des Indes Occidentales*, stated as follows:

> Seront les juges établis en tous lesdits lieux, tenus de juger suivant les loix et ordonnances du royaume, et les officiers de suivre et se conformer à la coutume de la prévôté et vicomté de Paris, suivant laquelle les habitans pourront contracter sans que l'on puisse introduire aucune coutume pour éviter la diversité.[319]

Some scholars argue that the terms of the 1663 charter were sufficient to introduce the *coutume*;[320] while others argue that this charter meant simply that the new court was to follow the procedure of the *Parlement de Paris*, the law being left uncertain and vague as "les loix et ordonnances de notre royaume". These scholars believe that only the 1664 Édit introduced the *Coutume de Paris*.[321] It is not necessary to decide this matter, although the latter view seems preferable.

As already discussed,[322] the *Coutume* did not provide a complete system of rules.[323] Thus, it had provisions neither on the general law of obligations nor on the law of special contracts. Roman law was used extensively to fill in gaps and interpret the *Coutume*, although this conception of Roman law as a residual common law was rejected by adherents of the notion of a *droit commun coutumier*.[324] Royal ordinances were of vital importance too. The *Coutume* was developed into a comprehensive system of laws using Roman law and royal ordinances. There is a long- running dispute over whether or not the series of "grandes ordonnances" under Louis XIV and Louis XV were valid in Quebec if not registered by the Sovereign Council. This debate is mainly technical in nature, as the courts frequently applied the provisions of these *ordonnances* without questioning their validity in Quebec. Indeed, it seems that it was only after the British conquest that the matter was first considered. Thus, we need not attempt to decide this point, it being sufficient to point out that these ordinances

---

318 Quoted J.G. Castel, *The Civil Law System of the Province of Quebec*, Toronto, Butterworths, 1962, pp. 9–11 and in Doutre and Lareau, *op. cit supra* note 289, pp. 116–118.
319 Text found quoted in Munro, *op. cit. supra* note 292, p. 136 n. 3 (art. 33 of the *Édit.*)
320 See Castel, *op. cit supra* note 318, pp. 9–11; Doutre and Lareau, *op. cit supra* note 289, pp. 116–118.
321 Munro, *op. cit. supra* note 292, pp. 136–137 n. 4; Deleury et al., *op. cit. supra* note 286, pp. 815–816 n. 96, and Gérin-Lajoie, *op. cit. supra* note 292 , pp. 63–64.
322 See *supra*, text at notes 17–19 and 30–36.
323 See *supra*, note 18 for contents.
324 See *supra*, text at notes 33–36.

provided a possible source of law for the Quebec redactors, ignoring the legal niceties of their validity in Quebec.[325]

The sources of the law used in New France, therefore, were the *Coutume de Paris*, royal ordinances, colonial legislation and Roman law. It appears that not all the provisions of the *Coutume* were applied in New France.[326] Munro believes there to have been very little influence of Roman law in the colony under the French regime.[327] His arguments are not convincing. He states that the law introduced was the Custom of Paris, and that the Custom of Paris was not based on Roman law.[328] He also recognizes as sources of law for Canada under France royal ordinance[329] and colonial legislation.[330] He points out that the *Code Napoléon*, unlike the *Coutume de Paris*, contains rules of Roman origin,[331] and that the Quebec code copied the French code. He concludes that, rules of Roman origin were adopted in Quebec through copying the *Code Napoléon*.[332] Munro indicates the role played by Roman law in customary law France,[333] but then, curiously enough, denies it any validity in New France. He does not consider that the colonists or traders would need a law of contracts. Further, Munro does not take into consideration that the *Édit* of 1664 stated that the judges were to follow not only the *Coutume* and ordinances, but also more generally "les loix . . . du royaume". This would surely include the subjects normally covered by Roman law in the jurisdiction of the *Parlement de Paris*. It is possible that, in the early colonial period, the more refined areas of the law of obligations would have little practical importance; but this does not matter. The Roman-based aspects of the law of northern France were introduced, at least as a potentiality. Thus, the later elaboration of these Roman rules, and their eventual incorporation in the 1866 Code, can be ascribed to the 1664 introduction of the law as practised in the *Vicomté* and *Prévôté* of *Paris*.[334] Thus, Roman law, as

---

[325] On this question, see, e.g., Doutre and Lareau, *op. cit. supra* note 289, pp. 115–129; Munro, *op. cit. supra* note 292, pp. 139–143; L. St. Laurent, "The Law of Quebec", 10 *Can. Bar. Rev.* (1932), pp. 442–455 at p. 446.

[326] See *An Abstract of Those Parts of the Custom of the Viscounty and Provostship of Paris, Which Were Received and Practised in the Province of Quebec, in the Time of the French Government. Drawn up by a Select Committee of Canadian Gentlemen, well skilled in the Laws of France and of that Province. By the Desire of The Honourable Guy Carleton, Esquire, Governour in Chief of the said Province*, London, C. Eyre and W. Strahan, 1772, pp. i and ii. On p. ii is a note of the articles revoked in whole or in part. See also *The Sequel to the Abstract of Those Parts of the Custom of the Viscounty and Provostship of Paris, Which Were Received and Practised in the Province of Quebec, in the Time of the French Government: Containing the Thirteen Latter Titles of the Said Abstract*, London, C. Eyre and W. Strahan, 1773.

[327] Munro, *op. cit. supra* note 292, *passim*, esp. at pp. 132–133, 135, 143.

[328] *Ibid.*, pp. 133–136.

[329] *Ibid.*, pp. 139–142.

[330] *Ibid.*, pp. 142–143.

[331] *Ibid.*, p. 148.

[332] *Ibid.*, pp. 147–148.

[333] *Ibid.*, pp. 135–136.

[334] I should not be understood to mean that there were no innovations on the old law in the 1866 Code taken from the French code. Obviously many provisions of importance were borrowed from the French code. What I wish to stress is that there was a potential role for Roman law in Quebec

received in the *pays du droit coutumier*, was a live source of law in New France, along with the *Coutume de Paris*, royal ordinances and colonial legislation.[335]

The British Period

Britain captured New France in 1760, in the course of the Seven Years War. Britain's possession of the colony was confirmed in 1763 by the Treaty of Paris.[336] The subsequent legal history of the province is complex, and there will be no attempt here to discuss it in any detail, as this is unnecessary here. It is sufficient to outline some of the main events relating to the British desire to introduce the English common law, and to note the reforms undertaken before codification.

In 1763, the British Crown issued a Royal Proclamation providing a system of government for various newly conquered colonies, including Canada (which was renamed Quebec).[337] In providing for the establishment of courts, the Proclamation stated that the courts were to determine "all Causes, as well criminal as civil, according to Law and Equity, and as near as may be agreeable to the Laws of England".[338] Provision was made for legislation "as near as may be agreeable to the Laws of England",[339] and, furthermore, "all Persons Inhabiting in or resorting to. . . ." Quebec could expect royal protection "for the Enjoyment of the Benefit of the Laws of our Realm of England".[340] Although the point has been argued, there can be no doubt that the British government intended to abolish the Canadian law and introduce the English.[341] There have been doubts as to whether the British Government could validly introduce English

before any borrowing from the French code. The law was of necessity more than the few provisions of the *Coutume de Paris*.

[335] On Roman law and the *droit coutumier*, see *supra*, text at notes 19–36.

[336] See Lanctôt, *op. cit. supra* note 282, vol. 3, *passim*; G.F.G. Stanley, *New France, The Last Phase, 1744–1760*, Toronto, McClelland and Stewart, 1968, *passim*.

[337] For the text, see Public Archives of Canada, *Documents Relating to the History of Canada, 1759–1791*, ed. by A. Shortt and A.G. Doughty, 2nd ed., Ottawa, J. de L. Taché, 1918, pp. 163–168.

[338] *Ibid.*, p. 165.

[339] *Ibid.*, p. 165.

[340] *Ibid.*, p. 165.

[341] Lord Hillsborough, Secretary of State, later claimed that this had *not* been the government's intention: letter, *ibid.*, p. 297. This is unconvincing given the overwhelming contrary evidence. The commissions of the first two Chief-Justices, Gregory (Doutre and Lareau, *op. cit. supra* note 289, pp. 585–587) and Hey, (*Documents 1759–1791 supra* note 337, pp. 273–276) instructed them to judge according to common law. The first Governor and his administration obviously thought they were instructed to introduce the common law. For the arguments on the Royal Proclamation, see Doutre and Lareau, *op. cit. supra* note 289, pp. 310–354.

law in this fashion.[342] It seems that for ten years the two systems of private law existed uneasily side by side.[343]

In 1774, the British Parliament passed the Quebec Act (14 Geo. III, ch. 83), intending to settle various unsatisfactory matters relating to the government of the Province. The Act also attempted to end the confusion caused by the semi-introduction of English law.[344] With certain (important) exceptions, this Act reinstated the French Canadian law. First, the English criminal law was retained. Second, the free disposal of property by testament was extended.[345] Third, the Act stated in a proviso that nothing in it should be taken to apply to lands granted in free and common socage (an English tenure).[346] The interpretation of this proviso was to cause problems, as was the general wording of the Act, which stated it was to apply to "all His Majesty's *Canadian* subjects": Canadian at this period meant French Canadian. This point was considered in 1785 in the case of *Gray* v *Grant*. The new Chief Justice of Quebec, William Smith, decided that the Canadian laws were introduced by the Act only as applicable to the French Canadians, and that in disputes between others, the "old subjects", English common law should be applied.[347] Many—including other judges—opposed this interpretation, and indeed, after Smith's death in 1793, it seems to have been forgotten.[348]

---

[342] Further on the Proclamation, see Munro, *op. cit. supra* note 292, p. 144; F.P. Walton, *The Scope and Interpretation of the Civil Code of Lower Canada*, Montreal, Wilson and Lafleur, 1907, pp. 12–19; Lamarche, "French Civil Law under British Rule", 31 *Canadian Law Times* (1911), pp. 420–441, *passim*; Doutre and Lareau, *op. cit. supra* note 289, pp. 310–354.

[343] Probably the best published account of the confusion over the laws and of French Canadian reactions is A. Morel, "La réaction des Canadiens devant l'administration de la justice de 1764 à 1774", 20 *R.duB.* (1960), pp. 53–63, who shows that the French Canadians boycotted the courts. H.M. Neatby, *Quebec: The Revolutionary Age, 1760–1791*, Toronto, McClelland and Stewart, 1968, p. 52 points out that the Court of Common Pleas tended to employ French law. W. Smith, "The Struggle over the Laws of Canada, 1763–1783", 1 *Can. Hist. Rev.* (1920), pp. 166–186, may be found useful, though it should be read with caution, being a fairly slight work, containing some inaccuracies and written before all documentary sources were available.

[344] For the relevant sections relating to the law, see *Documents 1759–1791 supra* note 337, pp. 573–574.

[345] On the development of this area of the law, see A. Morel, "L'apparition de la succession testamentaire", 26 *R.du B.* (1966), p. 499–511, esp. at pp. 503 and 506–510. Morel mainly deals with subsequent jurisprudence.

[346] "Socage" is the usual spelling, although the 1774 Act itself spells the word "soccage". On this form of tenure, see e.g. W. Blackstone, *Commentaries on the Laws of England*, Chicago, Chicago University Press, 1979 (reprint of 1st ed., Oxford, Clarendon Press, 1765–1769), vol. 2, pp. 79–82; a concise explanation may be found in D.M. Walker, *The Oxford Companion to Law*, Oxford, Clarendon Press, 1980, p. 1151, s.v. "socage"; *Jowitt's Dictionary of English Law*, 2nd ed. by J. Burke, London, Sweet and Maxwell, 1977, vol. 2, p. 1669.

[347] For text of judgement, see *The Diary and Selected Papers of Chief Justice William Smith 1784–1793*, ed. by L.F.S. Upton, Toronto, Champlain Society, 1963–1965, vol. 2, pp. 209–210.

[348] See H. Neatby, *The Administration of Justice under the Quebec Act*, London, H. Milford, Oxford University Press, 1937, p. 331 and pp. 320–322. On the opposition to Smith's view, see *ibid.*, p. 227; *Diary of William Smith supra* note 347, vol. 2, p. 163 n. 2. The downfall of Smith's interpretation is shown with fine irony by the fact that, on his death, his widow had to go to court

In 1791, the Constitutional Act (31 Geo. III, ch. 31) was passed by the British Parliament.[349] This Act split the province of Quebec into two new provinces—Upper and Lower Canada. Each new province had a new constitution, involving an elective legislative assembly.[350] No change was made in the laws of Lower Canada, although Upper Canada quickly introduced common law.[351] The Act had originally been intended to have provisions introducing English-style commercial laws, and provisions granting the holder of lands directly from the Crown *en seigneurie* the power to surrender them and have them regranted in free and common socage.[352] For various technical reasons these provisions had been excluded from the final bill.[353]

The early 1800s saw some changes in the law and increasing confusion generally in the state of the law. The Provincial Act, 41 Geo. III, ch. 4 (1801), extended the freedom of testamentary disposition of property introduced in 1774.[354] The proviso to the 1774 Act, apparently exempting land held in free and common socage from its provisions,[355] caused considerable confusion at this period, because it was unclear whether the English law was to be used only to define socage and its incidents, or whether the English laws on conveyancing, dower, and succession were to be applied to such land rather than the French equivalents. An added problem was that if, as some thought,[356] the 1763 Proclamation could not and did not validly introduce English law, then it was doubtful if English law could be introduced by way of exception in a proviso to the 1774 Act. At this period, many English holders of seigneurial land in Canada wished to change their tenure from seigneurial to socage.[357] The English law officers decided that such a change would require legislative authority.[358] We need not discuss the dispute over the abolition of seigneurial tenure in any detail:[359] it is sufficient to point out that in the early 1800s the merchant class

---

to request the election of a tutor under French law for their minor daughter, Harriet. See Neatby, *op. cit.*, p. 227.

[349] On the development of the Act, and background, see V. Harlow, *The Founding of the Second British Empire, 1763–1793:New Continents and Changing Values*, London, Longmans, 1964, pp. 751–773; A. Burt, *The Old Province of Quebec*, Toronto, Ryerson Press, 1933, pp. 487–494; Neatby, *op. cit. supra* note 343, pp. 249–263.

[350] *Documents 1759–1791 supra* note 337, pp. 1031–1051.

[351] See the provincial "Act introducing English Civil Law into Upper Canada", quoted in Public Archives of Canada, *Documents Relating to the Constitutional History of Canada, 1791–1819*, ed. by A.G. Doughty and D.A. MacArthur, Ottawa, C.H. Parmalee, 1914, pp. 83–84.

[352] See the 1789 first draft of the bill, *Documents 1759–1791 supra* note 337, pp. 992–1002 at pp. 999–1001, on the surrender of seignueurial land, and the letter Grenville to Dorchester, 20 Oct. 1789, *ibid.*, p. 991 on commercial regulations.

[353] Grenville to Dorchester, 5 June 1790, *Documents 1759–1791 supra* note 337, pp. 1024–1027 at p. 1026 and pp. 1026–1027.

[354] See A. Mayrand, *Les successions ab Intestat*, Montreal, Presses de l'université de Montréal, 1971, pp. 5–6; Morel, *op. cit. supra* note 345, pp. 503–510.

[355] See *supra*, text at note 346.

[356] See *supra*, references in note 342.

[357] Munro, *op. cit. supra* note 290, pp. 221–223.

[358] See their report in *Documents 1791–1819 supra* note 351, pp. 501–502 on this point.

[359] See Munro, *op. cit. supra* note 290, pp. 224–251. His account is still the only complete one. For the background see F. Ouellet, "L'abolition du régime seigneurial et l'idée de propriété", 14

wished for abolition of seigneurial tenure, while, in general, the French Canadians resisted any attempt at abolition.[360] In 1822, the British Parliament passed the Canada Trade Act.[361] This Act provided[362] that anyone holding land directly from the Crown, either *en fief et seigneurie or en censive*, and having power to alienate the same, could surrender such land to the Crown, and have it regranted in free and common socage.[363] This Act was ineffective in helping commute tenure and ending confusion over the laws in force, as it did not allow for commutation by the *censitaires* of a *seigneur* and did not settle which law was applicable to land held in free and common socage. In 1825, the British Parliament enacted the Canada Tenures Act,[364] which continued the provisions of the 1822 Act, but bound a *seigneur*, who had himself commuted his tenure, to commute that of his *censitaires*, should they demand that he do so.[365] The commuted land would be held in free and common socage as in England. The eighth section is of great interest, since it stated that, in land held in socage, all matters of conveyancing, succession and rights of married women were to be governed by the laws of England. This section attempted to settle the doubts over the meaning of the 1774 proviso.[366] It thus appears that, by 1825, English law was to govern important areas of social life in a substantial part of Lower Canada, as, in the Eastern Townships, land was already held in free and common socage, and there was a prospect of large areas of the *seigneuries* being held in socage.

This was an obviously unsatisfactory state for the law. Not only were two systems of law existing side by side in the same jurisdiction, but also many past land transactions would seem to have been overturned because the eighth section of the 1825 Act was declaratory in nature. There were doubts about the effect of this section, and, in 1829, the Provincial legislature passed an Act rendering it only prospective in effect; but the validity and scope of this Act were also doubtful.[367] In fact, the problem of the applicability of English law to

---

Hermès (1954), pp. 21–36; F. Ouellet, *Éléments d'histoire sociale du Bas-Canada*, Montreal, Hurtubise, 1972, pp. 91–110 ("Le régime seigneurial dans le Québec"). See also, M.Séguin, "Le régime seigneurial au Pays de Québec, 1760–1854", 1 *R.H.A.F.* (1947), pp. 382–402, (1948), pp. 519–532. Also, see *supra*, chap. 2 "Quebec".

[360] See F. Ouellet, *Histoire économique et sociale du Québec, 1760–1850: structures et conjuncture*, Montreal, Fides, 1966, pp. 199–200 on seigneurialism retarding economic development; see *supra*, chap. 2, text at notes 101–106.

[361] 3 Geo. IV, ch. 119. For text see Public Archives of Canada, *Documents Relating to the Constitutional History of Canada, 1819–1825*, ed. by A.G. Doughty and N. Story, Ottawa, J.O. Pautenaude, 1935, pp. 106–120; *Statutes at Large*, vol. 8, 1819–22.

[362] By ss. 31 and 32.

[363] See Munro, *op. cit. supra* note 290, pp. 224–225; Séguin, *op. cit. supra* note 359, pp. 391–392. This Act, s. 31, also abolished the need, in making such a regrant, of reserving land for the use of the Protestant clergy—a necessity which had caused problems in previous attempts at changing tenure, and which originated in s. 36 of the Constitutional Act of 1791.

[364] 6 Geo. IV, ch. 59, *Statutes at Large*, vol. 10, 1825–1826, pp. 151–156.

[365] By ss. 3 and 4.

[366] See *supra*, text at note 346.

[367] On the problems as regards this Act, see St. Laurent, *op. cit. supra* note 325, pp. 452–453; and also the case of *Stuart* v. *Bowman*, 3 Lower Canada Reports 309 (1853), esp. at pp. 369–77 (Panet

large areas of Lower Canada remained unsettled until the 1850s.[368] In 1857, the Provincial legislature[369] passed "An Act for settling the Law covering Lands held in Free and Common Soccage in Lower Canada",[370] which removed the anomaly of English law and rendered the Lower Canadian law uniform.

In 1840, the two provinces of Upper and Lower Canada had been reunited as part of the political settlement of the rebellions of 1837 and 1838.[371] Although the British government wished to introduce the English laws,[372] under the Union there was no serious attempt to assimilate the laws of the formerly separate provinces, both retaining their own laws and court structure.[373]

The period of Union was one of major reforms in the Lower Canadian law, reforms which commenced under the Special Council, even before the Act of Union came into effect. Thus, in 1841, there were major reforms of the law on customary dower and hypothecs, reforms making for greater security of transactions, especially through registration.[374] In 1843 and 1849 there were major reforms of the Court of Appeal of Lower Canada.[375] The bar and notaries of Lower Canada were incorporated, in 1849 and 1847 respectively.[376] During this period, university teaching of law became regular, with the organization of law faculties in the universities of McGill and Laval.[377] In 1857 came an

---

J.) and 392–396 (Alwyn J.). See also the case of *Wilcox* v. *Wilcox* 8 Lower Canada Reports 34 (1857) esp. at pp. 94–98.

[368] The differing opinions of the judges in *Wilcox* show that, even in 1857, the meaning of the 1763 Proclamation, the Quebec Act etc. could still be a matter of dispute.

[369] Just prior to the decision in *Wilcox*.

[370] 20 Vict. S.C. 1857, ch. 45. "Soccage" so spelt in title.

[371] On the rebellions, see, e.g. H.T. Manning, *The Revolt of French Canada, 1800–1835: A Chapter in the History of the British Commonwealth*, London, MacMillan, 1962; H. Wade, *The French Canadians*, rev. ed., Toronto, Macmillan, 1968, vol. 1, pp. 152–219. On the settlement, see *Lord Durham's Report on the Affairs of British North America*, ed. by C.P. Lucas, Oxford, Clarendon Press, 1912, vol. 1, introduction; on Union, see J.M.S. Careless, *The Union of the Canadas: The Growth of Canadian Institutions, 1844–1857*, Toronto, McClelland and Stewart, 1968.

[372] See L. Groulx, *Histoire du Canada français*, 4th ed., Montreal, Fides, 1968, p. 190.

[373] For the text of the Act of Union, 3 & 4 Vict. ch. 35, see *Statutes, Treaties and Documents of the Canadian Constitution*, ed. by W.P.M. Kennedy, 2nd ed., London, Oxford University Press, 1930, pp. 433–445 at pp. 442–443. The existing laws of both Provinces were maintained by s. 46, and by s. 47 the separate courts and law officers.

[374] These reforms will be found in C.S.L.C., ch. 37. On these reforms, see A. Perrault, "Le conseil spécial, 1838–1841", 3 *R.duB.* (1943), pp. 130–144, 213–230, 265–274, 299–307 at pp. 269–72; Y.F. Zoltvany, "Esquisse de la Coutume de Paris", 25 *R.H.A.F.* (1971), pp. 365–384 at pp. 371, 375. There were later attempts to reform the law on hypothecs, on one such failure, see "J.C.", "De la publicité des hypothèques dans le Bas-Canada", 3 *Revue de législation et de jurisprudence* (1847), pp. 24–33.

[375] See L. Renaud, "La Cour d'appel à l'aube de l'Union (1839–1849)", 8 (new ser.) *La revue juridique Thémis* (1973), pp. 465–499. Ms Renaud gives the acts in appendices at pp. 492–494.

[376] An Act to Incorporate the Bar of Lower Canada, 12 Vict. S.C. 1849, ch. 46; An Act for the Organization of the Notarial Profession in that part of this Province called Lower Canada, 10–11 Vict. S.C. 1847, ch. 1. See A. Sinclair, "L'avocat au Québec: 209 ans d'histoire", 16 *Les cahiers de droit* (1975), pp. 689–702 at pp. pp. 693–701. See also Brierley, "Codification", p. 523 and n. 6.

[377] See L. Lortie, "The Early Teaching of Law in French Canada", 2 *Dalhousie Law Journal* (1975), pp. 521–532 at pp. 527–531, especially p. 529; Sinclair, *op. cit. supra* note 376, pp. 696–697. University study of law only become necessary for an *avocet* in 1937: *ibid.*, p. 697.

important restructuring of judicial organization.[378] A reform of major importance accomplished under the Union was the abolition of the seigneurial system. The moves to achieve this started in 1841 with the appointment of a commission to investigate the system of land tenure. In its report of 1843,[379] the commission condemned the seigneurial system and recommended its abolition.[380] As a result of this report, in 1845, the provincial legislature passed an act "to facilitate optional Commutation of the Tenure of Lands".[381] This act was amended in 1849, but commutation was still optional. In 1850, the Legislative Assembly resolved that commutation be made obligatory,[382] and, in 1854, was eventually passed an "Act for the Abolition of Feudal Rights and Duties in Lower Canada".[383] The work of commutation was completed in 1859, the new tenure being a free one of French origin, not the English one of free and common socage.

The period of Union was one of major reform in the Quebec law. The anomalies of the semi-introduction of English law were removed;[384] the court structure was reformed; the legal profession was reorganized; university teaching of law started; and the substantive law was modernized. As part of this reform movement, in 1857, the legislature passed An Act to provide for the Codification of the Laws of Lower Canada relative to Civil Matters and Procedure.[385] This Act resulted in the 1866 Code.

The legal history of Quebec or Lower Canada after cession to Britain has some important implications for codification. It is obvious that the British government had wished to introduce English common law, although attempts to do so had met with failure. English law had been applied in the period 1764 to 1774, and had apparently been applicable to large areas of land after that date. English law obviously would be well known in Lower Canada, and thus a possible source for the Commissioners for Codification to draw on. The French Canadian resistance to the common law would suggest that, as a source for the code, it would not readily be used, especially in the traditional areas of family, property and obligations. Furthermore, the reforms of the law (sketched in above), carried out prior to codification, modernized the law while maintaining it as a cohesive system based on the old French law. This would suggest that arguments for introducing English law because of its "modernity" would not

---

378 An Act to amend the Judicature Acts of Lower Canada, 20 Vict. S.C. 1857, ch. 44: see Brierley, "Codification", p. 522 and n. 3.

379 See *Documents Relating to the Seigniorial Tenure in Canada: With a Historical Introduction and Explanatory Notes*, ed. by W.B. Munro, Toronto, Champlain Society, 1908, pp. 308–357.

380 *Ibid.* p. 353.

381 See Munro, *op. cit. supra* note 290, pp. 242–244 for discussion of this Act.

382 See *ibid.*, pp. 243–244.

383 For text, see *Statutes, Treaties and Documents supra* note 373, pp. 519–532. On this Act and its operation, see Munro, *op. cit. supra* note 290, pp. 245–251.

384 See *supra*, text at notes 369–370.

385 20 Vict. S.C. 1857, ch. 43, in C.S.L.C., ch. 2; *The Civil Code of Lower Canada*, ed. T. McCord, Montreal, Dawson Bros., 1867, pp. XXXIII–XXXVII; Castel, *op. cit. supra* note 318, pp. 24–26.

carry much weight. Likewise, if new provisions were required for modernization, the codifiers would be likely to turn to civilian compilations, such as the Code Napoléon, in search of rules consistent with the general tenor of the indigenous law.

Codification

The background to the 1866 codification has already carefully been investigated by J.E.C. Brierley.[386] This section, therefore, will be devoted merely to extracting, from the whole complex process of codification, those elements which help explain the sources selected on codification, and their relevance to conditions in Quebec. Four topics will be examined: first, the immediate background to codification; second, the legislature's instructions to the codification Commissioners; third, the characters of the codification Commissioners; and fourth, the Commissioners' interpretation of their instructions and their method of working.

Immediate Background to Codification

The Act enabling codification was passed in 1857.[387] The code was completed and came into force in 1866, just one year prior to confederation in Canada. Some writers[388] have been inclined to infer that the two events of codification and confederation are connected in some way other than by closeness in time, and conjecture that codification was a means of preserving the Quebec civil law from common law encroachment after confederation. Brierley has shown that the original motive for codification could not have been this one of preservation, since codification was proposed before confederation became a policy of the provincial government.[389] Further, in all the negotiations leading up to confederation, the special status of the Quebec civil law had been recognized.[390] Even without codification, the Quebec laws would seem to have been secure on entering the confederation. The "preservation" conjecture seems to be based almost entirely on the coincidence in time of codification and confederation, and on the following statement of McCord:

> In view of a union of the British American provinces, the codification of our laws is perhaps better calculated than any other available means to secure to Lower Canada an advantage which the proposed plan of confederation appears to have contemplated, that of being the standard of assimilation and unity, and

---

[386] Brierley, "Codification".
[387] 20 Vict. S.C. 1857, ch. 43, in C.S.L.C., ch. 2. See *supra*, text at note 385.
[388] See Brierley, "Codification", pp. 527–528 and n. 18. See *supra*, chap. 1 note 51.
[389] Brierley, "Codification", pp. 527–533.
[390] See the Quebec Resolutions of 1864, clause 43, parts 15, 17 and 18 on preserving local laws in *Statutes, Treaties and Documents supra* note 373, pp. 541–547 at p. 547; London Resolutions of 4 Dec. 1866 on the same in *ibid.*, pp. 611–617 at p. 615.

of entering into new political relations without undergoing disturbing alterations in her laws or institutions.[391]

The British North America Act of 1867, s. 94, provided for the possible unification of private law in the confederation, but specifically excluded Quebec. This had been a policy in confederation from 1864,[392] and makes McCord's remarks seem strange. His comment seems to have two possible meanings. First, codification meant that the Quebec laws could serve as a model for the possible assimilation or unification of the Canadian laws.[393] Second, if there were an assimilation, codification would prevent the Quebec laws from being much altered. That Lower Canada had insisted on control of her own private laws must render McCord's statement fairly pointless, and it is difficult to decide how much reliance should be placed on it. The statement may reflect an erroneous fear among the French Canadians that their laws would be infiltrated by the common law. As Brierley suggests,[394] it is possible that during the process of codification, as confederation approached, there developed the notion of codification as preserving the Quebec laws: it must be accepted, however, that the prime motive for codification was not a political desire to preserve the Quebec laws and to affirm the existence of a francophone population with their unique laws and institutions. If preservation of the integrity of Lower Canadian law had been an aim of codification, it would suggest that common law sources would not be used.

Brierley identifies as the main motive for codification in Quebec the desire to solve three legal and technical problems: the diversity of the sources of law; the problem of language; and the absence of any legislative or doctrinal synthesis. A spur to codification was the ready availability of foreign models.[395] The bulk of the laws were of French origin: codification in France had stopped the reprinting of these sources, and the vital commentaries upon them, making access difficult to the sources of Quebec law.[396] A considerable amount of provincial legislation and court decisions had been added to these French sources. While many inhabitants were monolingual, parts of the law were written in French, parts in English. Some provisions of English law had been introduced. All was obvious confusion.[397] The Code Napoléon and the

---

[391] McCord, Synopsis, pp. I–II.
[392] See *supra*, note 390.
[393] See Brierley, "Codification", p. 531, on proposed assimilation of the laws of Upper and Lower Canada in 1857—not necessarily to the detriment of Lower Canadian law.
[394] *Ibid.*, p. 528.
[395] *Ibid.*, pp. 533–542. These were also the reasons given in the preamble to the 1857 enabling statute. See *supra*, note 385 *supra*.
[396] See *supra*, text at notes 320–335 on French sources.
[397] See *supra*, "The French Period" and "The British Period". Castel, *op. cit. supra* note 318, gives a simple review of the sources at pp. 14–15, 17–18, and 20–23 with excerpts from some of the source material.

Louisiana Code of 1825[398] both offered examples of a synthesis of the law, and of the benefits accruing on codification. Brierley concludes that:

> The essential reasons . . . motivating the proposed codification . . . were rooted in this fact: the actual *content* of the legal system of Lower Canada was not easily ascertainable, by way of reference to either an official compilation or suitable doctrinal synthesis. The difficulty existed on two levels: the *substance* of the law was only to be gathered from a multiplicity of different sources which, themselves, existed in a language not always accessible to all portions of the population. The classification and organization of the law, to be exposed in the systematic fashion of a code along the lines of the two obvious models available, were thus the aims of the new compilation.[399]

Instructions to the Codification Commission

The 1857 Act[400] laid down in its various sections an outline method of operation for the Codification Commission. Under ss. 1 and 2, three Commissioners, who had to be barristers and could be judges, and two secretaries (one francophone the other anglophone, each with a good knowledge of the other's language) were to be appointed. The Commissioners were instructed by s. 4 to reduce the whole of the civil law to one code composed of laws of "a general and permanent character", but excluding any laws relating to seigneurial tenure. By s. 6, only laws actually in force were to be embodied in the code, while proposed amendments had to be stated separately and distinctly, with reasons given for their suggested adoption. The code was to be framed on the same general plan and was to contain a similar amount of detail as the French code (s. 7). Reports to the Governor were to be made periodically, and could be submitted to the Lower Canadian judges for their comments and advice on amendments or the accuracy of the statement of the actual law (ss. 8–12). Under s. 15, the code was to be "framed and made in the French and English languages", and when printed, the two texts were to be next to each other. Any two Commissioners could frame a report, but the third could frame a separate report or enter his dissent into the minutes of the proceedings of the Commission (s. 16). From the Commission's instructions, it is clear that the primary task was to reduce the vast mass of source material of Quebec law into one concise code, using the French *Code civil* as a plan and example; while

---

398 On the role of the 1825 Civil Code of Louisiana, see J.P. Richert and E.S. Richert, "The Impact of the Civil Code of Louisiana upon the Civil Code of Quebec of 1866", 8 (new ser.) *La revue juridique Thémis* (1973), pp. 501–520.

399 Brierley, "Codification", p. 542. (It is clear that the C.N. and C.L. offered new alternative provisions.) R. Taschereau gave the same explanation for codification: "Le Bas-Canada conservait cependant les lois françaises, mais ces lois étaient devenues tellement compliquées, tellement mêlées, qu'en 1857 Sir Georges Etienne Cartier proposait la codification pour des lois françaises pour le Bas-Canada", in "La Codification de Nos Lois Civiles", in *Le droit civil français: livre souvenir des journées du droit civil français. (Montréal–31 août –2 septembre, 1934)*, Paris, Sirey, 1936, pp. 657–671 at p. 662.

400 20 Vict. S.C. 1857, ch. 43, in C.S.L.C., ch. 2. See *supra*, note 385.

amendments were allowed, they had to be stated separately with arguments in support. It appears that the Commission was not given a totally free hand and that the redaction was to be of a basically conservative nature.

That the Commission was instructed to draw up the code on the basis of the law in force does not mean that there would be no element of selection present in this, the primary task. As has been pointed out, the law in force would have to be gathered from many, and possibly conflicting, sources. Doctrinal writers, for example, could have differing views of the meaning of the law; statutes could conflict; and cases could give contradictory decisions. The potentially doubtful nature of much of the Lower Canadian law would mean that, in deciding what was the law actually in force, the Commission would inevitably be involved in selecting among competing possible sources in areas of the law that were unclear or unsettled. The process of selection would likely be guided by the Commissioners' views on what the law ought to be, taking into account matters such as purity of principle, reform needed in view of changing social circumstances, and the like. Indeed, the Commissioners were well aware of the necessity of their making selections between competing sources in deciding what the law actually was, and they left on record their views as to what should guide their decisions.[401] Proposing amendments, the secondary task of the codifiers, obviously allowed them freedom to innovate wherever they thought necessary. They, of course, would use their freedom in a restricted way. That is, they would be likely to innovate by using obvious and traditional sources, and they would be unlikely to attempt to frame a completely new provision, given the obvious tendency of those with the task of reforming the law to borrow provisions from other systems.[402]

Characters of the Individual Commissioners

It is appropriate briefly to examine the background and careers of the three Commissioners, as it is possible that their political views and general character could predispose them to favour a particular view of the law and to adopt particular provisions. Although the Act enabling codification had been passed in 1857, not until 1859 was the Commission appointed.[403] On 4th February of that year, René-Edouard Caron,[404] puisné judge of the Court of Queen's Bench, Charles Dewey Day,[405] and Augustin-Norbert Morin,[406] puisné judges of the Lower Canadian Superior Court, were appointed as Commissioners for

---

[401] See *infra*, text at notes 423–424.

[402] See *supra*, chap. 1, text at notes 34–37 and 51–53. The purpose of this study is, of course, to see *why* the codifiers chose a particular source and rule for use in Quebec.

[403] In 1857, Cartier had offered the position of President of the Commission to L.H. LaFontaine, Chief-Justice of Lower Canada, who had declined on grounds of ill health. See Brierley, "Codification", appendix II, p. 581.

[404] 1800–1876.

[405] 1806–1884.

[406] 1803–1865.

Codifications. On the 10th of the same month, J.U. Baudry and T.K. Ramsey, both members of the bar, were appointed as the bilingual secretaries. On 25th October, 1862, Ramsey was replaced as secretary with Thomas G. McCord; while in 1865, on A.N. Morin's death, Baudry replaced him as Commissioner—one L.S. Morin taking the latter's position as secretary. Out of this group, we need discuss only the three judges originally appointed as Commissioners, as theirs was the task of codifications. When A.N. Morin died, the work was effectively finished, as the draft code was already being examined by the legislature;[407] and thus Baudry, appointed to replace Morin, would have no determining influence on the provisions of the civil code.[408]

Morin and Caron were francophone, while Day was anglophone. Day had been born in Vermont; but his family had come in 1812 to Montreal where he had been educated. All three were called to the bar in the late 1820s and had a common training in the Quebec civil law. All had had active political careers prior to elevation to the bench. Thus Day had been solicitor-general prior to his 1842 appointment to Queen's Bench. (He had transferred to the Superior Court in 1849.) Caron had been active as a moderate and liberal, and had been mayor of Quebec,[409] speaker of the Legislative Council,[410] and had held ministerial position under the Hincks-Morin liberal coalition (see below) before his 1853 appointment to the Superior Court, from which, in 1855, he was appointed to Queen's Bench. Of all three, Morin had the liveliest political background.[411] In 1830 he had been elected to the Legislative Assembly of Lower Canada, and he took a prominent part in all the troubles during the 1830s. He was entrusted by L.J. Papineau with drawing up the famous Ninety-Two Resolutions of 1834, on which the Assembly had taken its stand against the Provincial administration and Imperial government.[412] During the *Patriote* rebellions of 1837–1838, Morin was charged with high treason, but escaped arrest by going into hiding.[413] During the Union he had returned to political life, being elected to the Assembly in 1841, being the Assembly's Speaker from 1848 to 1851, in which latter year he joined with Hincks of Upper Canada to head the liberal coalition ministry which bears their names. He held various ministerial posts until his 1855 appointment to the Superior Court.

All three Commissioners had had ministerial responsibility and had played an important part in the events of their time. The three were men of learning and practical experience, undoubtedly familiar with the intellectual movements of their period. They would seem to be suitable candidates for the work of redaction, to which they could apply their knowledge of intellectual and

---

[407] See Brierley, "Codification", appendix II, p. 588.

[408] On this, see the McCord, Preface, pp. v–vi; and Brierley, "Codification", appendix II pp. 581–589.

[409] See Careless, *op. cit. supra* note 371, p. 47.

[410] See *ibid.*, p. 100.

[411] It is undoubtedly due to this that he has attracted the interest of more than one biographer.

[412] See G. Parizeau, *La société canadienne française au XIXe siècle*, Montreal, Fides, 1975, pp. 465 and 474–476. Parizeau devotes a whole chapter to Morin (pp. 465–519).

[413] See *ibid.*, pp. 465–467.

material life.[414] Though deeply versed in Lower Canadian law, by virtue of education and linguistic ability, all three would have access to sources written in languages not their own. While there is nothing in Day's background to suggest he would favour the introduction of common law notions, the strong commitment of both Caron and Morin to the French Canadian cause suggests that they would be zealous in preserving the integrity of the French Canadian law. This does not mean they would favour the retention of archaic provisions; on the contrary, the legal practices all had had before elevation to the bench, and their judicial positions themselves, would mean that all three would be well aware of any deficiencies in the Lower Canadian law, and the need for corresponding revision and modernization.[415]

The Commission's Interpretation of its Instructions and its Manner of Working

Since Brierley has given a very full account of the *modus operandi* of the Commission, and McCord a brief but important one, only certain aspects of the Commission's work need be touched on here.[416] Caron acted as *de facto* president of the Commission, and early in 1859 gave thought to how the Legislature's instructions were to be implemented. Turning his attention first to determining what exactly were the laws in force in Lower Canada,[417] he set down his thoughts in a *Mémoire*, in which he classified all the possible sources of the existing law.[418] The list of sources in the *Mémoire* is comprehensive and exhaustive,[419] and includes the *Coutume de Paris*, French ordinances and edicts, provincial legislation, juristic writers on French law of the *ancien régime*, such as Pothier, and those who wrote on the Roman law as adapted to France, notably Domat.[420] Although the writings of jurists were only given a brief mention towards the end of the list, they in fact constituted the most important and fruitful source;[421] the bulk of the other sources being found of little relevance.[422]

---

[414] From 1852 until his death, Day was Chancellor of McGill University. Morin was, first, Professor of Law at Laval, and then Dean of Laval's Law Faculty: Parizeau, *op. cit. supra* note 412, pp. 503–505.

[415] For further information on all three, see the entries in *Dictionary of Canadian Biography*, ed. by G.W. Brown, Toronto, University of Toronto Press, 1966; H.J. Morgan, *Sketches of Celebrated Canadians*, Quebec, Hunter, Rose, 1862, pp. 351–352 (Morin), pp. 472–473 (Caron); *The MacMillan Dictionary of Canadian Biography*, ed. by W.S. Wallace, 4th ed., Toronto, MacMillan, 1978, These works are the sources of information in the text not attributed in a note. Further biographies of Morin are cited by Brierley, "Codification", pp. 581–582 n. 7.

[416] See Brierley, "Codification", pp. 542–573; McCord, Preface, pp. v–ix, and Castel, *op. cit. supra* note 318, p. 29, who gives a brief account, apparently taken entirely from McCord.

[417] Brierley, "Codification", pp. 544–545.

[418] Further comprehensive lists of sources were proposed; but seemingly never drawn up: ibid. p. 546.

[419] See *ibid.*, pp. 547–552 for list, with notes for commentary.

[420] *Ibid.*, pp. 550–552.

[421] Brierley, *ibid.*, p. 553 remarks: "The vast bulk of actual law to be included in the provisions of the future code was thus contained in a myriad of French writers of the seventeenth and eighteenth centuries."

As well as the sources of the *ancien droit*, the codifiers examined the provisions of the Code Napoléon and the Louisiana Code for a concise expression of the old law. The latter code was especially useful, having both an English and French text.

The codifiers commented on the task of sifting through the sources in order to discover the laws actually in force. They stated that: "on an infinity of points there is uncertainty and difference of opinion. The legislature is silent, the courts do not concur, the authors disagree, and yet in all these cases a decision must be come to . . ."[423] The codifiers had already outlined in an earlier *Report*, some of the criteria by which they decided on any particular rule as being the law in force:

> The Commissioners would remark that in all cases of doubt and conflicting opinions upon the law, and in the oases of suggested amendments, they have not been governed by the mere weight of authority upon the one side or the other, but have preferred the rules likely to be found practically the most convenient and beneficial.[424]

It is obvious that the codifiers recognized that in deciding what was the law in force they were involved in a creative act, as they often had to choose between competing potential provisions. This statement indicates that in exercising such choices, they were concerned to fit law to what they saw as the requirements of their society.

When it came to amending the law, the codifiers apparently examined many and varied sources in a search for provisions suitable for borrowing.[425] The Code Napoléon and the 1825 Louisiana Code would often offer potential amendments. Caron believed that the latter, completed after the French code, might well contain provisions suitable for adoption in Quebec.[426] The Louisiana Code was also specifically mentioned in the preamble to the 1857 Act, and Cartier had been warm in recommending it in the debate over the codification bill.[427] Fortunately, the Commission left in its *Reports* details of sources consulted, and this renders comparatively easy ascertainment of sources consulted, and provisions accepted and rejected. McCord states (and as one of the secretaries to the Commission his evidence is very valuable) that in their amendments, the Commissioners consciously sought to fit the law to the

---

422 See *ibid.*, pp. 552–554.

423 *Second Report*, pp. 139–143, esp. at pp. 141–143 for these general statements made by the codifiers on their work. They also remarked, *ibid.*, that the sources were "so varied, and more numerous perhaps with us than in any other country and the long enumeration of which would be out of place here." On mode of citation of these *Reports*, see *supra*, chap. 1, note 34. These important general remarks at the beginning of the *Second Report*, may also be found quoted in Castel, *op. cit. supra* note 318, pp. 27–29.

424 *First Report*, p. 32. On p. 32 of their *First Report*, the Commissioners make several remarks of interest on the nature of law and codification.

425 See the list of abbreviations in McCord, Synopsis, pp. XLIII–LI for an idea of the range of sources consulted. See also Brierley, "Codification", p. 552, where he gives a count of over 350 different sources; and Morel, *op. cit. supra* note 345, p. 501 counts more than 300 "titres".

426 Brierley, "Codification", p. 545.

427 *Ibid.*, pp. 541–542 and n. 54.

existing society: "[The amendments are] intended for the most part to improve our law as a system, and to adapt it more perfectly to our present state of society."[428] He adds that the amendments: "[A]re . . . of a nature to harmonize with the ideas of the present day, and to adapt our ancient laws to the changes which since their date society itself has undergone."[429] These statements by McCord are confirmed by the Commissioners themselves in the passage already quoted from their *First Report*.[430] Thus, the Commissioners were actively seeking provisions suited to the state of society, and the sources they consulted, the provisions accepted or rejected, and the reasons they gave for doing the same, will obviously reflect on the influences on them in their task of creatively developing and modernizing the law.

The work of drafting individual books and titles of the code was split among the three Commissioners, and it is possible to ascertain which parts were originally drafted in French and which in English (obviously by Day).[431] The drafts were translated into the other language by the secretaries, checked by the Commissioner who drew them up, and then carefully examined by all three.[432] Both texts are thus of equal authority.[433] The especial prominence given to the French code is clearly shown by the method of working adopted in drawing up individual articles. The Commission worked using *cahiers*, each double page of which was divided into four columns, headed: "Existing law", "Corresponding Article of the Civil Code of France", "Proposed Amendment" and "Remarks".[434] The intention was to utilize, as instructed by the Legislature, the expression and wording of the French code in drawing up articles to encapsulate the existing law.[435] It is obvious that this method, involving comparison with the French code, would cause the Commissioners to reflect critically on the existing law, and would inevitably mean that, in considering a possible amendment, the French provision would always be the one most convenient and obvious to borrow.

Conclusion on the Background to Codification in Quebec

French colonization of New France had resulted in the introduction of the law of the customary-law north of France, specifically, the *Coutume de Paris*. Right up until codification, the Quebec private law remained firmly based in the law of *ancien régime* France (the *Coutume de Paris*, royal ordinances, and the received Roman law) despite the attempted introduction of Anglo-American

---

[428] McCord, Synopsis, p. II.
[429] *Ibid.*
[430] See *supra*, quotation in text at note 424.
[431] See McCord, Preface, pp. viii–ix; Brierley, "Codification", p. 537.
[432] McCord, Preface, pp. viii–ix; Brierley, "Codification", p. 537.
[433] McCord, Preface, p. ix, tells us that to overcome difficulties attendant upon the translation of French texts into English, Scots legal terminology was often used.
[434] See Brierley, "Codification", appendix I, pp. 577–580 on *cahiers*.
[435] See *ibid.*, pp. 563–564.

common law, and the application of aspects of the common law to some areas of the province.[436]

Although the legal culture of Quebec was firmly based in the French law of the *ancien régime*, with the inclusion of some common law, the large amount of source material apparently available in Quebec for consultation meant that the codifiers, in so far as they chose to modernize the law, could choose among many differing sources and provisions. The codifiers had access to the doctrinal writers on the old and new French law, writers on the Roman law, the *Corpus iuris civilis* itself, English law, American law and Scots law. From their *Reports*, it is clear that the Commissioners made full use of these sources, as well as of the Code Napoléon and Code of Louisiana.

The strong commitment of the codifiers to the French Canadian law and the conservative instructions of the legislature, would both tend to suggest that the sources most used would be the traditional ones, although, as pointed out by the codifiers themselves,[437] even in constructing the code out of the traditional sources, to embody the law presently in force, the codifiers would be involved in choosing between different provisions. The same conservative tendencies would suggest that in modernizing the law, the sources most likely to be used by the codifiers, especially in the traditional fields of family, property and obligations, would be the modern French ones, as being the ones closest in outlook to the traditional Quebec law. The *method* used in drawing up the code would also mean that the provisions of the Code Napoléon were those most convenient and obvious to borrow.

---

[436] The *droit commercial* is rather different from the *droit civil* in Quebec. See the conclusions on codification in Quebec in the final part of the thesis.

[437] See *supra*, text at notes 423–424.

Louis Casimir Elisabeth Moreau Lislet,
Codifier of the 1808 Digest and 1825 Civil Code
(*Courtesy of The Grand Lodge of Louisiana F.& A.M..*)

Part II

4

Family Law in the Louisiana Digest and Quebec Code

INTRODUCTION

The Family

It is notoriously difficult to define the term "family" in a satisfactory fashion. Mark Poster has remarked that "social science does not have an adequate definition of the family, or a coherent set of categories from which to analyze it, or a rigorous conceptual scheme to specify what is important about it."[1] To some extent, this is because, until recently, there has not been much research into the historical development of the family. Most of those scholars who were interested in the history of the family had generally accepted the nineteenth-century views of Frédéric Le Play, who considered that the past had been dominated by extended families, while modern nuclear families had developed under the impact of industrialization.[2] But the theories of Le Play have now been questioned and most vigorously rejected, especially by the Cambridge Group for the History of Population and Social Structure, the attack being led by Peter Laslett.[3] The work of the Cambridge Group has itself been questioned. There is, therefore, a revived and continuing debate over the nature of the family as an historical phenomenon, and over the appropriate method to study it.[4] Ariès

---

[1] M. Poster, *Critical Theory of the Family*, London, Pluto Press, 1978, p. ix.
[2] A good account of Le Play's work and the reasons for rejecting it may be found in J.-L. Flandarin, *Families in Former Times. Kinship, Household and Sexuality*, Cambridge, Cambridge University Press, 1979, pp. 50–68.
[3] See *infra*, text at notes 15–39.
[4] C. Middleton, "The Sexual Division of Labour in Feudal England", pp. 113–114 *New Left Review* (1979), pp. 147–168, remarked at p. 148: "Whereas a decade ago 'the family' was regarded as one of the most boring topics on the sociology curriculum … it is now the subject of an intense controversy." The method of investigation is very controversial: new theoretical concepts are constantly being developed to further analysis: e.g. the new approach based on the "life cycle" (of individuals) rather than "family cycle", to be found in T.K. Hareven, "Introduction", in T.K. Hareven (ed.), *Transitions: The Family and Life Course in Historical Perspective*, New York, Academic Press, 1978, pp. 1–15; G. Elder, "Family History and the Life Course", in Hareven (ed.), *Transitions supra*, pp. 17–56. On another recent contribution to the debate, see M. Verdon, "The Stem Family: Toward a General Theory", 10 *Journal of Interdisciplinary History*

found it necessary to ask: have we any right to talk of a history of the family? Is the family a phenomenon any more subject to history than instinct is?"[5] While Tamara Hareven remarked: "As a new field the history of the family is broadly interpreted, its boundaries undefined."[6]

The very term "family" is indeed ambiguous, with a meaning varying historically and from place to place, reflecting the growth and change of "family" as a concept.[7] Thus the term can be linked with household and hence has been taken to cover servants, slaves and apprentices. The seventh *Partida* gives a very wide definition of family;[8] and Laslett remarks: "servants were workers in the position of sons and daughters, the sons and daughters of the house were workers too."[9] Family organization varied also according to class: nobles, peasants, and town dwellers all had differing family and household structures.[10]

From the nineteenth century until recently, it was accepted that the family had progressed in a linear manner from an extended cohesive kin group (Middle Ages) to the modern nuclear family, which, it was thought, developed under the impact of industrialization.[11] This notion has been refuted by modern research which has shown that the history of the family is infinitely more complex than this simple linear model suggested. Whereas previously the rise of the "privatized" nuclear family was directly linked to the economic changes in the structure of society caused by the development of capitalism, with "a tendency ... to collapse into a single category ('pre-industrial' or 'pre-capitalist'society) periods of history ... quite distinct in time and character",[12] it is now thought that the development of changes in the family structure has a certain autonomy within the overall social structure. Thus Ariès has shown that the concepts of "childhood" and "family" which are associated with bourgeois society from the nineteenth century onwards developed before the onset of industrialization gave

---

(1979), pp. 87–105. See also L. Stone, *The Family, Sex and Marriage in England, 1500–1800*, London, Weidenfeld and Nicolson, 1977, pp. 21–41.

[5] P. Ariès, *Centuries of Childhood*, trans. by R. Baldwick, London, Jonathan Cape, 1962, p. 9.

[6] T.K. Hareven, "The History of the Family as an Interdisciplinary Field", in T.K. Rabb and R.I. Rotberg (eds.), *The Family History*, 1973, pp. 211–226 at p. 211.

[7] On this, see R. Williams, *Keywords*, Glasgow, Fontana, 1976, pp. 108–111; and Flandrin, *op. cit. supra* note 2, pp. 4–10 for an excellent conceptual analysis covering the 17th and 18th centuries.

[8] See *infra*, text at note 166.

[9] P. Laslett, *World We Have Lost*, 2nd ed., London, Methuen, 1971, p. 3.

[10] Poster, *op. cit. supra* note 1, pp. 166–205 develops 4 "models" of family structure in Europe. The notion of class variation of family structure is implicit in Laslett, *World supra* note 9, pp. 2 and 6 where he shows the different households of a baker (artisan, towndweller) and peasants. Stone, *op. cit. supra* note 4, pp. 9-10, discusses the variation of family types according to social stratification. He also takes such into account in the discussion of change in the nature of the family, *passim*.

[11] This is, of course, the analysis of Le Play: see Flandarin, *op. cit. supra* note 2, pp. 50–68. See also, Stone, *op. cit. supra* note 4, pp. 661–665.

[12] Middleton, *op. cit. supra* note 4, p. 148.

rise to that particular society.[13] The work of others confirms his view.[14] The notion, that before the development of the "bourgeois" family, people tended to live in extended kin groups has been seriously challenged by Laslett, who, on the basis of his demographic studies analysing parish registers, concludes:

> It is simply untrue as far as we can yet tell that there was ever a time or place when the complex family was the universal background to the ordinary lives of ordinary people.[15]

Laslett argued that family size had remained constant through the ages, but with a shift from high fertility and high mortality to low fertility and low mortality. Laslett's views have given rise to an extended controversy. It has been pointed out that the family has a "cycle"[16] and that often the married child who was to inherit the peasant farm lived with his parents (until they died or retired) and his own children, along with any unmarried siblings. This form of organization has been called the stem family;[17] the family being conceived of as going through a cycle of stem family, nuclear family to stem family as generations died out and were replaced.[18] The position thus becomes rather more complex than Laslett has argued. Flandrin has shown that Laslett's analysis of the statistics of household size is misleading: by a reanalysis of Laslett's own findings, he shows that, in one village, although 4.47 was the average size of the household, 65% of the population lived in exceptionally large households. The households of the gentry and wealthier yeomen were very large indeed.[19] In other words, in this village, the majority of the population lived in a few very large households, while the minority lived in a large number of tiny households. Flandrin shows, as Ariès had already shown, that households of the elite could be huge.[20] Further complexities are introduced by consideration of the nature of the relationships within the family, the relationships of the family to the wider community, and of the way in which the family is viewed.

---

[13] Laslett, *op. cit. supra* note 9, pp. 365–404, esp. at pp. 398–403.

[14] Stone, *op. cit. supra* note 4, pp. 661–665.

[15] P. Laslett, "Preface to the First Impression", in P. Laslett and R. Wall (eds.), *Household and Family in Past Time*, Cambridge, Cambridge University Press, 1972, pp. ix–xi at p. xi. See also P. Laslett, "Introduction: The History of the Family", in *ibid.*, pp. 1–90, esp. at pp. 16–23; Peter Laslett, "Mean Household Size in England since the Sixteenth Century", in *ibid.*, pp. 125–158. He restated his views in P. Laslett, *Family Life and Illicit Love in Earlier Generations: Essays in Historical Sociology*, Cambridge, Cambridge University Press, 1977, pp. 12–49; see esp. p. 14 n. 2.

[16] See *supra*, note 4 for discussion.

[17] On the problems of definition of this term, see L.K. Berkner, "Inheritance, Land Tenure and Peasant Family Structure: A German Regional Comparison", in J. Goody, J. Thirsk and E.P. Thomson (eds.), *Family and Inheritance. Rural Society in Western Europe 1200–1800*, Cambridge, Cambridge University Press, 1976, pp. 71–95 at pp. 84–85 and works cited in n. 31. See also Verdon, *op. cit. supra* note 4.

[18] See Berkner, *op. cit. supra* note 17, pp. 86–87 for a discussion of the cycle of the stem family, and its possible variations.

[19] See Flandrin, *op. cit. supra* note 2, pp. 53–58, 65–74.

[20] See Ariès, *op. cit. supra* note 5, pp. 391–392; Flandrin, *op. cit. supra* note 2, pp. 59–65.

Even were Laslett correct that in the past families lived in "nuclear-style" households, it must still be stressed that the structure of the relationships within the family was different, and hence the structure of the family was different (at least on an ideological level). The relationships of the members of the family with the wider society were also different.

In village societies of peasant farmers, individual members of the family owed allegiance to peer groups outwith the family. Shorter has argued that the meaningful relationships of peasants under the ancien régime were with the village as a whole, the wider community of the village intervening to a very great extent in family life, regulating the rituals of courtship, marriage and death, with the result that social authority over family members was exercised collectively, and not by the father and husband.[21] He contrasts the modern nuclear family with the old-style peasant family by stating that "[t]he locus of meaningful ties … shifted from without the family to within".[22] After reviewing the literature and research on the topic, Poster reaches the same conclusion.[23] Noble families were also radically different from the modern nuclear family. The households within which they were situated could be huge, with the size of the household increasing with the status of the family.[24] Ariès remarks that "the houses of the rich sheltered, apart from the family proper, a whole population of servants, employees, clerics, clerks, shopkeepers, apprentices and so on."[25] It must be admitted that after the development of the modern-style family in the eighteenth century, the noble family would still share its house with a considerable number of servants; but the circumstances were rather different. Ariès shows this brilliantly, by pointing out the change in the organization of the dwellinghouse, and by reviewing literary sources. Up to the seventeenth century, rooms were general purpose, and communicated with one another, as there were no corridors. Tables and beds were collapsible and could be moved from room to room.[26] The noble and bourgeois families were perforce on intimate terms with their servants. "In those rooms intended for no special purpose, where people ate, slept and received visitors, servants never left their masters…. This was not only true of the middle class, but of the nobility as well."[27] It must also be recalled that the place of business of an artisan, a merchant or a lawyer was his home: there was no separation of home and work. From the eighteenth century onwards this closeness of master and servant no longer existed. Rooms became specialized, corridors developed, as did an

---

[21] E. Shorter, *The Making of the Modern Family*, Glasgow, Collins, 1976, pp. 213–227.
[22] *Ibid.*, p. 230.
[23] Poster, *op. cit.* note 1 *supra*, p. 185: "The basic unit of early modern peasant life was not the conjugal family … but the village. The village was the peasant's family."
[24] A household of 200 was not unknown. See *ibid.*, p. 178 and n. 13 on p. 225. See Flandrin, *op. cit. supra* note 2, pp. 53–65, esp. at pp. 61–65.
[25] Ariès, *op. cit. supra* note 5, p. 392.
[26] *Ibid.*, pp. 393–395.
[27] *Ibid.*, p. 396. See the anecdote about the Princesse de Condé, her page and her footman, which well illustrates the familiarity between even the highest nobility and their servants: *ibid.*, p. 397.

elaborate system of bells. The family was able to isolate itself physically from the outside world.[28] Ariès concludes that:

> The rearrangement of the house and the reform of manners left more room for private life; and this was taken up by a family reduced to parents and children, a family from which servants, clients and friends were excluded.[29]

Thus, we can see that the family (narrow sense) under the ancien régime was very different from the modern. It may have consisted of parents and children, but there was a qualitative difference in that the family was not an isolated unit. Peasant families were influenced by the village as a community. Nobles and other wealthy groups lived constantly surrounded by servants, friends and the like. For all classes of society, up to the period around the end of the seventeenth century and the beginning of the eighteenth, life was conducted in public gaze. The family was not a private place. Further, Flandrin has shown that in rural society, the small households were dependent on the dominant large ones. Disagreeing with Laslett and the Cambridge Group, he states:

> It is this co-existence and this association that characterized western society in former times. The averages calculated on the basis of the parishes can give no indication of this.[30]

Corresponding to the above, and, of course, interdependent with it, there was a change in relationships within the family. These relationships arguably became more intense. Parents became much more concerned with their children. Ariès argues this thoroughly.[31] He suggests that the present concept of "childhood" is a modern one for Western Europe. Previously children were not separated from adults, but with the development of schooling and the growing intensity of parent-child relationships a new concept of childhood developed, with children no longer being regarded as little adults, but as a special group in whom parents invested a good deal of time and emotion. Formerly, he argues, children up to the age of seven or nine were treated virtually as "non-persons", and, if the families could afford it, were sent away to be nursed, with, apparently, no great interest taken in them. After the age of seven or so, children played a full part in the adult world, often being sent to live in other households as "apprentices" in order to learn useful social skills.[32] In the seventeenth century, this way of life was changing, and in the eighteenth, the modern notion of childhood and family developed. The wealthy might still employ wetnurses; but the child was no longer sent away to nurse, the wetnurse stayed in the family home. Parents started to take an intense interest in their children, around whom

---

[28] *Ibid.*, p. 399: "This specialization of rooms ...was...one of the greatest changes in everyday life. It satisfied a new desire for isolation."
[29] *Ibid.*, p. 400.
[30] Flandrin, *op. cit. supra* note 2, p. 65.
[31] Ariès, *op. cit. supra* note 5, pp. 365–404.
[32] See *ibid.*, pp. 71–81 and 128–133.

family life now pivoted.[33] The family no longer was only a method of transferring inherited property and privilege: it became a sanctuary of close emotion away from the outside world. The middle classes withdrew into the family, and physically separated themselves from the rest of humanity.[34] There are very considerable doubts as to Ariès' accuracy in stating that childhood itself was a new discovery;[35] nonetheless, his argument is correct in so far as he shows that the *modern* concept of childhood developed in the seventeenth and eighteenth centuries. Not all classes were affected by this change in the relationship between parent and child. The peasantry continued to live much as they had always done; the new working classes in the towns of the nineteenth century did not adopt bourgeois family organization. For the latter class, for example, childhood was not a prolonged experience, as children worked alongside adults from an early age.

The same time as there arose the new concept of childhood, the husband-wife relationship changed. Ties between husband and wife grew closer; affection between a married couple came to be thought more necessary. In short, there developed what Stone has called the companionate marriage.[36] However, this brought in its train some disadvantages, notably isolation.[37] The married couple was denied external support from kin groups and neighbours, as marriage came to be thought to be a more personal affair between the partners.

This suggests that Laslett's thesis requires amendment. The emotional structure of the old-style family was arguably quite different from that of the modern. Parents and children did not have the same intense relationship. The family took a full part in wider social life, from which it was not hermetically sealed away.

In conclusion, it may be said that the seventeenth and eighteenth centuries saw the development of the modern conception of family. Before the modern period, people did not oppose family to society: the two were inseparable. The family existed; but the conception of the family as a privatized area of life did not. While there had been no rigid separation of business from family as Ariès shows, with the privatization of the family such a separation developed. The old social contacts of work, friends and neighbours were devalued, while the "family" was valued more and more. Parents came to care for their children *qua* their children, not as representatives of the family line or as a means of improving the family's status or helpers with the farm. With the growth of the concept of childhood came the growth of the notion of caring within the family. Parental (especially paternal) authority grew; but its nature changed. It was no longer based on the power of a father over those subject to him, but rather on notions of care and protection. The

---

[33] See *ibid.*, pp. 71–81 and 128–133.

[34] An obvious example of this is the building of the eighteenth-century New Town in Edinburgh.

[35] D.E. Stannard, *The Puritan Way of Death: A Study in Religion, Culture and Social Change*, New York, Oxford University Press, 1979, pp. 44–47 questions the accuracy of Ariès' work for New England. But see also *ibid.*, pp. 168–169.

[36] Stone *op. cit. supra* note 4, pp. 325–326.

[37] *Ibid.*, pp. 396–404.

husband-wife tie grew closer, revolving around domesticity. Companionship and affection became much more important in marriage than hitherto. The closeness of the husband and wife bond paradoxically resulted in the early nineteenth century in the repression of wives, as the nuclear family became the emotional focus of the lives of its members.[38] That is, under notions of care for the weaker wife and children, the husband's authority grew. The old-style family was not the sole source of social contact and emotion, but with the growth of the close and exclusive modern family, the family became almost the sole source of emotion and affection based on care for the children. Thus, there can be traced a change from the old hierarchical style family, based on the power and authority of its head, to a modern associative or affective family, composed of individuals held together by notions of care and affection.[39]

Quebec and Louisiana

The above discussion, arguing for a qualitative change in parent-child and husband-wife relationships in the course of the seventeenth and eighteenth centuries, relies on works dealing with the family in Europe (especially France). Unfortunately, there is no equivalent detailed systematic research for Louisiana and Quebec;[40] but from the survey in chapter 2, it is clear that a similar pattern emerges.[41] In that chapter it was argued that by the time of the respective codifications in Louisiana and Quebec the nature of family relationships had changed vis-à-vis the countries from which they drew their laws.[42] In both it appears that families were no longer conceived of as patriarchal in the sense of being grouped under the authority of a father, with other members of the family being dependent on him because of his power over them as head of the household. It must be remembered that servants were regarded as under his power in the same type of relationship as sons. Rather, by the time of their respective codifications, in both Louisiana and Quebec, family structure was associative rather than hierarchical. The physical circumstances of life (abundant land) and the intellectual movements of the period (individualism) had tended to produce greater independence for children.[43] Commentators on both Louisiana and Quebec stressed the closeness of family ties in both; but, it must be stressed, this was a closeness based on affection, not authority. The husband-wife relationship is rather more difficult to assess. Early commentators on New France remarked on the independence of

---

[38] Stone shows this particularly well. See *ibid.*, pp. 666–673.

[39] See *ibid.*, pp. 221 et seq for the term "affective".

[40] But see L. Dechêne, *Habitants et marchands de Montréal au XVIIe Siècle*, Paris, Plon, 1974, pp. 433–449.

[41] See *supra*, chap. 2, esp. text at notes 46–57, and 107–120.

[42] R.L. Kagan, *Students and Society in Early Modern Spain*, Baltimore, Johns Hopkins, 1974, pp. 5–9, makes some relevant remarks on patriarchal family organization. He points to the lack of research on the history of the Spanish family.

[43] Dechêne, *op. cit. supra* note 40, p. 443 gives examples of the ease with which children could gain independence from their parents.

women, and, conceivably, this independence existed for them in early Louisiana; but this is no reason to suppose that such independence existed at the time of codification. Given, however, the general social conditions, both material and ideological, we can suppose a close tie between the husband and wife based on domesticity, with the husband in a position of superiority.

In Quebec we know that the French-Canadian population put a very great emphasis on the family: not the family in the sense of lineage, but as an emotional unit. In the basically peasant communities of much of nineteenth-century Quebec, there was doubtless a great interaction of communal and family life and the situation among, for example, the Acadians in Louisiana, was presumably similar. The life of town dwellers of the middle class would be different, corresponding to what above has been called the bourgeois family. Given the middle class origins of both sets of redactors, we can fairly expect that they would perceive the family as being the bourgeois family; or, at least, if they recognized differences of family organization, they would favour the bourgeois family as superior. Dechêne argues that colonial circumstances accelerated the growth of the modern family;[44] if she is correct, it is possible that there was less variety of family types in North America than in Europe.

Elements Important for the Law

From the foregoing discussion it is clear that from the historical view of the family what is important is to investigate changing relationships within the family. This is not to deny the importance of relationships of the family with the outside wider society, both are interconnected; but while the changing social structure initiates changes within the family organization, it is the family organization and relationships within it that structure the relationships of individual family members with outside society. This is so given that it appears that the historical development of the family is to some extent independent of that of the wider social structure.[45]

Hence, the investigation of changes in the law on codification and their connection with the changing concept of family should be centred round relationships within the family as revealed by the law. Thus, we should attempt to identify legal change or stasis and assess its significance. A note of caution should be added. While in the above discussion of the history of the family, the changes in its nature have been emphasized, it will have been noticed that many of these changes were not such as necessarily to call for any particularly dramatic change in the law, since these changes were mainly of an internal, qualitative nature. On the other hand, we are dealing here with the selection of rules from among competing potential sources, and some of these sources (for

---

[44] *Ibid.*, p. 434, where, after discussing the work of Ariès, she states, "La famille canadienne du XVIIe siècle s'inscrit dans ce mouvement général, mais les circonstances particulières du milieu colonial accélèrent son modernisation."

[45] See *supra*, text at notes 11–14.

example the old Castilian law), might well suppose a rather different family structure, or have individual inappropriate provisions, while some of the modern sources might suggest important reforms. The selection among these sources, and the reasons for it are what is important. If the formal law in force were particularly inapt, codification provided (potentially) an opportunity for reform. Whether or not that opportunity was taken (if necessary) and why (if not) are of great importance.

Since what is important is the shifting nature of relationships within the family, as regulated by law, we must study the law relating to husband and wife and parent and child in the two codes. (Other close relatives will be occasionally referred to, because, as Shorter points out,[46] with the withdrawal of the family from social life in general, not only parent-child relationships became more intense, but also those with other close kin.)[47] The law on these relationships provides the central core on family law in the two codes. This has the effect of limiting the body of research (excluding, for example, that on guardianship). This is unfortunate, but to cover every aspect of the law relating to the family would be a huge task, while it is clear that in concentrating on these two relationships we are covering what is most important. Thus, succession as it reflects on the family will be excluded. Matrimonial property will be touched on in so far as it illuminates the husband-wife relationship. The French law provides two concepts around which it is useful to centre the discussion—that of *puissance maritale* (or *puissance du mari*) and that of *puissance paternelle*.[48] These two concepts deal with the two significant relationships that are the central core of law on the family and provide a useful way of structuring the study by examining the way each power arises, its content and significance, and how it comes to an end. In the next section these two powers will be explained and the general civilian background to the family set out.

In the above discussion the exclusion of the servant from the family was mentioned. This is a theme that will be taken up and developed later.[49]

The Civilian Background

The Notion of "Puissance Maritale"

Neither the Quebec Code nor the Louisiana Digest of 1808 articulate a coherent concept of the *puissance du mari*, which was carefully described by authors of the *ancien régime* in France;[50] yet, as will be seen, the notion is implicit in both codes, each of which mentions the actual term (*puissance*

---

[46] See Shorter, *op. cit. supra* note 21, pp. 213–227.

[47] This is of most relevance with regard to children, as will be seen *infra*.

[48] In concentrating on paternal *power* or authority, we will ignore reciprocal duties of aliment between parent and child as not being of prime importance. We will also ignore illegitimate children. These omissions are unfortunate, but inevitable, especially considering time.

[49] See *infra*, chap. 5.

[50] See, e.g., Pothier, *T.P.M.*, pp. 1–2 (no. 1).

maritale) in one of their articles.[51] The actual extent of the power in both codes will be shown later. The notion of the *puissance du mari* over his wife is not of Roman origin, apparently having originated in the old German *mundium*, whereby the patriarchal head of the household had control over the persons and possessions of all the members of his household, including his wife.[52] In the process of the Reception of Roman law in Europe, the Roman principles of the husband and wife relationship appear to have contested this area of the law with the concept of *puissance du mari*. Accordingly, to explain the development of the law it is appropriate to discuss the Roman rules, then the provisions of the old French law—both *droit coutumier* and *droit écrit*—and then discuss the control over wives exercised by husbands, as can be gathered from the old Castilian law. Details will not be entered into, as these will be developed in discussing the selection of sources by the redactors of the C.Q. and the D.O. What exactly was meant by *puissance maritale* will be explained below; but to make the following discussion comprehensible, it should be pointed out that it referred to the contractual and proprietary capacity of women being restricted simply because they were married.

Husband and Wife in Roman Law

During the long history of Roman law, from the Republic to the Justinianic compilation, the status of wives changed. During the early Republic (at least) it had been common for wives to be married *cum manu*. Marriage *cum manu* meant that the wife left her own family and entered that of her husband, to whom she was in the position of a daughter *in potestate*.[53] Marriage *cum manu* disappeared entirely in the early Empire, and marriage generally became *liberum matrimonium*. This meant that the wife did not enter her husband's family, but stayed within her own, which meant that if she were *alieni iuris*, she continued in the power of her own *paterfamilias*, or if *sui iuris*, she was independent, although until late in the Empire there was nominal tutelage of all women (*tutela perpetua mulierum*). As Corbett states, "Free marriage had no effect on the general proprietary and contractual capacity of the wife."[54] In Roman law, it was supposed that a wife generally brought a dowry (*dos*) to her husband, and, indeed, with the very different concept of marriage in Roman law and society from our own, *dos* was one of the most important ways of proving *liberum matrimonium* existed between the couple rather than concubinage.[55]

---

[51] C.Q. 1259; D.O. 4 (p. 325); both have taken their wording from C.N. 1388.

[52] See Brissaud, *History*, pp. 84–86, 163–177.

[53] See P. Corbett, *The Roman Law of Marriage*, Oxford, Clarendon Press, 1930, p. 108.

[54] *Ibid.*, p. 113. The Roman law terms relating to *patria potestas*, and the institution itself, will be briefly explained *infra* in discussing *puissance paternelle*.

[55] On *dos* generally, see W.W. Buckland, *Textbook of Roman Law*, 3rd ed. rev. by P. Stein, Cambridge, Cambridge University Press, 1963, pp. 107–110; Corbett, *op. cit. supra* note 53, pp. 147–204. A helpful account of the Roman concept of marriage and family in its social context may

Dos became the property of the husband (or of his *pater* if he were a *filius familias*) who administered it, but it had to be accounted for at the end of the marriage.[56] The other property of the wife (if she were *sui iuris*) constituted her *parapherna*, which she administered herself, unless there were a specific agreement to the contrary, and we know from legal texts of circumstances where her husband had control of it.[57]

As pointed out above, in general, marriage had no effect on the wife's contractual or proprietary capacity (although both of these could be affected by her being a *filia familias*). One exception to this was the *Lex Julia de fundo dotali*, which, as amended by Justinian in a constitution of 530 A.D., forbade the alienation or hypothecation of dotal land, even with the consent of the wife, "ne fragilitate naturae suae in repentinam deducatur inopiam."[58] The capacity of women in general (not just wives) was limited by the *Senatusconsultum Velleianum* of 46 A.D., which forbade women to undertake liability for others, but not on their own account.[59] One final point to be made is that, to speak broadly, by Novel 61 of 537 A.D., Justinian applied the rules established for *donatio propter nuptias* to *dos*, with the result that dotal land could be validly alienated or pledged, if the wife consented and repeated her consent after two years, and provided that the husband continued to have resources to meet her lawful claims to her dowry.[60] It is not proposed to enter further into the question of matrimonial property in Roman law, as it is outwith the scope of this discussion.[61] What must be stressed is that Roman law in general did not reduce the capacity of women to any great extent because they were wives. The origins of the French *puissance du mari* cannot be traced to the Roman law.

Husband and Wife in the Droit Coutumier and Droit Écrit

In Rome, a wife who was *alieni iuris* was in the power of her *pater*, not of her husband. In the customary law north of France, the position was different. As Loisel laconically put it: "Femmes franches sont en la puissance de leurs

---

be found in J.A. Crook, *Law and Life of Rome*, London, Thames and Hudson, 1967, pp. 98–138. On ownership and administration of dowry, see Corbett, *op. cit. supra* note 53, pp. 177–182.

56 See D.23.3.75: "quamvis in bonis mariti dos sit, tamen mulieris est."

57 On *parapherna*, see Corbett, *op. cit. supra* note 53, pp. 202–204. On marriage and matrimonial property, see H.F. Jolowicz, *Roman Foundations of Modern Law*, Oxford, Clarendon Press, 1957, pp. 141–160, 161–177.

58 C. 5.13.1.15–15C. The original *lex Julia de fundo dotali* was part of the *lex Julia de adulteris* according to Corbett, *op. cit. supra* note 53, p. 180, and prohibited on pain of nullity the alienation of rustic or urban *praedia* in Italy without the wife's consent, or their hypothecation even with her consent. Justinian extended this to all dotal land wherever situated, and forbade alienation even with her consent, lest, as stated in Inst. II.8 pr., "sexus muliebris fragilitas in perniciem substantiae earum converteretur."

59 See Buckland, *op. cit. supra* note 55, pp. 448–449.

60 See Corbett, *op. cit. supra* note 53, p. 180; A.-J. Boyé, "Les destinées de la Novelle 61 chez les romanistes et les canonistes du moyen âge", 3 (4th ser.) *R.H.D.F.E.* (1924), pp. 473–514.

61 See *supra*, works cited in notes 53–60.

maris, et non de leurs peres."[62] As has been pointed out above,[63] this notion of the power of the husband originated in the German *mundium*, but, by the period towards the end of the *ancien régime*, the power in general meant only that the husband had a certain control over his wife's person and property, with the result that she lacked capacity in certain matters. It is unnecessary here to trace the historical development of this incapacity of the married woman, but it seems that in the customary law north of France its extent had varied greatly, with at some periods the wife having more capacity at others less.[64] There was also variation from one *coutume* to another. In the Roman law, the restrictions on the capacity of women were generally ascribed to notions of *fragilitas sexus*; but the foundation of the incapacity due to the *puissance du mari* was necessarily quite different, because unmarried women and widows had full contractual and proprietary capacity. Claude de Ferrière stated that:

> Cette disposition n'est pas fondée sur le foiblesse du sexe puisque les filles majeures et usantes de leurs droits peuvent disposer de leurs biens à leur volonté de même que les hommes: mais sur la puissance maritale établie par le mariage. . . .[65]

This was the crucial point: according to the commentators on the *ancien droit*, the *puissance maritale*, justified by natural and divine law, was necessary so that the society between husband and wife be given a firm and unified direction.[66] Ferrière explained it thus:

> Dieu les [i.e. les femmes] y a assujetties par une puissante raison, que l'homme et la femme étant mis ensemble par le mariage, par une union qui ne peut se rompre que par la mort de l'un d'eux, il étoit nécessaire que l'un fût soumis à l'autre pour le gouvernement et l'administration des affaires communes.[67]

Pothier argued thus:

---

[62] A. Loisel, *Institutes coustumieres ou manuel de plusieurs et diverses reigles . . . du droit coustumier et plus ordinaire de la France*, ed. by M. Reulos, based on 3rd ed. of 1611, Paris, Sirey, 1935, p. 30 (bk. 1, tit. 2, rule 20).

[63] See *supra*, text at note 52.

[64] See Brissaud, *History*, pp. 163–177.

[65] Ferrière, *Corps et Comp.*, vol. 3, col. 141, no. 2, discussing *Coutume de Paris*, art. 233: "La femme mariée ne peut vendre, aliéner, ni hypotéquer ses héritages, sans l'autorité et consentement exprès de son dit mari: et si elle fait aucun contrat sans l'autorité et consentement de son dit mari tel contrat est nul, tant pour le regard d'elle, que de son mari, et n'en peut être poursuivie par ses héritiers après le decès de son dit mari."

[66] See J. B. Denisart, *Collection de décisions nouvelles et de notions relatives à la jurisprudence actuelle*, 7th ed., Paris, veuve Desaint, 1771, vol. 3, s.v. *mariage*, p. 254: "L'autorité du mari sur la femme est du droit des gens et même du droit divin." See also Pothier, *T.P.M.*, p. 1 (no. 1): "La puissance du mari sur la personne de la femme, consiste, par le droit naturel, dans le droit qu'a le mari d'exiger d'elle tous les devoirs de soumission qui sont dus à un supérieur."

[67] Ferrière, *Corps. et Comp.*, vol. 3, col. 141 no. 2.

> Le mariage, en formant une société entre le mari et la femme, dont le mari est le chef, donne au mari, en la qualité qu'il a de chef de cette société, un droit de puissance sur la personne de la femme, qui s'étand aussi sur ses biens.[68]

The individual rules of this power will be described in discussing the codes, but these statements give an idea of the ideology underpinning the rules. The notion of marriage implicit in the statements is obviously very different from the Roman one, and is based on Christian ideas of conjugal union. In the *droit coutumier*, these Christian notions of matrimony have been used to rationalize and justify the incapacity of wives inherited from the German *mundium*. The wife is incapacitated so that the conjugal association can have a unified direction by the natural head: the husband.[69] Thus, by the eighteenth century, the leading commentators on the *droit coutumier* had rationalized a theory of the *puissance du mari*, which resulted logically in provisions relating to control over a wife's person, and property, and restriction of her administrative and contractual capacity.

The *puissance du mari* in this form did not *generally* exist in the *pays du droit écrit*. The law there was much more Roman in cast. The useful work of Serres shows this clearly.[70] Further, in the south in most areas, the paternal power retained an almost Roman extent, despite in some instances, provisions to the contrary in local *coutumes*.[71] Marriage in the south did not necessarily emancipate.[72] Thus, d'Espeisses remarks that:

> Le mariage ne délivre pas l'enfant de la puissance paternelle. . . . Ainsi la fille de famille ne peut tester de sa Dot, bien que sa Dot soit adventice. . . .[73]

If a son or daughter lived away from home for ten years, tacit emancipation was normally presumed. D'Espeisses comments on this:

---

[68] Pothier, *T.P.M.*, p. 1 (art. prél.).

[69] "Vir caput est mulieris", said the Vulgate Bible: Paul, *Ephesians*, 5.23. Theologians taught that for a woman to disobey her husband was a mortal sin. See Brissaud, *History*, pp. 165–166; A. Esmein, *Le mariage en droit canonique*, Paris, Larose et Forcel, 1891, vol. 2, pp. 4–8.

[70] Cl. Serres, *Les institutions du droit françois, suivant l'ordre de celles de Justinien*, Paris, veuve Cavelier & fils, 1753, p. 25 (I.viii). Serres was referring to the law as applied by the Parlement de Toulouse. He was an *avocat* and a *professeur* at Montpellier.

[71] Thus both the Coutume de la Ville de Montpellier and that of the Ville de Toulouse provided that marriage emancipated. Neither of these provisions was followed. See Serres, *op. cit. supra*, note 70, pp. 28 (I.ix), 65 (I.xii).

[72] See *supra*, references in note 71; also, see *infra*.

[73] *Œuvres de M. Antoine d'Espeisses, avocat et jurisconsulte de Montpellier où toutes les plus importantes matières du droit romain sont méthodiquement expliquées et accommodées au droit françois. Confirmées par les arrêts des cours souverains, et enrichies des plus utiles doctrines des auteurs anciens et modernes*, ed. by G. du Rousseaud de la Combe, Lyons, frères Bruyset, 1750, vol. 2, p. 13 (part. 1, tit. 1, sect. 1, no. 17). (The 1750 edition of his work is generally taken to be the best.) In *ibid.*, vol. 2, pp. 13–14, Rousseaud de la Combe remarks that, in those areas of *droit écrit* under the jurisdiction of the *Parlement de Paris*, marriage emancipates both sons and daughters. On the areas of *droit écrit* in the jurisdiction of the *Parlement de Paris*, see *infra*, note 77. The main *parlements* in the south were at Aix, Toulouse, and Bordeaux.

> Il en est autrement de la fille mariée; car bien qu'elle ait demeuré dix ans mariée hors de la maison de son père, elle n'est pas censée emancipée, comme il a été juge au Parlement de Toulouse. . . .[74]

Thus, the northern concept of *puissance maritale* was not applicable in most areas of *droit écrit*, because of the more Roman concept of *puissance paternelle*; as Argou said, "dans le ressort du parlement de Thoulouse, . . . le mariage n'emancipe pas les enfans de l'un ni de l'autre sexe. . . ."[75]

The legal capacity of women was limited, however, by the *Senatusconsultum Velleianum*, and that of wives by the *Lex Julia de fundo dotali*, in its 530 A.D. version.[76] A royal edict of August 1606 repealed the *Senatusconsultum*; but, as the *Parlements* of the south refused to register this edict, the *Senatusconsultum* remained in force.[77] (From this it will be obvious that the south followed the Roman law on dowry.) Thus, we may conclude that, in the *pays du droit écrit*, a wife was not under the power of her husband in the sense of the customary law, and did not require authorization for almost every action as she did in the *droit coutumier*.[78] Her *dot* would of course be controlled by her husband,

---

[74] D'Espeisses, *Œuvres supra* note 73, vol. 2, p. 15 (part 1, tit. 1, sect.1, no. 17). Rousseaud de la Combe, in his note on *ibid.*, vol. 2, p. 16, remarks that this usage of the *Parlement de Toulouse* was not followed by the *Parlement de Paris* as regards those areas of written law under its jurisdiction. He points out, though that the *Parlements* of Aix, Bordeaux and Toulouse all here followed the same rule. Serres, *op. cit. supra* note 70, p. 65 (I.xii) explains the rule here as regards married women: "il faut que la séparation de dix ans ait été volontaire de part at d'autre et non une séparation de nécessité; car une fille qui auroit demeuré dix ans mariée et séparée de son père comme étant obligée de suivre son mari, ne seroit pas censée emancipée."

[75] G. Argou, *Institution au droit françois*, ed. by B.J. Bretonnier and E.J. Barkier, Paris, Pierre Emery, 1719, vol. 2, p. 76 (bk. III, chap. VIII). The effect of the marriage of sons and daughters on *puissance paternelle* is more complex than here stated; we will return to it later in discussing *puissance paternelle* in the *droit écrit*. There seems to have been a good deal of uncertainty among scholars over the point. See *infra*, text at notes 111–124.

[76] On the fate of Novel 61, see Boyé, *op. cit. supra* note 60, pp. 513–514, where he remarks that the commentators generally refused to apply this Novel to *dot*. I certainly could find no trace in the works I consulted.

[77] See Serres, *op. cit. supra* note 70, p. 487, and Brissaud, *History*, p. 229, n. 5. Delaporte and Riffé-Caubray, *Pan. fran.*, vol. 3 pp. 378–379, n. 1, remark: "Les édits d'août 1606, et avril 1664, en abrogeant la loi *Julia*, rendaient cette autorisation (i.e. par le mari) assez commune, dans les pays de Droit écrit, du ressort du Parlement de Paris." The edict of 1606, of course, repealed the *Sc. Velleianum*, while that of 1664 repealed the *Lex Julia de fundo dotali* as regards the districts of Lyonnais, Mâconnais, Beaujolais and Forez, all districts of written law within the jurisdiction of the *Parlement de Paris*. Because of the restricted nature of the 1664 edict, and because of the failure of the southern *Parlements* to register the 1606 edict, the southern law remained untouched. In general, what Delaporte and Riffé-Caubray say is correct, though somewhat unclear. Serres and Brissaud, as cited *supra*, make the position certain. The *Sc. Velleianum* was particularly tenacious in the south: thus, it was applied in Toulouse, even though an article of that town's *Coutume* specifically stated it was inapplicable: see Serres, *op. cit. supra* note 70, pp. 487–488. This suggests how powerful Roman law was in the south.

[78] Olivier-Martin, *Histoire*, p. 654 (no. 490) states: "L'autorité marital s'est même étendue en pays du droit écrit, malgré la grande liberté de disposer de ses biens paraphernaux traditionnellement reconnue à la femme." This is stated too broadly. Obviously, some areas were more influenced by

and she had to live with him, be faithful to him and the like; but, if she had administration of her *parapherna* (*biens paraphernaux*), her actions as regards it were untrammeled.[79] Thus, it is clear that the general concept of *puissance du mari* was specific to customary-law France.

Husband and Wife in the Old Castilian Law

Only some general remarks need be made here, as the details of the relationship between husband and wife will be shown in discussing the 1808 Digest. The Castilian law operated a community of property system, with the husband controlling the community. There was also a system of dowry and *parapherna*, and the *Senatusconsultum Velleianum* had been received into the law.[80] In the *Siete Partidas*, the most important Castilian law book for the Louisiana redactors,[81] there was no treatment of community property,[82] probably because of the Romanizing tendencies of the work: the *Fuero real*, however, dealt with the matter.[83]

Despite the Roman cast of the law, it would be wrong to think there is no trace of a husband's authority over his wife. The *Partidas* does not indeed treat of the question,[84] but elements of such an authority over the wife's capacity to act can be found. Thus, under *Part.* 4.11.7, the husband has control over his wife's property, but he cannot alienate or squander it ("non puede el marido vender, nin enagenar nin malmeter mientre que durare el matrimonio la donación que él dió á la muger, nin la dote que él rescibiese della. . ."). *Part.* 4.11.17, on the wife's *parapherna*, presupposes that she will hand it to her husband to administer, but does not demand that she do so. What is clear

---

the northern law than others: see *Pan. fran.* vol. 3, pp. 378–379, n. 1: "[L]a puissance maritale n'était pas absolument étrangère dans notre Droit français à plusieurs provinces régies par le Droit écrit. Quelques coutumes locales exigeaient cette autorisation du mari." But the statements of d'Espeisses and Serres allow us to be certain that in general a wife in the south did not come under a northern-style marital authority. See Brissaud, *History*, p. 166.

[79] See E. Chénon, *Histoire générale du droit français, public et privé, des origines à 1815*, Paris, Sirey, 1926–1929, vol. 2, p. 128.

[80] By *Part.* 5.12.2. *Ley* 3 of the same title allowed for the exceptions permitted by contemporary commentators: a wife could thus renounce this protection (or prohibition). *Ley* 61 *de Toro* changed the position slightly. See R. Altamira, "Spain", in *A General Survey of Events Sources Persons and Movements in Continental Legal History*, ed. by J.H. Wigmore, Continental Legal History Series, vol. 1, London, John Murray, 1912, pp. 578–702 at p. 629 and 633; see also N.N. Pugh, "The Spanish Community of Gains in 1803: *Sociedad de Gananciales*", 30 *La. L. Rev.* (1969), pp. 1–43 at pp. 22–23. The reception of this *senatusconsultum* was no doubt due to the "Romanizing" tendencies of the *Partidas*. On the reception of Roman law in Castile, see *supra*, chap. 3, text at notes 61–115.

[81] See *supra*, chap. 3.

[82] *Part.* 4.11.24 and 30 allow the making of marriage contracts and communities, although there is no attempt to regulate them.

[83] See *infra*, text at notes 302–306.

[84] Cf. S. Minguijón, *Historia del derecho español*, Barcelona, Editorial Labor, 1927, vol. 1 p. 127. See discussion *infra*, text at notes 87–88.

though, is that, in the *Partidas*, a wife, *merely because she was a wife*, did not suffer lack of legal capacity and require authorization by her husband to contract, appear in court and the like. Some examples show this clearly. The *Tercera Partida, titulos* 1 to 27 deals with procedure. *Part*. 3. 7.3. states an exception to who can be summoned to appear personally in court. This exception applies to all women, there is no distinction made for wives: "Dueña casada, ó vibda, ó doncella ó otra muger que viva honestamente en su casa, non debe seer emplazada ninguna dellas de manera que sea tenuda de venir personalmente ante les jugadores. . . ."[85] I have located only one text which gives a *generalized* description of marital authority conceived of as power, *Part*. 3.2.5: a *ley* on whether husband and wife can sue one another. It starts as follows:

> Marido at muger son una compaña que ayuntó nuestro señor Dios, entre quien debe seer siempre muy verdadero amor et grant avencia: et por ende tovieron por bien los sabios antiguos que los maridos usasen de los bienes de sus mugeres et se acorriesen delles do les fuese meester; et otrosi que gobernasen á ellas at que les diesen lo que les conviniese segunt el poderio et la riqueza que hobiesen.

The text continues that what one has taken from the goods (*cosas*) of the other cannot be claimed in court.[86] There arise from this text some points meriting discussion. The *poderio* referred to means something akin to status (not *puissance du mari*), as is indicated by, *inter alia*, its conjunction with *riqueza* (wealth). The husband can aid himself with the use of his wife's goods when nessessary.[87] Generally, however, the husband has authority over his wife (*gobernar*). Further, the passage is intended primarily to provide the premise on which the prohibition of husband and wife suing each other is based. Thus, if this passage is considered in its particular context, it is clear that it does provide some *generalized* statement of marital authority, but this statement is not rigorously conceptualized nor, in the general context of the whole *Partidas*, are any particular rules logically derived from it. It provides a particular, localized statement of marital authority in general terms, (possibly revealing popular sentiment) but there is no general concept of marital authority (similar to that in northern France) working through the Partidas, influencing the particular legal provisions.

Minguijón relies on this passage to make a general statement about the husband-wife relationship in the *Partidas*.[88] This is misleading for the reasons given above. Further, he neither mentions the particular context of the passage in *ley* 5

---

[85] Cf. *Part*. 3.7.6.

[86] This is a Roman rule—in Roman law there could be no *actio furti* between spouses, although there could be an *actio rerum amotarum*: D. 25.2; C. 5.21.

[87] The subjunctive mood of the verb "to be" & *me[n]ester* following on from *acorrer* shows this clearly.

[88] Minguijón, *op. cit. supra* note 84, vol. 1, p. 127. His quotation is slightly different (due to his using a different edition), but identical in meaning.

of the second title of the third *Partida* (he does not even state a reference or give any indication of from where he has plucked his quotation) nor does he attempt to locate the passage within the general context of husband and wife in all seven *Partidas*. Had he said that the passage was symptomatic of a general trend within Castilian life he might very well have been correct; but he does not. The passage clearly does not reveal the attitude taken by the *Partidas* towards wives *qua* wives. Hence we can conclude that the *Partidas* provide no general concept of marital authority.

Despite the *Partidas*' neglect of marital authority, provisions can be found in the old Castilian law that reflect such an authority. A good example of this is provided by the 1505 *Leyes de Toro*. The specific provisions will be discussed *infra*;[89] but a few general statements may be made, the accuracy of which can be checked later. A sequence of individual *leyes*, from *ley* 54 onwards, enacts principles of the incapacity of married women because of their status as wives. These provisions were reaffirmed in the later *Recopilación de las leyes destos reynos* of 1567, commonly called the *Nueva recopilación*.[90] Similarly to the French *droit coutumier*, these *leyes* require that a wife be authorized by her husband to contract and appear in court (*estar en juicio*); but this requirement of authorization is not as extensive as in the *droit coutumier*, and is rather more flexible, while there is no statement of a general *concept* of marital authority from which these individual legal provisions flow, (although, of course, such a concept could be developed inductively from the individual provisions, and given an ideological foundation on, for example, divine or natural law).[91] Some specific differences from the *droit coutumier* may be pointed out. Two major differences were that, in the Castilian law, a husband could give a general authorization to his wife for future actions,[92] and he could subsequently ratify unauthorized actions.[93] The *droit coutumier* permitted neither of these.[94] Further, in the customary law there are provisions excepting from authorization wives who are public traders:[95] there are no equivalents in the *Leyes de Toro*.[96] Since, however, the Castilian law permitted *general* authorizations, a wife as a public trader could presumably be so authorized. In the *droit coutumier*, unauthorized actions by the wife were radically null, and the provisions of *Toro* apparently provide the same, but with the possibility of the husband ratifying unauthorized actions by his wife.

---

[89] See *infra*, on the D.O. in Louisiana.

[90] On the *Nueva recopilación* [*Rec. Cast.*], see *supra*, chap. 3, note 77. I shall cite the *Leyes de Toro* y *Toro* and the number of the *ley*, e.g. *Toro*, 54. The relevant provisions of the *Leyes de Toro* may be found in *Rec. Cast.* 5.3.1 *et seq*. They may also be found in the *Nov. Rec. Cast.* 10.1.10 *et seq.*

[91] We need not concern ourselves with the historical origins of these rules of the *Leyes de Toro*, given that we are primarily concerned with developing the general legal background that the D.O. redactors could draw on.

[92] *Toro*, 56; *Rec. Cast.* 5.3.3.

[93] *Toro*, 58; *Rec. Cast.* 5.3.5.

[94] See *infra*.

[95] See *infra*, esp. under Quebec.

[96] But cf. *Fuero real*, 3.20.13 (bk 3, tit. 20, law 13.

The treatment of the incapacity of married women by the legal writers is most instructive. Asso and Manuel,[97] in their *Instituciones*,[98] discuss nothing remotely resembling *puissance maritale*, which, as a legal concept, obviously did not exist for them, although they occasionally refer to the incapacity of married women. Had they so chosen, they could easily have fitted such a concept into their natural law scheme. Llamas y Molina in his commentary on the *Leyes de Toro* makes no attempt to develop a general theory of the incapacity of married women,[99] nor does Gomez.[100] Febrero[101] discusses frequently the contractual capacity of married women (an obviously important topic given that his work was intended for notaries); but he too gives no general theoretical statement analogous to that of Pothier,[102] even though he does provide some reasons for the limitation of the capacity of married women.[103] It will be shown later that the jurists interpreted these provisions restricting the capacity of married women in such a way as to minimize their effect.[104] The provisions were already less restrictive than those of the *droit coutumier*, but the Castilian jurists rendered them even less restrictive. This helps explain why the jurists never developed a concept of *puissance maritale*. They followed the tradition established by the *Partidas*, influenced by the Roman law.

In sum, in the Castilian law, there existed some measure of marital authority, both in control over a wife's property and over those of her actions that had legal consequences. The *Siete Partidas*, the main legal text providing a coherent account of all the law (that is, the account most important for the Louisiana

---

[97] I. Jordan de Asso y del Rio and M. de Manuel y Rodriguez.

[98] *Instituciones del derecho Civil de Castilla*, 7th ed. by Joaquin Maria Palacios, Madrid, 1806. This edition was the only one available to me. This work was one of the books written to meet the need arising out of the introduction of the teaching of the national law in Spain. L.F.C. Johnston translated it as *Institutes of the Civil Law of Spain*, London, J. Butterworth & Son, 1825, intending it to be useful in former Spanish colonies now governed by Britain.

[99] S. de Llamas y Molina, *Comentario critico-juridico-literal á las ochenta y tres leyes de Toro*, Madrid, Repullés, 1827: see his commentaries on *leyes* 54–59.

[100] A. Gomez, *Ad leges Tauri commentarius, cui accesserunt Doctoris Diegi Gomezij, ... annotationes vtilissimae, & pernecessariae*, Antwerp, Petrus et Joannes Belleri, 1624, pp. 503–504, commentaries on *leyes* 54–59. Gomez was a 16th-century jurist, and his was probably the most respected commentary on the *Leyes de Toro*.

[101] References are to the edition J. Febrero, *Librería de escribanos, é instrucción juridíca theórico práctica de principiantes*, Madrid, Imp. de P. Marin, 1789–1790. This is divided into two parts, *Contratos*, vols. 1–3 and *Juicios* (vols. 4–7); the volumes of the latter will be cited thus: 4(1). This one conforms in structure to that cited in the D.L.V., which states its references are to the third edition, which is that of 1783, which may suggest that this was the one to which the compilers had access. Batiza, "Sources", p. 34 cites the *Febrero adicionado*, 5th ed., 1806, 1808. I have been unable to carry out a careful comparison, but there seems little textual variation of juridical significance.

[102] See supra, note 50.

[103] See e.g. Febrero, *Contratos*, ch. 1, § V no. 75 (vol. 1, p. 87), on *Toro*, 55, where he states motive is not "imbecilidad, ó fragilidad de la muger", but because the husband is the legitimate administrator of her property during marriage, with responsibility for it; see also *Contratos*, ch. 4 § IV, no. 107 (vol. 2, p. 86), on women being prohibited as guarantors, because of the "imbecilidad de su sexo", never thinking of the future, and easily persuaded etc.

[104] See *infra*, text at notes 430–437 and 450–455.

redactors), provided no adequate statement of such marital authority, either as to individual provisions, or as to a generalized concept. Other legal sources provided an account of individual provisions, but no coherent concept of marital authority, while the jurists interpreted the provisions as restrictively as possible.

The Code Napoléon, and General Remarks

The C.N. and its *projet* of 1800 provided further legal provisions among which the Louisiana and Quebec redactors could select.[105] The relevant individual provisions will be made clear in the discussion of both codifications; but it may be noted that, in general, the C.N. followed the *droit coutumier* on *puissance maritale*, though with some modification, rationalization, and modernization of the provisions. The C.N. also included provisions on the dotal regime of matrimonial property. During the Revolutionary period, there had been moves to abolish marital authority, and put spouses on an equal footing;[106] but there was, however, a return to the traditional customary-law notion of the subjection of a wife to her husband.

The redactors of the C.Q. could draw on the *ancien droit* and the C.N., while the D.O. redactors could draw on both these sources and on the Castilian law in force. Thus, from the existing sources, both sets of redactors, could develop a scheme of marital authority which could vary on a continuum from very slight to very great. They could change the existing law or keep it, affecting either minor details or the totality of provisions.

Puissance Paternelle

Puissance paternelle refers to that power and control which a father has over the persons and property of his children. Here the Roman *patria potestas*, the French analogous provisions in the *droit écrit* and *droit coutumier*, and the Castilian *patria potestad* will be discussed. The position taken by the C.N. will be indicated.

The institution of *patria potestas*, which effectively defined the family, pervades Roman law:[107] the members of the family being those (including slaves)

---

[105] For the *Projet de l'an VIII* I have used the edition in P.A. Fenet, *Recueil complet des travaux préparatoires du Code civil*, Osnabrück, O. Zeller, 1968 (repr. of ed. of 1827), vol. 2, citing it by book, title, and article, e.g., *Proj. An VIII*, 1.3.5. Year VIII was the Revolutionary Calendar's name for 1800.

[106] See A.H. Huussen Jr., "Le droit du mariage au cours de la Révolution Française", 47 *Tijdschrift Voor Rechtsgeschiedenis* (1979), pp. 9–51 (1st. part) and 99–127 (2nd. part.) at pp. 114–115 and 118–119. See also Brissaud, *History*, p. 166 and nn. 4 and 5.

[107] Buckland, *op. cit. supra* note 55, pp. 101–104; Jolowicz, *op.cit. supra* note 57, pp. 181–203. I will not bother to give references for specific aspects of the Roman law. In general outline, this area of the law is uncontentious, and any standard textbook will confirm what is said in the text. The Romans recognized the uniqueness of their conception of *patria potestas*. See Gaius, *Inst.* 1.55: "quod ius proprium civium Romanorum est. Fere enim nulli alii sunt homines qui talem in filios suos habent potestatem qualem nos habemus."

in *potestate* of the *paterfamilias*, the head of the household. The *paterfamilias* had an almost total legal control over his descendants in the male line. He alone owned the family's property, and anything his *filiifamilias* or *filiaefamilias* acquired, they acquired for him. In classical times, a *filius* could acquire a *peculium castrense* (as the name suggests, it consisted of property acquired while soldiering), which was his own property,[108] and he could be granted a *peculium* (*profecticium*); that is, property given him by his father to control, which, in theory, remained the father's and could be taken back. In the later Empire, a son's proprietary capacity increased. The *peculium quasi-castrense* was introduced, permitting the son to control property gained in certain non-military forms of employment. The Emperor Constantine limited to a usufruct a *pater's* interest in property his *filius* inherited from his mother (*bona materna*). This principle was extended, first, to all acquisitions coming to the *filius* from his mother and her family, and, eventually, to all acquisitions. These were called *bona adventicia*. This class of property is sometimes called *peculium adventicium*.

The power of the *pater* over his descendants in the male line (or those adopted into the family) lasted until his death, or he emancipated them. On his death his descendants either became *sui iuris* or remained *alieni iuris*. Those who became *sui iuris* were freed from power, and, if male, became *patres familias* in their own right, although if *impuberes* they were under tutelage, and if women, they were (originally) likewise under tutelage because of the *tutela perpetua mulierum*. Those who remained *alieni iuris* fell into the power of their ascendant who was now a *paterfamilias* through having been freed by the death of the *pater*.[109]

In France, under the *ancien régime*, the north and the south had very different conceptions of *puissance paternelle* because of the different historical origins of their laws on paternal authority. The south had received the Roman *patria potestas*, while the north followed a law derived from the Germanic concept of *mundium*.[110]

In the *droit écrit*, the Roman rules were in almost full vigour. In the past there has been some confusion over *puissance paternelle* in the south. It is, therefore, important to discuss it fairly fully here, more especially to support statements already made about married women in the south.[111]

First, paternal power lasted until the father died, or he emancipated his children. As already indicated, there could be a tacit emancipation.[112] The thirteenth-century local *coutumes* of Toulouse and Montpellier provided that

---

[108] Originally, at the end of a campaign, such property would go to the father.

[109] The operation of *patria potestas* in Roman society is of no direct relevance here; but, see, e.g., D. Daube, *Roman Law: Linguistic, Social and Philosophical Aspects*, Edinburgh, Edinburgh University Press, 1969, pp. 75–91; Watson, *Society*, pp. 23–29.

[110] On the origins of *mundium*, and its similarity to *patria potestas*, see Brissaud, *History*, pp. 179–185.

[111] See *supra*, text at notes 70–79.

[112] See *supra*, text at notes 73–75 (and notes themselves).

marriage should emancipate:[113] however, with the revival of Roman law these provisions were not followed.[114] (Indeed, before the reception of Roman law in the south, the law on husband and wife was very similar to that of the north.)[115] This point was controversial: it appears that some authors asserted that marriage emancipated in the whole of France (Henrys for example),[116] and they appear to have based this statement on a knowledge of the *droit écrit* within the jurisdiction of the *Parlement de Paris*. Even more controversial than whether marriage emancipated generally was whether marriage emancipated *daughters*: for, if daughters were not emancipated from paternal power by marriage, then the northern-style *puissance maritale* could not exist. Bretonnier on Henrys discussed the confusion, and dealt with each area of the written laws. He concluded that, except for areas of *droit écrit* within the jurisdiction of the *Parlement de Paris*, marriage generally did not emancipate either sex.[117] Argou reached the same conciusion.[118] Indeed it was only in the course of the sixteenth century that it was decided that, in the *droit écrit* in the jurisdiction of the *Parlement de Paris*, marriage emancipated.[119] This change in the law, "excita de grands murmures à Lyon", according to Argou, but the change in the law remained.[120] The *Parlement* of Toulouse later considered the same point in a case in which at

---

[113] Chénon, *op. cit. supra*, note 79, vol. 1, p. 133, nn. 2 and 3, quotes the relevant provisions.

[114] See Serres, *op. cit. supra* note 70, pp. 65 (I.xii) and 28 (I.ix), where he states, "on n'observe pas même en Languedoc les articles de la Coutume de Toulouse et de celle de Montpellier, qui veulent que les enfans soient émancipés par le mariage ...."

[115] See Ch. Lefebvre, *Le droit des gens mariés aux pays de droit écrit et de Normandie*, Paris, Sirey, 1912, p. 10, where the author states that, in the pre-reception, southern customs, one finds "une donnée d'autorité et de direction maritale, analogue à notre puissance maritale des pays coutumiers, nonobstant certains vestiges alors fort attenues de la *patria potestas*". Also for this period, he states, *ibid.*, p. 12: "Pour ce qui regarde la vie conjugale, au Midi comme au Nord, nulle autorité dans le ménage que celle du mari." Of the local customs, he states, *ibid.*, p. 9, that they suffered a "desuetude de plus en plus marquée en face de droit romain. . . ." (The copy of Lefebvre's work used was that bound at the end of *Le droit des gens mariés*, part of his *Cours de doctorat sur l'histoire du droit matrimonial français*.)

[116] See *Œuvres de M. Claude Henrys conseiller du roi; ... contenant son recuëil d'arrêts, ses plaidoiers et harangues, et vingt-deux questions postumes tirées des écrits de l'auteur trouvés après son decès. Avec des observations sur les changemens de la jurisprudence arrivés depuis la mort de l'auteur. Une conference de la jurisprudence de tous les païs du droit écrit du Roiaume. Et des moiens faciles et sures pour la rendre certaine & uniforme dans tous les tribunaux*, ed. by B.J. Bretonnier, Paris, Michel Brunet, 1708, vol. 2, pp. 338–339 (bk. IV, quest. XIII).

[117] Bretonnier, comment on Henrys, *op. cit. supra* note 116, p. 340.

[118] See *supra*, quotation in text at note 75; also, *supra*, the remarks drawn from d'Espeisses in notes 73–74.

[119] Bretonnier, comment on Henrys, *op. cit. supra* note 116, p. 340; Argou, *op. cit. supra* note 75, vol. 2, p. 78 (bk. III, ch. 8). This case was considered in the Toulouse case; see *infra*, note 121.

[120] Argou, *op. cit. supra* note 75, vol. 2, p. 78. Of the principle in the areas within the jurisdiction of Paris, Argou states, *ibid.*, that it "n'a été établi à l'égard des filles que vers la fin du dernier siècle; et les auteurs qui en rapportent les arrêts, remarquent que ce changement de jurisprudence excita de grands murmures à Lyon, que les états de la province dresserent des memoires pour s'opposer au premier arrêts mais les troubles du royaume en ayant empêché l'effet, la jurisprudence de nouveaux arrêts a prevalu à l'ancien usage." Bretonnier, comment on Henrys, *op. cit. supra* note 116, p. 340, reports that there were three relevant *arrest*, in 1540, 1595 and 1597.

issue was whether or not a married woman could validly make a will without the consent of her father. It was decided that she could not.[121] Hence, paternal power over women continued after their marriage.[122] The case report notes that the jurisprudence on the *droit écrit* within the jurisdiction of the *Parlement de Paris* is not generally followed.[123] It must be concluded that in all areas of *droit écrit* within the jurisdiction of the southern *Parlements*, neither sex was emancipated by marriage.[124]

The *droit écrit* gave the *père de famille* a usufruct in his children's own property, that is, in their *biens adventices*;[125] as regards the *biens profectices* of children in power, "le père a non seulement l'Usufruit, mais aussi la propriété . . .", as d'Espeisses said.[126] This usufruct did not need to be relinquished on the marriage of the child, unless the child was emancipated, although Serres did point out that if a father made a gift in the marriage contract to his son on the occasion of the son's marriage, there would not be a usufruct in the gift, even should the son not be emancipated.[127] As in the late Roman law, sons could have a *peculium castrense* or *quasi-castrense*.[128]

---

[121] Maynard reports the case. I used the 1611 Latin edition of his collection of cases, entitled: *Illustres controversiae forenses, secundum iuris civilis Romanorum normas in amplissimo Senatu Tholosano decisae, quas collegit . . . Dn. Gerardus de Maynard, I.C. consiliarum regius et Suprema Curiae Tholosano senator, atque e Gallico sermone in Latinum transtullit . . . Hieronymus Bruckner*, Cologne, Alexander Pernet, 1611, bk V, *decisio* II, cols. 1067–1071. For the reasoning, see the *summaria* at col. 1067: "1. Glossa vulgaris Accursii quo ad exemptionem a patria potestate liberum Gallicorum explicatur. 2. In qua Glossa, quemadmodum vulgo accipitur, Accursius deceptus fuit. 3. Filius emancipatus aut pro emancipato vigore consuetudinis habitus valide testatur. 4. In provinciis iuris scripti, nisi peculiaris consuetudo aut statutum in contrarium extet, filiaefamilias nuptae testari aut etiam sine patris consensu mortis causa donare nequeunt. 5. Arresta contraria suprema curiae Parisiensis haud generaliter accipienda sunt. 6. Testamentum tamen, quod a filio coram quinque testibus patre consentiente factum fuit et clausulam codicillarem habet, subsistere potest."

[122] It should be noted the question of paternal authority over married a woman was discussed in the case as it touched on her capacity to dispose of property. The point would always arise in this manner, as it would only be as regards her property rights, that the question of *authority* would arise. The wife would live with and follow her husband. This is in tune with the Roman notion of *patria potestas*.

[123] See *supra*, note 121.

[124] Lefebvre, *op. cit. supra*, note 115, pp. 35–46, does not unfortunately, directly address the point we have considered. He only alludes to the question on *ibid.*, p. 46 and n. 1; but he does state, *ibid.*, p. 43, that: "Une autre conséquence de la Renaissance romaine fut l'abandon du principled autorisation maritale aux pays de droit écrit, parce quo'n n'en trouvait pas de trace et de précédents dans le droit romain." He is not aware, or at least does not state, that one of the reasons behind the abandonment of marital authorization was the revival of the contradictory concept of *patria potestas*.

[125] Argou, *op. cit. supra* note 75, vol. 1, pp. 18–19 (bk.1, ch.3); d'Espeisses, *Œuvres supra* note 73, vol. 1, p. 607 (part II, tit. 1, preliminary art., no. 2); Serres, *op. cit. supra* note 70, pp. 26 (I.ix) and 203–204 (II.ix).

[126] D'Espeisses, *Œuvres supra* note 73, vol. 1, p. 606 (part II, tit. 1, prel. art., no. 2); Serres, *op. cit. supra* note 70, pp. 203–204 (II.ix).

[127] Serres, *op. cit. supra* note 70, p. 210 (II.ix); Maleville, *Analyse*, vol. 1, p. 337, states that in the *pays de droit écrit*, paternal power continued as in Roman law, bar two modifications. The first was tacit emancipation after ten years separation (see *supra*, text at notes 73–75.); the second was

We may conclude that in the *pays du droit écrit*, except for those areas under the jurisdiction of the *Parlement de Paris*, the Roman *patria potestas* had been received, and continued in full vigour.

In northern France, the puissance paternelle had a very different appearance. Some *coutumes* explicitly recognized it;[129] but their particular provisions and the general law in the *pays du droit coutumier* were such that Loisel could assert as a general maxim: "Droict de puissance paternelle n'a lieu."[130] The maxim, however, is stated in too general terms. The Quebec codifiers state correctly: "it is certain that, under the customs in France, there was formerly a species of paternal authority."[131] The individual provisions on this paternal authority varied from *coutume* to *coutume*, but the following general remarks may be made. The paternal power was of limited duration, ending on the minor's reaching the age of majority or his emancipation by marriage.[132] On the death of the father, the minor did not come under the control of any ascendant, but rather under that of a tutor.[133] The father had particular rights over the child as to, *inter alia*, his marriage and had some powers of correction. The child could, of course, hold property in his own right, but the father had certain rights in that property.

"que le père était obligé de se départir de l'usufruit des biens de see enfans à leur mariage, sauf à s'en reserver ce qui lui était nécessaire pour sa subsistence et celles de ses autres enfans, s'il n'avait pas d'autres moyens pour y pourvoir. *Lapeyrère, letter D, n.* 115. Il ne parle, il est vrai, que du mariage de la fille, mais les mêmes raisons s'appliquent au fils . . . . Il faut bien en effet pourvoir aux besoins de la nouvelle famille qui se forme." The author cited is A. de la Peyrère. Maleville's accuracy is questionable: see Serres, *op. cit. supra* note 70, pp. 205–209 (II.ix); Argou, *op. cit. supra* note 75, vol. 1, pp. 18–19 (bk.1, ch.3). The *Parlement de Toulouse* had decided differently to the proposition stated by Maleville; see Maynard, *Illustres controversiae forenses supra* note 121, bk. II, *decisio* 73, col. 308, where, in the case of Austry *filius contra* Austry *pater*, the *Parlement de Toulouse* said, first, that in the areas of written law, the father has a usufruct of his children's property, and, second, that this usufruct does not end on the marriage of the children, since in the event, the father is bound to assign to them, on the decision of the near relations, fixed alimentary payments and certain moveables, in proportion to the property belonging to them. Both Serres, *op. cit. supra* note 70, pp. 205–210 (II.ix), and Argou, *op. cit. supra* note 75, vol. 1, pp. 18–19 (bk.1, ch.3), would agree. On Abraham de la Peyrère, see *Biographie Universelle*, vol. 32, which states that, though an advocate in Bordeaux, he was noted for not distinguishing clearly or adequately between the *droit écrit* and *droit coutumier.*

[128] See, e.g. Argou, *op. cit. supra* note 75, vol. 1, p. 19 (bk. 1, ch. 3); Serres, *op. cit. supra* note 70, p. 206 (II.ix).

[129] See, e.g., discussion in Maleville, *Analyse*, vol. 1, pp. 335–336.

[130] Loisel, *op. cit. supra* note 62, bk. 1, tit. 1, rule 36 (borrowed from the *Coutume de Senlis*, art. 221).

[131] *Second Report*, p. 203.

[132] Loisel, *op. cit. supra* note 62, bk. 1, tit. 2, rule 37: "Feu et leu font mancipation ce dict Brassas, et enfans mariez sont tenus pour hors de pain et pot, c'est-à dire emancipez."

[133] *Henrys, op. cit. supra* note 116, vol. 2, p. 338 (bk. IV, quest. XIII): "[O]n peut dire, que parce qu'en France le mariage émancipe, le fils marié sort de la puissance du père est fait père de famille, et par consequent a ses enfans en sa puissance, lesquels autrement par le Droit Romain seroient aussibien que le père en la puissance de l'ayeul." See also *ibid.* vol. 2, p. 339: "Concluons donc, que c'est une erreur de croire que le père mort, les enfans qu'il laisse retombent en la puissance de leur ayeul paternel, et que cet ayeul ait l'usufruit de leurs biens." His remarks should be taken to apply only to the north of France.

These rights of the father varied from *coutume* to *coutume*; sometimes he had a right of administration, sometimes he had a right of usufruct.[134] In *coutumes* where there was no mention of a right of usufruct, the father would not have one:[135] the fruits of the property would belong to the child, although rights of *garde noble* and *garde bourgeoise* could complicate the situation.[136] Further, the customary law gave authority to the mother as well as the father; but it was the father who exercised the authority during the marriage.

In sum, in the *pays du droit coutumier*, the concept of paternal power was very different from that in the southern regions. The customary law limited severely a father's rights in his children's property, and, in general, his authority ended on their marriage or reaching the age of majority.

The Castilian law on paternal authority is rendered complex by its uneasy mix of customary and Roman law, although the law is essentially more Roman than customary. It is therefore necessary to look at the main, rather contradictory, sources of the law. The *Siete Partidas* provide most material on *patria potestad. Titulo* XVII of the fourth *Partida* is devoted to the "Poder que han los padres sobre los fijos".[137] The *Partidas* here follow the Roman law very closely indeed, leading Llamas y Molina to remark: "El derecho real de las partidas siguió las disposiciones del derecho Romano."[138] The *Partidas'* provisions will be discussed at length in dealing with Louisiana, but the following general points may be made. The *Partidas* granted the power to the paternal male ascendant: grandfathers would have both sons and grandsons in the male line in their power. Things gained by a son using the property of his father belonged to the father, and were called *peculium profectitium*.[139] Gains which a son made due to his own work, or by using property not his father's, belonged to the son, while the father had a usufruct in them: this is called in Latin *adventitia*, explains the *Partidas*, "porque [esta ganancia] viene de fuera, et non por los bienes del padre".[140] The *Partidas* even allowed a father to sell his son, but only as a last resort.[141]

A different version of paternal power is found in the *Fuero real*, however, though it is also the work of Alfonso *el sabio*. "El Fuero Real limita claramente la potestad paterna", Minguijón accurately points out.[142] The *Fuero* contradicted

---

134 See generally Ferrière, *Corps et Comp.*, vol. 3, cols. 497–498, nos. 18–22.

135 *Ibid.*: the *père* could keep the fruits under the following *coutumes*: Rheims (art. 8); Laon (art. 56); Châlons (art. 8); Sedan (art. 7); and Bourbonnais (art. 174). He could not under the *Coutume de Paris*.

136 These two forms of *garde* cause some problems. The position of a father's rights in his children's property under the *Coutume de Paris* is unclear; but see *infra*. On *garde*, see Ferrière, *Corps et Comp.*, vol. 3, esp. cols. 945–948; Pothier, *T.G.N.B.*; *Ancien Denisart*, vol. 2, pp. 503–510, s.v. *garde*.

137 The 18th. title is on how the power comes to an end.

138 Llamas y Molina, *op. cit. supra* note 99, vol. 2, pp. 118–125, commentary on *Toro*, 47, no. 5.

139 *Part.* 4.17.5. The property provisions (*leyes* 5–7) are very Roman.

140 *Part.* 4.17.5. *Leyes* 6 and 7 regulated *peculium castrense* and *peculium quasi-castrense*.

141 *Part.* 4.17.8.

142 Minguijón, *op. cit. supra* note 84, vol. 1, p. 135.

the provision on the sale of sons.[143] In the *Partidas*, the paternal power could never pass to the mother, whereas the *Fuero real* allowed a widowed mother (in certain circumstances) to exercise authority over her children.[144] In a different *ley*, the same *Fuero* again implies that the mother may have her children in power, though the gloss of Montalvo states that this is wrong.[145] Minguijón states that some municipal *fueros* allowed the mother exercise of the *patria potestad* along with the father, for which he says there is a precedent in the Visigothic law.[146] Although the *Fuero real* said nothing explicitly about marriage freeing sons from *patria potestad*, one text implies very strongly that such was the law.[147] The significant text is *ley* 47 *de Toro*, which states:

> El hijo ó hija casado y velado, sea avido por emancipado, en todas cosas para siempre.

It is obvious that the provisions of the *Partidas* and those of the *Fuero real* are contradictory.

Here the Romanizing tendencies of the *Partidas* vanquished the customary law tradition. The *patria potestad* of Castile was of a Roman nature. The only notable difference was the provision of *ley* 47 of Toro: marriage emancipated. The treatment of the whole of the law on *patria potestad* by the Castilian jurists is of importance in indicating the extent of the influence of the Roman conception of *patria potestad* in Castile. Asso and Manuel provided a clear and logical account of the law, very firmly based on the *Partidas* in their *Instituciones*.[148] In the section on the modes of ending *patria potestad*, they stated that the first method is by the death of the *pater*:

> El primer modo se entiendo, si el padre que murió no estaba al tiempo de morir baxo el poder de su proprio padre; porque en este caso, el hijo que dexabo racaeria baxo la potestad del abuelo, segun la l.1 tit. 18. part. 4.

They then added, rather lamely, that the *Recopilación* provides differently, "as we shall see".[149] The fourth mode of ending paternal power, according to Asso and Manuel, was emancipation, one method of which they state to be marriage, adding that children do not, therefore, fall into the power of their grandfather

---

[143] *Fuero real*, 3.10.8.

[144] *Fuero real*, 3.7.2 and 3 (cf. *Fuero viejo* 5.4.1). Minguijón, *op. cit. supra* note 84, vol. 1, p. 136, states that both these *Fueros* "dan a entender que la patria potestad corresponde no sólo al padre sino también a la madre viuda, pues sólo a falta de ésta llaman a los parientes a que se encarguen de los menores."

[145] *Fuero real*, 1.11.8. The gloss to consult is that on *si padre* by Montalvo.

[146] Minguijón, *op. cit. supra* note 84, vol. 1, p. 136 and also pp. 53–54. Of the Visigothic laws generally, he says, *ibid.* vol. 1, p. 53: "No tenía la patria potestad entre los visigodos un carácter absoluto ni inhumano."

[147] *Fuero real*, 1.11.8. See Llamas y Molina, *op. cit. supra* note 99, commentary on *Toro*, 47, no. 8. What of the same *ley*'s mention of 25 years of age?

[148] *Asso y Manuel*, vol. 1, pp. 115–123 (book 1, tit. 8, cap. 2 - accidentally printed as cap. 3 in edition used.)

[149] *Ibid.*, vol. l, pp. 119–120. They refer to *Rec. Cast.* 5.1.8 (*Nov. Rec. Cast.* 10.5.3), i.e. *Toro*, 47.

when their father dies, because the act of marriage has freed their father from his father's powers.[150] This is a very curious procedure on the part of Asso and Manuel: to state the out-of-date rule and then later contradict it. They betray a confusion of purpose. They seem to indicate that they regarded the 47th law of Toro as inconsistent with the Castilian concept of *patria potestad*. Whatever their motives, Asso and Manuel clearly adopted an entirely Roman concept of *patria potestad*, viewing *ley* 47 of Toro as a minor variation of the Roman rules, along with some other minor differences.[151]

Gomez' discussion of the *ley* 47 of Toro is also interesting.[152] At the end of his commentary, he deals with "velado". The meaning of this term—which seems to have been problematic— need not concern us;[153] but Gomez states that if a grandchild is born to a son:

> desponsato per verba de praesenti et non velato, erit in potestate avi, sicut de iure communi, cum non sit natus ex filio coniugato et velato ut nostra lex requirit, et in hoc nepote habebunt locum et verificabuntur omnes effectus patriae potestatis.[154]

(It should be recalled that the *Leyes de Toro* date from before the Council of Trent and the decree *Tametsi*.)[155] Thus, Gomez interpreted the law in such a way that if the son was *casado*, but not *velado* (whatever this technicality may have been), then he was not freed from *patria potestad*, and the grandson too came under the power of his grandfather as in the Roman law—the *ius commune* as Gomez terms it. Gomez thus narrowly interpreted the *ley* so as to retain much of the Roman rule.

Despite the limited customary law concept of paternal power in Castile, the Roman law was received through the medium of the *Partidas* and the actions of the Castilian jurists.[156] So thoroughly Roman was the concept of paternal power that jurists could treat the 47th law of Toro almost as an aberration. The *Partidas*' version of *patria potestad* was probably so successful because they provided a thorough account with clear and logical rules, whereas the other provisions with contradictory concepts were scattered through various

[150] *Asso y Manuel*, vol. 1, p. 121.
[151] On some differences between the Roman rules and those of the *Partidas*, see Llamas y Molina, *op. cit supra* note 99, vol. 2, pp. 118–125, commentary on *Toro*, 47, no. 5.
[152] Gomez, *op. cit. supra* note 100, pp. 436 et seq., commentary on *Toro*, 47.
[153] See Llamas y Molina, *op. cit. supra* note 99, commentary on *Toro*, 47, nos. 11–18. "Velado" means "veiled". The *Leyes de Toro* date from before the Council of Trent, and there were few requirements of ceremony for a marriage to be valid.
[154] Gomez, *op. cit. supra* note 100, p. 438, commentary on *Toro*, 47, no. 3.
[155] See *supra*, note 153. See *infra*, text at notes 181–197 on the Council of Trent.
[156] *Patria potestad* in the Roman or Castilian style did not exist in Aragon: see *Asso y Manuel*, vol. 1, pp. 122–123: "En Aragon no se conoce la patria potestad."

sources,[157] and because the Castilian jurists, trained in the Roman law (the *ius commune*), would find in the *Partidas* rules with which they were familiar.

In France, the Revolutionary law attacked paternal power. *Puissance paternelle* over adults was abolished on 28th August, 1792.[158] The age of majority was lowered to 21, and other limitations on paternal authority were introduced.[159] There was a reaction against this liberalization, and, from 1800 onwards, it was proposed to reassert and extend *puissance paternelle*. What motivated this revival can be gathered from the statements of some of the legal writers. Maleville, for example, wrote:

> Il serait peut-être important d'examiner si maintenant que la France est bien lassé de révolutions, qu'elle n'aspire qu'à conserver la tranquillité intérieure que le gouvernement d'un seul lui a enfin procurée les mêmes raisons qui ont fait abolir la puissance paternelle, ne devraient pas aujourd'hui la faire rétablir.[160]

Again, summarizing the arguments of the *tribunal d'appel de Montpellier*, he stated:

> La puissance paternelle est dans la famille ce que le gouvernement est dans la société. . . . Si le maintien de l'ordre social dépend de la force du Gouvernement, le maintien de l'ordre domestique tient à l'efficacité de la puissance paternelle. . . .[161]

He continued in like vein, mentioning that all that parents do for their children requires that children respect them and that it is insufficient for a father to be regarded a mere guardian of their property, liable to account for his husbandry when the children come of age. The affection of parents will prevent them from abusing their authority. He next discussed Montesquieu writing that "toujours est-il constant qu'il a reconnu partout l'efficacité de la puissance paternelle pour le maintien des moeurs."[162] The authors of the *Pandectes françaises* held similar views:

---

[157] On the reception of Roman law in Castile, see chap. 3 *supra*, at notes 61–115. According to the *Ordenamiento de Alcalá*, the *Fuero Real* should have taken precedence over the *Partidas*; see chap. 3 *supra*, at notes 68–76.

[158] See Huussen, *op. cit. supra*, note 106, p. 43; Brissaud, *History*, p. 199; and Maleville, *Analyse*, vol. 1, p. 339.

[159] See e.g. Huussen, *op. cit. supra* note 106, pp. 34, 35, 37, 41–43, 115–116; Brissaud, *History*, pp. 34, pp. 199–200. Maleville, *Analyse*, vol. 1, pp. 338–339, comments thus: "Quelque modérée fût la puissance paternelle, dans les pays où elle s'était conservée, il restait cependant aux pères de grands moyens pour contenir leurs enfans, et cette puissance paternelle devait nécessairement déplaire à ceux qui avaient envie de renverser l'ordre des choses alors établi. Ils n'ignoraient pas que la conservation et le repos sont les deux grands objets de la vieillesse, que ce n'était pas parmi les hommes d'un âge mûr qu'ils devaient trouver beaucoup de partisans, qu'il fallait en conséquence dégager de ses liens, et abandonner à sa fougue la jeunesse toujours avide de nouveautés, toujours ouverte à l'espérance."

[160] Maleville, *Analyse*, vol. 1, p. 339.

[161] *Ibid.*

[162] *Ibid.* p. 341.

> Dans quel temps était-il plus nécessaire de répéter ce précepte divin [i.e. that children should honour and respect their parents], que dans celui où tous les liens de la subordination sont encore relâchés; où l'on sent la nécessité de rétablir le gouvernement des families pour fortifier celui de l'État?[163]

Such examples could be multiplied, but these few will suffice to indicate the atmosphere within which were drawn up the C.N. provisions on *puissance paternelle.*

Thus, it is hardly surprising that the articles of the C.N. restored and reinforced *puissance paternelle*, given the date when they were definitively drafted; but the concept of *puissance paternelle* from which these articles were drawn was essentially that of the *pays du droit coutumier*. A father, failing whom the mother, had great powers over the persons and property of his children—indeed including a usufruct in the property. Some Roman principles were included, however: emancipation, for example. In some respects, close relatives were given a new importance.[164]

The redactors of the D.O. and C.Q. both had fairly similar material to hand for the construction of their provisions on paternal authority. Both had access to the two types or models of *puissance paternelle*: first the Castilian and that of the *droit écrit*; second that of the customary law and C.N. Of course, between these two models, and indeed between the versions of each model, there were differences, and many alternative possibilities would face the redactors in Louisiana and Quebec.

The General Civilian Notion of "Family"

As already seen, the Roman conception of marriage was radically different from that of modern times.[165] The contemporary idea of marriage as a legal institution originates not in the Roman law, but in the Canon. This must be taken into consideration when we reflect on how marital authority arises. The Roman concept of "family", however, has been influential. It will be recalled that *familia* consisted of all those *in potestate* of the patriarchal paterfamilias:

---

[163] *Pan. fran.*, vol. 4, p. 318. The authors feel threatened not only by young people, but also by utilitarianism: they continue, *ibid.*, pp. 318–319, answering their own question: "Que dans un temps, où la nouvelle philosophie vient encore semer ses poisons mortels; où l'on s'érige audacieusement en Législateur, pour détruire tous les principes de législation; où l'on vient jeter, au sein de la dépravation effrayante des moeurs, de nouveaux fermens de corruption; enseigner dogmatiquement, qu'il a ni droit naturel ni vices, ni vertus; que ces sont des mote vides de sans faits pour amuser les enfans; que les deux seules principes de la conduite des hommes, sont le plaisir et la peine; qu'ils ont le droit de faire tout ce qui peut leur procurer l'un et de repousser tout ce qui peut leur faire souffrir l'autre; et qu'enfin, toute loi eat un attentat à la liberté." This attack on Bentham and Utilitarianism (incidentally neither being named) may strike as quaint; but it is important in revealing an attitude of mind, and a desire to restore old principles. Bentham's writings were very influential in France.

[164] See *supra*, text at notes 46–47.

[165] See *supra*, text at notes 53–61. Jolowicz, *op. cit. supra* note 57, pp. 141–160 may be consulted.

children born in *iustum matrimonium*, those adopted, and slaves. The *Partidas* give a neat description or definition of family:

> Et aun decimos que por esta palabra familia se entiende el señor de la casa et su muger, et todos los que viven con él sobre que ha mandamiento, asi como los fijos, et los servientes, et los siervos et los otros criados. Et familia es dicha aquella, en que viven mas de dos homes á mandamiento del señor, mas dende ayuso non serie familia. Et aquel es dicho *paterfamilias*, el que es señor de la casa, maguer non haya fijos: et *materfamilias* es dicha la muger que vive honestamente en su casa, ó es de buenas maneras.[166]

Here again the family is hierarchical and defined by power or authority, and, following the Roman law, it includes all those over whom the *padre* has authority. As will be seen, as a general definition of family, this text had some influence on the D.O., as indeed had a similar text of Domat.[167]

The French customary law, in the modern period, had a more restricted notion of family. The *Nouveau Denisart* states: "Dans le sens le plus ordinaire, la famille signifie le père la mère et les enfans."[168] Henrys defines the family through marriage, and, taking a somewhat Hobbesian view of society,[169] states as follows:

> Disons donc qu'il faut avoüer que sans la société civile, le monde ne serait qu'un vaste et affreux desert, que les hommes y seroient pires que les animaux, et que comme ils auroient plus d'industrie pour se nuire on n'y verroit aussi qu'un perpetual brigandage, et coupe-gorge; mais que s'il faut avo ü er cela, il faut aussi qu'on avoüe, que le principal lien de la société civile est le mariage, que comme c'est lui qui l'établit, c'est aussi lui qui la maintient, et que qui le voudroit ôter ou confondre, causeroit aussi-tôt la ruine du monde: En effet ce sont les mariages qui forment les familles et les distinguent, ce sont eux qui en les séparant ne laissent pas de les unir par les alliances.[170]

This notion of marriage as defining the family was operative during codification; thus we find the following statement in 1806:

---

[166] *Part.* 7.33.6. (The text in Lopez' edition is different in part; but this difference is not significant here.) T.W. Tucker, "Sources of Louisiana's Law of Persons: Blackstone, Domat and the French Codes", 44 *Tul. L. Rev.* (1970), pp. 264–295 gives the reference for a translation of this passage as *Part.* 7.1.6., in *ibid.* p. 285 n. 108. The D.L.V. refers to it as *Part.* 7.3.6. (D.O. 7 (p. 127) on interleaf), while Batiza, "Sources", p. 68, in his appendix C, p. 68 (same article as D.L.V.), gives the reference as *Part.* 7.23.6. They are all obviously referring to this passage, but, curiously enough, all three have given a wrong different reference. *Part.* 3.31.21 gives us a similar account of the links of dependency between the father and those in his power.

[167] Domat, *Loix civiles*, vol. 1, p. 14 (prel. bk., tit. 2, sect. 2, no. 5).

[168] *Nouveau Denisart*, vol. 8, p. 439. The other meanings of "famille" alluded to were "synonime de race ou maison".

[169] I am thinking of Hobbes' view of man in a state of nature: T. Hobbes, *Leviathan*, ed. by M. Oakeshott, Oxford, Basil Blackwell, 1946, pp. 80–84, where he envisages (at p. 42) that the life of man in a state of nature as "solitary, poor, nasty, brutish, and short".

[170] Henrys, *op cit.* supra note 116, vol. 1, p. 987: diaeresis over "u" of "avouer" his.

> Les familles commencent par le mariage, et c'est la nature elle-mêne qui invite les hommes à cette union.[171]

Both sets of redactors were presented with two models for the family: one based on marriage (northern France); one based on paternal authority (southern France and Castile). The two models were perhaps in some ways not particularly far apart and were capable of reconciliation; but there were significant differences nonetheless. In this section, we have been concentrating on the family as a unified concept; but one important point should be made clear. Neither the C.N. nor the D.O. nor the C.Q. presents us with a unified system of family law in the modern sense, and indeed, their legal sources did not present them with such a system. Provisions on the family are scattered throughout the codes; for example, in the sections on persons and obligations. The codes simply dealt with two separate relationships: husband and wife, and parent and child. The two were obviously connected, since it was marriage that resulted in legitimate filiation for the children of the union. The main method for unification of the law into a whole is clearly through the one person, in his different aspects as husband and father, who controlled the other members of the family. The *Nouveau Denisart* expressed this clearly:

> Le gouvernement d'une famille, et celui d'un corps politique doivent rouler sur les mêmes principes; l'une est en petit l'image de l'autre.... La puissance domestique représente en quelque manière la souveraineté....[172]

The law was concerned with the person who was the sovereign of the family, who governed the other members through his *puissance domestique* in its two aspects of *puissance maritale* (*puissance du mari*) and *puissance paternelle*.[173] This stress by the law on the two relationships of spouses and parents ties in with the argument of treating the family historically by studying the changes in the relationships within;[174] it further justifies the approach to the family through the two different *puissances*, that of the husband and that of the father. We will examine each *puissance* in turn by studying how they arise, their scope, and how they end, taking Louisiana and Quebec in turn.

---

[171] *Nouveau Denisart*, vol. 13, p. 495 (1806).

[172] *Ibid.*, vol. 13, p. 496 (1806).

[173] The theme of comparing the organization of the family to that of the nation state was a very common one. We find that, in the discussion of the first Cambacérès *projet*, many revolutionary leaders argued that *puissance maritale* was a creation of despotic governments and husband and wife were equal, so the wife should be freed from her bondage: see Huussen, *op. cit. supra* note 106, p. 199.

[174] See supra, esp. text at notes 45–49.

Part One

LOUISIANA

THE 1808 DIGEST OF THE TERRITORY OF ORLEANS

Puissance Maritale

How *Puissance Maritale* Arises in the D.O.

In this subsection we shall be concerned with the forms of marriage and their requirements for validity. Hence we shall examine the following chapters of title IV (entitled "Du mari et de la femme") of Book One of the D.O.: Chapitre Premier, "Du Mariage"; and Chapitre II, "Comment les Mariages peuvent être contractés". The third chapter of the title, "Des Demandes en nullité de Mariage" will not be examined (except for one aspect later)[175] because the provisions relate closely to the provisions of chapter II and are not directly relevant for the general theme of this section; one or two relevant remarks on the provisions will be made, however, when appropriate.

The equivalent title in the C.N. is V. It is entitled "Du Mariage", and is divided thus into relevant chapters: first, "Des qualités et conditions requises pour pouvoir contracter mariage"; second, "Des formalités relatives à la célébration du mariage;" third, "Des oppositions au mariage"; and fourth, "Des demandes en nullité de mariage". As well as the heading, the scheme of division is obviously different. The third chapter of the C.N. has provisions on who can oppose an intended marriage; there is no equivalent in the D.O. The C.N. carefully regulated oppositions to marriage, in reaction to the *ancien droit* where, following the Canon law, any person claiming the right to do so could oppose a marriage.[176] Although the D.O. had no provisions on the matter, oppositions in fact were regulated by an Act of 1807, ch. 17.[177] This Act, by its sections 42, 43 and 44, limited the class of those who could oppose a marriage to exactly the same persons as permitted by the C.N., with the difference that, in the D.O., ascendants could not oppose the marriage of those over twenty-one.[178]

---

[175] See *infra*, text at notes 656–662 on paternal authority.

[176] The relevant C.N. articles were 172, 173, and 174. On the *ancien droit*, see Brissaud, *History*, pp. 129–130, and Esmein, *op. cit. supra* note 69, vol. 1, pp. 421–427.

[177] Louisiana Acts, 1807, ch.17 (6 Apr. 1807), "An Act Concerning the Celebration of Marriages". Hereafter referred to as Act 1807, ch. 17.

[178] The equivalent sections of the Act 1807, ch. 17 and articles of the C.N. are as follows. C.N. 172: "Le droit de former opposition à la célébration du mariage, appartient à la personne engagée par mariage avec l'une des deux parties contractantes." S. 43: "A person already married to either of the parties proposing to intermarry, may oppose the marriage." C.N. 173: "Le père, et à défaut du père, la mère, les aieuls et aieules, peuvent former opposition au mariage de leurs enfans et descendans, encore que ceux-ci aient vingt-cinq ans accomplis." Act 1807, ch. 17, s. 42: "The

The Louisiana Act's provisions are obviously based on the work of the French codifiers. Thus, although there are no provisions in the D.O., the Louisiana and French laws were similar.

The C.L. of 1825 did regulate oppositions. By article 110 it provided:

> Toute personne peut former opposition à un mariage; mais dans le ces où l'opposition est rejetée, l'opposant doit payer les frais de la procédure.

This is obviously an amendment of the law. The compilers of the 1823 *Projet* had merely stated (of a whole series of articles including this one) that this chapter of their proposed amended code was extracted from the 1807 Act.[179] C.L. 110, however, broadened the class of those entitled to oppose to the state of the old law, that is, the Canon law. Why the redactors of the C.L. should have changed the law, while claiming to be enacting the provisions of the 1807 Act is unclear.[180]

The D.O. provisions in the three relevant chapters consist of 18 articles, while in the C.N., excluding the provisions on oppositions, the equivalent chapters contain 50 articles. The D.O. redactors are obviously not following the C.N. This said, it must be admitted that, in general, the thrust of the provisions of the D.O. is very similar to that of those of the C.N. A major difference does exist, however, in regards to the marriage of minors: this will be discussed

---

father and mother or the surviving parent, the grandfather and grandmother or the survivor, may oppose the marriage of such of their descendants, as have not completed their twenty-first year." C.N. 174, "A défaut d'aucune ascendant, le frère ou la soeur, l'oncle ou la tante, le cousin ou la cousine germains, majeurs, ne peuvent former aucune opposition que dans les deux cas suivans: 1. Lorsque le consentement du conseil de famille, requis par l'article 160, n'a pas été obtenu; 2. Lorsque l'opposition est fondée sur l'état de démence du futur époux: cette opposition, dont le tribunal pourra prononcer main-levée pure et simple, ne sera jamais reçue qu'à la charge, par l'opposant de provoquer l'interdiction, et d'y faire statuer dans le délai qui sera fixé par le jugement." Act 1807, ch. 17, s. 44: "If there are no relations in the ascending line, the brother or the sister, the uncle or the aunt, the cousin germain, having attained the age of majority, can oppose the marriage in the two following cases only: 1st. When the consent of the family required by the nineteenth section has not been duly obtained; 2nd., When the opposition is grounded upon the madness or insanity of the person whose marriage is opposed." The *Proj. An VIII*, 1.5.28–30 covers the same situations, and possibly has exercised some influence on the sections of the Act 1807, ch. 17: notably, the order of the Act follows that of the *Projet* rather than of the C.N. But s. 44 of the Act is closer to C.N. 174 than to *Proj. An VIII*, 1.5.30. There are, of course, significant differences between the French and Louisiana provisions.

[179] *1823 Projet*, comment on p. 8, proposed article on p. 9.

[180] There is little point here in speculating on this curious reversal of the law. R. Batiza, "The Actual Sources of the Louisiana *Projet* of 1823: A General Analytical Survey", 47 *Tul. L. Rev.* (1972), pp. 1–115, appendix B at p. 32 states that C.L. 110 was "substantially influenced" by Act 1807 ch. 17, s. 46. This section reads: "If the opposition is rejected, the party petitioning shall pay costs and damages, unless such party be a father or mother, or grand father or grand mother to one of the contracting parties." Note that, first, s. 46 is only analogous to half of C.L. 110, and that, second, the legal provision is different, the 1807 Act exempting parents and grandparents. This is a neat example of how Batiza's work may sometimes be misleading. Act 1807 ch. 17, s. 46 is almost identical in provision to C.N. 179.

below in the context of paternal authority. There are some other differences which will also be pointed out in discussing the relevant D.O. articles (e.g. age of marriage). Given that, in general, the D.O. redactors were very influenced by the C.N., why have they here departed from its organization of the material? The answer is simple. It was brought about by the existence of the 1807 Act, ch. 17, on the celebration of marriages. This recent Act of the territorial legislature covered the topics we are here concerned with in great detail, and many of its provisions are the sources of the relevant D.O. articles. The Act restricted the operations of the redactors; given its nature as a recent statute, they could hardly depart from it. It is nevertheless clear that the redactors have done their best to mold the statutory provisions into a form equivalent to the C.N. and the *Proj. An VIII*. Indeed, the first chapter of this title of the D.O., containing articles 1 to 3 (p. 25), follows the *Proj. An VIII*, 1.5.1–3 in both form and intent, and lays down provisions of a general, very abstract and indeed didactic nature, not found in the C.N., and from which the more specific provisions of the following chapter flow logically. Despite following the *Proj. An VIII* in this, the articles are nonetheless firmly based on the 1807 Act, though rearranged to the scheme of the *Proj. An. VIII*.

The 1807 Act thus explains why there are the differences between the C.N. and its *Projet*. The specific provisions of the Act will be dealt with in discussing the D.O. articles, but it is relevant here to give a rough indication of the law prior to the Act during the Spanish government of Louisiana. A recent article by Hans Baade has explored this area of the law, and the following remarks are based on his work.[181] Baade is concerned to show whether the provisions of the Council of Trent on the form of marriage were in force in Spanish North America. In the pre-Tridentine Canon law there were no formal requirements for the validity of marriage other than the mutual expression of consent on the part of the spouses.[182] This state of the law is found expressed in, for example, the *Partidas*.[183] In 1563, the Council of Trent changed this and prescribed that all marriages take place with the assistance of a priest and the presence of witnesses. One of the aims of this provision was to prevent clandestine marriages by requiring all valid marriages to be *in facie ecclesiae*.[184] In any area where the decrees of the Council had been promulgated, any marriage not in Tridentine form was invalid, even if the marriage was of non-Catholics.[185] (By the so-called Benedictine Declaration of 1741, the rules for the marriages of non-Catholics were changed;[186] but since this was never in force in Spain or her American Empire, we can ignore it.)[187] The application of this provision of the

---

[181] Baade, "Form".
[182] *Ibid.*, p. 20.
[183] *Part.* 4.1.4; see also *Fuero real*, 3.1.1.
[184] See Baade, "Form", pp. 20–21. On clandestine marriages, and those *in facie ecclesiae*, see *infra*.
[185] Baade, "Form", p. 21.
[186] *Ibid.*
[187] *Ibid.*, p. 28.

Council of Trent in the Spanish dominions was dependent on the authority of the King, who could extend its scope.[188] A royal *cédula* of 1564 applied the Tridentine legislation to all the Spanish realms.[189] Although the matter was previously obscure, Baade shows conclusively that "the legislation of the Council of Trent simply was the law of the land in Spanish North America."[190]

There were, however, some uncertainties about Louisiana, arising both from its late acquisition by Spain and the existence of a protestant population (although the vast majority was Catholic). Further, during the Spanish régime, the government had encouraged American immigration.[191] Under France, the substance of the Tridentine law had been in force in Louisiana.[192] Baade shows that, certainly in theory, the Tridentine law was in force in Spanish Louisiana as part of the general law,[193] and that there is strong evidence that it actually was enforced.[194] This said, Baade points out that there was in fact general contemporary uncertainty about the applicability of the Tridentine Canon law, even among the upper ranks of the Roman Catholic hierarchy.[195] This confusion was exacerbated beacuse two texts of primary importance were not available: the *Cédula* of 1564 was not republished until the *Novísima recopilacón* of 1805, and a Royal Order of 1792,[196] which directed the enforcement of the Tridentine law in Louisiana, was not published until 1845.[197]

This account of the Spanish background helps place the 1807 Louisiana Act in perspective. The law before was uncertain and this Act provided definitively for the forms and conditions of marriage. In so far as the previous law was not obscure, it provided for marriage by a Roman Catholic priest. This would have been unacceptable to the new immigrants from the U.S.A. In the other states and territories of the Union, marriage was, in theory, a civil contract, capable of being solemnized either by magistrates or by ministers of religion.[198] The 1807 Act stated that only marriages celebrated by one licensed for that purpose by any parish judge of Louisiana would be valid.[199] Any priest or minister of the gospel ordained or admitted into any religious society could obtain such a

---

[188] *Ibid.*, pp. 28–30.

[189] *Ibid.*, p. 29.

[190] *Ibid.*, p. 46.

[191] See *supra*, chap. 2.

[192] See Baade, "Form", p. 49, and on the Council of Trent and the French law see *infra*.

[193] Baade, "Form", pp. 46–55.

[194] *Ibid.*, pp. 54–55 and p. 74.

[195] *Ibid.*, p. 55 and *passim*.

[196] *Nov. Rec. Cast.* 1.1.13. The Royal Order may be found quoted in Baade, "Form", p. 51.

[197] Baade, "Form", p. 62.

[198] See L.M. Friedman, *A History of American Law*, New York, Simon and Schuster, 1973, p. 179. G.L. Haskins, "The Legal Heritage of Plymouth Colony", in D.H. Flaherty (ed.), *Essays in the History of Early American Law*, Chapel Hill, University of North Carolina Press, 1969, pp. 121–134 at p. 130, points out that the civil form of marriage was an innovation of the Plymouth Colony. The so-called "common law" marriages found in some of the common law states were apparently not introduced to Louisiana. On them, see Friedman, op. cit., pp. 179–181. Baade, "Form", *passim*, makes some relevant remarks.

[199] 1807 Act, ch 17, s. 27.

licence.[200] The parish judge, if he thought there were insufficient licensed ministers or priests, could license justices of the peace to solemnize marriages.[201] There was a special provision for Quakers and Menonists.[202] Thus, to a large extent, the 1807 Act brought the Louisiana law into line with that of the Union as to who could solemnize marriages. We need not consider whether the 1807 Act was influenced by other American law;[203] it is sufficient to point out that, the provisions, as to who might celebrate marriages, were only sensible given the heterogeneity of Louisiania society with its variety of religious adherence.[204]

Having set out the background, it is appropriate now to turn to the D.O. provisions. The first article of the first chapter of this title, D.O. 1 (p. 25), states that "La loi ne considère le mariage que comme un contrat civil." The D.L.V. refers to s. 1 of the 1807 Act, while Batiza claims that this Act is the "almost verbatim" source of the article with *Proj. An VIII*, 1.5.1 and 3 as subsidiary sources.[205] "La loi ne reconnaît que les mariages qui sont contractés et solemnisés conformément au règles qu'elle prescrit," states D.O. 2 (p. 25). The D.L.V. refers to s. 3 of the 1807 Act, which Batiza claims as the "verbatim" source with *Proj. An VIII*, 1.5.2 as a subsidiary. D.O. 3 (p. 25) provides that "Le mariage est un contrat qui, dans son origine, est destiné a durer jusqu'à la mort de l'une des parties contractantes, néanmoins ce contrat peut être dissous avant la mort de l'un ou de l'autre des epoux, pour des causes déterminées par la loi." The D.L.V. refers here to Pothier,[206] *Part.* 4.2.3 and 7, and the 1807 Act, s. 4. Batiza claims *Proj. An VIII*, 1.5.3, as the "almost verbatim" source.

These three articles of the D.O. clearly originated in the provisions of the 1807 Act indicated by the D.L.V., that is: ss. 1, 3 and 4. (The 1825 C.L. included s. 2 of the Act at this point as article 88.) The provisions of the *Proj. An. VIII* are broadly similar in expression, and probably suggested this organization of the statutory material (the exclusion of s. 2 would support this).[207] Further, although the wording of 1.5.3 of the *Proj. An VIII* is similar to that of D.O. 3 (p. 25), it should be recalled that the *Proj. An VIII* intended divorce to be included as one means of dissolving marriage before the death of one of the spouses, whereas the D.O. did not, and was only referring to nullification of the marriage.

---

[200] *Ibid.*, s. 28.

[201] *Ibid.*, s. 29.

[202] *Ibid.*, s. 37.

[203] A point that would be worth exploring to help understand the origins of the Louisiana law.

[204] See *supra*, chap. 2, text at notes 46–61.

[205] All further mentions of Batiza in the text without any specific, pin-point citations of one of his publications, are to be understood as to appendix C of Batiza, "Sources", referring to the relevant article of the D.O.

[206] Pothier, *T.C.M.*, p. 201 (no. 442).

[207] *Proj. An VIII*, 1.5.1: "La loi ne considère le manage que sous ses rapports civils et politiques;" 1.5.2: "Elle ne reconnaît que le mariage contracté conformément à ce qu'elle prescript;" 1.5.3: "Le mariage est un contrat dont la durée est dans l'intention des époux, celle de la vie de l'un d'eux: ce contrat peut néanmoins être résolu avant la mort de l'un des époux, dans les cas ou pour les causes déterminés par la loi." Note the possibly significant differences from the D.O. equivalents.

The *Partidas*' provisions referred to by the D.L.V. are again very roughly similar to those of the D.O., as are the statements by Pothier. The strongly religious bias of Pothier and the *Partidas* to some extent makes their provisions incompatible with D.O. 1 (p. 25); but, nonetheless, in considering that marriage lasts until death, and can only be ended before that by annulment on the grounds of invalidity, they are closer to the D.O. than is the *Proj. An VIII*. In fact, however, the provisions of the D.O. are of such generality that they are inevitably similar to the provisions found in other legal authorities, and it is only in the details dependent on these generalities that meaningful differences and similarities can be indicated. The discussion of divorce in the *Proj. An VIII* shows this. Further, we know that the *Partidas* envisaged the pre-Tridentive form of marriage, Pothier the Tridentine (as applied in France), and the *Proj. An VIII* a purely civil form: all three are different from the D.O. and the relevant 1807 Act. Since in their details the laws are all different, all that can be said about these articles is that they are of a very general nature, originate in the 1807 Act and that their resemblance to the *Proj. An VIII* is of a literary rather than a legal nature, based on the organization of the material.

The next chapter of the D.O. deals with how marriage may be contracted. The first article, D.O. 4 (p. 25), states that, since the law only considers marriage as a civil contract, it sanctions as valid all those marriages where, at the time of contracting, the parties were willing to contract, able to contract, and did contract according to the formalities and solemnities prescribed by the law. This article is taken directly from the 1807 Act, ch. 17, s. 5, which Batiza states to be the "almost verbatim" source. The D.L.V., as well as citing the Act, refers to *Part*. 4.2.5, 6 and 7, and to Pothier.[208] *Part*. 4.2.5 states that: "Consentimiento solo con voluntad de casar face matrimonio entre el varon et la muger." It develops this theme by discussing, for example, how deaf and dumb people may signify consent. *Ley* 6 discusses who has the capacity to marry, and provides that they must be of sound mind (*entendimiento sano*), capable of lying with women, and of sufficient age to understand to what they are consenting. Further, castrated men and those debilitated in their sexual organs cannot marry since they are incapable of coupling carnally with their wives to father children, despite the fact they have sufficient understanding to consent. Finally, those who are mad (*loco*) cannot marry, unless they have lucid intervals during which they signify consent. *Ley* 7 is not directly relevant. It should be noted that the *Partidas* are only envisaging mutual consent as required, and no other formalities; in this, and also in stressing *copula carnalis*, they are, of course, following the pre-Tridentine Canon law. The D.O. left other formalities to be found in the 1807 Act. Pothier, as referred to, gives an extended discussion of the requirements of marriage, who can marry, impediments and the relevant formalities. We need not consider his discussion further than to remark that he is providing an exegesis of the French law based on the contemporary Canon law. Again his comments are relevant; but the details differ from those of the D.O. and the

[208] Pothier, *T.C.M.*, pp. 36–173 (nos. 85–378).

1807 Act. We can conclude by stressing that this D.O. provision comes directly from the 1807 Act, to which it alludes (indirectly) for the required forms and solemnities of marriage. These detailed formalities were not included in the D.O., whereas they were inserted as a new chapter in the 1825 C.L., on the recommendation of the latter's redactors.[209]

D.O. 5 (p. 25) states that marriage is only valid if consent has been given freely, and that consent has not been given freely: first, if given to a ravisher,[210] unless given by the person ravished after completely recovering her liberty; second, when extorted by violence; and third, when there has been error as to the person whom one of the parties intended to marry. This article is taken directly from the 1807 Act, s. 6, which Batiza gives as the "verbatim" source, with *Proj. An VIII* 1.5.5 as a subsidiary source. The D.L.V. refers to the Act, *Part.* 4.2.10 and 15, and Pothier.[211] The *Proj. An VIII* is very similar in wording and meaning. (It was possibly—probably—the source of s. 6 of the Act.) *Part.* 4.2.10 states that error as to person invalidates a marriage, while 4.2.15 states (*inter alia*) that force (*fuerza*) or fear (*miedo*) invalidate a marriage. Thus these provisions are the same as that of the D.O. It must be pointed out, however, that the *Partidas* provide for no less than fifteen circumstances that prevent a marriage,[212] some of which are covered in later articles of the D.O., although many are not. Pothier covers similar material to the D.O.: error, violence and seduction. Again we conclude that the D.O. is following the 1807 Act; but it must be pointed out that lack of free consent for the three reasons stated would invalidate the marriage in all systems derived from Roman or Canon law. Hence this provision is not particularly relevant for our purposes.

The next article, D.O. 6 (p. 25), states that ministers of the gospel (*ministres du culte*) and magistrates authorized to celebrate marriages in the Territory are forbidden to solemnize the marriages of boys under fourteen years and girls under twelve, on the pain of the former having the right to celebrate marriages withdrawn and of the latter being dismissed from office. Batiza gives no source. The D.L.V. refers to *Part.* 4.1.6, and the formalities on the marriage of minors found in the 1807 Act. The C.N., article 144, states that men cannot marry before eighteen nor women before fifteen. (C.N. 156 provides penalties for public officers who marry people below age.) The provision of the C.N. is the result of amending legislation during the Revolution and Directory, while under the *ancien régime*, the ages of marriage for the two sexes were as is stated in the

---

[209] See the *1823 Projet*, pp. 8–9; see also *supra*, text at notes 176–180.

[210] In the old sense of abductor.

[211] Pothier, *T.C.M.*, pp. 132–138 (nos. 306–319).

[212] *Part.* 4.2.10–18, thus: *ley* 10: 1) error; *ley* 11: 2) servile condition: 3) vows of celibacy; *ley* 12: 4) relationship; *leyes* 13 and 14: 5) having committed a grievous sin, e.g. incest; *ley* 15: 6) cannot marry heretic or non-Christian, 7) force and fear; *ley* 16: 8) being in the last 3 of the 9 gradations of holy orders (subdeacon, deacon, priest); 9) having certain afflictions as the result of sin (venereal disease?); *ley* 17: 10) when against honour of church or people; 11) relationship; 12) when man of too cold a nature to lie with a woman; 13) madness; 14) nonage and impotency; *ley* 18: 15) when church prohibits and during religious holidays. This ragbag of provisions is repetitious and shows the analytical imperfections of the *Partidas*.

D.O.[213] These ages were fixed by the Canon law (and were the same in the Roman law) as the presumed age of puberty, and those who were *impuber*, not being able to have sexual intercourse with their spouses and thus procreate, could not validly marry. *Part.* 4.1.6 states this by saying that if a man below fourteen and a girl below twelve give consent to marry, the status they achieve is not one of marriage but of betrothal. It should be noticed that this D.O. article penalizes those who conduct the marriage ceremony, but does not state that the marriage is necessarily invalid in the definite manner of C.N. 144. Is there any significance in this? It could reflect the Canon law stress on puberty and *copula carnalis*.[214] First, under chapter 3 of this title on nullity, nullity has to be sued for, otherwise the marriage is valid: D.O. 16 (p. 27). Second, the Canon law, although prohibiting marriage before the (legal) age of puberty, rendered such a marriage valid if the spouses were capable of sexual intercourse. Esmein puts it thus:

> Le droit canonique défendait bien de contracter mariage avant la puberté; mais si, en fait, cette prohibition n'avait pas été respectée et que l'impubère marié eut été, d'un côté physiquement capable d'établir les relations sexuelles avec son conjoint, et, d'autre part moralement capable de bien comprendre l'acte qu'il accomplissait, doli capax, le mariage était reconnu valable; la présomption cédait devant la vérité.[215]

Third, this recognition of the Canon law of physical capacity rebutting the presumption of a party below the legal age being *impuber* would be known to the D.O. redactors: it is to be found, for example, in Pothier.[216] The careful phrasing of D.O. 6 (p. 25) would suggest they are intending to allow this defence to an action of nullity on grounds of the parties, or one of them, being below the age of puberty. Be that as it may, however, this D.O. article provides for the traditional age of marriage, following the Canon and Roman law. The D.L.V. referred to the 1807 Act, ch.17. This Act has no specific provisions on the minimum age of marriage, although its ss. 16–20 regulate the marriage of minors.

D.O. 7 (p. 25) provides that those who are legally married cannot contract another marriage until the dissolution of the first, under the penalties prescribed by statute. This provision is taken directly from the 1807 Act, s.10, to which it also alludes. The D.L.V. refers to the Act as does Batiza who claims it as the "almost verbatim" source, and who gives as subsidiary sources C.N. 147 and *Proj. An VIII*, 1.5.8. These two latter are indeed similar: "On ne peut contracter un second mariage avant la dissolution du premier," says C.N. 147; but it must be

---

[213] See Pothier, *T.C.M.*, p. 39 (no. 94). This will be explored further, *infra*, on Quebec.

[214] See Esmein, *op. cit. supra* note 69, vol. l, p. 83: "Le droit canonique assigne aux rapports sexuels, à la *copula carnalis*, une importance particulière: aucune autre législation, je le crois, n'est entrée aussi loin dans cette voie." See also, *ibid.*, vol. 1, pp. 83–85 generally.

[215] *Ibid.*, vol. 1, p. 283.

[216] Pothier, *T.C.M.*, p. 40 (no. 94). He quotes Pope Alexander III: "Si ita fuerint aetati proximi, quod potuerint copula carnali coniungi minoris aetatis intuitu separari non debent, quum in eis aetatem supplevisse malitia videtur."

borne in mind that the C.N. and its *projet* both envisage the possibility of dissolution by divorce, while the D.O. does not. Further, no Christian countries have allowed polygamy, so the "source" of the article is largely irrelevant; but Batiza, in claiming these two "subsidiary" sources, is being misleading, especially when there are not even strong literary resemblances between them and D.O. 7 (p. 25).

D.O. 8 (p. 25) is of rather more interest:

> Les personnes libres et les esclaves ne peuvent contracter mariage ensemble; la célébration de ces mariages est défendue et le mariage est nul; il en est de même du mariage des blancs ou blanches avec les personnes de couleur, libres.

This article forbidding marriage between blacks and whites and free and enslaved was the inevitable product of prevailing *mores*. The Act 1807, ch. 17, s. 13 provides:

> Free persons and slaves are incapable of contracting marriage together, the celebration of such is forbidden, and the marriage is void.

Batiza states this is the "almost verbatim, first part" source of the article. The D.L.V. also refers to this section of the Act, and to *Part*. 4.2.11 and 4.5.1. The second part of the article is not derived from the 1807 Act, ch. 17; but it probably correctly represents the law in Louisiana prior to the Digest.[217] The references to the *Partidas* are of great interest. Slavery is provided for in the *Partidas*; but, of course, no account is taken of specifically black slavery.[218] *Part*. 4.2.11 states that, if the free person marrying the slave did not know the latter was unfree, then the marriage is invalid; but if the former knew of the latter's unfree status and still married the latter then the marriage is valid, and cannot be annulled for that reason. *Part*. 4.5.1 provides the same, but regulates slave marriages in greater detail. Both parties must be Christian. A slave can marry another slave, and such a marriage is valid even if their masters (*señores*) prohibit the marriage; but they are not released from bondage to their master. Masters have to sell married slaves in such a manner that they can continue to live together. Further if a free person (of either sex) marries a slave with the knowledge or permission of the latter's owner, the slave becomes free. These provisions are obviously very different from those of the D.O., and considerably more humane.[219] (They are also radically different from the Roman law.) According to Van Kleffens, in thirteenth- century Spain, "slavery was still of frequent occurrence";[220] but it was not approved of, as is shown by the introduction to title 5 of the *Quartena Partida*, named "De los casamientos de los

---

[217] The French *Code Noir* of 1724 provided the same as the relevant article: see D.E. Everett, "Free Persons of Color in Colonial Louisiana", 7 *Louisiana History* (1966), pp. 21–50 at p. 22. The French Prefect, de Laussat, had attempted ot restore the 1724 French law on slavery in late 1803: E.G. Brown, "Law and Government in the 'Louisiana Purchase': 1803–1804", 2 *Wayne Law Review* (1956), pp. 169–189 at p. 186.

[218] S.E. van Kleffens, *Hispanic Law until the End of the Middle Ages*, Edinburgh, Edinburgh University Press, 1968, pp. 199–200.

[219] See D.O. 15–27 (pp. 39–43), bk. 1, tit. 6, chap. 3.

[220] Van Kleffens, *op. cit supra* note 218, p. 199.

servios." The title starts thus: "Servidumbre es la mas vil et la mas despreciada cosa que entre los homes puede seer," because man "es la mas noble et libre criatura entre todas las otras criaturas que Dios fizo." This attitude towards slavery was not that prevalent in Territorial Louisiana, where there existed not only contempt for slaves, but colour prejudice against blacks. Thus, the 1806 Act, ch. 33, s. 40 provided:

> *And be it further enacted,* That free people of colour ought never to insult or strike white people, nor presume to conceive themselves equal to the white; but on the contrary that they ought to yield to them in every occasion, and never speak or answer to them but with respect, under the penalty of imprisonment according to the nature of the offence.[221]

Hence, given opinion in Louisiana, the humaner provisions of the *Partidas*, although known to the redactors, would not be likely to find favour. Thus, given the current ideology and conditions, the D.O. article is readily explained.[222]

D.O. 9 (p. 25) and 10 (p. 27) lay down the prohibited degrees of marriage. The first prohibits marriage between those in direct ascending and descending line, including those born illegitimate, while the second prohibits marriage in the collateral line between brother and sister (whether of whole or half blood, illegitimate or not) and between uncle and niece and aunt and nephew. These two articles are taken directly from the 1807 Act, ss. 14 and 15, which Batiza classes as their "verbatim" sources. He also includes C.N. 161, 162 and 163 and *Proj. An VIII*, 1.5.17 and 18 as subsidiary sources, and these are indeed roughly similar to the D.O. articles; but this is hardly surprising. The D.L.V. also refers to these sections of the 1807 Act: it also refers on D.O. 9 (p. 25) to *Part.* 4.2.12 and 4.6.4 and Pothier,[223] and on D.O. 10 (p. 27) to the *Partidas* again (same *leyes*) and once more to Pothier.[224] *Part.* 4.2.12 states:

> Parentesco et cuñadia fasta el quarto grado . . . embarga el casamiento que se non faga, et si fuere fecho débenlo desfacer: otrosi el parentesco espiritual . . . embarga el casamiento. . . . Otrosi porfijando algunt home a alguna muger, non debe el casar con ella nin ninguno de sue fijos mientre que durase el porfijamiento. . . .

Thus, relationship or affinity to the fourth degree prohibited marriage, as did the spiritual relationship between godparents, between godparents and godchildren, and between godchildren and their godparents' children who were "hermanos espirituales". Finally, adoptive relationships prevented marriage. *Part.* 4.6.4 describes clearly how relationships to the fourth degree are to be computed according to the Canon law. In effect, these provisions of the *Partidas* are

---

[221] Louisiana Acts, 1806, ch. 33 (7 June 1806), "Black Code. An Act Prescribing the rules and conduct to be observed with respect to Negroes and other Slaves of this Territory".

[222] The Spanish laws of the Indies did not specifically forbid the marriage of free blacks with white people, but generally discouraged interracial marriage: see *Rec. Ind.* 5.5.7.

[223] Pothier, *T.C.M.*, p. 63 (no. 132).

[224] *Ibid.*, pp. 63–74 (nos. 133–149).

stating the Canon law as laid down in 1215 by the Fourth Lateran Council.[225] The Council of Trent to some extent limited the *cognatio spiritualis*, that is, the prohibitions on the marriage between those connected through godparents;[226] but, in general, the provisions of the *Partidas* would be in force on this matter in Louisiana under Spanish government. As the references to Pothier show, the law on this matter in France under the *ancien régime* was almost exactly the same.[227] Since this is so, it can be seen that the Louisiana Act of 1807, ss. 14 and 15, introduced a very significant restriction of the prohibited degrees of relationship. We need not concern ourselves with the sources of these sections of the Act: it is sufficient to point out that, as re-enacted in the D.O., they provided a very useful reform. It is quite conceivable that, in a small rural community without easy means of transport, it would be difficult to meet a marriageable person who was not within the very extended prohibited degrees of the Canon law. In a frontier community this might well be an acute problem.[228] To search for sources is not important, as the prohibitions in these two articles are fairly universal, conforming to the Roman law, and, indeed, to Leviticus, chapter eighteen. This explains why they are so similar to C.N. 161–163.[229] They also differ from the C.N. in that the latter by its article 164 states that the government can for "causes graves" dispense from the prohibition of marriage between uncle and niece, aunt and nephew.[230] This facility to grant such a dispensation would doubtless be thought unnecessary in Louisiana, and indeed contrary to tradition and popular sentiment.

Hence these articles were only reasonable and sensible reforms, given the nature of the territory at the period. One very interesting point arises out of them in connection with the 1825 C.L. The *1823 Projet* had recommended the inclusion of a new article, which became C.L. 98.[231] It states: "Tout autre empêchement, pour raison de parenté ou d'affinité, est aboli." This article must have been included because of fears of an attempt to revive the old law on prohibited degrees, fears arising out of decisions such as *Cottin*.[232] This relates to the discussion of whether or not the 1808 D.O. is a "true" code. It was argued in chapter three that the D.O. was a true code, and that attempts after 1808 to revive the Spanish law arose out of factors other than the D.O. not being an

---

[225] See Esmein, *op. cit. supra* note 69, vol. 1, p. 355, and vol. 2, p. 130 (*cognatio spiritualis*); Pothier, *T.C.M.*, pp. 73–74 (nos. 146–149). For an impression of the social effects of the prohibitions before and after Lateran IV, see Flandrin, *op. cit. supra* note 2, pp. 24–26. On the development of the Canon law on prohibited degrees, see Pothier, *T.C.M.*, pp. 63–74 (nos. 133–149), where he also discusses the Roman law, and Esmein, *op. cit. supra* note 69, vol. 1, pp. 335–383, and vol. 2, pp. 258–266.

[226] See Esmein, *op. cit. supra* note 69, vol. 2, pp. 261–262.

[227] Pothier, *T.C.M.*, pp. 63–74 (nos. 132–149).

[228] See Flandrin, *op. cit. supra* note 2, pp. 24–26.

[229] See on the C.N., Maleville, *Analyse*, vol. 1, pp. 156–159.

[230] See *infra*, where these matters will be canvassed on Quebec.

[231] *1823 Projet*, p. 8.

[232] See *supra*, chap. 3, text at notes 208–227.

authoritative legislative statement, superseding what had gone before.[233] The inclusion of this new article in the C.L. supports this, since the old law on prohibited degrees had been abolished by the 1807 statute *before* the redaction of the D.O. Even those who tend to reject the D.O. as a "true" code must accept that this statute is more than a consolidating statement of the existing law.

The next article, D.O. 11 (p. 27), relates to the marriage of minors, and will be discussed *infra*;[234] but it should be pointed out that it also is to some extent founded in the 1807 Act, s. 16.

D.O. 12 (p. 27), the final article of this chapter, states that, as well as the above general rules, the formalities relating to the publication and celebration of marriages will be found in a special law of the legislature. This is a direct reference to the 1807 Act, to which the D.L.V. here also refers. Batiza states that in *Proj. An VIII*, 1.5.24 this article of the D.O. has a "substantially influencing" source. Any correspondence between the two, however, is only a coincidence based on linguistic similarity. How can an article referring to an 1807 territorial statute be in any way based on an 1800 French provision? These sections of the 1807 Act were included in the 1825 C.L. as articles 100–110.[235] Finally, C.L. 111 forbade marriages by procuration which the Spanish laws had permitted.[236] This C.L. article is again undoubtedly the result of fears aroused by *Cottin*.[237]

The above provisions are all that the D.O. contains on the nature and formalities requisite for marriage. The redactors intended that their general statements be supplemented by recourse to the detailed provisions of the 1807 Act. It is notable that neither in the requisites for marriage nor in the section on nullity is impotency mentioned as a ground for invalidating the marriage. Why is this so? Before considering this question it is first appropriate to mention that the 1823 *Projet* intended that the revised C.L. should include an article stating that all causes of nullity that existed by the old laws were abolished, apart from that of the impotency of one of the parties, caused either by defective anatomy or an accident before the marriage.[238] The first part of this provision is again the result of *Cottin*.[239] The second attempts to reassert impotency as a ground of nullity. In fact, this section was excluded from the final redaction of this article, which became C.L. 116. Impotency was a ground of nullity in the Canon law and, as such a ground, is found in the *Partidas*.[240] It is, however, not included in the C.N., and it may be suggested (but only suggested) that it was excluded from the D.O. in copying the C.N. in this respect. (The C.N. excluded it on the grounds

---

[233] See *supra*, chap. 3, text at notes 171–239.

[234] On *puissance paternelle*, see *infra*, text at notes 645–653.

[235] See *1823 Projet*, pp. 8–9. The redactors there said that "The Chapter relative to the celebration of marriages, is extracted from the Act of the 6th, April, 1807, . . . and contains all the material dispositions concerning them, which were not inserted in the code." But see *supra*, text at notes 176–180.

[236] See *1823 Projet*, p. 9.

[237] See *supra*, notes 232–233 with the text.

[238] See *1823 Projet*, pp. 9–10.

[239] This is obvious from the interesting comment at *1823 Projet*, p. 10.

[240] *Part*. 4.2.6 and 4.2.17 show this.

of difficulty of proof.)[241] By the time of the drawing up of the 1823 *Projet*, the redactors might well have been aware of the problems this exclusion was causing in the operation of the law in France,[242] and they might have sought to rectify the situation. This is, of course, only a plausible speculation. A further explanation could be that, in this area of the D.O., the redactors were closely following the 1807 Act, which also did not mention impotency. Both of these suggestions could be correct, but want of evidence necessitates leaving the question posed above without definite answer.[243]

The following points may conclude this discussion of how, according to the D.O., a valid marriage is contracted. First, Professor Baade's conclusions on the law in force under Spain have already been discussed.[244] He demonstrated that, in theory, and to some extent in fact, the Tridentine law on the form of marriage was in force. He also showed that the legal sources proving this would have been difficult to acquire in Louisiana. Neither Moreau Lislet nor James Brown came to Louisiana until after the cession to the United States.[245] Perhaps they did not know that the Tridentine law was formally in force. This could explain why, in this section of the D.L.V., the only references to the Castilian law are to the *Partidas*. Against this, however, it can be suggested that it is quite possible that Moreau and Brown would simply assume the Tridentine law was in force, and that this was the reason for the D.L.V. referring to Pothier who gives the substance of the Tridentine law. Be this as it may, the 1807 Act introduced, for the celebration of marriages, a system similar to that of the law arising out of the French revolution, and similar, in some ways, to the laws of the states of the Union.

In the redaction of this section of the 1808 Digest, the codifiers were aware of the pre-Tridentine Canon Law, the Tridentine Canon Law, the law of *ancien régime* France, of Castile, the common law as applied in the U.S.A., and the C.N. and its *projet*. The existence of the 1807 Act, however, prevented any great eclectic innovation. The overall structure of the two chapters of the title which have been considered in depth may have been, to some extent, based on that of the *Proj. An VIII*, or the C.N. (though much more likely the former), but there can be no doubt that the provisions of the D.O. are here very firmly based on the 1807 Act. Moreover, the redactors conceived of their code and the relevant sections of the Act being read together to give the full law. Professor Batiza refers frequently to the *Proj. An VIII* as an influence on individual articles;[246] but it is clear that any influence exerted is on style. The D.O. provides for religious and civil forms of marriage (although the law considers marriage only as a civil contract), while the French code and its *projet* only envisage only a purely civil form of marriage. Further, the C.N. and its *projet* contain provisions

---

[241] See *infra*, text at notes 720–724.
[242] See *infra*, text at notes 715–737.
[243] It would be interesting to know why the enacted version of C.L. 116 excluded impotency as a ground of nullity. C.L. 116, or rather the *1823 Projet*'s version, was intended "to follow article 16".
[244] See *supra*, text at notes 181–197.
[245] See *supra*, chap. 3, text at notes 254–265.
[246] Usually only as an "indirect" source.

on divorce, whereas the D.O. does not deal with it at all; although the 1807 Act does mention it, but without regulating it in any way.[247] It was earlier pointed out that the C.N. contains a great many more articles than the D.O.[248] The reasons for this should now be obvious. The D.O., unlike the C.N., excluded the *minutiae* of the formalities of publication and of parental consent to children's marriages.[249] These topics were instead covered in the 1807 Act. Perhaps Brown and Moreau believed that such precise details were best excluded from a code, and were encouraged in this belief by the existence of the very recent act. A reading of Batiza's appendix C might lead one to suppose that the Louisiana Digest is, in this section, virtually identical to the French code or its *projet*. The appendix, however, is here misleading. This impression is given purely because of Batiza's comparison of individual article with individual article, ignoring the fact that there are far more articles in the French codification. The French and Louisiana codes are, indeed, similar, and there is some influence on general form; but the source for the provisions of this section of the Digest is the 1807 Act, and much of the similarity between the individual articles of the D.O. and of the French code and its *projet* is due to the similarity of the Act to the French materials.

The redactors of the D.O. here had to provide clear, concise rules on the nature of marriage and the requirements for formal validity. This they did, basing their provisions on the 1807 Act. They had no chance to innovate, as the Act restricted their operations. Further, they had no need to innovate, as, given the material conditions of the territory and its heterogeneous society, the law embodied in the Act adequately regulated the formalities and requirements for marriage.

Puissance Maritale and the Property Aspects of the Husband-Wife Relationship

Marriage, when validly contracted according to the provisions of the D.O. and 1807 Act ch. 17, had certain consequences as to property. The D.O. provides for a community of gains (*sociedad de gananciales* or *communauté d'acquêts ou de gains*) between the husband and wife, and regulates control over property belonging to them as individuals. The origins of the Digest's provisions on matrimonial property are very controversial.[250] Professor Pascal has maintained that the origins are in the Castilian law;[251] Professor Batiza claims on the contrary that:

---

[247] In 1807 Act, ch. 17, s. 70: on which see *infra*, text at notes 497–503.

[248] See *supra*, text between notes 180 and 181.

[249] On parental consent, see *infra* on *puissance paternelle*. See 1807 Act, ch. 17, ss.16–25.

[250] See Batiza, "Rejoinder", pp. 641–642; Pascal, "Reply", pp. 616–620; Baade, "Marriage Contracts"; R. Batiza, "The Actual Sources of the Marriage Contract Provisions of the Louisiana Civil Code of 1808: the Textual Evidence," 54 *Tul. L. Rev.* (1979) pp. 77–116. Pugh, *op. cit. supra* note 80, adopts Pascal's position; but her useful article does not discuss the D.O., although she makes some relevant remarks in passing.

[251] Pascal, "Reply", pp. 616–620; R. Pascal, "The Work of the Louisiana Appellate Courts for the 1974–1975 Term–Matrimonial Regimes", 36 *La. L. Rev.* (1976), pp. 409–416 at p. 410.

> The Spanish system of community of acquets or gains (*sociedad de ganancias*) that appears in the Code, rather than being opposed to the French system of *communauté*, supplements it.[252]

He explains this as:

> the adoption by the drafter of the Spanish system of gains as one partial aspect of the general concept of conjugal partnership in a French inspired background of rules, irrespective of differences in their original metropolitan settlings.[253]

Professor Batiza later reasserted his view, stating that, of the ninety-seven articles of Title V of Book III of the Digest containing a "real rule",[254] fifty-six were taken from the C.N., nine from the *Proj. An VIII*, three from Pothier, two from Domat, three from Febrero, and the rest from combinations of various sources, namely: Domat, Pothier, Febrero, the *Fuero real*, the *Siete Partidas*, the *Nueva recopilación*, the *Fuero juzgo*, and the *Leyes de Toro*.[255] Essentially, Batiza is arguing the law on the point is basically French with some Castilian additions.

Professor Baade has recently engaged in this debate.[256] He sets out the socio-legal context and explains social and legal practice (legal folkways) at the period of codification. He points to the French legal folk custom of making marriage contracts which was transplanted to Louisiana along with the *Coutume de Paris*.[257] In Castile there was no equivalent folk custom of drawing up such contracts.[258] One reason for the difference is that the French *coutume* allowed marriage contracts to be used to provide for the future transmission of wealth, whereas the Castilian law did not, a will and testament being used instead for such future transmissions of property.[259] Baade goes on to show that the French legal folkway of concluding marriage contracts continued in Louisiana under Spanish rule, although there can be no doubt that Castilian law was introduced.[260] (The Castilian law did allow for the making of such contracts.)[261] Professor Baade classifies the two legal approaches thus: the old French approach as "notarial" or "contractual"; the old Castilian as "statutory".[262] By this he means that, in France, the accepted folkway was to draw up a marriage contract using the services of a notary, while in Castile it was normal to accept the provisions of the *sociedad de gananciales* without varying them in a contract.

---

[252] Batiza, "Sources", p. 29.
[253] Batiza, "Rejoinder", p. 642.
[254] Batiza, "Textual Evidence", p. 105 and see *passim*. He states that one article does not contain a "real rule": there are 98 relevant articles in total.
[255] *Ibid.*, p. 105 and n. 113.
[256] Baade, "Marriage Contracts", *passim*.
[257] *Ibid.*, pp. 15–30.
[258] *Ibid.*, pp. 45–49.
[259] *Ibid.*, pp. 47–48.
[260] *Ibid.*, pp. 73–75.
[261] *Part.* 4.11.24 and 30.
[262] Baade, "Marriage Contracts", pp. 44–48.

He argues that the northern French law was based around the concept of the marriage contract, while the Castilian was not.[263] He then goes on to show that the D.O. redactors chose to follow the French "contractual" model of matrimonial property, rather than the Castilian "statutory" one.[264] His evidence is the prominence given to the marriage contract in the D.O. (a prominence which Castilian law would have denied), the general scheme of the relevant D.O. provisions, and certain important articles which contradict the Castilian law.[265]

Turning to Pascal's view that the D.O. inevitably was based on Castilian law,[266] Baade points out that, to some limited extent, there had been a revival of the French law on marriage contracts between 1803 and 1808. He bases this conclusion on an examination of marriage contracts of the period.[267] Further, the folkway of concluding such contracts had continued even under Spain.[268] He then points out that the adopting of the French "contractual" régime from the French sources was hardly a surprising act on the part of the Digest redactors:

> the codification had to reflect *enacted* law previously in effect, for any reliance on customary law was bound to be exploited by the champions of the 'new' customary law of the United States, the common law.[269]
>
> Further:
> since time was of the essence, extant French-language legislative precedent had to be followed.[270]

Since the "living law" was of the "contractual" model, any choice of provisions on matrimonial property other than those basically French would have been very surprising.[271]

That the basic model adopted was the French "contractual" one does not mean that individual articles could not be of Castilian origin. Baade himself points out that the 1808 redactors adopted as the "statutory" regime the Castilian *ganancial* community, whereas the C.N. had adopted the community of moveables and acquests of the *Coutume de Paris*.[272] As he shows, the redactors could have adopted the French *communauté réduite aux acquêts* as the statutory regime.[273]

Batiza has recently challenged Baade's work.[274] Alleging that Baade argues that the marriage contract provisions of the Digest originated in the "living law"

---

[263] *Ibid. passim*, but especially pp. 84–85.
[264] *Ibid.*, pp. 85–86.
[265] *Ibid.*, pp. 85–89.
[266] See *supra*, chap. 3, text at notes 132–170; and Pascal, "Reply", *passim*.
[267] Baade, "Marriage Contracts".
[268] *Ibid.* pp. 73–75; see *supra*, text at notes 260–261.
[269] Baade, "Marriage Contracts", p. 83.
[270] *Ibid.*, pp. 83–84.
[271] *Ibid.*, p. 87.
[272] See *ibid.*, pp. 87–88; on the C.N. and *Coutume de Paris* see *infra*.
[273] Baade, "Marriage Contracts", pp. 87–89; but cf. Batiza, "Textual Evidence", p. 97 note 75.
[274] Batiza, "Textual Evidence".

of the Orleans Territory,[275] Batiza points out that none of the relevant articles have a source in the "living law", but only in materials such as the French code.[276] Batiza seems to have misunderstood Baade's argument. Nowhere does Baade state that any individual article had an origin in the "living law". He merely states that the "living law" being of a "contractual" model, the adoption in the D.O. of the "contractual" model of the French materials is hardly surprising.[277] Batiza claims Baade is being inconsistent in stating that the code had to reflect enacted law while its "source" was the living law.[278] Identification of this supposed inconsistency is again the product of Batiza's misunderstanding of Baade's argument, for, as just pointed out, Baade does not claim the "living law" anywhere as a "source" in the sense Batiza alleges.[279] Batiza claims that Baade has failed to show a "key relationship"[280] between D.O. 9 (p. 325) and the "living law" of marriage contracts and that this invalidates the latter's hypothesis.[281] This article provides thus:

> Les conventions les plus ordinaires, dans le contrat de mariage, sont:
> La constitution de dot;
> Et les diverses donations que les époux peuvent se faire, soit réciproquement, soit l'un à l'autre, ou qu'ils peuvent recevoir d'autrui, en considération du mariage.

Batiza argues that, since Baade has failed to show that these were the most ordinary clauses of a marriage contract in Louisiana prior to the Digest, in the "living law", Baade's argument should be rejected.[282] This argument of Batiza's is once more based on a misunderstanding. Baade does not allege that this article represents notarial practice in Louisiana: he states that this article should be read with the articles (found in chapters 8 and 9 of the title on Donations) on interspousal donations and donations by third parties to the spouses or their children.[283] He states that the combined effect of these articles was to allow

> spouses when there were no children of the marriage to make irrevocable reciprocal donations of their future shares of the community to each other in full property by marriage contract, but not otherwise.[284]

This was contrary to Castilian law. Baade uses this article to show that, *when taken with the other relevant articles*, it indicates that the D.O. redactors were

---

[275] *Ibid.*, pp. 77 and 97.
[276] *Ibid.*, pp. 97–105.
[277] See *supra*, text at notes 256–271.
[278] Batiza, "Textual Evidence", p. 107. He quotes the passage from Baade's article partially quoted *supra*, at notes 269 and 270.
[279] See *supra*, text at notes 256–271 and 277.
[280] Batiza's term: "Textual Evidence", p. 107.
[281] *Ibid.*, pp. 106–107. This is Book 3, Title 5, art. 9.
[282] Batiza, "Textual Evidence", pp. 106–107 and n. 116.
[283] The relevant articles are D.O. 222 (p. 257) and D.O. 210–218 (pp. 255–257). The relevant articles in Title 2 (Donations) in Book 3 are 222 and 210–218.
[284] Baade, "Marriage Contracts", p. 87.

adopting French substantive laws on marriage contracts.[285] He does not argue that this *individual* article was based on the "living law", nor that this *individual* article could be only of French origin: this means that Batiza's point, that Castilian equivalent statements may be found, is quite irrelevant.[286] We may conclude that the arguments Batiza puts forward on the grounds that the "sources" of the 1808 Digest marriage contract provisions are not the "living law" should be dismissed, as based on a complete misunderstanding of Baade's argument.

Baade adduces ample evidence to show that the making of a marriage contract was not a Castilian legal folkway.[287] Batiza develops a second line of attack on Baade's argument, by taking two quotations the latter uses, attempting to refute Baade's interpretation of them,[288] and, on the basis of this refutation, claiming that Baade "went too far in minimizing the importance of marriage contracts in Castile".[289] It must be stressed that, even were Batiza's interpretation of these quotations correct, Baade's argument would not be seriously affected. A contemporary Spanish author cited by Baade states: "In Castille such contracts were not known in practice."[290] Batiza refers to the following statement by Baade:

> As late as 1851, Garcia Goyena observed that in contradistinction to France, the use of marriage contracts in (non-foral) Spain was likely to be '*rarisimo*' even with full freedom to contract.[291]

Batiza states that Baade has "misread and mistranslated" Garcia Goyena's remark. Batiza provides the following translation. After referring to the French position, Goyena states:

> among us, despite the freedom that always has existed to modify the partnership by special pacts, the case will be extremely rare in which that freedom has been used.[292]

Professor Batiza obviously gives the better version;[293] but this interpretation of Goyena is, however, unjustified. He states that Goyena means that:

---

[285] *Ibid.*, pp. 86–87.
[286] Batiza, "Textual Evidence", p. 107. As will have been seen, on its own, D.O. 9 (p. 325) is not really a rule of any significance.
[287] Baade, "Marriage Contracts", pp. 45–47, p. 85.
[288] Batiza, "Textual Evidence", pp. 94–95.
[289] *Ibid.*, p. 94.
[290] Nagore Yarnoz, found quoted in Baade, "Marriage Contracts", p. 45, translation in n. 222.
[291] Baade, "Marriage Contracts", p. 85; Batiza, "Textual Evidence", p. 94.
[292] Batiza, "Textual Evidence", p. 94 and n. 69.
[293] The relevant passage from Goyena reads: "Nuestra posicion en este punto es mas ventajosa que la del Código Frances y otros, donde la comunion ó sociedad se halta modificada por muchas clausulas ó pactos que ha sido preciso consignar en los mismos Códigos, por ser de uso muy frecuente: entre nosotros, á pesar de la libertad que siempre ha habido para modificar la sociedad por pactos especiales, sera rarisimo el caso en que se haya hecho uso de ella." Professor Batiza points out that the feminine pronoun *ella* refers to *libertad*, whereas Professor Baade has taken it

> while marriage agreements in Castile were seldom modified by the parties, the marriage agreements themselves were of normal occurrence.[294]

Goyena simply does not say that such marriage contracts were of normal occurrence. Although Baade has here mistranslated Goyena's remark, his argument is not affected. Baade points out that, contrary to French attitudes, Febrero did not seem to consider marriage contracts as the most important civil transaction;[295] while of testaments Febrero wrote:

> Ninguna cosa pide mas cuidado, mas sabiduria y claridad que la disposicion de un Testamento.[296]

Batiza states that this is correct, but that the reason why Febrero regarded a testament as so important was not to do with *capitulaciones matrimoniales*, but because, by its very nature, a testament cannot be improved, as it takes effect after the testator's death.[297] This does not really affect Baade's point: Febrero does appear to put more stress on testaments than on marriage contracts. Batiza's allegation, that Baade unjustifiably minimizes the importance of marriage contracts in Castile, is wrong.

Batiza has a third line of argument against Baade's views. He argues that the 1808 redactors did not make a clear choice of the French "contractual" prototype.[298] He points out that in the *droit coutumier* it was possible, by contract, to modify the community or exclude it.[299] This was also allowed by the French code. He argues that the only way provided in the D.O. to escape the legal community was to use D.O. 2 (pp. 323–325) to stipulate that their matrimonial agreement should be regulated by the law of another state or territory.[300] That this should be so does not really affect Baade's argument. He argues that the model of matrimonial regime adopted in the D.O. was the "contractual" one: he does not state, nor need he state, that all the provisions of the D.O. are founded on the customary law of northern France. That some aspects of the provisions in the D.O. are of Castilian or other non-French origin does not matter: the overall conception of the law in the Digest and the whole thrust of that law are derived from the northern

---

to refer to *sociedad*. See Batiza, "Textual Evidence", p. 94 n. 69 where Batiza quotes Goyena and where, in the text, he gives a translation of the whole passage.

[294] Batiza, "Textual Evidence", pp. 94–95.

[295] Baade, "Marriage Contracts", p. 47.

[296] Quoted in *ibid.*, p. 47.

[297] Batiza, "Textual Evidence", p. 95. The relevant text of Febrero reads, as cited by Batiza, *ibid.*, p. 95, n. 71: "El hombre miéntras vive puede corregir sus yerros; pero quando dexa de exîstir y no puede evitar las contiendas, y los funestos efectos que causen la ignorancia y la obscuridad de su Testamento. Para evitar estas fatales consequencias debe otorgarle estando sano: debe consultarlo con personas doctas y timoratas: debe sobre todo implorar los auxilios divinos, y de esta suerte descaragará su conciencia y conseguirá el acierto haciendo á sus herederos el bien que les desea."

[298] Batiza, "Textual Evidence", pp. 95–97.

[299] *Ibid.*, pp. 96–97.

[300] *Ibid.*, p. 96.

French "contractual" conception of matrimonial regime. Batiza's third, and strongest, argument should be dismissed.

In sum, Baade's argument must be upheld. The 1808 redactors have adopted a "contractual" model of the matrimonial regime, a model derived from the *droit coutumier*. The overall tenor of the articles of the code is of French origin, and, while several articles have Castilian origin, the Digest incorporates some key provisions which, in a fundamental way, are antithetical to the Castilian substantive law.[301]

The above discussion of the controversy over the provisions on matrimonial property helps ground the following account of the authority of the husband over the property. At issue in this section of the book is not the matrimonial property system as such, but rather the authority of the husband over the community property, and the separate property of his wife. The following discussion will be concerned with whether or not this authority has changed with codification, when the redactors adopted a French "contractual" model of matrimonial property, though with the intercalation of some rules of Castilian origin.

The important role of matrimonial property in preserving and transmitting wealth and securing protection for wives and children is not at issue here; but, in order to facilitate discussion of marital authority, it is necessary to give a brief outline of the system provided in the 1808 Digest.

D.O. 1 (p. 323) permits a husband and wife to regulate matrimonial agreements in any way they wish, so long as they do not contravene good morals, and provided they follow the modifications prescribed in the code. Under D.O. 15 (p. 327), in a marriage contract spouses can make reciprocally, or one to another, or receive from others, in consideration of their marriage, all kinds of donations *inter vivos* or *mortis causa*. (*Mortis causa* donations in a marriage contract were invalid under Castilian law.)[302] Under D.O. 16 (p. 327) a wife can bring a dowry to support the expenses of the marriage. Under D.O. 56 (p. 335) all the effects belonging to the wife that have not been settled on her as dowry belong to her *parapherna*. D.O. 63 (p. 337) provides that any marriage contracted in the territory brings about *communauté d'acquêts ou de gains*, and this is so, whether or not there is a marriage contract, and should there be one, if it is silent on *communauté*. D.O. 9 and 10 (p. 325) state the same principle. D.O. 64. (p. 337) describes the composition of the community, which is stated to consist of: first, the fruits of all the effects of which the husband has administration or enjoyment; second, the produce of the reciprocal labour and industry of both husband and wife; and third, the *biens* which they may acquire during marriage, either by donation made jointly to them both, or by purchase, or in any other similar way, even though the purchase be made only in the name of one of the two, because what is relevant is the time of purchase, and not the purchaser.

---

[301] Baade, "Marriage Contracts", pp. 85–89; see *supra*, text at notes 280–286. Note that Batiza's original position is not far removed from that of Baade: see *supra*, text at note 253.
[302] See Baade, "Marriage Contracts", p. 86.

This last article, D.O. 64 (p. 337), involves a change from the Castilian law. It refers to the fruits of the property which the husband administers and enjoys: hence, if a wife administered her *parapherna*, the fruits would not fall into the community. The *Fuero real*, 3.3.3., provided thus:

> Maguer que el marido [h]aya mas que la muger, o la muger [mas] que el marido: quier en heredad, quier en mueble, los frutos sean communales de ambos a dos: y la heredad y las otras cosas do vienen los frutos [h]ayalas el marido o la muger cuyas antes eran, a sus heredos.[303]

This text was included in the *Nueva recopilación*;[304] it was interpreted to mean that the fruits of a wife's *parapherna* belong to the *sociedad*, whether or not she administered it. This was the view, for example, of Azevedo.[305] Thus, this provision of the D.O. includes a minor amendment of the old law.[306] Whether this change amounts to a conscious freeing of the wife from marital authority would seem doubtful: perhaps it is merely the result of an oversight of the redactors, although this also would seem doubtful. The matter will be discussed below.

One article, not directly on matrimonial property, should be mentioned. This is D.O. 4 (p. 325), which sets out what cannot be done in a marriage contract, as being (presumably) *contra bonos mores*. It states thus:

> Les époux ne peuvent, non plus, déroger par leurs conventions matrimoniales, ni aux droits résultant de la puissance maritale sur la personne de la femme et des enfans, ou qui appartient au mari, comme chef, ni aux droits conférés aux survivant des époux, par le titre des pères et des enfans, et par le titre des mineurs, de leurs tuteurs et curateurs, ni aux dispositions prohibitives du présent code.

Batiza gives as the "almost verbatim" source C.N. 1388. The D.L.V. refers to Pothier.[307] C.N. 1388 is indeed almost identical. The Pothier reference found in the D.L.V. is of considerably more interest. The French author states that since God has made man "le chef de la femme, Vir est caput mulieris", any marriage contract making the woman head of the matrimonial community is contrary to good morals and public orders.[308] He continues:

> Les conventions qui paraissent tendre à soustraire la femme à la puissance que notre droit municipal à accordée au mari sur elle, sont aussi regardées comme étant, dans nos moeurs, contraires à la bienseance publique, et en conséquence nulles.

---

303 I have quoted from a 1544 edition of the *Fuero real* which contains the Latin gloss of Montalvo. The spelling has been modernized slightly and the text clarified as indicated by the square brackets. Abbreviations have been extended.

304 *Rec. Cast.* 5.9.4; *Nov. Rec. Cast.* 10.4.3.

305 A. de Azevedo, *Commentarium juris civilis in Hispaniae regis constitutiones*, no. 22 on this text of the *Rec. Cast.*, found quoted in translation in W. de Funiak, *Principles of Community Property*, Chicago, Callaghan, 1943, vol. 2, appendix 3, pp. 261–262.

306 Pugh, *op. cit. supra* note 80, p. 8 recognizes this.

307 Pothier, *T. Comm.*, pp. 50–51 (introd., nos. 4. and 5).

308 *Ibid.* pp. 50–51 (no. 4).

> C'est pour cette raison que la jurisprudence a déclaré nulles les autorisations générales dans les contrats de mariage, c'est-à-dire, les clauses par lesquelles il était porté que le mari, par le contrat de mariage, autorisait sa femme, non-seulement pour administrer, mais même pour aliéner à son gré ses héritages, à quelque titre que ce soit, sans qu'elle eût besoin d'avoir recours pour cela à une autorisation particulière.[309]

The introduction to this chapter pointed out that, in the Castilian law, a husband could give his wife a general authorization, which was contrary to the *droit coutumier*.[310] If in the provisions on authorization (discussed later) in the D.O., we find that the redactors have followed D.O. 4 (p. 325) to the logical conclusion indicated by Pothier, and forbidden such general authorizations, then such a change would indicate the adoption of the French concept of *puissance maritale* and the rejection of the rather more limited Castilian conception. If so, then this article, D.O. 4 (p. 325), will be crucial in demonstrating the change in concepts of marital authority. The fact that the D.L.V. makes no reference to a Spanish source suggests that in the redaction of this article the redactors have adopted the French law. This matter will be discussed in the next subsection. Further, the use of the term "puissance maritale", along with the reference to Pothier, both suggest that the redactors are working with a much more rigorous conception of *puissance maritale* than that found in the Castilian law.

It is now appropriate to turn to the articles on exercise of authority over property. If we start with the control over the *société* or *communauté de gains ou acquêts*, the relevant article is D.O. 66 (p. 337). It states thus:

> Le mari est chef et maître de la société, ou communauté d'acquêts; il en administre les biens, dispose des revenus qu'ils produisent, et peut les vendre, et même les donner, sans le consentement, ni la permission de son épouse, parce que celle-ci n'y a aucun droit, jusqu'à ce que son mari meure.
>
> Mais s'il était prouvé que le mari n'a aliéné lesdits biens, ou n'en a autrement disposé que par dol pour porter préjudice à la femme, elle pourrait avoir son action contre les héritiers de son mari, en répétition de sa moitié desdits biens, en par elle, justifiant du dol.

Batiza gives as the "substantially influencing" sources: Pothier, *Communauté*, nos. 3, 467 and 480,[311] the *Coutume de Paris*, art. 225, the *Nueva recopilación*, 5.9.5, and Febrero.[312] The D.L.V. also refers to *Rec. Cast.* 5.9.5, *Leyes de Estilo*, *ley* 205,[313] and Febrero.[314] Pothier, as cited by Batiza, makes statements broadly similar to those of the D.O. The article of the *Coutume de Paris* also provides

---

[309] *Ibid.* p. 51 (no. 5).

[310] See *supra*, text at notes 90–93.

[311] Pothier, *T. Comm*, pp. 57 (no. 3), 258 (no. 467), 264 (no. 480).

[312] Cited as Febrero, 1 *Adicionado*, Part. 1. cap. II, no. 10 (p. 234). In the edition I have used, the equivalent reference is the same, but with the page being p. 206.

[313] On these *Leyes*, see *supra*, chap. 3 text at note 79.

[314] Febrero, *Contratos*, ch. 1, § 22 no. 240 (vol. 1, p. 202); Febrero, *Juicios*, bk. 1, ch. 4, § 1 nos. 29 & 30 and § 2 nos. 60, 63–66 (vol. 4(1), pp. 256–257, 276–281).

similarly, although it refers to "meubles et conquêts immeubles", in line with its community of moveables and acquests. Febrero, as cited by Batiza, sets out, at great length, a rule very similar to that of D.O. 66 (p. 237).[315] *Ley* 205 of *Estilo* provides that if any married man buys an "eredad ó otra cosa", which he gains while living with his wife, then he can sell it, even though the wife owns half of the "ganancia", provided he does not do so in fraud of his wife.[316] The *Nueva recopilación*, as cited, provides that a husband may dispose of property gained during the marriage, "sin licencia ni otorgamiento de su muger", and this disposition will be valid, unless it is proved he has alienated the property "por defraudar ó damnificar á la muger".[317] Thus, these two Castilian sources allow a husband to sell or alienate ganancial property, provided he is not acting fraudulently to deprive his wife of her rightful claims. Febrero, as cited by the D.L.V., states that the wife owns half the gains made by her and her husband during the marriage.[318] The husband administers them, however, and may dispose of them as he wills, provided he is not acting to defraud his wife.[319] Febrero reports that there was a dispute over whether the husband could give away the *gananciales* or consume them in a frivolous way.[320] He himself favoured the view that a husband could make modest donations, if there were just cause, to relations, domestics, or friends.[321] It is obvious that the whole thrust of the Castilian law on this point is very similar, or indeed identical, to that of the D.O. The husband is the administrator of the community and can do with it as he wishes, provided he does not act in such a way as to defraud his wife. The French law to which Batiza refers is substantially the same. Thus, the redactors introduced no change in this aspect of the husband's authority.

It will have been noted that no reference was made by Batiza to the C.N. or its *projet*. From our perspective, however, the French code has articles of great importance. The C.N. provides as follows:

> 1421. Le mari administre seul les biens de la communauté. Il peut les vendre, aliéner et hypothéquer sans le concours de la femme. 1422. Il ne peut disposer entre-vifs à titre gratuit des immeubles de la communauté, ni d'universalité ou d'une quotité de mobilier, si ce n'est pour l'établissement des enfans communs.
>
> Il peut néanmoins disposer des effets mobiliers à titre gratuit et particulier au profit de toutes personnes, pourvu qu'il ne s'en réserve pas l'usufruit.

Thus, the C.N. restricted the husband's right to make donations. Maleville characterized as *abusif* the powers under the *ancien droit* of the husband to

---

[315] See *supra*, note 312.
[316] Found quoted in de Funiak, *op. cit. supra* note 305, vol. 2, appendix 1, pp. 7–8, where he cites *ley* 205.
[317] This became *Nov. Rec. Cast.* 10.4.5. The *ley* points out that a wife will forfeit her share of the *ganancias* if she lives *luxuriosamente* as a widow.
[318] Febrero, *Juicios*, bk. 1, ch. 4, § 1 no. 29 (vol. 4(1), pp. 256–257).
[319] *Ibid.*, bk. 1, ch. 4, § 1 no. 30 and § 2 nos. 60 and 63 (vol. 4(1), pp. 256–257, 276–281).
[320] *Ibid.*, bk. 1, ch. 4, § 1 no. 30 and § 2 nos. 64 and 65 (vol. 4(1), pp. 256–257, 276–281) for the differing views.
[321] *Ibid.*, bk. 1, ch. 4, § 1 no. 30 and § 2 no. 66 (vol. 4(1), pp. 256–257, 276–281).

make donations:[322] this was the reason for the change in the C.N. (It should be pointed out that it was a change from the provisions of the *Coutume de Paris*: some other *coutumes* had a provision similar to that selected in the C.N.)[323] Would such a reform have been useful in Louisiana? It is difficult to say. First, under the C.N., a husband could still sell an immoveable and then dissipate its proceeds, thus causing his wife to suffer. Second, excessive donations might well amount to fraud, and the wife could gain restitution from her husband's property after the dissolution of the community. If these two reasons are taken into account, it appears that perhaps the reform of the C.N. is not quite as radical as might appear. Further, a wife could petition for separation of property under the D.O. if her husband was maladministering such property. (This is something that will be considered later.)[324] The D.O. redactors, since to some extent they were strengthening the husband's authority, might have felt that to derogate from his control over the community property would be illogical and inconsistent. All this is, of course, speculation. The innovation of the C.N. could well have been useful, and the reasons for its rejection must be a combination of traditionalism in law and a preference for strong marital authority: the latter can reasonably be inferred when it is considered (as will be shown) that the D.O. redactors strengthened the marital authority of the husband. We can conclude discussion of this D.O. article by remarking that the redactors followed the old law, and rejected a possibly useful innovation of the C.N.

If we next turn to consideration of dowry in the D.O., we find, not surprisingly, very traditional provisions. Thus D.O. 16 (p. 327) states that by dowry are meant the effects the wife brings to the husband to support the charges of marriage; and D.O. 17 (p. 327) states that everything the wife settles upon herself or which is given her is included as dowry, unless there be a stipulation to the contrary. D.O. 29 (p. 329) states as follows:

> Le mari a seul l'administration de la dot, et sa femme ne peut la lui ôter; il peut agir seul en justice pour la conservation et le recouvrement de la dot contre ceux qui en sont débiteurs ou détenteurs, ce qui n'empêche pas que la femme ne demeure propriétaire des biens qu'elle a apportés en dot.

This is again a traditional statement: by the very nature of dowry, the husband had the administration of it. No innovation would be possible, thus we need not examine the relevant source material.[325] The statement at the end that the wife is

---

[322] Maleville, *Analyse*, vol. 3 p. 202. Note that *Proj. An VIII*, 3.10.31 is phrased to appear more restrictive than C.N. 1422.

[323] See *infra*, text at notes 792–813 on Quebec.

[324] See *infra*, text at notes 465–475.

[325] See e.g. C.N. 1549; Domat, *Loix civiles*, vol. 1, p. 93 (pt. 1, bk. 1, tit. 9, sect. 1, no. 3); Febrero, *Contratos*, ch. 2, § 1 no. 6 (vol. 1, p. 297). See also Brissaud, *History*, pp. 802–803. Batiza, "Sources", appendix 3, gives as the "source" of this article C.N. 1549, first paragraph, classed as a "substantial influence". He later changed his mind and correctly identified Domat and the C.N. as the source: Batiza, "Textual Evidence", pp. 85–86 and n. 40.

owner of the dowry is again traditional: "quamvis in bonis mariti dos sit, tamen mulieris est", said Justinian's Digest.[326]

D.O. 30 (p. 329) is of more interest:

> La femme peut cependant agir en justice pour ses biens dotaux, soit lorsqu'elle est séparée de biens d'avec son mari ou lorsqu'elle est autorisée à cet effet par lui, ou à son refus, par justice.

The probable "source" of this article is a footnote in Domat.[327] The D.L.V. gives no references. There is no equivalent article in the C.N. Domat points out that this provision is contrary to Roman law. There is no equivalent provision in the *Partidas*. The notion of *séparation de biens*, as found in the D.O., was not found in the Castilian law as regards mismanagement by the husband, although a wife had remedies to stop her husband dissipating her dowry.[328] It seems that this article of the D.O. had no equivalent in the old Castilian law.[329] Since there is no citation in the D.L.V., it possibly is fair to suggest that no equivalent Castilian provision was known to the redactors of the D.O. Thus, the D.O. redactors would appear to have increased the wife's power over her dowry by borrowing a provision from Domat, in order to allow her to protect her interest. This to some extent might appear to derogate from marital authority, since it increases a wife's power over her dowry. This change is, however, consistent with marital authority in the D.O. in general, since the wife needs the authorization of her husband or of a judge to act, when she is not separated as to property.

Alienation of dotal land deserves some remarks. D.O. 36 (p. 329) provides:

> Les immeubles constitués en dot, ne peuvent être aliénés on hypothéqués pendant le mariage, ni par le mari, ni par la femme, ni par les deux conjointement; sauf les exceptions qui suivent.

Batiza gives C.N. 1554 as the "verbatim" source; and, indeed, the two articles are identical. The D.L.V. refers to *Part.* 4.11.7, Domat,[330] and Febrero.[331] Before considering this article, it is necessary to set out the exceptions to the general rule. D.O. 37 (p. 329) states that a wife, with the authorization of her husband, or, on his refusal, of the court, may give dotal effects to establish children she has had by a previous marriage; but if the authorization is by the court, she must reserve the enjoyment of the effects for her husband. This article is identical to

---

[326] D. 23.3.75.

[327] Domat, *Loix civiles*, vol. 1, p. 93, n. *d* (pt. 1, bk. 1, tit. 9, sect. 1, no. 3). Batiza, "Sources", appendix C, originally gave no "source" for this article; but now he has reached the same conclusion: see Batiza, "Textual Evidence", pp. 108–109.

[328] See Pugh, *op. cit. supra* note 80, p. 30. On the wife's remedies to stop the dissipation of her dowry: see Febrero, *Contratos*, ch. 2, § 1 no. 10 (vol. 1, p. 299).

[329] At least none that I have been able to find. The *Partidas* on dowry were very Roman in approach.

[330] Domat, *Loix civiles*, vol. 1, pp. 94–95 (pt. 1, bk. 1, tit. 9, sect. 1, nos. 13 and 14).

[331] Febrero, *Contratos*, ch. 2, § 1 no. 8 (vol. 1, p. 298); Febrero, *Juicios*, bk. 1, ch. 3, § 1 no. 39 (vol. 4(1), p. 205).

C.N. 1555, which Batiza classes as its "verbatim" source. The D.L.V. gives no references. D.O. 38 (p. 329) states that the wife, with the authorization of her husband, may give her dotal effects to establish their common children. This is identical to C.N. 1556, which Batiza claims as the "verbatim" source: once more the D.L.V. makes no references. D.O. 39 (p. 329) states that a dotal immoveable may be alienated when this is permitted by the marriage contract: this is a provision identical to C.N. 1557, the "source" according to Batiza, while the D.L.V. gives no references. Finally D.O. 40 (p. 331) states that a dotal immoveable may be sold with the judge's authorization after certain formalities for certain specific limited purposes. Any moneys left over from such transactions remain dotal effects, and should be employed as such to the wife's benefit.[332] Batiza claims C.N. 1558 as the "almost verbatim" source, and indeed it is almost identical, while the D.L.V. refers to Domat.[333]

The provisions will now be discussed in turn. To some extent D.O. 36 is merely the restatement of the traditional principle of the inalienability of dotal immoveables, and follows the Justinianic pre-Novel 61 version of the *lex Julia de fundo dotali*. What is curious is the stress on the *wife*. The received Roman law forbade the *husband* to alienate even with the consent of his wife. The D.O. has pushed the wife into equal prominence with her husband. Domat, as cited, follows the Roman rule, and does not give the wife such prominence; nor does the fourth *Partida*, which states as follows: "non puede el marido vender, nin enagenar nin malmeter mientre que durare el matrimonio ... la dote que el rescebiese de la mugger. . . ."[334] Febrero states, similarly, that the husband "no los [i.e. dotal immoveables] puede enagenar, obligar, ni hipotecar aunque su muger lo consienta. . . ."[335] He does, however, add the exception that if the wife:

> concurra à la celebracion del contrato, se obliga espontáneamente con juramento à no reclamarlo ni contravenirlo, y renuncie (como puede) el derecho, y accion hipotecaria que la compete contra los bienes de él; pues contiendo estos requisitos, valdró su enagenacion y gravamen.[336]

Febrero does allow then for the alienation of dotal immoveables if the wife takes part in the contract, and on oath renounces her rights of hypothec over the husband's goods for the relevant dotal property. After consideration of the exceptions to D.O. 36 (p. 329), the signficance of this statement of Febrero's will more readily be evaluated. It may be noted, however, that the greater stress the D.O. appears to place on the rights of a wife over her dowry originates in the C.N.: Febrero does not envisage the wife disposing of her dowry. The C.N.

---

[332] The English version is rather curious; but this is unimportant.
[333] Domat, *Loix civiles*, vol. 1, p. 95 (pt. 1, bk. 1, tit. 9, sect. 1, no. 15).
[334] *Part.* 4.11.7.
[335] Febrero, *Contratos*, ch. 2, § 1 no. 8 (vol. 1, p. 298). Febrero, *Juicios*, bk. 1, ch. 3, § 1 no. 39 (vol. 4(1), p. 205), states: "No puede enagenar el marido los bienes dotales immeubles, ò raices de su muger, aunque ésta lo consienta verbalmente."
[336] Febrero, *Contratos*, ch. 2, § 1 no. 8 (vol. 1, p. 298). Febrero, *Juicios*, bk. 1, ch. 3, § 1 no. 39 (vol. 4(1), p. 205 makes a similar statement.

considers the husband as having only a right of usufruct in the dowry: C.N. 1562. The *Partidas*, following the Roman law, regard the husband more as some kind of owner: though with a fairly limited ownership. Febrero considers that in dotal property the husband's right is a usufruct.[337] If the above is correct, then the D.O. redactors, in adopting the C.N.'s stress or emphasis on the wife's actings as regards her dowry, have altered, in a subtle fashion, the balance of the law, since the Castilian sources appear only to conceive of the husband alienating or hypothecating the dowry.

The next article, D.O. 37 (p. 329), has again obviously been copied from the C.N. The *Partidas* contain no such provision; the same can be said for the *Nueva recopilación,* the *Leyes de Toro*, and Domat. Again, this article is predicated on the wife having a greater right over the dowry than her husband. It is not surprising, perhaps, that there are no Castilian sources, as the C.N. here has adopted and, to some extent, amended the *jurisprudence* of some of the regions of *droit écrit.*[338] Thus, this exception to the inalienability of dowry is again of French provenance. It is incompatible with the *Partidas*' notion of the husband's absolute control over the dowry. Although it derogates from that control, the D.O. provision, following the C.N., requires the wife to be authorized, and the article thus fits into the general notion of the incapacity of married women. The stress on the wife is dependent on the existence of the previous article. D.O. 38 (p. 329) is again copied from the C.N. I can trace no equivalent Castilian provision. The D.O. article is again contradicts the *Partidas*' conception of inalienability and the husband's control (though the Castilian law did permit alienation in certain circumstances). In changing the law, the principles of marital authority have been adhered to. D.O. 39 (p. 329) is copied from the C.N. Since by D.O. 1 (p. 323) husbands and wives have been allowed to regulate their property as they wish within certain limits, the existence of the article under discussion is hardly surprising. Again there is no Castilian equivalent and again the French nature of this article is obvious. (D.O. 1 itself is very "French".)[339] D.O. 40 (p. 331) is copied reasonably closely from the C.N. 1558. Domat as cited[340] enunciates a provision fairly similar to the D.O. Once more I can find no Castilian equivalent. This article is not really relevant for the purpose of examining marital authority, but I have included it for completeness.

It is now appropriate to sum up this discussion of these articles by relating them to marital authority. The D.O. redactors, by adopting these C.N. provisions, have altered the law in a subtle way. In so far as they have stressed the interest of the wife in the dowry, they have reduced the husband's control. Nevertheless, they have asserted marital authority by requiring the wife's

---

[337] Febrero, *Contratos*, ch. 2, § 1 no. 6 (vol. 1, p. 297), states that the wife is owner of the dowry and the husband the usufructuary. The dowry is intended (he says) to support the charges of the marriage.

[338] See Maleville, *Analyse*, vol. 3, p. 274.

[339] See supra, text at notes 199–200.

[340] See Domat, *Loix civiles*, vol. 1, p. 95 (pt. 1, bk. 1, tit. 9, sect. 1, no. 15), with the note appended to his provision.

authorization by her husband or the court. This renders the provisions congruent with the other articles on authorization. In the discussion I have stressed the difference of the D.O. articles from the Castilian law; but it should be pointed out that these articles could be regarded more as a development of that law rather than a complete break. The Castilian law showed the same ambiguity over the ownership of dowry, an ambiguity inherited from the Roman law. Febrero shows that dotal property may be alienated with the concurrence of the wife; but, in contradistinction to the French law, it is the husband who is envisaged as actually alienating the property. It may be asserted, therefore, that these articles are of specifically French provenance, and show a weakening of the husband's control over his wife's dowry, along with an assertion of marital authorization of the wife.

It is now convenient to turn to the question of the control over the wife's other property. D.O. 56 (p. 335) states that all the effects of the wife which are not settled as dowry are paraphernal. This is identical to C.N. 1574, which Batiza classes as the "verbatim" source. The D.L.V. refers to *Part.* 4.11.17, Domat,[341] and Febrero.[342] *Part.* 4.11.17 states: "Paraferna son llamadas en griego todos los bienes et las cosas, quier sean muebles ó raices que retienen los mugeres para si apartadamiente et non entran en cuento de dote." This is an identical rule. Domat, section 1, no. 7 as cited, states similarly; his section 4 no. 1 is again compatible and the same section's number 6 states that paraphernal property is distinguished from dowry by the marriage contract. The similarity of all these provisions is hardly surprising, given their common foundation in Roman law. Febrero defines paraphernal bienes as "los que la muger lleva al matrimonio sin incluirlos en las dotales".[343] He also states the difference between *parapherna* and *extradotales*, but opines that "esta diferencia es puramente verbal, y el derecho lo llama indistintamenta *parafernales* segun el idioma Griego, y *extradotales* segun el Latino, y Castellano".[344] Febrero's definition of the wife's *parapherna*, as cited by the D.L.V., is identical to that of the D.O.

A point of some, if minor, interest is that under the Castilian law a wife could have a third class of property-*bienes propios*. Gomez states of the wife:

> [N]am primo potest habere bona dotalia que, fuerunt data in dotem marito, in quibus solus maritus agit tanquam dominus . . . . Secundo potest habere bona paraphernalia, quorum dominium est penes eam, administratio vero penes maritum, in quibis maritus agit sine mandato. Tertio potest habere alia bona propria quorum dominium et administratio est penes eam, in quibis sola uxor potest agere, vel maritus praestita cautione tanquam coniuncta persona. . . .[345]

---

[341] Domat, *Loix civiles*, vol. 1, p. 94 (pt. 1, bk. 1, tit. 9, sect. 1, no. 7), pp. 99–100 (pt. 1, bk. 1, tit. 9, sect. 4, nos. 1 and 6).

[342] Febrero, *Contratos*, ch. 2, § 1 no. 11 (vol. 1, pp. 299–300); Febrero, *Juicios*, bk. 1, ch. 3, § 1 nos. 42 and 54 (vol. 4(1), pp. 206–207, 211–212).

[343] Febrero, *Contratos*, ch. 2, § 1 no. 11 (vol. 1, pp. 299–300).

[344] Febrero, *Juicios*, bk. 1, ch. 3, § 1 nos. 42 (vol. 4(1), pp. 206–207).

[345] Gomez, *op. cit. supra* note 100, pp. 503–504, commentary on *Toro*, 54–59, no. 1.

What is the relationship between this third form of property and the *paraphernal*? Paraphernal property was property brought to the marriage, but not as dowry, and, as will be seen, the husband might, but need not, have been granted administration of it.[346] *Bienes propios* appear to have been property not brought to the marriage, and over which the wife always had control. Thus, *bienes propios* were in the same position as *parapherna* of which the husband had not been granted administration. The difference is perhaps not of importance, and certainly the D.O. redactors have not incorporated it in the Digest. The disappearance of this third class of property would appear (potentially at least) to extend the sphere of a husband's interest in his wife's property. Could this be an unknowing change on the part of the redactors? Febrero does discuss the class of property called *propios*, but, as regards the wife, he classes them with *bienes parafernales*.[347] We may conclude that this class of property might have been known to the redactors. As a class, however, it was not readily distinguishable from the parapherna, and the difference was, perhaps, mainly one of terminology. As regards *bienes propios*, just as *parapherna*, a wife would require authorization to act.[348]

D.O. 58 (p. 335) provides:

> La femme a l'administration et la jouissance de ses biens paraphernaux, mais elle ne peut les aliéner, ni paraître en jugement, à raison desdits biens, sans l'autorisation du mari, ou à son défaut, sans permission de la justice.

Batiza gives C.N. 1576 as the "almost verbatim" source, and the two articles are indeed virtually identical. The D.L.V. cites Domat[349] and Febrero.[350] Domat, as cited, differs from the D.O., as he does not require the wife to be authorized in her dealings with her *parapherna*. Febrero, as cited, mentions the two possibilities, first of the husband having control of the *parapherna*, and second, of the wife having control. In the second case, he points out that the husband has no responsibility.[351] He does not expressly point out that the wife would require authorization for her administration; but, for contracts, she would indeed require authorization under the *Leyes de Toro*, as will be shown.[352] Thus, the Castilian law here would

---

[346] See *infra*, text at notes 349–356.

[347] Febrero, *Contratos*, ch. 2, § 1 no. 13 (vol. 1, p. 300): "Otros se llaman *Propios*, y son los que cada conyuge lleva al matrimonio, y hereda, ò adquirere durante él por ultima voluntad, ò por contrato lucrativo, y à estos llaman tambien hereditarios; en todos tiene su dueño la propriedad y dominio natural, pero en los de la muger toca à su marido el civil para administrarlos, y mantener con sus frutos las cargas del matrimonio, si al tiempo de casarse no se pactó expresamente otra cosa entre los dos en cuanto à los parafernales, como pueden hacerlo."

[348] See generally, de Funiak, *op. cit. supra* note 305, vol. 1, pp. 317–319.

[349] Domat, *Loix civiles*, vol. 1, p. 99 (pt. 1, bk. 1, tit. 9, sect. 4, nos. 2 and 3).

[350] Febrero, *Contratos*, ch. 2, § 1 no. 11 (vol. 1, pp. 299–300); Febrero, *Juicios*, bk. 1, ch. 3, § 1 nos. 46–54 (vol. 4(1), pp. 208–212).

[351] Febrero, *Contratos*, ch. 2, § 1 no. 11 (vol. 1, pp. 299–300); Febrero, *Juicios*, bk. 1, ch. 3, § 1 nos. 46–54 (vol. 4(1), pp. 208–212).

[352] See *infra*, text at notes 392–400; see *supra*, text at notes 80–104.

be roughly identical with the D.O.; it should be noted, however, that authorization in Castilian law was very different from that in the French law.[353]

D.O. 59 (p. 335) states:

> La femme peut donner sa procuration à son mari, comme à toute autre personne, pour administrer ses biens paraphernaux, et dans ce cas, il sera tenu vis-a-vis d'elle, comme toute autre mandataire.

C.N. 1577 is almost identical (and is the source according to Batiza). The D.L.V. refers to Domat[354] and Febrero.[355] Domat and Febrero both allow the wife to grant to her husband administration of her *parapherna*, and he is responsible for it, although neither describe this responsibility as that of a mandatary. In the Castilian law, as in D.O. 62 (pp. 335–337), a husband's estate is tacitly hypothecated for the return of the wife's *parapherna*.[356] This tacit hypothec is preferred, in Castile, to prior personal creditors, and to later creditors whether or not they have an express hypothec, but not to prior creditors with express special or general hypothecs.[357] A further point arises out of D.O. 62; it will be considered below.

D.O. 57 (p. 335) is of some interest. It states that if all the wife's goods are paraphernal, and there is no provision in the marriage contract, then she shall contribute a third of her income to support the charges of the marriage. This is drawn from C.N. 1575. The D.L.V. cites no authorities. This is not surprising, since the C.N. article was a new arbitrary provision.[358] There was no Castilian equivalent. For the Castilian law, it is appropriate to refer back to the discussion above of D.O. 64 (p. 337), which described the composition of the community.[359] It was pointed out that D.O. 64 excluded from the community the fruits of the wife's separate assets; such fruits, under the Castilian law, went to the community and hence to support the charges of the marriage. The article at present under discussion, D.O. 57, helps explain the change in the law contained in D.O. 64. D.O. 57 (which preceeds D.O. 64 in the code) copied the provision of the C.N., and thus necessitated the change in the law on composition of the ganancial community. What the D.O. redactors have done is hand the fruits of her *parapherna* to the wife (unless her husband administers it under D.O. 59) and thus substitute for the sensible Castilian provision the arbitrary one of the C.N. The only reason that can be ascribed for such a change is one of desire to copy the C.N. (or ignorance of the Castilian law, which seems unlikely).

---

353 See *supra*, text at notes 62–104; see *infra*, text at notes 452–455.

354 Domat, *Loix civiles*, vol. 1, p. 99 (pt. 1, bk. 1, tit. 9, sect. 4, nos. 3 and 5).

355 Febrero, *Contratos*, ch. 2, § 1 no. 11 (vol. 1, pp. 299–300); Febrero, *Juicios*, bk. 1, ch. 3, § 1 no. 43 (vol. 4(1), pp. 207–208).

356 See Febrero, *Contratos*, ch. 2, § 1 no. 11 (vol. 1, pp. 299–300).

357 *Ibid.*

358 See for discussion, *infra* on Quebec. See also Maleville, *Analyse*, vol. 3, pp. 287–288. Note that this article arose out of the *droit écrit*, which differed from the Castilian law on community and ownership of the fruits of a wife's *parapherna*.

359 See *supra*, texts at notes 302–306.

Further, D.O. 57 does not make an exception for the husband's administration of the *parapherna*; whereas under D.O. 64 if he has administration and enjoyment of them the fruits go into the community. The law is clearly confused. Whether or not this article has any bearing on *puissance maritale* is difficult to say. It is clear, however, that the redactors were here very influenced by the French code, and readily copied its dispositions.

D.O. 62 (pp. 335–337) has already been referred to.[360] As well as the point already discussed, this article states that, if a husband enjoys the *parapherna*, he is bound by all the obligations of a usufructuary. This part of the article appears to have been copied from C.N. 1580.[361] It raises the question of the nature of the husband's interest in the dowry and *parapherna*. D.O. 43 (p. 331) classes the husband as a usufructuary, and D.O. 29 (p. 329) classes the wife as owner. Both of these articles take these views from French sources: first the C.N., article 1562, and second, Domat.[362] In D.O. 62, the C.N. has again been followed, as the logic of the code required. The statement that the wife is owner of the dowry is traditional.[363] To classify the husband as a usufructuary is rather more problematic. As seen, Febrero did so.[364] In Roman law, according to some sources, *dos* became the property of the husband, but he had to restore it.[365] In fact, throughout the *ancien régime*, the authors disputed over the exact nature of the rights of husband and wife in the dowry.[366] The C.N. chose one solution, the same as Febrero had chosen, and the D.O. redactors did the same. The *Siete Partidas*, reflecting the juristic thought of their period, do not class the husband as a usufructuary. The relevant provisions of the D.O. are obviously strongly influenced by the C.N.: the redactors are copying the French code rather than Febrero. Further, as already pointed out,[367] the C.N. puts a new stress on the wife's interest in the dowry, a stress copied by the D.O. The differences between the C.N. and the Castilian law on this point are more differences of approach or of attitude rather than of anything more significant; but the adoption of the C.N. provisions in the D.O. indicates that it is the French attitude that has been followed.

In summing up the discussion of control over property during marriage, and its consequences for marital authority, the first point to be made is that the whole approach of the D.O. to matrimonial property is, in nature, French rather than Castilian. This is shown by the accent on ante-nuptial marriage contracts and the pervasive influence of French sources in the substance of the law. Some aspects of the Castilian law have been overturned; other areas of the law, which have been left as compatible with the French provisions, have been given a different empha-

---

360 See *supra*, text at notes 354–357.
361 According to Batiza the "almost verbatim" source, first part.
362 See *supra*, text at notes 325–326.
363 See *supra*, text at note 326.
364 See *supra*, text at note 337.
365 See, e.g. Buckland, *Textbook*, pp. 108–110; Corbett, *op. cit. supra* note 53, pp. 177–181.
366 See Brissaud, *History*, pp. 802–803.
367 See *supra*, text at notes 330–337.

sis, as a result of the adoption of French models. In both the D.O. and the Castilian law, the husband controls community property. He controls his wife's dowry. The D.O. redactors, by copying provisions from the C.N., have given greater prominence than is found in the Castilian law to the rights of the wife in her dowry. A wife controls her *parapherna* unless she hands control of it to her husband. The wife's actions with regards to her *parapherna* require authorization, according to both the Castilian law and the C.N. It must be noted, however, that the nature of the requirement of marital authorization in the C.N. and the Castilian law is rather different. The Castilian law was more liberal than the French *droit coutumier* and the C.N. Thus, when this is taken into account, the Castilian law and the C.N., in many ways apparently congruent, may not be as similar as the discussion has already suggested. It is relevant to recall D.O. 4 (p. 325),[368] which gave an account, derived from the *droit coutumier*, of *puissance maritale*, which Pothier described as logically preventing the general authorization of wives. Such general authorizations were permissible in Castille. If this is taken into consideration, it becomes apparent that authorization of the wife as regards her actions with her personal property was very different in the Castilian law and the C.N. Thus, apparently similar attitudes to the wife's actions may well be revealed to be radically different, when the provisions on authorization are examined.

It is worth stressing that the approach to dowry and *parapherna* is heavily influenced by the C.N., in that the wife's interest has been stressed vis-à-vis that of her husoand. This might appear to have lessened a husband's authority over his wife's property; but it should be noted that, along with the apparent technical increase of the wife's interest, the requirements of his authorization have also been emphasized. Although this change is arguably more one of terminology than one with real effects, it is important in revealing the attitude of the redactors in Louisiana. Further, although the Castilian *sociedad de gananciales* has been adopted as the "statutory" matrimonial regime, the composition of the ganancial community has been affected by the reception of C.N. 1575 as D.O. 57 (p. 335): a reception which seems to have caused confusion.[369]

Puissance Maritale: Aspects other than Property

In this subsection we turn to consideration of the non-property aspects of the husband wife relationship, and consider the disposition of authority within the marriage. We shall examine the articles in chapter 4, "Des Droits et Devoirs respectifs des Époux", of the fourth title of Book one of the D.O. This chapter is very similar in form to that of the C.N., and chapter 6 of the fifth title of its first Book has the same rubric. The relevant C.N. chapter contains fifteen articles, however, while that of the D.O. has eleven. In the discussion of the D.O. articles, the nature of the "absent" C.N. provisions will be indicated; but it can straightaway be pointed out that these "absences" are not too significant, and

---

[368] See *supra*, text at notes 306–311.
[369] See *supra*, text at notes 357–360.

that the influence of the C.N. on this chapter is obvious. In this chapter, all of the D.O. provisions, bar the last, are drawing on the 1807 Act, ss. 60–69 inclusive.[370] Linguistically, the D.O. articles are sometimes closer to the C.N., sometimes closer to the Act. In the introduction to this chapter, it was pointed out that the Castilian law was rather more liberal than the C.N. or *droit coutumier* on the question of authorization.[371] Full discussion of the D.O. articles will reveal their attitude; but it can be pointed out that, if they depart from the Castilian law, they are following the 1807 Act, and that this act changed the law, not the D.O. This brings us back to the point above: the absences in the D.O. of articles equivalent to some of the C.N. provisions can tentatively be ascribed to the redactors' following of the Act. The Act did not have sections equivalent to the excluded C.N. provisions. In one sense this is an obviously inadequate explanation: the redactors could depart from the Act, as they did in including C.N. 226 as D.O. 29 (p. 29). Because of this, the excluded C.N. provisions will be examined to see if any reason, other than copying the Act, can be given for the redactor's rejection of them.

In the conclusion to this subsection, we will discuss the 1807 Act, its relation to the D.O. and the previous Castilian law, and its likely source of inspiration on these matters. In the discussion of the articles, it will be shown that the D.O. here embodies a primarily northern French conception of *puissance maritale*, a conception rather different from that of the Castilian law. The Castilian provisions that mean that the nature of *puissance maritale* in that law is radically different will be discussed (mainly) in the concluding remarks to this subsection.

The first article to be examined is D.O. 19 (p. 27), which states that "Le mari et la femme se doivent mutuellement fidélité, secours et assistance." This is identical to s. 60 of the 1807 Act (the source according to Batiza) and very nearly identical to C.N. 212. The D.L.V. cites Pothier[372] and *Part.* 4.2.7 at its end. Pothier, as cited, is roughly congruous with the D.O.: he stresses the reciprocity of these marital duties;[373] he also stresses the duty of the husband to receive and support his wife,[374] and that of the wife to live with her husband (provided he does not leave the *royaume*).[375] *Part.* 4.2.7 is again similar, and stresses the duties of loyalty as promised in marriage supported by the church. This D.O. article is on the lines of a moral precept, and is not really relevant from our point of view, except in so far as infidelity could ground an action for separation.[376]

C.N. 213 is one of the "absences" in the D.O. In the C.N. it is the article following from the above. It states that the husband owes protection to his wife

---

[370] See *supra*, note 177.
[371] See *supra*, text at notes 90–104.
[372] Pothier, *T.C.M.*, pp. 174–175 (nos. 379, 380, 382–383).
[373] Pothier, *T.C.M.*, p. 174 (no. 379).
[374] Pothier, *T.C.M.*, p. 174 (no. 380).
[375] Pothier, *T.C.M.*, p. 175 (nos. 382–383).
[376] See *infra*.

and the wife obedience to her husband. Why would this be excluded? It is a provision compatible with the others of the D.O. and indeed with the Castilian law: the wife's obedience was promised during the religious marriage ceremony. It cannot have been excluded on ideological grounds: the D.O. redactors were hardly champions of women's equality and rights. The only plausible reason that can be given is that here the redactors were following the 1807 Act closely, and it had no equivalent section.

D.O. 20 (pp. 27–29) is as follows:

> La femme est tenue d'habiter avec son mari et de le suivre partout où il juge à propos de resider; le mari est obligé de la recevoir et de lui fournir tout ce qui est nécessaire pour les besoins de la vie, selon ses facultés et son état.

This is almost identical to s. 61 of the 1807 Act, and indeed to both C.N. 214 and the *Proj. An. VIII*, 1.5.64.[377] The D.L.V. refers to Pothier's treatises on *Puissance du Mari*[378] and *Marriage*.[379] In the first treatise cited, he states that a wife has to follow her husband except out of the kingdom, while in the second, as cited, he states a husband has to receive and support his wife, and the wife has to follow him, except out of the kingdom. The D.L.V. makes no reference to Castilian law; but it is obvious that the position there would be the same. Again, this article of the D.O. is typical of its period, and is not significant for our purposes. It should be noted that the D.O. phrases these two duties as equal and reciprocal, but in effect they are not. The wife is in a lesser position. As Pothier says explicitly the duty to follow her husband is part of "les devoirs de soumission qui sont dus à un supérieur".[380]

The next article, D.O. 21 (p. 29) is of more interest:

> La femme ne peut *ester* en jugement sans l'autorisation de son mari, quand même elle serait marchande publique, ou serait séparée de biens d'avec son mari.
>
> (The wife cannot appear in court, without the authority of her husband, although she may be a public merchant or possess her goods separate from her husband (p. 28).

Thus, a wife requires authorization to be either plaintiff or defendant. The Act of 1807, s. 62 was very slightly different:

> La femme ne peut *ester* en jugement sans l'autorisation de son mari, quand même elle serait marchande publique, ou posséderait des biens séparées de son mari.
>
> (The wife cannot appear in court as plaintiff without the authority of her husband, although she may be a public merchant or possess her goods separate from her husband.)

---

[377] Batiza claims these three as equal "almost verbatim" sources.

[378] Pothier, *T.P.M.*, pp. 1–2 (no. 1).

[379] Pothier, *T.C.M.*, pp. 174–175 (nos. 380, 382).

[380] Pothier, *T.P.M.* p. 1 (no. 1).

D.O. 21 has got rid of an apparent difference between the English- and French-language texts of the Act of 1807, which, in its French text had closely followed C.N. 215.[381] (C.N. 215 also refers to wives *non-commune*; this is not applicable given the regime of matrimonial property in the D.O.)[382] This again indicates the extent to which the D.O. redactors were adopting the French conception of *puissance maritale*. The D.L.V. refers to the *Nueva recopilación* and the *Leyes de Toro*,[383] Pothier,[384] and Febrero.[385] Pothier states that a wife cannot appear in count unless authorized. The specific references of the D.L.V. to Febrero are to the ramifications of the Castilian law, rather than to the equivalent provisions, although in one cited section Febrero does state that authorization is required even after separation *e mensa e thoro*.[386] Elsewhere, however, Febrero does give an account of restrictions on the wife's capacity under the *Leyes de Toro*.[387] The *Nueva recopilación* and *Toro* provide thus:

> La muger durante el matrimonio, sin licencia de su marido, como no puede fazer contrato alguno, assi mismo no se puede apartar, ni desistir de ningun contrato que à ella toque, ni dar por quito à nadie del; ni puede fazer casi contrato, ni estar en juizio, faziendo, ni defendiendo, sin la dicha licencia de su marido: y si estuviere por si, ò por su procurador, mandamos, que ne vala lo que fiziere.

Under *Toro* 57, the judge, "con conocimiento de causa legitima ò necessaria", could give the wife authorization, or force the husband to give his.[388] In relevant part, these Castilian provisions might seem very similar to those of the D.O. or C.N. The Castilian law does differ greatly, however, when it is considered that a husband can ratify his wife's unauthorized actions,[389] and can give her a general authorization.[390] Note that the provision just quoted does not mention separation of property. Further, it does not mention wives who are public traders. In the D.O., following the C.N. and the 1807 Act, wives who are public traders require authorization to litigate. The most relevant Castilian *ley* (not cited in the D.L.V. in this connection) is *Fuero real* 3.20.13:

---

[381] Batiza claims these as equal "almost verbatim" sources with *Proj. An. VIII*, 1.5.65, as a subsidiary.

[382] See *infra* on Quebec.

[383] *Rec. Cast.* 5.3.2; *Toro*, 55.

[384] Pothier, *T.P.M.*, p. 22 (no. 55).

[385] Febrero, *Contratos*, ch. 4, § 4 nos. 109–111 (vol. 2, pp. 87–90); Febrero, *Juicios*, bk. 3, ch. 1, § 1 no. 27 (vol. 6(3), p. 38).

[386] Febrero, *Contratos*, ch. 4, § 4 no. 109 (vol. 2, p. 87).

[387] *Ibid.*, ch. 1, § 5 nos. 75–76 (vol. 1, pp. 65–66).

[388] Also *Rec. Cast.* 5.3.4.

[389] *Toro,* 58; *Rec. Cast.* 5.3.5: "El marido puede ratificar lo que su muger oviere fecho sin su licencia, no embargante que le dicha licencia no aya precidido ora la ratificacion sea general ò especial."

[390] *Toro*, 56; Rec. Cast. 5.3.3: "Mandamos, que el marido puede dar licencia general à su muger para contraher, y para hazer todo aquello que no podia fazer sin su licencia: y si el marido se la diere, vala todo lo que su muger hiziere por virtud de la dicha licencia."

> Maguer que muger de su marido no puede fiar ni fazer deuda sin otorgamiento de su marido: pero si fuere muger que vende o compra, por si o aya menester de mercaderia vala todo deuda y toda cosa que fiziere en quanto pertenesce a su menester.

Thus, a wife who was a public trader could contract without authorization. The *ley* does not mention court appearances; nor do Gomez, Febrero and Montalvo in their discussions of wives contracting as public traders.[391] Thus, it would appear that the Castilian authorities do not consider the point. If the general rule, as in *ley* 55 of *Toro*, were applied, then the Castilian law would be as that of the D.O., except for the matter of ratification and general authorization. The width of the phrase "toda cosa que fiziere" might suggest the interpretation that she should be allowed *estar en juicio*, in matters of her trade, without being authorized. What is more important, perhaps, is to understand that the Castilian law and authorities were not so interested as were the French and the D.O. in the point at issue Overall, it would appear that in this article the D.O. has increased the authority of the husband.

We may conclude discussion of this article by pointing out that the D.O. redactors, by following the French text of the Act of 1807, based on C.N. 215, have increased *puissance maritale* in comparison with the Castilian law. The French conception of marital authority, found in both the D.O. and the Act, is wider than the Castilian.

At this point, the redactors of the D.O. have chosen to omit a C.N. provision: C.N. 216. This article states that the husband's authorization is not necessary when the wife is pursued in a police or criminal action. This absence in the D.O. is not very important, and we need not consider it.

D.O. 22 (p. 29):

> La femme même lorsqu'elle est séparée de biens de son mari, ne peut donner, aliéner, hypothéquer ou acquérir à titre onéreux ou gratuit, sans le concours de son mari dans l'acte, ou son consentement par écrit.

This article is virtually identical to s. 63 of the 1807 Act, and C.N. 217.[392] The D.L.V. refers to the *Nueva recopilación* (as quoted in text above) and the *Leyes de Toro*,[393] as well as Pothier[394] and Febrero.[395] The provision of the *Leyes de*

---

[391] Febrero, *Contratos*, ch. 4, § 4 no. 111 (vol. 2, pp. 89–90); Gomez, *op. cit. supra* note 100, pp. 503–504, commentary on *Toro*, 54–59, no. 7; *Fuero real*, 3.20.13 gloss "d" by Montalvo (1544 edition). See *infra*, note 411, where Gomez is quoted.

[392] Curiously enough, the 1807 Act, ch. 17, s. 63 and C.N. 217 are closer to each other than either is to D.O. 22 (p. 29). This is because s. 63 starts "The wife even where there is not a community of goods between her and her husband, or where she holds her property separate . . . ." C.N. 217 starts: "La femme non commune ou séparée de biens . . . ." Both continue thereafter as does D.O. 22 (p. 29). Note that the D.O. makes no allowance for absence of community.

[393] *Toro*, 55, quoted *supra*, text at notes 387–388.

[394] Pothier, *T.P.M.*, pp. 3–9 (nos, 3–14, 15–19). The D.L.V. cites the sections and subsections; the reference here conforms to that generally used in this book.

[395] Febrero, *Contratos*, ch. 4, § 4 nos. 119–112 (vol. 2, pp. 87–91); *ibid.*, ch. 7, § 1 no. 2 (vol. 2, pp. 348–349).

Toro and the *Nueva* is broadly similar to that of the D.O., although they do not mention *séparation de biens*; but the proviso to the discussion of the previous D.O. article must be recalled—the Castilian law allowed general authorization and validation after the act. Thus, although apparently similar, the law was in fact different. Pothier gives an extended discussion of authorization, how it is given, and of women *séparées de biens*. It should be noted that, since Pothier is discussing the pre-Code customary law, authorization, as he describes it, is a much more formal affair than in the C.N. or D.O. articles.[396] Febrero states that a wife requires authorization if separated *e mensa e thoro*,[397] and generally discusses the requirements of authorization from the point of view of notarial practice.[398] It should be pointed out that *séparation de biens*, without *séparation de corps*, did not really exist in Castilian law.[399] The Castilian requirements for authorization were laxer than in the *droit coutumier*.[400] It would be wrong, however, to argue that here the D.O. redactors have adopted the C.N. provisions as a near equivalent to the Castilian law. The D.O. redactors are following the 1807 Act, which has adopted a northern French conception of marital authority, rather different from that of the Castilian law. This article follows the 1807 Act's departure from the Castilian law. *Proj. An. VIII*, 1.5.66, the equivalent article to C.N. 217, is interesting in that it has an extra paragraph stating that "Le consentement du mari, quoique postérieur à l'acte, suffit pour le valider." Thus, the 1800 *Projet* allowed retrospective validation of deeds. This is similar to the Castilian law, and the D.O. redactors have obviously rejected this provision (if they considered it) for the same reasons as they rejected the Castilian equivalents.

D.O. 23 (p. 29) states that: "Si le mari refuse d'autoriser sa femme à *ester* en jugement, le juge peut donner l'autorisation." This is identical to C.N. 218. The English text of the 1807 Act, s. 64, in line with its version of s. 62, only mentions wives as plaintiffs;[401] the French text has "ester en jugement"—both texts specify the judges to whom the wife should apply for authorization.[402] The redactors have adopted the rule of the C.N., essentially the same as the French text of the Act. D.O. 24 (p. 29) provides that:

> Si le mari refuse d'autoriser sa femme à passer un acte, la femme peut le faire citer devant le juge qui peut l'autoriser, à passer cet acte ou lui refuser cette autorisation, après que le mari aura été dûment entendu ou appelé devant lui.

---

[396] Pothier, *T.P.M.*, pp. 3–4 (nos. 3–6 esp. no. 6). On the formalities of authorization in the *ancien droit*, see *infra*, Quebec.
[397] Febrero, *Contratos*, ch. 4, § 4 no. 118 (vol. 2, pp. 96–97).
[398] *Ibid.*, ch. 4, § 4 nos. 110–118 (vol. 2, pp. 88–97).
[399] See *infra*, text at notes 465–473.
[400] See *infra*, text at notes 450–453.
[401] See *supra*, text at notes 380–382.
[402] Batiza classes the C.N. article as the "verbatim" source, and the 1807 Act as a subsidiary, along with *Proj. An. VIII*, 1.5.6.7, first part. 1807 Act, ch. 17, s. 62: "Si le mari refuse d'autoriser sa femme à ester en jugement, tout Juge de la Cour supérieure, ou le Juge de la paroisse où le mari a son domicile puet lui donner l'autorisation."

C.N. 219 is broadly similar in effect, but enters into greater deal about the judge and proceedings.[403] The 1807 Act, by its s. 65, provides similarly to the D.O.; although, as with s. 64, more precise procedural details are given, in this rather resembling the C.N. On both these articles of the D.O., the D.L.V. refers to the same texts, the *Nueva recopilación*, 5.3.4., Pothier,[404] and Febrero.[405] The *Nueva recopilación*, taking its provision from *Toro* 57, provides:

> El juez, con conocimiento de causa legitima, ò necessaria, compela al marido que de licencia à su muger para todo aquello que ella no podria fazer sin licencia de su marido: y si compelido no se la diere, el juez solo se la puede dar.

The effect of this *ley* is broadly similar to that of the D.O. provisions, although the judge's first action is to compel the husband to consent, and only if the husband does not obey, does the judge give authorization. Pothier, as cited, gives the same rule as the D.O. and C.N. Febrero also, of course, recognizes this power of the judge.[406] This article could appear to be an example of Pascal's notion of the D.O. redactors using the C.N. as an expression of the Castilian rules, considering that the Castilian provision is similar in substance to the D.O. and C.N. articles.[407] However, if the context of the provision is borne in mind, it will be obvious that this article is another expression of the importance of northern French *puissance maritale*, as adopted in the 1807 Act and D.O.

D.O. 25 (p. 29) is as follows:

> La femme, si elle est marchande publique, peut, sans l'autorisation de son mari, s'obliger pour ce qui concerne son négoce, et audit cas, elle oblige aussi son mari, s'il y communauté de biens entre eux.
>
> La femme n'est pas réputée marchande publique, si elle ne fait que détailler les marchandises du commerce de son mari, mais seulement quand elle fait un commerce séparé.

C.N. 220 is almost identical, while s. 66 of the 1807 Act is of the same substance.[408] The D.L.V. refers only to Pothier, who does indeed lay down a similar principle.[409] Although the D.L.V. does not cite any Castilian law, it is necessary here to see if we can recover what its provisions would be. (An interesting point is *why* the D.L.V. referred to no Castilian provisions.) A basic text is *Fuero real*, 3.20.13, already quoted.[410] This provides that a wife who is a public trader can

---

[403] Batiza classes C.N. 219 as the "almost verbatim, first part" source, with *Proj. An. VIII*, 1.5.67, second part, as a subsidiary. He ignores the 1807 Act, ch. 17, s. 65.

[404] Pothier, *T.P.M.*, p. 5 (no. 12).

[405] Febrero, *Contratos*, ch. 4 § 4, no. 110 (vol. 2, pp. 88–89); Febrero, *Juicios*, bk. 3, ch 1, § 1 no. 27 (vol. 6(3), p. 38).

[406] See, e.g., Febrero, *Contratos*, ch. 4 § 4, no. 110 (vol. 2, pp. 88–89).

[407] See Pascal, "Reply", pp. 605–607.

[408] Batiza classes the former as the "almost verbatim" source, and the latter and *Proj. An. VIII*, 1.5.68 as subsidiary sources.

[409] Pothier, *T.P.M.*, pp. 9–10 (nos. 20–22), Bug. 7, pp. 9–10. I have amended the D.L.V. citations: see *supra*, note 394.

[410] See *supra*, text after note 391.

oblige herself in the course of that trade, as regards that trade. This is the same as the first part of the first paragraph of D.O. 25. Febrero and Gomez state that a wife who is a public merchant does not require authorization.[411] The Castilian law can also be assumed to be the same as the second paragraph of D.O. 25, since otherwise the wife would not be acting as a public trader, but as an agent for her husband. In the Castilian law, would the wife also obligate her husband if there were community between them? This is more difficult to say, primarily because the most utilized sources, the *Nueva recopilación* and the *Leyes de Toro*, do not directly envisage the situation. Nor do the provisions of the *Fuero real* on the *sociedad de gananciales* (the quoted text is appended to title 20, "De las deudas y de las pagas", almost in the manner of an afterthought). This lack of relevant provisions is undoubtedly the result of the Castilian law's lack of interest (in comparison to the *droit coutumier*) in marital authority. The French *droit coutumier* had a tradition of commentary on the *puissance maritale*, and the question of wives as public traders had frequently been discussed.[412] One point can be made; the profits of the wife's trade would have accrued to the ganancial community.[413] It must be supposed that the wife as public trader was using her own property, since if she were using *sociedad* property, it is doubtful if, given the husband's control, this would have amounted to a separate trade. Thus we must assume that a wife was using her separate property. Thus, the debts she would contract would seem to be separate debts not community debts, although this is unclear. To give an example of the uncertainty, it is convenient to quote de Funiak:

> . . . debts contracted by a spouse in a matter not concerning the actual marriage and the conjugal partnership and not for its benefit were not payable from the community property.[414]
>
> In the Spanish law, on the other hand, the income etc., from the separate property or business interest of either spouse was community property. Hence contracts or transactions in connection with such separate property or separate interests of the spouse which raised obligation on the part of the spouse would usually be transactions to assure or further interests or property rights, the returns from which would belong to the community. Even though the debts or obligations might arise from transactions relating to interests or property belonging individually to the spouse, it would be highly probable that the community had been or would be benefited in some way. And any debt or obliga-

---

[411] Febrero, *Contratos*, ch. 4, § 4 no. 111 (vol. 2, pp. 89–90); and Gomez, *op. cit. supra* note 100, pp. 503–504, commentary on *Toro*, 54–59, no. 7: "Sexto quaero, si uxor sit praeposita alicui officio vel negatiationi sciente et patiente marito, ut quia sit posita mercantiae, vel officio obstetricis, vel chirurgiae vel simili officio, an requiratur licentia mariti in contractibus eius: et breviter et resolutive dico et teneo, quod non, quia eo ipso, quod de voluntate mariti est posita in illo officio visus est licentiam et consensum sibi praestare . . . ." In gloss "d" on *Fuero real*, 3.20.13, Montalvo also talks of *officium obstetricis, vel chirurgiae*. Gomez is either following Montalvo's gloss fairly closely, or these are stock examples.

[412] See *infra*, on Quebec.

[413] See *supra*, discussion at notes 302–306 and 358–360; Pugh, *op. cit. supra* note 80, p. 6.

[414] De Funiak, *op. cit. supra* note 305, vol. 1 p. 448.

> tion relating to the community affairs and the success of the conjugal partnership would come under the head of a community debt.[415]

Note de Funiak's uncertainty. The Castilian law in this point was simply unclear. If de Funiak is correct, and he is plausible, then the *sociedad* would be obligated for the wife's debts arising out of her separate trade. Would her husband be liable? Again the Castilian sources do not envisage this question or deal with it in any way. One can infer that he is liable as regards his share of the community property. It is clear that we need not pursue this line of enquiry any further, as to do so would be pointless. Perhaps if we prosecuted the investigation to its logical end we might come up with a proposition similar to that of D.O. 25 (p. 29) and C.N. 220.

That we might result with a provision similar to D.O. 25 is not any support for Pascal.[416] What is important from the above discussion is that the Castilian sources just simply *do not deal* with the question on hand. The long quotation from de Funiak above is not based on any legal sources: it is his inference from the known provisions of the law. He is extending the law by a process of logical deduction. The Castilian law, just as it did not properly consider the question of wives as public traders, so it did not consider husbands' liability for debts arising out of their wives' trade. From this we must conclude that D.O. 25 (p. 29) is indeed a very French provision: the Castilian law, in the sources used, simply did not regulate the matter. The French law, because of its academic discussions of *puissance maritale*, regulated the question: its developed concept of marital authority had been worked out to include propositions of law such as that embodied in D.O. 25 (p. 29) and C.N. 220. This explains why the D.L.V. referred to no Castilian provisions: apart from *Fuero real* 3.20.13 there were none in point. This article of the D.O. is therefore of particular importance in showing that the Castilian approach to this area of the law was entirely superseded by the French, even if this supersession came from the 1807 Act rather than the D.O. itself. It should also be pointed out that this article might well usefully fill a gap in the old law.

The next D.O. article to be discussed is article 26 (p. 29): "Si le mari est interdit ou absent, le juge peut en connaissance de cause, autoriser la femme, soit pour *ester* en jugement, soit pour contracter." This is identical to C.N. 222,[417] and the same principle is enunciated in s. 67 of the 1807 Act.[418] The D.L.V. cites the *Nueva recopilación*, 5.3.6, Febrero[419] and Pothier.[420] Here the English text of the 1807 Act also includes the wife as defendant as well as

---

[415] *Ibid.*, p. 450.

[416] See *supra*, note 407.

[417] C.N. 221 has been excluded from the D.O.: it is not relevant here.

[418] The former is the "verbatim" source according to Batiza, with the latter and *Proj. An. VIII*, 1.5.70 as subsidiary sources.

[419] Febrero, *Contratos*, ch. 4, § 4 no. 110 (vol. 2, pp. 88–89); Febrero, *Juicios*, bk. 3, ch. 1, § 1 no. 26 (vol. 6(3), p. 38) (the last is a mistake in the D.L.V. for no. 27).

[420] Pothier, *T.P.M.*, pp. 11–12 (nos. 25–27). The D.L.V. cites these sections in a different way: see *supra*, note 394.

plaintiff, in contrast to ss. 62 and 64.[421] The *Nueva recopilación* (the relevant passage being the 59th *ley de Toro*) states that when "el marido estuviere ausente, y no se espera de proximo venier, ò corre peligro en la tardenza", then the court, "con conocimiento de causa", when such cause is legitimate or necessary, may authorize the wife to act, such authorization being as valid as one from the husband. This is broadly similar to the provision of the D.O., except that interdicted husbands are not mentioned. Febrero states:

> La muger casada no puede comparecer en juicio, ni elegir Procurador sin licencia de su marido, à menos que esté ausente del Pueblo donde se ha de litigar, y no espere su pronto regreso, que en este caso puede el Juez concedérsela con prévio conocimiento de causa, ò que el marido sea loco, furioso, mudo, ò mentecato, pues aunque esté presente, se le estima por ausente. . . .[422]

Thus, although interdiction is not specifically mentioned, the circumstances in which a wife could go to court for authorization were much the same as in D.O. 26 (p. 29).[423] Like Febrero, Pothier, as cited, discusses the authorization of wives whose husbands have succumbed to madness or have disappeared: two obviously related topics, which are included in the D.O. article's more general terms. Thus, the Castilian law and the French law were similar to each other and to the D.O. The article of the D.O. is, however, of a French cast, and its phrasing and terminology suggest the influence of the concept of *puissance maritale* found in the *droit coutumier*. It should always be remembered that in Castile a wife's capacity to act was always greater, and the laws interpreted liberally.

D.O. 27 (p. 29) states as follows:

> Toute autorisation générale, même stipulée par contrat de mariage, n'est valable que quant à l'administration des biens de la femme.

C.N. 223 and the 1807 Act, s. 68 are identical.[424] The D.L.V. comments that this article is a "dérogation" from *ley* 56 of *Toro*, the *Nueva recopilación*, 5.3.3,[425] and a statement of Febrero.[426] This is correct: Castilian law allowed general authorizations. This article of the D.O., and this section of the 1807 Act, overturn the Castilian law. They import, into Louisiana, the much stricter French conception of *puissance maritale*. The implications of this will more fully be worked out later; but it should be noted that it was such general authorizations that Pothier considered to be contrary to the *puissance du mari*.[427]

---

[421] Why there should be these differences between the sections of this Act is unclear.

[422] Febrero, *Juicios*, bk. 3, ch. 1, § 1 no. 27 (vol. 6(3), p. 238).

[423] Note that Febrero, following the Roman law, includes deaf mutes among those interdicted. The modern French law and the D.O. would not do so: Maleville, *Analyse*, vol. 1, pp. 433–434; Inst. 1.23.4.

[424] The "verbatim" sources according to Batiza, with *Proj. An. VIII*, 1.5.70 as a subsidiary source.

[425] See *supra*, note 390.

[426] Febrero, *Contratos*, ch. 4, § 4 no. 110 (vol. 2, pp. 88–89).

[427] See *supra*, text at notes 307–310.

The redactors of the D.O. decided not to include C.N. 224 or some equivalent. This is an interesting article in this context and it will be discussed later.[428]

D.O. 28 (p. 29) states that:

> La nullité fondée sur le défaut d'autorisation, ne peut être opposée que par la femme, par le mari, ou par leurs hêritiers.

C.N. 225 is identical; the 1807 Act, s. 69 provides the same.[429] The D.L.V. gives no references. This article embodies a notion of the relative nullity of the unauthorized actions of wives, following the C.N., which had here innovated, the old *droit coutumier* having rendered unauthorized actions absolutely null.[430] The Castilian law was as follows. *Ley* 55 of *Toro* stated that unauthorized actions of wives were invalid.[431] One point should again be recalled: husbands could give a general authorization, so individual authorizations were not so crucial. *Ley* 58 of *Toro*[432] allowed a husband to validate retrospectively, in general or in particular, actions of his wife. These are the only relevant legal provisions. It would appear that unauthorized actions were invalid until ratified, which is obviously unsatisfactory. Llamas y Molina (who was not a potential source for the D.O.) pointed out the confusion caused by the contradictory nature of the two laws.[433] Further, the *Leyes de Toro* did not consider who had the right to have declared a concluded contract (*ex facie* valid) null and void on the grounds of want of authorization. This is presumably because of the lack of juristic attention devoted to marital authority in general. What this amounts to, in effect, is that on this question the *Leyes de Toro* are unsatisfactory. D.O. 28 (p. 29) can thus be declared to be firmly rooted in the French tradition, not the Castilian.

Having said that the provisions of *Toro* were unsatisfactory, it is necessary briefly to examine the attitude of the Spanish authorities to the interpretation of this question. The typical attitude was that of Antonio Gomez,[434] and in his commentary on *Leyes* 54–59 *de Toro* he addressed himself to the question: "si contractus sit utilis ipsi mulieri, an possit fieri et valere sine licentia viri?" The way in which he argued the point, and the conclusion he came to, are both instructive. It should first be noted that he had already admitted the incapacity of married women to contract without *licentia mariti*.[435] He first points out that it is

---

[428] See *infra*, text at notes 441–449.

[429] Batiza states that the former is the "verbatim" source, with the latter and *Proj. An. VIII*, 1.5.73 as subsidiary sources.

[430] See *infra* on Quebec.

[431] See *supra*, text between notes 387 and 388.

[432] See *supra*, note 389.

[433] Llamas y Molina, *op. cit. supra* note 99, commentary on *Toro*, 58, no. 7: "Como la ley establece por regla general que en vertud de la ratificacion general ò especial subsista el acto que habia celebrado la muger sin licencia de su marido, y entre los actos de esta especie se prohiba la comparencia en juicio, bien sea demandado ò respondiendo, segun la ley 55, se sigue claramente que tambien esta especie de actos celebrados por la muger sin licencia de su marido son comprendidos en la presente ley, y se revalidan por la ratification."

[434] Gomez, *op. cit. supra* note 100, pp. 503–504, commentaries on *Toro*, 54–59.

[435] See *ibid.*, the six *conclusiones* at the start of his first commentary on *Toro*, 54–59.

open to the husband not to ratify the unauthorized contract. He then gives an extended discussion of the position of the contracts of unauthorized minors, pointing out the circumstances in which their contracts would be valid despite want of authorization from their tutors or curators, and, with much citation of Justinian's Code and Digest, and of jurists such as Baldus, Bartolus and Albericus, he concludes that the general view was that the contracts of minors, unauthorized by tutors or curators, were valid, if the contracts were to the benefit of the minors. Following the obvious analogy, he turns to the provisions of *Toro* on the contracts of married women; what he says is worth quoting in full:

> [U]bi habetur, quod quando maritus est absens et non speratur venire de proximo, et contractus appareat utiles mulieri, potest adiri iudex ut praestet licentiam in defectum mariti: ergo sentit clare, quod etiam, si contractus sit utilis, non valet, nec potest fieri sine licentia mariti: quia notabiliter respondeo et intelligo ut requiratur licentia, ut semper et perpetuo valeat et teneat, licet postea deficiat utilitas contractus: sed in nostro casu et quaestione utilitas debet durare et probari ut valeat et teneat contractus, quo casu valebit et tenebit contractus sine aliqua licentia mariti vel iudicis.[436]

In other words, if the *utilitas* of the contract (that is its benefit) lasts and can be proved, then the contract is valid and adhered to without any authorization, whether from the husband or the judge. Febrero stated the law to be that, when the wife contracted unauthorized, then the contract was valid "quando hace contrato es util".[437]

The Castilian law may thus be seen to have been rather different from that in the C.N., D.O., and Act of 1807. What is most telling, however, is the very different way in which Gomez conceived of the problem. The C.N. provisions considered unauthorized acts as null *ab initio*, whereas the Castilian law did not. Ultimately, the effect of the Castilian law and of the C.N. might broadly be the same; but the whole approach to marital authority on this question was different. Authorization under the Castilian law lacked the rigour it had in northern France. Here the D.O. and 1807 Act imported the French conception of *puissance du mari*.

The final D.O. article to be discussed in this subsection is D.O. 29 (p. 29): "La femme peut tester sans l'autorisation de son mari." This is identical to C.N. 226.[438] The D.L.V. cites no works or statutes. There is no equivalent provision in the 1807 Act. This article was included in the C.N. because several *coutumes*—such as those of Burgundy and Normandy—had taken *puissance maritale* to the extent of requiring a husband to authorize his wife to make a will.[439] C.N. 226 is thus the product of specifically French circumstances and the extended scope of *puissance maritale* in the *droit coutumier*. The D.L.V. cites no Castilian sources: this is hardly surprising, again because the whole thrust of marital

---

[436] *Ibid.*, commentary no. 2 on *Toro*, 54–59.

[437] Febrero, *Contratos*, ch. 4, § 4 no. 102 (vol. 2, pp. 89–90).

[438] According to Batiza, the "verbatim" source, with *Proj. An. VIII*, 1.5.74 as a subsidiary source.

[439] See Maleville, *Analyse*, vol. 1, pp. 208–209; see *infra*, on Quebec.

authorization in Castille was so radically different from that in France that in the *Leyes de Toro*, for example, it would never have been considered that a wife might need her husband's authorization to make a will. Such an authorization would have been the antithesis of the general Castilian approach. In so far as this is the case, one can say that D.O. 29 indeed expresses the pre-codification Castilian law; but the fact that it was thought necessary to insert such a provision shows the extent to which the French concept of *puissance maritale*, its individual provisions and modes of expression, had been adopted into Louisiana by the 1807 Act and the Digest. Gomez, in commenting on *ley* 3 of *Toro* (a general provision on testation), does say: "Ex quo infero quod licet mulier coniugata hodie in nostro regno, non possit contrahere sine licentia mariti, tamen bene poterit testari."[440] The fact that this is the *only* statement he makes on the question, and that it comes in a discussion on testaments, not in the discussion on authorization, shows the extent to which such a conception would have been contrary to the approach of the Castilian law. D.O. 29 (p. 29) originates in the French conception of *puissance maritale*: the fact that the individual provision coincides with the Castilian law is fortuitous.

Before going on to discuss the conclusions to be drawn from the discussion in this subsection, it is appropriate to return to the exclusion of C.N. 244 from the D.O. It provided: "Si le mari est mineur, l'autorisation du juge est nécessaire à la femme, soit pour ester en jugement, soit pour contracter." This provision in the C.N. removed an absurdity from the old customary law,[441] to some extent reduced—if slightly—marital authority, and, in strict theory, was illogical.[442] There are two points at issue here. First, would such a provision have been useful in Louisiana? Second, why was it not adopted? The first question is not easily answered. There does seem something curious in allowing a minor to authorize his major wife to do something he himself might not be able to do. This brings up points of law which will be discussed in answering the second question. In fact, the question as to suitability must be left open: there can really be no definitive answer. As to the second question there are some relevant points to be made. The Castilian law did not consider the question of minor husbands as separate from that of adult ones: the laws of *Toro* spoke of husbands generally. Further, the *Siete Partidas* had introduced into the Castilian law the Roman distinction between pupillage and minority, minors having greater capacity than pupils and acting along with their curators.[443] The French customary law and the C.N. did not make this distinction: anyone below the age of majority was a minor in a unified notion of minority. In the French customary law and the C.N., the question of minors authorizing their wives was an acute

---

440 Gomez, *op. cit. supra* note 100, p. 12, commentary on *Toro*, 3, no. 5.
441 Maleville, *Analyse*, vol. 1, p. 208; see *infra*, on Quebec.
442 See *infra*, on Quebec for a full discussion.
443 See *Part.* 6.16 generally, esp. *leyes* 1 and 13. Minguijón, *op. cit. supra* note 84, vol. 1, p. 139, states: "En las *Partidas* la institución única, que el derecho germano y nuestros fueros establecián para la guarda de los menores, se ve sustituída por el doble sistema romano de la tutela y la curatela."

problem, because of the minor's very limited contractual capacity. On the other hand, in Castilian law as expressed in the *Partidas* (although the latter did not treat of authorization), this problem would not be acute, as minors, following the Roman law, would have a greater capacity to act for themselves. Only those who were minors under curators could marry, as only they were above the age of puberty.[444] There would be no conflict with *potestad paterna*, because, under *ley* 47 *de Toro*, marriage emancipated.[445] This explains why the Castilian sources, in contradistinction to the *droit coutumier*,[446] ignored this question: it simply did not arise. Further, the fact that Gomez, for example, did not discuss this question is also a reflection of the relative unimportance and lax nature of marital authorization in the Castilian law when compared to the northern French. In other words, in the Castilian law, the dealings of married minors would be dealt with under the general law on minority. Instructive in this respect is Febrero's discussion of *Part.* 6.17.3: this *ley* stated that a husband ought not to be *guardador* of the goods of his minor wife, lest the wife, because of her love for her husband, not demand the correction of his mismanagement. Instead the husband should go to the judge for the appointment of a *guardador* of his wife's goods, a *guardador* who will be above suspicion. Febrero concluded that if a wife was under twenty-five, then the validation of her contract required the intervention of a judge and a curator.[447] This restriction did not apply to a husband appearing in court for his wife, nor to his actions with *bienes dotales*. Febrero did not mention minor husbands. The Castilian law dealt with this matter from the perspective of minority, rather than from that of marital authority. The emphasis of the law was different from that of the *droit coutumier*, reflecting the different outlooks on authorization by the husband, and on minority. In the D.O., the redactors have followed the Castilian divisions of nonage into pupillage and minority, which might well explain why the C.N. provision has not been followed.

There are two further potential explanations of why the C.N. has not been followed here. First, the C.N. provision was an intrusion into the customary law conception of *puissance du mari*, which it rendered illogical in part.[448] Pothier said:

> Un mari, quoique mineur, a le droit de puissance maritale sur la personne de sa femme, quoiqu'elle soit majeure; d'où il suit qu'un mari, quoique mineur, a le

---

[444] See *supra*, text at notes 212–216 for discussion of D.O. 6 (p. 25).

[445] "El hijo o hija casada y velado sea avido por emancipado, en todas cosas para siempre." See *infra* on paternal power.

[446] Loisel, *op. cit. supra* note 62, bk. 1, tit. 2, rule 21, said: "Un mari mineur peut auctoriser sa femme majeure sans qu'elle s'en puisse faire relever: mais bien luy." The whole question of authorization by minors in the *droit coutumier* will be canvassed *infra* on Quebec. Some commentators had thought they could not so authorize their wives; but by the eighteenth century, it was firm law that they could.

[447] Febrero, *Contratos*, ch. 4, § 4 no. 112 (vol. 2, pp. 90–91).

[448] See *infra*, on Quebec, especially the reasoning of the redactors of the Quebec code.

> pouvoir d'autoriser sa femme, soit qu'elle soit mineure, soit qu'elle soit majeure, ce pouvoir étant un effet et une dépendance de la puissance qu'il a sur elle.
>
> Un mari mineur, quoiqu'il n'ait pas le pouvoir d'aliéner ses propres biens immeubles, a néanmoins le pouvoir d'autoriser sa femme majeure pour l'aliénation des immeubles de cette femme.[449]

Hence, in the *droit coutumier*, the *puissance du mari* was such that a minor husband could validly authorize his adult wife. The C.N. provision under consideration detracted from the logic of the traditional *puissance*. The D.O. redactors, in excluding this C.N. provision, were following the premisses of the *puissance maritale* of northern France to their logical conclusion. They had introduced in every aspect so far the rigorous customary law conception; Pothier's views were well known to them. By omitting the C.N. provision, they allowed the customary law notion to remain logical. The D.L.V. contains no specific reference to Pothier's relevant provisions; but this is inevitable given the fact that specific references could only be made in connection with specific articles. Their omission of this article allowed the old French law to be in force and prevented specific reference to that law in the D.L.V. The desire to introduce the rigours of the customary law *puissance maritale* provides another explanation of this absence of C.N. 224 in the D.O. The final point in connection with this omission in the D.O. is to do with the 1807 Act. In all the articles of the chapter under consideration, with the exception of D.O. 29 (p. 29), the redactors have followed ss. 60–69 of the Act in sequence, even if they have sometimes preferred the expression of the C.N. to that of the Act.

There are thus three possible reasons for the omission of a version of C.N. 224 from the D.O. The omission might well have been the result of all three possible influences acting together. The redactors, following the lead of the 1807 Act, throughout this chapter have introduced the concept of *puissance maritale* found in the *droit coutumier*. The inclusion of C.N. 224 would have destroyed the pure logic of their innovation.[450] The exclusion of this article found precedent in the 1807 Act: the redactors' examination of the *Nueva recopilación* would have shown that no equivalent provision was contained therein. Hence, everything would indicate to the redactors that C.N. 224 should not be copied in their code. That the redactors have copied so completely the concept of *puissance du mari* would strongly suggest that their prime motive in excluding C.N. 224 was the desire to follow this concept in all its ramifications. Following the Castilian law could have been no more than an added—and quite

---

[449] Pothier, *T.P.M.*, p. 12 (nos. 29–30).

[450] This interpretation of the exclusion of C.N. 224 is supported by the actions of the redactors of the 1825 C.L., who, in the section of their code on the emancipation of minors, recommended, in the *1823 Projet*, p. 29, the inclusion of an article, which became C.L. 368, which read: "Le mari mineur peut non seulement ester en justice sans l'assistance d'un curateur mais même autoriser sa femme à y paraître." The inclusion of this article amounts to a recognition that the Louisiana code, whether that of 1808 or of 1825, included a conception of *puissance du mari* deriving from the *droit coutumier*.

incidental—bonus, since the redactors had already so vigorously departed from its general approach and provisions on marital authorization.

By now it should be clear that this aspect of the D.O. is radically different from the equivalent Castilian provisions. These articles, following the 1807 Act, amounted to a significant restriction of the capacity of married women under that law. The equivalent Castilian laws were less comprehensive: wives could be given a general authorization and their actions retrospectively validated, even by a judge. Further, the provisions were liberally interpreted. Another example from Gomez can be adduced to show the liberal interpretation of the *leyes de Toro*. In the *droit coutumier*, authorization had to be very formal; it had to express, and it was disputed whether it had to be in the deed itself or could be in a preceding "acte".[451] C.N. 217 (as followed by D.O. 22 (p. 29)) mitigated this somewhat; but the husband still had to consent in writing or concur in the deed. The *leyes de Toro* did not regulate how authorization should be indicated; but Gomez was of no doubt but that the mere presence of the husband, without his speaking a word, when his wife contracted, was sufficient to render the contract validly authorized.[452] Febrero too was of this opinion.[453]

In sum, there is an obvious and radical difference in attitude between the Castilian and French laws: here the 1807 Act adopted the French approach and the D.O. followed it. It has already been explained that Pothier considered the possibility of general authorizations, even in the marriage contract, as contradicting the basic premisses of puissance maritale, namely that *vir est caput mulieris* and was, by virtue of his superiority, the necessary guide and controller of the conjugal association as regards person and property.[454] In the Castilian law, however, general authorizations were permissible, contracts could be retrospectively validated either in particular or general by either the husband or the judge;[455] in the opinion of one of the leading jurists (and he was not alone in his opinion) unauthorized contracts, if beneficial to the wife, were valid. Clearly, the whole concept of marital authority and its concomitant, married women's incapacity, was, in the Castilian law, radically different from that in the French customary law and the C.N. In short, married women had effectively much greater capacity under the *Leyes de Toro*.

---

[451] See e.g., the *Coutume de Paris*, art. 223 on the formalities of the old law. See *infra* on Quebec for a full discussion of the old law; some *coutumes* were not so rigorous as that of Paris.

[452] Gomez, *op. cit. supra* note 100, p. 505, commentary on *Toro*, 54–59, no. 5: "Quarto quaero, si uxor contrahat cum alio in praesentia mariti, an sufficiat eius taciturnitas? Et videtur quod non, sed requiritur consensus expressus [he here cites various authorities including Baldus] quia verba statuti debent intelligi proprie, et ideo non sufficit sola praesentia mariti cum tacurnitate: quia est fictus et improprius consensus. Sed certe ego tenerem contrarium, quia praedictae leges regni non requirunt consensum mariti pro forma et solemnitate actus sed pro evitando damno et praeiudicio eius."

[453] Febrero, *Contratos*, ch. 4, § 4 no. 111 (vol. 2, pp. 89–90).

[454] See *supra*, text at notes 307–311, and 424–427. It will be recalled that the D.L.V. referred specifically to this passage of Pothier.

[455] See Llamas y Molina, *op. cit. supra* note 99, commentary on *Toro*, 59, no. 3; Febrero, *Contratos*, ch. 4, § 4 no. 110 (vol. 2, pp. 88–89).

It is thus quite certain that the redactors of the D.O. have accepted the French concept of *puissance du mari*. It is important to try to recover their reasons for doing so, in order to explore the causes for these changes in the law. The existence of the 1807 Act has to be taken into account: it was this Act which originally introduced the *puissance du mari* of the *droit coutumier* into the territory. Further, the similarity of this Act to the C.N. and its *projet* (to which it is closer does not matter here) is far too great to be coincidental. The Act must have been, at the least, strongly influenced by the French law, and it thus caused a radical departure from the Castilian model of *puissance maritale*. The existence of this recent legislation inevitably tied the hands of the redactors. Nonetheless, whatever the motives of the legislature, it is certain that the D.O. redactors approved of this change in the law.[456] This is easily demonstrated. First, their articles on matrimonial property, none of which were affected by this Act, embodied the French conception of *puissance du mari*.[457] Second, they ensured that the limitations on the capacity of married women found in the Act, ss. 62 and 64, were made to conform directly to the articles of the C.N., thus ensuring that they exactly matched those found in the *droit coutumier*. The inclusion of D.O. 29 (p. 29) also shows the extent to which the redactors were copying the C.N. on this point. Third, the exclusion of C.N. 224 (which could have been included without disturbing the 1807 Act), given the close attention paid by the redactors to the French code, shows how closely they were adhering to the customary law conception of *puissance du mari*, as presented, for example, by Pothier.[458] Fourth, the redactors, without departing from the individual sections of the 1807 Act, could have defeated the policy of its provisions by inserting articles equivalent to *leyes* 56 or 59 of *Toro*. Such articles would have redirected the law towards the Castilian model. Instead, they chose to ensure the provisions in ss. 62 and 64 were made the same as the French law. Fifth, the redactors could have openly amended the law provided in the 1807 Act. The title of the Digest acknowledged that some amendments were included in the provisions. It would always have been open to the legislature to reject such amendments. There can be no doubt, however, that the redactors preferred the French provisions, and that they deliberately extended the 1807 Act's introduction of the French concept of *puissance du mari*.

Some points should be made on the redactors' reasons for adopting the French provisions, and the suitability of such provisions for Louisiana. First, it is obvious that the redactors did not adopt these provisions through ignorance of

---

[456] It would be of great interest to know the circumstances surrounding the specific background to the passing of the Act. Who drafted it? Why did it change the law in this way? Is it evidence of an ongoing revival of French law in the early territorial period? Consider James Brown's remark, quoted Dargo, *Jefferson's Louisiana*, p. 115, that the future House of Representatives in the territory would be dominated by French inhabitants "attached to French Law . . . [passing] only acts resembling the Civil Law and the Spanish Ordinances formerly in force here".

[457] These articles, in the sequence of the D.O., of course follow long after those presently under discussion.

[458] That is, if my argument is correct. See *supra*, text between notes 441–449.

the Castilian law. The Castilian provisions were readily ascertainable in the *Nueva recopilación*; and the liberal juristic interpretation of these provisions could be found in Febrero, whose work was extremely popular in Spanish America.[459] Second, that the redactors were using the Code Napoléon as a model did not require the adoption of these provisions. The general scheme of the French code (or its *projet*) could have been followed, but with minor changes made in the text to render the provisions on authorization like those in the *Leyes de Toro*. This would still have been a rapid method of redaction.[460] The redactors clearly preferred the *puissance maritale* of the *droit coutumier*. There remain two (compatible) possibilities. The redactors were swayed by the legal-technical excellence of the Code Napoléon, and they approved of the very great incapacity of married women. The thinking of the period favoured the husband as controller of the household,[461] and, indeed, at the time of Louisiana's codification, there appears to have been an intensification of the social authority of the husband, in comparison to the eighteenth century (at least among middle class families).[462] The *Leyes de Toro* cannot be described as favouring the emancipation of women—the husband was clearly the head of the household; but the wife's capacity was less circumscribed. The ideology of the husband as head of the household did not necessitate the adoption of the French provisions, because the *Leyes de Toro* themselves gave sufficient symbolic assertion of that ideology. It is possible that the Castilian provisions would have been more useful, in facilitating economic activity and making for greater contractual certainty. Married women's property could have been dealt with much more simply. Only in New Orleans would it have been relatively easy for a woman to go to court to obtain judicial authorization for each act, were her husband away. A system of general authorization and the possibility of the ratification of unauthorized actions would have been, potentially at least, useful. The French provisions on women as public traders made more economic sense in that they were more thoroughly worked out and systematic. Women separated from bed and board still required authorization. Separation from bed and board will be discussed later; but it may be pointed out that this provision was amended in the 1825 C.L.[463] The only "improvement" (in a functional sense) made by following the C.N. was in D.O. 25 (p. 29), which decided that a woman who was a public trader obligated her husband, if they were in community of property.[464] We may conclude that these changes in the law were not introduced because they

---

[459] De Funiak, *op. cit. supra* note 305, vol. 1, pp. 277–281, expresses regret that Febrero was used so much in America, since he was not a jurist. The use of Febrero's work is not really strange; it was reasonably concise and clear, it was written in the vernacular, and, above all, it was practice-oriented. He reports the decisions of the great jurists, but gives instructions as to how, for example, contracts should be drawn up to be valid. De Funiak in particular regrets the use of Febrero in early U.S. cases; but his work was used extensively throughout Spanish America.

[460] And was one the redactors adopted in many instances.

[461] See *supra*, text at notes 37–38 and 169–174.

[462] See *supra*, text at notes 37–38 and 105–106.

[463] See *1823 Projet*, p. 10.

[464] See *supra*, text at notes 408–416.

brought about an improvement in the economic functioning of society. It is a fair surmise that as regards most (if not all) of these provisions, the redactors did not really consider the potential economic impact.

That the ideology of the subjection of women to their husbands was very influential in Louisiana is suggested by the passing of the 1807 Act, the provisions of which gave expression to the views of the Louisiana legislators. This ideology was one cause of the adoption of the provisions of the French law. Another, perhaps more important cause was the prestige and modernity of the French code, taken along with the trend set by the 1807 Act itself. Further, although it might possibly be argued that the Castilian law was more sensible in a functional manner, the C.N. provisions were not such as to impede in any way the functioning of Louisiana society, while at the same time they asserted the social aspirations of Louisiana's élite and middle classes.

Effect of *Séparation de Corps* or *Séparation de Biens* on the Husband and Wife Relationship

Having discussed the *puissance du mari* over the property and person of his wife, it is appropriate now to examine separation of property and separation from bed and board, in order to ascertain the effect these had on the *puissance du mari*. Discussed in turn will be: first, how separation of property comes about; second, how that from bed and board comes about; and third, the effect of both of these on *puissance maritale*. Both have the same effect on marital authority over property, as under D.O. 17 (p. 35), *séparation de corps* results in separation of property.

D.O. 86 (pp. 341–343) states thus:

> La femme peut, pendant le mariage, former contre le mari une demande en séparation de biens, toutes les fois que sa dot est mise en péril par le mauvaise conduite du mari, ou autrement, ou lorsque le désordre de ses affaires fait craindre que ses biens ne soient pas suffisans pour remplir les droits et reprises de sa femme.

(D.O. 87–89 (p. 343) lay down the procedure for *séparation de biens*.) D.O. 86 (pp. 341–343) is very similar in substance and phrasing to C.N. 1443 (first paragraph) and *Proj. An. VIII*, 3.10.57.[465] On this article, the D.L.V. refers to *Part.* 4.11.29, Domat,[466] Febrero[467] and Pothier.[468] *Part.* 4.11.29 states that a wife can demand restitution of her dowry if she fears that her husband's mismanagement will result in its loss; however, if her husband has always made good provision in managing that which he has, and has not misused that which has been placed in his care, but has come to poverty for different reasons (that is, not by reason of his own mismanagement) then she cannot demand restitu-

---

[465] According to Batiza, the latter is the "almost verbatim" source, the former a subsidiary one.
[466] Domat, *Loix civiles*, vol. 1, p. 100 (pt. 1, bk. 1, tit. 9, sect. 5, nos. 1 and 2).
[467] Pothier, *T. Comm.*, pp. 275–276 (nos. 510–512).
[468] Febrero, *Contratos*, ch. 2, § 1 no. 10 (vol. 1, p. 299).

tion of her dowry during the marriage.[469] The cited passage of Febrero provides for the restitution of the dowry of the wife if her husband dissipates or fritters away her dowry; for success in the action, however, the husband must be coming "à inopia por su culpa".[470] Like the *Partidas*, Febrero required there to be fault on the part of the husband. Domat defines separation of property, and states that it can only take place when the husband's affairs are in such disorder, and his estate so small, that his wife's property is in danger. Pothier makes similar statements; but it is interesting to note the following:

> Il n'est pas nécessaire que le mauvais état des affaires du mari soit arrivé par sa faute ou par sa mauvaise conduit. Quoique le dérangement de ses affaires s'est arrivé sans sa faute . . . il suffit, pour obtenir la séparation, que les biens du mari ne soient plus suffisants pour répondre de la dot de la femme.[471]

This seems rather different from the *Partidas*' provision, which apparently requires fault on the part of the husband. As a protection, a wife had a tacit hypothec over her husband's property for the return of her dowry.[472] The Castilian and French laws were essentially the same in allowing a wife to sue for the restitution of her dowry, were it at risk due to her husband's financial difficulties; but an important difference was that the Castilian law seems to have required such financial difficulties to be the fault of the husband, before the wife could succeed in gaining restitution. Thus, separation of property, in the sense of return of the dowry, would be more readily obtained under the D.O. and the French law than under the Castilian.

In the D.O., if a wife petitioned successfully for separation of property, she brought about dissolution of the community. No article states this specifically; but it is implicit in the provisions for separation of property: see, for example, D.O. 90 (p. 343). This was not possible in the Castilian law, where a wife could obtain restitution of her dowry, but not the dissolution of the *sociedad de gananciales*.[473] Thus, in permitting dissolution of the community while the spouses continued to live together, the D.O. has adopted the C.N. concept of "séparation de biens" rather than the Castilian law, which only allowed dissolution of the *sociedad* if there were separation from bed and board ending cohabitation. The Castilian law only allowed restitution of the dowry (and the paraphernalia, if under the husband's control).

Hence, the 1808 Digest, following the French law but not the Castilian, permitted a wife to seek separation of property, should her husband be mismanaging the property. This separation resulted in return of her dowry and para-

---

[469] "Et en tal razon como esta se entiende lo que dice el derecho, que la muger que mete su cuerpo en poder de su marido, que nol debe desapoderar de la dote quel dió."

[470] *Contratos*, ch. 2, § 1 no. 10 (vol. 1, p. 299).

[471] Pothier, *T. Comm.*, p. 276 (no. 510).

[472] *Part.* 4.11.17; D.O. 53 (p. 333) and 62 (p. 335). For the same in ancien droit français, see Brissaud, *History*, pp. 806–807.

[473] I can certainly trace no texts to that effect; neither apparently could de Funiak, *op. cit. supra* note 305, vol. 1, pp. 374–375, nor Pugh, *op. cit. supra* note 80, p. 30 and n. 185.

phernalia (if not under her own control) and dissolution of the *communauté d'acquêts ou de gains*. Before discussing the results of such *séparation* on marital authority, *séparation de corps* must be discussed, as it also resulted in separation of property.

The fifth title of the first book of the D.O., is called "De la séparation de corps." The C.N. has no exactly equivalent title because of its recognition of judicial divorce; but the D.O. title is obviously modelled after the French code, and the grounds given for the action are very similar to those found in the C.N. and the *Proj. An. VIII* for divorce and *séparation de corps*.[474] The D.O. does not regulate divorce.[475] Though what is at issue is the effect of such separation on the *puissance du mari*, the grounds for separation are of interest for the insight they give into the relative status of husband and wife.

D.O. 1–5 (p. 31) state:

> La séparation de corps qui existait d'après les anciennes lois du pays, aura lieu pour les causes suivantes:
>
> Le mari pourra demander la séparation pour cause d'adultère de sa femme.
>
> La femme pourra demander la séparation pour cause d'adultère de son mari, lorsqu'il aura tenu sa concubine dans la maison commune.
>
> Les époux pourront réciproquement demander la séparation pour excès, sévices, ou injures graves de l'un deux envers l'autre, si ces mauvais traitements sont d'une nature à rendre celui-ci, la vie commune insupportable.
> La séparation pout être également demandé réciproquement dans les cas
> 1. De diffamation publique de l'un des époux envers l'autre;
> 2. D'abandonnement du mari par la femme, ou de la femme par le mari;
> 3. D'attentat d'un époux à la vie de l'autre.

These provisions seem to have been borrowed from the French code and its *projet*.[476] For the fourth and fifth articles, the D.L.V. gives no references; for the first to the third it refers to *Part.* 4.10.2, while for the second and third, it refers to Pothier.[477]

Examination of Pothier and the *Partidas* show that there can be no doubt that the redactors here followed the French code and its *projet*. Pothier states that a husband may demand separation on the grounds of his wife's adultery, with the result that, on her conviction of adultery, she may be secluded in a convent.[478] Although the D.L.V. does not cite the section, Pothier states that a

---

[474] See *infra*, note 476.
[475] See *infra*, notes 497–503.
[476] For article 1, Batiza gives *Proj. An. VIII*, 1.6.1. as the "partially influencing" source; for article 2, he gives C.N. 229 as the "almost verbatim" source; for article 3, he gives C.N. 230 as the "almost verbatim" source; for article 4, he gives C.N, 231 as the "almost verbatim in part" source; and for article 5, he gives *Proj. An. VIII*, 1.5.3, 3d. to 5th. paragraphs, as the "almost verbatim" sources. See Febrero, *Juicios*, ch. 4, § 11 nos. 53–56 (vol. 4(1), pp. 269–274.
[477] D.O. 2: Pothier, *T.C.M.*, p. 242 (no. 525); D.O. 3: Pothier, *T.C.M.*, pp. 242–243 (nos. 526–527).
[478] Pothier, *T.C.M.*, pp. 242–243 (no. 525–527).

wife cannot ground an action for separation on the adultery of her husband.[479] Further, again uncited, Pothier allowed only the wife to sue on the grounds of *sévices* or *excès*.[480] (Though Pothier is not necessarily correct in his opinion on this last point, given the lack of other references in the D.L.V., it seems likely that, the redactors took him as accurately representing the law of the *ancien régime*.)[481] The *Partidas* allowed only one relevant ground for separation: the adultery of *either* spouse.[482] *Part.* 4.10.2 might suggest that only the wife's adultery was relevant;[483] *Part.* 4.9.2, however, shows that this was probably not the case.[484] Canon law allowed separation on the grounds of a husband's adultery.[485] The *Partidas* are closely following Canon law here, even submitting such questions to the ecclesiastical courts;[486] this suggests that such adultery was a relevant ground for separation. It appears that other grounds for separation were recognized later;[487] but the D.L.V. refers to no source other than the *Partidas*. The D.O. redactors obviously conceived of the grounds for separation entirely within the limits set by the C.N. and its *projet*, the provisions of which they preferred to those of Pothier and the *Partidas*. Thus, the redactors preferred to make the husband and wife unequal as to the effects of their adultery. Although the redactors gave more attention to the adultery of the husband than did Pothier, they must have agreed with him that the adultery of the wife was more reprehensible, since it could introduce illegitimate children into the family.[488] The adoption of the provisions on ill-treatment, defamation, abandonment and attempted murder need occasion no surprise.[489]

Chapter five of this title of the D.O. lists the effects of *séparation de corps*. The only article we need consider is D.O. 17 (p. 35): "La séparation de corps entraîne toujours celle de biens." This is copied from C.N. 311. The position and approach adopted by the Castilian law on the effects of separation (*divorcio*) was rather different from those of the French law. We need not discuss it, other than to

---

[479] *Ibid.* p. 238 (no. 516).

[480] *Ibid.* pp. 235–236 (nos. 508–510).

[481] Cf., for example, Huussen, *op. cit. supra* note 106, pp. 110–111, on the separation of citizen Jacquotot and his wife. The complex history of the grounds for separation will be discussed *infra* in considering Quebec, where the discussion is more relevant.

[482] *Part.* 4.10.2: separation was also permitted for a spouse entering a religious order.

[483] "Otrosi faciendo la muger contra su marido pecado de fornicio ó de adulterio, es la otra razon que deximos por que se face propriamente el divorcio." For the first reason, see *supra*, note 482.

[484] "Acusarse pueden aun et otra manera sin las que deximos en la ley ante desta el marido et la muger; et esta es por razon de adulterio. Et si la acusacion fuere fecha para departirlos que non vivan en uno nin se ayuntan carnalmiente, por tal razon non los puede otro ninguno acusar sinon ellos mesmos uno a otro."

[485] Esmein, *op. cit. supra* note 69, vol. 2, pp. 90–91.

[486] *Part.* 4.9.2; *Asso y Manuel*, vol. 1, p. 76.

[487] See de Funiak, *op. cit. supra* note 305, vol. 1, p. 626, where he suggests that *Fuero real*, 4.5.5, was used for separation on the grounds of desertion, and that cruelty and dangerous insanity were later admitted as grounds.

[488] See Pothier, *T.C.M.*, p. 238 (no. 516).

[489] They were not adopted because they, in some way, expressed the Castilian law, *pace* Pascal; that they were similar to other Castilian provisions is fortuitous: see *supra*, note 487.

point out that in substance, context, and mode of expression, D.O. 17 is firmly rooted in the French tradition.[490]

It is now possible to discuss the effect *séparation de corps* and that *de biens* had on the capacity of the wife, and the extent to which either liberated her from *puissance maritale*. First, and most obviously, *séparation de corps* released the wife from her obligation to live with her husband. Second, *séparation de biens* alone obliged the wife to contribute to the expenses of the still joint household and the education of the common children. This was a contribution to be proportional to her and her husband's means; but if he had none, she had to support all the expenses.[491]

The most important article here is D.O. 97 (p. 343):

> La femme séparée, soit de corps et de biens, soit de biens seulement, en reprend la libre administration. Elle peut disposer de son mobilier et l'aliéner. Elle ne peut l'aliéner ses immeubles sans le consentement de son mari, ou sans être autorisée en justice, à son refus.

This is copied from C.N. 1449.[492] The D.L.V. has no references. Before going on to consider the Castilian law on this, it is as well to indicate the effects of this provision on the wife's capacity. She could administer her property unauthorized, and did not require authorization to dispose of moveables. D.O. 21 and 22 (p. 29) would still apply.[493] Thus she would require authorization to appear in court as well as to alienate or to dispose otherwise of her immoveables. Thus, the requirement of authorization was only relaxed to a slight extent. Her capacity was still reduced by the *puissance du mari*. The D.L.V. makes virtually no references to Castilan law on this point, because there were no relevant provisions. The commentators simply did not discuss the question of authorization and control over property after separation.[494] This is the result of the different approach taken to separation, to marital authorization, and to the incapacity of married women. Pugh attempts to reconstruct what the law should have been, at least as regards ganancial property, dowry and paraphema; this need not concern us, as what is important is that the matter simply was not dealt with. The D.O. redactors could not have followed any Castilian provisions, as the logic of their articles on *puissance du mari* required the adoption of provisions, at the least, similar to those of the French code or its *projet*. The D.O. redactors had adopted the rigorous northern French conception of *puissance du*

---

[490] On the approach taken by Castilian law, see Pugh, *op. cit. supra* note 80, pp. 34–39, and de Funiak, *op. cit. supra* note 305, vol. 1, pp. 626–633. It is no doubt significant that in title five, the D.L.V. has very few references opposite the articles.

[491] See D.O. 96 (p. 343).

[492] According to Batiza, this is the "verbatim" source, with *Proj. An. VIII*, 3.10.67 as a subsidiary. The whole of this section the D.O. is copied, in general, from the French law, both in substance and in spirit. See *supra*, note 490.

[493] See *supra*, text at notes 380–400 *supra*.

[494] At least so far as I can discover. Pugh, *op. cit. supra* note 80, pp. 38–39 reaches the same conclusion.

mari, with its requirements of authorization, which rendered acute the problem of administration and authorization after separation. The Castilian law did not render separation and its effects such a problem, since it had a much laxer attitude to authorization in general: hence, it had no provisions in point, and no doctrines developed by the jurists. The adoption of the *puissance du mari* of the *droit coutumier* required provision to be made to cover authority after separation, so the D.O. redactors also borrowed the French provisions on this.

An interesting point is why the redactors adopted the French provisions without amendment. As regards separation, the redactors were innovating freely: they could easily have amended the C.N. provisions, and indeed some amendments might well have been very appropriate. First, it seems quite inapproriate that, after a wife has separated from her husband on the grounds of, for example, his cruelty, she should have to go to him to seek authorization before alienating an immoveable, and, indeed, before seeking authorization from the judge. If the requirement of authorization was to be maintained, because of the logic of the system, it would have been more suitable to confine it to judicial authorization in these circumstances.[495] Second, if the separation was of property only, and hence on the grounds of the husband's financial incapability, was he a suitable person to authorize his wife to alienate immoveable property, an alienation with potentially disastrous consequences? In both these sets of circumstances if authorization were thought to be necessary, judicial authorization would have been better. Further, given the geographical circumstances of much of Louisiana, it might well have been better to dispense completely with the requirement of authorization, if a woman were separated either as to property, or as to bed and board. A woman living in an isolated community might not find it convenient to go to court to seek authorization. The redactors of the 1825 C.L. acknowledged the inappropriateness of aspects of this requirement of authorization.[496]

Despite this, the D.O. redactors followed the C.N., and embodied the whole of the *droit coutumier*'s *puissance maritale* in their provisions on authorization of women separated from their husbands, either as regards property or bed and board. They could not have followed the Castilian law, because it had no relevant provisions. Nonetheless, they need not have copied the C.N. here, as innovation would have been easy, as the 1825 C.L. shows. One can only conclude that a combination of haste, admiration for the C.N., and the ease of borrowing from the latter resulted in the enactment of these provisions on authorization of separated women. The general ideology of the period supported the law adopted, without necessitating its adoption. These provisions were an innovation: the redactors were not including in the code the law in force—no Castilian law nor territorial act enjoined these provisions.

---

[495] *1823 Projet*, p. 10.

[496] See *ibid.*, p. 10: "It appeared to us, improper to oblige the wife separated from bed and board, generally in consequence of bad treatment, to address herself to her husband to obtain permission to conduct her own affairs."

Separation thus did not end a husband's authority over his wife, but merely reduced it slightly: here the D.O. redactors have copied the French concepts of *séparation de biens*, *séparation de corps*, and *puissance du mari*.

The Dissolution of Marriage, and the Ending of *Puissance Maritale*

Only the dissolution of the marriage ended the husband's authority over his wife. The 1808 Digest has one relevant provision, D.O. 30 (p. 29):

> Le lien du mariage se dissout,
> 1. Par la mort de l'un des époux;
> 2. Lorsque le mariage s'est déclaré nul par l'une des causes exprimées au chapitre 3 du présent titre, ou lorsqu'il en est contracté un autre, en raison de l'absence d'un des époux dans les cas autorisés par la loi.
>
> Les séparations de corps n'opèrent pas la dissolution du lien de mariage, puisque les époux séparés ne peuvent pas se marier à d'autres personnes, mais elles mettent fin à la cohabitation conjugale, ainsi qu'aux intérêts communs qui pouvaient exister entre les epoux.

Thus, according to the D.O., death alone ended marriage, except for special provisions on nullity or absence. In mode of expression, to a limited extent, this passage is modelled on C.N. 227;[497] but the C.N., of course, regulated divorce, whereas the D.O. did not. The D.L.V. refers to *Part.* 4.9.9. and 4.12.3, and Pothier.[498] *Part.* 4.9.9. regulated annulment of marriage, while 4.12.3 was on the second marriages of widows. Pothier, as cited, enunciated principles similar to D.O. 30 (p. 29). In the *Partidas*, a marriage validly contracted, and with no impediments, was for life; divorce in the modern sense was not allowed, only separation.[499]

The 1807 Act, ch. 17, provided as follows in its final section (70):

> Marriages are dissolved,
> 1stly, By the death of the husband or wife.
> 2ndly, By a sentence of divorce legally pronounced.

This refers to legislative divorces; these had been granted by the territorial legislature as early as 1805.[500] Such legislative divorces were apparently fairly common in the U.S.A. in the early nineteenth century.[501] Why did the redactors of the D.O. not mention this? D.O. 30 (p. 29) was altered on the recommenda-

---

497 Batiza classes it as the "substantially influencing first part" source in its first paragraph, along with the first paragraph of *Proj. An. VIII*, 1.5.15 as a subsidiary.
498 Pothier, *T.C.M.*, pp. 211 and 235 (nos. 462 and 506).
499 See *Part.* 4.10.1; "divorcio" in Castilian signified separation.
500 See A.L. Dart, "Adultery as a Defense to a Divorce Action in Louisiana", 11 *Tul. L. Rev.* (1936), pp. 95–112 at p. 106.
501 See Friedman, *op. cit. supra* note 198, pp. 181–184.

tion of the 1823 *Projet*,[502] so that article 133 of the 1825 C.L. stated that marriage would be dissolved by a divorce legally pronounced. The 1825 Act made no further mention of divorce. Presumably, the 1808 redactors excluded any mention of divorce because each individual divorce was an act of the legislature. There was certainly no need to regulate divorce as each was a specialized legislative act intended to apply only to the parties, and not altering the general provisions of the law. Whatever were the reasons for excluding mention of the divorce (and the exclusion must have been deliberate, since the sources in front of the redactors—the C.N. and the 1807 Act—mentioned it), the redactors would probably have done better to have mentioned divorce as was done in the 1825 C.L., because the statement in D.O. 30 (p. 29) is not quite accurate. Judicial divorce being impossible, there was no need on the topic for any articles such as those found in the C.N. or its *projet*.

Thus, *puissance maritale* only ended on the dissolution of the marriage, whether by death or legislative divorce. Separation from bed and board only reduced this *puissance*, and did not free the wife from it.[503]

Conclusion on the Relationship between Husband and Wife in the 1808 Digest

In this subsection, conclusions on the changes in the various areas of the law will be drawn together, in order to gain an overall impression of the provisions of the D.O. on the relationship of husband and wife, and on how these provisions as a whole relate to the C.N., its *projet*, the French customary law as revealed by Pothier, and the Castilian law. Also at issue is how the provisions relate to the relationship between husband and wife when considered from a social rather than a legal perspective.

---

[502] *1823 Projet*, p. 10: "Among the causes of the dissolution of marriages mentioned in art. 30, divorce is not mentioned, as if it were not known among us."

[503] One article of the D.O. not touched on as not really relevant here, but still deserving some mention, is D.O. 31 (p. 29), which states that a widow cannot remarry until 10 months after the dissolution of the marriage. This is copied exactly from C.N. 228. (Note that the *droit coutumier* had no provision forbidding such remarriage.) The D.L.V. refers to *Part.* 4.12.3, *Fuero real*, 3.1.13 and Febrero, *Juicios*, bk 2, ch. 5, § 1 nos. 1–3 (vol. 5(2), pp. 322–324). Drawing on the Roman law, the *Partidas* and the *Fuero real* state that a widow cannot remarry within a *year* of her husband's death (unless with a dispensation from the king) without suffering certain penalties. The Canon law did not disallow remarriage within any period, though disapproving of remarriage in general: see Esmein, *op. cit. supra* note 69, vol. 1, p. 107, pp. 401–402, vol. 2, pp. 99–104, and Pothier, *T.C.M.*, pp. 244–245 (nos. 528–531). Febrero points out that in Spain the law was now changed: there was no prohibition on remarriage within a certain period (see, e.g. *Nov. Rec. Cast.* 10.2.4, or *Rec. Cast.* 5.3.1 and *Asso y Manuel*, vol. 1, pp. 76–77). Why, given that the Castilian law was found in sources known to them, did the redactors here change the law? The C.N. article was (according to Maleville, *Analyse*, vol. 1, pp. 209–210) intended to avoid *turbatio sanguinis*. It was an innovation on the *droit coutumier*, but not in the *droit écrit*, where a 1-year period applied. The D.O. redactors can only have copied the C.N. article because it was in the C.N., and part of the civil law tradition.

The D.O. articles on the method of contracting marriage are closely based on the territorial Act of 1807, ch. 17, though with some traceable influence from the C.N. and *Proj. An. VIII.* The 1807 Act itself has been significantly influenced by the French codification.[504] The nature of the rules on the contract of marriage embodied in the D.O. is different from that of those in the *Proj. An. VIII* or C.N., in that the latter two envisage a purely civil ceremony and consider marriage terminable by divorce, which they carefully regulate. Although there could be legislative divorce in Louisiana, in principle a valid marriage was only terminated by the death of one of the spouses. This aspect of the D.O. also differs from the rules of the pre-Tridentine and Tridentine Canon law. The D.O. articles, based on the 1807 Act, are clear and concise, providing suitable provisions for the territory, given the heterogeneous nature of Louisiana society.

The property aspects of the husband and wife relationship are conceived of in a French manner, even though some Castilian notions have been intercalated in the text of the D.O.: notably, the "statutory" matrimonial regime is based on the *sociedad de gananciales*. There can be no doubt that the overall conception is French, given that, as in the *droit coutumier* and C.N., and not as in the Castilian law, marriage contracts can be used to regulate the future disposition of family wealth.

It is clear that the Castilian notion of the legal relationship between husband and wife has been replaced in the territory with the *puissance maritale* of the *droit coutumier*. The Castilian law had a very limited, underdeveloped concept of marital authority. Montalvo states that a wife is in the power of her husband in so far as she ought to live with him and obey him, but: "In aliis autem non dicitur esse in viri potestate."[505] Gomez, in the only general statement he makes on the nature of the husband's authority, says:

> nam licet vere et proprie quoad omnia non sit uxor in potestate mariti sicut filius et servus, tamen quo ad tria bene est in eius potestate. Primo ad residentiam et cohabitationem quam debet uxor facere cum viro, et inde est quod potest intentare maritus contra eam detinentam utile interdictum de liberis exhibendis ut in ... [D. 43.30.1.5].[506] Secundo quo ad operas quas debet reddere et praestare marito. Tertio quo ad iurisdictionem: quia efficitur de iurisdictione et domicilio mariti, ut in ... [D. 5.1.65][507] et tenet et declarat magistraliter Bal[dus].[508]

Thus, for Gomez, a wife is only in the power of her husband in so far as she should live with him, owed him certain *operae* and was domiciled with him.

---

[504] See *supra*, discussion at notes 177–180, esp. of 1807 Act, ch. 17, ss. 42–44.

[505] Gloss "b" *Fuero real*, 3.20.13 (1544).

[506] The text of the Digest provision cited by Gomez states that a father cannot succeed in an *actio de exhibendis liberorum* to recover his daughter from her husband. He cannot exercise his *patria potestas* harshly and overturn the marriage. Gomez also refers to C. 8.8.3 on the same topic, and states this is the common opinion of the learned. I have modernized the references.

[507] This provision states that a woman ought to exact her dowry where her husband is domiciled.

[508] Gomez, *op. cit. supra* note 100, p. 504, commentary on *Toro*, 54–59, no. 1. The reference to Baldus is to his commentary on C. 6.46.5

This is very different from the extensive and comprehensive conception of *puissance du mari* found in the *droit coutumier*, and which pervaded all the law on husband and wife. Some of the provisions of the Castilian law were contradictory to the French concept of *puissance maritale*, notably those on general authorizations and ratifications. The Castilian law provided a much laxer conception of marital authority, which, was, moreover, interpreted by the Castilian jurists in such a way as to give a wife considerable freedom of action. Further, because the Castilian law, in comparison to the French, had a minimal notion of marital authority—and one to which scant juristic attention was devoted—it simply failed to regulate areas of social life, potentially involving marital authority, that were regulated in great detail by the *droit coutumier* and C.N. In some of these areas, the approach of the Castilian law was so radically different that its provisions cannot readily be compared to those of the C.N. or *droit coutumier*. The attempts by Pugh and de Funiak to reconstruct the Castilian law on such apparently unregulated areas of social life show this clearly; they both fail to give a satisfactory account of what the law had been.[509] The reason for their failure is obvious: they are approaching the old Castilian law from the perspective of the modern French law, and they fail to appreciate that, for the Castilian law, the problems they pose either do not exist or are conceived of in a different way. They both attempt to impose on the Castilian law a structure derived from the modern law. This relates to the provisions on *puissance du mari* in the D.O. The structure (and concept) of marital authority in the C.N. was very different from that in the Castilian law, causing both laws to have different and (in some cases) antithetical provisions: some provisions did correspond; but the existence or not of some essential provisions caused both laws to have a different appearance and substance.

The D.O. has adopted the concept of *puissance maritale* found in the C.N. and the northern French *droit coutumier*; and, indeed, has adopted it so rigorously as to reject C.N. 224, which was an illogical provision, given the premisses of this *puissance*.[510] From the adoption of the basic promises of *puissance maritale*, various consequences flow. This adoption, along with the borrowing of the scheme of the C.N., entails provision being made for contingencies not covered by the Castilian law. This explains the absence in the D.L.V. of references to Castilian provisions for many of the articles in point: there were no such provisions because of the different structure of the law. *Leyes* 56 and 58 of Toro are of major importance:[511] by providing for general authorizations and *ex post facto* validation, they render the Castilian law very different from the *droit coutumier*. They are incompatible with the *puissance du mari* of the *droit coutumier*, as Pothier states explicitly.[512] These two *leyes* were rejected for the D.O., in which there is a complete acceptance of the conception of marital authority found in the C.N. and the French customary law. Further,

---

[509] See *supra*, text at notes 413–416, 490 and 494–495.
[510] See *supra*, text at notes 441–449.
[511] See *supra*, quoted in notes 389 and 390.
[512] See *supra*, text at notes 307–310, 424–427 and 454.

the D.O. rejects the very liberal interpretation given by the Castilian law to the provisions on authorization. Some of the articles of the D.O. are compatible with some of the provisions of the Castilian law; but the absence of these two *leyes* shows how radically different the law in the D.O. is from the Castilian. Indeed, any correspondence on this matter between *individual* provisions of the *Leyes de Toro* and *individual* articles of the D.O. is unimportant or, indeed, irrelevant, as both sets of provisions, when regarded as a whole, are quite different on marital authority.

Given that, in the the D.O., basic premisses on northern French *puissance maritale* were accepted in articles such as D.O. 4 (p. 325) and 27 (p. 29), there was no particular reason for the redactors to have accepted all the individual provisions of the C.N., its *projet*, or the *droit coutumier*. Yet, by and large, this they did. As already noted, the adoption of the conceptual scheme of the C.N. necessitated the redaction of provisions for contingencies not perceived of in the Castilian law. In these areas, the D.O. redactors simply copied the C.N. provisions. Some points should be made about this. As previously argued, in the provisions on authorization, the D.O. redactors had generally to follow sections 61–69 of the 1807 Act.[513] Perhaps, to some extent, the redactors could have circumvented these sections, while remaining faithful to their individual provisions; but given that the Act was recent, it would be implausible to suggest that the D.O. redactors might have chosen effectively to repeal some of these sections. It is certain that the D.O. redactors followed the provisions of this Act, and the trend thus set, not only because they felt compelled to do so, but also because they approved of them. Thus, they extended some of the provisions of the Act,[514] and included the whole of the French conception of *puissance maritale* in the individual provisions of the D.O., and without possible amendments: consider the rules on authorizations after *separation de corps*.[515]

Hence, it may be concluded that the D.O. redactors imported provisions on marital authority from the French law. The 1807 Act prompted this, and, to some extent, had already done so itself; but it did not necessitate the wholesale borrowing undertaken by the redactors. Further, this major change in the law can have been neither accidental nor occasioned by ignorance of the Castilian law, which was easily ascertainable, in so far as it extended, in the *Nueva recopilación* and Febrero's work, both of which were known to and used by the redactors. Thus, this reversal of the law was conscious and deliberate. This leads on to consideration of the change in the law in relation to the social context, and whether or not the change was the result of changes in Louisiana society.

As already argued, at the period in which codification was undertaken in Louisiana, there was a general trend, especially among bourgeois families, towards closer family relationships, with the tie of husband to wife becoming closer, based around domesticity and child care, and, at the same time, the

---

[513] See *supra*, text at notes 456–459.

[514] See 1807 Act ch. 17, ss. 62 and 64, and *supra*, text at notes 377–391, 401–402 and 457–459.

[515] See *supra*, text at notes 492–496.

authority of the husband grew.[516] This qualitative change in the nature of husband and wife relationships would not necessitate a drastic curtailment of the proprietary and contractual capacities of married women, though it would certainly support such curtailment. The alteration in the capacity of married women was possibly not desirable in an economic sense, although the economic disadvantages most certainly were not prohibitive.[517] Although the ideology of supremacy of the husband would definitely support such an increase in marital authority, on its own it might not necessitate it, because the Castilian law also clearly asserted such supremacy.

This factor, the ideology of male dominance in marriage, on its own would not have necessitated change: however, the facts surrounding codification made for the expression of this ideology in the new Digest. First, there existed convenient, prestigious and readily borrowed French texts, all containing an extended concept of *puissance du mari*. The redactors were already following fairly closely the scheme of the C.N. and/or its *projet*. They were drawing up their code in French. The French law had, rather confusingly, been stated by the court, in 1805, to be part of the law of Louisiana;[518] and there had, in part, already been a revival of French law and French legal folkways in Louisiana after 1803.[519] The 1807 Act itself seems to have imported French legal notions into the Louisiana law. The civilian tradition and codification both facilitated borrowing from foreign sources.[520] The prestige of the Code Napoléon would make its articles very attractive to the redactors.

Thus, it may be concluded that the changes in the law on the relationship of husband and wife were the result of the process of codification, combined with the civilian tradition and the existence of the French texts, all of which together permitted the redactors to assert, in a series of legal provisions, the current ideology of the husband as head of the conjugal association. Undoubtedly the redactors would have included provisions in some way asserting this ideology, even if only on a symbolic level; but the extent of the *puissance du mari*, and the form of its expression were, more than anything, the direct result of the redactors' use of the French sources.

Puissance Paternelle

In the first title of the first book of the D.O., some fundamental statements are made on *puissance paternelle*. This title is taken almost word for word from Domat's *Livre Préliminaire*.[521] D.O. 3 (p. 9) says that under natural law, by the

---

[516] See *supra*, text at notes 36–43, 45–49.
[517] See *supra*, text at notes 461–463.
[518] See *supra*, chap. 3, text at note 169.
[519] See *supra*, chap. 3, text at notes 156–160; Baade, *Marriage Contracts*, pp. 79–89.
[520] See *supra*, chap. 1, text at notes 51–53; *supra*, chap. three, text at notes 136–155.
[521] Batiza, "Sources", appendix C, pp. 46–47 shows this clearly.

fact of birth, children are subject to the power and authority of those to whom they are born. D.O. 16 (p. 11) states that, according to civil law:

> Les fils et filles de famille, sont les personnes qui sont sous la puissance paternelle; et les pères ou mères de famille, qu'on appelle aussi chefs de famille, sont les personnes qui ne sont pas sous cette puissance, soit qu'ils aient des enfans ou non, et soit qu'ils aient été dégagés de la puissance paternelle par l'émancipation ou par la mort du père.

D.O. 17 (p. 11) states that emancipation and the other methods of freeing children affect only the civil law aspects of paternal power, but not the natural law aspects. The inclusion of this title, of which there is no equivalent in the C.N., was obviously suggested to the D.O. redactors by Domat's work. With the division into distinctions between persons established by nature, and those established by law (*loi*), this title indicates the influence of natural law theories on the D.O. redactors. Though Domat was obviously the inspiration for this title and for its substance, similar statements may be found elsewhere. Thus, the *Quarta Partida*, in the introduction to *titulo* XVII, states:

> Poderio et señorio han los padres sobre los fijos segunt razon natural et segunt derecho: lo uno porque nascen dellos, et lo al porque han de heredar lo suyo.

The D.O., in fact, bears much more of an imprint of natural law than does the C.N. These articles provide the theoretical foundation for the more specific provisions on *puissance paternelle* found elsewhere in the D.O.

How *Puissance Paternelle* Arises

The first and most common method of a child coming under paternal power is through legitimate birth. Chapter two of the seventh title of the first book of the D.O. provides for legitimacy if born within marriage, and sets out the manner of proving such legitimacy. We need not discuss these articles, since they are purely incidental to the subject matter of this section, and do not reflect on the relationship of father and child. In general, the articles embody the ancient maxim: *pater is est quem nuptiae demonstrant*. "Les enfans légitimes sont ceux qui sont nés dans le mariage", states D.O. 2 (p. 45), while D.O. 7 (p. 47) states that "L'enfant conçu pendant le mariage a pour père le mari." The D.O. rules are basically similar to those in Castile and France, though with some differences which are not particularly important. Pothier states that:

> La puissance paternelle sur les enfants qui naissent du mariage est . . . un des effets civils du mariage . . . .[522]

Though their concepts of paternal power differed, his remark holds good for Castile, France and Louisiana.

---

[522] Pothier, *T.C.M.*, p. 181 (no. 399).

The second method of a child coming under *puissance paternelle* is legitimation. D.O. 21 (p. 49) states:

> Les enfans nés hors du mariage, autres que ceux nés d'un commerce incestueux ou adultérin, pourront être légitimés par le mariage subséquent de leur père et mère, lorsque ceux-ci les auront légalement reconnu avant leur mariage, ou qu'ils les reconnaîtront par leur contrat de mariage.

This is very similar to C.N. 331, which Batiza classes as the "almost verbatim" source. The D.L.V. refers to *Part.* 4.13.1 and 2, 6, *Part.* 4.15.2 and Febrero.[523] Although the last clause of the C.N. article reads: "ou qu'ils reconnaîtront dans l'acte même de célébration", it is obvious that the D.O. redactors have copied their provision from the C.N. Thus, both the D.O. and the C.N. required a strict, formal recognition of the child for legitimation to take place by subsequent marriage. Under the Canon law[524] and the *ancien droit* in France,[525] such recognition was not necessary: marriage *ipso facto* legitimated natural children, that is, those who were born of neither incestuous nor adulterous intercourse. The position under the Castilian law is more complex. But the work of Enrique Gacto Fernandez, in a valuable historical study, permits the easy ascertainment of the Castilian provisions.[526]

Legitimation by subsequent marriage was permitted in the Roman law of Justinian's time only in the case of a marriage of a man to his concubine, where there was an *instrumentum dotis*, and where, at the time of conception of the children, the parents could have married.[527] Concubinage was a recognized relationship in Roman law,[528] and only children born of such concubinage were classed as natural children, *liberi naturales*, other illegitimate children were *spurii*.[529] The mediaeval Castilian law recognized the institution of concubinage (*barraganía*),[530] and, contrary to the Canon law, it seems that the *Partidas* gave the status of natural child only to a child of such a union.[531] Here the *Partidas* were obviously following the Roman law, since Canon law granted the status of

---

[523] Febrero, *Contratos*, ch. 1, § 7 no. 109 (vol. 1, p. 94) [D.L.V. lists no. 108 in error]; *ibid.*, ch. 12, § 2 nos. 7–15 (vol. 3, pp. 273–276); Febrero, *Juicios*, bk. 2, ch. 1, no. 74, ch. 7, nos. 6–7 (vol. 5(2), pp. 57–58, 429–430).

[524] See Esmein, *op. cit. supra* note 69, vol. 1, pp. 39–44.

[525] See, e.g. Pothier, *T.C.M.*, pp. 183–194 (nos. 409–425); Maleville, *Analyse*, vol. 1, pp. 294–295; and *infra*, on Quebec.

[526] Enrique Gacto Fernández, *La filiación no legítima en el derecho histórico español*, Seville, publicaciones de la Universidad de Sevilla, 1969.

[527] See C. 5.27.8, 10 and 11. See Buckland, *Textbook*, p. 129. Constantine had originally allowed such legitimation for present but not future cases of concubinage, with certain requirements to be fulfilled. Anastasius allowed such legitimation for future cases of concubinage. This had subsequently been repealed: see *ibid.*

[528] See Buckland, *Textbook*, pp. 128–129, and D. 25.7.3 pr.

[529] See, e.g. M. Kaser, *Roman Private Law*, trans. R. Dannenbring, Durban, Butterworths, 1965, pp. 265–266; Esmein, *op. cit. supra* note 69, vol. 2, pp. 37–39.

[530] See *Part.* 4.14, which regulates *barraganía*; Gacto Fernández, *op. cit. supra* note 526, pp. 4–55.

[531] See, for Canon law, Esmein, *op. cit. supra* note 69, vol. 2, pp. 37–44; and, for Castilian law, Gacto Fernández, *op. cit. supra* note 526, pp. 70–72, 75.

natural child to any illegitimate child born of a union that was neither adulterous nor incestuous, that is, one where the parents had been free to marry at the time of conception.[532] Gacto points out, however, that although the rules in the *Partidas* on legitimation by subsequent marriage refer to sons born to a *barragania* (concubine), it was not necessary for the child to have been born of a stable union for him to be legitimated, it was sufficient that the Canon law requirements on the status of natural child be fulfilled.[533] Thus, legitimation by subsequent marriage comes about by the law of *Partidas* in the same circumstances as it would in Canon law. Although the laws of Toro expanded the class of *liberi naturales*,[534] they did not affect legitimation by subsequent marriage.[535] Thus, the rules in Castilian law stayed the same as those in Canon law.

The authorities cited by the D.L.V. provide as follows. *Part*. 4.13.1 states that, if a man has children by a concubine (*barragana*), and he subsequently marries this concubine, the children will be legitimated. *Part*. 4.13.2 lists the advantages of legitimacy. *Part*. 4.15.2 states that children born of a union prohibited by the church are illegitimate (that is, incestuous children); likewise those a man fathered on his concubine while his wife was alive are not capable of legitimation by the subsequent marriage of the father and concubine, since they were conceived in adultery. Febrero sets out the later Castilian position on legitimation by subsequent marriage.[536]

The redactors of the D.O. have not copied C.N. 331 because it expresses the Castilian law. In the Castilian law, marriage *ipso facto* legitimated *liberi naturales*, and *reconocimiento* was just one possible way of proving the status of *liber naturalis*,[537] rather than a requirement of legitimation, as it was in the C.N. Since the redactors have copied C.N. 331 for some reason other than belief it embodied the existing law, they must have approved of the change it wrought in the Canon law and the *ancien droit* of France.

Maleville states that one reason for the change in the C.N. was that *recherche de paternité* had been abolished; with such abolition, proof of parentage was rendered very difficult, and C.N. 331, by limiting legitimation, allowed for certainty as to the children legitimated.[538] This would not apply in Louisiana,

---

[532] Esmein, *op. cit. supra* note 69, vol. 2, pp. 37–44. Febrero, *Contratos*, ch. 1 § 7 nos. 134–135 (vol.1, pp. 113–114) gives en account of the law on natural children, and *espurios*. See also *Asso y Manuel*, p. 113.

[533] Gacto Fernández, *op. cit. supra* note 526, pp. 96–97, where he demonstrates how closely the *Partidas* here are following Canon law.

[534] *Toro*, 11: "Y porque no se pueda dudar quales son hijos naturales: ordenamos y mandamos que entonces se digan ser los hijos naturales, quando al tiempo que nascieren, o fueran concebidos, sus padres podían casar con sus madres justamente sin dispensacion: con tanto que el padre lo reconozca por su hijo, puesto que no haya tenido muger de quien lo uvo en su casa, ni sea una sola: ca concurriendo en el hijo las calidades suso dichas, mandamos que sea hijo natural." See Gacto Fernández, *op. cit. supra* note 526, p. 75.

[535] See Gacto Fernández, *op. cit. supra* note 526, p. 100.

[536] Febrero, *Juicios*, bk 2, ch.1, no. 74 (vol. 2(5), pp. 57–58; *ibid*., ch.7, nos. 6 and 7, (vol. 2(5), pp. 429–430). See *supra*, note 523, for references to other methods of legitimation.

[537] See *supra*, note 534.

[538] Maleville, *Analyse*, vol. 1, p. 294.

because the D.O. allowed such a *recherche* for free white children.[539] Maleville does give the following explanation. In answer to the criticism that this article might prevent a woman of strict parents from legitimating her children—since she would have to acknowledge publicly her *faute*—and, further, that it was unnecessary to forbid legitimation by recognition *after* the marriage, when C.N. 337 allowed one spouse to recognize a natural child (though without prejudicing the interests of the other spouse and their common children) with resulting rights of succession, hee states that "On répondit qu'il fallait tranquilliser les familles, et ne pas s'arrêter à la répugnance d'une fausse pudeur."[540] Thus, given the social circumstances of the period, such a change as that in D.O. 21 (p. 49) becomes understandable: it made the family unit more certain. This notion seems likely to have influenced the redactors. Further, the article avoided difficult problems of proof of parenthood, and so rendered the law rather simpler—though this does not quite match the permission of legal *recherche de paternité*.[541] Finally, the D.O. redactors seem always ready to borrow from the C.N. or its *projet*. In conclusion, three factors would seem to have affected the redactors' decision: a social one, a legal-technical one, and a legal-cultural one.

One last point on D.O. 21 (p. 49) relates to its statement that incestuous children may not be legitimated by the subsequent marriage of their parents. Supposing that by incest is meant sexual intercourse within the prohibited degrees of marriage laid down in D.O. 9 and 10 (pp. 25–27), such parents of incestuous children would never be able to marry. Article 164 of the C.N. did permit dispensations; the D.O. did not. It would seem likely that the D.O. redactors on this minor point have unthinkingly copied a provision of the C.N. This would not be of great importance here, as the D.O. phrase is merely unnecessary, having no legal effect. The point is more important in relation to the Quebec code and will be discussed there. The relationship of the C.N. provision to the *ancien droit* and the Canon law is of interest.

Legitimatio per subsequens matrimonium is the only form of legitimation mentioned in the D.O.; yet others had existed according to the Castilian law: Febrero, for example, lists them all, as do *Asso y Manuel*.[542] Thus, fathers could legitimate children in written public deeds; a natural daughter would be legitimated by marriage with an *hombre illustre*; a natural son would be legitimated by his father offering him in the service of the king or of a municipal council; a natural child could be legitimated in a testament which was confirmed by the king; and, finally, children could be legitimated by favour of the king or of the Pope. Obviously, not all of these would have been applicable in Louisiana, and, from the point of view of this study, not all would have given rise to paternal

---

[539] See D.O. 30–32 (p. 51).

[540] Maleville, *Analyse*, vol. 1, p. 295.

[541] Thus, a child could prove his paternity by *recherche*, yet not be legitimated by subsequent marriage if not formally acknowledged: here there would have been no problems of proof.

[542] Febrero, *Contratos*, ch. 1, § 7 nos. 107–109 (vol. 1, pp. 91–93); *ibid*., ch.12, § 2 nos. 7–15 (vol. 3, pp. 273–276); *Asso y Manuel*, vol. 1, p. 114; Gacto Fernández, *op. cit. supra* note 526, pp. 109–129.

power over the legitimated child. However, some of these forms of legitimation could have been useful. Thus, *legitimatio per rescriptum principis* was used in Texas in the middle of the nineteenth century, when one of the parents had died before they could legitimate their children by marriage.[543]

The redactors must have chosen to exclude these other forms of legitimation. Some of them were obviously inapplicable; but others might have been useful, as that *per rescriptum principis* was found to be in Texas. In the 1825 Code, however, a new paragraph was added to D.O. 21 (p. 49) stating that "Tout autre mode de légitimation est aboli."[544] The C.L. redactors remarked:

> The 7th law, tit. 5, part. 4, published by the translators as being in force, permits the father to legitimate his children by a simple declaration under his hand, or received by a Notary before three witnesses. We propose to suppress this law.[545]

The reference to "the translators" is to the translation of the *Partidas* by Moreau Lislet and Carleton.[546] Obviously, the decision in *Cottin* has influenced the redactors of the 1825 C.L.[547] What this suggests is that the 1808 redactors copied the provisions of the C.N. and rejected the Castilian provisions because they thought them inapplicable and because they did not appear in the C.N. or its *projet*.

One other obvious method of acquiring *puissance paternelle* over another is adoption. The D.O. redactors devote the whole of chapter IV of this title to one article on adoption, D.O. 35 (p. 51), which states:

> L'adoption qui était autorisée par les lois du pays, est, et demeure abolie.

The French code allowed adoption,[548] as did the Castilian laws.[549] In *Part.* 4.17.4 adoption is specifically stated to be a method of gaining *potestas* over another. We need not discuss the specific rules, bar to point out that the Castilian rules on adoption were derived from the Roman, to the extent of having the Roman distinction between *adrogatio* and *adoptio*.[550] This distinction is logical, given the Castilian law's very Roman conception of *patria potestad*. Adoption had not been possible under the *droit coutumier*.

There is no indication as to why the redactors abolished adoption. They perhaps considered it contrary to the "true" conception of marriage and family

---

543 See Baade, "Form", p. 9 and n. 37.

544 C.L. 217.

545 *1823 Projet*, p. 17. The redactors meant *Part.* 4.15.7. There is an obvious slip in printing.

546 See *supra*, chap. 3, text at notes 221–222.

547 See *supra*, chap. 3, text at notes 208–227.

548 See C.N. 343 *et seq.*

549 The D.L.V. refers to the 16th title of the fourth *Partida*, which is devoted entirely to adoption, and to Febrero, *Contratos*, ch. 12, § 1 nos. 1–6 (vol. 3, pp. 270–273). See also *Asso y Manuel*, vol. 1, pp. 117–119.

550 Febrero, *Contratos*, ch. 12, § 1 nos. 1–6 (vol. 3, pp. 270–273); *Asso y Manuel*, vol. 1, pp. 117–119. On the Roman law, see Buckland, *Textbook*, pp. 121–128.

according to the Christian tradition.[551] Further, other social circumstances might render adoption unnecessary. Adoption, according to Roman law, appears to have served the purpose of preventing families dying out, lest the religious duties of the family no longer be carried out.[552] The Canon law did not recognize adoption and Brissaud suggests that the revival of adoption in Revolutionary France was in imitation of antiquity,[553] while Baudouin speculates the revival was prompted by the gaps left in families by the Revolutionary and Napoleonic wars.[554] None of these reasons would have called for the continuance of adoption in Louisiana.

It must be assumed that, in the absence of any obvious need for adoption, the D.O. redactors abolished the institution which they considered contrary to their conception of family. The Roman reasons for adoption were hardly applicable. Further, although technically in force, one may doubt that the Castilian provisions on adoption were much used, if at all.[555] Certainly the Castilian law and the Code Napoléon were exceptional, in the legal systems of the period, in permitting adoption, and it is clear from Maleville's discussion that there was opposition to adoption in the redaction of the French code.[556] Adoption was certainly contrary to the traditional Canon law conception of marriage and family.

The Castilian sources mention a fourth method of acquiring *patria potestas* over another: the ingratitude of an emancipated son returns him to the potestad of his father.[557] There is no equivalent provision in the D.O., nor in the C.N. or its *projet*. The Castilian rule is of Roman origin.[558] The Castilian rule is the result of the Roman concept of *patria potestas* in the Castilian law, even though children are emancipated by marriage.[559] The C.N. has no need of such a rule, considering that most aspects of paternal power ended with the child's reaching the age of majority. The D.O. redactors have here followed the C.N. and excluded any such rule, just as they have adopted the *droit coutumier*'s conception of *puissance paternelle* (as will be demonstrated). Thus, the adoption by the

---

[551] L. Baudouin, *Le droit civil de la province de Québec: modèle vivant de droit comparé*, Montreal, Wilson and Lafleur, 1953, p. 244: "Si l'on considère la morale comme le fondement des relations de famille, il est hors de doute que l'adoption doit être vue avec défaveur. N'est-il pas immoral qu'une personne ayant la puissance paternelle sur son enfant, puisse en faire abandon à une autre comme si l'enfant était une marchandise cessible? Il est également difficile d'admettre qu'une personne n'ayant pas d'enfant puisse s'en donner fictivement. L'adoption parait ainsi contraire à toutes les normes légales de l'organisation de la famille, en ce qu'elle fait de la puissance paternelle un élément de négociabilité et en ce qu'elle détourne du mariage, dont la finalité selon la doctrine chrétienne, est la procreation."

[552] See Jolowicz, *op. cit. supra* note 57, pp. 194–197.

[553] Brissaud, *History*, pp. 218–219.

[554] Baudouin, *op. cit. supra* note 551, pp. 250–251.

[555] Examination of the colonial archives, especially those of notaries, might help establish this.

[556] Maleville, *Analyse*, vol. 1, pp. 301–309.

[557] *Part.* 4.18.19; *Asso y Manuel*, vol. 1, p. 117; Febrero, *Contratos*, ch. 12, § 3 no. 17 (vol. 3, pp. 276–277).

[558] C. 8.49.1, cf. D. 1.7.12.

[559] See *supra*, text at notes 137–157.

D.O. redactors of the northern French concept of *puissance paternelle* renders unnecessary a rule such as this Castilian one.

Thus, under the D.O., *puissance paternelle* was acquired over those born in legitimate marriage or those legitimated by subsequent marriage. Adoption was rejected as a method of creating family ties. The subjection of ungrateful emancipated children to *puissance paternelle* was irrelevant given the concept of paternal authority found in the D.O. The redactors have copied the C.N.'s conception of legitimation, and rejected that of the Castilian law. Overall, the D.O. redactors have restricted the possibilities for the creation of legitimate ties of parent to child; they have limited the possibilities of operation of paternal authority by restricting the class of those who may be subject to such authority. The restriction of legitimation and abolition of adoption show this clearly. Such limitation seems to have been the result of both social and legal-technical factors, being in accord with the growth of the close affective nuclear family unit, and permitting easy proof of legitimation. The C.N. was obviously influential in the restriction of legitimation; but, although the French code's influence is pervasive, it was not enough to prevent the abolition of adoption, though found in both the C.N. and the Castilian law.

Scope of *Puissance Paternelle*

Rules in Chapter V, title 7 of Book 1

This chapter—articles 36–58—deals with *puissance paternelle*. It is equivalent to title 9 of the C.N.'s first book: C.N. 371–387. The title and the chapter, however, do not correspond completely; this is because, from D.O. 46 (p. 53) onwards, the D.O. deals with reciprocal rights and duties (for example, aliment) of parents and children. The C.N. dealt with these earlier, in chapter V of its fifth title. These articles of the D.O. (46–58 (pp. 53–55)) will not be discussed here, as they do not deal directly with the notion of paternal power.[560] The remaining articles, D.O. 36–45 (p. 53), are the equivalents of the corresponding C.N. title, though there are differences between the two codes, as will be seen from the fact that the C.N. title contains articles 371–387, seventeen in all, while the D.O., in the part to be discussed, contains only ten. The reason for this difference will be shown *infra*; but it may be pointed out that the same situations are being regulated.

D.O. 36 (p. 53) states:

> L'enfant à tout âge doit honneur et respect à ses père et mère.

---

[560] These articles undopubtedly would illuminate the parent-child relationship; but considerations of space dictate a choice.

This is identical to C.N. 371.[561] The D.L.V. refers to *Part.* 4.19.1, which states that an upbringing (*crianza*) is one of the greatest benefits one man can give another, and such upbringing causes the natural love of a son for his father to grow:

> Otrosi el fijo es mas tenudo de amar et de obedescer al padre, porque él mesmo quiso levar el afan en criarle ante que darle á otri.

Thus, the *Partidas*' provision is similar to that in the D.O.; but this article is not particularly significant juridically and no conclusions of interest may be drawn from it.

D.O. 37 (p. 53) states:

> L'enfant reste sous l'autorité de ses père et mère, jusqu'à son majorité, ou à son emancipation.

C.N. 372 provides much the same.[562] C.N. 373 states that, during the marriage, the father alone exercises this authority. There is no equivalent article in the D.O., though, in the *1823 Projet* of the 1825 C.L., it was recommended that there be added to D.O. 37 the sentence: "En cas de dissentiment, l'autorité de père prévaut."[563] The D.L.V. refers to *Part.* 4.17.1, 2 and 3 and to Pothier.[564] *Ley* 1 of the *Partidas*' title states that *patria potestas* is the power a father has over his sons, grandsons and all who descend from him in the direct line. *Ley* 2 describes those sons not under a father's power, and repeats that the *padre* has in his power all his legitimate descendants in the male lines. *Ley* 3 defines what is meant by *potestas* or *poder*. The Pothier reference is to a passage that states that *puissance paternelle* ends, not only on the natural or civil death of the child, but also on his majority, marriage, or emancipation. Pothier also remarks that *puissance paternelle* belongs to the mother as well as the father, but that the mother only exercises the power when the father is unable to do so, otherwise she is excluded, being herself under the power of her husband.

The D.O. redactors have based their article on C.N. 372. They have thus overturned the Castilian law, where the *patria potestad* belonged to the father alone. The provision of the C.N. originates in the *droit coutumier* of France, whereas the Castilian provision originates in the *Partidas*' reception of Roman law.[565] The D.O. follows the *droit coutumier* in permitting majority to emancipate, whereas the Castilian law does not. (It should be recalled that contrary to the *Partidas*, in the Castilian law of a later date, marriage emancipated.)[566] The redactors of the D.O., however, have declined to adopt C.N. 373, and—in theory—have put the mother and father in a position of equality. Their reasons for overturning the Castilian concept of *patria potestad* will be canvassed *infra*;

---

[561] According to Batiza, the "verbatim" source.
[562] According to Batiza, the "almost verbatim" source.
[563] *1823 Projet*, p. 18: C.L. 234.
[564] Pothier, *T.P.C.*, p. 52 (no. 134).
[565] See *supra*, text at notes 137–157.
[566] See *supra*, text at notes 147–155.

but the reasons behind the rejection of C.N. 373 need to be discussed here. A first point is that the 1807 Act, ch. 17, on the celebration of marriages, by s. 16, on the consents of parents to the marriage of minor children, stated that both mother and father should consent; but if they disagreed, the consent of the father sufficed. Thus, this attitude in the D.O. was not dictated by an anterior statute. Nor can the rejection of C.N. 373 have been accidental: given how closely the D.O. redactors were following the C.N., the rejection must have been a deliberate choice. One must assume that the D.O. redactors felt that such sharing of the authority over children was appropriate: and, indeed, all the rest of the articles of this section give the parents an apparently equal authority, only in a later article is it stated that the father alone has the *administration* of his children's property, although both parents have an equal right to the enjoyment of such property. That such equal authority might be thought as being likely to lead to conflicts would explain the amendment of D.O. 37 (p. 53) in the 1825 C.L. This article, then, in both allowing majority to emancipate, and giving equal authority to the parents, signifies a rejection of the Castilian concept of *patria potestad* in favour of the *droit coutumier*'s concept of *puissance paternelle*.

D.O. 38 (p. 53) states:

> Tant que l'enfant reste sous la puissance de ses père et mère, il doit leur obéir dans tout ce qui n'est pas contraire à la religion et aux lois.

Batiza states that a passage of Pothier was the "substantially influencing" source.[567] This must be correct. There is no equivalent provision in the C.N., nor are any references given by the D.L.V. It should be noted that Pothier only states that children should obey their parents in all matters bar those contrary to "la loi de Dieu". The D.O. refines this statement; but the difference is unlikely to be important. The statement on obedience is an obvious one, given the nature of *puissance paternelle*, and holds no great significance.

D.O. 39 (p. 53) is more interesting:

> L'enfant au dessous de l'âge de puberté, ne peut quitter la maison paternelle, sans la permission de ses père et mère et ceux-ci ont le droit de le corriger, *pourvu* que ce soit d'une manière raisonnable.

Batiza gives, as the equal "substantially influencing" sources, both Pothier[568] and C.N. 374. The D.L.V. has no references. C.N. 374 states:

> L'enfant ne peut quitter la maison paternelle sans la permission de son père, si ce n'est pour enrôlement voluntaire, après l'âge de dix-huit ans révolus.

Pothier, *mutatis mutandis*, gives a roughly equivalent statement to that in the C.N. There are two obvious differences from the D.O.: the latter applies only to children under puberty, while the C.N. and Pothier refer to any child under paternal authority; second, the C.N. and Pothier make an exception for volun-

---

567 Pothier, *T.C.M.*, p. 177 (no. 389).
568 Pothier, *T.P.C.*, pp. 50–51 (no. 131).

tary enlistment, an exception not necessary in Louisiana, given that the D.O. refers only to pre-pubertal children. The D.O. retained the Castilian division of nonage into minority and pupillage.[569] It is because of this that the redactors have made their article apply only to pupils, that is, those under puberty. The Castilian law allowed fathers to compel their children to stay with them: such a right is implicit in the notion of paternal power being the *ligamiento* of *reverencia, subyeccion* and *castigamiento*, as defined by the *Quarta Partida.*[570] *Part.* 4.17.10 allows a father to demand of the judge that his son be returned into his power, should the son be *vagando por la tierra*, not wishing to obey his father. Asso and Manuel also point out that vagrant children may be compelled to return to their father.[571] The D.O. has thus lessened the *puissance paternelle* in comparison to the *droit coutumier*, the C.N., and Castilian law, since it only compels pupil children to remain with their parents. Given that, in the D.O., majority emancipated, that the division of nonage into pupillage and minority did not necessitate this D.O. provision, and that the redactors were not copying any obvious source, it must be assumed that the redactors considered this restriction of *puissance paternelle* appropriate for Louisiana. Perhaps they thought that the social circumstances of the New World favoured the early freeing of children from parental restrictions.

This article of the D.O. allows parents a power of reasonable chastisement. Neither of the "sources" cited by Batiza includes such a provision: they do have, however, elaborate provisions on "correction" of the child. Thus, in its articles 375–383, the C.N. permits and regulates the imprisonment of the child by the parents. Pothier states that parents have a "*droit d'une correction* modérée ... sur leurs enfants", adding that this "droit de correction dans la personne du père va jusqu'à pouvoir de sa seule autorité faire enfermer ses enfants dans des maisons de force".[572] If, however, a father had remarried, he required a judicial decree for the imprisonment of his son; while mothers, because of the "faiblesse de leur jugement, et le caractère d'emportement, assez ordinaire à ce sexe", always required judicial authorization for the imprisonment of their children.[573] Although the C.N.'s provisions differ in details from those of Pothier, the essential idea is the same: parents may demand the imprisonment of their children.[574] The D.O. gives no such draconian powers to parents. Maleville claims that the principle behind these articles is taken from a constitution of the Emperor Alexander found in Justinian's code.[575] The provisions of the C.N., however, are much more closely related to the *ancien droit* as stated by Pothier than to this imperial constitution. The Castilian law permitted the chastisement of children

---

[569] See *supra*, text at notes 443–448; *Asso y Manuel*, vol. 1, pp. 4–5 and 6–7.
[570] *Part.* 4.17.3.
[571] *Asso y Manuel*, vol. 1, p. 116.
[572] Pothier, *T.P.C.*, p. 51 (no. 132).
[573] *Ibid.*, pp. 51–52 (no. 133).
[574] See *infra*, on Quebec for further discussion.
[575] Maleville, *Analyse*, vol. 1, pp. 332 and 346; C. 8.46.3.

(*Part.* 4.17.3, as already cited, shows this),[576] but had no detailed provisions on imprisonment on the demand of fathers. Blackstone states that a father "may lawfully correct his child, being under age, in a reasonable manner".[577] The D.O. rather echoes this in its provision; but this has, for us, no signifance. The D.O. has excluded the C.N.'s regulation of imprisonment. Given the noticeable liberalization of *puissance paternelle* in the D.O., to have included such severe powers of imprisonment would have been to violate the obvious policy of the redactors. Further, there would be no facilities in Louisiana for such imprisonment of disobedient children; in France the tradition of such imprisonment meant there were facilities available. Similarly, severe misconduct on the part of children would usually mean they had committed some criminal offence, and the penal law could be left to deal with them. Circumstances would not favour the adoption of provisions such as those in the C.N., especially when there were no Castilian equivalents.

In conclusion, this article seems to be an amalgam of the French and Castilian law; but with a liberalization of both, and a rejection of the harsh powers of correction granted by the French law. The form of the article seems prompted by the sources, though the content is explicable in terms of contemporary society in Louisiana. Even if the wording of the right of reasonable correction has been adopted from Blackstone, there has been no importation of a common law principle: the expression of Blackstone has been adopted as congruent with the principles of the civil law, and offering a refined statement suitable for borrowing.

D.O. 40 (p. 53) states:

> Les père et mère ont le droit de nommer des tuteurs à leurs enfans, ainsi qu'il est prescrit au titre *des mineurs, etc.* et de leur transmettre leur autorité pour l'exercer même après leur mort.[578]

Batiza states that the "substantially influencing" source of this article is Domat.[579] The D.L.V. refers to *Part.* 6.16.3 and 6. The provision of Domat is roughly in accord with that of the 1808 Digest. *Part.* 6.16.3 states that a father or grandfather may by testament appoint a tutor to his son or grandson. *Part.* 6.16.6 adds that a mother may appoint a tutor to her son in her testament, if she has made her son her heir, and if there be no father to appoint a tutor. This tutor is controlled and directed by the local judge. If a mother does not so appoint her son as her heir, she may not name a tutor for him; but if she nevertheless does so

---

[576] See *supra*, text at note 570.

[577] W. Blackstone, *Commentaries on the Laws of England*, 9th ed., London, W. Strahan, 1783, vol. 1, p. 452. This edition is relied on as that used by Batiza and by Tucker, *op. cit. supra* note 166. Neither Batiza nor Tucker noticed this *possible* influence from Blackstone.

[578] Note that the spelling of *enfants* has changed; in this article the spelling *enfans* is used. The two spellings appear to vary at random in the (only) edition of the D.O.; it is just conceivable that the spelling used indicates a source copied. If this hypothesis is correct, then such variation could be used to help pinpoint sources even more precisely.

[579] Domat, *Loix civiles*, vol. 1, p. 145 (pt. 1, bk. 2, tit. 1, sect. 1, no. 4).

name a tutor, the judge has discretion to confirm him. T.W. Tucker suggests that Blackstone is the source of this article.[580] In relevant part Blackstone states:

> The legal power of a father (for a mother, as such is entitled to no power, but only to reverence and respect) the power of a father, I say, over the persons of his children ceases at the age of twenty-one. . . . Yet till that age arrives this empire of the father continues even after his death; for he may by his will appoint a guardian to his children.[581]

The last sentence of this quotation seems to have exercised some influence on D.O. 43 (p. 53), since there is no equivalent in Domat. In form, the article would seem to be an amalgam of Blackstone and Domat. This has, however, little significance for the rule enunciated, which is a traditional rule of the *droit coutumier* of France. Further, if as directed by the article, the relevant part of the title *des mineurs* is examined, the rules on testamentary tutors in the D.O. and C.N. are very similar.[582] Thus, this article, though possibly an amalgam of Domat and Blackstone in form, contains a traditional civilian rule in content. The wording may in part be influenced by Blackstone—but the *rule* is different.

The rule in the D.O. is of French origin, since the mother has certain rights to appoint a testamentary tutor, whereas, in the Castilian law, her right to do so was very limited indeed.[583] On the other hand, in the D.O., as in the Castilian law, tutorship ends when the child reaches puberty; thereafter there may be a curator, but curatorship is always dative, never testamentary. Thus, the rule in the D.O. is rather more restricted than would initially appear, and is an amalgam of the French concept of *puissance paternelle*, as shared between the mother and father, and the Castilian division of pupillage and minority.[584] The only influence Blackstone has had is on the expression of D.O. 40 (p. 53). Thus, this provision of the D.O. is the result of the inclusion in the 1808 Digest of the Castilian division of nonage into pupillage and minority combined with the French concept of *puissance paternelle* shared between father and mother. The increased rôle given to the wife and mother is consistent with the rest of the provisions on paternal power.

D.O. 41 (p. 52) states:

> Fathers and mothers may, during their life, delegate a part of their authority to teachers, schoolmasters and other persons to whom they entrust their children for their education, such as the power of restraint and correction, as far as may be necessary to answer the purposes for which they employ them.

---

[580] Tucker, *op. cit. supra* note 166, pp. 271–272 and n. 40.

[581] Blackstone, *op. cit. supra* note 577, vol. 1, p. 453.

[582] Compare C.N. 397–401 with D.O. 11–14 (p. 61).

[583] See e.g. *Asso y Manuel*, vol. 1, p. 9.

[584] Book 1, tit. 8 is interesting. It is entitled "Des mineurs, de leur tutelle, curatelle et de leur emancipation". There is an uneasy mixture of French and Castilian concepts: notably the French concepts of *puissance paternelle* and emancipation, and the Castilian division of pupils and minors, these Castilian rules being, to some extent, predicated on the concept of a *patria potestad*.

Batiza claims Pothier as the "partially influencing" source of this article.[585] The French author states that a father and mother have a right to retain their children with them, "ou les envoyer dans tel collège, ou autre endroit ou ils jugent à propos de les envoyer pour leur éducation". Pothier says nothing of a licence to delegate paternal powers; but such would exist. This delegation of paternal power is made explicit in Blackstone, who says, in a text bearing a very strong resemblance to the English version of the D.O. article:

> He [i.e. the father] may also delegate part of his parental authority, during his life, to the tutor or schoolmaster of his child; who is then *in loco parentis*, and has as such a portion of the power of the parent committed to his charge, *viz.* that of restraint and correction, as may be necessary to answer the purposes for which he is employed.[586]

Tucker claims this as the source of the D.O. article.[587] The D.L.V. refers to Febrero, who states:

> En consecuencia de esta oblicion, y dominio pueden los padres servirse de sus hijos, sin que éstos tengan accion à pedirles salarios; por lo que cumplen con mantenerlos, y educarlos segun su esfera, y possibilidad. Pueden asimismo ponerlos à pupilage con Maestros que los enseñen, y estos deben hacerlo, sin ocultarles cosa alguna de la ciencia, arte, ù oficio que profesan, à fin de que se instruyan à satisfacion de inteligentes, y à este efecto se les permite castigarlos de suerte que no los elisien en sus cuerpos, pena de los daños (2) [*Part.* 5.8.11].[588]

There can be no doubt that the actual wording and expression of D.O. 41 (p. 52) is taken from Blackstone; as regards the rule contained, that the mode of expression which should have been adopted is that of Blackstone is of little signifance, in so far as similar rules may be found in other sources: there has been no importation of a rule of the common law. Blackstone has provided a useful expression of the rule, and his expression has been appropriated. It should be noted that, consistent with the general trend of this title, this power has been given by the D.O. redactors to both the mother and father.

D.O. 42 (p. 53) states that:

> Les père et mère auront, durant leur mariage, la jouissance des biens de leurs enfans jusqu'à leur majorité ou émancipation.

Batiza states that C.N. 384 is the "substantially influencing" source of the D.O. article, while *Proj. An. VIII*, 1.8.12 is a subsidiary source. The D.L.V. refers to Domat[589] and *Part.* 4.17.5. C.N. 384 states:

---

[585] Pothier, *T.P.C.*, p. 50 (no. 131).

[586] Blackstone, *op. cit. supra* note 577, p. 453.

[587] Tucker, *op. cit. supra* note 166, pp. 271–272, n. 40.

[588] Febrero, *Contratos*, ch. 12, § 4 no. 32 (vol. 3, pp. 284–285). The footnotes cite *Part.* 2.20.3, and 5.8.11.

[589] Domat, *Loix Civiles*, vol. 1, p. 369 (pt. 2, bk. 2, tit. 2, sect. 2, no. 2).

> Le père, durant le mariage, et après la dissolution du mariage, le survivant des père et mère auront la jouissance des biens de leurs enfans, jusqu'à l'âge de dix-huit ans accomplis, ou jusqu'à l'émancipation qui pourrait avoir lieu avant l'âge de dix-huit ans.

The *Proj. An. VIII* is, in relevant part, substantially the same as C.N. 384, except that, unlike the latter, the enjoyment ends at the majority (or emancipation) of the children, not on their reaching eighteen. This difference is the result of a decision during the redaction of the Code Napoléon to lower the age of this ending of the enjoyment of the usufruct, lest parents, desirous of keeping this usufruct, unreasonably refused either to allow their child to marry or to emancipate him or her.[590] Domat states that the father, during his life, has a usufruct of the goods which may have been acquired by his unemancipated children. *Part.* 4.17.5 states that those gains made by sons using the goods of their fathers belong to their fathers, while those gains made by sons through their own industry or by, *inter alia*, finding a treasure or by donations to them *mortis causa* or *inter vivos* belong to the sons; but the usufruct of this last class of goods belongs to the father, by reason of his power, while he is alive. In other words, the *Partidas*' provision follows the Roman law on *bona adventicia* and *bona profecticia*.[591]

Once more, the provision in the *Partidas* has not been followed because it is contradictory to the much more restricted conception of *puissance paternelle* found in the D.O., where, for example, majority ended paternal authority. Further, in line with their policy of giving wives equal rights with their husbands in such authority, the D.O. redactors have given both parents equal enjoyment, whereas the C.N. and its *projet* state that, during the marriage, the father alone enjoys the property. The D.O. redactors have followed the *Proj. An. VIII* in providing that the parental usufruct should last until the children reached the age of majority. The French codifiers' fear that parents would unreasonably refuse permission to their children to marry might not have been relevant in Louisiana, where lack of parental consent was not a ground for annulling a marriage. Further, the more traditional view adopted by the D.O. redactors was more in line with the theory of family implicit in their conception of *puissance paternelle*, since it assumed that parents would be acting in the best interests of their children, and that their usufruct of the children's property was reasonable given the parental tasks of care, control and upbringing. In the D.O., the usufruct ends at the dissolution of the marriage, because the surviving parent is entitled to become the natural tutor of the child.[592] Under D.O. 44 (p. 53)

---

[590] See Maleville, *Analyse*, vol. 1, pp. 351–353; Maleville thoroughly disapproved of the C.N. provision. See also M. Planiol, *Treatise on the Civil Law*, trans. by Louisiana State Law Institute, St. Paul, MN, West Pub. Co., 1959, vol. 1,2, pp. 48–49 (no. 1704) Note that this article of the 1800 *projet* also states that this usufruct does not cover children's earnings. C.N. 387 contains the same rule, copied by the D.O. See *infra*, text at notes 599–604.

[591] Buckland, *Textbook*, pp. 280–281; see *supra*, text at notes 107–109.

[592] D.O. 6 (p. 59).

(discussed below), in the event of separation from bed and board, the right of usufruct goes to the parent who sued for the separation.

D.O. 43 (p. 53) provides thus:

> Les charges de cette jouissance seront:
> 1. Celles auxquelles sont tenus les usufruitiers;
> 2. La nourriture, l'entretien, et l'education des enfans, selon leur fortune.

Batiza states the "verbatim" source of this article to be the first two paragraphs of C.N. 385. The D.L.V. cites *Part.* 4.17.5 and Domat.[593] Domat sets out the duty of a father in connection with his usufruct, and the provisions are much as those in the D.O.;[594] he also states that parents are obliged to nourish and maintain their children, not only because of the usufruct, but also because of the blood tie.[595] He generalizes this into a reciprocal duty between ascendants and descendants. *Part.* 4.17.5 is not really equivalent to the D.O. article, merely stating that a father has a usufruct of the *bona adventicia.*[596] *Part.* 4.19.1 and 2, however, do contain provisions on the care of children. *Ley* 1 states that fathers should look after their children, *ley* 2 giving the reasons why. No statement is made to the effect that this is a reciprocal duty correlative to the parental right of usufruct; instead, the relevant *ley* states that this duty is the result of the natural law that makes all creatures nourish and guard their offspring, of the natural love parents have towards their children, and of the spiritual and temporal laws enjoining parents so to do. The Digest's article, following the C.N., has formed the parental right of usufruct and the duties of upbringing into the mold of reciprocal obligations. A connection has been made between the two not found in the old Castilian law, which regarded the paternal usufruct as a right resulting from the natural and civil power of parents over children, while the duty of care and upbringing was the result also of natural and civil law. The C.N. and D.O. here conceive of family relationships as those between individuals with reciprocal—if not always equal—rights and duties, while the *Partidas* conceive of such relationships as the result of the natural power of the ascendant over his descendants, though tempered by the natural love he has for them: that is, family relationships are regarded as those of dependency. That the D.O. does not copy the last two paragraphs of C.N. 385 has no significance for the above argument.[597]

D.O. 44 (p. 53) states that:

> Cet usufruit, en cas de séparation de corps, aura lieu pour la totalité, au profit de celui des père et mère qui aura obtenu la séparation, aux charges prescrites dans l'article précedent *et l'autre époux en sera privé.*[598]

---

[593] Domat, *Loix Civiles*, vol. 1, pp. 369–370 (pt. 2, bk. 2, tit. 2, sect. 2, nos. 7 and 11).

[594] *Ibid.*, vol. 1, p. 369 (pt. 2, bk. 2, tit. 2, sect. 2, no. 7).

[595] *Ibid.*, vol. 1, p. 369 (pt. 2, bk. 2, tit. 2, sect. 2, no. 11).

[596] See *supra*, text at note 591.

[597] The fourth paragraph of the C.N. article on the usufruct is taken from the northern conception of *garde*, and there was no equivalent in the *droit écrit*: see Maleville, *Analyse*, vol. 1, pp. 353–354. An argument that this was excluded as contrary to the Castilian law would be doubtful.

[598] Emphasis added: these words are not found in the English version.

Batiza claims C.N. 386 to be a "partially influencing" source. The D.L.V. gives no references. C.N. 386 is as follows:

> Cette jouissance n'aura pas lieu au profit de celui des père et mère, contre lequel le divorce aurait été pronounce; et elle cessera à l'égard de la mère, dans le cas d'un second mariage.

Although the C.N. mentions divorce, *mutatis mutandis*, the general drift of the two articles is indeed the same: the usufruct goes to the innocent party who wins the action. Given the notion of one party being guilty, given that the wife has equal rights of authority, the D.O. provision is hardly surprising. The D.L.V. makes no reference to Castilian law. And indeed the concept of *patria potestad* in the Castilian law is so Roman that such power could never be exercised by the mother. The usufruct always belongs to the father alone: separation *a mensa et a thoro* would have no effect on his rights. An important difference between the D.O. and the C.N. is that, in the latter code, the mother did not enjoy the usufruct during the marriage, so that, if her husband divorced her, as regards the usufruct, she lost nothing.

D.O. 45 (p. 53) provides thus:

> Cet usufruit ne s'étendra pas aux biens que les enfants pourront acquérir par un travail et une industrie séparée, et à ceux gui leur seront donnés et légués, sous la condition expresse que les père et mère n'en jouiront pas.

The English version of this article reads:

> This usufruct shall not extend to any estate which the children may acquire by their own labour or industry, *whilst they live apart from their father and mother*, nor to such estate as is given or left them under the express condition that the father and mother shall not enjoy such usufruct.

The clause emphasised does not appear in the French text, and significantly alters the meaning of the article. Though there was no mention in the 1823 *Projet*, this clause was removed from the English text in the 1825 Code (C.L. 242), and the French was altered by changing "séparée" to "séparés." The French text of D.O. 45 (p. 53) is very similar to C.N. 387:[599]

> Elle ne s'étendra pas aux biens que les enfans pourront acquérir par un travail et une industrie séparés, ni à ceux qui leur seront donnés ou légués sous la condition expresse que les père et mère n'en jouiront pas.

The D.L.V. refers to *Part.* 4.17.6 and 7, and to Febrero.[600] The two *leyes* of the *Partidas* deal with *peculium castrense* and *peculium quasi castrense*, following the provisions of the Roman law, though the categories are adapted for medieval

---

[599] According to Batiza, the "almost verbatim" source. This point is covered in *Proj. An. VIII*, 1.8.12. See *supra*, note 590.

[600] Febrero, *Juicios*, bk 2, ch. 3 § 2 no. 38 (vol. 5(2), p. 510).

Castile.[601] The father is stated to have no rights in such acquisitions. *Part.* 4.17.5, though uncited here, provided that *bona adventicia* (all property acquired other than from the father's goods) belonged to the son, but the father had a usufruct: such property included gains made "por obra de sus manos".[602] Febrero, as cited, defines *bienes castrenses* and *cuasi castrenees*, much as do *leyes* 6 and 7 discussed above. The categories include gains made in war, at the court and palace of the king (either for services or from royal munificence and liberality), what is gained as the salary or stipend paid for the public teaching of some science, and also gains from ecclesiastical benefices and dignities.

If the *English* text of D.O. 45 (p. 53) were taken as the correct one, it would result that the parental usufruet would extend to acquisitions made by children by their own labour while living *with* their parents. This would seem to be similar to *Part.* 4.17.5. If whatever children acquired while living *away* from their parents were regarded as the modern equivalent of *peculium castrense* and *quasi castrense*, it might perhaps be argued that D.O.45 (p. 53) embodied a modernized version of the Castilian law, and that this chapter had obviously been drawn up in English, as the similarity to Blackstone of some of the English versions of the articles would suggest. This argument, however, would be wrong. Although the addition of an extra clause would seem an odd error to make in translating, it is obvious that the translators have taken "séparée" to refer to the children themselves, rather than to "travail" and "industrie". It is indeed a strange error to have made, given that "séparée" is feminine singular (to agree with "industrie") while "enfants" is masculine plural. One may surmise that hasty translation resulted in the mistake. That the difference is the result of error is suggested by the removal of the clause in the 1825 C.L. without any comment having been made. Further, to regard the *English* text as embodying the Castilian law would be rather too fanciful.

It is clear that, in D.O. 45 (p. 53), the redactors have followed the C.N. and overturned the Castilian law with its categories of *bona profecticia*, *bona adventicia*, *peculium castrense* and *peculium quasi castrense*. Thus the Roman rules of Castile have not been favoured, and this is in line with the general actions of the redactors in this chapter.

As already indicated, the remaining articles of this chapter of the D.O. will not be discussed. Title VIII of Book One does have a relevant article, however, which should be discussed here here. This is D.O. 5 (p. 59), which states:

> Le père est, durant le mariage, administrateur des biens de ses enfans mineurs.
>
> Il est comptable quant à la propriété et aux revenus, des biens dont il n'a pas la jouissance; et quant à la propriété seulement, de ceux des biens dont la loi lui donne l'usufruit.
>
> Cette administration, cesse lors de la majorité ou de l'émancipation desdits enfans.

---

[601] See *supra*, text at notes 107–109 and 137–141.

[602] See *supra*, text at notes 590–591.

This is nearly identical to C.N. 389.[603] The D.L.V. gives no references. The Castilian position was that the father was administrator of the *bona adventicia*, that is, of the property of which he had a usufruct. He owned the *bona profecticia*. He had no interest in any *peculium castrense* and *quasi-castrense* which his son might have.[604] It should be recalled that more classes of property were subject to the paternal usufruct in Castile, and that such usufruct lasted until the death of the *padre* or the emancipation of the son.

The above articles contain the core of the provisions on *puissance paternelle* in the D.O.; thus, although there will be further discussion of relevant provisions, it is useful here to form some conclusions on the foregoing. Although not all the articles of the C.N. have been adopted, and although not all of those which have been introduced have been followed exactly, there can be no doubt that the conception of *puissance paternelle* found in the D.O. is that of the C.N. The Castilian law had permitted more control over property, and had envisaged a form of authority which was not ended by the child reaching majority. In both these aspects of the power (control over property, and emancipating majority) the D.O. has followed the C.N. The Castilian law only gave the power to fathers. The D.O. gives it equally to mothers and fathers. Though the father administers the property of the children, the D.O. redactors have gone farther than the C.N. in granting equality to the mother. The D.O., following the C.N., has given the parents a usufruct in the property of their minor children. This was not generally the position in the *droit coutumier*, where, unless the relevant *coutume* specified that such a usufruct existed, the parents would not have had one. It would be wrong to argue that the D.O. redactors have here copied the C.N. because it provided similarly to the law of Castile: in other aspects of this chapter of their code, the Louisiana redactors have not hesitated to overturn the Castilian provisions. The C.N. provisions were copied because they were in the C.N., not because they were similar to the Castilian. (Reasons derived from Louisiana society will be discussed below.)

In the above discussion, little attention has been paid to the *Proj. An. VIII*. Title VIII of its first book was devoted to *puissance paternelle*. The articles of this title have exerted no real influence over the D.O. equivalent. The title of the *Projet* is divided into three chapters, with an initial general provision (*Proj. An. VIII*, 1.8.1) which states:

> La puissance paternelle est un droit fondé sur la nature et confirmé par la loi, qui donne au père et à la mère la surveillance de la personne et l'administration des biens de leurs enfans mineurs et non émancipés par mariage.

This article apparently puts the husband and wife on an equal footing; but the specific provisions of the *Projet* on detention of children in a *maison de correction* (*Proj. An. VIII*, 1.8.2–11, all of chapter one) and on the administration and

---

[603] According to Batiza the source, classed as "almost verbatim, first paragraph", and "verbatim second paragraph".

[604] See *Asso y Manuel*, vol. 1, p. 116.

jouissance of the property of the children—other than that earned by their own labour and industry (*Proj. An. VIII*, 1.8.12–14, all of chapter two)—show that during the marriage the father alone exercised these rights. Thus, in this respect, the provisions of the *Proj. An. VIII* are the same as those of the C.N. and *droit coutumier*: the equality of husband and wife found in the D.O. cannot have been borrowed from the *Proj. An. VIII*; at the most, such equality could have been inspired by *Proj. An. VIII*, 1.8.1, though this would seem so oblique an influence as not to be worth considering. The third and final chapter of title VIII of the 1800 *Projet* is on *disposition officieuse*;[605] there is no equivalent in either the C.N. or D.O. and it need not be further considered here. Thus, it may be concluded that the 1800 Projet's title on *puissance paternelle* has had no significant influence on the D.O.: the influence of the work of the French redactors on this area of the D.O. came from the C.N. itself.

An important aspect of this chapter of the D.O. is the influence of Blackstone, who seems to have exerted some sway on the wording of D.O. 39, 40 and 41 (p. 53). A first point to make is that these same articles express rules that may be traced elsewhere in civilian sources. That Blackstone was copied here does not mean that principles of the common law were introduced. Further, Blackstone's rules were modified in the redaction of the chapter, since he only gave authority to the father. The wording of Blackstone was adapted to serve the purposes of the redactors in parts of D.O. 39 and 40 (p. 53). One may surmise that the inclusion of D.O. 41 (p. 53) was prompted by the redactors' examination of Blackstone. (Indeed, the inclusion of D.O. 40 (p. 53) may also have been prompted by Blackstone—as well as his wording being adopted and adapted—as there is no C.N. equivalent.) The D.O. redactors obviously used Blackstone where they considered he might put forward a useful or borrowable proposition. These articles in part are the result of such consultation: they do not denote an introduction of common law principles, and they are congruent with the civil law. Blackstone merely prompted some provisions, and his mode of expression to some extent was borrowed.

These articles demonstrate the rejection of the Castilian model of *patria potestad* in favour of the Napoleonic version of *puissance paternelle*, though the D.O. redactors have apparently increased the authority of the mother in comparison to that found in the C.N. This change in the law—the borrowing of the essentially French concept of *puissance paternelle*—is not the result of slavish copying of the C.N.: there are too many differences between the codes for that to be a plausible claim, though some specific provisions must have been prompted by the C.N. The D.O. redactors evidently approved of the general thrust of the C.N.'s provisions on *puissance paternelle*. The Castilian concept of *patria potestad* was based on a notion of family where the patriarchal head of the household has his descendants in his power, and they are dependent on him by virtue of such power and his control over the family property. The C.N.'s concept of *puissance paternelle* to a large extent was based on the notion that

---

[605] On *disposition officieuse*, see *infra*, note 627.

children are in the authority of their parents for their own protection and care: their parents look after them and their property. Such authority ends, in most of its aspects, on the children's reaching majority, because the necessity for care and protection no longer exists. Further, the C.N. conceives of the family as nuclear and composed of individuals bound together by reciprocal rights and duties, based on affection, while the Castilian law conceives of the family as based on the authority and power of the head of the household. The difference on this point between the two is shown over the attitudes to the parental usufruct and education and rearing of the children.[606] The D.O. redactors selected the version of family found in the C.N., as regards the articles already discussed. They modified the C.N. provisions, and denied fathers any rights of imprisonment; but the model of *puissance paternelle* adopted is that of the C.N. Given that the redactors had a choice to exercise, to have exercised it in any other way would have been unthinkable, since the C.N. provided provisions which reflected the modern, affective, companionate family. Children were to be controlled by their parents for their own good while minors; they were not, as adults, to be subject to the authority of a *paterfamilias* simply because they were descended from him.

The Marriage of *Enfants de Famille*

Pothier states that the right of parents to exact from their children certain duties of respect was one aspect of paternal power.[607] He adds that this aspect of paternal power only ended with the natural death of the child or his parents.[608] From this aspect of paternal power derived the obligation of children to gain the consent of their parents to marry.[609] The rules of the *ancien droit* in France will be discussed below; but it may be pointed out that the 1808 Louisiana Digest requires parental consent only for the marriage of minors. This necessity of parental consent to the marriage of children raised a number of problems or questions: first, that of oppositions to a proposed marriage; second, that of the possibility of nullification of a marriage where parental consent had not been gained; and third, that of who, if anyone, was required to consent in default of parents. To discuss these issues in relation to Louisiana, it is appropriate to set out: first, the Canon law, second, the French *ancien droit* and codified law, third, the Castilian law as applicable in Spanish North America, and fourth the Louisiania provisions. This allows ascertainment of the sources of the Louisiana provisions.

The Canon law on the marriage of *enfants de famille* is simple: there was no requirement of parental consent to the marriage of minors, even after the

---

606 See *supra*, text at notes 593–597.
607 Pothier, *T.P.C.*, p. 50 (no. 130).
608 *Ibid.*, p. 52 (no. 135).
609 *Ibid.*

Council of Trent (1563).[610] It had originally been proposed in the Council that marriages would be null if, without the consent of parents, they were contracted by sons under eighteen years and daughters under sixteen;[611] but this proposal was ultimately rejected, though, *pro futuro*, the Council decreed the nullity of clandestine marriages, while, for the past, clandestine marriages were valid if free consent of the contracting parties had existed. Thus, under Tridentine Canon law, the marriage of *enfants de famille* was valid, although contracted without the consent of parents.[612]

It appears that there were initially no restrictions on the marriage of minors without parental consent in the *ancien droit*, such restrictions as there once had been having fallen into desuetude.[613] The policy of the Canon law was contrary to that of the French Crown, and, in 1556, Henri II stated in an edict that *enfants de familles* who married clandestinely against the wishes of their parents could be disinherited, and their parents could also revoke any donations made to such children. If such children were disinherited, they were deprived of the advantages they would otherwise have received under their marriage contracts, or local *coutumes*. Sons over thirty years of age and daughters over twenty-five could avoid these penalties, if, before marrying, they had sought the advice and consent of their mother and father.[614] This ordinance was confirmed by article 41 of the *Ordonnance* of Blois of 1579, which, by its article 40, provided that priests, who celebrated the marriages of *enfants de famille ou en puissance d'autrui*, were punishable as *fauteurs du crime de rapt*, if such *enfants* did not show the requisite consent of their father, mother, tutor or curator.[615] Subsequent royal legislation at various times confirmed and extended these provisions.[616]

Although it was nowhere stated that the marriages of minor children were null for lack of parental consent, this was the position taken by the *jurisprudence* and *doctrine* in the *ancien droit*. It was argued that, since the priest, under article 40 of the *Ordonnance* of Blois, was guilty as *fauteur du crime de rapt*, the marriage of the minor was rendered null by such *crime de rapt* (abduction),

---

[610] Esmein, *op. cit. supra* note 69, vol. 1, pp. 153–163 (pre-Tridentine law); and vol. 2, pp. 155–156, 163–164 and 167–170 (Tridentine law).

[611] *Ibid.*, vol. 2, p. 156.

[612] The Council decreed thus: "Tametsi dubitandum non est clandestina matrimonia libero consensu contrahentium facta, rata et vera esse matrimonia, quamdiu Ecclesia ea irrita non fecit, proinde jure damnandi sint, ut eos sancta synodus anathemate damnat, qui ea vera et rata esse negant, quique falso affirmant matrimonia a filiis-familias sine consensu parentum contracta irrita esse, et parentes ea rata et irrita facere posse; nihilominus sancta Dei Ecclesia, ex iustissimis causis illa semper detestata est atque prohibuit." On the necessity of future marriages being *in facie ecclesiae*, the Council said: "Qui aliter, quam praesente parocho, vel alio sacerdote de ipsius parochi seu ordinarii licentia, et duobus vel tribus testibus matrimonium contrahere attentabunt, eos sancta synodus ad sic contrahendum omnino inhabiles reddit, et huiusmodi contractus irritos et nullos esse decernit, prout eos praesenti decreto irritos facit et annullat." See Baade, "Form", pp. 20–21 and n. 100; Pothier, *T.C.M.*, pp. 138–139 (no. 321).

[613] According to Pothier, *T.C.M.*, p. 140 (nos. 323–324,); and *Pan fran.*, vol. 3, pp. 164–165.

[614] Quoted in relevant part in Pothier, *T.C.M.*, p. 141 (no. 324).

[615] *Ibid.*, p. 141 (no. 325).

[616] *Ibid.*, pp. 141–142 (nos. 325–326); Esmein, *op. cit. supra* note 69, vol. 2, pp. 200–207.

because abduction was contrary to freedom of consent, which was of the essence of marriage.[617] The presumption that the marriage of a minor without parental consent had been procured by abduction was irrebutable.[618] But the marriages of sons over thirty years and daughters over twenty-five years were considered valid, there being no presumption of *crime de rapt*. By the Royal edict of 26th November, 1639, such sons and daughters could only be disinherited if they had not sent an "acte de sommation respectueuse" as provided for under the 1556 edict, asking for permission to marry.[619] A 1692 *arrêt de règlement* of the *Parlement de Paris* stated that a child had to go in person to his father and mother's house to make the *summation respectueuse*.[620]

Thus, in the *ancien droit* minor children required the consent of their father and mother to marry, and if they did not have such consent, their marriages were annullable. Their parents could always oppose such a marriage.[621] Sons over thirty, and daughters over twenty-five could validly marry without the consent of their parents; but they could be disinherited unless they had sent an *acte de sommation respectueuse*.[622] If the mother or father were dead, the tutor or curator of the minor child had to consent to such child's marriage, after having taken the advice of the nearest relatives, following article 43 of the *Ordonnance* of Blois. There was no such procedure for adults whose parents were dead, since they would not have tutors and curators.

The *Code Napoléon* states in article 148 that sons under twenty-five years and daughters under twenty-one years cannot marry without the consent of their parents; if their parents disagree, the consent of the father suffices. C.N. 149 states that if one parent is dead or incapable of consenting, the consent of the other suffices. C.N. 150 states that if both parents are dead or incapable of consenting, then the grandparents should consent. If the grandparents of one line disagree, then the consent of the grandfather suffices; while if there is disagreement between the grandparents of the maternal line and the paternal line, then this taken to amount to consent. C.N. 160 states that if there be no father, mother, grandfather or grandmother, or if such are incapable of consenting, then sons and daughters under twenty-one years cannot marry without the consent of the family council. Thus, the C.N. differs significantly from the *ancien droit* in replacing the consent of the tutor with that of the grandparents or of the family council. The 1800 *projet* of the C.N. had stipulated that children of either sex up to the age of twenty-five required parental consent; if the parents disagreed, then that of the father sufficed (*Proj. An. VIII*, 1.5.10). *Proj. An. VIII*, 1.5.11 provided

---

617 Pothier, *T.C.M.*, pp. 100–101, 142 (no. 225, 228 and 326).
618 *Ibid.*, p. 142 (no. 326); Brissaud, *History*, p. 117.
619 Pothier, *T.C.M.*, pp. 141–144 (nos. 324–326); Loisel, *op. cit supra* note 62, bk. 1, tit. 2, rule 5; C. Pocquet de Livonnière, *Règles du droit françois*, 3rd ed., Paris, chez P.G. le Mercier, 1737, bk.1, tit. 2, s. 1, art. 7.
620 *Arrêt* of 27th August, 1692: see Maleville, *Analyse*, vol. 1, p. 154.
621 See Brissaud, *History*, pp. 129–30; *supra*, text at notes 176–180.
622 Loisel, *op. cit supra* note 62, bk. 1, tit. 2, rule 5; Pocquet de Livonnière, *op. cit supra* note 619, bk.1, tit. 2, s. 1, art. VII.

that if one parent was dead or otherwise incapable, the consent of the other sufficed, "bien qu'il ait contracté un second mariage".[623] *Proj. An. VIII*, 1.5.13 stated that if the father or mother be dead or incapable, then the grandparents replace them: if the grandparents disagree, then the majority decision rules; while if they are evenly divided, then the family council should decide.[624] *Proj. An. VIII*, 1.5.14 stated that should there be no parents or grandparents, then the family council is required to consent to the marriage of children under twenty-five years.[625] The rules of the 1800 *projet* are thus basically the same as those of the C.N. in having replaced the tutor with the grandparents and family council.

During the Revolution, the requirements of *sommations respectueuses* from adult children had been abolished.[626] Such *sommations* accordingly did not appear in the *Proj. An. VIII*, which provided that children can never be disinherited.[627] In the C.N., however, in articles 151 to 154, a similar institution was reintroduced, with the name of the formal request changed to *acte respectueuse*. Sons between 25 and 30 years had to send three such *actes* to their parents, or should their parents be dead, their grandparents. One *acte* had to be sent a month for three months, and then the son had to wait a further month before being able to marry without parental (or grandparental) consent. Daughters between twenty-one and twenty-five had to do likewise. Under C.N. 153, sons over thirty could marry without parental consent after having sent one such *acte*, and having waited one month. Daughters over twenty-five were not mentioned, but the same rule was taken to apply to them.[628] The C.N. provided no penalty of disinheritance if the child failed to send such *actes*: only the *officier de l'état civil* could be punished (C.N. 157). The authors of the *Pandectes françaises* argued that the father could still disinherit his children for not sending such *actes* on the grounds that, first, though the code was silent on the matter, there is little point in a prohibition without a penalty, and second, the silence of the code must mean the *ancien droit* on this point continues to exist.[629] These authors are presumably the *auteur récent* to whom Maleville refers and with whom he disagrees, arguing that there no longer can be disinheritance.[630] Maleville's view was the one followed.[631] Thus, with the C.N., there is the reintroduction of the

---

[623] This clause was dropped from the C.N. to avoid prejudging in cases of divorce: Maleville, *Analyse*, vol. 1, p. 148; but see *Proj. An. VIII*, 1.5.12 on controls on consent in cases of divorce.

[624] *Proj. An. VIII*, 1.5.12 is not strictly relevant here, see *supra*, note 623.

[625] Contrary to C.N., the age for males and females is the same in all these articles. *Proj. An. VIII*, 1.5.15 deals with when child and family council persist in different views.

[626] By the *loi* of 20th Sept. 1792: see Huussen, *op. cit. supra* note 106, pp. 42–44. It was this law that replaced the consent of the tutor with that of the family council.

[627] See *Proj. An. VIII*, 1.8.15–20 on *disposition officieuse* where, by testamentary acts, parents can by-pass married children who were notorious *dissipateurs*, but only by leaving property to the *dissipateur*'s children or further descendants.

[628] See C.B.M. Toullier, *Le droit civil français suivant l'ordre du Code… continué et complété par J.B. Duvergier*, 6th ed., Paris, F. Cotillon, 1844–1848, vol. 1, p. 326 and n. 2 thereon (no. 548).

[629] *Pan. fran.*, vol. 3, pp. 173–174.

[630] Maleville, *Analyse*, vol. 1, pp. 153–154; he does not specifically refer to the *Pandectes françaises*, but it is fairly certain this is the work he means.

[631] See Toullier, *op. cit. supra* note 628, p. 327 (no. 550).

requirement of the seeking of parental consent to the marriage of adult children, though adult children may no longer be disinherited for failing to comply with this requirement. In line with other C.N. provisions in this area of the law, failing the mother and father, grandparental consent should be sought.

The relevant Castilian law is contained in a royal *Pragmática* of 1776.[632] Minor children (those under twenty-five years), no matter what their rank or social position, must seek and obtain consent and counsel for betrothal or marriage.[633] They require such consent and counsel from their father, whom failing from their mother. If both their parents fail, then they require the consent and counsel of both of the grandparents, by both lines respectively. Failing grandparents, minors require the consent and counsel of the two nearest adult relatives who have no interest in such marriage: if such relatives have not the capacity to give consent and counsel, then the consent and counsel of tutors or curators is required. In this matter, however, the actions of the said close relatives and of the tutors and curators are subject to the supervision of the courts.[634] If minors celebrate their marriage without such consent and counsel, although the marriage is valid, it is deprived of civil effects such as the right to claim dowry. The contracting party may be disinherited completely, and even excluded from entailed property. This disinheritance and exclusion affects all his descendants.[635] There still would exist, however, a right for suitable necessary aliment.[636] Adults of twenty-five years are said by this *Pragmática* to comply with its provisions by seeking paternal counsel only when they wish to marry. If they fail to seek such parental counsel, then they are subject to the established penalties.[637] Note that adults are only required to seek parental counsel; unlike minors, they are not required to *gain* parental consent. The

---

[632] Don Carlos III por pragmática de 23 Marzo de 1776 publicada en 27 el mismo: "Consentimiento paterno para la contraccion de esponsales y matrimonio por los hijos de familia": *Nov. Rec. Cast.* 10.2.9. This *Pragmática* is divided into 19 sections, and I will refer in the notes to the relevant section.

[633] See *Pragmática supra* note 632, s. 2 on rank and social class. There were further restrictions, of course, on the marriages of Princes and certain public functionaries. See ss. 11–19.

[634] *Ibid.*, s. 21, in the relevant part, reads: " . . . los hijos é hijas de familia menores de veinte y cinco años . . . dehan, para celebrar el contrato de esponsales, pedir y obtener el consejo y consentimiento de su padre, y en su defecto de la madre, y á falto de ambos de los abuelos, por ambos lineas respectivamente y no teniendolos, de los dos parientes mas cercanos que se hallen en la mayor edad, y no sean interesadod ó aspirantes al tal matrimonio, y no habiendolos capaces de darle de los tutores ó curadores; bien entendido, que prestando los expresados parientes, tutores ó curadores su consentimiento, deberan executarlo con aprobacion del Juez Real é interviniendo su autoridad, simó fuese interesado; y siéndolo, se devolvera esta autoridad al Corregidor ó Alcalde mayor Realengo mas cercano." Although the start of the above quotation only refers to betrothals, marriages are also intended to be covered.

[635] *Ibid.*, ss. 3–5.

[636] *Ibid.*, ss. 3 and 5 at end of each.

[637] *Ibid.*, s. 6: "Los mayores de veinte y cinco años cumplen con pedir el consejo paterno para colocarse en estado de matrimonio, que en aquella edad ya no admite dilacion, como está prevenido en otras leyes; pero si contravinieren, dexando, de pedir este consejo paterno, incurriran en las mismas penas que quedan establecidas, así en quanto ó los bienes libres como en los vinculados."

Pragmática has provisions to guard against the abuse of these powers by parents and relatives.[638]

Thus, in Castilian law, minors had to seek and obtain paternal consent to their marriages. If they had not obtained such consent, they were subject to severe penalties, though their marriage was valid. That the marriage was not invalidated was because any such legislation by the king would be an interference with the authority of the spiritual powers: as the *Pragmática* itself said, only the civil effects of marriage could be dealt with by the king.[639] The decree *Tametsi* of the Council of Trent anathematized those who stated that the marriages of minor sons of families were invalid for want of paternal consent.[640] (This is, of course, why the *ancien droit* in France adopted such an indirect method to invalidate such marriages.)[641] Failing their father, minors had, in turn, to gain the consent of their mother, grandparents, near relatives, tutors or curators. That relatives should come before tutors and curators indicates that this provision was more concerned with the protection and welfare of the minors than with the fact that the death of the father had liberated the child from paternal power. As regards adults, only the paternal counsel is mentioned. Failing the father, an adult son would be a *paterfamilias* himself, and without need for protection. Adult children need to seek only paternal counsel to avoid disinheritance: consent to the marriage was not necessary.

For this *Pragmática* to be valid in Spanish North America (the Indies) and hence in *Luisiana*, it had to be approved by the Council of the Indies and then sent to the Spanish Indies.[642] It appears that this was done.[643] Thus, this *Pragmática* was the basis of the law on this point in Louisiana at the time of the cession to the United States. A *pragmática* of 10th April, 1803 altered the Castilian law on these matters. It is probable that this would not have been received and become applicable in Louisiana before the cession to the U.S.A. It is certainly unlikely that the redactors of the D.O. would have known of it, and there is no reference to it in the D.L.V.[644]

In Louisiana, the 1807 Act, ch. 17, on the celebration of marriages regulated consents to marriage.[645] Its sixteenth section stated:

> A minor who has not yet compleated [*sic*] his or her twenty-first year, shall previous to obtaining a licence to be married in the manner hereinafter directed, have received the consent of his or her father and mother, if alive and

---

[638] *Ibid.*, ss. 7–10.

[639] *Ibid.*, s. 1, where the authority of the church over the sacrament of marriage is mentioned.

[640] Quoted *supra*, note 612.

[641] See *supra*, text at notes 612–623.

[642] See *supra*, chap. 3, text at note 68; *Rec. Ind.* 2.1.39 and 40; Baade, "Marriage Contracts", pp. 40–41.

[643] *Nov. Rec. Cast.* 10.2.18, contains a *Pragmática* of 1803 amending that of 1776. This new *pragmática* was promulgated on the advice of the Council of the Indies: see first sentence of the *Pragmática*. This strongly suggests that the 1776 *Pragmática* was applied in the Indies.

[644] *Nov. Rec. Cast.* 10.2.18.

[645] See *supra*, note 177.

> capable of consenting; in case of a difference of opinion between them the consent of the father shall be sufficient.

Section 17 provided:

> If either of the parents is dead, or is incapable of consenting, the consent of the other shall be sufficient, even although he or she may have contracted a second marriage.

Section 18 said:

> If the father and mother are both dead or incapable of giving a consent, the grand father and grand mother shall supply their places as to this consent, and in case of difference of opinion a majority shall prevail; when they are equally divided in their opinions, the council of the family is convoked to decide.

Section 19 stated:

> If there be neither father nor mother, nor grand father nor grand mother alive and capable of consent, then the minor under twenty-one years of age cannot obtain a licence to marry without the consent of the council of the family, legally convoked for that purpose.

Section 20 said that such a family council had to decide within one month of being convoked and their consent requested. After the delay of a month, if the consent had neither been granted nor been refused, the marriage could be celebrated. It is obvious that these rules are taken from the *Proj. An. VIII* and perhaps the C.N.[646]

The 1808 Louisiana Digest states thus (D.O. 11, p. 27):

> Tout mineur des deux sexes qui a atteint l'âge compétent pour se marier, est tenu de prendre le consentement de ses père et mère s'ils sont vivans, ou du survivant d'entre eux, s'il y en a un de mort.

This is all the D.O. states on this matter, although D.O. 12 (p. 27) does refer to the 1807 Act for details of the formalities to be followed. The 1808 redactors intended that on this point the 1807 Act should be followed, so that, failing the mother and father, sections 17–20 would be applied. It has already been pointed out that in this part of the D.O. (that on the celebration of marriages) the D.O. redactors have incorporated far fewer provisions than the C.N. has, mainly because the D.O. redactors have deliberately left the detailed provisions on marriage in the 1807 Act.[647]

---

[646] See *supra*, text at notes 622–631. Note that s. 17 is closer to the 1800 *Projet* than to the C.N.: see *supra*, note 623.

[647] See *supra*, text at notes 246–250, and between notes 180 and 181.

The redactors of the 1823 *Projet* inserted such detailed provisions their revised code.[648] D.O. 11 (p. 27) was amended by them,[649] and in the 1825 C.L. became C.L. 99. It reads thus:

> Tout mineur des deux sexes, qui a atteint l'âge compétent pour se marier est tenu de prendre le consentement de ses père et mère, ou du survivant d'entre eux; et si tous les deux sont morts, celui de son curateurs.
>
> Il doit fournir la preuve de ce consentement au juge à qu'il s'adresse pour obtenir une permission de mariage.

Thus, the law has been reformed radically in the 1825 Code. The redactors unfortunately give no indication as to why they have reformed the law in this way.[650] The redactors of the C.L. have returned the law on consents to the marriages of minors to what it was under the *ancien droit* of France. Why they have done so need not be considered here, as we are more concerned with the actions of the D.O. redactors.[651] It should be stressed that the actions of the redactors of the C.L. do not provide evidence of the intentions of the redactors of the D.O. The D.O. redactors (as D.O. 12 (p. 27) indicates) intended the relevant sections of the 1807 Act to be applied.

On D.O. 11 (p. 27), the D.L.V. refers to the *Pragmática* of 1776, already discussed,[652] to the 1807 Act, s. 16, and to Pothier.[653] Pothier gives an extended account of the *ancien droit* as already indicated. Batiza gives s. 16 of the 1807 Act as the "substantially influencing" source, with C.N. 148 and *Proj. An. VIII*, 1.5.10 as subsidiary sources.

Along with the relevant sections of the 1807 Act, the redactors of the 1808 D.O. provide a series of rules originating in the work of codification in France. Before discussing their reasons for doing so, it is useful to look at rights to oppose the marriage of minor children and the effect of lack of consent on the validity of such a marriage.

As pointed out, the 1808 D.O. contains no provisions on oppositions to marriages.[654] The 1807 Act, yet again following the work of the French codifiers, restricts the class of those who can oppose the marriages of minors. Here the old law has been overturned by the Act, since the Canon law allowed anyone to

---

648 *1823 Projet*, p. 8, comment on ch. 3.

649 *1823 Projet*, p. 8. Note that in the *projet*, *tuteur* is used; *curateur* is more accurately used in the C.L. itself.

650 See *1823 Projet*, p. 8.

651 See *supra*, text at notes 176–180 for a discussion of the similar actions of the C.L. redactors.

652 *Pragmática supra* note 632. The D.L.V. cites it from A.X. Pérez y López, *Teatro de legislación universal de España é Indias, por orden cronológico de sus cuerpos y decisiones no recopiladas y alfabético de sus títulos y principales materias*, Madrid, En la Imprenta de Don Antonio Espinosa, 1791–1798. The D.L.V. never cites the *Novísima recopilación*.

653 Pothier, *T.C.M.*, pp. 138–148 (nos. 321–336).

654 See *supra*, text and notes at notes 175–180.

oppose a marriage.[655] The D.O. redactors have evidently intended that the Act's provisions should remain in force: this is in line with their actions on who was required to consent to a marriage. The redactors of the C.L. here restored the Canon law, and allowed anyone to oppose a marriage: as with consents, the 1825 redactors have overturned the joint provisions of the 1808 Digest and the 1807 Act.[656]

On the validity of a marriage by a minor without the required consent, the 1808 Louisiana Digest states thus, at D.O. 15 (p. 27):

> Le mariage des mineurs qui a été contracté sans le consentement de leur père et mère, n'est pas nul pour cela, s'il est d'ailleurs revêtu des autres formalités prescrites par la loi mais ce défaut de consentement est une juste raison pour les père et mère, de deshériter leurs enfans ainsi mariés, s'ils le trouvent convenable.

Section 49 of the 1807 Act had provided:

> A marriage contracted without the consent of the father and mother, the relations in the direct ascending line, or the council of the family, cannot for that cause be annulled, but the relatives whose consent was wanting, shall have a right to sue upon the bonds of the person issuing the licence, or of the person celebrating the marriage, and to recover damages. They may also direct the public prosecutor to sue for the fines and penalties imposed on that offence by law. Parents also, on account of such marriage, have the right of disinheriting such children.

On this article of the D.O., the D.L.V. referred to the 1807 Act, s. 49 as well as the *Pragmática*, "cidessus citée art. 3".[657] Batiza claims that s. 49 of the Act and a text of Pothier[658] are equal "substantially influencing" sources. The *Pragmática* in relevant part, allowed the disinheritance of minor children who had not obtained consent, while not nullifying their marriage.[659] Pothier, as cited, states:

> Une fille qui, avant l'âge de vingt-cinq ans, un garçon qui, avant l'âge de trente ans, se marient sans le consentement de leurs père et mère, sont sujets à la peine d'exhérédation. Après cet age, ils peuvent se marier, malgré leurs père et mère, pourvu qu'ils aient requis leur consentement par des sommations respectueuses faites en présence de notaire, qui leur en donne acte, faute de quoi, ils seraient pareillement sujets à la peine de l'exhérédation.[660]

Although it is not obvious in this text, lack of parental consent to the marriage of minors could, in the *ancien droit*, lead to the annullment of the marriage.[661]

---

[655] See *supra*, text and notes at notes 176–180. The relevant provisions of the Act, and those of the French code are quoted *supra*, note 178. On Canon law and *ancien droit* on oppositions, see Brissaud, *History*, pp. 129–130; Esmein, *op. cit. supra* note 69, vol. 1, pp. 421–427.

[656] See *supra*, text at notes 178–180.

[657] *Pragmática supra* note 632, s. 3.

[658] Pothier, *T.S.*, p. 26 (ch. 1, s. 2, art. 4 § I q. 1, 14.)

[659] *Pragmática supra* note 632, s. 3; *supra*, text at note 635.

[660] Pothier, *T.S.*, p. 26 (ch. 1, s. 2, art. 4 § I q. 1, 14.); he goes on to refer to the 1556 Edict, the *Ordonnance* of Blois and the 1639 Declaration.

[661] See *supra*, text at notes 612–622.

The C.N., article 182, states that if a marriage had been contracted without the consent of the father and mother, ascendants or family council, where such consent was necessary, then the validity of the marriage may be attacked by those whose consent was required, or by the spouse who had required such consent. The *Proj. An. VIII*, 1.5.38 allowed parents and ascendants to sue for the nullity of a marriage to which their consent had been required, such consent not having been gained. Thus, the C.N. and its *projet* allowed the annullment of the marriages of minors who had not gained the requisite consent. In this aspect of the law, the D.O. redactors and the 1807 Act have not followed the example of the French codification, but have perpetuated the provision found, as regards the marriage of minors, in the Castilian law and the Canon law. Despite Batiza's citation of Pothier, the *ancien droit* of France has not been followed, since the *ancien droit* (though by an indirect method) rendered annullable the marriages of minors who had not gained the requisite consents. The D.O. redactors could hardly have reversed s. 49 of the Act; but it is probable that they approved of this provision. It seems likely that the redactors allowed such marriages to be valid because to do so was in line with their policy of restricting *puissance paternelle*. Given that minors above the age of puberty in Louisiana were able to leave home and could not be forced to return,[662] to have annulled the marriages of other minors might have seemed absurd and contrary to principle.

So far, it has been assumed that the two relevant provisions in the D.O. on consents to the marriages of minors were intended to be read with the 1807 Act, even though that Act had considerably more detailed and rather broader provisions than the D.O. Any argument that, since the 1825 C.L. expanded the D.O. provisions, but in a way different from the provisions of the 1807 Act, it is likely that the D.O. redactors had intended these two provisions completely to replace the relevant sections of the 1807 Act, is clearly wrong. The D.O. did not intend to repeal these parts of the Act. One or two arguments have already shown that such an approach to the D.O. provisions would be wrong. First, the D.O., having no provisions on oppositions, referred specifically to the 1807 Act.[663] The Act's provisions on oppositions were in line with those on consents and disinheritance. Second, the whole of this title of the 1808 D.O. is intended to be read along with the 1807 Act. None of the necessary detail on the procedures for marrying, opposing a marriage, or annulling a marriage is included. The D.O. redactors intended that these be governed by the Act. It seems likely that this was their intention as regards the further rules on consents to marriages. Third, the rules in the D.O. were manifestly incomplete, since D.O. 11 (p. 27) makes no attempt to regulate the potential disagreements between parents.[664] This article is, of course, directly followed by the article referring to the Act. This again indicates that the D.O. redactors intended the 1807 Act's rules to govern. Thus, it is clear that the 1808 redactors intended their provisions to be

---

[662] See *supra*, text at notes 568–572.
[663] D.O. 12 (p. 27): see *supra*, text at notes 646–647.
[664] Quoted *supra*, text between notes 646 and 647.

read along with those in the 1807 Act. The major change in the law would then have been introduced by the 1825 redactors: this would be in line with the 1825 C.L.'s obvious reversal of the law relating to oppositions to a marriage. The redactors of the 1825 C.L. have, in effect, introduced the *ancien droit français* on the marriages of minors—anyone can oppose, failing parents, curators[665] are to consent—without, however, allowing such marriages to be annulled.

The Castilian law in the 1776 *Pragmática* had a certain similarity to the system in the 1807 Act and D.O. The Castilian law did not invalidate the marriages; mothers, grandparents and other relatives also had some control over the marriage of minors. It would be wrong, however, to argue that the 1807 Act and the D.O. had here followed the C.N. or its *projet* because the rules in the French codification were similar to the Castilian: it is likely that the similarity between the Louisianian rules and those of the *Pragmática* is here fortuitous. (This is so, even though one might surmise that similar social circumstances gave rise to the rules of the French code and the *Pragmática*.)[666] The 1807 Act and the D.O. are, in this whole area of the law, strongly influenced by the work of the French codifiers. Since the influence of the French codifiers' provisions on the Louisianian law on the marriages of minors is so great (though in Louisiana such marriages may not be annulled), it is important to explore the reasons why the redactors in Lousiana copied the French laws.

The D.O. and the Act have rejected any control over the marriages of adult children, while giving control over the marriages of minor children to the family as a whole, rather than to tutors or curators.[667] That the *family*, in the sense of close relatives, has control over such marriages indicates a new stress on the care of minors for their own good, with such care being exercised by close relatives, failing the mother and father. Adult marriages are not controlled, because adults are presumed not to need such protection. Adult marriages need only be controlled by ascendants when the family is conceived of as more than a domestic unit for the care and nurture of children. If paternal power is conceived of in the Roman sense, the marriages of adult *filiifamilias* are subject to the authority of the *pater* by virtue of their dependency on him and subjection to his authority. In such a system of paternal power, a minor with no ascendants is himself a *pater*, subject to no one. The only consent that could possibly be needed would be that of a curator who has been appointed to advise him. On the other hand, if paternal authority is conceived of as being for the protection of the child, then in the event of the parents being dead, other relatives become important, because of the affection they are supposed to have for the minor. Marriage becomes a matter for such relatives, because their care and affection

---

[665] Note that in the *1823 Projet*, p. 8, the redactors used the term *tuteurs*: this term is appropriate for the French law, but not the D.O. or Castilian, which both have a division into pupillage and minority. See *supra*, note 649.

[666] The eighteenth century is arguably the period of change in law towards the modern nuclear-style family based on affection rather than the power of the head of the household. Note that the Castilian provisions do not go so far in this direction as those of Louisiana.

[667] In the 1825 C.L., of course, curators have replaced close relatives.

for the minor are taken to be the best protection. One must conclude that a strong motive for the adoption of the provisions of the 1808 D.O. and 1807 Act on the marriage of minors must have been the development of the new vision of family as based on marriage and centred on care and affection for the children. This new style family also brought close relatives into greater prominence than hitherto.[668] The exact expression of the Louisiana rules obviously was influenced by the work of the French redactors; but a desire and tendency to copy the provisions of the French codification cannot have been the sole motive underlyingthe choice of the Louisiana provisions, since the latter differ in many crucial respects from those of the C.N. and *Proj. An. VIII.* (In not controlling the marriage of adults, the Louisiana provisions are closer to those of the 1800 *Projet* than those of the C.N. itself, though there are still sufficient differences for it to be clear that the D.O. redactors are not simply copying the *Proj. An. VIII*'s articles.) Thus, these provisions of the early Louisiana law are the result of the growth of the modern affective or associative family, with much of their expression borrowed from and suggested by the work of the French redactors.

How *Puissance Paternelle* Ends

The most obvious method of ending paternal authority is the death of the parent exercising authority over the child. In Louisiana, the mother was granted equal authority with the father. Some aspects of parental control lasted only so long as the marriage (notably, *jouissance* of the property of the child), but other aspects of parental authority survived the end of the marriage, so long as the child was still a minor. Certain rights deriving from paternal power (those relating to the marriage of minors) on the death of both parents, devolved on other close relatives. In general, the Louisiana law has here followed the French codal versions of *puissance paternelle*, rather than the Castilian. The Castilian law granted *patria potestad* to the father alone: the death of only the father was required to end this *potestad.* The consents to the marriage of minors were a special case in Castilian law in giving some of the paternal authority over minors to the mother, grandparents and other close relatives; but, even in this aspect of the law, the person conceived of as having the authority was the father, and the others who exercised such authority after the father's death did so because, in the words of the 1776 *Pragmática*, they were "en lugar de padres".[669]

The second way whereby a child would be freed from power was his reaching the age of majority, which, in Louisiana, was twenty-one years. Majority in the Castilian law did not end *patria potestad.* Here the Louisianian redactors have followed the law of the French code and the *droit coutumier*, presumably because it was more in keeping with their conception of paternal authority as being for the welfare of the minor child, rather than the institution defining the family of the head of the household. Emancipating majority was suited to the

---

[668] See *supra*, text at notes 46 and 47 on the greater role allotted to close relatives.
[669] *Pragmática supra* note 632, s. 1.

close affective family composed of individuals bound together by ties of care and affection. That majority should not emancipate is appropriate for the family conceived of as a hierarchy bound together by the power of the head of the household.

The third method of freeing children from paternal power was emancipation. The eighth title of the first book of the D.O. devoted its third chapter to emancipation, articles 87–97.[670] It is not necessary to deal here with D.O. 90–97 (p. 77), as these articles are concerned with matters of accounting and administration. D.O. 89 (p. 75) concerns the emancipation of a minor by the judge, when the minor has no mother and father: this is not emancipation from paternal power, but a method of allowing a minor control of his own property.[671] This leaves D.O. 87 and 88 (p. 75).

D.O. 87 (p. 75) states thus: "Le mineur est émancipé de plein droit par le mariage." This is identical to C.N. 476.[672] It is, of course, the rule of the *droit coutumier*.[673] The D.L.V. here refers to *Ley* 47 of Toro, the *Recopilación* of Castile[674] and Febrero.[675] The Castilian rule referred to is that marriage emancipates children from paternal power.[676] This rule has been discussed already, and it has been argued that the Castilian jurists treated this rule as an illogical addition to the concept of *patria potestad*;[677] Gomez even limited its applicability.[678] The *Partidas* did not permit marriage to emancipate.[679] The Castilian rule and the Louisiania rule here correspond; but it is obvious that the D.O. has copied the French rule because of the new conception of paternal authority that has been introduced.

D.O. 88 (p. 75) is as follows:

> Le mineur même non marié, pourra être êmancipé par son père, ou à défaut de son père, par sa mère, lorsqu'il aura quinze ans révolus.
>
> Cette émancipation s'opère par la seule déclaration du père ou de la mère reçue par un notaire, en présence de deux temoins.

C.N. 477 is very similar, with the difference that the *déclaration* should be made to the *juge de paix* assisted by his clerk, no further witnesses being required.[680] The D.L.V. here refers to *Part.* 4.18.15, 16 and 17, and to Febrero.[681] Febrero

---

[670] At D.O. p. 75–77.

[671] This is, of course, the Roman *venia aetatis*. See Jolowicz, *op. cit. supra* note 57, p. 203.

[672] According to Batiza the "verbatim" source. He also gives *Proj. An. VIII*, 1.9.106 as a subsidiary source; but this last article is more concerned with *venia aetatis*.

[673] See *supra*, text at notes 130–136.

[674] *Rec. Cast.* 5.1.8. This is *Toro*, 47.

[675] Febrero, *Contratos*, ch. 4, § 4 no. 94 (vol. 2, pp. 77–78) [the D.L.V. has ch. 1 in error]; *ibid.*, ch 12, § 3 nos. 16 and 23 (vol. 3, pp. 276 and 280).

[676] *Ley* 47, quoted *supra*, text between notes 147 and 148.

[677] See *supra*, text at notes 148–157.

[678] See *supra*, text at notes 152–157.

[679] See *supra*, text at notes 563–566.

[680] According to Batiza, the "almost verbatim" source.

[681] Febrero, *Contratos*, ch. 12, § 3 no. 24 (vol. 3, p. 281).

states that for emancipation there are three requirements. The first is that the child be fully seven years of age. If the child is under such age, then royal permission is required for emancipation. Second, judicial approval of the emancipation is necessary. Third, in the presence of the *juez ordinario*, the father emancipates the son and the son accepts. Thus, the child must be above seven, must consent to be emancipated, and judicial authority is necessary for the validity of the emancipation.[682] *Part.* 4.18.15 provides for judicial emancipation. *Ley* 16 allows for emancipation be letters from the king, while *ley* 17 states that a father may emancipate his son if both wish it.

In the *droit écrit* in France, as in the D.O. article, emancipations could be made before notaries;[683] there is probably little significance in the departure of the D.O. here from the C.N. The emancipation provided for in the D.O. (and C.N.) is rather different from that in the Castilian law. The difference in the ages at which such emancipation becomes possible is very important. The purpose underlying the French and Louisiania provisions is to give a fairly mature minor independence from his father and control over his property. The presumption behind this is that care and protection are no longer necessary. In Castile, on the other hand, although the intention is to render the *hijo* independent, since the *hijo* may be emancipated from seven years of age, the reasoning behind the emancipation cannot have been that the son was able and competent to manage his own affairs. The effect of emancipation in Castile was to render the son a *paterfamilias* in his own right, and to make him legally independent of his father's family, of which he was no longer formally a member. The Castilian rules betray their Roman origin, and demonstrate the Castilian idea that the family was the group connected to the head of the household by virtue of being under his *potestad*. The C.N. provisions have been followed in the D.O. as more in keeping with the Louisiania conception of *puissance paternelle* being for the care and protection of children; this meant that children could be freed from paternal authority only when they no longer required such care and protection.

The Castilian law had additional methods of emancipating children from *patria potestad*. Febrero, for example, stated that there were seven methods of ending paternal authority.[684] These included natural death of the *padre*, the marriage of the son *en faz de la Sante Madre Iglesia*, and emancipation. Other methods were the civil death of the father, through perpetual banishment, condemnation to the mines, or permanent outlawry.[685] The eighteenth title of the *Quarta Partida*, in its *leyes* 7 to 15, provided for the ending of *patria potestad* on the son's achieving certain dignities (many of which indicate the late-Roman origin of the rule)[686]. Asso and Manuel state that many of these dignities are no longer recognized; but, arguing from them, they think that every *dignidad* which may have jurisdiction attached to it and every ecclesiastical dignity are suffi-

---

[682] *Asso y Manuel*, vol. 1, p. 121 give the same account as Febrero.
[683] Maleville, *Analyse*, vol. 1, p. 426.
[684] Febrero, *Contratos*, ch.12, § 3 nos. 21–24 (vol. 3, pp. 279–281).
[685] *Ibid.*, ch.12, § 3 nos. 21 and 22 (vol. 3, p. 279). See also *Asso y Manuel*, vol. 1, pp. 119–120.
[686] Consider that the proconsulship and the praetorian prefecture are stated to end paternal power.

cient to end power over the *hijo*.[687] This rule is unnecessary in Louisiana where majority emancipated, and would only be required where paternal power in general lasted until the death of the father.

In Castilian law, a judge could force a father to emancipate his children for four reasons: first, if the father cruelly chastised them; second, if he prostituted his daughters; third, if be had taken possession of property bequeathed to him on condition he emancipate the child, and had not done so; and fourth, if he were misspending the property of or misconducting himself towards an adopted child.[688] The D.O. contained no such provisions. The 1823 *Projet*, however, recommended the inclusion of an article stating thus:

> Le mineur peut être émancipé contre la volonté de ses père et mère, lorsqu'ils le maltraitent outre mesure, lui refusent des alimens, ou lui donnent des exemples corrupteurs.[689]

This recommended article became C.L. 371. This article, though of Castilian origin, conforms to the conception of the purpose of paternal power found in the D.O.: care and protection of the child. The D.O. redactors do not appear to have included such a provision because there was no equivalent in the French code, and the D.O. redactors appear to have been here following the French code very closely indeed. There were certainly no social reasons for the exclusion of a provision such as this.

A final important point relates to the effect of emancipation on the paternal usufruct. In the D.O. and C.N. this usufruct ended on emancipation.[690] This is only logical given that the enjoyment of the child's property was a right corresponding with and derived from the duty of caring for the child.[691] The Castilian law was different. Febrero states:

> En premio de la emancipacion puede el padre retener para sí la mitad del usufructo de los bienes adventicios que su hijo tenia antes de ser emancipado, y no de los que despues adquiera; antes bien, si su hijo se casa luego, deberá bolverle la mitad que se reservó, porque por legal disposicion le pertenecen enteramente los bienes adventicios, sin que su padre pueda retenerselos, ni su usufructo.[692]

This is a revised version of the Justinianic Roman rule. The difference between the Castilian law and the D.O. and C.N. is once more derived from their different ideas about the purpose and extent of paternal power: in the D.O. and C.N. the power is considered as necessary for the care and protection of minor children, and the usufruct is a recompense for the attention and upbringing the

---

[687] *Asso y Manuel*, vol. 1, p. 120.
[688] *Ibid.*, vol. 1, p. 122; Febrero, *Contratos*, ch.12, § 3 no. 26 (vol. 3, pp. 282).
[689] *1823 Projet*, p. 29. The redactors state that their recommended article conforms to *Part.* 4.18.18.
[690] See *supra*, text at notes 589–604.
[691] See *supra*, text at notes 589–591.
[692] Febrero, *Contratos*, ch. 12, § 3 no. 25 (vol. 3, p. 282).

parents give their children. In the Castilian law, the usufruct derives from the father's power and authority as head of the household. The D.O. redactors have adopted the C.N.'s version of paternal power.

The methods of ending paternal power in the 1808 Louisiana code are derived from the French code. Some of them have corresponding Castilian provisions, but there can be no doubt that the D.O. redactors were following the French provisions, and such correspondence is fortuitous. This action on the part of the D.O. redactors was necessary given their introduction of the northern French concept of paternal power. The Castilian provisions on ending *patria potestad* are dependent on the extended power given to fathers in Castile. The one Castilian rule, excluded from the D.O., that is included in the 1825 C.L., is one consistent with the D.O.'s conception of *puissance paternelle* as existing for the care and protection of minor children.

Conclusion on Paternal Power in Louisiana

The provisions of the D.O. on the acquisition of *puissance paternelle* are taken from the French code. The D.O. redactors have limited the methods of acquiring such power over children, and have thus restricted the family grouping. The number of forms of legitimating children has been reduced to one only—*legitimatio per subsequens matrimonium*. That form of legitimation itself has been rendered more complex. It is possible to be quite certain that the D.O. redactors were deliberately shaping the law for reasons other than an observable tendency to copy the French code, since the D.O. redactors abolished adoption, permitted by the C.N. as by the Castilian law. The D.O. redactors here appear to have a deliberate policy of restricting the family of the married couple to those children definitely born from the marriage. They seem to be attempting to render the nuclear family unit more secure. Obviously they were influenced by the work of the French redactors; but the articles of the French codification also allowed them to express an ideology of which they approved.

That the actions of the D.O. redactors were not dictated by a desire to copy unthinkingly the Code Napoléon is also shown by the title specifically devoted to *puissance paternelle*.[693] Although there are obvious influences from the C.N., many of the articles are derived from other sources. Clearly, the redactors were consciously shaping the law, using the materials to hand. This said, it is obvious that the redactors have introduced the concept of paternal power found in the *droit coutumier* of northern France. They have rejected the Roman concept of *patria potestad* found in the Castilian law. The D.O. redactors have gone further than the *droit coutumier* and Code Napoléon, however, since in all the relevant articles of the D.O., the wife is given equal status with the husband, and there is no article equivalent to C.N. 373.[694] The only article inconsistent with this total equality and

[693] Chap. 5 of the tit. 7 of the first book of the D.O. See *supra*, text at note 560.
[694] See *supra*, text at notes 562–563.

exercise of the power is D.O. 5 (p. 59),[695] which seems to assume that only the father has the enjoyment of the children's property, which is contrary to the statements in D.O. 42 and 44 (p. 53).[696] This inconsistency must be the result of the close copying of D.O. 5 (p. 59) from C.N. 389.[697] It seems correct to deduce that the D.O. redactors deliberately gave equality to the husband and wife, since C.N. 373 was known to them and before them as they worked.

As well as differing from the *droit coutumier* and C.N. (and indeed the Castilian law) in giving complete equality to mothers, the D.O. differed from them in giving more freedom to *fils* and *filles de famille*, who could, if above the age of puberty, leave home, and could also validly marry (though under penalty of disinheritance). To some extent, this difference is founded on the adoption of the Castilian division of nonage into pupillage and minority. But this division really only permitted the redactors to provide that children over puberty not be compelled to stay with their parents;[698] it most certainly did not require such a provision, and in the Castilian law, no matter what their age, children in power could be compelled to return to their father if they had left home. Thus, the D.O. redactors, in comparison to their sources and models, heve liberalized paternal power. In comparison to the Castilian law, under the D.O. a father has fewer rights in the property of his children, and such rights end completely on emancipation.[699] He has a right of usufruct as in the C.N., but which most *coutumes* of northern France (notably that of Paris) did not give fathers. A right of usufruct as incorporated in the D.O., is quite consistent with the social circumstances of the period, and is stated to be reciprocal to the parental duty to feed, bring up and educate their children. The Castilian right of usufruct is declared to be a natural aspect of the dependency of the son on the *padre* who has him in his power.

The D.O., taken with the 1807 Act, ch. 17, extends control over the marriages of minors to grandparents and other close relatives. These provisions, adopted and adapted from the C.N. and its *projet*, are consistent with the current notion of the family as being based on care; and closer connections with near relatives are compatible with the development of the private nuclear family.[700] The C.N., the *droit coutumier*, and the Castilian law all allowed parents some measure of control over the marriage of their adult children. The D.O. and the 1807 Act denied such control to parents. This is quite consistent with the general liberalization of *puissance paternelle* by the D.O. redactors, who, as regards the marriage of minors, only permitted disinheritance of the minors, not annullment of their marriage, if the requisite consents had not been obtained.

The D.O. provisions on *puissance paternelle* thus mark a radical departure from the Castilian law. The D.O. provisions are obviously strongly influenced by the C.N. and its *projet*, and resemble those of the latter two codes; but the

---

[695] See *supra*, text at notes 603–604.
[696] See *supra*, text at notes 588–592 and 598.
[697] See *supra*, text at note 603.
[698] See *supra*, text at notes 568–571.
[699] Febrero, *Contratos*, ch. 12, § 3 no. 25 (vol. 3, p. 282).
[700] See *supra*, text at notes 45 and 47.

D.O. redactors themselves went beyond their models and source materials in liberalizing their provisions on paternal authority.

The Castilian rules on paternal authority presupposed a hierarchical family based on the authority of the *padre*. The link binding fathers and children was the subjection of the latter to the former by virtue of the former's *potestad* as head of the household. The Code Napoléon had a different conception of *puissance paternelle*. In the C.N., paternal power ended on the majority of the child, and was shared to some extent by the mother. The power was more limited than in Castilian law. The code phrased the rights of the parents as having corresponding duties towards the children. Parent and child were connected by links of reciprocal obligations. The paternal power was in many ways apparently for the benefit of the minor child, and was based on notions of care and protection. The rules of the Code Napoléon provided an expression of the affective, associative family, bound together by parental care for the children: *puissance paternelle* was to provide care and protection for the child, the usufruct of the child's property helping the parents make such provision, and preventing the awkward case of a father having to account for his administration of his child's property.

The D.O. redactors, no matter the sources they used, expressed in their code the same conception of *puissance paternelle* as providing care and protection for the child in the bosom of the family. The rules of the Castilian law would have been quite unsuitable in early-nineteenth-century Louisiana, being premissed on a mode of family organization not found in the territory. The possible restriction on the capacity of adults in the Castilian law would have been unthinkable in a commercial society where wealth was not based solely on land. Further, the restriction on the freedom of action of adults would have been unacceptable from an ideological viewpoint, and indeed impractical in a society such as that of early Louisiana. Although every article discussed has some minimal basis in another code, statute or doctrinal writing, the redactors of the 1808 Digest were using their varying source material to construct, on the relationship between parent and child, articles embodying their view of that relationship, and expressing the ideology of the close, affective family based on domesticity and childcare. The articles of the French code and its *projet* might have suggested this view of the tie of parent to child, while other sources may have suggested specific provisions; but it must be accepted that the D.O. redactors used these materials to express their own conception of paternal authority, especially since they went further than any of their sources in liberalizing the authority and in giving equality of control to the mother.

Part Two

QUEBEC

THE 1866 CIVIL CODE OF LOWER CANADA

Puissance Maritale

How *Puissance Maritale* Arises in the Quebec Code

In the Quebec code, as in those of France and Louisiana, and as in the *ancien droit coutumier*, the *puissance du mari* arose from the fact of marriage. Thus, though by an antenuptial marriage contract the spouses could vary the normal property consequences of marriage, by C.Q. 1259, the spouses could not derogate from the husband's rights over his wife and children, nor from his rights as head of the conjugal association. The C.N. and the *ancien droit* had imposed the same restriction.[701]

The fifth title of the first book of the C.Q. is entitled "Of Marriage". It is divided into seven chapters: "Of the qualities and conditions necessary for contracting marriage"; "Of the formalities relating to the solemnization of marriage"; "Of oppositions to marriage"; "Of actions for annulling a marriage"; "Of the obligations arising from marriage"; "Of the respective rights and duties of husband and wife"; and "Of the dissolution of marriage". This division of the title is closer to that of title five of the first book of the C.N., than is that of title four of the D.O.[702] Chapters 6 and 7 of this title of the C.Q. will be discussed later.[703]

This subsection will be devoted to the contracting of a valid marriage. As with the D.O., neither annulment of marriages[704] nor all of the more technical formalities will be discussed

The first article of this title is C.Q. 115 It states:

> A man cannot contract marriage before the full age of fourteen years, nor a woman before the full age of twelve years.

C.N. 144, the equivalent French article, made the age of marriage eighteen for men and fifteen for women, though C.N. 145 allowed dispensations for *motifs graves*. Here Quebec has followed the old law in fixing the age of puberty and

---

[701] See C.N. 1388 and Pothier, *T. Comm.*, pp. 50–51 (Introduction, nos. 4 and 5).

[702] The C.N. has, of course, an eighth chapter in this title, "Des Seconds Mariages", composed of one article, C.N. 228: see *supra*, note 503. The C.Q. redactors point out that this provision was not found in the *droit coutumier*: *Second Report*, p. 175. Chapter 5, "Of obligations arising from marriage", is, in the D.O., covered in the section on paternal power: see *supra*, text at 560.

[703] See *infra*, the subsections "*Puissance Maritale*: Aspects Other than Property" and "The Dissolution of Marriage, and the Ending of *Puissance Maritale*".

[704] Except as it relates to paternal power: see *infra*.

marriage at fourteen and twelve for males and females respectively.[705] One below the legal age of puberty was presumed *impuber* and incapable of marriage. The redactors state that they are here following the old rule.[706] Prior to codification in France, the age required to contract a valid marriage had already been raised by one year by the *loi* of 20th September, 1792.[707] In the final redaction of the C.N., the ages in C.N. 144 were decided on.[708] Maleville explained that there were two reasons for raising these ages. First:

> La climat influe d'une manière puissante sur la puberté; la loi qui la fixait à quatorze et à douze, avait été originairement faite pour Athènes, plus meridionale que Paris d'environ six degrés; elle pouvait être bonne encore à Rome et à Constantinople, mais elle était mauvaise pour nos climats plus septentrionaux. . . .[709]

Second (a social reason):

> Des époux trop jeunes, aujourd'hui émancipés par le mariage n'ont d'ailleurs pas la maturité d'esprit et l'expérience nécessaires pour conduire leur maison et élever des enfans; ces enfans eux-mêmes sont ordinairement d'une constitution faible.[710]

These two reasons would have been just as relevant for Quebec, and the raising of the minimum age for marriage just as appropriate. The codifiers give no reason for not suggesting a reform such as that in the French code. They merely remark that since they have retained the old rule, an article such as C.N. 145 is unnecessary; this also kept the rule in conformity with that of the rest of the British Empire, a practical consideration.[711] Their actions here reflect their conservative interpretation of their instructions.

C.Q. 116 provides: "There is no marriage when there is no consent." C.N. 146 is virtually identical. Pothier states that "consentement…est de l'essence du marriage".[712] Here the C.Q., the C.N., and the *ancien droit* were the same. Consent

---

[705] Pothier, *T.C.M.*, p. 39 (no. 94) states: "La procréation des enfants étant la fin principale du mariage… ceux qui ne sont pas habiles à la génération… ne sont pas habiles au mariage." Inst. 1.10: "justas nuptias contrahunt masculi quidem puberes, feminae vero viripotentes." The Canon law had followed the Roman: Esmein, *op. cit. supra* note 69, vol. 1, pp. 212–216.

[706] *Second Report*, p. 177. In the *ancien droit* the presumption that a person below the required ages was *impuber* could be overturned if "la vigueur avait devancé en âge en cette personne, et qu'elle eut donné des preuves de puberté". Pothier *T.C.M.*, p. 40 (no. 94). This could only be proved if the party below the legal age had already married, and pregnancy resulted. It was thus, in fact, a means of contesting an action for annulment on the ground of nonage. It is included as such a defence in the C.Q. as art. 145.

[707] See Huussen, *op. cit. supra* note 106, pp. 40–41.

[708] *Proj. An. VIII*, 1.5.4 still gave the required ages as 15 and 13 years.

[709] Maleville, *Analyse*, vol. 1, p. 143.

[710] *Ibid.*

[711] *Second Report*, p. 177; W. Burge, *Commentaries on Colonial and Foreign Laws Generally, and in Their Conflict with Each Other and with the Law of England*, London, Saunders and Benning, 1838, vol. 1, p. 140.

[712] Pothier, *T.C.M.*, p. 38 (no. 92).

was nullified by violence, seduction or error.[713] Pothier comments that those entirely deprived of the power of reason because of *folie* or *imbécillité* could not contract marriage, being incapable of consent.[714] The same would apply in Quebec. The position on the consent of deaf mutes is rather more complex; neither the Quebec nor French codes explicitly deal with it. Pothier states:

> Il ne faut pas non plus mettre au rang des personnes privées de l'usage de la raison, les sourds et muets de naissance. Ces personnes non-seulement jouissent de leur raison, mais elles font entendre par des signes leurs pensées, et on leur fait pareillement entendre par des signes ce qu'on veut leur faire entendre; c'est pourquoi, pouvant faire entendre le consentement qu'elles donneraient à un mariage, elles ne sont point incapables de le contracter.[715]

Delaporte and Riffé-Caubray state that those who cannot indicate their will are incapable of contracting marriage:

> En conséquence les sourds-muets étaient autrefois dans l'impossibilité de se marier, parce qu'ils ne pouvaient, d'aucune manière, faire connaître leur consentement.[716]

They continue, mentioning that it had been intended to include an article on the marriage of deaf mutes, but that since this was not done, the law must still be the same, and deaf mutes cannot marry.[717] Their statement of the *ancien droit* is incorrect. If deaf mutes could indicate their consent by signs they could marry; and, indeed, this seems to be the position taken by doctrine in both Quebec and France.[718] The proposed article, referred to by Delaporte and Riffé-Caubray, had stated that madmen, imbeciles, those condemned to civil death, and deaf mutes could not marry; with the exception that deaf mutes could marry if they could indicate their wishes. There was a lengthy dispute over this article when it was discussed, and it was proposed to replace it with one in the chapter "des actes de mariage" of the title "des actes de l'état civil", explaining how deaf mutes could express consent; but this was not done.[719] Although the C.Q. redactors were aware of the potential problems with consents in the marriage of deaf mutes, they chose to follow the C.N. and make no special provision.

C.Q. 117 is as follows:

---

[713] See C.Q. 148–151; C.N. 180–183. *Pan. fran.* vol. 3, pp. 141–152 discusses violence nullifying consent, seduction having the same result, and error.
[714] Pothier, *T.C.M.*, p. 38 (no. 92).
[715] Pothier, *T.C.M.*, p. 39 (no. 93).
[716] *Pan. fran.*, vol. 3, p. 153.
[717] *Ibid.*, pp. 153–154.
[718] P. Mignault, *Le droit civil canadien*, Montreal, Whiteford & Théoret, 1895–1916, vol. 1, p. 345; Toullier, *op. cit. supra* note 628, vol. 1, p. 306. For his statement of the *ancien droit*, Pothier, *T.C.M.*, p. 39 (no. 93) relied on an *arrêt* of 16th Jan., 1658. Buckland, *Textbook*, p. 113, n. 4 states that under Roman law deaf mutes could marry.
[719] See Maleville, *Analyse*, vol. 1, pp. 144–145.

> Impotency, natural or accidental, existing at the time of the marriage, renders it null; but only if such impotency be apparent and manifest.
>
> This nullity cannot be invoked by any one but the party who has contracted with the impotent person nor at any time after three years from the marriage.

There is no equivalent article in the C.N., which apparently rejected this form of annulling a marriage because "la preuve en est difficile et scandaleuse".[720] After the redaction of the C.N., however, both *jurisprudence* and *doctrine* in France had allowed the annulment of the marriage of an impotent, on the grounds of error as to person.[721] The Quebec codifiers did not follow the example of the C.N.: they provided a specific article on *impuissance*.[722] In their remarks on their proposed article, the C.Q. redactors remark that they thought the old law should be preserved, and that impotency should be grounds for invalidating a marriage; but they also thought there should be a restriction to impotency at the time of marriage, such impotency being apparent and manifest. That the impotency be apparent and manifest means that it must be capable of being demonstrated by a simple inspection of the alleged impotent, and must result from some demonstrable malformation:[723] mere refusal to have sexual intercourse due to repugnance for the act is also insufficient.[724]

The rule in the Quebec code is a response to the problems and difficulties with both the *ancien droit* and the French new law. The *ancien droit* merely required that impotency be incurable and existing from the time of marriage for it to be an effective ground for annulling a marriage. Pothier states thus:

> Pour que l'impuissance soit un empêchement de mariage... il n'importe qu'elle soit de naissance ou qu'elle lui soit survenue depuis. ...
>
> Mais il n'y a qu'une impuissance perpétuelle et incurable, telle que celle qui résulte de la privation de quelqu'une des parties nécessaire à la génération, qui forme un empêchement de marriage... .
>
> L'impuissance est un empêchement dirimant de mariage, lorsque celui-ci existe au temps auquel le mariage se contracts; mais s'il n'est survenu que depuis le mariage, il ne le rompt pas.[725]

---

[720] *Pan. fran.*, vol. 3, p. 276. See also *infra*, note 730.

[721] See, e.g., *Pan. fran.*, vol. 3, pp. 275–276; Toullier, *op. cit. supra* note 628, vol. 1, pp. 315–317 (nos. 525–526); [imprint varies], vol. 4, pp. 406–411, no. 254; Merlin, *Répertoire* (5), vol. 16, s.v. *Impuissance*.

[722] *Second Report*, p. 177.

[723] See *T.D.C.Q.*, vol. 1, p. 359 ("[l]a seule debilité des organes est insuffisante pour fonder la nullité"); Mignault, *op. cit. supra* note 718, vol. 1, p. 357; Baudouin, *op. cit. supra* note 551, pp. 152–153.

[724] In relatively recent years, however, *Scholes* v. *Warlow* (1927) 65 C.S. p. 6, decided that "invincible repugnance to this act of consommation resulting in a paralysis of the will" was sufficient to found an action for nullity on the grounds of impotency: Trudel, *T.D.C.Q.*, vol. 1, p. 359; Baudouin, *op. cit. supra* note 551, pp. 152–153.

[725] Pothier, *T.C.M.*, p. 41 (nos. 97–98). *Ancien Denisart*, vol. 2, p. 700, s.v. *Impuissance*, no. 6 states: "Comme l'impuissance est un obstacle à la principale fin du mariage, elle la rend nul si elle est perpétuelle, ou si elle existoit au temps de la célébration, mais quoiqu'elle soit perpétuelle, le mariage est bon si elle n'est survenue que depuis le mariage."

The problem of proof was rendered acute by the rule that, to be an effective ground for annulment, impotency had merely to be incurable and exist from the time of marriage. Up to 1677, proof of impotency was through a procedure known as *Congrès*; but this method was abolished because it was considered "aussi équivoque qu'indécente et contraire à la pudeur".[726] In the eighteenth century, modesty restrained proof of impotency to the following procedure described by Denisart:

> On ne peut donc actuellement acquérir le preuve d'impuissance que par la vote de l'interrogatoire et des visites par des experts; car nos tribunaux ne consentent pas du serment des parties, ni de l'enquête per septimam manum, et le congrès et aboli: aussi c'est par la visite des parties et sur le rapport des experts, qui font cette visite, que les juges doivent porter leur jugement.[727]

Pothier points out that the experts were *chirurgeons* or *matrones*;[728] he also remarks that:

> Il suffit aujourd'hui qu'il résulte de la visite, que les parties extérieures sont bien conformées, pour que la personne ne soit pas réputée impuissante.[729]

This is perhaps not far removed from the position in the Quebec code, despite the difference in phrasing. This statement no doubt also reflects the eighteenth-century French embarrassment with this topic and the difficulties of proof.[730]

The second paragraph of C.Q. 117 states that only the party with whom the impotent has contracted marriage can found an action for nullity on such impotency. The *ancien droit* was the same, for to permit otherwise would be to

---

[726] Pothier, *T.C.M.*, p. 210 (no. 458). *Congrès* was a procedure instituted around 1550 by the *Parlement de Paris* whereby the couple were put to bed with witnesses in the room, and it was for the alleged impotent to prove his potency. There are obvious problems with this procedure. See *Ancien Denisart*, vol. 2, pp. 702–703, s.v. *Impuissance*, nos. 19–21. In Merlin, *Répertoire* (4), vol. 2, s.v. *Congrès*, n. 3, it is stated: "On attribue l'origine du Congrès à l'effronterie d'un jeune homme qui étant accusé d'impuissance, offrit de prouver le contraire en présence de chirurgiens et de matrones. L'official eut l'indiscretion d'admettre ce nouveau genre de preuve." In Merlin, *Répertoire*, (4), vol. 6, s.v. *Impuissance* there is a long discussion of all the problems of proving or disproving impotency. The explanation of the origin of *congrès* originates in the writings of Hotman: see Esmein, *op. cit. supra*, note 69, vol. 2, p. 280 and n. 2. Esmein, *op. cit. supra*, note 69, vol. 2, pp. 275–284 gives a good discussion of this institution.

[727] *Ancien Denisart*, vol. 2, p. 703, s.v. *Impuissance*, no. 23. Pocquet de Livonnière, *op. cit. supra* note 619, p. 25 (bk. 1, tit. 1, sect. 6, no. 58) states thus: "La preuve d'impuissance ne se peut faire que par l'interrogatoire et la visite, celle du Congrès a été abolie."

[728] Pothier, *T.C.M.*, p. 210 (no. 458).

[729] *Ibid.*

[730] See P.J.J.G. Guyot, *Répertoire universel et raisonné de jurisprudence ...; ouvrage de plusieurs jurisconsultes*, new ed., Paris, Visse, 1784–1785, vol. 9, p. 86, s.v. *Impuissance*: "Le jurisconsulte, qui doit être chaste et pur comme la loi, se trouve embarrassé en traitant ces matières, qui peuvent reveiller des images voluptueuses: mais en se rendant l'interprête de la loi, il s'oblige à parler avec autant de courage que le legislateur des mystères de la nature; et ce n'est pas, sans doute, dans un livre de jurisprudence que l'imagination viendra chercher ce qui peut inflammer les sens. Ici tout est épuré par la justice, qui est à la fois le guide et l'objet de nos recherches." This is a neat statement of the attitude that culminated in the exclusion of an article on *impuissance* from the C.N.

permit someone to allege his own "turpitude".[731] The Canon law, however, had allowed impotent persons to sue for annulment, alleging their own impotency.[732] The C.Q. redactors maintained the rule of the *ancien droit*.

The second paragraph of C.Q. 117 also states that the action of nullity could not be brought if three years had elapsed from the date of the marriage. This is new law: the *ancien droit* was not so precise, merely providing that, after cohabitation for "un grand nombre d'années", the marriage could not be attacked on the grounds of the impotency of one of the spouses.[733] The number of years which would bar such an action would vary according to the circumstances. Denisart, for example, reports an *arrêt* where a wife was allowed to seek the annulment of her marriage on the grounds of her husband's impotency eight years after the marriage had been celebrated.[734]

In C.Q. 117, the Quebec redactors have followed the *ancien droit*, though reforming it, while rejecting the position taken by the C.N. The Quebec redactors knew that the C.N. had no article on impotency as ground for annulling marriage simply because proof was considered difficult and improper.[735] They would also know from the French commentaries on the C.N. that actions to annul a marriage on the grounds of impotency were successfully brought in France, alleging error as to person.[736] They would realise that the same would be likely to happen in Quebec were there not a specific provision on impotency. Further, the introduction of a specific article on impotency would permit useful reforms of the law. Proof of impotency had caused many problems in the *ancien droit*: the C.Q. redactors provided that such impotency had to be "apparent and manifest" in order to found an action. Another reform was the limitation to three years after the marriage of the period within which such an action could be brought.[737] Thus, this article of the C.Q. is the result of the redactors' desire to follow the *ancien droit*. Experience of the interpretation of the C.N. would support this approach. Further, the inclusion of a specific article allowed useful reforms of the law as regards mode of proof and time within which the relevant action should be brought.

---

[731] Pothier, *T.C.M.*,. p. 203 (no. 445): "[I]l n'y a que la partie avec qui l'impuissant a contracté mariage qui soit recevable à intenter la demande en cassation de mariage pour raison de l'empêchement d'impuissance; et l'impuissant n'est pas reçu à attaquer son mariage pour cause de ce prétendu vice, lorsque la personne avec qui il a contracté mariage ne s'en plaint pas." D'Espeisses, *Œuvres supra* note 73, vol. 1, p. 275 (part 1, tit. 13 no. 3): "Le marié impuissant n'est reçu à poursuivre le cassation du Mariage, contre celui qui est puissant; car c'est alléguer sa turpitude.... [S]eulement il est reçu en ladite poursuite, lorsque le marié puissant y consent."

[732] See Esmein, *op. cit. supra*, note 69, vol. 1, pp. 232–267, vol. 2, pp. 273–286.

[733] Pothier, *T.C.M.*, p. 203 (no. 445).

[734] *Ancien Denisart*, vol. 2, p. 704, s.v. *Impuissance*, no. 32.

[735] See *supra*, text at note 720.

[736] See *supra*, text at note 721 and references in note 721.

[737] The period in France under the C.N. would be different. *Doctrine* had applied C.N. 180 (error as to person) to impotency. C.N. 181 stated that the wronged person had only six months to demand nullity "depuis que l'erreur a été par lui reconnue".

C.Q. 118 states that: "A second marriage cannot be contracted before the dissolution of the first." C.N. 147 states the same; the *ancien droit* provided similarly. Any other provision would have been unthinkable.[738]

Articles 119–123 of the C.Q. concern the necessary consents to the marriage of minors and will be discussed below. C.Q. 124–126 lay down the prohibited degrees of relationship. They are the same as in C.N. 161–163, though C.N. 164 allowed the government to grant dispensations from C.N. 163. The C.Q. redactors merely remarked that a power to grant dispensations as in C.N. 164 did not exist in Quebec.[739] The prohibited degrees as laid down by the C.Q. are those of Leviticus and of the Roman law.[740] They are the minimum prohibited degrees of most Christian societies and are not of great interest here. The *ancien droit* of France followed the Canon law and accordingly had much wider prohibitions.[741] We need not consider the difficult question of what the law in Quebec would have been on the prohibited degrees of relationship prior to codification.[742] The redactors, however, included the following article, C.Q. 127, in their code:

> The other impediments recognized according to the different religious persuasions, as resulting from relationships or affinity or from other causes, remain subject to the rules hitherto followed in the different churches and religious communities.
>
> The right, likewise, of granting dispensations from such impediments appertains, as heretofore, to those who have hitherto enjoyed it.

The second paragraph of C.Q. 129 states that no priest or minister can be compelled to solemnize a marriage to which an impediment exists according to his religion. There is no equivalent to C.Q. 127 in the C.N., where marriage is purely secular. C.Q. 127 has been the subject of lively controversy; and it has been much disputed whether this article introduces into the law of Quebec Canon law impediments as regards the marriage of Roman Catholics.[743]

The redactors of the C.Q. state that there are certain impediments applicable only to members of particular religions; and since these impediments could not

---

[738] *Pan. fran.*, vol. 3, pp. 154–162 has an interesting discussion on this point. There it is argued that polygyny is not contrary to natural law or the essence of marriage (pp. 155–156); but (at *ibid.*, p. 156) polyandry is stated to be contrary to natural law: "Si une femme avait plusieurs maris on ne pourrait pas savoir qui serait le père des enfants qu'elle mettrait au monde. On ne pourrait pas non plus déterminer auquel de ces maris elle devrait obéir."

[739] *Second Report*, p. 179.

[740] Leviticus, ch. 18; Inst., 1.10.1–11; Corbett, *op. cit. supra* note 53, pp. 47–51.

[741] See Maleville, *Analyse*, vol. 1, p. 160; Pothier, *T.C.M*, pp. 57–96 (nos. 120–211); Esmein, *op. cit. supra*, note 69, vol. 1, pp. 335–383. See *supra*, text at notes 222–230, where this has been discussed in relation to Louisiana.

[742] See C. Lemesurier, "The Marriage Law of Quebec", in *Le droit civil français: livre-souvenir des journées du droit civil (Montréal, 31 août-2 Septembre 1934)*, Paris, Sirey, 1936, pp. 135–154 at p. 150.

[743] See *ibid.*; Baudouin, *op. cit. supra* note 551, pp. 160–167; *T.D.C.Q.*, vol. 1, 380–385; and J.E.C. Brierley, "Husband and wife in the Law of Quebec: A 1970 Conspectus", in D. Mendes da Costa (ed.) *Studies in Canadian Family Law*, Toronto, Butterworths, 1972, vol. 2, pp. 795–844 at pp. 806 and 807–809.

be governed by general provisions, the redactors included this article, leaving the members of such religions governed by the rules of their religion.[744] It seems likely that the redactors intended to introduce these impediments as the law of Quebec as regards the members of particular religions.[745] The Privy Council decided otherwise, however, in *Despatie* v. *Tremblay*.[746] What cannot be doubted, however, is that the redactors were attempting to give suitable recognition to the religious diversity of the Province. In the introduction to their title on marriage, the redactors had admitted that circumstances in Quebec prevented:

> the adoption on the subject of marriage of uniform and specific rules, applicable to all the inhabitants of the province where such variety of usages, religions and religious associations are to be met with, having different customs and practices, and having ministers authorized to celebrate marriages, and to make acts of their celebration.[747]

On this particular article, the C.Q. redactors refer to the noted English author, Stephen, who, in the relevant section of his work, remarks that there are two kinds of impediments to marriage: "first, such as are canonical; secondly, such as are municipal or civil," before discussing the differences between them.[748] The redactors have accepted this division, permitting them to recognize the religious diversity of the Province.

C.Q. 127 completes the first chapter of this title of the Code. The next article, C.Q. 128, the first of the second chapter, states thus:

> Marriage must be solemnized openly, by a competent officer recognized by law.

The first paragraph of C.Q. 129 states thus:

> All priests, rectors, ministers and other officers authorized by law to keep registers of acts of civil status are competent to solemnize marriage.[749]

C.N. 165 states thus:

> Le mariage sera célébré publiquement devant l'Officier civil du domicile de l'une des parties.

The *ancien droit* in France had followed the Tridentine Canon law, though the decrees of the Council of Trent had in themselves no validity in France.[750] Especially crucial was the December, 1606, Edict of Henri IV which, following

---

[744] *Second Report*, p. 179.
[745] So certainly is the opinion of Brierley, *op. cit. supra* note 743, p. 806.
[746] 1921 A.C. 702.
[747] *Second Report*, p. 175.
[748] H.J. Stephen, *New Commentaries on the Law of England*, 3rd ed., London, Butterworths, 1853, vol. 2, p. 239.
[749] The second paragraph, referred to already in connection with C.Q. 127 states: "But none of the officers thus authorized, can be compelled to solemnize a marriage to which any impediment exists according to the doctrine and belief of his religion, and the discipline of the church to which he belongs."
[750] See Pothier, *T.C.M.*, pp. 158–159 (no. 349).

article 40 of the Ordonnance of Blois, declared that marriages not celebrated in church were null.[751] Thus, the only valid marriage was that celebrated by a Roman Catholic priest, and the parties had to go to church to receive the nuptial benediction and to celebrate the marriage "en face d'Eglise". (An Edict of Louis XVI of 1787 allowed non-Catholics to marry in front of an officer of civil justice.)[752] The Tridentine law as enacted in France would be unacceptable in Quebec under British rule. Although there was no legislation on the point, it is evident that from the time of the cession to Britain onwards, Protestant clergymen (certainly those of the Anglican faith) could solemnize marriages in Quebec.[753] The first legislation on marriage came in 1795, when a provincial Act (35 Geo. III, ch. 4) required clergymen in charge of parishes to keep official registers of civil status.[754] This applied to Protestant and Catholic clerics. Lemesurier points out that no express power to conduct marriages is granted: it is merely assumed.[755] It was doubtful if this Act applied to Church of Scotland ministers, but an Act of 1827 (7 Geo. IV, ch. 2) provided that any marriages which had been celebrated and any which were to be celebrated by a Church of Scotland minister were to be valid.[756] The power to solemnize marriages and to keep registers of civil status was gradually extended to ministers of other Protestant denominations, and this series of statutes was consolidated in 1860.[757] This is basically the law contained in these provisions of the Quebec code.[758] Thus, these articles stated the existing law of the Province, which already recognized the religious diversity of the inhabitants. The redactors point out that in *ancien régime* France uniform rules on the solemnization of marriage were practicable, there being only one recognized religion:[759] after the Revolution, all religions being recognized, marriage was made a purely civil act to secure uniformity in the celebration of marriages.[760] They continue:

---

[751] See Pothier, *T.C.M.*, p. 159 (no. 349). Generally on the French law, see Pothier, *T.C.M.*, p. 155, pp. 157–159 (no. 346, and nos. 348–349).

[752] See Toullier, *op. cit. supra* note 628, vol. 1, p. 301, no. 492.

[753] See Lemesurier, *op. cit. supra* note 742, pp. 147–148.

[754] See *ibid.*, p. 148. I have not seen these statutes, and am relying on Lemesurier's account of and quotation from them.

[755] *Ibid.*

[756] *Ibid.*

[757] See *ibid.*, pp. 148–149: C.S.L.C., ch. 20.

[758] On these articles the Commissioners made the following references. On C.Q. 128, they refer only to C.N. 165. On C.Q. 129 they referred to Pothier, *T.C.M.*, p. 159 (no. 349); 35 Geo III ch. 4, s.1; C.S.L.C. ch. 20, ss.16 and 17; and W.O. Russell, *A Treatise on Crimes and Misdemeanors*, vol. 1, p. 192. The C.Q. redactors do not indicate which edition of Russell they were referring to: I consulted the second, London, Butterworths, 1826–1828, the third, London, Saunders and Benning, 1843, and the Philadelphia, T. and J.W. Johnson, 1853, editions, each of 2 vols. The section the redactors cite is a discussion of marriage law in England, in Russell's chapter 23 on bigamy: it contains nothing of direct relevance here. They also referred to C.N. 75, which deals with the celebration of marriages.

[759] However, see *supra*, text at note 752.

[760] *Second Report*, pp. 175–177.

> A change of such a nature, not appearing in any way desirable in this country, it became necessary to renounce the idea of establishing here, as to the formalities of marriage, uniform and detailed rules, and of following the Code Napoleon in the new system it has adopted.[761]

The term "openly" ("publiquement") in C.Q. 128 was the subject of a dispute between the redactors. Commissioner Day feared that this term might be interpreted to mean "in church" (*en face d'Eglise*) as it had been understood in *ancien régime* France. He pointed out that Protestants generally did not marry in church. The other Commissioners, Caron and Morin, considered the term to be sufficiently elastic to cover the variations in mode and place of celebration among the several religious denominations.[762] This dispute indicates once more the extent to which the redactors were concerned, in these articles, to take account of the diversity of religions and practices in the Province.

The remaining articles of chapter two of this title do not provide material of interest here. Articles 130–134 deal with banns and their publication.[763] C.Q. 135 is a provision on conflict of laws. The only point to be made on these articles is that C.Q. 134, consistent with C.Q. 127 and 129, states that those "who have hitherto held the right to grant licenses or dispensations for marriage", may grant exemptions from the publication of banns.

The third chapter of title five is concerned with oppositions to marriage; it consists of twelve articles, C.Q. 136–147. It follows the equivalent chapter of the C.N. fairly closely. C.Q. 137–142 deal with oppositions to the marriages of children, and will be discussed later.[764] Publication of banns permitted the making of oppositions:[765] C.Q. 144 refers to the Code of Civil Procedure which lays down the method of making oppositions, while C.Q. 145 states before which court such actions of opposition are to be brought. C.Q. 146 states that proceedings on appeal from a judgment under C.Q. 144 and 145 are to be summary, and to be given precedence.

In general, the Quebec code has followed here the provisions of the C.N. in so far as the code only provides for a restricted class of persons to have the right to make formal opposition to a marriage. In the *ancien droit*, following the Canon law, any person claiming a right to do so could oppose a marriage.[766] Opposition was made by writing intimated to the parish priest who had published the bans. The opposition, no matter how ill-founded, prevented celebra-

---

[761] *Ibid.*, p. 177.

[762] *Ibid.*, pp. 179–81.

[763] On the *ancien droit*, see Pothier, *T.C.M.*, pp. 27–33 (nos. 66–80). The C.N. deals with this matter in articles 165–169.

[764] See *infra*, on paternal authority.

[765] See the *Second Report*, p. 181. Pothier, *T.C.M.*, p. 33 (no. 81) states that: "Les personnes qui prétendent avoir droit d'empêcher le mariage dont on a publié les bans, peuvent former opposition aux bans." Bugnet, in his n. 1 on p. 33, points out that Pothier is really referring to oppositions to marriage.

[766] See Pothier *T.C.M.*, p. 33 (no. 81), especially sentence quoted in note 765 *supra*; Brissaud, *History*, pp. 129–30; and also Esmein, *op. cit. supra* note 69, vol. 1, pp. 421–427.

tion of the marriage by the priest, until the opposition had been withdrawn by the party making it or had been set aside by the judge.[767] If the court lifted the opposition, and the person opposing the marriage appealed, the priest still could not celebrate the marriage.[768] The system was obviously open to abuse, because of, first, the lack of clear regulation of who had a right to oppose, and, second, the want of adequately defined grounds for making opposition. Further, the system involved long delays and apparently thus ultimately prevented from taking place marriages to which there could be no valid objection. The church had made it a sin to oppose a marriage maliciously and unreasonably; but this measure was of doubtful efficacy as remedy for the problem.[769]

Towards the end of the *ancien régime*, an *arrêt* of the *Parlement de Paris* had to some extent improved the position. This *arrêt*, of 28th April, 1778, forbade anyone, other than fathers, mothers, tutors, curators, brothers, sisters, uncles, and aunts, from making oppositions to marriages.[770] The *loi* on marriage of 20th September, 1792, devoted the third section of its fourth title to marriage. This enactment solved the problems, noted above, relating to oppositions by limiting to a small number of persons the right of making opposition, and by compelling judges to decide on oppositions with despatch.[771] The French code adopted the system of this *loi*, and, in turn, the C.Q. generally followed the system of the C.N.[772] Thus, it would appear that the C.Q. restricted the class of those who could oppose a marriage.[773] The benefits of so doing are obvious.

C.Q. 136 states thus:

> The solemnizing of a marriage may be opposed by any person already married to one of the parties intending to contract.

C.N. 172 provides the same. Pothier states the same, and adds that opposition may even be made by a person affianced to one of the persons whose bans have been proclaimed.[774] (The *ancien droit* was less restrictive, and, as shown, anyone claiming the right could make an opposition; whether that opposition would be successful is a different question.)[775] Neither the C.N. nor the C.Q. states that a fiancé may make an opposition. Maleville remarks that if a fiancé

---

[767] The technical term used was *donner mainlevée*.

[768] On this whole procedure, see Pothier, *T.C.M.*, pp. 34–35 (no. 82).

[769] See Brissaud, *History*, p. 130. If a priest celebrated a marriage without the opposition having been lifted, he was subject to severe penalties: Order of 5th June, 1691: Pothier, *T.C.M.*, p. 34 (no. 82).

[770] See Merlin, *Répertoire* (4), vol. 8, s.v. *Oppositions à Mariage*.

[771] See Brissaud, *History*, p. 130. Huussen, *op. cit. supra* note 106, p. 43 points out that this particular section of the highly contentious *loi* of 1792 was passed easily.

[772] With some exceptions, which will be noted *infra* in discussing paternal authority.

[773] It should be noted that the *arrêt* of the *Parlement de Paris* would be of no validity in Quebec. Note that none of the relevant articles here of the C.Q. purport to be reforming the law. Indeed, all their provisions had precedents in the *ancien droit*; but because they are restrictive, the law is quite changed.

[774] Pothier, *T.C.M.*, p. 33 (no. 81).

[775] See *supra*, text at notes 765–769.

attempts to oppose a marriage the court has to give *main-levée*.[776] He debates whether the court ought to condemn the opposant to pay damages as authorized under C.N. 179 (C.Q. 147). He refers to a recent author (probably an allusion to Delaporte and Riffé-Caubray),[777] who was of the opinion that in such circumstances, a *fiancé* could make opposition, and the person against whom the opposition had been made should pay damages to the opposant (for breach of promise to marry). Maleville disagreed, arguing that a person to whom a promise of marriage had been made could not make an opposition not permitted by law, and the only remedy such person would have would be to sue, independently, for damages.[778] In the *Pandectes françaises* Delaporte and Riffé-Caubray argue that, if A has made a promise of marriage to B, there is sufficient ground for B to oppose A's marriage to a third party; if, however, A persists in marrying the third party—they add—the judge must lift the opposition and merely cause A to pay damages to B.[779] Here the *Pandectes françaises* are closely following the *ancien droit*, especially as found in Pothier.[780] The Commissioners referred to this section of the *Pandectes françaises* in connection with C.Q. 136; but it seems most unlikely that they would have accepted the authors' views on this issue. The C.Q. makes no reference to fiancés opposing marriages, and they must not have been granted this right. Here it is importany to note that C.Q. 62, though placed in a different section of the Code, supports this:

> If, however, the opposition be founded on a simple promise of marriage, it is of no effect, and the marriage is proceeded with as if no such opposition had been made.

There is no equivalent article in the C.N.; and, indeed, the article originates in provincial legislation.[781] This supports the interpretation here given of the C.Q.'s failure to mention fiancés, though, as Trudel and Mignault point out, there is a difference between a mere promise to marry and a formal betrothal (*fiançailles*), the latter having an effect under Canon law.[782]

---

[776] See *supra*, note 767 on this term.

[777] See *infra*, text at notes 778–780.

[778] Maleville, *Analyse*, vol. 1, pp. 165–166.

[779] *Pan. fran.*, vol. 3, p. 241.

[780] Pothier, *T.C.M.*, p. 35 (no. 83) states: "Lorsque ce ne sont que des fiançailles qui font le sujet de l'opposition, si l'opposant en fait la preuve, l'official les déclare bonnes et valables, et il exhorte l'autre partie à les accomplir. Si elle persiste en son refus, après lui avoir imposé une pénitence, il prononce la dissolution des fiançailles, et en conséquence fait mainlevée de l'opposition." In the *ancien droit*, oppositions on the grounds of marriage or betrothal were in the jurisdiction of the ecclesiastical courts: hence the penalty of penance. This was because they referred to spiritual matters; other oppositions were in the jurisdiction of temporal courts.

[781] 12 Vict. ch. 53, s.1 (C.S.L.C. ch. 34, s. 4). See *T.D.C.Q.*, vol. 1, pp. 196–197, and Mignault, *op. cit. supra* note 718, vol. 1, pp. 409–410.

[782] See *T.D.C.Q.*, vol. 1, pp. 196–197; Mignault, *op. cit. supra* note 718, vol. 1, pp. 409–410. See *supra*, note 780, where it is pointed out that oppositions on the grounds of marriage or betrothal were heard by ecclesiastical courts.

The next article to be considered,[783] C.Q. 143, states as follows:

> Whatever may be the quality of the opposant, it is his duty to adopt and follow up the formalities and proceedings necessary to have his opposition brought before the court and decided within the legal delays, a demand for its dismissal not being required; in default of his so doing the opposition is regarded as never having been made, and the marriage ceremony is proceeded with, notwithstanding.

This is new law, and stated to be such by the redactors. There is no exact equivalent in the C.N. C.N. 176, read along with C.N. 66, lays down the form of the opposition to be given to the *Officier de l'état civil*; there is no statement that the onus is on the opposant to take the opposition to court. C.N. 177 and 178 lay down time limits for the courts' decisions on actions for *main-levée* brought by the couple intending to marry. In the *ancien droit*, it was the couple to whose marriage opposition had been made who had to seek *main-levée*,[784] and there was no provision for an especially speedy decision. The C.N. improved on the *ancien droit* here by providing for a speedier court decision. The C.Q. improved on the C.N. by enacting that a demand for *main-levée* was not required: the opposant had to go to court and justify his opposition, and, if he failed to do so, his opposition was ignored. Given the criticisms of the right of opposition under the old law, it is obvious why the Quebec codifiers reversed the old law, and made the procedure quicker. (Artciles 144, 145 and 146 of the C.Q. set out the relevant procedure; they contain no matter of interest to us.)

C.N. 147 states that:

> If the opposition be rejected, the opposants, other than the father and mother, may be condemned to pay costs, and are liable for damages according to circumstances.

C.N. 179 is similar in purport:

> Si l'opposition est rejetée, les opposans, autre néanmoins que les ascendans, pourront être condamnés à des dommages-intérêts.

The *Pandectes françaises* explain why parents (and ascendants in the C.N.)[785] are exempted from liability in damages:

> [L]a loi, par la grande confiance qu'elle a dans leur [i.e. parents and ascendants] tendresse pour leurs enfants, suppose toujours qu'ils ont agi par des motifs raisonnables; et que, d'ailleurs, les enfants doivent toujours respecter leurs actions.[786]

---

783 On exclusion of C.Q. 137–142, see *supra*, text at note 764.

784 Pothier, *T.C.M.*, p. 35 (no. 83): "La partie qui veut avoir mainlevée de l'opposition faite à ses bans de mariage, doit assigner l'opposant devant le juge qui est compétent pour en connaître."

785 On this difference between the C.N. and the C.Q., see *infra* on paternal power.

786 *Pan. fran.*, vol. 3, pp. 255–256.

Thus, in their provisions on oppositions to marriage, the Quebec redactors have radically amended the law. They have reduced the categories of persons entitled formally to oppose a marriage; and they have done so without indicating they have changed the law. They must be taken to have restricted the making of oppositions to the persons named in the articles: if any other person purports to make an opposition, it may be ignored completely. Under the *ancien droit* on oppositions, because of its broad scope, all the persons specifically named in the C.Q. could make oppositions: it is this that enables the redactors to avoid stating these articles as new law. But the expressions used in these articles leave no doubt that other persons may not make oppositions, even although this is nowhere explicitly stated.[787] The restriction of the class of persons entitled to oppose a marriage was only reasonable, given that the *ancien droit* had been "un moyen de vexation".[788] The only opposition that could be made under the C.Q. to the marriage of a sane adult was that by a person purporting to be married to such adult.[789]

The C.Q. redactors must be taken as having restricted the class of potential opposants because they considered that no others could have, or claim, any real interest in the marriage of adults in a modern society. To have allowed others to make an opposition, even if such oppositions would be rejected ultimately, would have been to bring about unjustifiable delays in the marriage of independent individuals: a result unacceptable given the liberal individualist conception of society current in nineteenth-century Quebec. This must explain why the redactors have followed the scheme of the C.N. One of the problems connected with the old law had been delay in the court hearings on oppositions. The C.Q. provided a speedy procedure. Further, the C.Q. required the person opposing the marriage to go to court to make good his case; if he did not go to court, his opposition automatically lapsed. The C.N. and the *ancien droit* both required the person whose marriage had been opposed to go to court to gain *main-levée*. The action here of the C.Q. redactors seems just, and reflects their notion that oppositions to marriage should be restricted and should not be allowed to hinder or inconvenience couples proposing to marry. Although the chapter of the code on anulling marriages will not be discussed here,[790] it may be pointed out that the C.Q. redactors, following the C.N., have adopted the view of Pothier that, if a marriage, to which opposition has been made, is celebrated without such opposition having been lifted, the marriage is nonetheless incapable of annul-

---

[787] See Mignault, *op. cit. supra* note 718, vol. 1, pp. 406–408.

[788] *Ibid.*, vol. 1, p. 393.

[789] *Ibid.*, vol. 1, p. 394.

[790] Generally a marriage could only be annulled if invalid due to a defect or lack in the meeting of the conditions set out in the discussion above, if such defect or lack was in relation to more than a mere formality. The C.Q. articles do not contain any major departure from the *ancien droit* or C.N. except as regards the marriages of minors, and these differences will be discussed *infra* on paternal authority. See C.Q. 148–164, C.N. 180–202; Pothier, *T.C.M.*, pp. 201–208 (nos. 442–451). See also the discussion in *Second Report*, pp. 183–185. Day disagreed with C.Q. 149, taken from C.N. 181, preferring the *ancien droit*; he also disapproved of the fines under C.N. 157 and 158.

ment, if otherwise valid. Lamoignon had been of the opposite opinion.[791] Neither of the two codes state that a marriage may be annulled simply because there had been an opposition to it.

Thus, comparison with the C.N. and the *ancient droit* shows that the work of the redactors of the C.Q. on the requirements for contracting marriage is a mixture of conservatism and innovation. The redactors have preserved the ages of marriage as provided under the Canon law, though there might well have been an argument in favour of raising such ages, thoughthis might have raised a conflicts issue with other British colonies. They have preserved impotency as a factor rendering marriage null, though amended in light of the criticisms of the *ancien droit*. The exclusion of an equivalent article from the C.N. had not resulted in the disappearance of impotency as a ground for annulling a marriage. Obviously, the inclusion of C.Q. 117 on impotency may be ascribed to the redactors' knowledge of the interpretation of the C.N., and the necessity of reforms of the *ancien droit* to render proof easier with an acceptable method of acquiring that proof. It is important to note that the redactors gave due recognition to the diversity of religions in the Province, allowing the solemnization of marriages, according to their various forms of doctrine, by clergymen authorized to keep registers of civil status. These provisions are founded in provincial statutes, and do not connote any massive innovation, though the intention behind C.Q. 127, on impediments not recognized by the code but recognized by other religions, is rather more problematic. The C.Q. redactors have significantly innovated in their provisions on oppositions to marriage. Following the C.N., they have restricted the class of persons who may oppose a marriage (although the class of persons in the C.Q. is not exactly the same as that in the C.N.). There were obvious reasons of social policy for doing so: to have allowed simply any one to oppose the marriage of a sane adult would have been unthinkable in mid-nineteenth-century Quebec. In here following the C.N., the redactors were knowingly importing a restriction on the class of those who could oppose marriages. Again for reasons of social policy, the Quebec redactors have required the person opposing to bring his opposition to court, failing which his opposition automatically falls: similarly, the court procedure is particularly expeditious.

In this section of the code, the redactors had to provide clear concise rules on the requirements for marriage. This they did, using the French code as a model. The French code has exerted some influence on the substance, though the C.Q. redactors were both independent (consider their rules on oppositions and the reform of the law on impotency) and conservative (consider their rules on the ages required for marriage and the inclusion of a rule on impotency). The redactors also had to recognize the diversity of religions in the Province, and had to follow the Acts of the legislature on who was authorized to celebrate marriages. The relevant articles fulfilled these functions, being adapted to Quebec society. As regards the preservation of the Canonical ages for marriage, it should be recalled that the instructions of the legislature were essentially

---

[791] Pothier, *T.C.M.*, p. 35 (no. 82).

conservative, and that there would be no obvious or pressing need for reform of a rule that presumably caused no problems in practice, and which matched the position throughout the British Empire.

Puissance Maritale and the Property Aspects of the Husband-Wife Relationship

At issue here, just as in the discussion of the provisions of the D.O. on the property relations of spouses, is not so much such property relationships in themselves, but rather their effect on the relationship between husband and wife. It is important to note that the nature of matrimonial property in the Quebec code is much less controversial than in that of Louisiana.

The rubric of the fourth title of the third book of the C.Q. is: "Of marriage covenants and of the effect of marriage upon the property of the consorts." The Quebec redactors preferred this to the C.N.'s "Du contrat de Mariage, et des Droits respectifs des Epoux", which they considered to be ambiguous.[792] Indeed, Toullier remarks that "le contrat de mariage proprement dit" is matrimony, the marital union, rather than the conventions regulating the property relations of the spouses.[793] There is a major difference between these provisions of the C.Q. and those of the C.N., since the latter includes the dotal regime of property and excludes dower, whereas the former, following the *Coutume de Paris*, contains no provisions on dowry but does regulate dower.[794]

C.Q. 1257 states that:

> All kinds of agreements, may be lawfully made in contracts of marriage, even those which, in any other act *inter vivos*, would be void; such as the renunciation of successions which have not yet devolved, the gift of future property, the conventional appointment of an heir, and other dispositions in contemplation of death.

This is followed by C.Q. 1258:

> All covenants contrary to public order or to good morals, or forbidden by any prohibitory law, are, however, excepted from the above rule.

C.Q. 1259 has already been mentioned;[795] it states that one example of covenants struck at by C.Q. 1258 would be those derogating from the power of the husband over the persons of his wife and children, or from that power belonging to the husband as head of the conjugal association. C.Q. 1260 provides that if no covenants have been made, or if the contrary has not been stipulated, then the consorts are presumed to have subjected themselves to the general law of the country, and in particular to the legal community of property and to customary

---

[792] *Fifth Report*, p. 201.
[793] See Toullier, *op. cit. supra* note 628, vol. 12, p. 2, and n. 1.
[794] See *Fifth Report*, pp. 201–203.
[795] See *supra*, text at note 701.

or legal dower in favour of the wife and children.[796] C.Q. 1270 gives a neat definition of legal community as

> that which the law, in the absence of stipulation to the contrary, establishes between consorts, by the mere fact of their marriage, in respect of certain descriptions of property, which they are presumed to have intended to subject to it.

These articles of the C.Q. express the *ancien droit coutumier* of Paris, and make no change in the law of Quebec.[797]

According to C.Q. 1272, the legal community consists of the following property: all moveable property possessed by the consorts on the day of their marriage; all moveable property they acquire during marriage or which comes to them by succession or gift, unless the testator or donor has otherwise provided; all the fruits, revenues, interests and arrears of whatever nature, which fall due or are received during the marriage, and arise from property which belonged to the consorts at the time of marriage, or from property which has accrued to them during marriage, by any title whatsoever; and, finally, all immoveable property acquired during marriage. The rules on immoveables are further refined in C.Q. 1273–1279; but we need not consider these here. The C.N. provided similarly to C.Q. 1272 in its article 1401. The *Coutume de Paris* stated thus in its article 220:

> Homme et femme conjoints ensemble par mariage, sont communs en biens meubles, et conquêts immeubles faits durant et constant ledit mariage, et commence le communauté du jour des épousailles et benediction nuptial.

Thus, C.Q. 1272 follows the *ancien droit.*[798] There has been no change in the composition of the legal community.

C.Q. 1292 is important:

> The husband alone administers the property of the community. He may sell, alienate, or hypothecate it without the concurrence of his wife.
>
> He may even alone dispose of it, either by gifts or otherwise *inter vivos*, provided it is in favour of persons who are legally capable, and without fraud.

C.N. 1421 provides the same as the first paragraph of C.Q. 1292:

> Le mari administre seul les biens de la communauté. Il peut les vendre, aliéner et hypothéquer sans le concours de la femme.

C.N. 1422 is, however, different from the second paragraph of C.Q. 1292:

> Il ne peut disposer entre-vifs, à titre gratuit, des immeubles de la communauté, ni de l'universalité ou d'une quotité du mobilier, si ce nest pour l'établissement des enfans communs.

---

[796] It is not proposed to deal with dower here.

[797] See, e.g. Pothier, *T.Comm.*, pp. 49–52 (introd., nos. 1–10), pp. 58–60 (nos. 4, and 9–11).

[798] Among the numerous authorities that could be cited (see the references of the C.Q. redactors), see, e.g., Pothier, *T.Comm.*, pp. 65–66 (nos. 24–26).

> Il peut néanmoins disposer des objets mobiliers, à titre gratuit et particulier, au profit de toutes personnes, pourvu qu'il ne s'en réserve pas l'usufruit.

Quebec is here following the *ancien droit* as found in the *Coutume de Paris*, article 225 of which stated thus:

> Le mari est seigneur des meubles et conquêts immeubles par lui faits durant et constant le mariage de lui et de sa femme. En telle manière qu'il peut les vendre, aliéner ou hypothéquer, et en faire et disposer par donation ou autre disposition, entre-vifs, à son plaisir et volonté, sans le consentement de sadite femme, à personne capable, et sans fraude.

That this article of the *Coutume* mentions only "conquêts immeubles par *lui* faits", does not limit the husband's power of alienation to immoveables he himself has acquired during the marriage. Included in the power of alienation, according to most of the commentators, were all the immoveables of the *communauté*.[799]

The provisions of the *Coutume de Paris*, expressed in C.N. 1421 and the first half of C.Q. 1292, were *droit commun coutumier*; but those expressed in the second half of C.Q. 1292 were not. While, for example, the *Coutume d'Orléans* had a provision almost identical to that of Paris,[800] the *Coutumes* of Anjou (art. 289), of Maine (art. 304), and of Lodunois (chap. 26, art. 6) allowed the husband to sell, hypothecate and exchange the goods of the *communauté*, but not to donate them *inter vivos*. The *Coutume* of Saintonge (tit. 8, art. 68) allowed the husband alone to dispose of *meubles* and *conquêts*, while excepting from this general power those which had been acquired by the husband and wife *contractants ensemble*; whereas the *Coutumes* of Bayonne (tit. 9, art. 29) and of Labour (tit. 9, art. 2) excepted, from this general power of disposal granted to the husband, any property acquired by the wife or gained by her work.[801]

The French code restricted the husband's power of donating community property.[802] The redactors of the C.Q. did not choose to adopt the innovation of the C.N.—if "innovation" be correct, since there was precedent in some of the *coutumes*— and kept to dispositions of the *Coutume de Paris*. They retained the *ancien droit* of Paris which they considered to be "more consonant with the

---

[799] See Pothier, *T. Comm.*, p. 258 (no. 468). Lebrun had been of the contrary opinion; but his views were not accepted. See Ferrière, *Corps et Comp.*, vol. 3, col. 209, n. 1 on art. 225: "La Coûtume en cet article rend le mari maître absolu de *tous* les biens de la Communauté, meubles ou immeubles, pour en pouvoir disposer à sa volonté, sans le consentement de sa femme." Note *Coutume de Paris*, art. 233: "Le mari est seigneur des actions mobilières et possessoires, posé qu'elles procèdent du côté de sa femme; et peut le mari agir et déduire lesdits droits et actions en jugement sans sadite femme."

[800] Pothier, *C. d'Orl.*, Art. 193: "Le mari est seigneur des meubles et conquests immeubles par lui faits durant le mariage de lui et de sa femme; en telle manière qu'il les peut vendre, aliéner ou hypothéquer, et en faire et disposer par disposition ou donation faite entre-vifs à son plaisir et volonté, sans le consentement de sadite femme à personne capable et sans fraude."

[801] Pothier, *T. Comm.*, p. 259 (no. 472).

[802] See Maleville, *Analyse*, vol. 3, pp. 202–203.

fundamental principles of conjugal community. . . ".[803] They argued that given that the husband could sell an immoveable belonging to the *communauté*, and dissipate the proceeds, it was pointless to refuse him power to donate it, provided that he should not do so with intent to defraud his wife or her heirs.[804] Toullier had also stressed the inefficacy of the C.N.'s provision in restraining the husband from dissipating community property.[805] In both the *ancien droit* and the C.Q., excessive donations could amount to fraud.[806] Lebrun had stated that the time when a donation was made could amount to fraud on the wife; Pothier agreed.[807] Pothier also considered that a husband could donate a *conquêt inter-vivos* and retain the usufruct "à lui seul" without fraud resulting; Lebrun disagreed.[808] Here, as Toullier points out, the C.N. redactors have followed the view of Lebrun.[809] On this point, the redactors of the C.Q. were rather more cautious than Pothier, while not adopting the explicit rule of the C.N.: they stated that C.Q. 1292 does not go so far as Pothier, and that they felt it best left to doctrine to decide whether such a usufruct of property donated would amount to fraud, according to the circumstances.[810] Donations by the husband, amounting to fraud, would usually be the result of an attempt by the husband to advantage himself or his heirs at the expense of his wife and her heirs.[811]

The C.Q. redactors have rejected the rule of C.N. 1422, and have asserted the traditional rule on the husband's control of community property because of his *puissance maritale*: "La puissance qu'a le mari, le rend maître absolu de tous les *biens de la communauté*. . . ."[812] Undoubtedly this rule is consistent with the social views of the period. The argument the C.Q. redactors put forward for rejecting the provision of C.N. 1422 is, however, not very satisfactory. They state that: since the husband may sell an immoveable and dissipate the proceeds, why not let him donate such an immoveable? Certainly the French code's provision does not necessarily prevent a prodigal husband from wasting the community property; but it does render more indirect the method of dissipation. Even though the husband has the potentially disastrous power of selling an immoveable and dissipating the proceeds, there is no reason why he should have a second method of frittering away community property. Further, although the French article is imperfect, the redactors could have

---

803 *Fifth Report*, p. 211.
804 *Ibid.*
805 Toullier, *op. cit. supra* note 628, vol. 12, pp. 275–276, no. 311.
806 See Pothier, *T. Comm.*, p. 264 (no. 480). This rule is articulated precisely by the *Coutume de Poitou*, art. 244, and the *Coutume de Saintonge*, tit. 8, art. 67. See also *Fifth Report*, p. 211.
807 Pothier, *T. Comm.*, p. 264 (no. 480) citing Lebrun, *Traite de la communauté*, bk. 2, ch. 2, sect. 1, no. 33.
808 Pothier, *T. Comm.*, p. 264 (no. 480) citing Lebrun, *Traite de la communauté*, bk. 2, ch. 2, sect. 1, no. 33.
809 Toullier, *op. cit. supra* note 628, vol. 12, p. 276, no. 312.
810 *Fifth Report*, p. 211.
811 See Pothier, *T.Comm.*, pp. 264–265 (nos. 481–483). Pothier cites Dumoulin, who was also of this opinion, on the *ancienne coutume* of Paris.
812 Pothier, *T.P.M.*, p. 32 (no. 82) (Pothier's emphasis). See also his edition of the *C. d'Orl.*, p. 258, introd. to tit. X (no. 158).

improved on it, and further protected the interests of the wife. Thus, it seems likely that the reason for the rejection of the innovation in C.N. 1422 is the desire, as expressed by the redactors, to preserve intact the traditional control of the husband over the community, as an important aspect of his *puissance maritale*.[813] The redactors in C.Q. 1292 asserted that traditional control, supporting contemporary social values.

Various other articles expand on this power of the husband over the *communauté*, some of which, as they relate to the authorization of the wife, will be returned to later. It is unnecessary here to discuss control over community property any further; instead, it is convenient to turn to the control exercised by the husband over his wife's property that did not fall into the community, when legal or customary (as distinct from conventional) community existed between them. C.Q. 1298 is as follows:

> The husband has the administration of all the private property of his wife.
>
> He may exercise, alone, all the moveable and possessory actions which belong to his wife.
>
> He cannot, without her consent, dispose of the immoveables which belong to her.
>
> He is responsible for all deteriorations which his wife's private property may suffer for want of conservatory acts.

C.N. 1428 provides identically. This follows the *ancien droit coutumier*, in which the husband administered the *biens propres* of his wife,[814] and alone could exercise all his wife's moveable and possessory actions.[815] He could not dispose of her immoveables without her consent:

> Le mari ne peut vendre, échanger, faire partage ou licitation, charger, obliger, ni hypothéquer le propre heritage de sa femme sans le consentement de sadite femme et icelle par lui autorisée à cette fin.[816]

Finally, the *ancien droit* also provided that the husband had to conserve his wife's property; if he did not, or acted negligently, he would have been liable for damages.[817]

C.Q. 1299 gives a further refinement of the power of the husband over a wife's private property when they are *communes en biens*:

---

[813] See *supra*, text at note 803.

[814] See Pothier, *T.P.M.*, p. 34 (no. 91); Pothier, *C. d'Orl.*, p. 257, introd. to tit. X (no. 153).

[815] See *Coutume de Paris*, art. 233, quoted *supra*, note 799.

[816] *Coutume de Paris*, art. 226.

[817] Pothier, *C. d'Orl.*, pp. 246, 258, introd. to tit. X (nos. 114 and 157). In his laconic style, Loisel, *op. cit.* supra note 62, bk. 1, tit. 2, rules 16, 17, and 12, described the powers of the husband over his wife's property thus: "Le mary est maistre de la communauté, possession et jouissance des propres, de sa femme et non de la propriété d'iceux." "Car quant à ce qui concerne la propriété des propres de la femme: il faut que tous deux y parlent, selon la coustume de la France, remarquée Jean Faure." "Le mary ne pouvant directement, ny indirectement obliger les propres de sa femme."

> Leases of the wife's property, made by her husband alone, cannot exceed nine years; she is not bound, after the dissolution of the community, to maintain those which have been made for a longer term.

C.N. 1429, the equivalent provision, is different:

> Les baux que le mari seul a faits des biens de sa femme pour un tems qui excède neuf ans, ne sont, en cas de dissolution de la communauté, obligatoires vis-à-vis de la femme ou de ses héritiers que pour le tems qui, reste à courir, soit de la première période de neuf ans, si les parties s'y trouvent encore, soit de la seconde, et ainsi de suite, de manière que le fermier n'ait que le droit d'achever la jouissance de la période de neuf ans ou il se trouvée.

The system under the C.N. is that if a husband has granted a lease for more than nine years, when the community is dissolved, the whole term of the lease is divided into periods of nine years, and the wife will have to respect the lease for the period of nine years that is running at the time of dissolution of the community. This is perhaps best understood by an example. Thus, if a husband has granted a lease of his wife's property for twenty-seven years, and the community is dissolved in the twelfth year of the lease, the lease is divided into three periods of nine years. At the time of dissolution of the community, the lease is in the third year of the second period of nine years, and hence the lessee is entitled to the property for another six years, which brings the second period of nine years to an end. The *ancien droit*, on the other hand, essentially was as in the C.Q. Under article 79 of the *Ordonnance de Blois*, leases of more than nine years were regarded as amounting to alienation; a husband could not alienate his wife's immoveable property.[818] Article 227 of the *Coutume de Paris* states the rule explicitly:

> Peut toutefois le mari faire baux à loyer ou à moison à six ans, pour héritages assis à Paris; et neuf ans, pour héritages assis aux champs; et au-dessous, sans fraude.

(The restriction to six years was peculiar to houses in the town of Paris; houses in other towns governed by the *Coutume de Paris* were not affected.[819] Indeed, the writers of the *Pandectes françaises* state, that by the end of the *ancien régime*, the distinction in the *Coutume de Paris* between houses in Paris and other immoveables had fallen into desuetude, so that husbands could make a nine-year lease of town houses.)[820] Thus, it was *droit commun coutumier* that the husband could lease out his wife's property for up to nine years, except for those *coutumes* that explicitly forbade husbands to make leases, without the consent of their wives, which would extend beyond the period of the marriage.[821] The wife was not obliged to maintain leases of over nine years after the

---

[818] Pothier, *T.P.M.*, pp. 34-35 (nos. 92–93); Maleville, *Analyse*, vol. 3, p. 206.
[819] Pothier, *T.P.M.*, pp. 34–35 (nos. 92–93).
[820] *Pan. fran.*, vol. 11, p. 375.
[821] E.g., the *Coutume de Blois*, art. 179: see Pothier, *T.P.M.*, p. 34 (no. 92).

dissolution of the community, even if very few years were left to run.[822] The C.N. innovated here. Maleville points out that, now that article 79 of the *Ordonnance de Blois* was no longer followed, and leases of over nine years were no longer regarded as alienation, it was necessary to determine afresh the effect of long leases made by a husband of his wife's property.[823] The redactors of the C.N. chose the provision now embodied in their article 1429.[824] The Quebec codifiers did not adopt this reform found in the C.N. They remarked that they followed the old rule as embodied in the *Coutume de Paris* and enunciated by Pothier. The change contained in C.N. 1429, they said, had not been regarded by some commentators as an improvement.[825] The Quebec redactors probably considered that the old law provided adequate security for lessees, while giving more protection to the interests of the wife. A provision permitting the granting of longer leases by a husband might have been useful in Quebec, in encouraging lessees to improve the land in the knowledge that they would have a certain time in which to enjoy the benefits of the improvements: under the Quebec provision, a lessee would not be likely to initiate major improvements or invest much capital in the land. This is not necessarily an unimportant point when the backward nature of Quebec agriculture in the nineteenth century is considered.[826] It is nonetheless clear that such considerations were not taken into account by the C.Q. redactors. Given the rather arbitrary nature of the C.N. provision itself, it is unlikely anyway that it would have fulfilled the function here suggested. The redactors of the C.Q. believed there to be no reason for changing the rule of the *ancien droit*.

As already indicated, spouses in Quebec, within certain limits, could in a marriage contract avoid or vary the legal community.[827] That is, they could provide that there be no community of property between the spouses, or provide for a conventional community. It is important to see what effect such marriage contracts could have on the husband's control of his wife's property.

C.Q. 1416 states as follows:

> The clause which declares that the consorts marry without community does not give the wife the right to administer her property, nor to receive the fruits thereof; these are deemed to be contributed to her husband to enable him to bear the charges of marriage.

---

[822] Pothier, *T.P.M.*, p. 35 (no. 93).

[823] Maleville, *Analyse*, vol. 3, p. 206.

[824] On the C.N. provision, see Maleville, *Analyse*, vol. 3, p. 206; Toullier, *op. cit. supra* note 628, vol. 12, pp. 351–356, nos. 403–410; *Pan. fran.*, vol. 11, pp. 376–379.

[825] *Fifth Report*, pp. 213–215. This is possibly an allusion to *Pan. fran.*, vol. 11, pp. 376–379.

[826] See *supra*, chap. 2, text at notes 89–91.

[827] See *supra*, text at notes 793–797.

C.N. 1530 provides identically. The rule of the *ancien droit* was the same.[828] Maleville, following the doctrine of Philippe Renusson, *Traité de la communauté des biens entre l'homme et la femme conjoints par mariage*, wrote as follows:

> C'est . . . la puissance maritale et non la communauté, qui donne au mari le droit d'administrer les revenus des biens de sa femme, et les employer aux besoins de la famille.[829]

C.Q. 1417 states further on the clause simply excluding community:

> The husband retains the administration of the moveable and immoveable property of his wife, and as a consequence the right to receive all the moveable property she brings with her, or which accrues to her during the marriage; saving the restitution he is bound to make after its dissolution, or after a separation of property judicially pronounced.

C.N. 1531 is the same in meaning, though using the term "dot". The *ancien droit* made the same provision as the C.Q.[830]

The next two articles, C.Q. 1418 and 1419, are more interesting. The former states thus:

> If, amongst the moveable property brought by the wife or which accrues to her during marriage, there be things which cannot be used without being consumed, an appreciatory statement must be joined to the contract of marriage, or an inventory must be made of them at the time when they so accrue to her, and the husband is bound to give back their value according to the valuation.

C.Q. 1419 adds that:

> The husband, with regard to such property, has all the rights and is subject to all the obligations of a usufructuary.

On C.Q. 1418, the codifiers cite no authority from the *ancien régime*. They refer to commentators on the modern French law—as they have copied C.N. 1532—and to Justinian's Digest.[831] With C.Q. 1419, again they refer to commentators

---

[828] See Pothier, *T. Comm.*, pp. 254–255 (nos. 461–462); Pothier, *T.P.M.*, p. 36 (no. 97); Pothier, *C. d'Orl.*, p. 235, introd. to tit. X (no. 83).

[829] Maleville, *Analyse*, vol. 3, pp. 258–259. Delaporte and Riffé-Caubray, *Pan. fran.*, vol. 12, p. 145, state: "La clause d'exclusion de communauté ne change rien aux effets ordinaires du mariage. Un des effets étant la puissance que la loi accorde au mari sur la personne et sur les biens de la femme, laquelle puissance ne peut être restreinte que par un exception expresse, et seulement dans les cas prévus par la loi, il s'ensuit que la simple exclusion de la communauté laisse subsister cette puissance dans toute son étendue."

[830] See e.g. Pothier, *T. Comm.*, p. 255 (no. 463); Pothier, *T.P.M.* p. 36 (no. 97).

[831] D. 23.3.42 "Res in dotem datae, quae pondere numero mensura constant, mariti periculo sunt, quia in hoc dantur, ut eas maritus ad arbitrium suum distrahat et quandoque soluto matrimonio eiusdem, generis et qualitatis alias restituat vel ipse vel heres eius." They also refer to Maleville, *Analyse*, vol. 3, p. 259; *Pan. fran.* vol. 12, p. 147, and some authors, including Toullier, who will be mentioned below.

on the modern French law and to the Digest.[832] C.Q. 1419 probably derives from C.N. 1553. On C.Q. 1418, the codifiers remark that no such rule is found in Pothier, but that the rule they have borrowed from the French code is just and conformable to principle.[833] This comment is fair. The *ancien droit coutumier* does not seem specifically to have dealt with this point. On C.Q. 1419, the redactors again cite no author of the *ancien régime*. Again, this provision, putting the husband in the position of a usufructuary, is obviously just.

It is interesting to examine the statements of authors of the *ancien droit* to establish the attitude they took to the husband's control over his wife's separate property. Pothier remarks that:

> La puissance maritale ne donne pas à la vérité au mari *jus dominii* sur les immeubles propres de sa femme; mais elle lui donne, par rapport auxdits biens, une espèce de droit de bail et de gouvernement. . . .[834]

Under this "espèce de droit de bail et de gouvernement", the husband exercised the feudal rights and carried out the duties of any *seigneurie* belonging to his wife.[835] Pothier, in discussing a husband's powers of administration of his wife's property, remarks that they are greater than those of a usufructuary.[836] He contrasts the husband's position with that of a usufructuary in so far as a husband may grant a lease of his wife's property which will be effective after his administration has ended: a usufructuary could not.[837]

Pothier describes the husband's right as an "espèce de droit de bail et de gouvernement". Elsewhere he stated: "*Garde* et *bail*, sont des termes qui, dans nos coutumes, signifient gouvernement, administration avec autorité."[838] Again in a different work he wrote: "Ces noms [i.e. *garde* et *bail*] sont synonymes et signifient *gouvernement, administration.*"[839] As the terminology suggests, the husband's right has an obvious analogy and connection with the right called in some *coutumes garde-noble* and in others *bail.*[840] *Garde-noble* originated in the requirement that someone carry out the military and other duties attached to a *fief* or *seigneurie* if such *fief* or *seigneurie* had devolved by the law of succession to a minor, who, by reason of nonage, was unable to carry them out himself.[841] Under this institution, the *gardien* or *baillistre* had the right to enjoy

---

[832] D. 25.1.13, 15 & 16; D. 24.1.28.1. The modern authors are those as for C.Q. 1418. The Digest texts relate to necessary expenses taken from dowries: none makes a direct statement such as found in the C.Q. article: they seem a random choice.
[833] *Fifth Report*, p. 235.
[834] Pothier, *T.P.M.*, p. 33 (no. 86).
[835] *Ibid.* pp. 33–34 (nos. 87–89).
[836] *Ibid.* pp. 34–35 (nos. 91–92).
[837] *Ibid.*
[838] Pothier, *C. d'Orl.*, p. 126, introd. to tit. I (no. 313).
[839] Pothier, *T.G.N.B.*, p. 500 (no. 5).
[840] *Ibid.*, pp. 499–500 (nos. 1–7). See *infra*, where *garde-noble* will be discussed further in connection with paternal power.
[841] See Pothier, *T.G.N.B*, pp. 500–501 (nos. 8–10).

and to apply to his own use all the immoveable property that had come to the person under his *garde*.

Pothier obviously linked the rights of a husband in his wife's immoveable property with the rights of the *gardien* in *garde-noble*. The two institutions are very similar. Both indeed have historical origins in the feudal system of tenure, as the husband carried out the duties connected with *seigneuries* belonging to his wife, she herself being incapable in this respect. The feudal origins of these rights of the husband are reflected in Pothier's terminology. The fact that there was no community did not alter the situation, since this right of the husband's was considered an aspect of his *puissance maritale* and not a corollary of the *communauté de biens*: this last decision being, as Toullier shows, also a consequence of feudalism.[842]

It will be recalled, from the discussion of dowry in Louisiana, that the C.N. placed the husband in the position of a usufructuary of his wife's dowry.[843] The property relations between spouses when they were simply *non-communs* were obviously analogous to those of spouses married under the dotal regime.[844] Given that the categories of *bail* or *garde* could no longer be used to define the authority of a husband over his wife's property, it was an obvious solution for the redactors of the C.N. to place the husband here in the category of a usufructuary. Although Pothier contrasts the husband with a usufructuary, it should be noted that the example he gives of the difference still holds good: husbands, unlike usufructuaries, could grant leases which could last, in certain circumstances, beyond the husband's enjoyment and administration of the property. The assimilation, on this point, to the law on dowry is eminently reasonable, and it is unlikely that it brought about any change in the details of the law about.[845] Thus, the C.Q. redactors, although there is no provision for dowry in their code,[846] were probably embodying the provisions of the *ancien droit*, if not its mode of expression, by following C.N. 1533.

C.Q. 1420 states thus:

> The clause which declares that the consorts marry without community, does not prevent its being agreed that the wife, for her support and personal wants, shall receive her revenues in whole or in part, upon her own acquittances.

C.N. 1534 made similar provision, as did the *ancien droit*.[847] This article is of no great interest here. C.Q. 1421 provides the following:

---

[842] Toullier, *op. cit. supra* note 628, vol. 14, pp. 9–11, no. 14.

[843] See *supra*, text at notes 360–367.

[844] See, e.g. Toullier, *op. cit. supra* note 628, vol. 14, pp. 12–23, nos. 16–30, esp. p. 15, no. 21.

[845] See Maleville, *Analyse*, vol. 3, pp. 259–260. Maleville did not think the assimilation of the husband to a usufructuary was particularly happy.

[846] Note that the Digest references under C.Q. 1418 and 1419 are to passages on dowry.

[847] See Pothier, *T.Comm.*, pp. 256–257 (no. 646). There was a dispute between Pothier and Bourjon on a related point that need not concern us. See 12 *Pan. fran.*, vol. 12, pp. 149–150 – the authors disagree with Pothier.

> The immoveables of the wife which are excluded from the community in the cases of the preceeding articles are not inalienable.
> Nevertheless, they cannot be alienated without the consent of the husband, or, upon his refusal without judical authorization.

This is taken from C.N. 1535. This article is unnecessary in the Quebec code, as such property would never be inalienable in Quebec law, whether the parties were in community or not. The sole effect of this article is to restate the principle that the wife requires authorization to alienate her immoveable property. Although there is no harm in restating the law thus, it is likely that the main reason behind the inclusion of C.Q. 1421 is simple copying of the French code. In the C.N., this article was required, because the code provided for a dotal regime of matrimonial property (unlike the Quebec code), under which, if adopted, the wife's *dot* was inalienable, following the Roman law of the *pays du droit écrit*. In the articles on spouses marrying without community, the C.N. referred to the wife's property as *dot*, so that C.N. 1535 was necessary to avoid confusion.[848]

As well as simply not being in community, spouses could live under a matrimonial regime of total separation of property, regulated by articles 1422–1425 of the C.Q. This had certain effects on the husband's rights over his wife's property. The first relevant article is C.Q. 1422. This states that when the marriage contract stipulates separation of property, the wife retains the complete administration of her property, both moveable and immoveable, and the free enjoyment of her revenues. C.N. 1536 made a similar provision. The *ancien droit* of most of the *pays du droit coutumier* was the same,[849] though some *coutumes* stated that the wife separate as to property was in the position of an unmarried woman.[850] The C.Q. redactors made no change in the law here. Their reading of Pothier would have made them well aware that some *coutumes* denied the husband any powers over the property of the wife separate as to property. They chose to maintain the existing rule. Reasons for the redactors' actions here will be discussed below.

C.Q. 1423 provides that the spouses contribute to the expenses of the marriage according to the terms of their marriage contract, or if there be no such regulation in the contract, and the parties cannot agree on appropriate contributions, then the court determines the amount each shall contribute according to his or her wealth. The equivalent provision of the French code is quite different: C.N. 1537 states that spouses should contribute to the expenses of their marriage according to the terms of their marriage contract; but if there be none, then the wife should contribute up to a third of her revenues. Quebec has here followed the *ancien droit* which stated that, failing regulation in the marriage contract, or

---

[848] C.N. 1554–1563 are on the inalienability of dowry under the dotal regime, except in certain specific carefully defined instances. See on this point *Pan. fran.*, vol. 12, pp. 150–151; Toullier, *op. cit. supra* note 628, vol. 14, pp. 21–22, no. 29.
[849] See Pothier, *T.P.M.*, pp. 7, 36–37 (nos. 15 and 98); Pothier, *T. Comm.*, p. 255 (no. 464).
[850] See Pothier, *T.P.M.*, p. 8 (no. 16).

agreement between the parties, the judge should decide how much the wife should contribute, according to her means and circumstances, both to the expenses of the marriage and the aliment and education of the common children.[851] The Quebec redactors chose to reject the innovation of the C.N. and to follow the *ancien droit*: they considered the new French provision as arbitrary and preferred the *ancien droit* as enunciated by Pothier.[852] The criticism of C.N. 1537 is to the point.[853] The only advantage of the C.N. is that it avoided the necessity of going to court. It could, however, be very unfair if the wife were wealthy and the husband poor.[854]

C.Q. 1424, the next article on spouses separate as to property, provides that the wife still cannot alienate her immoveables without the consent of her husband, or, on his refusal, judicial authorization: any general authorization to alienate immoveables, whether given in the marriage contract or otherwise, is void. C.N. 1538 provides likewise, and so generally did the *ancien droit*:[855] though some *coutumes* provided that a wife separate as to property had the capacity of an unmarried woman.[856]

The final article of this section, C.Q. 1425, states thus:

> When the wife who is separated as to property has left the enjoyment of her property to her husband, the latter upon the demand which his wife may make or upon the dissolution of the marriage, is bound to give up only the fruits which are then existing, and is not accountable for those which, up to such time, have been consumed.

This is taken from C.N. 1539. The Quebec redactors cite no source of the *ancien droit coutumier*. They state that their article conforms to the Roman law and the French code.[857] All that they cite is a provision of the Justinianic *corpus*, and various modern commentators on the C.N.[858] Though there be no equivalent specific provision in the *droit coutumier*, the article is eminently sensible. The provision of the C.N. here is consistent with its articles on the husband's enjoyment of the wife's paraphernal property under the dotal regime.[859] Given that the C.Q. redactors considered a rule such as this filled a *lacuna* in the law,

---

[851] Pothier, *T. Comm.*, p. 255 (no. 464).
[852] *Fifth Report*, p. 237.
[853] Note that C.N. 1537 conforms to C.N. 1575. This latter article covered the situation where, under the dotal regime, all of the wife's property was paraphernal. This, too, is a new rule.
[854] Cf. *Pan. fran.*, vol. 12, pp. 153–154.
[855] See Pothier, *T.P.M.*, pp. 36–37 (no. 98); Pothier, *T. Comm.*, p. 255 (no. 464); *Coutume de Paris*, art. 223.
[856] See Pothier, *T.P.M.*, p. 8 (no. 16).
[857] *Fifth Report*, p. 237.
[858] E.g. Maleville, *Analyse*, vol. 3, p. 264 (who refers to pp. 289–290 of his own work); *Pan. fran.*, vol. 12, pp. 155–156. The Justinianic provision is C. 5.14.11.
[859] See C.N. 1577–1579; Maleville, *Analyse*, vol. 3, pp. 289–290; Toullier, *op. cit. supra* note 628, vol. 14, pp. 259–265, nos. 361–369. As the C.N. provisions on a clause simply excluding community were seen as, in some ways, analogous to the dotal regime's rules on dowry, so a clause bringing about complete separation as to property was seen as analogous to the provisions of the dotal regime where all the wife's property was paraphernal.

the C.N. provided a useful article for borrowing, even though it perhaps originated in the Roman rules on *parapherna*.

Before going on to conclude this subsection on the property aspects of the *puissance du mari*, it is appropriate to comment generally on the section of the C.Q., "Of the clause of separation of property", that has just been discussed. The redactors remark that by this clause the powers of the husband are severely restricted, though not destroyed.[860] As pointed out already, the redactors would be aware that in some *coutumes*, such a clause would, as regards her property, give a wife the capacity of an unmarried woman, allowing her to deal with her property as she wished. The redactors chose to follow the existing law of Quebec, copying the expression of the C.N.: they saw no reason for reducing here the traditional *puissance du mari*, and, indeed, there is no indication in their *Fifth Report* that they ever considered changing the law of Quebec in this respect. They presumably saw no pressing or obvious reason for altering the law here, which was the same as in the C.N. and which asserted the beliefs of the peridod: the conservative instructions of the legislature would reinforce this attitude.

This area of the C.Q. is obviously closely modelled on the equivalent sections of the French code. The rules on what constitutes community property should there be no marriage contract are those of the existing law in Quebec, which was also the same as the rules in the French code on this point. The husband's authority over the community property under the rules of the C.Q. was as in the *ancien droit*. As head of the conjugal association, he was in control of the communal property. The C.N. had reduced the husband's authority over the community by limiting his power to make donations of community property. If the argument above is accepted as correct,[861] then the reason for rejecting this innovation was not so much that the husband would still be able to dissipate the community property, but rather that the old law was more consistent with the community property being controlled by the husband as head of the conjugal association by virtue of his *puissance maritale*. The redactors of the C.Q. saw the innovation contained in C.N. 1422 as an unnecessary restriction of the husband's authority. Should there be no stipulation in a marriage contract to the contrary, the husband, under the regime of legal community, by virtue of his *puissance maritale*, had control of his wife's separate property, though he could not alienate such property without her consent. This rule is consistent with the customary law conception of the *puissance du mari*, and follows the provisions of the *ancien droit*. The redactors' support for this authority of the husband's meant that no change was made or even considered.

Following the *ancien droit* once more, if the spouses concluded a marriage contract to govern their property relations, they could not, by such a contract, derogate from the husband's power over his wife and children, nor from his power as head of the conjugal association: *puissance maritale* inevitably

---

[860] *Fifth Report*, p. 235.

[861] See *supra*, text at notes 802–813.

resulted from the marriage and could not be reduced or avoided by contract. If the spouses simply excluded community of property, the husband had administration of his wife's property, the revenues of which went to him to help bear the expenses of the marriage: this was because the husband's authority over his wife's property was taken to be the result of his *puissance maritale*, rather than a corollary of the existence of community of property. If by a marriage contract there were complete separation of property, the husband did not have the right to administer his wife's property or receive the revenues therefrom: she would continue to administer it herself. As Toullier shows, the difference between these two situations can be explained as resulting from feudal law.[862] Though the wife completely separate as to property could administer her property, she could not alienate her immoveables without the authorization of her husband or of the judge: furthermore, any purported general authorization to alienate immoveables was invalid. This requirement of authorization to alienate was the result of the *puissance du mari*: the C.Q. redactors would have known that some *coutumes* considered the wife, separate as to property, as having the capacity of an unmarried woman. They made no change in the Quebec law, preferring to perpetuate the system of *puissance maritale* followed in most of northern France and, indeed, adopted by the French code. This action on the part of the Quebec redactors is consistent with their attitudes towards the other property aspects of *puissance maritale*.

The redactors of the C.Q. asserted the traditional *puissance du mari* in their provisions on the property relations of husband and wife: in so doing, they asserted current perceptions of the proper nature of the husband and wife relationship. Some restrictions on the husband's authority in this area of the law might have been useful: notably, it might have been advantageous to have let a wife separated as to property alienate her immoveables without authorization, as some *coutumes* had in fact permitted. The C.Q. redactors did not consider this. It is unlikely that there would have seemed to them any reason for so weakening the husband's authority, especially when their instructions were very conservative. Further, they had already rejected more minor reforms introduced by the C.N. For the C.Q. redactors to have acted other than they did would have been most improbable. The only articles here in which they perhaps incorporated new law into their code were C.Q. 1418 and 1425. These articles embodied useful rules and did not detract from the principles of *puissance maritale*.[863]

---

[862] Toullier, *op. cit. supra* note 628, vol. 14, pp. 9–11, nos. 14 and 15.

[863] It should be noted that in C.Q. 1418, 1419 and 1425 the redactors cite texts of the Roman law. These Roman provisions are on dowry. The C.Q. articles are on community property. In these three articles, the redactors have departed from the terms of the *ancien droit*, and copied the new French code. They appear to cite the Roman texts and stress their articles' conformity to the Roman law, to support their copying of the C.N.: they seem to believe that the Roman texts give extra authority to their work.

Puissance Maritale

Aspects Other than Property

The sixth chapter of title five of the first book of the C.Q. is named: "Of the respective rights and duties of husband and wife."[864] It contains legal provisions which the *ancien droit* regarded as deriving from the *puissance du mari*. Despite the heading of the chapter, most of the rights belong to the husband, to whom most of the duties are owed by the wife. It follows closely the sixth chapter of the C.N.'s fifth title: there are, however, significant differences between the C.Q. and its model.

C.Q. 173 states: "Husband and wife mutually owe each other fidelity, succour and assistance." C.N. 212 provides the same. The *ancien droit* took a similar attitude.[865] Although this article has the appearance of being an essentially moral precept, infidelity could ground an action for separation from bed and board, while wives usually had a right to be maintained by their husbands, as C.Q. 175 points out.

C.Q. 174 provides: "A husband owes protection to his wife; a wife obedience to her husband." C.N. 213 states the same. The *ancien droit* made similar provision.[866] Maleville remarks thus:

> *Protection, obéissance*, ces mots sont durs, ils sont pourtant pris de St.-Paul, et cette autorité en vaut bien une autre.[867]

On the duty of wifely obedience, the *ancien droit*, as would the new, limited the obedience to all things not "contraires à la loi de Dieu", and which were reasonable.[868] For the C.Q. redactors not to have adopted such a provision would have been unthinkable. Toullier expresses the opinions of the period when he states:

> La femme doit obéissance à son mari. La société conjugale ne pourrait subsister, si l'un des époux n'était subordonné à l'autre.[869]

That the husband should command his wife was axiomatic.

C.Q. 175 states as follows.

> A wife is obliged to live with her husband, and to follow him wherever he thinks fit to reside. The husband is obliged to receive her and to supply her with all the necessaries of life, according to his means and condition.

C.N. 214 states likewise. Pothier remarks that:

---

[864] See *supra*, text at notes 701–703.
[865] See e.g. Pothier, *T.C.M.*, pp. 174–175 (nos. 380 and 382).
[866] See e.g. Pothier, *T.C.M.*, pp. 1, 175 (nos. 1 and 382).
[867] Maleville, *Analyse*, vol. 1, p. 201.
[868] See Pothier, *T.C.M.*, p. 174 (no. 382); Pothier, *C. d'Orl.*, p. 255, introd. to tit. X (no. 143).
[869] Toullier, *op. cit. supra* note 628, vol. 2, p. 9, no. 615.

> La femme . . . contracte envers son mari l'obligation de le suivre partout où il jugera à propos d'établir sa résidence ou sa demeure, pourvu néanmoins que ce ne soit pas hors *du royaume*.[870]

It had originally been proposed to add to the article which became C.N. 214 a section stating that a husband could not oblige his wife to follow him out of the Republic unless he was on a government mission: on the opposition of Napoleon, this proposed qualification of the husband's authority was withdrawn.[871] Napoleon, notoriously, upheld the principle of the husband's authority over his wife.[872] The Quebec redactors considered an addition to C.Q. 175 along the lines of the proposed addition to C.N. 214: they decided, however, to follow C.N. 214, arguing that a derogation from the power of the husband to compel his wife to follow him to where he chose to reside, if it had existed in the old law, was part of the public law, and not of the private, and hence was not relevant in a civil code, since it only gave rise to questions of allegiance and whether a husband could compel his wife to change her allegiance and abdicate her native land.[873] The C.Q. redactors appear to be, to some extent, avoiding the issue: presumably they considered that the general principle was best left to stand without qualification, as a proper assertion of the husband's authority. They may also have been mindful of the circumstances of the British Empire. The duties of a husband towards his wife as set out in C.Q. 175 were the same in the *ancien droit*.[874]

These first three articles contain no provisions to cause surprise. They are a fairly faithful translation of the substance of the *ancien droit*, and though the various rights and duties are stated to be reciprocal, it is obvious that the wife is under the authority of her husband: she has *to obey* him, *to live with* him, and *to follow* him; he has *to receive* her, *to protect* her, and *to supply* her with the necessities of life. The husband and wife, in accordance with the prevailing *mores*, are not of an equal status. Perhaps what is most interesting about these articles is that the rights and duties are stated to be reciprocal, as if in a contract reached through a series of bargains: the wife has given up her independence in return for certain benefits, but the parties are viewed as free and equal agents. Pothier, for example, merely states that:

---

[870] Pothier, *T.C.M.*, p. 175 (no. 382). See also Pothier, *T.P.M.*, pp. 1–2 (no. 1); Pothier, *C. d'Orl.*, p. 255, introd. to tit. X (no. 143). See *Pan. fran.*, vol. 3, p. 176: "Autrefois le mari ne pouvait point obliger sa femme à le suivre hors du royaume."

[871] Maleville, *Analyse*, vol. 1, p. 201.

[872] [A.-C. Thibaudeau], *Mémoires sur le Consulat, 1799 à 1804: par un ancien conseiller d'état*, Paris, Ponthieu et Cie., 1827, pp. 433–436, reports Napoleon as remarking: "Est-ce que vous ne ferez pas promettre obéissance par la femme? ... Il faut qu'elle sache qu'en sortant de la tutelle de sa famille, elle passe sous la tutelle de son mari. . . . Ce mot-là [obeisance] est bon pour Paris surtout où les femmes se croient [u]n droit de faire ce qu'elles veulent."

[873] *Second Report*, p. 187.

[874] See Pothier, *T.C.M.*, p. 174 (no. 380).

> La *puissance du mari* sur la personne de la femme, consiste, par le droit naturel, dans le droit qu'a le mari d'exiger d'elle tous les devoirs de soumission qui sont dus un à un supérieur. . . .
>
> Le droit civil a beaucoup augmenté la puissance du mari sur la personne de sa femme.[875]

For Pothier, the husband's authority derives from natural law; he is his wife's natural superior: she has not bargained away her independence for his protection. The rights are not stated in the contractual form of reciprocal duties and obligations. Although Pothier regards these obligations of both spouses as being a consequence of the contracting of marriage, such obligations are not put into the form of mutually interdependent reciprocal rights and duties, but are regarded as separate obligations depending from marriage and governed by the husband's natural superiority.[876]

The next article, C.Q. 176, states thus:

> A wife cannot appear in judicial proceedings, without her husband or his authorization, even if she be a public trader or not common as to property; nor can she, when separate as to property, except in matters of simple administration.

The equivalent French article, C.N. 215 is rather different:

> La femme ne peut ester en jugement sans l'autorisation de son mari, quand même elle serait marchande publique, ou non commune, ou séparée de biens.

The *ancien droit* was as follows. The *Coutume de Paris*, in articles 224 and 234, said thus:

> Femme ne peut ester en jugement sans le consentement de son mari, si elle n'est autorisée ou séparée par Justice, et ladite séparation executée. (224)

> Une femme mariée ne se peut obliger sans le consentement de son mari, si elle n'est séparée par effet, ou marchande publique, auquel cas étant marchande publique, elle s'oblige et son mari, touchant le fait et dependances de ladite marchandise publique. (234)

The wife who was simply *non-commune* still has her property administered by her husband, and for the reasons already described.[877] As Ferrière said, "La

---

[875] See *T.P.M.*, pp. 1–2 (no. 1).

[876] See Pothier, *T.P.M.*, pp. 174–175 (nos. 379–383).

[877] See *supra*, text at notes 827–848. Ferrière, *Corps et Comp.*, vol. 3, col. 171, nos. 2 and 4, states: "La raison de la règle est que la femme entrant en la puissance de son mary par le mariage; et transmettant en sa personne l'administration et jouissance de ses biens, . . . elle ne peut point disposer de ses biens par actes entre-vifs, ni s'obliger sans son consentement." "[S]'il le réfuse, le juge y supplée en l'autorisant sur l'exposé d'une requête pour cause legitime, c'est-à-dire, pour agir ou défendre, pour la conservation de ses droits, et non pour aliéner ses biens." The *Coutume de Sedan*, tit. 4, art. 96 said that a wife could be authorized by justice "pour son profit et cause raisonnable", that of Bounbonnais, "au refus du mari sans cause legitime", and that of Peronne, "au cas qu'il [i.e. le mari] fût refusant sans cause raisonnable". See Pothier, *T.P.M.*, p. 23 (no. 58).

femme n'est pas moins sous l'autorité de son mary, quoiqu'elle ne soit point commune avec luy."[878] Thus, a wife who was simply *non-commune* with her husband, like a wife who was *commune*, required her husband's or the judge's consent to appear in court proceedings. From this requirement of authorization to sue or be sued, article 224 exempted the wife separated as to property. Ferrière commented:

> C'est une maxime generalement reçûë, en pays coutumier, que la femme separée d'avec son mary peut ester en jugement sans être ni par luy autorisée, ni par Justice.
>
> La raison est, que le mary n'étant pas maître des meubles et effets mobiliaires de sa femme, et n'ayant plus d'administration et la joüissance de ses biens, il semble être sans intégrêt.[879]

Pothier expands on this point:

> Ce pouvoir que la coutume [de Paris] donne aux femmes séparées, d'ester en jugement sans l'assistance de leurs maris, étant une suite du pouvoir que la séparation donne aux femmes d'administrer leurs biens, sans avoir besoin pour cela de leurs maris, il est évident que cette exception pour les femmes séparées, ne doit s'entendre que des actions qui concernent l'administration de leurs biens, qu'elles peuvent intenter, et auquelles elles peuvent défendre sans leurs maris.
>
> A l'égard de celles qui concernent la propriété de leurs immeubles les femmes quoique séparées, ne peuvent les intenter ni y défendre sans l'assistance de leur mari, ou l'autorisation du juge.[880]

Thus, the *ancien droit* on the authorization of wives *communes*, *non-communes*, and *séparées*, whether by justice or by contract,[881] was the same as the law expressed in C.Q. 176; though C.Q. 210, discussed below, changed the law on wives *séparées de corps*. The Quebec redactors followed the *ancien droit* here, whereas the C.N. did not. The question of wives *marchandes publiques* has still to be discussed; but before doing so, it is convenient to discuss the reasons behind the difference here between the C.N. and the C.Q.

In the *Pandectes françaises*, the authors explain why the C.N. changed the *ancien droit*, so that wives *séparées de biens* now would require authorization to appear in judicial proceedings: they state that under the *ancien droit*, though not required by law, it was legal practice ("dans l'usage") to adjoin the husband's name for regularity of procedure.[882] The Quebec codifiers did not adopt this reasoning, and argued that, given the powers of administration granted to a wife separated as to property by justice or contract, it would be quite inconsistent to forbid her to appear in judicial proceedings: they expressly supported the

---

[878] Ferrière, *Corps et Comp.*, vol. 3, col. 176, no. 14.
[879] *Ibid.*, vol. 3, col. 181, no. 1.
[880] Pothier, *T.P.M.*, pp. 23–24 (no. 61). See generally Pothier, *ibid.*, pp. 22–25 (nos. 55–66).
[881] See Pothier, *T.P.M.*, p. 24 (no. 61).
[882] *Pan fran.*, vol. 3, p. 385. Note that the authors of this work are confused about the position of wives who were *non-communes* and of those who were *séparées* in the *ancien droit*, as regards appearing in court proceedings: *ibid.*

reasoning of Pothier.[883] The Quebec position is logical. Given that a wife *séparée* could administer her property, there seems to be no convincing reason why she should not be able to appear unauthorized in court in actions relating to that administration. There was certainly no social reason for restricting further the capacity of wives *séparées de biens*; though there was also no social reason for not so restricting wives' capacities.

Neither C.Q. 176 nor C.N. 215 permit wives who are public traders to appear unauthorized in court, even in matters relating to their trade. In the *ancien droit coutumier*, some *coutumes* had a specific provision permitting wives who were public traders to bring and defend actions relating to their trade.[884] It was always a matter of controversy whether those *coutumes* with no explicit provision to this effect allowed a wife who was a public trader to do likewise;[885] the general opinion, however, was that, if there were no specific provision in the *coutume*, then wives who were public traders required authorization to appear in court proceedings. Pothier, in discussing article 224 of the *Coutume de Paris*, argues that had it been wished in the *Coutume* to give this power to wives who were *marchandes publiques*, they would have been specifically mentioned in the exception to article 224 along with wives separated as to property and those authorized by justice, in the same way as they were specifically mentioned in article 234 of the same *Coutume*.[886] The C.N. and the C.Q. adopted the law as followed under the *Coutume de Paris*. The reasons why the C.N. and the C.Q. kept to the law as under the *Coutume de Paris* were presumably the reasons given by Pothier for the difference between wives *séparées* and wives *marchandes publiques*. The relevant passage of Pothier is referred to by the C.Q. redactors and by the *Pandectes françaises*, the latter work citing the passage approvingly.[887] Pothier states that separation gives the wife power to administer her goods and to enjoy them on her own account, the right of suing or defending on such administration deriving from her enjoyment of the goods, in which her husband had no interest. On the other hand, a wife who was a public trader exercised her trade for the benefit of the community, and the fact that her husband, having authorized her to carry on a trade, is taken to have permitted her to contract relative to such trade without further authorization from him, does not mean that to sue or to defend concerning such trade is a necessary consequence of such permission.[888] This argument is tenable; but to have concluded the opposite from a husband's permitting his wife to carry on a

---

[883] *Second Report*, pp. 187–189. The reasoning of Pothier to which they refer is that in Pothier, *T.P.M.*, pp. 23–24 (no. 61), the bulk of which is quoted *supra*, text at note 880.

[884] E.g. the *coutumes* of Dourdan, tit. 6, art. 80, and of Mantes, art. 125: Pothier, *T.P.M.*, p. 24 (no. 62).

[885] See *Pan. fran.*, vol. 3, p. 385.

[886] Pothier, *T.P.M.*, p. 24 (no. 62). Art. 234 is quoted *supra*, text between notes 876 and 877. A problem with Pothier's argument here is that *Coutume de Paris*, art. 234 does not mention wives authorized by justice: Pothier's argument should here have the result that wives could not be authorized by justice to contract. This, of course, was not the case. See Pothier, *T.P.M.*, pp. 5–6 (nos. 12–14). See further *infra*.

[887] *Pan. fran.*, vol. 3, p. 387.

[888] Pothier, *T.P.M.*, p. 24 (no. 62).

separate trade would have been as plausible. Pothier's argument is derived directly from the omission of an exception in favour of *marchandes publiques* in article 224 of the *Coutume de Paris*. Neither the Quebec nor the French redactors were bound any more necessarily to follow the exact provisions of the *Coutume*. The C.N. redactors had already departed from article 224 of the *Coutume* in restricting the capacity of wives separated as to property; but their adoption of the *Coutume's* provision prohibiting wives *marchandes publiques* from appearing in court proceedings without authorization is consistent with that departure. Under C.N. 215, a wife, be she *non commune en biens*, *séparée en biens* or *marchande publique*, could not appear in court without her husband or his authorization. C.Q. 176 lacked this consistent denial of capacity to take part in court proceedings. The redactors are merely following exactly the *ancien droit* in the whole of their article. The reasons for their rejection of the C.N.'s innovation on wives *séparée* have been discussed above; their refusal here to amend the *ancien droit* on *marchandes publiques* seems to have been dictated by legal conservatism. The redactors did not consider an amendment, though an amendment might have been useful. To have allowed a wife to sue or defend concerning her trade might have expedited legal proceedings. Clearly, the redactors did not consider this, and rejected the examples of some of the *coutumes*.[889] Their legal conservatism preserved the *status quo*.

C.N. 216 states that authorization by the husband is not necessary when the wife is pursued "en matière criminelle ou de police". There is no equivalent in the C.Q. The redactors probably did not consider this matter appropriate for a civil oode.[890] Some *coutumes* allowed a wife to appear alone in certain cases;[891] but the C.Q. redactors obviously wished to retain the law as laid down by the *Coutume de Paris*.

C.Q. 177 states thus:

> A wife even when not common as to property, cannot give nor accept, alienate, nor dispose of property *inter vivos*, nor otherwise enter into contracts or obligations, unless her husband becomes a party to the deed, or gives his consent in writing; saving the provisions contained in the act 25 Vict., chap. 66.
>
> If, however, she be separate as to property, she may do and make alone all acts and contracts connected with the administration of her property.

C.N. 217 differs from C.Q. 177, and provides as follows:

> La femme même non commune, ou séparée de biens, ne peut donner, aliéner, hypothéquer, acquérir, à titre onéreux ou gratuit, sans le concours de son mari dans l'acte, ou son consentement par écrit.

---

[889] See *supra*, text at note 884 and note 884 itself.

[890] See *supra*, text at notes 872–873 the redactors' remarks on C.N. 214. The *ancien droit* was as in the C.N.: see Pothier, *T.P.M.*, p. 24 (no. 63).

[891] See Pothier, *T.P.M.*, p. 25 (nos. 65–66).

Two matters require discussion here: first, the method of authorization, and, second, when authorization is required. Following the C.N. on method of authorization, the C.Q. merely requires that the husband be a party to the deed or consent to it in writing. The old law was quite different. Most *coutumes* required express and explicit authorization, using the verb "autoriser".[892] Ferrière, in discussing the law under the *Coutume de Paris*, said as follows:

> Le consentement du mary ne suffit pas, il faut une autorisation expresse. . . .
> Le mary doit declarer en termes exprès qu'il autorise sa femme à l'effet et pour la validité du present acte. . . .
> Ces termes *autorisation, autoriser*, sont solemnels et consacrez par un usage tres-ancien dans nos Coûtumes, pour rendre valables les contrâts passez par les femmes mariées; et ces termes *consentement*, *consentir*, n'ont pas la même force. . . .[893]

It was disputed in the *ancien droit* whether or not the authorization was required to be in the deed itself.[894] Some *coutumes* provided that the mere concurrence of the husband in the deed was sufficient to make it valid;[895] but the majority followed the law as set out above.[896] The reasoning behind the Quebec adoption of the rule found in the C.N. is obvious. The old law was complex and over-subtle.[897] There was no need for such formality, which could only cause problems by resulting in delay in concluding a contract or by bringing about unnecessary nullities if there were some minor mistake in form.[898]

It is appropriate now to turn to the second point: under which circumstances authorization is required. C.N. 217 is differently worded from C.Q. 177. The French article lacks the sentence allowing a wife separate as to property to make alone all contracts and acts connected with the administration of her property. Before considering the significance of this, it is useful to set out the *ancien droit*. The *Coutume de Paris* stated that, no matter a wife's property relations with her husband, she could neither alienate, nor hypothecate nor in any way dispose of her immoveable property (*héritages*);[899] nor, under article 234, could

---

[892] *Pan. fran.*, vol. 3, p. 381: "L'autorisation, suivant la plupart des coutumes, était si rigoureusement exigée que le terme *autorisée*, était sacramental."

[893] Ferrière, *Corps et Comp.*, vol. 3, col. 147, nos. 23 and 24. He goes on to cite the authors who agree with him.

[894] An *acte de notoriété* of the Châtelet de Paris of 25th February, 1708, required that the authorization be given in the deed: see Ferrière, *Corps et Comp.*, vol. 3, cols. 198–203, where this *acte* is quoted: see on authorization especially his nos. 4, 5 and 6. Pothier, *T.P.M.*, p. 27 (no. 71) was of the opposite opinion: "[L]e mari peut valablement autoriser sa femme par un acte qui précède celui pour lequel il l'autorise, et il n'importe quel intervalle de temps il y ait entre l'acte d'autorisation et le contrat pour lequel la femme a été autorisée."

[895] Those of Sens, Bar, Lamarche and Rheims: see *Pan. fran.*, vol. 3, p. 381.

[896] Brissaud, *History*, pp. 173–174, no. 149 states that this requirement of express authorization was not found in the early law.

[897] See Maleville, *Analyse*, vol. 1, p. 205.

[898] See *Second Report*, p. 189.

[899] *Coutume de Paris*, art. 223: "La femme mariée ne peut vendre, aliéner ni hypothéquer ses héritages, sans l'autorité et consentement exprès de son mari, et si elle fait aucun contrat sans

she place herself under any obligation unless she were separate as to property.[900] Article 234 of the *Coutume* might suggest that a wife *séparée* could obligate herself to any extent. This was not so, as Ferrière points out:

> Enfin telle est la disposition de nôtre Coûtume, que la femme *séparée* ne peut faire aucun acte emportant alienation de ses biens, si elle n'est autorisée suivant l'article 223, mais qu'elle peut s'obliger par de simples obligations, pour sommes mediocres de deniers, qui se peuvent acquitter sur ses meubles ou sur le revenu de ses immeubles.[901]

Pothier summed up the law thus:

> [L]a femme qui n'est pas séparée, ne peut faire valablement aucun acte, aucun contrat, quel qu'il soit, sans autorisation de son mari, ou du juge. Au contraire, la femme séparée ayant, par sa séparation, le droit d'administrer, elle-même, ses biens, les coutumes l'ont dispensée de l'autorisation pour tous les actes qui ne concernent que la simple administration de ses biens.[902]

Although the husband had no apparent or immediate interest in her property, such authorization was still necessary, because authorization was a requirement of the *puissance du mari*, not a result of the existence of *communauté de biens*.[903] Ferrière also points out that a husband has an interest by virtue of the children born and to be born of the marriage.[904] Some *coutumes* did allow wives separated as to property to contract and to dispose of their moveable and immoveable property as if they were not married;[905] but the general *droit coutumier* was as under the *Coutume de Paris*. Further, under article 9 of the *Ordonnance des Donations* of 1731, a wife could not accept donations unless authorized.[906]

It is obvious that C.Q. 177 has followed the *ancien droit*; the import of C.N. 217 is rather more problematic. C.N. 217 does not contain the exception permitting a wife, who is separate as to property, to contract as regards the administration of her property. It might be concluded from this that such a wife

---

l'autorité et consentement de sondit mari, tel contrat est nul, tant pour le regard d'elle que de son mari; et n'en peut être poursuivie, ni ses héritiers après le décès de sondit mari."

[900] *Coutume de Paris*, art. 234, quoted *supra*, text at notes 876–877.

[901] Ferrière, *Corps et Comp.*, vol. 3, col. 355, no. 16. He explains further, *ibid.*, no. 19: "Il paroît assez que l'esprit de (la) notre [*coutume*], en cet article est de donner à la femme separée le pouvoir de s'obliger indefiniment et indistinctement pour quelque cause que ce soit. Mais la Cour a jugé le contraire, quoique la separation elle soit, *soluta a lege mariti*, à cause de l'interêt du mary par l'esperance qu'Il a de se reconcilier avec elle: ainsi elle ne peut s'obliger que par de simples obligations dont la cause soit juste et legitime, comme pour le besoin de sa maison."

[902] Pothier, *T.P.M.*, p. 7 (no. 15).

[903] *Ibid.*; Ferrière, *Corps et Comp.*, vol. 3, cols. 357–358, no. 23.

[904] Ferrière, *Corps et Comp.*, vol. 3, cols. 357–358, no. 23. He points out that Duplessis doubted if a wife *séparée* required authorization: Ferrière disagreed with Duplessis for the reasons in the text.

[905] Ferrière, *Corps et Comp.* vol. 3, col. 355, no. 18; Pothier, *T.P.M.*, p. 8 (no. 16); and *Pan. fran.*, vol. 3, p. 397.

[906] Pothier, *T.P.M.*, p. 17 (no. 42); Pothier, *T.O.*, p. 30 (no. 52).

suffered the same complete incapacity to contract as a wife not so separated. C.N. 1538, already discussed,[907] stated that a wife, separate as to property, might administer her property: all that was forbidden her being alienation of her immoveables. C.N. 217, if interpreted literally, would contradict C.N. 1538:[908] the article, however, has not been given this literal interpretation. The authors of the *Pandectes françaises* state that C.N. 217 deals solely with disposing of immoveables, simple administration not being governed by it, and therefore not being excluded. Thus, a wife separate as to property could contract as regards simple administration following C.N. 1538, while a wife *commune en biens* could not.[909] Ingenious though this argument is, Maleville is no doubt correct when he suggests that the reason why the prohibition in C.N. 217 is so wide is that the redactors of the code simply forgot to mitigate its rigours in favour of the wife separate as to property.[910]

If the above argument be correct, then, despite the differences in expression, the law on the subject matter covered in C.Q. 177 is the same as in C.N. 217 and the *ancien droit*. No doubt the C.Q. redactors departed from the wording of C.N. 217 because they were well aware of the problems it entailed. It was always open for the C.Q. redactors to suggest reform of the law here, and perhaps allow a woman separate as to property to act in any manner towards her property without requiring authorization: if the redactors had done so, they would have followed the views of Duplessis,[911] Dumoulin,[912] and the provisions of various *coutumes*.[913] They chose not to do so. They preferred to keep to the traditional rule, and seemed unable to see any reason for a change in the law here. They probably considered that there was no need to enhance the capacity of a wife.

C.Q. 178 states as follows:

> If a husband refuse to authorize his wife to appear in judicial proceedings or to make a deed, the judge may give the necessary authorization.

C.N. 218 provides: "Si le mari refuse d'autoriser sa femme à ester en jugement, le Juge peut donner l'autorisation." C.N. 219 dealt with authorization, by the court, of the wife to make a deed: this article goes into greater detail than C.Q. 178 on the point. These two articles of the C.N. provide in principle the same rule as C.Q. 178. The *ancien droit* was the same.[914] No conclusions relevant here may be drawn from this article on its own: it merely enacts a necessary rule given the general requirement of authorization by the husband.

---

[907] See *supra*, text at notes 849–856.

[908] Maleville, *Analyse*, vol. 1, p. 204, states that the difference between the two articles "lève tout équivoque".

[909] *Pan. fran.*, vol. 3, pp. 390–391.

[910] Maleville, *Analyse*, vol. 1, p. 204.

[911] See *supra*, note 904.

[912] See Brissaud, *History*, p. 175.

[913] See *supra*, note 905 and relevant text.

[914] See *Coutume de Paris*, art. 224; *Coutume d'Orléans*, art. 201; Pothier, *T.P.M.*, pp. 5, 23 (nos. 12, 57 and 59).

C.Q. 179 provides:

> A wife who is a public trader may, without the authorization of her husband, obligate herself for all that relates to her commerce; and in such case she also binds her husband, if there be community between them.
>
> She cannot become a public trader without such authorization express or implied.

The first paragraph of C.N. 220 has a provision identical to that of the first paragraph of C.Q. 179. The second paragraph of C.N. 220 reads as follows:

> Elle n'est pas réputée marchande publique, si elle ne fait que détailler les marchandises du commerce de son mari; mais seulement quand elle fait un commerce séparé.

Article 4 of the French *Code de commerce* states: "La femme ne peut être marchande publique sans le consentement de son mari." The relevant provisions of the *ancien droit* in Quebec are articles 234, 235 and 236 of the *Coutume de Paris*. The first of these has been quoted already;[915] the other two are as follows:

> La femme n'est pas réputée marchande publique, pour debiter la marchandise dont son mari se mêle; mais elle est réputée marchande publique, quand elle fait marchandise séparée, et autre que celle de son mari. (235)

> La femme marchande publique, se peut s'obliger sans son mari, touchant le fait et dépendance de ladite merchandise. (236)[916]

The Coutume d'Orléans, articles 196 and 197, provides similarly. Thus, under the *Coutume de Paris*, a wife was a *marchande publique* if she had a trade separate from that of her husband; such a wife, *marchande publique*, could oblige herself without authorization as regards her trade, and she would also oblige her husband.[917] Although these articles of the *Coutume de Paris* do not mention the point, to be a *marchande publique*, a wife required the consent of her husband.[918] Of course, a wife who was a public trader would require authorization for contracts not concerning her trade:

> Ce qui est fondé sur cette raison, sçavoir, que le consentement exprés ou tacite du mary, ne regarde que le negoce dont sa femme se mêle. . . .[919]

---

[915] See *supra*, text between notes 876 and 877.
[916] Art. 236 was added when the *Coutume* was reformed. Ferrière, *Corps et Comp.*, vol. 3, cols. 373–374, comment on art. 236, points out that it is a mere repetition of the rules of 234 and 235.
[917] See Ferrière, *Corps et Comp.* vol. 3, col. 362, no. 11; Pothier, *T.P.M.*, pp. 9–10 (nos. 20–21).
[918] See Ferrière, *Corps et Comp.*, vol. 3, col. 359, no. 1: "La femme marchande publique peut valablement s'obliger sans l'autorisation de son mary, suivant la disposition précise de cet article. Ce qui est fondé sur la faveur du commerce et sur la foy publique, qui requiert, que la femme s'oblige en conséquence de la seule liberté, que le mary luy donne de trafiquer publiquement: c'est pourquoy il faut qu'il le sçache et en ait connoissance."
[919] Ferrière, *Corps et Comp.*, vol. 3, col. 363.

The *ancien droit* was the same as that in the C.N. and in the C.Q.

The C.Q. article does not state that the wife's trade should be separate from that of her husband; this, however, is implied, as she would otherwise be acting as his agent, not as a trader on her own account. The requirement that the wife have permission to be a public trader is included in the C.Q. article, while not in the equivalent of the C.N.; under the French system, this requirement was stated in the *Code de commerce*. Quebec, however, having no separate commercial code, the provision was necessarily included here. C.Q. 179 thus contained no reform of the law. That the wife could contract on her own without specific authorization was sufficient to meet the demands of trade and to favour commerce and maintain public confidence in the contractual capacity of married women carrying on a trade. That she should be authorized to be a public trader is logical given that the premisses of authorization by the husband have been accepted.

Here the C.N. has an article, 221, for which the Quebec code has no equivalent There is no obvious significance in the omission of this article from the C.Q.: presumably the redactors considered the issues covered by C.N. 221 adequately dealt with by the general rules.

Article 180 of the Quebec code states:

> If a husband be interdicted or absent, the judge may authorize his wife, either to appear in judicial proceedings or to contract.

C.N. 222 provides the same, though pointing out that the judge can only give authorization "en connaissance de cause". The omission of this phrase from the C.Q. is unimportant: in Quebec, as in the *ancien droit*, the judge would obviously give authorization only "en connaissance de cause".[920] A difficult point arises out of the meaning of the term "absent" in the C.N.; but before dealing with this, the *ancien droit* should be set out. Pothier states that if the husband has fallen into a state of *démence*, then the wife requires the authorization of the judge.[921] If it is unknown where the husband is, or uncertain if he is living or dead, again the wife requires the authorization of the judge.[922] He adds, however:

> Néanmoins, comme il n'est guère possible que la femme ait recours à l'autorisation du juge pour chacun des actes qui sont à faire pour l'administration des biens tant de son mari que d'elle, j'aurais de la peine à ne pas regarder comme valables tous les actes et contrats de pure administration, quoique faits sans autorisation. Il est pourtant plus sûr que cette femme se fasse autoriser par le juge pour cette administration.[923]

---

[920] See Pothier, *T.P.M.*, p. 5 (no. 12).

[921] See *ibid.*, p. 11 (no. 25). At *ibid.*, p. 11 (no. 26) Pothier states that if the wife has been appointed curatrix by the judge of her husband's person and property, she needs no farther authorization to administer the property; but for alienation of heritage, acceptance or refusal of an inheritance, and anything outwith the bounds of administration, she requires authorization.

[922] *Ibid.*, p. 11 (no. 27).

[923] *Ibid.*, pp. 11–12 (no. 27).

Pothier is also of the opinion, that if a woman's husband is publicly accepted as dead, and she acts without authorization, then her acts are valid, even if her husband later returns.[924] He also states that:

> Comme un mari . . . pourrait être trop éloigné pour donner cette autorisation aussi promptement que le cas l'exige, nos coutumes ont pourvu à cela, en permettant en ce cas à la femme de se faire autoriser par le juge . . . pour l'absence de son mari.[925]

The *ancien droit* is thus apparently the same as law in the C.N. and C.Q., with the exception that wives may, in some circumstances, carry out unauthorized acts of administration.

It has been noted that there is a problem concerning the import of the word "absent" in the C.N. For Pothier, there can be no doubt that absence permitting authorization by the judge meant merely *non-présence*.[926] Some commentators on the C.N., however, were of the opinion that in its article 222 the term "absent" had the technical meaning ascribed to it in title four of the C.N., "Des Absens".[927] Thus Marcadé, in his commentary on C.N. 222, said the following:

> C'est de l'absence proprement dite, et non de la simple non-présence, qu'il s'agit ici .... Il est vrai que lors de la discussion de cet art. 222, quelques membres du Conseil d'Etat parurent l'entendre dans le sens de la non-présence; mais quand même il aurait été écrit et voté dans ce sens, tout ce qu'il en faudrait conclure, c'est que l'art. 863 du Code de Procédure serait venu y déroger. La femme devra donc, dans le cas de simple non-présence, ou attendre le retour du mari, ou lui demander une autorisation par lettre.[928]

Demolombe disagreed with Marcadé's interpretation, which he quoted before remarking:

> Cette proposition toutefois me semble trop absolue: Pothier n'hésitait pas à dire que 'la femme peut recourir à la justice lorsque le mari est trop éloigné pour donner l'autorisation aussi promptement que le cas exige . . .' . . . Pourquoi en serait-il autrement aujourd'hui? Il est vrai que l'article 863 du Code de procédure ne s'occupe que de l'absence proprement dite; maie la généralité des termes de l'article 222 du Code civil peut s'appliquer même au cas de simple

---

[924] *Ibid.*, p. 12 (no. 28).
[925] *Ibid.*, p. 5 (no. 12).
[926] See *supra*, text at note 925.
[927] Maleville, *Analyse*, vol. 1, pp. 111–112: "Le mot absent, dans le langage des lois, a une acception bien différente de celle qu'il a dans l'usage ordinaire; on dit communément qu'un homme est absent, pour exprimer qu'il n'est pas dans le lieu où il demeure; mais dans les lois, et particulièrement dans ce titre, l'absent est celui qui a disparu de son domicile, sans qu'on alt eu depuis aucune nouvelle de son existence."
[928] V. Marcadé, *Explication théorique et pratique du Code Napoléon*, 5th ed., Paris, Cotillon, 1859, vol. 1, pp. 561–562, no. 744. *Code de procédure*, art. 863 stated: "Dans le cas de l'absence présumée du mari, ou lorsqu'elle aura été déclarée, la femme qui voudra se faire autoriser à la poursuite de ses droits, présentera également requête au président du tribunal, qui ordonnera la communication au ministère public, et commettra un juge pour faire son rapport à jour indiqué."

> éloignement. . . . Car le mot *absence* n'a pas toujours dans nos lois son acception techique et spéciale.[929]

Toullier was also of the opinion that "absence" was not meant in any technical sense: merely that the husband should be away and not readily accessible.[930] There is some evidence of the intention behind the redaction of C.N. 222, since, as Marcadé pointed out, it appears from the discussion of the article in the *Conseil d'État* that the article was considered to refer to husbands too far away to be readily accessible.[931] Maleville naturally repeats this.[932]

Had the C.Q. redactors studied the French books, it would have been obvious to them that the wording of C.N. 222 had caused problems: nonetheless, the C.Q. redactors themselves used the term "absent". In their references after C.Q. 180, the redactors refer to the following works: Pothier's treatise on the *puissance du mari*, numbers 25 to 28; the *Pandectes françaises*;[933] Fenet's work relating Pothier's treatises to the Code Napoléon;[934] and C.N. 222 itself. The *Pandectes françaises* say nothing relevant to the point under discussion. Fenet on Pothier cites numbers 25 to 28 of the latter's treatise on the *puissance du mari*, and does not discuss the import of the term "absent".[935] Pothier's account has been set out above;[936] but it should be noted that the C.Q. redactors do not cite the passage of Pothier where he states that wives whose husbands are too far away for it to be practicable for them to give authorization may be authorized by the judge.[937] It is difficult to see any significance in this exclusion of number 12 of Pothier's treatise: it would seem unlikely that it had been excluded from the references because the C.Q. redactors did not intend their article to cover the situation where a husband was away but not "absent" in the technical sense. In fact, the most likely reason for the exclusion of a reference to number 12 of Pothier's treatise is that the C.Q. redactors have simply followed the references given by Fenet, and have not considered referring to other parts of the relevant work. The passage of Pothier was presumably known to the redactors, since they cite it under C.Q. 178. That the redactors did not intend "absent" in C.Q. 180 to have its technical sense is strongly suggested: they do not indicate in their *Second Report* that they are changing the law here, nor do they refer to any of the modern commentators who were of the opinion that "absent" in C.N. 222 was used in its strict technical sense.[938]

---

929 Demolombe, *op. cit. supra* note 721, pp. 264–265, no. 214.

930 Toullier, *op. cit. supra* note 628, vol. 2, pp. 17–18, no. 651.

931 Fenet, *op. cit. supra* note 105, vol. 9, p. 78.

932 Maleville, *Analyse*, vol. 1, p. 207: "Le mot *absent* n'est pas pris ici dans la signification qu'il a au titre 4; il se prend dans l'acception ordinaire, c'est-à-dire, que si le mari, n'est pas à portée d'autoriser sa femme, et qu'il s'agisse d'une affaire urgente, le juge peut s'autoriser.

933 *Pan. fran.*, vol. 3, p. 397.

934 P.A. Fenet, *Pothier analysé dans ses Rapports avec le Code civil, et mis en ordre sous chacun des articles de ce Code*, 2nd ed., Paris, Au dépot ... et chez Alex-Gobelet, 1829, p. 57, on art. 222.

935 *Ibid.*, p. 57.

936 See *supra*, text at notes 920–926.

937 Quoted *supra*, text at note 925.

938 *Second Report*, p. 189.

If it is accepted that the word "absent" was not intended to bear its technical sense, the Quebec redactors were still using a potentially ambiguous term; one indeed that was to cause the same problems of interpretation in Quebec as in France.[939] Why should they have done so? It is notable that under C.Q. 180, the redactors make no reference to any of the French works where this point is discussed, though they referred quite often to Marcadé, Demolombe and Toullier. Indeed were to cite these very authors in connection with C.Q. 183. It would therefore seem unwise to deduce that they were unaware of the debate: the frequency with which the redactors referred to these authors would suggest that they consulted them regularly on the interpretation and menaing of the articles of the C.N., while the method of working followed by the redactors would have made it advisable to consult such works of doctrine.[940] It is probably correct to assume that the redactors knew of the problems caused by the use of the word "absent". Despite this, they copied the unsatisfactory wording of the C.N., though they could easily have amended the expression to avoid the difficulty. Perhaps they preferred the concise, terse expression of the French article, and assumed that "absent" would be given its ordinary meaning, and not the technical one.[941] If this is correct, the redactors were misled by the apparent technical perfection of the C.N., which they were generally copying fairly closely. They accordingly failed to make an appropriate alteration in the wording of the article.

There is one final point to note about C.Q. 180. As indicated, Pothier thought that, if a husband were away, a wife probably could carry out simple acts of administration without being authorized.[942] Neither the C.N. nor the C.Q. supports this interpretation. To have followed Pothier's suggestion might well have provided a useful reform, in that the wife of an interdicted or absent man would have been able to act speedily in dealing with property, and would have been spared the necessity of seeking judicial authorization for fairly trivial actions.[943] The Quebec redactors chose to assert the incapacity of the married woman, who would require the authorization of the judge if her husband could not authorize her, because even were a husband absent or interdicted, the *puissance du mari* over his wife continues.

C.Q. 181, the next article, states:

> All general authorizations, even those stipulated by marriage contract, are only valid in so far as regards the administration of the wife's property.

---

[939] See Mignault, *op. cit. supra* note 718, vol. 1, p. 526.

[940] See *supra*, chap. 3, text at notes 432–435.

[941] This criticism of the C.Q. redactors holds good, even if, contrary to the argument above, they had intended "absence" to have its technical meaning.

[942] See *supra*, text at note 923.

[943] It appears that in an earlier period of French law, a wife could so act: Brissaud, *History*, p. 174, no. 150.

C.N. 223 provides identically. The *ancien droit coutumier* was the same,[944] unless a *coutume* had a specific provision allowing wider general authorizations.[945] No doubt the redactors, in theory, could have departed from the *droit commun coutumier*, and permitted general authorizations to alienate property; but, given that the redactors were upholding the *ancien droit*, they would have thought such a general authorization inconsistent with the principles of the *puissance du mari*, despite the odd example or opinion to the contrary. It must be concluded that the redactors approved of the *ancien droit* on authorizations as expressed by Pothier.[946]

C.Q. 182 states:

> A husband although a minor may, in all cases, authorize his wife who is of age; if the wife be a minor, the authorization of her husband, whether he is of age or a minor, is sufficient for those cases only in which an emancipated minor might act alone.

C.N. 224, the equivalent article, is quite different:

> Si le mari est mineur, l'autorisation du juge est nécessaire à la femme, soit pour ester en jugement, soit pour contracter.

Quebec is here following the *ancien droit*, under which a minor husband could authorize his adult wife to contract, because her incapacity was the result of the *puissance du mari*, the majority or minority of the husband being irrelevant.[947] Ferrière explains this clearly:

> La raison pour laquelle un mary mineur peut autoriser sa femme majeure ou mineure, est que le droit d'autorisation ne dépend pas de l'âge et de

---

[944] See Pothier, *T.P.M.*, pp. 25–26 (no. 67): Pothier, *T. Comm.*, p. 51 (Introd. no. 5). Pothier quotes from and refers to the cases cited by the C.Q. redactors, as does *Pan. fran.*, vol. 3, pp. 435–436.

[945] François Bourjon, *Le droit commun de la France et la coutume de Paris réduits en principes tires des ordonnances, des arrêts, des loix civiles, des auteurs*, Paris, Grangé, Rouy, 1747, vol. 1, p. 37, nos. 14 and 15: "Cependant elle [i.e. l'autorisation générale] est valable lorsqu'elle est portée par contrat de mariage, c'est le seul cas dans lequel l'autorisation générale vaut." "En ce cas la femme non-seulement administrer, mais encore aliéner, et même à titre de liberalité; telle autorisation mettant ses biens hors la dépendance de son mari." He repeats the same in *ibid.*, vol. 1, pp. 509–510, nos. 33 to 37, where he develops the principle more thoroughly. Bourjon was thus of the opinion that there could be general authorizations in marriage contracts, *even to alienate property*, provided there was contractual separation of property. Among the more modern writers on the *ancien droit*, his was definitely not a commonly held view.

[946] Although in some circumstances the Quebec redactors refer to Bourjon, *op. cit. supra* note 945, it would seem unlikely, given their likely working method (see *supra*, text at notes 936–938 and *infra* text at notes 954–945), that the redactors consulted Bourjon on this point. Accordingly, one cannot say that they rejected Bourjon's version of the law; nonetheless, given that Bourjon's opinion was one readily imagined, the C.Q. redactors may be said to be rejecting such an opinion: the wording of C.Q. 181, though following C.N. 223, by specifically mentioning marriage contracts, immediately suggests the opposite to its own opinion.

[947] See Pothier, *T.P.M.*, pp. 12–14 (nos. 29–32).

> l'experience du mary, mais de sa qualité et de l'autorité que la Loy luy donne sur sa femme.
>
> * * *
>
> La Coûtume de Paris dans tous les articles où elle parle de l'autorisation, et toutes les autres Coûtumes ne distinguent point entre le mary majeur ou mineur.
>
> La raison est, que l'effet de l'autorisation est de rendre la femme habile à contracter comme elle n'étoit point sous la puissance du mary, elle ôte l'inhabilité provenante de la dépendance; et parconsequent l'acte fait par la femme autorisée par son mary mineur, comme il pourroit valoir si elle étoit independante.[948]

If a minor husband suffered loss, he could seek to rescind the authorization.[949] Dumoulin, in his commentary on the *ancienne Coutume* of Paris, argued that a minor husband could not authorize his adult wife: "qui ipse vendere non potest, autorare non potest." Others, for example Chopin and Tiraqueau, had been of the same opinion.[950] By the eighteenth century, however, it was settled law that a minor husband could authorize his adult wife.[951] An apparent illogicality noted by some commentators on the *ancien droit* was that, although a minor could authorize his adult wife to contract, he could not authorize her to appear in court:[952] "ce qui était absurde", remarks Maleville.[953] A minor wife's capacity was determined by her minority, not by her husband's capacity: thus, an adult husband could not authorize his minor wife to alienate her *propres*.[954]

The Quebec redactors have here followed the *ancien droit*: the acts of which a wife authorized by her husband was capable depended upon her age, not that of her husband. The wife did not lack capacity; she was merely prevented from exercising her capacity because of the *puissance du mari*. The codifiers have rationalized the *ancien droit* by rejecting the authority which rendered a minor husband incapable of authorizing his wife to appear in court: it is likely that, agreeing with Maleville, they considered this exception to the general principle of the *ancien droit* as somewhat absurd. It is interesting to note that Pothier does not mention this exception to the *ancien droit*: the law as stated by the Quebec redactors in their article is the law as given by Pothier. It is likely that the C.Q. redactors were here able to cite Rousseaud de la Combe's collection of *juris-*

---

948 Ferrière, *Corps et Comp.*, vol. 3, col. 144, no. 18.

949 *Ibid.*; Pothier, *T.P.M.*, p. 13 (no. 30); Bourjon, *op. cit. supra* note 945, vol. 1, p. 37, no. 11.

950 See Ferrière, *Corps et Comp.*, vol. 3, col. 144, no. 18.

951 Loisel, *op. cit. supra* note 62, bk. 1, tit. 2, rule 21 had been of this opinion: "Un mary mineur peut auctoriser sa femme majeure, sans qu'elle s'en puisse faire relever: mais bien luy."

952 Guy du Rousseaud de la Combe, *Recueil de jurisprudence civile du pays de droit écrit et coutumier par ordre alphabétique*, 4th. ed., Paris, Veuve Savoye, 1769, p. 57, s.v. *Autorisation*, sect. II, no. 6: "Mari mineur ne peut autoriser sa femme majeure pour ester en jugement . . . mais bien pour contracter . . . ."

953 Maleville, *Analyse*, vol. 1, p. 208.

954 Pothier, *T.P.M.*, pp. 13–14 (nos. 31–32); Rousseaud de la Combe, *op. cit. supra* note 952, p. 57, s.v. "Autorisation", sect. II, no. 6: "Femme mineure, quoiqu' autorisée de son mari, ne peut intenter action concernant ses propres, sans curateur . . . ."

prudence because they were referred to it by Maleville; and it is thus because of Maleville's reference that the C.Q. redactors were aware of Rousseaud de la Combe's statement, on the basis of various *arrêts*, that minors could not advise their wives to appear in court.[955] The Quebec code has again followed the *ancien droit* in providing that, if the wife be a minor, on the authorization of her husband, she could only act as an emancipated minor: her husband's authorization did not make up for her own lack of capacity. In sum, in the C.Q., the capacity of the authorized wife depends on her status as either a minor or an adult, and not on that of her husband. Authorization was intended to remove the restriction on her capacity, a restriction resulting from the *puissance du mari*.

The French code innovated, and seems to have altered the conception of the *puissance du mari* to one different from that of the *ancien droit*. Under the *ancien droit*, wives did not lack capacity; they were merely prevented from exercising that capacity by the authority their husbands had over them, an authority grounded in the respect a wife was judged to owe her husband. This article of the French code, C.N. 224, seems to imply the adoption of the Roman notion that incapacity resulted from *fragilitas sexus*: wives required protection due to their inevitable weakness as women. This is, of course, illogical, since neither unmarried women nor widows suffered from incapacity by virtue of their sex. In fact, this change raised intellectual problems for some commentators on the Code Napoléon; Marcadé, for example, devotes a lot of time to attempting to resolve the apparent contradiction.[956] His argument is interesting. He points out that wives, during their marriage, are under the care of their husbands; accordingly, as is only natural, such wives occupy themselves less with business affairs than with the upbringing of children and care of the household, while their husbands look after the family patrimony. He states:

> Donc, la femme, tout en conservant au fond, et de manière à s'en servir encore au besoin, sa pleine capacité, la voit sommeiller, s'evanouir, sous la force des circonstances, et elle tombe, pour les cas généraux et ordinaires, presques dans l'état où nous place la minorité même: il y a pour ainsi dire, de la part de la femme, démission forcée de sa capacité.[957]

Thus, wives require the assistance of their husbands, not merely because they owe respect to their husbands, but because the social facts resulting from marriage render them unaccustomed to business. Authorization accordingly is no longer to remove the barrier to the wife exercising her capacity, but rather to assist one unused to transaction to act. Therefore, if husbands are unable to assist their wives, then the wives require assistance from elsewhere. A minor husband, himself requiring assistance, accordingly cannot authorize and assist

---

[955] Maleville refers to this author as "Rousseau", while in the abbreviations used by the Quebec redactors he appears as "Lac."; this is one instance of the readily observable fact that the C.Q. redactors tended to consult only a few works and then followed any interesting references these works gave.

[956] Marcadé, *op. cit. supra* note 928, vol. 1, pp. 562–566, nos. 746–748, esp. no. 747.

[957] *Ibid.*, p. 564, no. 747 bis.

his wife in the circumstances envisaged in the C.N. article. Marcadé is able to conclude:

> Ainsi donc, la nécessité de l'autorisation maritale se fonde sur deux causes simultanées, dont l'une le respect du au mari, existe toujours, tandis que l'autre, l'inhabilité purement accidentelle de la femme, disparait dans certaines circonstances.[958]

Marcadé's argument may or may not reflect the thoughts of the redactors of the French code. It is tempting to suggest that the French redactors enacted the provision in C.N. 224 because, at some level, they considered it ridiculous that a minor should be able to authorize his wife to act in a way he himself could not act. Indeed, if such had been their opinion, motivating it must have been the idea, as expressed by Marcadé, that wives required their husbands' aid. The redactors of the C.N. certainly have incorporated a notion of *surveillance* not found in the *ancien droit.* As Marcadé has pointed out, this notion of *surveillance*, required by the seclusion of the wife in the marital home occupied with education of the children and running the household, reflects the social practice of the day; but this social practice is one to be associated with the middle classes rather than other sectors of society.[959] It also seems a retrospective rationalization of the law enacted rather than the reason underlying its enactment.

The Quebec redactors have not followed the example of the French code; they described C.N. 224 as:

> a new rule to which the old one has been preferred as more in accordance with the principles of marital authority, and with the reasons upon which the necessity of authorization is founded.[960]

The C.Q. redactors are, of course, correct: the rule of C.Q. 182 is more in line with the principles of marital authority in the *ancien droit.* The redactors do not reveal themselves as having considered that C.N. 224, rather than merely being inconsistent with the rest of the articles of the French code, has resulted in a new conception of marital authority in line with some nineteenth-century ideal conception of the family. Though the redactors make no statements to that effect, they must have been aware of this new conception implicit in the C.N., if only because they had read Marcadé's commentary.[961] It must be concluded that in rejecting C.N. 224, the redactors were rejecting not so much a rule inconsistent with the principles of their Code, but a different conception of marital

---

[958] *Ibid.*, p. 565, no. 747 bis.

[959] See *supra*, text at notes 25–39, and chap. 2, text at notes 107–119.

[960] *Second Report*, p. 189.

[961] Thus, Demolombe, *op. cit. supra* note 721, vol. 4, p. 269, though he does not discuss the matter in as great a detail as Marcadé, implies a similar conception of marital authority: "Il ne s'agit plus seulement aujourd'hui d'une marque d'obéissance envers l'autorité maritale, que le mineur, aussi bien que le majeur, pouvait, en effet, reçevoir; c'est, de la part du mari, un acte de surveillance que son incapacité personnelle ne lui permet d'exercer. La loi n'a pas voulu qu'un incapable fût charger d'autoriser un autre incapable."

authority. The background of the Quebec redactors makes it implausible to suggest that they disapproved of the ideal of the relationship between husband and wife implicit in the C.N.[962] Nor does it seem likely that they rejected the provisions of the C.N. because they considered the relationship between husband and wife to be of a different nature for the majority of the inhabitants of the province: no remarks made by the redactors anywhere hint at recognition of variation of family organization according to social class, nor do their actions betray such a thought. Considering the statement made by the redactors on their article, it seems clear that they simply rejected the innovation of the C.N. because of their generally conservative outlook and behaviour. They saw no reason for changing the law here merely to reflect a prevailing ideal of family relationships, and thus preserved the disposition of the *ancien droit*, though rationalized to permit the authorization to appear in court of wives by their minor husbands.

The next article in this chapter of the Quebec code is C.Q. 183—an important article—which provides thus:

> The want of authorization by the husband, where it is necessary, constitutes a cause of nullity which nothing can cover, and which may be taken advantage of by all those who have an existing and actual interest in doing so.

C.N. 225 is quite different:

> La nullité fondée sur le défaut d'autorisation ne peut être opposée que par la femme, par le mari ou par leurs héritiers.

The Quebec code provides for an absolute nullity, while the C.N. enacts only a relative nullity. Here the C.Q. has followed one version of the *ancien droit*, rejecting the provisions of the C.N.

Pothier on this point states thus:

> À l'égard du défaut d'autorisation, l'effet est de rendre absolument nuls les actes de la femme mariée, dans lesquels l'autorisation n'est point intervenue.[963]

He points out that:

> il ne suffirait pas, pour que le contrat de la femme fût valable, que l'autorisation du mari fût intervenue depuis le contrat, quoique la femme, dans le contrat, se fût dite d'avance autorisée de son mari, dans la confiance qu'elle avait d'obtenir cette autorisation. Cet acte ayant été absolument nul, faute d'autorisation, n'a pu être confirmé par l'autorisation qui est survenue depuis. . . .[964]

Thus, for Pothier, an unauthorized *acte* was radically null, and could not be ratified by the husband's subsequent authorization. In two *arrêts* reported by Leprêtre, it was decided that authorization coming after an *acte* of the wife

---

[962] See *supra,* chap 3, text at notes 403–415.
[963] *T.P.M.* p. 30 (no. 78); see also *ibid.*, p. 4 (no. 5).
[964] *Ibid.*, p. 28 (no. 74).

could validate such *acte*: Pothier points out that both Lebrun and Leprêtre are of the opinion that these *arrêts* rendered the deed valid only from the date of authorization, and not from the date of the deed itself.[965] The Quebec redactors have not followed this authority; there seems to be no statement in their code allowing for any ratification by the husband of previous deeds, and, indeed, Quebec jurisprudence subsequently so decided.[966] Thus, the Quebec redactors have followed Pothier's principles without qualification, and not the *arrêts* reported by Leprêtre. The principle of absolute nullity is restated in C.Q. 1301.

The French article greatly restricts the class of those who may attack an unauthorized contract by a married woman, on the grounds of lack of such authorization. A wife's unauthorized act is no longer radically null, but can only be attacked by herself, her heirs, her husband or his heirs.[967] The limitation of the class of those entitled to seek the annullment of such a contract raises the question of whether or not a husband might subsequently ratify an unauthorized contract. Whether or not he could do so was the subject of a dispute among the commentators on the C.N. Marcadé was firmly of the opinion that, during the marriage, a husband could validate the posterior acts of his wife, even if she wished to annul them.[968] Demolombe took the contrary view,[969] as did Toullier.[970] We need not discuss this vexed question further, though it should be noted that the redactors of the C.Q. were well aware of this problem in the French law.[971]

The Quebec redactors have followed the *ancien droit* and rejected any restriction of the class of those entitled to seek the annulment of an unauthorized contract. They provided for an absolute nullity, and contracts might not be validated by the husband after they have been made by the wife. The article of the code states that ". . . the want of authorization . . . constitutes a nullity which nothing can cover . . ."; it is difficult to see this as anything other than a deliberate exclusion of the possibility of posterior ratification, an exclusion suggested by the debate in the French *doctrine*. This also means that the Quebec redactors have followed Pothier's view of the *ancien droit*. They state of the C.N.'s restriction of the class of those entitled to sue for annulment:

---

[965] *Ibid.*, p. 28 (no. 74), where the *arrêts* and the views of Leprêtre and Lebrun are discussed.

[966] The cases are *Pesant* v. *Robin* (1917) 23 R.J. 211 and *Saint-Pierre* v. *Dupont* (1934) 37 R.P. 14: I have not seen these cases, and am relying on Baudouin, *op. cit. supra* note 551, pp. 275–276. They referred to wives appearing in court; but the principle would be the same for wives contracting.

[967] Demolombe, *op. cit. supra* note 721, vol. 4, pp. 437–439, no. 342 argues that such an unauthorized contract may also be attacked by her creditors. Some authors have wondered why the husband's heirs could attack such an act, since they could not possibly have any pecuniary interest. See Toullier, *op. cit. supra* note 628, vol. 2, p. 20, no. 661, n. a. (provided by Duvergier); and Demolombe, *op. cit. supra* note 721, vol. 4, pp. 435–437, no. 341.

[968] Marcadé, *op. cit. supra* note 928, vol. 1, pp. 567–568, no. 749, n. I.

[969] Demolombe, *op. cit. supra* note 721, vol. 4, pp. 257–263, no. 211.

[970] Toullier, *op. cit. supra* note 628, vol. 2, pp. 17, 20–21, no. 648, no. 661.

[971] This is apparent from their citation of the relevant passages of doctrine. Marcadé, *op. cit. supra* note 928, vol. 1, p. 567, no. 749, n. 1 gives all the sources for the differing sides in the debate.

> There appears to be no good reason for adopting this change, contrary to principle and repelled by the old jurisprudence and by ours.[972]

Maleville remarks that C.N. 225 “a embrassé l’opinion le plus favorable à la femme”.[973] It is important to discover why the C.Q. redactors retained the *ancien droit.*

The French article allows an unauthorized contract to stand, unless the wife, husband or their heirs choose to challenge it: this would seem to support the principle of *pacta sunt servanda.* If a wife’s unauthorized contracts are advantageous, they may be allowed to remain unchallenged, and the person with whom she has contracted cannot seek their annulment. A motive for the requirement of authorization is preservation of family property, and, under C.N. 225, if the contract is advantageous, there need be no fear that such property is in jeopardy, so the contract may be maintained. Implicit in this view is the notion that authorization of the wife is required for her *protection* against her own inexperience and folly: if there be no disadvantage in the contract, there need be no nullity, since the purpose of authorization is to prevent her suffering loss, and she has not suffered loss. This is in line with C.N. 224.

C.N. 224 was rejected as contrary to the Quebec principles of *puissance maritale*; C.N. 225 has been rejected for the same reason. The Quebec redactors retained the *ancien droit*’s notion that authorization was required because of the respect due to a husband by his wife. C.N. 225 goes against this in rendering her unauthorized contracts only annullable by a restricted class of persons. C.Q. 183, on the other hand, by rendering all unauthorized contracts radically null upholds the principle of the *ancien droit*, while C.N. 225 follows C.N. 224 in implying that authorization is the result of the wife’s need of guidance. Though C.N. 225 might have had practical usefulness in allowing advantageous contracts to stand, and perhaps supported the principle of *pacta sunt servanda*, the C.Q. redactors preferred to maintain the *ancien droit*, upholding the traditional principle of the *puissance du mari*, whereby a wife’s incapacity to contract is, in general, absolute. Authorization is always required, and any unauthorized act is null and void, of which nullity anyone with an existing and actual interest may take advantage. Since an unauthorized act is a nullity, completely without legal effect, prescription does not serve to render an unauthorized contract incapable of being attacked after a certain period.[974]

The reform contained in C.N. 225, in restricting the class of those entitled to seek the nullity of an unauthorized contract, might have seemed useful in Quebec: it would be easy, however, to emphasize too much the advantages of such a reform. At the time of codification, most women in Quebec would marry *communes en biens*, so their moveable property would fall into the community administered by their husbands, who would also have the right to administer their wives’ immoveables. The wife would have little practical opportunity to

---

[972] *Second Report*, p. 189.
[973] Maleville, *Analyse*, vol. 1, p. 208.
[974] *T.D.C.Q.*, vol. 1, p. 561.

contract. Further, the likelihood of a wife selling an immoveable without consulting her husband would always be slight. Thus, though the reform in C.N. 225 might have been advantageous, not to introduce this reform could not be described as disadvantageous. Given the instructions to the Quebec codifiers, and given their own conservative attitudes to much of the law, the lack of reform here is not surprising.

The final article of this chapter of title V is C.Q. 184. It states:

> A wife may make a will without the authorization of her husband.

C.N. 226 provides the same. Certain of the *coutumes* of northern France had demanded that wives be authorized to dispose of property by testament; that of Paris was not one of thern.[975] There can be no surprise that the redactors here followed the *ancien droit* and the C.N. It should be remembered, however, that in Quebec there was much greater liberty to test on property than in the C.N. or the *ancien droit*.[976]

There are many articles in the C.Q. which duplicate or depend on the provisions discussed above; but because they duplicate these rules or depend on them, we need not consider them.[977] The principles outlined above are worked out throughout the code in relevant areas of the law.

To conclude discussion of the issue, it may be noted that chapter six contains the most important provisions relating to the husband's control over the person of his wife. Most of these rules follow the provisions of the *ancien droit* as applied under the *Coutume de Paris*, though molded into the form of the French code, many of provisions of which are also derived from the same *ancien droit*. Apart from one provision rationalizing the *ancien droit*,[978] the C.Q. here only introduces one reform of importance: C.Q. 177 no longer requires authorization to be in the strict form demanded by the *ancien droit*. This is an obviously useful reform, making for ease of contracting and rendering wives' contracts less prone to annulment because of a minor fault in complex requirements for valid authorization. This reform was adopted from the C.N.

The C.N. contains two other important reforms; but these were not adopted. These are the ones contained in C.N. 224 and 225. It has been argued above that these articles of the C.N. have resulted in a new understanding of the reasons for the necessity of the authorization of married women.[979] The C.N. has altered this requirement of authorization so that it appears to be the result from the necessity

---

975 See Pothier, *T.P.M.*, pp. 17–18 (no. 43); *Pan. fran.*, vol. 3, pp. 442–443; Maleville, *Analyse*, vol. 1, pp. 208–209.

976 See C.Q. 832, and A. Morel, "L'apparition de la succession testamentaire", 26 *R.d uB.* (1966), pp. 499–511. Under the *Coutume de Paris*, a testator could dispose by will of all his moveables and *acquêts*, but only of a fifth of his *propres*, *propres* being immoveables acquired by succession in the direct or collateral line, or by gift in the direct line; *acquêts* being immoveables acquired *à titre onéreux ou lucratif*, except those classed as *propres*. See Pothier, *T.D.T.*, pp. 273–274 (no. 180).

977 See e.g. C.Q. 643, on the acceptance of successions by wives.

978 In C.Q. 182, minor husbands may authorize their wives to appear in court.

979 See *supra*, text at notes 947–959 and 963–974.

to protect a wife who, by virtue of her domestic seclusion in the home, has become unable to cope adequately with the demands of business. Under the *ancien droit*, of course, authorization was required because a wife owed respect and obedience to her husband, not because she was judged to require protection from her own supposed lack of business acumen.

The C.Q. copied the reform of the C.N. on authorization, while rejecting those contained in C.N. 224 and 225. The reasons for the actions of the codifiers here appear to have been that the useful reform on authorization could be copied without doing violence to the traditional conception of the *puissance du mari*: those reforms in C.N. 224 and 225 could not be copied without changing the traditional notion of the *puissance du mari*. The C.N. provisions implied that wives, through remaining at home absorbed in domesticity, became generally out of touch with the world of affairs, and thus required guidance and help in their dealings with their property. The C.N. accordingly envisages a different form of relationship between husband and wife from that in the *ancien droit*. The *ancien droit coutumier* saw the requirement of authorization as resulting not from the wife's need for help, but from her duty to be respectful and to be obedient to her husband. The C.Q. redactors preferred the *ancien droit's* version of the relationship between husband and wife. This preference, however, seems to be the result, not so much of different ideals of the relationship between husband and wife, much less different family relationships, but rather of the conservatism of the redactors towards the law.

The Quebec codifiers obviously believed in the rightness of the incapacity of wives. For example, Pothier suggested that, in the absence of her husband, an unauthorized wife might carry out acts of administration.[980] The C.Q. redactors did not allow this. The C.N. reforms, however, do not detract from this incapacity, but put it on a different basis. Though the C.N.'s articles conformed more to the nineteenth century's ideal of the role of wives, the Quebec redactors, because of their strong conservative tendencies, undoubtedly saw no reason for change. The *ancien droit* adequately expressed an ideology of the supremacy of the husband: that the conception of husband and wife relationships underlying the C.N. articles was more in line with the ideals of the nineteenth century did not matter. The redactors saw no reason to justify a departure from the traditional version of the *puissance du mari*. Although Quebec society would have permitted such a departure from the *ancien droit*, it did not necessitate it, and there were no technical reasons for such a reform of the law; whereas the reforms in the C.Q. in this chapter, in C.Q. 177 and 182, though undoubtedly practical, were also technical improvements rendering the law more rational.

A final point relates to wives *séparées de biens* from their husbands. The C.Q. followed the C.N. and the *ancien droit* of Paris in still requiring such wives to be authorized. This has been referred to already in connection with contrac-

---

[980] Pothier, *T.P.M.*, pp. 11–12 (no. 27), quoted *supra*, text at note 923.

tual separation;[981] it will also be discussed in the next subsection in relation to judicial separation. All that need be said here is that the C.Q. redactors maintained the existing law, not following the examples of some *coutumes* which permitted wives separate as to property to act as if unmarried.

Effect of *Séparation de Corps* or *Séparation de Biens* on the Husband and Wife Relationship

The Quebec code permits judicial separation of property and also separation from bed and board. Both of these have an effect on the *puissance du mari* over his wife. Before going on to describe that effect, it is necessary to set out the grounds permitting each kind of separation, as they throw useful light on the changing nature of the husband and wife relationship.

C.Q. 1311 states:

> Separation of property can only be obtained judicially, before the court of the domicile, when the interests of the wife are imperiled and the disordered state of the husband's affairs gives reason to fear that his property will not be sufficient to satisfy what the wife has a right to receive or to get back.
>
> All voluntary separations are null.

Although this article comes in a section on the dissolution of the community—and indeed C.Q. 1310 provides that *séparation de biens* dissolves the community—its provision would also be applicable to a separation of property when the spouses were simply *non communs en biens*, without being *séparés de biens*, as C.Q. 1417 enacts. C.Q. 1311 follows C.N. 1443, and the *ancien jurisprudence*, as the Quebec redactors point out.[982] C.Q. 1312–1317 further regulate separation of property; we need not discuss them.

C.Q. 1318 governs the effect of *séparation de biens* on the relationship between husband and wife. Since *séparation de corps* also brings about *séparation de biens*, as C.Q. 1318 points out, and also ends the community (if there be one) under C.Q. 1310, it is as well to discuss *séparation de corps* and then return to C.Q. 1318.

The Quebec code devotes the whole of the sixth title of its first book to separation from bed and board. Here will only be discussed the causes of separation from bed and board, and those of the effects which are relevant to the theme.

---

[981] See *supra*, subsection "Puissance Maritale and the Property Aspects of the Husband-Wife Relationship", esp. text between notes 862–863 and 849–860.

[982] *Fifth Report*, p. 217. For the *ancien droit*, see Pothier, *T. Comm.*, pp. 275, 276, 277 and 278 (nos. 510, 512, 514, 517). At *ibid.*, p. 255 (no. 463), Pothier discusses spouses where community is excluded, but without separation of property. This last passage is cited neither by the C.Q. redactors, nor indeed by Fenet, *op. cit. supra* note 934, p. 449, no doubt because both the C.N. and C.Q. follow Pothier's organization of the material in these areas.

The causes of such separation are set out in C.Q. 186–191, which provide as follows:

> 186. Separation from bed and board can only be demanded for specific causes; it cannot be based on the mutual consent of the parties.
>
> 187. A husband may demand the separation on the ground of his wife's adultery.
>
> 188. A wife may demand the separation on the ground of her husband's adultery, if he keep his concubine in their common habitation.
>
> 189. Husband and wife may respectively demand this separation on the ground of outrage, ill-usage or grievous insult committed by one toward the other.
>
> 190. The grievous nature and sufficiency of such outrage, ill-usage and insult, are left to the discretion of the court which, in appreciating them, must take into consideration the rank, condition and other circumstances of the parties.
>
> 191. The refusal of a husband to receive his wife and to furnish her with the necessaries of life, according to his rank, means and condition, is another cause for which she may demand the separation.

Since the Code Napoléon provided for divorce, it was organized rather differently from this title of the C.Q., because the latter did not.[983] The C.N.'s title VI, however, as well as regulating divorce, also regulated separation from bed and board, its article 306 states:

> Dans les cas où il y a lieu à la demande en divorce, pour cause déterminée, il sera libre aux époux de former demande en séparation de corps.

Thus, the relevant grounds for *séparation de corps* in the C.N. are the same as those that ground an action for divorce, and they are contained in C.N. 229–233. C.N. 229 permits a husband to divorce his wife if she has committed adultery. C.N. 230 allows a wife to divorce her husband on the grounds of adultery if he has kept his concubine in the *maison commune*. C.N. 231 permits the spouses reciprocally to demand divorce on the grounds of outrage (*excès*), ill-usage (*sévices*) and grievous insult (*injures graves*). C.N. 232 states that there may be a divorce if one of the spouses has been condemned to a punishment importing infamy. C.N. 233 allows divorce on the grounds of mutual consent. The redactors of the C.Q. remark that the grounds for separation contained in C.N. 229–233 are all admitted in Quebec bar condemnation to an infamous punishment and mutual consent: the first being contrary to their article declaring that death alone disolves a marriage, and the second contrary to C.Q. 193, which does not allow the admission of allegations in an action for separation from bed and board, there always had to be proof.[984] Although the C.N. has no equivalent to C.Q. 191, the

---

[983] See *infra*, text at notes 1039–1042.

[984] *Second Report*, p. 191. Actually, contrary to what the C.Q. redactors say, C.N. 307 did not permit separation by mutual consent: see Toullier, *op. cit. supra* note 628, vol. 2, pp. 52–53, nos. 758–759.

circumstances envisaged in that article would permit an action for separation in the C.N. under article 231 for *injures graves*.[985]

With the exceptions noted above, it may be said that the Quebec redactors have followed the provisions of the French code on the causes giving rise to an action for *séparation de corps*. In the redactors' report, they state that their provisions "are conformable to the ancient jurisprudence, saving some exceptions which are indicated as they occur".[986] It is not indicated that any of the grounds for separation are not conformable to the *ancien droit*. But the Quebec redactors' statement that their provisions conform to the *ancien droit* is rather disingenuous as regards the causes for separation. The *ancien droit* differed in many significant respects. Pothier—and in this matter he is representative of the attitudes of most writers on the *ancien droit*—makes a strict separation between conduct allowing a wife to sue for separation and conduct permitting a husband to sue for the same.[987]

If we follow Pothier in dealing with the wife first, we find he makes the following statement:

> Elle est obligée, dans le for de la conscience, à s'attirer par sa douceur et par ses complaisances, les bonnes graces de son mari; et si, en faisant tout ce qui en son pouvoir, elle ne peut y réussir, elle ne doit opposer que la patience aux mauvaises manières de son mari, et même à ses mauvais traitements: elle doit regarder cela comme arrivant par l'ordre de Dieu et comme une croix qu'il lui envoie pour expier ses péchés.[988]

Although this statement deals with the *for de la conscience*, it indicates the tone of the provisions of the *ancien droit*. On the circumstances allowing a wife to separate from her husband, Pothier writes:

> À l'égard du for extérieur, les juges ne doivent pas trop facilement permettre à une femme de se séparer d'habitation de son mari . . . ; mais lorsqu'il y a de justes causes, ils doivent le lui permettre. . . .
>
> Quelles sont ces justes causes? C'est ce qui n'est pas facile à déterminer . . . .
>
> C'est pourquoi on doit laisser entièrement à l'arbitrage et à la prudence du juge les causes de separation. . . .[989]

The *ancien droit*, in contrast to the C.N. and C.Q., does not then give limited grounds for separation for the wife; but there was much discussion of what circumstances would permit her to separate, and, thus, by laying down the usual circumstances for separation and by stating which circumstances would not allow separation, the writers on the *ancien droit* gave some definition to the topic.

It was clear that a wife could seek separation if her husband refused to receive her, or to supply her with the necessaries of life.[990] A husband's mistreat-

---

[985] See e.g. Demolombe, *op. cit. supra* note 721, vol. 4, p. 490, no. 388.
[986] *Second Report*, p. 191.
[987] Pothier, *T.C.M.*, pp. 235–243 (nos. 506–527).
[988] *Ibid.*, p. 235 (no. 507).
[989] *Ibid.*, pp. 235–236 (no. 508).

ment of his wife was apparently the most common circumstance on which she could found an action for separation. What amounted to *mauvais traitements* sufficiently severe to ground such a separation would vary according to the circumstances and quality of the parties; thus the judge ought to take into consideration, for example, whether or not the wife had brought the mistreatment on herself by her own misbehaviour.[991] Pasquier considered that such *sévices* had to be *atroces*;[992] Rousseaud de la Combe thought that, though the Canon law required the wife to be in fear of her life, this was not a requirement of French custom, and he considered that "il suffit que les faits soient graves, qu'ils rendent la vie insupportable et infiniment triste et disgracieuse. . . ."[993]

The writers on the *ancien droit* believed *mauvais traitements* to be the most common reason for granting separation.[994] An *arrêt* of 1716 had decided that if the husband had defamed his wife by accusing her of a capital crime, she could justly separate from him.[995] Pothier states that a wife could not sue for separation on the grounds that her husband had contracted epilepsy, leprosy, or indeed any disease, no matter how contagious; nor, according to Pothier, could a husband separate from his wife if she had contracted any such disease.[996] A wife, according to Pothier and Ferrière, could not separate from her husband even if he was infected with venereal disease;[997] d'Espeisses, however, did allow *either* spouse to separate from the other if he or she had contracted venereal disease.[998]

Whether or not a wife could separate from her husband on the ground of his adultery is an interesting point. The general view of the authors on the *ancien droit* was that she could not. The courts had perhaps originally been uncertain; but it is clear that, by the eighteenth century at the latest, the courts normally

---

990 *Ibid.*, p. 237 (no. 511), p. 175 (no. 381).

991 *Ibid.*, p. 236 (nos. 509–510). Rousseaud de la Combe, *op. cit. supra* note 952, p. 639, s.v. *Séparation*, no. 9 states: "Il faut encore avoir égard aux personnes: car ce qui ne seroit pas un moyen de séparation entre gens du commun, en peut servir entre personnes d'une condition plus relevée."

992 Etienne Pasquier, *L'interprétation des Institutes de Justinien, avec la conférence de chasque paragraphe aux ordonnances royaux, arrestz de parlement et coustumes générales de la France*, Paris, Videcoq aîné, A. Durand, 1847, p. 95 (ch. 46).

993 Rousseaud de la Combe, *op. cit. supra* note 952, p. 639, s.v. *Séparation*, no. 9.

994 See Pothier, *T.C.M.*, p. 236 (no. 509); Ferrière, *Corps et Comp.*, vol. 3, col. 185, no. 19.

995 Pothier, *T.C.M.*, p. 237 (no. 512).

996 *Ibid.*, pp. 237–238 (no. 514). Ferrière, *Corps et Comp.* vol. 3, col. 185, nos. 20–22, states the same but says that the husband could separate from the wife if she has contracted leprosy and it could be communicated to the children.

997 Pothier, *T.C.M.*, p. 238 (no. 514); and Ferrière, *Corps et Comp.*, vol. 3, col. 185, no. 23.

998 D'Espeisses, *Œuvres supra* note 73, vol. 1, p. 310 (part 1, tit. XIII, sect. III, no. 3), makes the following interesting statement: "si l'un des mariés est affligé de la vérole, le sain n'est pas tenu de cohabiter avec lui, car cette maladie est contagieuse . . . et particulièrement, elle est plus contagieuse contre le mari sain, cohabitant avec sa femme vérolée, que contre la femme saine, cohabitant avec son mari vérolé."

would not allow a wife to separate from her husband on the grounds of his adultery.[999] Guyot sums up the matter thus:

> Plusieurs auteurs croient aussi que la femme du mari Adultère peut intenter contre lui l'action d'Adultère, non par la voie criminelle pour le faire punir, mais par la voie civile pour obtenir une séparation de corps et de biens, et le faire priver de la dot et des autres avantages qu'elle a pu lui faire par contrat de mariage. Mais d'autres pensent qui si la femme n'alleguoit que ce seul moyen, elle ne seroit point écoutée, et qu'il faut, pour que son action soit admise, que l'Adultère soit accompagné de scandale ou de mauvais traitemens, disipation, et autres choses semblables. Cette dernière opinion est suivie dans les tribunaux du royaume.[1000]

Pothier had absolutely no doubt that "Les adultères commis par le mari, ne peuvent servir à une femme de fondement pour une demande en séparation d'habitation. . . ."[1001] Thus, the better view, and the view followed by the courts, was that the adultery of the husband would not on its own give rise to an action for separation though some authors were of the contrary opinion.[1002]

Pothier allowed only one ground on which a husband could separate from his wife: her adultery.[1003] Though some authors were inclined to allow a husband to separate from his wife if she were suffering from some highly contagious disease,[1004] the only certain ground on which a husband could separate from his wife was her adultery. A wife convicted of adultery could suffer the Justinianic penalty of seclusion in a nunnery.[1005]

In short, the *ancien droit* in general was that a wife could only separate from her husband if he mistreated her, such mistreatment being fairly severe;[1006] a husband could separate from his wife if she had committed adultery. On why the husband's adultery was irrelevant, the reasoning of the jurists is instructive. Pasquier remarked that "la pudeur des femmes n'a jamais permis qu'elles eussent action pour cet effet contre leurs marys",[1007] while Pothier states:

---

[999] Ferrière, *Corps et Comp.* vol. 3, col. 185, nos. 23 & 24, reports one *arrêt* where a wife was refused separation, even though her husband had transmitted venereal disease to her: he points out that an *arrêt* of 14th June, 1561, had allowed such separation, but that since then the court had judged to the contrary in many cases.

[1000] Guyot, *op. cit. supra* note 730, vol. 1, p. 196, s.v. *Adultère*. Merlin, *Répertoire* (4), vol. 1, p. 144, s.v. *Adultère* is identical; his *Répertoire* was founded on that of Guyot.

[1001] Pothier, *T.C.M.*, p. 238 (no. 516).

[1002] See Rousseaud de la Combe, *op. cit. supra* note 952, p. 12, s.v. *Adultère*, no. 2 (note that he is relying on Spanish and Roman authorities, not French ones); d'Espeisses, *Œuvres supra* note 73, p. 310 (vol. 1, part 1, tit. XIII, sect. 3, no. 3).

[1003] Pothier, *T.C.M.*, pp. 242–243 (nos. 526–527).

[1004] See *supra*, text at notes 996–998.

[1005] Pothier, *T.C.M.*, p. 243 (no. 527); Merlin, *Répertoire* (4), vol. 1, p. 42 s.v. *Adultère*. Pothier notes a case of 1766 where a wife was sent to a nunnery.

[1006] Bourjon, *op. cit. supra* note 945, vol. 1, p. 526, no. 27 states: "La femme ne l'obtient que sur la preuve des faits graves qui font appréhender pour sa vie; ce qui recoit l'exception qu'on verra par la proposition qui suit." The proposition that follows (no. 28) is that if the wife is of high degree, "les procédés inhumains, même les mépris marqués" suffice.

[1007] Pasquier, *op. cit. supra* note 992, p. 96 (ch. 46).

> La raison de différence est évidente: l'adultère que commet la femme est infiniment plus contraire au bon ordre de la société civile, puisqu'il tend à dépouiller les familles, et à en faire passer les biens à des enfants adultérins qui y sont étrangers; au lieu que l'adultère commis par le mari, quoique très criminel en soi, est à cet égard sons conséquence. Ajoutez qu'il n'appartient pas à la femme, qui est une inférieure, d'avoir inspection sur la conduite de son mari, qui est son supérieur. Elle doit présumer qu'il lui est fidèle, et la jalousie ne doit pas porter à faire des recherches de sa conduite.[1008]

The adultery of the wife was thought to threaten the family and thence the social structure; that of the husband did not. The wife was her husband's inferior and, because of the respect she owed him, ought not to look into his affairs.

The Quebec code followed the French in laying down definite grounds for separation, and in applying all these grounds to either spouse. C.N. 308 still allowed for the seclusion of adulteresses;[1009] but there was no equivalent in the C.Q. However, both codes retained a difference between the adultery of the wife and that of the husband. For a wife to pursue an action for separation on the ground of her husband's adultery for adultery, he must have been maintaining his concubine in the marital home.

It is obvious that the provisions of the Quebec code here owe much more to the C.N. than to the *ancien droit*. The *ancien droit* left the decision as to what amounted to sufficient grounds for separation largely to the judge; but doctrinal writing and *jurisprudence* had refined the notions of what would be conduct sufficient to ground an action for separation. Moreover, it is clear that essentially there were only the grounds demonstrated above: the husband's mistreatment of his wife, and the wife's adultery. The fact that much was left to the individual judge, however, meant that there would be depatures from these two certain grounds.[1010] But, even though the redactors might find precedent for their provisions in the *ancien droit*, it is misleading of them to state they are following the *ancien jurisprudence*.

The works the redactors refer to on the *ancien droit* are those of Pothier, Rousseaud de la Combe, and Guyot and Merlin's *Répertoires*.[1011] These writers all stated the *ancien droit* as set out above, except for Rousseaud de la Combe, who allowed a wife to use her husband's adultery to prevent him having control of her property.[1012] Rousseaud de la Combe in fact relies on Spanish rather than

---

[1008] Pothier, *T.C.M.*, p. 238 (no. 516).

[1009] There had been doubts expressed in the debates on the code whether it was desirable that there should be separation without the seclusion of the adulterous wife, as, without such seclusion, "elle peut continuer à le [i.e. her husband] déshonorer, vivre même avec son séducteur." The issue was that she could no longer be sent to a convent, the convents having been suppressed, while the state was no longer being officially Roman Catholic, and the criminal code did not punish adultery. See Maleville, *Analyse*, vol. 1, pp. 226–227, 266–269 and 273.

[1010] See Huussen, *op. cit. supra* note 106, pp. 110–111.

[1011] Merlin's *Répertoire* dates after the *ancien régime*; but because it was based on that of Guyot, it gives an account of the *ancien droit*.

[1012] See *supra*, note 1002.

French authority.[1013] The C.Q. redactors must have been well aware that their articles did not embody the traditional rules on separation. It is possible that the Quebec courts had been granting *séparations de corps* in the circumstances envisaged in the C.Q. articles; but the redactors certainly do not cite any Quebec *jurisprudence* to support their articles.

For C.Q. 187, the redactors cite Pothier, a writer on the *nouveau droit*, and C.N. 229. On C.Q. 188, they cite Rousseaud de la Combe,[1014] Guyot,[1015] Merlin,[1016] C.N. 230, and a writer on the *nouveau droit*, and Roman texts. On C.Q. 189, they cite C.N. 231 and only writers on the *nouveau droit*. On C.Q. 190, they cite Pothier, and two writers on the *nouveau droit*. On C.Q. 191 they cite Pothier and a writer on the *nouveau droit*.[1017] That the provisions are taken from those of the C.N., the *nouveau droit*, rather than those of the *ancien droit*, is clear.

C.Q. 188's reference to Roman law is interesting. The redactors cite Justinian's Code and Novels.[1018] The relevant provisions state a wife could divorce her husband if he kept his concubine in the matrimonial home (or, under the Novel, even if he kept his concubine in the same city, were the offence repeated). Both the Code and the Novel allow *either* spouse to divorce the other on the grounds of adultery; adultery in the modern sense, however, did not necessarily amount to adultery in Roman law.[1019] It seems likely that the Quebec redactors used these Roman texts to give some support for their departure from the *ancien droit* here: it is clear that the provision was borrowed from the C.N. The redactors might also find some support in those statements of the jurists that, on its own, adultery was not enough; their provision only took into account a very aggravated form of adultery.

The redactors cited no writer on the *ancien droit* in connection with the C.Q. 189: and, indeed, none of the writers whom they seem to have consulted here on the *ancien droit* would have permitted a husband to separate from his wife in these circumstances. Indeed, the novelty of the C.N.'s rule was such that one commentator on the C.N., Pigeau, considered it necessary to stress that both could sue in these circumstances.[1020]

[1013] *Ibid.*

[1014] Rousseaud de la Combe, *op. cit. supra* note 952, p. 12, s.v. *Adultère*, no. 2.

[1015] Guyot, *op. cit. supra* note 730, vol. 1, p. 196, s.v. *Adultère*.

[1016] Merlin, *Répertoire* (4), vol. 1, p. 144, s.v. *Adultère*.

[1017] The Pothier references are those discussed above. The writers on the *ancien droit* vary; we need not consider them.

[1018] C. 5.17.8; Nov. 117.9.5.

[1019] See Corbett, *op. cit. supra* note 53, pp. 141–142. Both the constitution in the Code—one of Theodosius and Valentinian of 449 A.D.—and the Novel laid down many other grounds of divorce, none of which were adopted in Quebec. It would have been most surprising if the C.Q. had allowed separation if the husband were a brigand or a cattle thief, or if the wife attended theatres and games prohibited to her by her husband! It is obvious that the C.Q. redactors are using the Roman texts for purposes of giving authority to their propositions, rather than accepting the Roman rules.

[1020] E.N. Pigeau, *Notions élémentaires du nouveau droit civil, ou, exposé méthodique des dispositions du Code civil pour en faciliter l'intelligence*, Paris, Chez Rondonneau, 1803–1805, vol. 1, p. 67 states, discussing the article which became C.N. 231: "Mais sur cette troisième cause,

Given that the redactors are innovating here, what motivated their actions? First, the provisions of the C.N. themselves seem to have been influential: however, considering that the redactors altered the form of the articles, if not their substance, to make explicit aspects of the law left implicit in the C.N., it is clear that the C.Q. redactors were not thoughtlessly copying the C.N.'s rules. The rules of the C.N. were, however, fairly obviously derived from the *ancien droit*, though differing from it, and this also may have persuaded the redactors to copy them. It must be concluded that the Quebec redactors approved of the rules of the C.N. which they copied: they must have deliberately changed the law. The extension of *mauvais traitements* as a ground of separation to allow a husband to sue, seems an obvious sensible action needing no explanation. Allowing a wife to sue for separation on the grounds of her husband's adultery also seems sensible and equitable, given that, in a predominantly Catholic country such as Quebec, adultery was regarded as a sin. There was, of course, some authority from the *ancien régime* to the effect that, in some circumstances, wives could found on their husbands' adulteries. The question resolves itself into why should the only relevant adultery on the part of the husband be that committed when he keeps his concubine in the marital home. It seems likely that this specific qualication owes a great deal to the C.N.; the idea, however, that only certain adulteries should be taken into account must have been one of which the redactors approved. Maleville reports the following discussion of the French article during the redaction of the Code:

> [O]n a considéré que bien que l'adultère soit de la part des deux époux, une infraction aux lois du mariage, il a cependant des conséquences bien plus funestes lorsqu'il est commis par la femme, puisqu'il tend à introduire, dans la famille des enfans étrangers; que d'ailleurs l'adultère du mari était beaucoup plus difficile à prouver que celui de la femme, et l'on a fini par conserver la condition qu'on avait d'abord rejetée.[1021]

No doubt similar considerations swayed the Quebec redactors. Pothier also stressed the possibility of introducing *enfants étrangers* into the family.[1022] Demolombe gives the following fascinating explanation:

> Ce n'est point, sans doute, que l'adultère ne constitue aussi de la part du mari un très-répréhensible manquement à la morale et aux devoirs du mariage; mais on ne peut nier que l'adultère de la femme soit bien plus coupable encore: soit parce que la femme devant être plus retenue par la pudeur même de son sexe, l'adultère suppose en elle plus de dépravation; soit parce que, dans l'état de nos moeurs, ou si vous voulez, de nos préjugés, l'adultère de la femme porte à

---

deux observations importantes à faire 1. Tous deux le peuvent: ainsi, le mari en a le droit contre sa femme coupable d'excès, sévices et injures graves envers lui."

1021 Maleville, *Analyse*, vol. 1, pp. 221–222.

1022 See *supra*, text at note 1008.

> l'honneur du mari la plus grave atteinte; soit enfin parce qu'il peut avoir les plus funestes consequences et introduire dans la famille des enfants étrangers.[1023]

Demolombe, whose work the redactors used, wrote much nearer their time than did either Maleville or Pothier.

There is a definite and obvious shift in the rationalization of discrimination between the adultery of the husband and that of the wife. For Maleville and Pothier, the adultery of the wife introduced *enfants étrangers* into the family and dishonoured her husband;[1024] that of the husband had no such effects, and a wife, because she was linked to her husband by duties of respect and obedience, and was his inferior, should not inquire into his affairs. Demolombe indicates that rationalization on the grounds that the wife's adultery dishonoured her husband was no longer totally acceptable. The reason that adulterous bastards would be introduced into the family still held good. What is significant is Demolombe's stressing of the view that an adulterous wife was more depraved then an adulterous husband because of the natural modesty of the female sex. Given there could now be separation on the grounds of a husband's adultery, the argument that the wife ought not to look into his affairs because she was an inferior owing obedience and respect to him would no longer readily function as an acceptable justification for the discrimination.

The view of the respective roles of husband and wife propounded by Demolombe is one of which the C.Q. redactors would have approved. Their adoption of this provision of the C.N. would have been justified by their views of the husband and wife relationship. They might also have taken encouragement from the fact that they could be said to be following the *ancien droit* in so far as the only relevant adultery of the husband was that accompanied by an *injure grave*: the maintenance of his mistress in the conjugal home.

The fourth chapter of this title contains provisions on the effects of separation from bed and board. C.Q. 207 points out that the husband is no longer obliged to receive the wife, nor the wife to live with him. This is a reduction in the *puissance du mari* over the person of his wife, also obviously found in the *ancien droit.*[1025] Though the C.N. has no article equivalent to C.Q, 207, its provisions necessarily had the same result.[1026]

C.Q. 208 states:

> Separation from bed and board carries with it separation of property; it deprives the husband of the rights which he had over the property of his wife, and gives to the wife the right to obtain restitution of her dowry, and of the property that she brought in marriage.
>
> Unless by the judgement they are declared forfeited, which only takes place in the case of adultery, the separation also gives the wife the right to claim the benefit of all the gifts and advantages conferred on her by the marriage con-

---

[1023] Demolombe, *op. cit. supra* note 721, vol. 4, p. 470, no. 369.
[1024] Maleville, *Analyse*, vol. 1, p. 226.
[1025] See Pothier, *T.C.M.*, p. 240 (no. 522).
[1026] See e.g. Demolombe, *op. cit. supra* note 721, vol. 4, p. 599, no. 498.

tract; saving the rights of survivorship, to which such separation does not give rise, unless the contrary has been specially stipulated.

There is no problem with this article. The *ancien droit* and the C.N. provided the same.[1027] Separation from bed and board always ended the community, as, the next article, C.Q. 209, explicitly states, and thus the husband's control over the communal property.[1028]

The last article we need note here is C.Q. 210:

> The separation renders the wife capable of suing and being sued, and of contracting alone, for all that relates to the administration of her property; but for all acts and suits tending to alienate her immoveable property, she requires the authorization of a judge.

This article changes the law: under the *ancien droit*, the wife would have to seek authorization from her husband before requesting that of the judge, if there were *séparation de corps*.[1029] The C.N. still required the same. The *Pandectes françaises* explained thus:

> La nécessité d'autorisation pour l'aliénation des immeubles est fondée sur ce que la séparation ne détruit pas la puissance maritale.[1030]

The Quebec redactors justified their reform as one that would simplify proceedings and relieve the wife of a formality both useless and disagreeable.[1031] In fact, their motives are the same as those of the redactors of the 1825 C.L. who had introduced the same reform.[1032] There is no reason to attribute this change in the C.Q. to the redactors' study of the Louisiana code. The C.Q. redactors' reform is sensible, though, as the *Pandectes françaises* state, possibly contrary to the principles of *puissance maritale*. The Quebec redactors have, however, arguably maintained these principles in requiring the wife to be authorized by the judge. Marriage still has reducd her capacity, but, appropriately given the circumstances, authorization is given by the judge. In fact, that the Quebec redactors did not dispense with the necessity of authorization in these circumstances must be due to their obvious desire to preserve the traditional *puissance du mari*: they have rejected any notion that wives require authorization because of lack of ability.[1033]

We mentioned above that *séparation de biens* was obtainable if the husband's affairs were such that a wife feared her property to be at risk.[1034] The effect this form of separation has on the *puissance du mari* differs from that resulting from *séparation de corps*. C.Q. 1318 states thus:

1027 See Pothier, *T.C.M.*, pp. 240–241 (no. 522); C.N. 311, 1452. *T.D.C.Q.*, vol. 2, pp. 19–20 indicates some problems with this article: these are not relevant here.
1028 Pothier, *T.C.M.*, pp. 240–241 (no. 522); C.N. 311. See also C.Q. 1310.
1029 See Pothier, *T.C.M.*, p. 241 (no. 523).
1030 *Pan. fran.*, vol. 11, p. 420. See C.N. 1449 and also *Pan. fran.*, vol. 4, p. 164.
1031 *Second Report*, p. 195.
1032 C.L. 125. See 1823 *Projet*, p. 10. See *supra*, text at notes 495–496.
1033 See *supra*, text at notes 945–974.
1034 See *supra*, text at note 982.

> The wife, when separated either from bed and board or as to property only, regains the uncontrolled administration of her property. She may dispose of and alienate her moveable property. She cannot alienate her immoveables without the consent of her husband or, upon his refusal, without being judicially authorized.

This provision is identical to that in C.N. 1449. To some extent, however, it contradicts C.Q. 210 discussed above.[1035] This article seems to suggest that wives *séparées de corps* first require to seek authorization to alienate immoveable property from their husbands, before going to the judge. That this article should apparently provide so presumably results from an oversight caused by too close adherence to the C.N. here. The redactors make no relevant remarks on this article in their report.[1036] As it stands, the article basically follows the *ancien droit*.[1037] If it is accepted that the contradiction here of C.Q. 210 is an oversight, and that C.Q. 210 embodies the redactors' views on the authorization of women *séparées de corps*[1038]—the fact that under C.Q. 1318 only C.Q. 177, 178 and 206 are cited would support this hypothesis of error—then under C.Q. 1318 wives *séparées de biens*, but not *de corps*, would have to seek and to be refused their husband's authorization before they could request that of the judge. Given that the only ground for *séparation de biens* was that the husband's affairs were in sufficient disorder that the interests of the wife were endangered, this token gesture towards the *puissance du mari* seems unnecessary, and results in a cumbersome procedure. There can have been no social reason for the requirement other than that of preserving the facade of *puissance maritale*. Since the husband may well have been financially inept, he cannot have been considered as a person suitable to advise his wife. Here, despite the sensible reform in C.Q. 210, the redactors preferred to maintain the *status quo*, this being in line with their instructions and the probable lack of any obvious necessity for change.

The Dissolution of Marriage, and the Ending of *Puissance Maritale*

Neither *séparation de corps* nor *séparation de biens* ended the *puissance du mari*, though they both reduced its effects to a greater or lesser extent. Only the dissolution of the marriage ended the husband's authority over his wife. The seventh chapter of the fifth title of the first book of the Quebec code has only one article, C.Q. 185, and it is devoted to dissolution of marriage, providing as follows:

> Marriage can only be dissolved by the natural death of one of the parties; while both live it is indissoluble.

[1035] See *supra*, text at notes 1028–1032.

[1036] *Fifth Report*, p. 217.

[1037] See e.g. Pothier, *T. Comm.*, pp. 255 and p. 283 (nos. 464 and 522).

[1038] McCord, Synopsis, p. XIX picks out C.Q. 210 as one of the important reforms in the law. The Quebec statute, 39 Vict., c. 24, later amended C.Q. 210 to embody once more the *ancient droit*, removing this conflict.

The equivalent article of the French code, C.N. 227, states:

> Le mariage se dissout,
> 1. Par la mort de l'un des époux;
> 2. Par le divorce légalement prononcé;
> 3. Par la condemnation devenue définitive de l'un des époux à une peine emportant mort civile.

The Quebec redactors point out that divorce no longer exists in France, having been abolished in 1816, and that it had only recently been permitted in England other than by an Act of Parliament in each individual instance. They state that their civil laws do not recognize divorce, though, as formerly in England, the Canadian legislature considers itself authorized to pronounce divorce in individual cases. As to civil death, they point out that it also has been abolished in France (1854) and comment that the C.N. has innovated in allowing civil death to dissolve the marriage. Accordingly, they state that their article rejects the innovations of the C.N., and that only natural death dissolves the marriage tie.[1039] Their description of the *ancien droit* is correct.[1040]

To suggest that the redactors could have proposed the introduction of divorce would be wrong: circumstances in Quebec were such that judicial divorce was unthinkable. Quebec was a predominantly Roman Catholic province. That feelings on the subject of divorce were strong cannot be doubted: when confederation came, the British North America Act of 1867, s. 91, provided for "Marriage and Divorce" to be a topic within the legislative competency of the Federal Parliament, causing fears that "Protestant" divorce might be forced on French Canada.[1041] Everything would militate against the redactors even considering the introduction of divorce.[1042]

Thus, it is no surprise that only the natural death of one of the parties should end the marriage, and hence the *puissance maritale*. Quebec society of the period made inevitable the provision in C.Q. 185.

Conclusion on the Relationship between Husband and Wife in the 1866 Quebec Code

As in the equivalent subsection in the first part of this chapter,[1043] at issue here are the changes made in the various areas of the law discussed, considered

---

[1039] *Second Report*, pp. 189–191.
[1040] See Pothier, *T.C.M.*, p. 211 (no. 462). Maleville, *Analyse*, vol. 1, pp. 41–42 points out that it was a "maxime constante, avant la revolution", that civil death did not end marriage.
[1041] See J.E. Cauchon, *L'union des provinces de l'Amérique britannique du Nord*, Quebec, Imprimerie de A. Coté et Cie., 1865; reprint East Ardsley, Yorks., S.R. Publishers, 1968, pp. 92–101.
[1042] The French writers disagreed on divorce. Demolombe, *op. cit. supra* note 721, vol. 4, p. 462, no. 361 was opposed to its reintroduction. Bugnet, in Pothier, *Œuvres*, vol. 6, pp. 212–213, n. 1, thought it should be reintroduced. Maleville, *Analyse*, vol. 1, pp. 210–218, *passim*, criticizes divorce.
[1043] See *supra*, text at notes 503–520.

in connection with the possibilities for reform. The relationship of these provisions to Quebec society will also be assessed.

The redactors followed their instructions in their provisions on the method of contracting marriage. Thus, they molded the form of the Quebec law into that of the C.N. They retained the traditional ages at which marriage may be contracted. They included a specific article on impotency: the inclusion of this article, and the reforms contained in it, are attributable to the redactors' knowledge of the problems with the *ancien droit* and with the Code Napoléon. The Quebec redactors, however, included a major reform of one area of the law relating to the contracting of marriage. They radically changed the law on oppositions. As in the C.N.—and indeed there was precedent for the change from the last years of the *ancien régime* in France[1044]—the redactors restricted the class of those entitled to oppose a marriage. They also reversed the procedures on opposition, so that it is the opposant who has to take his action to court, and they have provided for a speedy court procedure: these reforms are not taken from the C.N. There was one obvious reason for restricting the class of people entitled to oppose a marriage: an unlimited class of potential opposants not only could cause great inconvenience, but was also contrary to the ideals of nineteenth-century liberal individualism. The articles in the French code recognized that marriage was a private affair, in which, if the contracting parties were adults, the wider society outside the family had no real interest. Reversing the procedure on who should take the action to court also furthered this notion that, in the absence of some very pressing reason, the marriages of adults should not be regulated in any way. A notable point is that the redactors do not claim to be reforming the law on who may make oppositions. They are able to do this because those who may oppose after their articles could have opposed before: their articles, however, inevitably have the result of excluding others from making oppositions. This must have been the intention of the redactors; for, although the class of opposants in the C.Q. is slightly different from that in the C.N., the redactors will have been well aware that the C.N.'s articles were exclusive in effect.[1045] A last point relates to C.Q. 127: it is possible that the redactors intended to introduce the Roman Catholic impediments to marriage into the law of Quebec for Roman Catholics. Whatever their intention, the redactors here clearly recognized the religious diversity of the Province. In respect of the other formalities and requirements, the redactors have made no change.

The redactors made no changes to the property relations between spouses that are relevant to *puissance du mari*. In fact, they firmly asserted such *puissance* in rejecting the potential reform contained in the *Code Napoléon* on the husband making donations from the community.[1046] Were there community between the spouses, the husband controlled the community, and also the separate property of his wife. Should the spouses simply be *non-communs*, the husband again controlled his wife's property. Were there contractual separation,

---

[1044] See *supra*, text at notes 770 and 764–791.

[1045] See *supra*, text at notes 787. From the commentators on the C.N., they would be aware of the interpretation.

[1046] See *supra*, text at notes 798–813.

though the wife controlled her property, she could not dispose of her immoveables without the consent of her husband or of the judge. In these articles the redactors maintained the traditional *puissance maritale*: indeed, the C.N. had generally done the same, and would not suggest possible reforms.

The effect on marital authority of the property relations between spouses links with the general need of the wife to be authorized to contract or to take part in court proceedings. In this area of the law, the redactors made no changes in the principles of the *ancien droit*, bar that contained in C.Q. 210 on wives *séparées de corps* from their husband; this article we will consider further below. The only change made in the details of the law is that in C.Q. 177 on the method of authorization, and this useful reform does not affect the traditional conception of the *puissance du mari*. Thus, the C.Q. maintains the conception of the *puissance du mari* found in Pothier. The requirement that the wife be authorized was not because she suffered from any supposed diminished ability to contract or to take part in court proceedings, whereby she required help and guidance, but because she owed a duty of obedience and respect to her husband: hence the provision in C.Q. 182. The only difference in the law here from the *ancien droit* is that resulting from C.Q. 210 (though indeed the actual articles on authorization do not hint at this difference) whereby women *séparées de corps* did not require to seek their husband's authorization before seeking that of the judge. Even this change, however, maintains the principle of the incapacity of wives, since the judge's authorization was necessary; such wives were not in the position of widows or unmarried women. Because of its article 224, the French code presents a rather different version of *puissance maritale*. In the C.N., the implicit theory behind the *puissance du mari* has shifted to one based on the idea that wives, because of their wifely duties and domestic seclusion in the home, require some assistance to make contracts, since they are unaccustomed to dealing with business matters, the care of the family patrimony being the lot of their husbands. This version of *puissance maritale* is one in line with the nineteenth-century ideal of the husband and wife relationship. The Quebec redactors, however, prefer the traditional version of the *ancien droit*: why they should have done so will be discussed below.

In relation to the articles on authorization, one final point is that the C.Q. redactors have maintained the principle that unauthorized actions are null, with a radical nullity that nothing could cure. C.N. 225 had provided for a relative nullity. This, to some extent, was in line with C.N. 224;[1047] but it probably was a more generally pragmatic "improvement" in the law. Here again the Quebec redactors preferred to assert the traditional law rather than accept the potentially useful change.

The rules on what conduct would be such as to give sufficient ground for an action of separation owe more to the Code Napoléon than to the *ancien droit*, though the Quebec redactors do not state that they are changing the law. The rules they have taken from the French law are, however, more in line with

---

[1047] See *supra*, text at notes 967–974.

nineteenth-century attitudes to the relationship between husband and wife than were those of the *ancien droit*; and, indeed, the actions of the Quebec redactors may be satisfactorily explained on those grounds.[1048] On the effects of separation from bed and board on the *puissance du mari*, the redactors have innovated by introducing C.Q. 210's rule that wives so separated need only seek the authorization of the judge. This is an obvious and useful reform. Wives judicially separated as to property still required to seek authorization from their husbands, which requirement was not perhaps satisfactory, though the disadvantages were obviously not major enough to have inspired the redactors in either France or Louisiana to make a change. The rule can be explained as a result of the Quebec redactors' desire to assert the traditional authority of the husband.

In all, the C.Q. redactors have made few changes in the law discussed in this section. They have obviously wished to maintain the traditional rules, though they reformed the law on oppositions to marriage, the method of authorizing, and the authorization of women separated from bed and board. The obvious question is: why were these reforms made and not others found in the C.N.? C.Q. 177 on the form of giving authority preserved the traditional *puissance du mari*, while introducing a useful reform. The reform on oppositions was again useful; but the redactors were able to fudge its appearance as a reform, while it was a change in tune with nineteenth-century liberal individualist conceptions of society. The only real alteration to the traditional *puissance maritale* was that in C.Q. 210, and even here the redactors still maintained the appearance of this authority since the wife still could not alienate her immoveables: *by virtue of being a wife* she could not alienate immoveable property and required judicial authorization, her husband, in the circumstances, being considered an unsuitable person to give authorization.

The period of codification in Quebec was the period when there was a trend towards the development of close family relationships based round domesticity and child-care, with the development of an affective or associative family rather than a hierarchical one. Though the provisions of the C.N. arguably presented a more accurate reflection of this new style of family, with stress being on the wife's inability outside the home, rather than on her legal incapacity being derived from her husband's authority, the provisions of the *ancien droit* still were such as to be compatible with such a conception of the respective roles of husband and wife. There was no *necessity* for change. Given then, the conservative instructions to the Codification Commission, it would be wrong to have expected the redactors to have enthusiastically espoused the new conception of *puissance maritale* implicit in the Code Napoléon. Bar some obvious pragmatically useful reforms, and some reforms that were disguised, the Quebec redactors preferred to assert here the continuity of the law, which still adequately asserted the traditional ideology of the husband's authority over his wife.

One point not yet mentioned here is that perhaps the major reform in this area of the code was in the form of the law, rather than in its substance. It has

---

[1048] See *supra*, text at notes 1011–1025.

been argued above that, in C.Q. 173, 174 and 175, the Quebec redactors have recast the traditional substance of the law as a series of reciprocal rights and duties between husband and wife: in this, the redactors have followed the French code.[1049] This has put these provisions into a contractual form, as if they were the results of bargaining between free individuals. In the *ancien droit*, these provisions were derived from the husband's natural authority and obligations arising from the fact of marriage. These articles conceive of the husband and wife, much more than do the provisions of the *ancien droit*, as being individuals connected by rights and duties rather than by links of authority in a hierarchy. They thus express the newer associative or affective conception of family, with the husband as the dominant partner.

Puissance Paternelle

How *Puissance Paternelle* Arises

As under the D.O. in Louisiana, in Quebec the most common method for a child becoming subject to paternal power would be uncontested legitimate birth. The provisions on the filiation of legitimate children are set out in C.Q. 218–227, the first chapter of Title Seventh, "Of Filiation", and are, in all relevant parts, the same as those contained in C.N. 312–318. Both C.Q. 218 and C.N. 312 provide that a child conceived during the marriage is legitimate, and taken to be the child of the husband. The Quebec redactors stress conception: "it is conception and not birth during marriage, which is the principle of legitimacy." They explain: "It is only a provision of positive law that legitimacy is presumed from birth during marriage."[1050] There is no need to discuss the detailed provisions of the Quebec code as they relate to the French code and the *ancien droit*: as in the D.O., these rules, at their least complex, embody the maxim *pater is est quem nuptiae demonstrant* and do not reflect over much on the nature and content of the relationship between father and child. Legitimate birth, under the C.Q., as under the C.N. and *ancien droit*, brings a child under the authority of his father, this being one of the civil effects of marriage.[1051]

The second method of acquiring paternal power is by the legitimation of children already born. C.Q. 237 states:

> Children born out of marriage, other than the issue of an incestuous or adulterous connection, are legitimated by the subsequent marriage of their father and mother.

[1049] See *supra*, text at notes 864–876.

[1050] *Second Report*, p. 197. As a result of this, they have given a rubric to this chapter different from that of the C.N. The C.N. reads: "De la filiation des enfants légitimes, ou nés durant le mariage." The C.Q. replaced the last clause with "or conceived during marriage". They have agreed with the criticism of Marcadé, *op. cit. supra* note 928, vol. 2, p. 2.

[1051] See Pothier, *T.C.M.*, p. 181 (no. 339), quoted *supra*, text at note 522.

C.N. 331 differs, stating that such children "pourront être légitimés", and adding that this would only take place if the mother and father had recognized the children as theirs before the marriage, or acknowledged them in the very "acte . . . de célébration". The Quebec redactors have rejected the reform expressed in the C.N., and have continued the rule that marriage *ipso facto* legitimated such children.[1052] The rule of the *ancien droit* was derived from the Canon law, not because the Canon law had had any civil force in France, but because, according to Pothier, it had been adopted to promote order and encourage marriage.[1053] Roman law had only legitimated by subsequent marriage children born *ex concubinatu*; but Canon law allowed the legitimation of those born of any illicit union which was neither incestuous nor adulterous.[1054] Lebrun stated thus the *ancien droit* (note that he is not using "concubinage" according to its meaning in Roman law):

> Enfin nostre Droit se contente de deux choses: La premiere, que le mariage ait pû se contracter au temps de concubinage; La seconde, qu'il soit actuellement celebré.[1055]

The attitude of the *ancien droit* was expressed by Pothier:

> Il n'est donc pas nécessaire que le consentement du père et de la mère intervienne pour cette légitimation; il n'est pas en leur pouvoir de priver leurs enfants du droit que la loi leur donne, par l'effet qu'elle donne au mariage de leurs père et mère de les légitimer.[1056]

Pothier also argued that children born of an incestuous union were legitimated if their parents subsequently married after obtaining the necessary dispensation: indeed this was a common view.[1057] It had once been the custom to place the children "sous le poêle" during the celebration of the marriage as a solemn recognition of the children by their parents;[1058] but this had died out relatively early, all that there was required was some form of recognition (not used in any technical sense) before or after the marriage, whereby the children could prove

---

[1052] *Second Report*, p. 201.
[1053] Pothier, *T.C.M.*, p. 186 (no. 412); see Esmein, *op. cit. supra* note 69, vol. 2, pp. 37–44.
[1054] See *supra*, text at notes 524–529.
[1055] *Traité des successions, divisé en quatre livres*, 3rd ed., Paris, Michel Guignard & Claude Robustel, 1714, p. 20 (bk. 1, chap. 2, sect. 1, dist. 1, no. 3).
[1056] Pothier, *T.C.M.*, p. 192 (no. 422).
[1057] Pothier, *T.C.M.*, p. 188 (no. 414); Pothier, *T.S.*, p. 22 (ch. 1, sect. 2, art. 3, § 5, quest. 1). Pocquet, *op. cit supra* note 619, p. 34 (bk. 1, tit. 1, sect. 6, art. 76), said thus: "Les bâtards adultérins ou incestueux ne peuvent être légitimés par mariage subséquent, à moins que l'inceste ne vienne de consanguinité et affinité, dont l'empêchement n'ait pas pû être levé et l'ait été par des dispenses antérieures au mariage." Pocquet cites two *arrêts* to this effect.
[1058] *Poêle* or *pallium* was a canopy held over the spouses at the celebration of marriages under the Gallican liturgy.

their status.[1059] In strict theory, in the *ancien droit*, as in the C.Q., marriage *ipso facto* legitimated, though proof of filiation might be a problem.

The Quebec redactors chose not to adopt the innovation of C.N. 331. Though they gave no reason for following the *ancien droit*, they must have made a policy decision in favour of legitimation, as favouring marriage and the family.[1060] Parents could relieve their illegitimate offspring from the disadvantages of bastardy simply by marrying. The Quebec redactors may have been in agreement with the argument put during the redaction of the C.N. that the requirement of public acknowledgement could deter parents from legitimating their children.[1061] Maleville points out that the C.N. has not permitted *recherche de la paternité*, and, therefore, some form of recognition would be necessary to allow proof of filiation.[1062] This would not apply in Quebec, as C.Q. 241 allowed illegitimate children to establish their paternity judicially.[1063]

A problem arises out of C.Q. 237's statement that children born of an incestuous marriage are not legitimated by the subsequent marriage of their parents. C.Q. 124–126 set out the prohibited degrees of marriage: under no circumstances could the parties so prohibited ever marry. The C.N., however, under its article 164, allowed dispensations to permit uncle and niece, aunt and nephew, to marry. Thus, the provision in C.N. 331 on incestuous children is understandable: there are circumstances in which the parents of such could marry. Who, then, are the children of an incestuous union who may not be legitimated by the subsequent marriage of their parents in terms of C.Q. 237? The terms of the 1808 Digest's article, D.O. 21 (p. 49), follow the C.N. in not allowing the legitimation *per subsequens matrimonium* of incestuous children: the D.O. admits no possibility of the parents of incestuous children marrying, assuming incest means sexual intercourse between those within the prohibited degrees of marriage. As pointed out, the D.O. redactors have copied the C.N. article without considering its full import; but this is unimportant, the provision merely being unnecessary.[1064] It is tempting to conclude that the Quebec redactors have likewise simply copied this statement of the C.N. without considering its import, and that there is no significance in the provision. C.Q. 127, however, should be considered. This article has already been discussed in a different context.[1065] Coming after those on the prohibited degrees, it states that the other impediments recognized by the various religions as resulting from relationship or affinity remained subject to the rules followed by the various churches, with

---

[1059] See Pothier, *T.C.M.*, pp. 192–193 (no. 422); *Ancien Denisart*, vol. 1, p. 297, s.v. *bâtards*, nos. 23–24. Loisel, *op. cit. supra* note 62, bk. 1, tit. 1, rule 39, states: "Enfans nais avant le mariage, mis soubs le poile sont legitimez." See *Pan. fran.*, vol. 2, pp. 82–84 for a brief outline of the history of *legitimatio per subsequens matrimonium*.

[1060] *Second Report*, p. 201.

[1061] See Maleville, *Analyse*, vol. 1, p. 295; *supra*, text at notes 539–540.

[1062] Maleville, *Analyse*, vol. 1, p. 294.

[1063] The C.Q. redactors in their *Second Report*, p. 201, point out that they have not introduced the C.N. rules on acknowledgement of children.

[1064] See *supra,* text between notes 541 and 542.

[1065] See *supra,* text at notes 742–748.

those already having the right to grant dispensations from such impediments retaining such the right. Should the clause on incestuous children in C.Q. 237 be taken as referring to this article? There are two separate issues here: first, the intention of the redactors, and second, the correct construction of the Quebec code. Here only the first issue is relevant, since we are dealing with the intentions of the codifiers.

The redactors gave several references for this article. First, they referred to Pothier,[1066] then to Fenet on Pothier,[1067] to C.L. 217, to C.N. 331, and to some commentators on the C.N.[1068] Some of these references relate to other aspects of C.Q. 237. It is worth noting that there are no references to other articles of the C.Q. itself—notably there is no reference to C.Q. 127.

The passages cited by the redactors from Pothier's treatise on the contract of marriage say nothing on the point in question.[1069] A passage cited from his treatise on persons and things, however, states:

> Les bâtards nés d'une conjonction incestueuse ou adultérine, sont d'une condition pire que les autres bâtards, en ce que – 1. ils ne peuvent devenir légitimes par le mariage subséquent de leurs père ou mère.[1070]

The passage cited from Pothier's treatise on successions states in relevant part:

> Il en est de même d'une simple conjonction passagère d'un homme avec une fille; s'il l'épouse par la suite, le mariage . . . rendra légitime l'enfant qui en est né; s'il y avait une parenté collaterale entre le garçon et la fille, qui ont habitude ensemble, le mariage célébré par la suite entre ces personnes légitimera-t-il les enfants nés de cette habitude? La raison de douter est que cette conjonction est entachée d'un vice d'inceste, qui la rend plus criminelle; néanmoins il faut décider que les enfants sont légitimés: la dispense obtenue depuis a un effet rétroactif qui purge ce vice d'inceste.[1071]

In an uncited passage of his treatise on marriage, Pothier states exactly the same.[1072] Fenet on Pothier states:

> Lorsqu'il s'agissait d'enfans nés d'un commerce incestueux, si le mariage s'ensuivait, la dispense avait un effet rétroactif et les légitimait... M. Merlin,

---

[1066] Pothier, *T.C.M.*, pp. 183, 185, 186, 188, and 192–193 (nos. 408, 411, 412, 415, and 422); Pothier, *T.P.C.*, pp. 46–47 (nos. 116 and 120); Pothier, *T.S.*, pp. 21–22 (ch. 1, sect. II, art. 3, § 5).
[1067] Fenet, *op. cit. supra* note 934, pp. 77–78, on art. 331.
[1068] *Pan. fran.*, vol. 2, p. 80; Toullier, *op. cit. supra* note 628, vol. 2, no. 924, p. 132; Marcadé, *op. cit. supra* note 928, vol. 2, p. 43; and one other commentator—Biret, whose work I have been unable to consult—but this is probably unimportant.
[1069] See Pothier, *T.C.M.*, pp. 183, 185, 186, 188, and 192–193 (nos. 408, 411, 412, 415, and 422): other sections of the *T.C.M.*, uncited, are relevant.
[1070] Pothier, *T.P.C.*, p. 47 (no. 120).
[1071] Pothier, *T.S.*, p. 22 (ch. 1, sect. II, art. 3, § 5).
[1072] Pothier, *T.C.M.*, p. 188 (no. 414). The redactors do not cite this, because it would seem they have copied their Pothier references from the first set of references Fenet gives on art. 331: Fenet, *op. cit. supra* note 934, p. 77. There is no reason to conclude that they have not read Pothier's work.

> Vo. *Légitimation*, pence qu'elle n'a plus cet effet sous l'empire de l'art. 331, et M. Toullier, tome 2, n. 933, semble d'un avis contraire.[1073]

The passage of Toullier cited by the C.Q. redactors does not bear on the topic at issue here; but, as Fenet points out (and the C.Q. redactors must have read Fenet) Toullier elsewhere said thus:

> L'ancienne jurisprudence distinguait entre les enfans nés de parens ou alliés dans les degrés où l'on obtenait des dispenses; ceux-la étaient légitimés par le mariage que leurs père et mère contractaient après les dispenses obtenues. On ne voit, dans le Code, aucune disposition contraire à cette distinction raisonnable; car, si l'art. 331 exclut en general, du bienfait de la légitimation enfans nés d'un commerce incestueux, il ne définit pas l'inceste.[1074]

He quotes Merlin (as cited above by Fenet) as being of the opposite opinion that now incestuous children were not legitimated.[1075] The C.Q. redactors also cite Marcadé, who stated that:

> Malgré la disposition si formelle et si absolue de notre article, quelques jurisconsultes, notamment Malleville [*sic*] (art. 331), Toullier (II-933) M. Pont . . . et M. Dupin ainé . . . ont enseigné que les enfants incestueux sont légitimés par le mariage subséquent que leurs père et mère contractent en vertu de dispenses. Mais cette doctrine est repoussée, avec raison, par le plupart des auteurs. Et en effet, bien loin que la prohibition de notre article ne soit pas faite pour cette classe d'enfants incestueux, elle n'est au contraire faite, *que pour elle*.
>
> L'impossibilité d'obtenir le bénéfice de la légitimation n'est écrite que pour ceux des enfants incestueux dont les parents se marient ensuite au moyen de dispenses, puisque ces dispenses sont le seul moyen de mariage, et que ce mariage est à son tour le seul moyen de légitimation. Ce n'est pas, apparement, à deux parents qui ne peuvent jamais se marier, que la loi dit: Je ne veux pas que le mariage que vous contracterez légitime vos enfants.[1076]

Toullier and Marcadé adequately represent the two views taken on C.N. 331: the most common being that C.N. 331's provision on incestuous children must be referring to the children of parents marrying under dispensation granted following C.N. 164, for otherwise the provision was pointless.[1077]

The C.Q. redactors must have been aware of this dispute: it is, for example, clearly pointed out by Fenet. Would their awareness of this dispute, and that the most common view was that of Marcadé, mean that they deliberately followed C.N. 331, intending this provision of their article to have some definite legal effect? Did they envisage circumstances wherein the parents of incestuous

---

[1073] Fenet, *op. cit. supra* note 934, p. 78, on art. 331. The ellipsis indicates omission of Fenet's references to Pothier's works.
[1074] Toullier, *op. cit. supra* note 628, vol. 2, pp. 135–136, no. 933.
[1075] *Ibid.*, p. 136. Duvergier disagreed with Toullier; see his note "a" on p. 136.
[1076] Marcadé, *op. cit. supra* note 928, vol. 2, pp. 44–45, on art. 331.
[1077] *Ibid.*, vol. 2, p. 45 n. 1, cites the various commentators and their views.

children could marry? Those prohibited from marrying under C.Q. 124, 125 and 126 could never marry. The C.Q. has no article equivalent to C.N. 164.

There are two possible answers to the above questions. The first is that the Quebec redactors intended the provision preventing the legitimation of incestuous children to apply in circumstances where the parties marrying were within degrees of relationship prohibiting marriage according to their religion, but from which prohibition, following C.Q. 127, dispensation could be granted, again according to the dispositions of their religion: the prohibited degrees concerned could not be those preventing marriage under C.Q. 124–126. Supporting this answer is the fact that the Quebec redactors must have been aware of the problems over the interpretation of C.N. 331; this would mean that they knew that most commentators considered C.N. 331 to apply to C.N. 164. The C.Q. redactors would thus have intended C.Q 237 to apply to C.Q. 127. This answer would make sense of the mention of incestuous children in C.Q. 237, interpreting incest to be sexual intercourse within the degrees prohibited not only by the Code, but also by the various religions.[1078] The second, and alternative, answer would be that the prohibition of the legitimation of incestuous children by the subsequent marriage of their parents is merely a conventional statement embodying a traditional precept, found also, for example, in Pothier,[1079] without it being intended to be construed along with C.Q. 127.

The following evidence supports the second answer. First, the redactors make no reference to C.Q. 127 or its provisions in connection with C.Q. 237. Second, C.Q. 237 could be construed to apply to the prior offspring of putative incestuous marriages, though the indirectness of the article suggests that this was not the intention of the redactors. Third, the view that C.Q. 237 was intended to apply to C.Q. 127 has ridiculous effects. It would mean that the redactors intended that if, for example, Roman Catholic first cousins, having had an illegitimate child, with the child not being conceived in adultery, later decided to marry, and, having gained the necessary dispensation from the appropriate ecclesiastical authority, did marry, their illegitimate child would not be legitimated according to the Quebec code, though both the Canon law itself and the *ancien droit* (according to most commentators) would have regarded the child as legitimated. It is difficult to accept that this was the intention of the codifiers here, no matter what they had intended by C.Q. 127. Fourth, were the first answer correct, then the redactors would have here probably changed the law, assuming that the Quebec courts, before codification, would have followed, as seems likely, the views of Pothier, Lebrun and Pocquet, rather than those of, for example, Dumoulin.[1080] The redactors give no indication that they have changed the law, and their study of the writers on the C.N. would have made them conscious of that code's change in the law on this point.

[1078] *T.D.C.Q.*, vol. 2, pp. 114–115; Baudouin, *op. cit. supra* note 551, pp. 244–248.

[1079] See *supra*, quotation in text at note 1070.

[1080] Pothier, *T.C.M.*, p. 188 (no. 414); Pothier, *T.S.*, p. 22 (ch. 1, sect. II, art. 3, § 5); *Pan. fran.*, vol. 4, p. 212, where the varying views of the writers on the *ancien droit* are mentioned. On the Canon law, see Esmein, *op. cit. supra* note 69, vol. 2, pp. 355–368.

It would seem likely that the second answer is the correct one: the redactors did not intend C.Q. 237's provision on incestuous children to apply to marriages prohibited by the various religions on the grounds of relationship, but not prohibited by C.Q. 124–126. It is likely that the redactors merely copied this provision of the C.N. without considering adequately its possible implications, and intended that it should stand as a general statement of policy. Pothier in his *Traité des Personnes et des Choses* makes an unqualified statement that incestuous children may not be legitimated by subsequent marriage,[1081] though, from his other writings, it is evident that he thought such children would be legitimated if their parents married with a dispensation.[1082] The redactors could have considered their provision as being of the nature of this statement of Pothier's, or indeed of C.L. 217, since the C.L. has no provisions for dispensation from its provisions on the prohibited degrees of marriage. The Quebec provision thus would have the meaning Toullier attributed to C.N. 331, and also would probably be following the *ancien droit*.[1083]

If the above argument—that the redactors here were only making a traditional statement without intending it to have a specific legal effect—be correct, their action in copying the wording of this part of C.N. 331 may be criticized in that, since they must have known of the problems of interpretation of the French article, they ought to have altered their own accordingly. (Indeed, this criticism is applicable even if the above argument be rejected.) Supposing that the argument given is correct, the C.Q. redactors had no reason to change the law here. There can have been no social reasons for preventing the legitimation of children whom only some of the Province's religions would have regarded as conceived in incest. There would indeed seem to be positive reasons for not changing the law: that the illegitimate child of Protestant first cousins should be legitimated by their subsequent marriage, but that of Roman Catholic first cousins should not is ridiculous.

Legitimation *per subsequens matrimonium* is the only form of legitimation found in the C.Q., though the *droit coutumier* had permitted legitimation *par lettres du roi*. This form of legitimation, rather different from the Roman *per rescriptum principis*, had only a limited effect.[1084] It was the only form of legitimation in the *ancien droit* other than that *per subsequens matrimonium*.[1085] Pothier remarks that such legitimation only allowed a child to use his father's name, and the family coat of arms, with a "brisure de gauche à droite" to signify the child was not born in marriage.[1086] Some authors stated that the child could

---

[1081] Pothier, *T.P.C.* p. 47 (no. 120).

[1082] Pothier, *T.C.M.*, p. 188 (no. 414); Pothier, *T.S.*, p. 22 (ch. 1, sect. II, art. 3, § 5).

[1083] *Pan. fran.*, vol. 4, p. 212, follows the opinion of Pothier, though the C.Q. redactors do not cite this passage.

[1084] See *supra*, text at notes 543–544.

[1085] D'Espeisses, *Œuvres supra* note 73, vol. 2, p. 446 (part II, tit. I, no. 66) states: "Aujourd'hui en France il n'y a que ces deux moyens de légitimation, sçavoir par mariage subsequent et par lettres du Prince. . . ."

[1086] Pothier, *T.P.C.*, p. 46 (no. 117); Pothier, *T.S.*, p. 24 (ch. 1, sect. 2, art. 3, § 6).

have certain limited rights of succession to his parents, if the other relatives agreed, and if the *Lettres du Roi* should contain a clause permitting succession.[1087] Pothier, however, stated that in his day a child so legitimated could not succeed at all, as *Lettres* with a "clause de succéder" were no longer used.[1088] *Légitimation par Lettres* did not give a minor, in Pothier's phrase, "droits de famille": he would not have come under his father's authority in the relevant sense. The main importance of this form of legitimation was that it relieved the child from some of the disabilities arising from bastardy, which could be very extensive under the *ancien régime*.[1089] This form of legitimation was not included in the French code. Maleville explained the exclusion thus:

> Aujourd'hui que les enfans naturels peuvent posséder des charges et des emplois commes les légitimes, on a moins besoin de cette espèce de légitimation.[1090]

The same reasoning would apply in Quebec. The redactors of the C.Q., however, make no reference to this institution, though it would seem most unlikely that they would not know of it. They presumably preferred here to follow the example of the C.N., and probably for the same reasons. There was perhaps no social reason for including such a form of legitimation, which could be regarded as discouraging marriage and encouraging fornication. Quebec would have no shortage of competent marriage officers, unlike Texas.[1091]

The 1866 Quebec code did not permit adoption, rejecting the example of the French code. The redactors remark that adoption had been unknown in the *ancien droit*.[1092] The arguments put forward on why Louisiana rejected adoption would apply here, but with one important difference: adoption had never been permitted by Quebec law.[1093] For the codifiers to have permitted adoption would have been to upset the *status quo*, and overturn the current conceptions of family: indeed, one writer has argued that adoption was contrary to the principles on the family embodied in the code.[1094] There can have been no obvious reason for changing the law here, and adoption was not introduced as a method of creating legal ties of *puissance paternelle*.

1087 See Lebrun, *op. cit. suopra* note 1055, pp. 24–29 at p. 25 (bk. 1, ch. 2, sect. 1, dist. 2, no. 5); Pocquet, *op. cit. supra* note 619, pp. 34–35 (bk. 1, tit. 1, sect. 6, art. 77); and *Ancien Denisart*, vol. 3, p. 91, s.v. *Légitimation*, nos. 23–25.

1088 Pothier, *T.P.C.*, p. 46 (no. 117); Pothier, *T.S.*, p. 24 (ch. 1, sect. 2, art. 3, § 6).

1089 See Brissaud, *History*, pp. 202–211.

1090 Maleville, *Analyse*, vol. 1, p. 296.

1091 See *supra*, text at notes 543–544.

1092 *Second Report*, p. 203.

1093 See *supra*, text at notes 547–556.

1094 H. Roch, *L'adoption dans la province de Québec*, Montreal, Wilson et Lafleur, 1951, p. 53 (not seen; found quoted by Baudouin, *op. cit. supra* note 551, p. 250, n. 3), in discussing the later provincial law on adoption said: "Le législateur a préféré la laisser comme loi statutaire et en dehors du Code, voulant, sans doute, ne pas associer aux principes fondamentaux et intangibles de celui-ci, une loi nouvelle qui les bouleverse à plus d'un pointe de vue." Maleville's discussion of the C.N. shows that there was opposition in France to adoption: Maleville, *Analyse*, vol. 1, pp. 301–309.

Thus, under the C.Q., paternal authority was brought into being in only two ways: first, by legitimate birth in marriage; and second, by legitimation by subsequent marriage. The redactors here closely followed the *ancien droit*, preserving the traditional legal concept of family. That there should be only these methods of creating ties of parent and child was appropriate given the development of the nineteenth-century close affective family. The continuation of the traditional law on legitimation, if the argument above be correct, may be explained by the traditional outlook of the redactors when there was no obvious reason for change. Certainly the C.N.'s innovation in requiring recognition for legitimation, while perhaps making it easier to ascertain legitimate parent and child relationships, was not at all necessary in Quebec, given the redactors' preservation of *recherche de paternité*.[1095] There is no need to summarize the problems over C.Q. 237's provision on incestuous children, bar to remark that it is obvious that the Quebec redactors were more intent on following the C.N. than in considering the implications, be they legal or social, of their article. As pointed out, such statements are traditional, and this may have obscured from the redactors the potential construction of their article.[1096]

Scope of *Puissance Paternelle*

The eighth title of the Quebec code's first book is entitled "Of Paternal Authority." It is a short title containing only four articles, C.Q. 242–245; but, as in Louisiana, provisions relating to *puissance paternelle* may be located in other parts of the code.[1097] The title is considerably shorter than that of the C.N. The articles from the latter's title on paternal authority, title nine of the first book, C.N. 371–387, which are not followed by the C.Q. redactors, will also be discussed, in order to reach an understanding of the actions of the Quebec codifiers.

Rules in Title Eighth of Book First

The Codification Commissioners made the following general remark on this title:

> The articles which follow give the rules of this authority, as admitted and practised within the jurisdiction of the Parliament of Paris; it has much analogy with that adopted by the Code of Louisiana. . . .[1098]

[1095] *Second Report*, p. 201.

[1096] See *supra*, text at notes 1079, 1081–1083.

[1097] Toullier, *op. cit. supra* note 628, vol. 2, p. 185, no. 1045 said: "On n'a point entendu réunir sous ce titre toutes les dispositions qui ont traité à la puissance paternelle, et qui se trouve mieu placées dans d'autres titres, d'où l'on ne pourrait les écarter, sans y laisser une lacune trop marquée." His remarks would apply not only to the C.N., but also to the C.Q. and D.O.

[1098] *Second Report*, p. 203.

It is useful here to discuss first the Quebec provisions and their origins, and then deal with the provisions of the C.N. differing from those of the C.Q.

C.Q. 242 states that:

> A child, whatever may be his age, owes honor and respect to his father and mother.

C.N. 371 and C.L. 233 state exactly the same. The Quebec redactors supplied a host of references.[1099] The provision is more moral precept (with obvious Biblical echoes) than one from which legal consequences may be derived, though Maleville reports that when, during the redaction of the C.N., it was proposed to remove this article as not containing a rule, the argument was put that this article enunciated the principle from which the others were derived.[1100] Equivalent statements by authors on the *ancien droit* are legion. Pothier, for example, states:

> Les enfants sont obligés, de leur côté, d'aimer et d'honorer leurs père et mère, de leur obéir, et de les assister dans leurs besoins, selon leurs moyens.[1101]

No great significance may be attached to this article.

C.Q. 243 is as follows:

> He remains subject to their authority until his majority or his emancipation, but the father alone exercises this authority during marriage; saving the provisions contained in the act 25 Vict., chap. 66.

Taken together, C.N. 372 and 373 provide much the same (bar, of course, the here unimportant reference to the Provincial Act). C.L. 234 is similar; it does not state, however, that the father *alone* exercises the authority during the marriage, but rather that if the parents disagree, the authority of the father prevails.[1102]

The redactors here embodied a traditional provision of the *ancien droit*.[1103] Again they gave a myriad of references to works consulted; but none of these are of interest here.[1104] The C.Q. redactors have chosen to follow the C.N.,

---

[1099] See, e.g., Pothier, *T.C.M.*, p. 177 (no. 389); *Pan. fran.*, vol. 4, 317. There are also references to Roman law, to D. 37.15.9, D. 2.4.6 and one mistaken reference to the Novels (the citation—McCord—is Nov. 12.c.9; there is no *caput* 9 in this Novel, nor can the reference be explained by consultation of a copy of Gothofredus' edition). D. 37.15.9 states: "Liberto et filio semper honesta et sancta persona patris ac patroni videri debet." D. 2.4.6: "Parentes naturales in ius vocare nemo potest: una et enim omnibus parentibus servanda reverentia." These references are analogous; the redactors may have felt these citations added on extra authority to their article.

[1100] Maleville, *Analyse*, vol. 1, p. 342.

[1101] Pothier, *T.C.M.*, p. 177 (no. 389).

[1102] See *supra*, text at notes 562–567.

[1103] Pothier, *T.C.M.*, pp. 177–178 (nos. 389–390); Pothier, *T.P.C.*, p. 52 (nos. 134–135).

[1104] See, e.g., Pothier, *T.C.M.*, p. 177 (nos. 388 and 389); *Pan. fran.*, vol.2, pp. 305, 324 and 327. Here the redactors also cite the C.I.C.: D. 50.16.196; Inst. 1.2 and 12. D. 50.16.196 states: "Familiae appellatione et ipse princeps familiae continetur. Feminarum liberos in familia earum non esse palam est, quia qui nascuntur patris familiam sequuntur." Inst. 1.2. is the title "De iure

which was in accord with the *ancien droit coutumier* on this point. Whether the wording of the Louisiania provision would have had a different effect is difficult to say: the Quebec provision follows C.N. 373 in saying the father *alone* exercises the authority during the marriage, and this would seem a clearer reflection of the former rule.

The next article, C.Q. 244, provides:

> An unemancipated minor cannot leave his father's house without his permission.

C.N. 374 is similar, though adding that the child could leave "pour enrôlement voluntaire", after having reached the full age of eighteen years. C.L. 236[1105] states:

> L'enfant au-dessous de l'âge de puberté, ne peut quitter la maison paternelle, sans la permission de ses père et mère, et ceux-ci ont le droit de la corriger, pourvu que ce soit manière raisonnable.

In the relevant part of this article, it is obvious that the rule is quite different from that of the C.Q.: C.L. 236 gives freedom to leave home to children over the age of puberty. The C.L. provision has been rejected: that of the C.Q., following the C.N., is the traditional rule of the *ancien droit.*[1106] The exception providing for voluntary enlistment in the army was included in the C.N. on the urging of Cambacérès, because the government intended to use conscription as little as possible as a method of recruiting the army. The exception in C.N. 374 was intended to encourage and to facilitate voluntary enlistment.[1107] Maleville states that "suivant les anciens réglemens, le fils mineur ne pouvait s'enrôler sans le consentement de son père. . . ."[1108] This is not quite correct. Pothier points out that:

> Il faut excepter de notre règle le service du roi, auquel les enfants de famille peuvent valablement s'engager contre le consentement de leurs père et mère. L'intérêt public l'emporte sur l'intérêt particulier de la *puissance paternelle.*[1109]

---

naturali, gentium et civili"; 1.12 is that "Quibus modis ius potestatis solvitur." See *supra,* remark in note 1099.

[1105] This is the same article as D.O. 39 (p. 53), bar an unimportant difference in punctuation. C.L. 235 has no equivalent in the C.Q.: this will be discussed below.

[1106] See e.g. Pothier, *T.P.C.*, pp. 50–51 (nos. 130–131); Merlin, *Répertoire* (5), vol. 10, s.v. *Puissance Paternelle*, sect. 3, § 6, discusses C.N. 374.

[1107] See *Pan. fran.*, vol. 4, pp. 329–330; Maleville, *Analyse*, vol. 1, p. 344; and Toullier, *op. cit. supra* note 628, vol. 2, p. 183, no. 1048. Art. 39, § 5, loi 21 Mars, 1832, raised the age to 20 years.

[1108] Maleville, *Analyse*, vol. 1, p. 344.

[1109] Pothier, *T.P.C.*, p. 51 (no. 131).

No actual provision in any *Coutume* or in royal legislation actually so provided; but the exception, as stated by Pothier, was followed nonetheless.[1110] Pothier, however, gives no age limit, unlike C.N. 374.[1111]

The Quebec redactors have followed the C.N. and *ancien droit*, apart from their sources' exceptions in favour of enlistment. Quebec had no need of such an exception to maintain a supply of army recruits. Unlike in Louisiana, minors above the age of puberty were not allowed to leave home without parental consent. The rejection of the C.L.'s rule conforms to the idea that the reason for *puissance paternelle* was the protection of the minor. The C.L., unlike the C.Q., laid more stress on the division of nonage into pupillage before puberty and minority after puberty, with those above the age of puberty having greater legal capacity. The C.Q. preserved the *ancien droit coutumier*'s unified notion of minority.

The final article of this title of the Code is C.Q. 245: it states:

> The father, and in his default, the mother of an unemancipated minor have over him a right of reasonable and moderate correction, which may be delegated to and exercised by those to whom his education has been entrusted.

There is no exactly equivalent article in the C.N., which did, however, provide the father and mother with powers to have their children imprisoned.[1112] C.L. 236, quoted above, allows parents to correct their children, "pourvu que ce soit d'une manière raisonnable". C.L. 238 allows parents to delegate their authority to those to whom they have entrusted their children.[1113] The Quebec redactors state:

> This article is new and is not to be found in the code; nevertheless it is conformable as well to the Roman as to the old French law. The code of Louisiana (art. 236) contains a similar provision. Instead of that right of moderate correction, the Code Napoleon (articles from 376 to 381) grants to the father and mother, under certain circumstances and with certain formalities more or less solemn, according to the age of the child and the position of the parents, the right to have him arrested and kept in custody, without being even obliged, in certain cases to give reasons therefor.[1114]

The C.Q. redactors obviously chose to adopt the "moderate" Louisiania provisions. The C.N. articles, and their relationship to the *ancien droit* will be

---

[1110] See *Pan. fran.*, vol. 4, p. 329, where, on C.N. 374, the authors state: "L'exception portée par cette article n'était pas exprimée par les Lois anciennes, mais elle s'observait de même. Le père réclamait vainement un fils en âge de porter les armes qui s'était enrôlé voluntairement. On ne l'écoutait pas."

[1111] Fenet, *op. cit. supra* note 934, p. 85, comments on art. 374: "Pothier ne fixe l'âge auquel l'enfant pouvait s'enrôler sans le consentement."

[1112] Discussed *infra*, text at notes 1127–1135.

[1113] C.L. 238 is identical to D.O. 41 (p. 53), except for the addition of an extra paragraph, which states: "Ils ont également le droit d'engager leurs enfans comme apprentis." D.O. 41, is quoted (in English) *supra*, between notes 584 and 585.

[1114] *Second Report*, p. 203.

discussed below; it is convenient here to quote one author on the *ancien droit*, to show its attitude:

> Les pères et les mères ont droit de correction sur leurs enfans; ils peuvent même, s'ils sont indociles, les faire renfermer dans des Maisons de force, en vertu d'une simple Ordonnance du juge.[1115]

Thus, there were *ancien droit* equivalents to the C.N. articles the redactors have rejected. The redactors' own article, however, had authority from the *ancien droit*. Pothier stated that parents had a "droit de correction modérée" over their children.[1116] It is sufficient here to comment that the redactors' article is eminently reasonable, and has been influenced by the C.L.; the reasons for their rejection of the C.N.'s provisions will be canvassed later.

It will be recalled that the Quebec redactors stated that their title of four articles on *puissance paternelle* "has much analogy with that adopted by the Code of Louisiana. . . ."[1117] They also claim that their provisions are closer to the *ancien droit coutumier* than are those of the C.N.[1118] In fact, this statement about the C.L. made by the C.Q. redactors is misleading. The title of the C.L. which contains articles on paternal power and the nature of that power are not particularly close to the title and provisions of the C.Q. In fact, the title of the C.L. is the same as that of the D.O. already discussed, except for some insignificant changes in the relevant articles. Thus, we discussed D.O. 36 (p. 53) to D.O. 45 (p. 53); C.L. 233 to C.L. 242 are essentially the same articles.[1119] Thus, C.L. 239 gives parents the enjoyment of their children's property: this, as will be seen, is not a right parents have in Quebec, though it is granted by the C.N. C.L. 237 allows parents to appoint tutors to their offspring: again the C.Q. does not grant this power, though the C.N. does. Further, as already shown,[1120] in Louisiana children could leave home after they had reached the age of puberty: this is contrary to the C.Q. These major differences in the *content* of paternal power show that the nature of *puissance paternelle* in the Quebec code differs from that of the Louisiana code.

[1115] Pocquet, *op. cit. supra* note 619, bk. 1, tit. 2, sect. 1, no. 5.

[1116] Pother, *T.P.C.*, p. 51 (no. 132). Note that Pothier considered that this right of moderate correction extended so far as the imprisonment of the child. Fenet, *op. cit. supra* note 934, p. 85 states on art. 375: "Les père et mère avaient sur leurs enfans, jusqu'à ce qu'ils fussent en âge de se gouverner eux-mêmes, le droit d'une correction modérée." This statement would seem to have had some influence on the redaction of the Quebec article, and the redactors certainly cite it. They also cite, *inter alia*, the *Nouveau Denisart*, vol. 9, pp. 183, 201, s.v. *Garde Noble et Bourgeoise*. The latter reference is probably a mistake for p. 204. At p. 204, § XI, no. 1, it is pointed out that a *gardien* has a duty to educate the minor, whether in his own house or by sending him away.

[1117] *Second Report*, p. 203.

[1118] *Ibid.*

[1119] See *supra*, text at notes 560–606. C.L. 234 contains the amendment of D.O. 37 (p. 53) already noted *supra*, notes 562–567. C.L. 235 contains a minor amendment of D.O. 38 (p. 53); see *infra*, text at notes 1122–1123. C.L. 237 amends slightly D.O. 40 (p. 53). C.L. 238 slightly amends D.O. 41 (p. 53) as noted *supra*, in note 1113.

[1120] See *supra*, text at notes 1105–1111.

Further, the *form* of the Louisiana title differs considerably: as in the D.O., the title containing articles on paternal authority discusses respective rights and duties of parents and children (rights such as aliment).[1121] Here the C.Q. follows the order of the C.N. The C.Q. redactors also did not copy a provision of the C.L. that was taken from the *ancien droit*. C.L. 235 states thus:

> Tant que l'enfant reste sous la puissance de ses père et mère, il doit leur obéir dans tout ce qui n'est pas contraire aux lois et aux bonnes moeurs.

This provision[1122] echoes statements made by writers on the *ancien droit*.[1123] From the rejection of C.L. 235 by the redactors of the C.Q., it is obvious that they were not even following the C.L. where it agreed with the *droit coutumier*, much less where it disagreed with the *droit coutumier*. In fact, it seems plausible to suggest that C.L. 235 was rejected because there was no equivalent in the C.N. The only influence from the C.L. traceable in the C.Q. here is in C.Q. 245:[1124] and even in this article the form of the C.L. has not been followed in any way.

The statement of the Quebec redactors that the paternal authority in their code "has much analogy" with that in Louisiana[1125] is misleading in so far as it implies that paternal authority is of the same nature in the two codes, when in fact it is not. In many ways, the nature of paternal authority in the C.L. is much closer to that of paternal authority in the C.N. than that of paternal authority in the C.Q. The only similarity between the C.L. and the C.Q. not found in the C.N. is in relation to powers of correction. Certainly, the C.Q. articles are analogous to those of the C.L. in so far as they deal with the same fact-situations; but the Quebec provisions are also analogous to those of the C.N. in exactly the same way: and the redactors are here contrasting the difference between the C.Q. and the C.N. (the former having purportedly followed the *ancien droit coutumier* of Paris) with the analogy between the paternal authority found in the C.Q. and that found in the C.L.[1126]

[1121] See *supra*, text at notes 560–561.
[1122] An amended version of D.O. 38 (p. 53): see *supra*, text at note 567.
[1123] See e.g. Pothier, *T.C.M.*, p. 177 (no. 389).
[1124] See *supra*, text at notes 1112–1116.
[1125] See *supra*, text at note 1117.
[1126] This may be clearly understood from the redactors' comments, *Second Report*, p. 203: "The title '*De la puissance paternelle*' in the Code Napoleon, contains provisions quite different from those of the Roman law, and foreign to the old French jurisprudence, particularly in the parts governed by customary law, where it was even pretended that paternal authority had never existed, so much so that Loysel (liv. 1, Tit.1, art. 37) has given it as a rule of French law that 'The right of paternal authority does not exist'. —Nevertheless it is certain that, under the customs in France, there was formerly a species of paternal authority, although different from that of the Roman law, and that of the code.—The articles which follow give the rules of this authority, as admitted and practised within the jurisdiction of the Parliament of Paris; it has much analogy with that adopted by the code of Louisiana. . . ."

Certain Napoleonic and Customary Laws on Puissance Paternelle *Not Found in the Quebec Code*

Both the *ancien droit coutumier* and the C.N. contain provisions on paternal authority which were not incorporated into the C.Q. The Quebec redactors rejected these rules for various reasons. In their *Second Report*, they stated that the French code's title on paternal authority "contains many provisions quite different from those of the Roman law, and foreign to the old French jurisprudence, particularly in the parts governed by customary law…."[1127] They imply that they have rejected these rules because they are not found in the *ancien droit.*[1128]

The first provisions to be noted here are those already mentioned: the parental powers of correction. C.N. 375 states that

> Le père qui aura des sujets de mécontentement très-graves sur la conduite d'un enfant, aura les moyens de correction suivans.

C.N. 376–382 then provide for powers of incarceration of children, even by a surviving mother; these powers are carefully regulated, though we need not discuss the details.[1129] A right of incarceration also existed in the *ancien droit*, though its exercise was less regulated, and its content different in significant ways.[1130] Pocquet de Livonnière, as quoted, sets out the general rule of the *ancien droit*;[1131] Pothier gives a more detailed elaboration of the procedure.[1132] On the French code's provisions, the Quebec Codification Commissioners said:

> These rigorous measures, which were not wholly foreign to the old jurisprudence, rather making part of the public and criminal than of the private law, have been suppressed by the commissioners, who regard as sufficient, for ordinary cases, the right of correction accorded by article 4 [i.e. C.Q. 245], leaving the criminal laws and those of the police to provide for cases of a grave and exceptional character.[1133]

Under the *ancien régime*, as well as according to the C.N., it was ultimately the state that incarcerated, not the father; but, despite the Quebec redactors' statement, this right of the father's to have his child imprisoned derived from his paternal power—the courts, to a greater or lesser extent, merely regulated the exercise of that power. Even under the C.N., in some circumstances, the father

---

[1127] *Second Report*, p. 203.

[1128] See *supra*, quotation in note 1126.

[1129] For a discussion of the C.N.'s rules, see Toullier, *op. cit. supra* note 628, vol. 2, pp. 184–186, nos. 1050–1058; Marcadé, *op. cit. supra* note 928, vol. 2, pp. 144–1452, nos. 136–142.

[1130] The differences between the C.N. and the *ancien droit* are most easily grasped by looking at Fenet, *op. cit. supra* note 934, pp. 85–87, on arts. 376–383. Some notable differences are: the C.N. makes a distinction between the ages of the child—the *ancien droit* did not; contrary to the C.N., the *ancien droit* did not provide time limits; the *ancien droit* only required the mother to have the authority of the judge—the C.N. required approval by paternal relatives.

[1131] See *supra*, text at note 1115.

[1132] Pothier, *T.P.C.*, pp. 51–52 (nos. 132–133). See *supra*, text at notes 572–575.

[1133] *Second Report*, p. 203.

did not need to give reasons for the incarceration of the child: he need only demand it.[1134] Thus, to a certain extent, the Quebec redactors are rationalizing their reasons for rejecting this aspect of traditional *puissance paternelle*: the circumstances envisaged by the *ancien droit* and the C.N. would not all be dealt with under the criminal law. The Quebec redactors have chosen to reduce the authority of fathers here because they considered that such powers of incarceration were contrary to the *mores* of Quebec. In this they were undoubtedly correct. The Province would also lack the institutional framework necessary to permit such incarceration. That parents should be able to imprison their children would be contrary to the prevailing attitude on the nature of the relationship between parent and child, an attitude deriving from the contemporary conception of the close affective nuclear family. Further, that parents should have such powers would be unthinkable in a country where, already in the eighteenth century, the discipline of children was reported to be lax.[1135]

Under C.N. 389, the father had a right to administer the goods of his unemancipated minor child; this has already been noted in discussing the D.O.[1136] There is no equivalent article in the C.Q., though the Commissioners said that "the father, and in his default, the mother, as a general rule, have the right to the tutorship of their minor children, a charge which in fact gives them the administration of the property so long as the minor is unemancipated. . . ."[1137] Under the C.Q., the right to administer children's property is not dependent on having paternal authority but on appointment as tutor. The father's powers to administer are rather more fettered by the C.Q. than by the C.N., because under the Quebec code he is liable for his administration in the way any tutor would be. The father might have "a right to the tutorship"; but the appointment is made by the court: "le père ou la mère qui détient la puissance paternelle n'exerce la tutelle que s'il le demande."[1138] This exclusion of the right of administration might seem rather strange, especially when it is considered that the family was regarded in nineteenth-century Quebec as a most important social and political institution. This point will be considered further *infra*.[1139]

Under C.N. 384–387, parents had a right of usufruct in their children's property. This right was not adopted in the C.Q., the redactors of which said:

> This draft omits also the articles 384, 385, 386 and 387 of the Code Napoleon, relating to the enjoyment, granted in its system to the fathers and mothers, of the property of their children, up to the age of eighteen years, or up to the period of their emancipation. This enjoyment, granted by the code, is nearly the *garde bourgeoise* of the article 266 of the Custom of Paris, which does not exist in this country, where it never was introduced nor observed. . . . This, after

---

[1134] Marcadé, *op. cit. supra* note 928, vol. 2 pp. 144–146.
[1135] P. Garigue, *La vie familiale des Canadiens français: précédée d'une critique*, Montreal, Presses de l'université de Montréal, 1970, p. 16; see *supra*, chap. 2, text at notes 107–120.
[1136] See *supra*, text at notes 603–604.
[1137] *Second Report*, p. 205.
[1138] Baudouin, *op. cit. supra* note 551, p. 289.
[1139] See *infra*, text at notes 1158–1161.

> all, is not surprising, since the article 266 of the Custom only grants the *garde bourgeoise* 'to the fathers and mothers, burgesses of Paris', thus excluding those who were not so.[1140]

The accuracy of this argument as to why the parental usufruct was not introduced has been doubted by one author;[1141] but the Codification Commissioners are correct in their statement. Some *coutumes* allowed fathers to keep the fruits of the property of their sons;[1142] but if a *coutume* did not explicitly and specifically grant this right to a father, he did not have it, unless under *garde noble* or *bourgeoise*.[1143] The *Coutume de Paris* did not grant such a right to fathers. Thus, under the *Coutume de Paris*, there was no right of parental usufruct, except under *garde*. The *Coutume de Paris* accorded *garde noble* to the survivor of the mother or father, or, in their default, to an ascendant, whether male or female, over minor children up to the age of twenty for males or fifteen for females. *Garde bourgeoise*, according to the same *Coutume*, was granted to the survivor of the mother or father (not to other ascendants) over their minor children up to the age of fourteen for boys and twelve for girls.[1144] Pothier defines thus the Parisian *garde bourgeoise*:

> [L]e droit que la loi municipale accorde au survivant de deux conjoints bourgeois de Paris, de percevoir, à son profit, le revenu des biens que ses mineurs ont eu de la succession du prédécédé, jusqu'à ce qu'ils aient atteint un certain âge, sous certaines charges qu'elle lui impose, et en récompense de l'éducation desdits enfants qu'elle lui confie.[1145]

Under article 266 of the *Coutume de Paris*, *garde bourgeoise* applied only to the *bourgeoisie* of Paris, not to those of other towns regulated by the *Coutume*.[1146] It therefore is obvious that the system of *garde bourgeoise* would not be applied in Quebec. In the 1772 *Abstract of Canadian Law*, it was pointed out that articles 265–271 of the *Coutume* (that is, those dealing with *garde*) were revoked for Quebec,[1147] and in place of these articles, the authors of the *Abstract* gave an

---

1140 *Second Report*, pp. 203–205.

1141 Baudouin, *op. cit. supra* note 551, p. 189.

1142 See, e.g. the coutumes of Rheims, art. 8, Laon, art. 56, Châlons, art. 8, Sedan, art. 7, Bourbonnais, art. 174; Ferrière, *Corps et Comp.*, vol. 3, cols. 497–498, nos. 20–21. See *supra*, text at notes 134–136.

1143 Ferrière, *Corps et Comp.*, vol. 3, col. 498, no. 22, states: "Dans les Coûtumes qui n'en parlent point, le père ne gagne point les fruits des héritages donnez à son fils ou qui luy appartiennent de quelque maniere que ce soit, si ce n'est en vertu de la garde noble."

1144 Ferrière, *Corps et Comp.* vol. 3, cols. 946–947.

1145 Pothier, *T.G.N.B.*, p. 501 (no. 12).

1146 *Ancien Denisart*, vol. 2, pp. 503–510, s.v. *Garde*, at p. 504, no. 7: "Les bourgeois des autres villes régies par la coutume de Paris, n'ont pas la garde bourgeoise." Denisart states (*ibid.*) that this privilege of the Parisian *bourgeoisie* originated in letters patent issued by Charles V on 9 Aug. 1371, and Charles VI on 5 Aug. 1390.

1147 *An Abstract of those Parts of the Custom of the Viscounty and Provostship of Paris, which were Received and Practiced in the Province of Quebec, in the Time of the French Government, Drawn up be a Select Committee of Canadian Gentlemen, Well Skilled in the Laws of France, and*

account of the law on *tutelle* and *curatelle* as applied in the Province.[1148] The *garde bourgeoise* of the *Coutume de Paris* was exceptional in the *droit coutumier*: in most *coutumes*, a *gardien bourgeois* was only in the position of a legitimate tutor, and had no right to receive the revenue of the property of the minor.[1149]

C.N. 384–387 innovated, as regards most of the *coutumes* of northern France, in granting parents a usufruct of their children's property: this went far beyond the *coutumes*' generally limited provisions on *garde*. The system of *garde* itself apparently had not been applied in Quebec, and, therefore, it is not surprising that the redactors did not introduce the right of usufruct found in the C.N., given their generally conservative approach to codification. Before this is finally decided on, however, it is appropriate to discuss *tutelle*. It may be pointed out that Maleville thoroughly approved of the French Code's system of parental usufruct, to the extent that he believed it should not end on the minor child's reaching the age of eighteen years.[1150]

C.N. 390 provided that a surviving parent was entitled, as of right, to the *tutelle* of any minor children of the marriage.[1151] C.N. 397 permitted surviving parents to appoint tutors to their minor children. Neither of these rights exist in the Quebec code, because under C.Q. 249 all tutorships are dative: in this, the C.Q. follows the *ancien droit coutumier*. The Roman law allowed testamentary, legitimate and dative tutorships, and the C.N. has adopted, adapted and expanded on the categories of the Roman law.[1152] Pothier said the following:

> Dans la plupart de nos coutumes, il n'y a qu'une espèce de tutelle, qui est la *dative*, c'est-à-dire celle qui est donnée par le magistrat, sur l'avis des parents des mineurs; et de ce nombre est la coutume de Paris."[1153]

According to the *droit coutumier*, if a father left a will in which he named a tutor to his minor child, great respect would be paid to his wishes, but the tutor's appointment would have to be confirmed by the judge on the advice of the

---

of that Province, by the Desire of the Honourable Guy Carleton, Esquire, Governor in Chief of the said Province, London, printed by Charles Eyre and William Strahan, 1772, p. ii.

[1148] *Ibid.*, pp. 97–99.

[1149] See Pothier, *T.G.N.B.*, p. 501 (nos. 11–13).

[1150] Maleville, *Analyse*, vol. 1, pp. 351–355.

[1151] C.N. 389 and 390 are not located in the title on paternal power, though they rightly belong there, as pointed out by Marcadé, *op. cit. supra* note 928, vol. 2, pp. 156–161, nos. 147–153. The D.O. is rather better organized in this respect.

[1152] See the remarks of the Quebec redactors in their *Second Report*, pp. 205–207. On the Roman law, see e.g. Buckland, *Textbook*, pp. 142–149. On the C.N., see Toullier, *op. cit. supra* note 628, vol. 2, p. 197, nos. 1085–1086, and Marcadé *op. cit. supra* note 928, vol. 2, pp. 285–297, resumé of tit. 10.

[1153] Pothier, *T.P.C.*, pp. 55–56 (no. 146). Pocquet, *op. cit. supra* note 619, pp. 45–46 (bk. 1, tit. 2, sect. 3, art. 21) stated: "Toutes les tutelles sont datives en France hors en quelques Coutumes, comme celles d'Anjou et du Maine, où il y a des tutelles naturelles et légitimes en faveur du père et de la mère seulement."

nearest relatives.[1154] Similarly, it was customary for the surviving parent to be appointed tutor;[1155] and if no election of tutor had been made, the survivor of the mother or father would be reputed tutor.[1156] The principle, however, was certain: all tutorships were dative.[1157] In C.Q. 249, the redactors have followed the *ancien droit*, and rejected innovations possibly suggested by the C.N.

It is now convenient to consider the implications of the preference shown for the old law over the provisions of C.N. 384–387, 389 and 390. It is important first of all to note that the Quebec redactors have a generally conservative outlook on the law, and are not usually concerned to introduce change unless absolutely necessary. Moreover, in Quebec, family ties were notably strong and close, the family being regarded as the foundation of the social fabric. This said, Maleville obviously regarded the provisions of these articles of the C.N. on parental usufruct, administration and tutorship as reflecting and asserting the importance and cohesion of the family;[1158] and he even believed that parental rights in these areas should be increased.[1159] Toullier, in discussing this topic stated:

> Le Code n'a voulu rétablir ni le droit de garde, ni la jurisprudence des pays de droit écrit, qui dépouillait les enfans pendant la vie de leurs pères, sans rien accorder aux mères; mais il a voulu accorder aux pères et aux mères une indemnité des peines, des soins et des responsabilités qu'entrainait l'éducation des enfans et l'administration de leurs biens. Il n'est pas juste que la garde des enfans ne soit, dans tous les cas, qu'une charge pour les pères et mères. D'un autre côté, il est contraire à la morale de ne présenter aux enfans le survivant de leur père et mère, que sous l'aspect d'un tuteur ou d'un homme d'affaires, dont les, comptes doivent être rendus de clerc à maitre et suîvis de discussions, souvent de procès, qui ne peuvent s'accorder avec la piété filiale, et qui exposent toujours les enfans à un très grand mal, la perte de la bienveillance et de l'affection de leurs père et mère.[1160]

This argument would be applicable in Quebec, where, the only form of tutorship being dative, a parent, as tutor, would be subject to all the liabilities and duties of any tutor. That parents' actions on their children's behalf should be controlled in this way would be contrary to the current conceptions of the parent and child tie. Further, the right of a parent to appoint a tutor to his or her minor child is a reflection of the value placed on the relationship between parent and child. These articles of the C.N. granting parental administration, usufruct and tutor-

---

[1154] Loisel, *op. cit. supra* note 62, bk. 1, tit. 4, rule 7: "Toutesfois quant par le testament y a tuteur nommé, il doit estre confirmé, si les parens n'allèguent cause légitime que le deffunct eust vraysemblablement ignoré." See also Maleville, *Analyse*, vol. 1, p. 360.

[1155] See the *Abstract of Canadian Law supra* note 1147, p. 97: "Le père ou la mère survivant est ordinairement préféré pour la tutelle, et à son défaut, un des plus proches parents. . . ."

[1156] *Ibid.*, p. 98; Ferrière, *Corps et Comp.*, vol. 3, col. 497, no. 19.

[1157] Loisel, *op. cit. supra* note 62, bk. 1, tit. 4, rule 6 concisely said: "Les tuteles sont datives." The humanist Pasquier, *op. cit. supra* note 992, p. 122 (ch. 47), disapproved of the application of the Roman term "dative" to a rather different legal institution.

[1158] Maleville, *Analyse*, vol. 1, pp. 351–353.

[1159] *Ibid.*, vol. 1, pp. 351–352.

[1160] Toullier, *op. cit. supra* note 628, vol. 2, pp. 187–188, no. 1060.

ship all asserted the special closeness of the domestic relationship between parents and their children, a closeness bound up with the growth of the affective family. Roman law had granted fathers great rights in their children's separate property; but such rights were derived from the power fathers had over their children in a hierarchical family. It seems likely that, given the stress placed on the family in Quebec, the rules of the C.N. would have asserted the contemporary values invested in family life more than those of the *ancien droit* in fact did. That this was so was not enough, however, to defeat the conservative attitude to codification taken by the redactors, who must have considered there to be no need for reform.

This part of the chapter has been devoted to explaining the reasons for the C.Q. redactors' rejection of some rules of the *ancien droit* and the C.N. on paternal power. A notable absence from the C.Q. is that no provision allows a father to emancipate his son: this will be discussed below.[1161] A right that parents had according to the *ancien droit* and the C.N. was that of consenting to or opposing the marriage of their *adult* children. The next part of this section will be devoted to paternal power and the marriage of *enfants de famille*.

The Marriage of Enfants de Famille

As in the discussion of Louisiana,[1162] at issue here are certain parental rights in relation to the marriage of their children: their right to oppose a marriage; and their right to seek the annulment of a marriage.

The Canon law and the *ancien droit* have been discussed above, and it is merely necessary here to point out that, for the validity of the marriages of minor children, the *ancien droit* required the consent of the parents: if the children did not have such consent, their marriages were annullable, and parents could always oppose such a marriage.[1163] Sons over thirty and daughters over twenty-five could validly marry without parental consent, but were liable to being disinherited, unless they had sent an *acte de sommation respectueuse* seeking consent to marry.[1164] If the mother or father of the minor child were dead, the tutor or curator had to consent to the marriage, after having taken the advice of the nearest relatives. Adults whose mother and father were dead had no restriction of any kind on their marriage.[1165]

The C.N. changed this. To recap what has been said in connection with the D.O., C.N. 148 provides that sons under twenty-five and daughters under twenty-one could not marry without the consent of their parents; if they disagreed, that of the father sufficed. C.N. 149 states that if one parent were dead or incapable, the consent of the other sufficed. C.N. 150 enacts that if there be

---

[1161] See *infra*, text at notes 1212–1227.

[1162] See *supra*, text at notes 607–668.

[1163] See *supra*, text at notes 610–618. The Canon law did not invalidate such marriages. The route of the *ancien droit* to reach invalidity was circuitous.

[1164] See *supra*, text at notes 619–620.

[1165] See *supra*, text after note 622.

no parents alive or capable of consenting, the grandparents' consent is required. If the grandparents of one line disagree, then the consent of the grandfather of that line suffices; while if there be disagreement between the lines, this amounts to consent. C.N. 160 provides that should there be no father, mother or other ascendant or should such be incapable of consenting, then sons and daughters under twenty-one years may not marry without the consent of the family council. As regards adult *enfants de famille*, C.N. 151–154 have a complex system of *actes respectueuses*, which children were required to send to their parents before they could marry without parental consent. If their parents were dead or incapable, then children had to send such *actes* to their grandparents, if alive.[1166] The C.N., however, attaches no penalty of disinheritance to the failure to send such *actes*.[1167]

The *ancien droit* on oppositions has been discussed above: essentially, any one claiming the right could bring an opposition to any marriage.[1168]

The Quebec code's rules on consent to the marriage of minors are contained in five articles, C.Q. 119–123:

> 119. Children who have not reached the age of twenty-one years must obtain the consent of their father and mother before contracting marriage; in case of disagreement, the consent of the father suffices.
>
> 120. If one of them be dead or unable to express his will, the consent of the other suffices.
>
> 122. If there be neither father nor mother, or if both be unable to express their will, minor children, before contracting marriage, must obtain the consent of their tutor, or, in cases of emancipation, their curator, who is bound, before giving such consent, to take the advice of a family council, duly called to deliberate on the subject.
>
> 123. Respectful requisitions to the father and mother are no longer necessary.[1169]

C.Q. 119 and 120 are essentially the same as C.N. 148 and 149, bar that, under the C.N., sons required consent until they reached twenty-five years.[1170] The rules in the Quebec code, allowing for the difference in the age of majority, follow those of the *ancien droit*.[1171]

[1166] See *supra*, text, at notes 626–631 for fuller account.

[1167] See *supra*, text at notes 626–31.

[1168] See *supra*, text at notes 764–790.

[1169] C.Q. 121 deals with the marriages of minor illegitimate children, and is omitted as not relevant here.

[1170] Maleville, *Analyse*, vol. 1, p. 147 explains thus the reason for the difference in the C.N: "la nature a rendu les filles plus précoces, et qu'il importe pour la conservation de moeurs de les marier plutôt."

[1171] Under the *ancien droit*, the right to have one's consent to one's children's marriages required was an aspect of *puissance paternelle*, belonging to both parents, but exercised during the marriage by the father. On default of the father, the mother's consent was required. In theory, as Pothier points out, the consent of both parents was required; but that of the father was the deciding one. See Pothier, *T.C.M.*, pp. 140–144 (nos. 324–328); Pothier, *T.P.C.*, p. 52 (nos. 134–135).

C.Q. 122, however, does not follow the French code. C.N. 150 grants to the ascendants the right to consent; there being no ascendants capable of consenting, under C.N. 160, the consent of the family council is required. Here the Quebec redactors have followed the *ancien droit*: failing the mother or father, the consent of the tutor or curator is to be required, and he has to have taken the advice of the nearest relatives, as provided by article 43 of the *Ordonnance de Blois*.[1172] In this area of the law, the Quebec Code has stayed closer to the old customary law notions of *puissance paternelle*, in so far as a minor, on the death of his parents, became himself a *père de famille*, outwith the control of his grandparents, though under certain legal disabilities because of his age.[1173] The French provisions in C.N. 150 and 160, by giving authority over the marriages of minors to grandparents and then to close relatives, juridically enhanced the status of the wider family. These provisions were also in accord with the modern notion that *puissance paternelle* was an institution designed for the protection and care of minors. Were a minor's parents dead, those who could generally be considered to have most affection and care for him would be his grandparents. The development of the affective family gave an increased importance to close relatives, joined to the smaller family unit by links of affection.[1174] C.N. 160, if there were no grandparents, and a family council had been called, makes no provision for the judicial regulation of the family council; its decision, however, could be reviewed.[1175] Under C.Q. 122, the family council has only to be consulted by the tutor for its opinion: again, this follows the *ancien droit*. The Quebec redactors took the term "family council", "conseil de famille", from the C.N.;[1176] but they kept, in general, the old procedures relating to the "assemblée de parents", which had to be called by the judge, the decision of which had to be accepted by the judge to have any force.[1177] Here, because of their legal conservatism, the Quebec redactors have rejected the enhanced role played by the family under the provisions of the C.N.: a role which the *mores* of Quebec and the values of the period might well have upheld.[1178]

C.Q. 123 provides that respectful requisitions (*sommations respectueuses*) are no longer required. The *ancien droit* and provisions of the C.N. have already been described.[1179] The Quebec codifiers have rejected this whole procedure.

[1172] See Pothier, *T.C.M.*, pp. 146–147 (nos. 333 and 336). The royal legislation referred to by the redactors may be found discussed in Pothier.

[1173] See Henrys, *op. cit. supra* note 116, vol. 2, pp. 338–339 (bk. IV, quest. 12): "c'est une erreur de croire que le père mort, les enfans qu'il laisse retombent en la puissance de leur ayeul paternel."

[1174] See *supra*, text at notes 46–47.

[1175] See Toullier, *op. cit. supra* note 628, vol. 1, p. 326, no. 547.

[1176] So they state in their *Second Report*, p. 207, in discussing *tutelle*.

[1177] See *Ancien Denisart*, vol. 1, pp. 216–217, s.v. *Avis de Parens*, esp. nos. 1, 2 and 8.

[1178] This rejection of the French code's stress on the family is visible in other Quebec provisions. Compare, e.g., C.Q. 121 with the second paragraph of C.N. 159. Compare also the following provisions on *tutelle*: C.Q. 249 with C.N. 405; C.Q. 290 with C.N. 450; C.Q. 293 with C.N. 452; C.Q. 296 with C.N. 456; C.Q. 297 with C.N. 457; C.Q. 309 with C.N. 470; C.Q. 315 with C.N. 477–478; C.Q. 318 with C.N. 480.

[1179] See *supra*, text at notes 618–620 and 626–631.

They stated that it had fallen into disuse in Quebec, and that the reason for its incorporation in the C.N. was "to inspire greater respect for the paternal authority, which the revolution had done much to weaken."[1180] They remarked that such *sommations* "are not consonant with our state of society, and are not only useless and without object, but are calculated to produce a result quite different from that desired."[1181] They explained:

> In reality these requisitions are only made after the consent has been asked and refused, that is to say, when the child is perfectly determined to marry, and the father equally determined to refuse his consent. In such a position can it be reasonably presumed that the child will abandon his project, or the father his opposition, in consequence of a step more insulting than respectful and more irritating than conciliatory.[1182]

The original intention of *sommations respectueuses* had been to prevent parents from being able, should they have so desired, to disinherit their adult children from marrying against their wishes. This was no longer important in Quebec, where free testation had been introduced;[1183] the French codifiers, however, had included a system of *actes respectueuses* in their code, without providing that failure to send such an *acte* should result in disinheritance. The aim of this revival of the necessity of adult children to request parental consent to their marriages was to encourage respect for paternal authority.[1184] Given the background to codification in Quebec, the same need to assert control over children would not be felt: the Province had not just been the scene of events as dramatic and destabilizing as the French Revolution. Further, the whole notion of *sommations respectueuses* would be one alien to the doctrines of liberal individualism that were influential in nineteenth-century Quebec, whereby adults were regarded as autonomous agents unless they were prodigals or insane.[1185]

Since oppositions to marriage have already been discussed, there is no need to do more here than sketch in the general system of the C.Q. The *ancien droit* had permitted anyone to oppose a marriage who claimed the right; the Quebec code, following the example of the C.N., but going farther than the latter, restricted to a very small class those entitled to make oppositions.[1186]

1180 *Second Report*, p. 177. This statement of the Quebec redactors obviously is taken from Maleville, *Analyse*, vol. 1, p. 152: "Leur objet est d'inspirer plus de respect pour l'autorité paternelle, que la révolution a beaucoup affaibli."

1181 *Second Report*, p. 179.

1182 *Ibid.*

1183 *Ibid.*, pp. 177–179; A. Morel, "L'apparition de la succession testamentaire", 26 *R.duB.* (1966), pp. 499–521.

1184 Maleville, *Analyse*, vol. 1, p. 152: see *supra*, note 1180.

1185 See *supra*, chap. 2, text at notes 93–120. Not every Quebec lawyer would have agreed with the C.Q. redactors that *sommations respectueuses* were not required: see E. Deleury, M. Rivet, and J.-M. Neault, "De la puissance paternelle à l'autorité parentelle: une institution en voie de trouver sa vraie finalité", 15 *Les Cahiers de Droit* (1974), pp. 779–870 at p. 859, n. 267.

1186 See *supra*, text at notes 764–790.

The provisions to be considered here are set out in articles 137 to 139 of the C.Q.:

> 137. The marriage of a minor may be opposed by his father, or in default of the latter, by his mother.
>
> 138. In default of both father and mother, the tutor or, in cases of emancipation, the curator may also oppose the marriage of such minor; but the court to which such opposition is submitted, cannot decide on its merits without the advice of a family council, which it must order to be called.
>
> 139. If there be neither father nor mother, tutor nor curator, or if the tutor or curator have consented without taking the advice of a family council, the grandfathers and grandmothers, the uncles and aunts, and the cousins-german, who are of full age, may oppose the marriage of their minor relative; but only in the two following cases:
>
> 1. When a family council, which, according to article 122, should have been consulted, has not been so;
> 2. When the party to be married is insane.

The equivalent provisions of the C.N. may be found quoted elsewhere, and it is not necessary to repeat them here.[1187] They restricted the class of those entitled to oppose a marriage, the intention being to prevent abuse of the right of opposition.[1188] All those named in the C.N. and the C.Q. could have opposed the marriage under the *ancien droit*.[1189]

The *ancien droit* was restricted by the French codifiers because it was open to abuse: the Quebec redactors followed the French code for the same reason, and they considered it a great improvement;[1190] but they did not adopt the particular rules of the C.N. First, in the C.Q. opposition is restricted to the marriage of minors;[1191] this is consistent with the law on consents. In the C.N., the marriage of adults might be opposed by their ascendants.[1192] Second, in the C.N., the right of tutors and curators to oppose was postponed to after that of ascendants and collaterals, and then they could only oppose on the authority of a meeting of the family council.[1193] In Quebec, the law was the opposite: in

---

[1187] C.N. 173–175: quoted *supra* in note 178, and *infra* in note 1193.

[1188] *Pan. fran.*, vol. 3, p. 245: "Autrefois, toute personne, quelle qu'elle fût, pouvait former opposition au mariage. Cette grande liberté était un abus qui servait merveilleusement la méchanceté, la jalousie et l'envie de nuire."

[1189] See Pothier, *T.P.M.*, p. 33 (no. 81).

[1190] *Second Report*, p. 185.

[1191] There is one exception. The marriage of an adult can be opposed on the grounds of insanity: C.Q. 141. There is no equivalent article in the C.N., as the proposed marriage of an insane adult could be opposed under the general articles on opposition. See also C.Q. 142 and C.N. 174, second paragraph.

[1192] C.N. 173.

[1193] C.N. 175 and 174. C.N. 175 states: "Dans les deux cas prévus par le précédant article, le tuteur ou curateur ne pourra, pendant la durée de la tutelle ou curatelle, former opposition qu'autant qu'il y aura été autorisé par un conseil de famille, qu'il pourra convoquer." C.N. 175 is the only article of C.N. 172–175 not quoted in note 178 *supra*.

default of parents, tutors and curators opposed, before other ascendants and collaterals, and such tutors and curators need only have consulted the family council. It was only after tutors and curators, and in very restricted circumstances, that ascendants and collaterals could oppose.[1194] The C.N. provision restricting the rights of tutors and curators to oppose was completely new law, as they had always been entitled to oppose the marriages of their charges; and at least one French commentary (referred to by the Quebec redactors) did not approve of these new provisions on tutors and curators.[1195] The French code's provisions arguably gave more importance to the family; while the Quebec redactors innovated by extending the *ancien droit* in a logical fashion, so that the right to oppose a marriage was restricted to coincide with the requirement of consent. On the death of the father and mother, the tutor became more important than grandparents, brothers, sisters, uncles or aunts. Baudouin remarked:

> Dans les familles aussi unies que le sont les familles québecoises, ou les plus veilles traditions semblent s'être maintenues, il est incontestable que les aieux jouent dans la domaine de l'autorité morale un rôle plus considérable que le tuteur ou le curateurs.[1196]

The redactors chose to innovate by restricting the right to oppose to tutors and curators, should the parents of a minor be dead: they rejected the French codifiers' stress on the importance of family relationships.

The final topic relevant here is the effect of lack of consent to the marriage of minors. C.Q. 150 states:

> A marriage contracted without the consent of the father or mother, tutor or curator, or without the advice of a family council, in cases where such consent or advice was necessary, can only be attacked by those whose consent or advice was required.

The *ancien droit* was the same as the rule in C.Q. 150. The father and mother could attack the marriage, or, if there were no father and mother, the tutor could attack the marriage as "présumé entaché de séduction".[1197] In the *ancien droit* the other relatives generally could not attack a marriage for any reason while the parties lived, as it was presumed that such relatives could have no interest in doing so; but after the death of one of the parties to the marriage, the other relatives could attack the validity of the marriage, but not for *vices respectifs*, only for *vices absolus*. Lack of parental consent was one of the *vices respectifs*: other relatives therefore could not attack a marriage should some necessary

---

[1194] Note that the C.N. includes brothers and sisters among collaterals, curiously omitted in the C.Q., probably because of oversight.

[1195] *Pan. fran.* vol. 3, p. 248: "C'est disposition est absolument neuve, elle est exorbitante du Droit commun. Elle est contraire à tout ce qui s'est pratiqué jusqu'à présent." The authors felt that since the tutor had the care of the person of a minor, he ought not to be deprived of the power of opposition.

[1196] Baudouin, *op. cit. supra* note 551, p. 178.

[1197] Pothier, *T.C.M.*, p 204 (no. 447).

consent be wanted. Thus, in the *ancien droit* only the mother, father, tutor or curator could attack a marriage should their consent have been required and not been given; other relatives could not attack on these grounds, since their consent could never be required.[1198] The equivalent article of the French code, C.N. 182, provides:

> Le mariage contracté sans le consentement des père et mère, des ascendans, ou du conseil de famille, dans les cas où ce consentement était nécessaire, ne pout étre attaqué que par ceux dont le consentement était requis, ou par celui des deux époux qui avait besoin de ce consentement.

The grounds on which the marriage might be attacked are the same as those determining whose consents were required. In contrast to the C.Q., the C.N. here places more importance on the family. The Quebec code excluded the family in favour of the tutor, who needed only *to consult* the family, whereas the French code provided that the family should sue for annulment, and when the tutor sued, he was acting *as directed* by the family council. An important difference in the C.N. is that the spouse who required such consent may sue on the grounds that it is wanting. This is an innovation on the system of the *ancien droit*. The C.Q. redactors gave no indication as to why they rejected this: presumably they saw no good reason for this change, which they alluded to in their discussion of the next article of the C.N., 183.[1199] The C.N. here permits a minor to annul a marriage he or she has contracted; this seems rather inconsistent, and there appears to be no good reason for allowing a minor to do this. The C.N. rule perhaps lays more stress on the minor's need for care: the minor requires the consent of his ascendants, for his own protection; if they be indifferent or neglectful, he may himself seek the annulment of his inappropriate marriage, should the required consent not have been given. Such at least is the explanation of Toullier for this rule.[1200] No such considerations have weighed with the Quebec redactors, who have preferred to preserve the *ancien droit*.[1201]

Toullier stated that:

[1198] See generally Pothier, *T.C.M.*, pp. 203–204 (nos. 446–448).

[1199] *Second Report*, p. 185. The redactors state that for C.Q. 151 they have adopted the new rule of C.N. 183, but struck off the last paragraph of the C.N. article, as they have kept old law that a minor cannot attack his own marriage for lack of necessary consent by parents or tutors.

[1200] Toullier, *op. cit. supra* note 628, vol. 1, p. 357, no. 613: "L'indifférence des ascendans ou de la famille ne doit pas priver du bénéfice de la loi celui des deux époux qui avait besoin de leur consentement. Si les plaintes d'un mineur qui a été surpris dans une convention peu importante, sont écoutée favorablement, on doit, à plus forte raison, lui accorder la même faveur, lorsqu'il demande à être restitué contre l'aliénation qu'il a faite de tous ses biens et de sa personne. Tel est le motif de la demande en nullité que le Code l'autorise à former." Note how far removed this is from the Canon law conception of marriage.

[1201] They have departed from the *ancien droit* in C.Q. 151, copying C.N. 183's provision of a time limit within which actions under C.N. 150 would have to be brought. The redactors regarded this as a useful improvement, and, taken with the reform in C.Q. 149 adopted from C.N. 181, the redactors obviously were seeking certainty. *Second Report*, p. 185.

> De toutes les actions de l'homme, le mariage est une de celles qui intéressent le plus sa destinée; et comme les facultés et les forces du corps se développent avant celles de l'esprit, l'homme se trouve habile à contracter mariage avant que l'âge ait muri sa raison, et qu'il soit en état de faire un choix éclair. Dans le premier âge des passions, la loi ne l'abandonne point à lui-même; elle lui donne un guide pour le diriger dans l'acte peut-être le plus important de sa vie.[1202]

The French code provided that, should there be no mother and father, the guides of an *enfant de famille* should be his ascendants or other close relatives. Ascendants even had some control over the marriages of *enfants de famille* who were adult. The Quebec code chose a different system: there could only be control over the marriages of minors, and should there be no mother and father to exercise such control, it passed to tutors and curators. To some extent the Quebec redactors were merely carrying out their instructions, and embodying in the code the rules of the *ancien droit*. Legal conservatism prevented them from embodying in their code rules giving more prominence to the family, a prominence the family probably merited in Quebec, given the strength and cohesion of family life in the Province at the period of redaction. In their rules on oppositions, however, the redactors were not following the *ancien droit*, but were innovating by restricting the class of those entitled to oppose a marriage. In their innovations, they did not recognize that grandparents and other close relatives undoubtedly were regarded as having much greater moral authority over their minor relatives than tutors or curators.[1203] The redactors here merely made a logical extension of the rules on consents: they provided that it was up to tutors and curators to oppose the marriages of their charges. Though the redactors here perhaps could have given more weight to the family, since they were already innovating, it is probably unrealistic to have expected them to do so. Given the nature of the code, it was obvious for the redactors to provide the rules they in fact did provide on oppositions, especially when tutors and curators were specifically mentioned by Pothier as being entitled to oppose their charges' marriages: and Pothier generally exercised great influence on the Quebec redactors.[1204] The Quebec rules here may all be attributed to legal factors, rather than any consideration of the nature of family life in the Province. The most effective reforms in this area of the law were perhaps those contained in C.Q. 149 and 151 laying down time limits within which should be brought actions seeking to annul a marriage on the grounds of want of the requisite consents. These reforms, adopted from C.N. 181 and 183, made for greater certainty as to

---

[1202] Toullier, *op. cit. supra* note 628, vol. 1, p. 322, no. 540.

[1203] Toullier, *op. cit. supra* note 628, vol. 1, pp. 325–326, no. 546, states: "La nécessité du consentement des père et mère ou ascendans au mariage de leurs enfans et petits enfans qui n'ont pas atteint l'âge de vingt-cinq ou vingt-et-un ans, est fondée sur l'amour des parens, sur leur raison, sur l'incertitude de celle des enfans, et surtout sur l'autorité de cette magistrature domestique que la loi donne aux pères et mères, et qui s'étend en ce point aux aïeuls at aïeules."

[1204] See Pothier, *T.C.M.* p. 33 (no. 81): "Ces oppositions sont aussi quelquefois formées par les parents, surtout par le père, mère tuteurs ou curateurs qui prétendent avoir droit d'empêcher le mariage de l'une des parties."

whether or not a marriage was valid.[1205] They were not motivated, however, by any consideration of the state of Quebec family life.

How *Puissance Paternelle* Ends

In general, the two most obvious ways in which *puissance paternelle* ended in Quebec were, first, by the child reaching majority, and, second, by the death of the parents, with the difference that, in the latter case, some of the authority came into the hands of a tutor or curator, though it could no longer properly be called paternal authority. This conformed to the *ancien droit coutumier.*[1206] Pothier, of course, pointed out that some aspects of *puissance paternelle* only ended on the death of the parents of the child. Thus, the necessity to seek parental approval to one's marriage continued.[1207] In Quebec, however, adults no longer were required to send *sommations respecteuses*. The French code's provisions were essentially similar, except that on the death of his parents, a child seemed to a certain extent to fall into a residuary power held by his grandparents. With the above qualifications, it may be said that the C.Q., the C.N., and the *droit coutumier* agreed: *puissance paternelle* ended on the death of the parents or the majority of the child. C.Q. 246 fixed the age of majority as twenty-one years; C.N. 388 did likewise. In the *ancien droit*, most *coutumes* fixed the age of majority at twenty-five years.[1208] In France, the law of September, 1792, fixed majority at twenty-one, and the Code preserved this.[1209] In Quebec, the age of majority had been lowered to twenty-one years in 1782 by an ordinance of the Governor, probably under the influence of English law, and to confirm with the general practice of the British Empire.[1210] The codifiers, not unnaturally, retained twenty-one years as the age of majority; it was also the age of majority for purposes of public law.[1211] The two articles which state the age of majority— C.Q. 246 and 324—borrow their expression from C.N. 388 and 488.

The third method of ending paternal authority in Quebec law was by emancipation, as C.Q. 243 states. The Quebec codifiers stated that the Roman form of

---

[1205] *Second Report*, p. 185; see *supra*, note 1201.

[1206] See C.Q. 243; Pothier, *T.P.C.*, p. 52 (no. 134).

[1207] See, e.g., Pothier, *T.P.C.*, p. 52 (nos. 134–1350.

[1208] Ferrière, *Corps et Comp.*, vol. 3, col. 499, no. 28: "C'est l'usage de la France coutumière que les enfans sortent de la puissance de leur père à l'âge de 25 ans accomplis." The fixing of the age of majority at 25 was, according to the *Pandectes françaises*, due to the influence of Roman law; before this happened, different *coutumes* had made differing provisions, depending on the status of the child as *noble* or *roturier*. "La découverte des Pandectes, et l'étude du droit Romain, qui s'étabit partout, introduisirent un changement dans les Coutumes. Lors de leur rédaction, on fixa généralement l'époque de majorité à vingt-cinq ans." Some *coutumes* kept to other ages for majority; e.g. Anjou, Maine and Normandy. On all this, see *Pan. fran.*, vol. 4, pp. 471–474; Ferrière, *Corps et Comp.*, vol. 3, col. 499, no. 28.

[1209] See Maleville, *Analyse*, vol. 1, pp. 356–357.

[1210] Found quoted in L. Saint-Laurent, "Majeurs et mineurs: quelques particularités du droit de Quebec à cet egard", in *Droit civil français supra* note 472, pp. 155–162 at p. 155. It became C.S.L.C. ch. 34, sec. 1.

[1211] Saint-Laurent, *op. cit. supra* note 1210, pp. 155–158.

emancipation was intended to release a son from his father's *potestas*, while emancipation in Quebec freed a minor from *tutelle*, and constituted him administrator of his own property under the protection of a curator charged to assist him.[1212] They stated that this form of emancipation differed from that of the C.N., which, admitting paternal power, necessarily permitted these to whom it belonged to liberate those subject to it.[1213] (This should not be taken to imply that there could be no emancipation ending paternal power as it exists in the Quebec code.) The codifiers added that the methods of emancipation recognized by Quebec are those found in the *Coutume de Paris*, namely, emancipation by marriage and letters of the Prince.[1214]

Before discussing the above, it is useful to review some aspects of the relationship between parent and child according to the Quebec law on *puissance paternelle*. First, the authority belongs to both parents, though the father exercises it during the marriage. Second, the father has a right to keep the children with him and to punish them, and they cannot marry without his consent. Third, the paternal power of Quebec does not give a father any rights over his children's property; he would only have rights over it and control were he also his children's tutor. Under the *Coutume de Paris*, as interpreted,[1215] a father would not have control over any of his children's property simply by virtue of his position as father; only under *garde noble* or *bourgeoise* would he have power over the property of his children. Fourth, in both the Quebec law and the *ancien droit*, the legal incapacities of children derive not from their being *fils de famille*, but from their status as minors: neither the C.Q. nor the *ancien droit* allow minors to administer their property unless emancipated, and, if emancipated, they can only freely use their moveables and administer their immoveables.[1216]

The commentators on the *ancien droit* noted that emancipation could end *puissance paternelle*. Pothier stated that, "La puissance paternelle, quant à la première partie, finit . . . par la majorité de l'enfant, par son mariage, . . . et par l'émancipation";[1217] while Ferrière remarked (on article 239 of the *Coutume de Paris*) that, by marriage, children "sont delivrez de la puissance paternelle, et de l'autorité de leurs tuteurs et curateurs, s'ils sont en tutelle."[1218] These authors were clear that emancipation brought about the end of paternal power; this was also the

---

[1212] *Second Report*, p. 219.

[1213] *Ibid.*, p. 221.

[1214] *Ibid.*, p. 221.

[1215] See Guyot, *op. cit. supra* note 730, vol. 14, p. 93, s.v. "puissance paternelle", where it is pointed out that at some time a more Roman paternal authority had been known at Paris.

[1216] See Ferrière, *Corps et Comp.*, vol. 3, col. 499, no. 29.

[1217] Pothier, *T.P.C.*, p. 52 (no. 134).

[1218] Ferrière, *Corps et Comp.*, vol. 3, col. 493, no. 1. At *ibid.*, vol. 3, col. 499, no. 29, he states thus: "[D]ans toute la France coutumiere le mariage délivre l'homme et la femme de la puissance du père..." He has already said that "Le mariage est aussi un moyen d'émanciper les enfans . . . ." Henrys, *op. cit. supra* note 116, vol. 2, p. 338 (bk. 4, quest.13) says: "[P]arce qu'en France le mariage émancipe, le fils marié sort de la puissance du père, est fait père de famille, et par consequent a ses enfans en sa puissance, lesquels autrement par le Droit Romain seroient aussi bien que le père en la puissance de l'ayeul."

position in Quebec. If we turn to consideration of the Quebec redactors' remarks on emancipation and *puissance paternelle*,[1219] it is now clear that what they meant is that both the C.N. and the Roman law permitted a father *as a father* to liberate his children from his own power, while the *puissance paternelle* of Quebec could not be ended in this way. In the Quebec law, emancipation is not a method used by a *père de famille* to liberate his children; but rather emancipation by the two methods considered below brings a father's power over his children to an end, as indeed C.Q. 243 expressly states: "He [i.e. the child] remains subject to their authority until his majority or emancipation. . . ."

C.Q. 314 states: "Every minor is, of right, emancipated by marriage." C.N. 476 has an identical provision. Thus, emancipation by marriage frees a child from *puissance paternelle*. The *ancien droit* was the same.[1220]

C.Q. 315 is an interesting article; it provides:

> An unmarried minor may, at his own request, or that of his tutor, or of any one related or allied to him, be emancipated by any court, judge or prothonotary having jurisdiction to confer tutorship, on the advice of a family council called and consulted as in the case of tutorship.

Although not immediately apparent, this article is the survival in Quebec of emancipation *par lettres du roi*.[1221] The *ancien droit coutumier* had borrowed this form of emancipation from the Roman law.[1222] It was similar to the Roman *venia aetatis*,[1223] and relieved the minor subject to *tutelle* from the legal disabilities he suffered. The procedure was well described by Denisart:

> On a recours au Prince pour en obtenir des lettres, par lesquelles il mande au juge du lieu de la tutelle, qu'après avoir pris l'avis de ses parens et amis, s'ils sont d'avis de l'émanciper, en ce cas il a l'habilité à jouir de ses meubles et à gérir et recevoir les revenue de ses immeubles, sans pouvoir les aliéner.[1224]

The Quebec article, like the rule of the *ancien droit*, was not designed to free children from the authority of their parents, that is, from *puissance paternelle*. Given that in the Quebec law *tutelle* was *separate* from *puissance paternelle*, it was, in theory, possible for a minor to have a tutor to look after his property and still to be under paternal power. In which case, emancipation from the *tutelle*

[1219] See *supra*, text at notes 1212–1214.

[1220] *Coutume de Paris*, art. 239: "Homme et femme conjoints par mariage, sont reputez usans de leurs droits, pour avoir administration de leurs biens, et non pour vendre, engager ou aliéner leurs immeubles pendant la minorité." Ferrière, *Corps et Comp.*, vol. 3, col. 502, no. 37 remarks: "Ces mots *usans de leurs droits* signifient ceux qui sont hors la puissance d'autruy . . . ." Loisel, *op. cit. supra* note 62, bk. 1, tit. 1, rule 37 states: "Feu et leu font mancipation ce dict Brassas, et enfans mariez sont tenus pour hors de pain et pot, c'est-à-dire emancipez." On emancipation, see further Brissaud, *History*, pp. 195–199.

[1221] See *T.D.C.Q.*, vol. 2, p. 361.

[1222] See Brissaud, *History*, p. 196.

[1223] See Pothier, *T.P.C.*, p. 71 (no. 187); Buckland, *Textbook*, p. 171; C. 2.44.2.

[1224] *Ancien Denisart*, vol. 2, p. 292, no. 3. See also Pothier, *C. d'Orl.*, p. 210 (introd. tit. 9, no. 21); Pothier, *T.P.C.*, p. 71 (no. 187).

would result in the ending of the *puissance paternelle*, under C.Q. 243. Emancipation *par lettres du roi* came to take on the appearance it has in the C.Q. because of two Provincial statutes, one placing this form of emancipation under the jurisdiction of the court, the other extending the power to judges and prothonotaries.[1225] The redactors declared themselves to be following the *ancien droit* as amended by Provincial legislation.

The system of the French code is rather different. C.N. 477 states that an unmarried minor may be emancipated by his father (or on his default his mother) by a declaration made by the person emancipating delivered to the *juge de paix* assisted by his clerk, provided the minor is fully fifteen years of age. This is a true emancipation from paternal authority. The Quebec redactors did not adopt this provision, as it was taken from the *droit écrit*, and was not generally found in the *droit coutumier*.[1226] According to C.N. 478, a minor who is an orphan, having reached eighteen years of age, may be emancipated if thought capable by the family council. This concerns solely emancipation from *tutelle*, and is a modern equivalent of *venia aetatis*. The authors of the *Pandectes françaises* remark: "Cet acte n'est point une veritable émancipation."[1227] C.N. 478 is obviously the French code's equivalent of C.Q. 315, except that the French article envisages that paternal power already be ended, both parents being dead, whereas the C.Q. completely separates *tutelle* from *puissance paternelle*.

The rules of the Quebec code on the ending of *puissance paternelle* follow the *ancien droit coutumier*: death of the parents (or the child),[1228] the child's reaching of the age of majority, the marriage of the child, and the child's emancipation from *tutelle* all end paternal authority. The rules of the C.N. are the same, except for those on emancipation other than by marriage. Here the C.N., because it permits parents, as of right, the administration and enjoyment of their children's property, allows parents to emancipate their children, to free them from *puissance paternelle*. This was not possible under the *ancien droit* as followed in Quebec, where emancipation, while ending paternal control in general, was intended to give minors control over their property. The Quebec redactors here chose not to follow C.N. 477, which allows parents to free children from paternal authority, because they must have considered such an emancipation unnecessary, since parents in Quebec would not have control and enjoyment of their children's property, and since it had not been possible in the *ancien droit coutumier*. The redactors preferred to keep the *ancien droit*.

[1225] 34 Geo. III. ch. 6 (1794); 12 Vict. ch. 38. See, e.g., *T.D.C.Q.*, vol. 2, p. 361; Mignault, *op. cit. supra* note 718, vol. 2, p. 258.

[1226] Cf. Brissaud, *History*, p. 196. In *Pan. fran.*, vol. 4, p. 612, the authors remark that in the *pays du droit coutumier* "elle y était absolument inconnue". See Maleville, *Analyse*, vol. 1, pp. 426–427. *Coutume d'Orléans*, art. 185: "Un père peut émanciper son enfant, tant en la présence que absence dudit enfant, en quelque age que ce soit." Pothier remarks, *C. d'Orl*, p. 214: "Cet article n'est plus d'usage."

[1227] *Pan. fran.*, vol. 4, p. 615.

[1228] This would include civil death, of course.

Conclusion on Paternal Power in Quebec

All of the articles of the Quebec code at which we have looked in connection with *puissance paternelle* demonstrate a profound conservatism. The provisions on the acquisition of paternal authority are those of the *ancien droit*. The redactors have kept the traditional rule on legitimation, rejecting the C.N.'s requirement of acknowledgement. There were not in Quebec the technical reasons for this change that there were in France: *recherche de paternité* was still possible. The redactors presumably felt that the old rule encouraged marriage, and that there were no reasons for the change.

The content of the paternal authority in the C.Q. is also very traditional. The Quebec redactors have followed the *ancien droit* as closely as they could. The first three articles of the C.Q. title on paternal authority, C.Q. 242–245, follow the first four articles of the C.N. title, C.N. 371–374, and are obviously based on them: and indeed this title of the C.Q. is obviously modelled on that of the C.N.[1229] The Quebec title, however, departs from that of the C.N. in two important respects. First, the C.Q. does not permit parents to seek the imprisonment of their children, and, second, it does not grant parents the enjoyment of their children's property. The C.Q. has been influenced by the C.L. on powers of punishment; indeed this is the only obvious influence of the C.L. on these articles of the C.Q.[1230] Parental powers to incarcerate children had existed under the *ancien droit*, though differing from those in the C.N. The institutional framework necessary for such powers had never existed in Quebec.[1231] The redactors, in not allowing parents to seek the imprisonment of their children, were not only following the law as applied in Quebec, but probably were also maintaining *puissance paternelle* as an institution considered primarily to be in the interests of the child for his care and protection. The C.Q. redactors rejected the C.N.'s grant to the parents of the enjoyment of the property of their children in their power. Here they were again enacting the *ancien droit coutumier* of Paris. Nor did the redactors follow the C.N. in giving parents the right to administer their children's property.[1232] In this, the codifiers also preserved the *ancien droit*. Likewise, the Quebec redactors did not give parents an automatic right to the tutorship of their children.[1233] The Quebec codifiers' actions here were all designed to preserve the *ancien droit coutumier* as they thought it had been received in the Province. This had the result that, if an *enfant de famille* had property of his own, for the administration of that property, his father would have to seek to be appointed tutor. In his actions as tutor, the father would be subject to the same scrutiny as any other tutor. He would have to give the same accounts of his tutorship. This is a fairly complex process, and is premissed on

---

[1229] See *supra*, text at notes 1098–1126.
[1230] See *supra*, text at 1117–1126.
[1231] See Deleury et al., *op. cit. supra* note 1185, p. 863.
[1232] This article is not of in the C.N.'s title on paternal authority, though it does, of course, belong there. See *supra*, note 1151.
[1233] See *supra*, note 1232.

the notion that fathers cannot be trusted to look after their children's property, without being subject to scrutiny. This might indeed be the case; however, such an idea is rather contrary to the nineteenth-century ideal of family. The Quebec redactors, however, did not consider this point, or, since some of the authors they used made it,[1234] did not consider it worth changing the law here, merely in order that the law should assert the contemporary vision of the relationship between parent and child. The Quebec provisions are also apparently fairer to the child. There was no obvious need for any change in the law here; and given both the instructions of the legislature, and the obvious conservatism of the redactors, the provisions are what might be expected.

As regards the requirement that parents should consent to the marriage of their minor children, the Quebec redactors have once more kept strictly to the *ancien droit*. Failing parents, tutors and curators have to consent. This provision follows the old rule. The C.N. here innovated, giving an enhanced importance to close relatives. The redactors rejected the C.N.'s innovation, an innovation which, in comparison to the C.Q. articles, would undoubtedly have reflected more accurately the importance placed on the close family circle in Quebec, where grandparents would most certainly have more moral authority than tutors. The rules in the C.Q. on who might seek annulment of the marriages of minors, if there had been no required consent, once more followed the *ancien droit*, and were consistent with the rules on consents. Only on oppositions to marriage did the Quebec redactors innovate. Following the example of the French code, the right to oppose a marriage was limited to a restricted class of people. Their innovations, however, logically extended the *ancien droit* on consents, so that those who had the right to consent had the right to oppose the marriage of minors. Consistent with their other articles, the Quebec redactors, as regards oppositions, rejected the French code's enhancement of the importance of the close family. The redactors were not influenced by the apparent appropriateness for Quebec of the C.N.'s innovations; they preferred to keep to the *ancien droit*, and, on the law on oppositions, where an innovation was obviously necessary, they extended the principle of the *ancien droit* to apply. That the provisions of the C.N. were arguably more suitable did not cause the redactors to reform the law, when the *ancien droit* would serve quite adequately. They thus obeyed their instructions to codify the law in force.

The redactors again kept to the *ancien droit* on the modes of ending *puissance paternelle*, there being no obvious need for change.

In sum, it is clear that the Quebec redactors have kept firmly to the *ancien droit* in their rules on *puissance paternelle*. They rejected all the French code's provisions that, in line with the nineteenth-century conception of the family, gave increased importance to close relatives, and asserted the affective nature of the modern family. What may be singled out as being of primary importance here is that the rules of the *ancien droit* were adequate to serve the purposes of the modern family of the nineteenth century. The C.N. may have seemed to

[1234] See, e.g., Toullier, *op. cit. supra* note 628, vol. 2 pp. 187–188, no. 1060.

express better the aspirations of the modern family; but the *ancien droit* sufficed. The adequacy of the *ancien droit*, and the conservative instructions given by the legislature, combined to produce no change. The redactors saw no reason to do other than preserve the *status quo*. Where the codifiers did change the law here, they acted because change was considered very necessary: the old law on oppositions was considered "un moyen de vexation".[1235]

CONCLUSION

The Family in the Two Codes

In this chapter have been studied the operations of the two sets of redactors in their tasks of providing articles to regulate the family. The codes, following the C.N., have no specific provisions on the family, but treat the husband and wife relationship and the parent and child relationship quite separately: there are no series of provisions which may be classed as "family law" in the modern sense. The connection between husband and wife and parent and child is made primarily through the father, through the two concepts of *puissance maritale* and *puissance paternelle*, even though the *puissance paternelle* may also be exercised by the mother.[1236] The Quebec code, the Louisiana Digest and the Code Napoléon all recognize the importance of these two *puissances* belonging to the husband and father, since they all state, with minor variation, as follows (in the wording of the French code, art. 1388):

> Les époux ne peuvent déroger ni aux droits résultant de la puissance maritale sur la personne de la femme et des enfans, ou qui appartient au mari comme chef, ni aux droits conférés au survivant des époux par le titre *de la Puissance paternelle* et par le titre *de la Minorité, de la Tutelle et de l'Émancipation*, ni aux dispositions prohibitives du présent code.

To derogate from these *puissances* would have been considered *contra bonos mores*.[1237] Although mothers under the three codes had varying degrees of

---

[1235] Mignault, *op. cit. supra* note 718, vol. 1, p. 393.

[1236] Jean Pineau, *Mariage, séparation, divorce: l'état du droit au Québec*, Montreal, presses de l'université de Montréal, 1978, p. 3: "Il est assez surprenant de constater, à la lecture du Code civil, que la famille ne tient nullement la place d'une véritable institution juridique alors qu'on s'accorde à la considérer comme un fait social méritant une protection particulière. Le Code civil, en effet, se borne à énoncer des règles juridiques qui gouvernent les relations familiales, c'est-à-dire le mariage, la separation de corps, la filiation, la puissance paternelle, les incapacités; il régit donc les rapports existant entre certains individus, sans prendre en considération les intérêts de la famille en tant que groupe." This would apply also to the C.N. and D.O. It is interesting to note in the new Draft Civil Code for Quebec that Book Two is devoted to the family. See Civil Code Revision Office, *Report on the Quebec Civil Code*, Quebec, Editeur officiel, 1978, vol. 1 Draft Civil Code, pp. 53–126; vol. 2, Commentary, tome 1, pp. 109–235.

[1237] C.N. 1387. See C.Q. 1258 and 1259; D.O. 1 (p. 323) and 4 (p. 325).

authority over their children, the figure unifying the family obviously was that of the husband and father.

Both the Quebec and Louisiana redactors were faced with two models of the family in the legal sources they consulted. First, there was a Roman model of family, based on the concept of paternal power; this model would be found not only in the texts of the *Corpus iuris civilis*, but also in the Castilian law, especially in the *Siete Partidas*, and in the *droit écrit* of the Midi. Second, there was the customary-law model of family, which was centred on marriage and immediate children, rather than on lineage and descent. This model of family was that discussed by various writers on the *ancien droit coutumier*, notably by Pothier. The family of the Code Napoléon conformed to this model (though fathers and mothers had greater rights in their children's property than in much of the *ancien droit coutumier*).

Both the C.Q. and the D.O. have adopted slightly differing versions of the customary law model of the family. But this adoption has had a different significance for each.

The D.O. contains a major change in the law on family. The law on marital and paternal authority in the 1808 Digest is—while having a measure of originality—largely that found in the C.N. and *droit coutumier*: the provisions on family conform to the customary-law model. This is a major change from the Castilian law, which conformed to the Roman model of family. The central feature of the Castilian law here was a modified version of *patria potestas*. Family was defined by the *padre*'s control over those in his power, rather than by an association of husband, wife and children. Because of the extent and strength of the reception of Roman law in Castile, the wife was accorded little importance in the legal family; and while her legal capacity was reduced by the mere fact of marriage, it was reduced to a considerably lesser extent than that of the wife under the *droit coutumier*. The D.O. increased the incapacity of the married woman by subjecting her to the full rigours of puissance maritale, while freeing children to a considerable extent by applying to them a form of *puissance paternelle* derived from the C.N. and the *droit coutumier*.

The C.Q., however, did not mark any dramatic change in this area of the law: indeed, the most significant aspect of codification, in so far as it related to the law on the family, was the casting of the law into a more modern form. The customary law versions of *puissance maritale* and *puissance paternelle* were preferred to those of the C.N., which were slightly—but significantly—different, in that they arguably expressed better than those of Quebec the ideals and reality of the nineteenth-century family. The C.N. had increased parental control over children's property, and given greater prominence to close relatives and grandparents than had the *ancien droit*. The C.N. changed the conception of *puissance maritale* in such a way as to reflect more thoroughly the nineteenth-century view of the role of women in marriage. The Quebec redactors rejected all these reforms, preserving the *status quo*; those reforms that they did make were more in the nature of technical improvements of the existing law rather than changes of significance marking a reorientation of the law.

The reasons why the D.O. preferred the provisions of the C.N. or the *droit coutumier* to those of the Castilian law and those why the C.Q. redactors preferred the *ancien droit coutumier* to the C.N. or *droit écrit* have already been sufficiently discussed, and it is unnecessary to repeat them here. It is helpful, however, to consider why the Louisiana redactors introduced radical changes into the law, while the Quebec redactors did not. The general conservatism of the Quebec redactors was such that they here rejected reforms suggested by the C.N. that would have expressed better than the rules they chose the ideals of family in nineteenth-century Quebec. Both societies had seen the development of a modern associative or affective family centred around marriage and care for children. This family was patriarchal in so far as the husband was the undoubted head of the conjugal association with greater moral authority than the wife; the wife ideally was confined to domestic duties. The Castilian law presupposed a different organization of family. The law was quite inappropriate for Louisiana in the early nineteenth century: Castilian *patria potestad* would be insupportable in a liberal, individualist society. It is obvious that a major reform would have been considered necessary. It would have been unthinkable for the redactors to have re-enacted the Castilian rules in their code; and the redactors' actions here would be supported by the ambiguity in their instructions and the ambiguity in the law in force.[1238] The restriction in the capacity of wives found in the D.O. must be the result of the attraction of the French texts and the changes already made by the 1807 Act on the celebration of marriages.[1239] It is obvious, too, that the redactors approved of this restriction (which asserted current visions of family life) even though the use of the French sources seems to have been of most importance here. In Quebec, on the other hand, the law in force before codification was not so obviously inappropriate. The *ancien droit coutumier* had a restricted conception of *puissance paternelle*. The notion of *puissance maritale* was similar to that of the C.N. There was no clear or immediate necessity for reform. Thus, though the C.N. contained rules which might well have asserted the contemporary ideology of family better than did those of the *ancien droit coutumier*, the rules of the *ancien droit* sufficed. The Quebec redactors had been instructed to codify the law in force, and in many ways their task was one of conservation.

The 1808 Digest's articles on the family changed Louisiana law; on the other hand, the 1866 Quebec code in large part merely restated in more modern form the *ancien droit* as applicable in Quebec. Few provisions in either code on this area of the law may be said to be truly original. The redactors of both codes utilized other codes and juristic writings in their work. The organization of the material on the family in the two codes derives from the Napoleonic model; though the 1808 Digest shows more originality in this than does the Quebec

---

[1238] I here refer to the fact that the redactors were instructed to base their code on the civil law in force, and to the problem of the applicability of French law in Louisiana prior to codification, though the Castilian law, in theory, should have been in force. Consider also the 1805 decision of Prevost. See *supra*, chap. 3, text at notes 136–170, 240–253.

[1239] Louisiana Acts, ch. 17, 6 Apr. 1807, "An Act Concerning the Celebration of Marriages".

code. Most provisions of both codes have a traceable historical source; but the rule may always have been altered in borrowing, and some sources may only have had influence on the phrasing of articles.

The redactors of the D.O. adopted the provisions of the French law on *puissance maritale* and the concept of *puissance paternelle* found in the French code. The C.Q. redactors followed the French code as much as possible while, in general, retaining the provisions of the *ancien droit coutumier*. The reasons for the difference between the actions of the codifiers would seem to be the following. First, the law in Louisiana on paternal authority was very outmoded, and the redactors borrowed from the French sources (and indeed Blackstone) to provide a series of articles they considered appropriate given their view of Louisiana society. Second, the C.N.'s provisions on much of paternal authority might have been more appropriate for Quebec than the *ancien droit* the redactors selected; nonetheless, the *ancien droit*'s rules on *puissance paternelle* were adequate and workable in a way that those of the Castilian law were not. Therefore, given the opportunity presented by codification, the Louisiana redactors innovated by selectively adopting rules from various sources, whereas the Quebec redactors saw no need to do so. Third, the D.O. redactors adopted the *droit coutumier*'s notion of *puissance maritale*, especially as found in the C.N.: they thus altered their law. This change seems to be due to very great extent to the seductiveness, for the redactors, of the Napoleonic texts; though there can be no doubt that the ideology of the period supported the change, and that the redactors themselves approved of the incapacity of married women. Fourth, the Quebec redactors maintained the *ancien droit* on *puissance maritale*, rejecting the innovations of the C.N. which were in line with the ideology of the period. The rules of the *ancien droit*, however, were also reasonably consonant with the ideals of the period. The C.Q. redactors here, therefore, generally obeyed their instructions, and maintained the *ancien droit*, bar for a technical improvement on mode of authorization. In conclusion, the actions of the Louisiana redactors in reforming the law were dictated by the usefulness of reform in some areas, and by the seductive ease of copying the modern French texts. The Quebec redactors preserved the *ancien droit*, though reformed in part, and rejected the innovations of the C.N. The innovation of the C.N. might have been closer to the contemporary ideal of the family, but the *ancien droit*, as expressed in the C.Q., adequately expressed the current ideals of family life. There was no obvious need for change, and the Quebec, redactors followed their conservative instructions.

Earlier it was remarked that neither of the two codes have general provisions on the family. Tucker, however, refers to two articles of the 1808 Digest, D.O. 16 (p. 11) and D.O. 78 (p. 127). The first of these states that:

> Les fils et filles de famille, sont les personnes qui sont sous la puissance paternelle; et les péres ou mères de famille qu'on appelle aussi chefs de famille, sont les personnes qui ne sont pas sous cette puissance, soit qu'ils aient des enfans ou non, et soit qu'ils aient été dégagés de la puissance paternelle par l'émancipation ou par la mort du père.

Tucker believes this article to contradict the other provisions of the code on the relationships between family members;[1240] he states that it "goes a long way toward re-establishing a quasi-Roman *familia*, with a *paterfamilias* at its head, as the unit of law".[1241] Tucker would seem to be reading too much into this article. It is taken from Domat,[1242] as are most of the articles of the title in which it appears: the first title of Book One of the code. The article is perfectly compatible with the other articles on *puissance paternelle*. Rather than regarding this article as a statement by the redactors on the nature of the family, it is better to regard the provision as a conventional definition included for reasons of tradition and because the rest of the title in which it appears is drawn from Domat. The article does not contradict the provisions of the D.O. regarding the family as the modern nuclear unit. All the effective provisions are drawn from the modern law. The second article Tucker mentions[1243]—D.O. 78 (p. 127)—is as follows:

> Le mot de famille employé dans cette section, doit s'entendre de la femme, des enfans et des domestiques de celui à qui le droit d'usage ou d'habitation est accordé.

This article is taken from Book 2, title 3, chapter 2, "De l'usage et de l'habitation", and only means that when a man is granted a right of habitation, he may take his servants. It does not affect the nature of the family in the D.O.; it merely shows that the D.O. redactors were aware of the possible ambiguities in the term "family", and that it was still possible to use "family" in the wider sense. That the redactors thought it necessary to state this indicates that the more limited usage was becoming predominant. This article is of more significance for the next chapter; it does not really affect the family as revealed in the articles on husband and wife and parent and child.

Thus, both the C.Q. and D.O. provide a series of modern provisions on the family, deriving ultimately from the model of family found in the *droit coutumier* of France. The extent of the changes in the law made by the two codes was dependent on both the state of the old law in the light of social organization, and the sources available to the redactors.

[1240] *Persons*, pp. 283–285.

[1241] *Ibid.*, p. 284.

[1242] Domat, *Loix civiles*, vol. 1, p. 14 (prel. bk., tit. 2, sect. 2, no. 5).

[1243] Tucker, *op. cit supra* note 166, p. 285, n. 107 and n. 108.

5

EMPLOYMENT IN THE LOUISIANA DIGEST AND QUEBEC CODE

INTRODUCTION

This chapter deals with the law relating to employment in the two codes. The provisions in each will be examined in their relationship both to the law before codification and to the sources drawn on by the codifiers. The preceding chapter has demonstrated that, up to the eighteenth century, relations between family and servant, artisan and apprentice had been close. There are three matters to be discussed: first, the exclusion of the servant from the family; second, the development of wage labour; and third, the particular social and economic circumstances of Louisiana and Quebec. All three have been touched on in describing Quebec and Louisiana society;[1] but here it is necessary to reformulate the material in order to confront more directly the three issues mentioned above, and to place the discussion of the law that follows in its appropriate context. The discussion of these three issues will be followed by an account of the civilian approach to them, as the received Roman law of Europe provided the basic material used by the redactors of the two codes.

The Exclusion of the Servant from the Family

In the introduction to chapter 4, the intimacy of masters and servants was touched on: it is now appropriate to expand on this and to show briefly how the servant came to be "excluded" from the family. Ariès's study once more permits us to explore this difficult area. Up to the seventeenth century, the notion of "service" was not necessarily connected with menial tasks. Thus, sons of noble families would wait at table or be sent off while young to serve another nobleman. But the seventeenth century was a period of transition with confusion over the role and status of servants, who were henceforth to become on the same

[1] See *supra*, chap. 2.

footing as manual labourers.[2] Ariès points out, however, that although in the seventeenth century the status of servants became degraded:

> There still remained between masters and servants something which went beyond respect for a contract or exploitation by an employer: an existing bond which did not exclude brutality on the one hand and cunning on the other, but which resulted from an almost perpetual community of life.[3]

Ariès surveys contemporary source material on masters and servants and concludes: "A servant was not paid, he was rewarded: a master's relationship with his servant was not based on justice but on patronage and pity, the same feeling that people had for children."[4] Flandrin also emphasizes this aspect of the master-servant relationship: "[T]he notion of wages was nebulous, it was by ensuring the material independence of a servant that one recompensed his services",[5] and he shows that servants were in a position similar to that of children in regard to the head of the household.[6] In other words, the master-servant relationship was not *regarded* as one based on contract, but as one of dependency analogous to the dependency of children on parents. (The legal relationship will be discussed below.) In the course of the eighteenth century this changed. The family (narrowly defined) withdrew into itself; servants were excluded, and their relationship to their masters or employers became more formal, and as such more skin to a strict contractual relationship.

The Development of Wage Labour

So far we have been discussing service in the household, a service which might be loosely termed "domestic". Another aspect of service is that in a workshop, one artisan employing another (or one being apprenticed to another). This form of service took place within what might conveniently be called "artisan production". That is, the independent artisan produced in his own workshop goods that he sold to the merchant: he was a small independent producer.[7] Artisan production existed along with the inclusion of servants in the family. Although there might appear to be a difference between service with or apprenticeship to an artisan and domestic service, it is not significant if the nature of society as a whole is considered. The place of production and hence of employment was the artisan's home: his servants in his labour and his apprentices would stay with him, and they formed part of his household. The

---

[2] P. Ariès, *Centuries of Childhood*, trans. by R. Baldwick, London, Jonathan Cape, 1962, p. 396.
[3] *Ibid.*
[4] *Ibid.*, p. 397.
[5] J.-L. Flandarin, *Families in Former Times. Kinship, Household and Sexuality*, Cambridge, Cambridge University Press, 1979, p. 142.
[6] *Ibid.*, pp. 140–150 and *passim.*
[7] Cf. A. Sohn-Rethel, *Intellectual and Manual Labour: a Critique of Epistemology*, London, MacMillan,1978, p. 117: "The artisan producer owned his means of production. . .[and] nominally sold his finished product to the merchant."

unit of production and that of consumption were co-terminous.[8] In the eighteenth century this "familial" relationship between the artisan and his "employees" was breaking down and re-forming along contractual lines. The employees and apprentices were excluded from the family and their status changed. At the same time, artisan production was in decline, to be replaced in the nineteenth century by industrial production. Industrial (factory) production involved the use of wage labour; that is, employees were in a formal contractual relationship with their employer, and sold their labour for wages. Employees were no longer part of the household of an artisan, and the artisan household disappeared as the primary unit of production. Of course, wage labour has always existed; but it did not predominate until industrialization.[9] Further, although servants had always been "employees", and perhaps, in some abstract formal sense, wage labourers, the content of the master-servant (employer-employee) relationship changed from one of domestic dependency to one of formal contract, empty of domestic association.

The Particular Circumstances of Louisiana and Quebec

The changing nature of the relationship between master and servant in Louisiana and Quebec was discussed in chapter 2. Allan Pred has pointed out that, in the United States generally, techniques of industrial production were not used until after the first decades of the nineteenth century. Up to then, production used handicraft techniques rather than machines, and was organized on a household and workshop basis rather than on that of the factory, while being marked by rural dispersion, rather than concentration in urban centres. Cities themselves were mercantile rather than industrial in character.[10] This amounts to what we have described as "artisan production"; Pred's description

---

[8] Cf. Flandrin, *op. cit. supra* note 5, pp. 62–63: "If a distinction has become established today between the worker and the domestic servant, the reason is that, with the exception of some 'agricultural workers', the worker today is no longer accommodated in the house of his employer. The co-terminous character of the unit of production and that of consumption, which was formerly customary, has become exceptional."

[9] Cf. these statements of H. Braverman, *Labour and Monopoly Capital*, New York, Monthly Review Press, 1974, p. 52: "It is important to note the historical character of this phenomenon. While the purchase and sale of labour power has existed from antiquity, a substantial class of wage-workers did not begin to form in Europe until the fourteenth century, and did not become numerically significant until the rise of industrial capitalism (that is, the *production* of commodities on a capitalist basis, as against mercantile capitalism, which merely *exchanged* the surplus products of prior forms of production) in the eighteenth century."

[10] A. Pred, "Manufacturing in the American Mercantile City, 1800–1840", in K.J. Jackson and S.K. Schultz (eds.), *Cities in American History*, New York, Knopf, 1972, pp. 111–142, esp. at p. 111. A useful study of the process of industrialization in North America is C.G. Steffens, "Changes in the Organisation of Artisan Production in Baltimore, 1790 to 1820", 36 *The William and Mary Quarterly* (3d. series) (1979), pp. 101–117. Steffens studies the structural changes in employment and labour in artisanal workshops in Baltimore, reflecting the movement towards concentration of capital in factory (industrial) production.

would fit economic life in Louisiana.[11] There was little or no industrial production; the economy was based on trade and agriculture. There would correspondingly be few opportunities for employment as a labourer, especially when the institution of slavery is considered.[12] Thus, the need for a developed law on employment would apparently be slight; although the developing individualist conceptions of society would suggest that employment would be regarded from a primarily contractual viewpoint, rather than from one of domestic dependency.

Quebec, however, is rather different: codification came only in 1866, and by then liberal capitalist notions of individualism had greatly affected the conception of the relationship between employer and employee, which was viewed from the perspective of classic contractual freedom. Artisans and journeymen were wage labourers; and there was a continuing transformation of the concept of employment or service.[13] This said, it should be remembered that in Quebec, out of the total population, the numbers so employed were slight, the majority remaining peasant farmers.

Hence, there was a difference between Louisiana and Quebec at the time of their respective first codifications: Quebec by 1866 had gone much farther in transforming the relationship between master and servant than had Louisiana by 1808.

The Civilian Background

The civilian legal systems have traditionally classed the contract for labour as one of hire: hire of labour being one aspect of the general contract of hire.[14] Both the C.N. and the C.Q. deal with employment as hire. The D.O. does so, too; but it also includes a title on master and servant in its first book. This being so, it is necessary to describe the Roman law on the subject, and then to discuss the reception of that law in Castile and in France; it is useful, too, to examine the manner in which these latter two systems treated servants in general. The provisions of the C.N. and *Proj. An. VIII* will also briefly be discussed, and some concluding remarks will complete this introduction before we consider the provisions of the D.O. and C.Q.

---

[11] See *supra*, chap. 2.

[12] Steffens, *op. cit.supra* note 10, p. 107, states about Baltimore: "Although slave labor contributed substantially to artisanal production in Baltimore, apprentices provided the chief source of workers."

[13] See R. Tremblay, "La formation matérielle de la classe ouvrière à Montréal entre 1790 et 1830", 33 *R.H.A.F.* (1979), pp. 39–50.

[14] The new draft Quebec code breaks this tradition. See the Civil Code Revision Office, *Report on The Québec Civil Code*, Quebec, Editeur Officiel, 1977, vol. 2/2, pp. 738–742 at p. 738: "It will be observed that the term 'lease and hire of services' is henceforth dispensed with to make way for a notion closer to contemporary reality."

THE ROMAN LEGAL BACKGROUND

In Roman law the hiring out of one's labour for gain was part of the general law on hire: it was thus one aspect of the consensual contract of *locatio conductio*. Some scholars have suggested that the hiring out of one's own labour developed from the hiring out of slaves. Thomas disagrees, arguing that the leasing of the labour of free men is easily as old: his argument is plausible; but we need not concern ourselves with this point.[15] *Locatio conductio* was a *bonae fidei* consensual contract with three requirements: consent, price (*merces*, which had to be certain and in money)[16] and the thing.[17] Modern commentators usually divide this contract into three main types (the trichotomy): *locatio conductio rei*; *locatio conductio operis faciendi*; and *locatio conductio operarum*. For the first and third of these the person who supplies the thing or services is the *locator*, the person who pays is the *conductor*; while for the second, the person who gives the order for the work to be done and who pays is the *locator*, the person who executes the work is the *conductor*. Although the terminology might appear confusing, if it is borne in mind that the *locator* is the one who "places" ("*locat*"), the reason for the difference in terminology will appear. *Locatio rei* needs no explanation: its meaning is obvious. *Locatio operis faciendi* is where the *locator* hands over something or which the *conductor* is to work, the latter being paid by the former: it is the putting out of work on contract. *Locatio operarum* was where a worker, the locator, is employed by the *conductor* as what we have termed a wage labourer.

One point should be stressed: the trichotomy is the product of modern commentators. The Romans did not make this clear distinction. Schulz, for example, describes the trichotomy as "a product of continental legal scholasticism" and argues for its rejection, stating that it "leads to unnecessary difficulties".[18] Thus, in D. 19.2., the title on this contract, texts relating to all three forms of *locatio* are scattered throughout the general discussion, no distinction being made as texts are fitted into the general scheme of the title. Further, the jurists did not stick closely to the terminology. Thus, in D. 19.2.22.2, an example of what we would call *locatio operis faciendi*, the jurist Paul starts off "correctly" according to the modern terminology, and then appends a clause stating that the *conductor* "locat . . . operam suam":

---

[15] See J.A.C. Thomas, "Locatio and Operae", 3 (3rd ser.) *Bullettino dell'Istituto di Diritto Romano "Vittoria Scialoja"*, (1961), pp. 231–247 at pp. 239–40. See also G. Lepointe and R. Monier, *Les obligations en droit romain et dans l'ancien droit français*, Paris, Recueil Sirey, 1954, pp. 262–264.
[16] On certainty of price, see Gaius, *Inst.* 3.142; cf.3.144. See also D. 19.2.2 pr.; h.t.19.3 (rent in produce). See also h.t.25.6 on *locatio partiaria*. Justinian is definite on rent being money: Inst. 3.24.2.
[17] See generally Buckland, *Textbook*, pp. 498–506.
[18] F. Schulz, *Classical Roman Law*, Oxford, Clarendon Press, 1951, pp. 542–544. F. Olivier-Martin "Des Divisions en Louage en Droit Romain", 15 *R.H.D.F.E.* (1936), pp. 419–475, credited Voet with the invention of the trichotomy.

> Cum insulam aedificandum loco, ut sua impensa conductor omnia faciet, proprietatem quidem eorum ad me transfert et tamen locatio est: locat enim artifex operam suam, id est faciendi necessitatem.

It must be concluded that for the Roman jurists the distinction was of minimal importance: there was one contract: *locatio conductio*. This is indeed sensible. Wage labour would not be of any particular importance in Rome because of slavery, and the patron-client system:[19] "the sphere of the hired free worker at a wage, the *locator operarum*, is very restricted."[20] The contract *operis faciendi* was probably of considerably more importance, and this would explain the greater attention paid to it.

Thomas puts forward an interesting argument which, if accepted, helps explain the lack of attention paid to *locatio operarum*. He argues that the worker was originally regarded as letting *himself* out, and not his *operae* as a separate entity. Thus, the worker *se locat* rather than *suas operas locat*.[21] He argues that *se locare* is found in the early texts,[22] and suggests that *locatio operarum* was not in use until the time of Hadrian (indeed, he conjectures that the term was invented by Julian).[23] He argues that this change reflects both an upgrading of the status of wage labourers (*mercennarii*) and juristic development: the result was the realization that what was concerned was not the leasing of an individual but of his services (*operae*).[24] Thomas himself admits that the evidence is slight; but, given the paucity of texts dealing with *locatio operarum*, this is inevitable.[25]

If he is correct (and his argument is plausible) his suggestion helps explain why the jurists did not consider *locatio operarum* as being in any way different from *locatio rei*. There was absolutely no difference between letting of an object and letting of oneself: one let oneself as an object. If, as Thomas suggests, there had been an upgrading of the status of the wage labourer in the early Empire, to change the terminology from *se locare* to *operas locare* would provide a satisfactory euphemism: a euphemism both in line with the new status and conceptually satisfactory. The jurists, however, while changing the terminology in cosmetic fashion, continued to treat *locatio operarum* in the traditional way as letting of oneself, and did not concern themselves overmuch with this aspect of the contract.[26]

This leads on to another point: upper class Romans despised the *mercennarius*, who was *mercede conductus*. (Lower class Romans, no doubt, did not despise the *mercennarius* in the same way; but, unfortunately for us,

---

[19] J.A. Crook, *Law and Life of Rome*, London, Thames and Hudson, 1967, pp. 192–205.
[20] *Ibid.*, p. 195.
[21] Thomas, *op. cit. supra* note 15, p. 234.
[22] D. 19.2.60.7 (Labeo): "Se ipse se locasset", referring to a slave letting himself out, rather than being let out by his master. See also D. 47.10.11.4 (Proculus).
[23] Thomas, *op. cit. supra* note 15, p. 234 and pp. 238–239.
[24] See *ibid.*, pp. 234–237.
[25] Buckland, *Textbook*, p. 505, n. 1 also stresses the lack of textual authority.
[26] It seems likely that much of the modern concern with *locatio operarum* arises out of the importance of this contract in the contemporary world: an importance it perhaps did not have for the Romans.

they have left no statements equivalent, for example, to those of Cicero.) The *artes liberales* could not be the subject of letting and hiring, although in some of the liberal professions it became possible to receive an *honorarium* as their work came to be regarded as mandate (a supposedly gratuitous contract).[27] The matter of the nature of the reward earned by members of the liberal professions is rather confused; but this need not concern us.[28] For our purposes, it is important to stress the menial nature of *locatio operarum* in the Roman law, the law from which the modern civilian systems drew many of their rules.

In law, the nature of the relationship between *locator* and *conductor* was a formal one of contract between abstract equals. Either party could be liable to the other for any damage done arising out of the former's *culpa*. Were the *locator* incompetent in the work he contracted to carry out, he would be liable for *culpa*.[29] Despite this formal equality the wage labourer (*mercennarius*) was in an inferior position. In the agricultural *familia*, he was described as being *in loco servorum*:[30] an obviously inferior status for a free born man. Indeed, the very silence of the legal texts on the subject of the *mercennarius* suggests his lowly status. Given Roman society, the nature of the contract would result in *mercennarii* always being of low status.[31] It would seem likely that, in some circumstances at least, the *conductor* would have the right of *levis castigatio*.[32]

We may conclude that *locatio conductio operarum* was not differentiated from the general law on *locatio conductio*: this was perhaps due to the historical origins of *locatio operarum* and its general unimportance (for the Roman jurists). The wage labourer was of low status; it is possible, however, that, in the second century A.D., the status of the *mercennarius* improved somewhat. Prestigious skills and tasks could not be the subject of *locatio conductio*. The *locator* and *conductor* were formally equal; but the evidence suggests that this equality was indeed only formal, and that the *locator* was in a dependent

---

[27] See A. Watson, *The Law of Obligations in the Later Roman Republic*, Oxford, Clarendon Press, 1965, pp. 109–110. On mandate and *honoraria*, see Buckland, *Textbook*, p. 515. For some work no reward could be collected: D. 50.13.1.4 & 5 (professors of philosophy and law). See also Thomas, *op. cit. supra* note 15, pp. 240–247. But cf. D. 2.38.1, in which Paul seems to class advocates among those who lease out their services.

[28] See Watson, *op. cit. supra*, note 27 pp. 109–110; Buckland, *Textbook*, p. 515; Thomas *op. cit. supra* note 15, pp. 240–247; and Crook, *op. cit. supra* note 19, pp. 203–205.

[29] D. 19.2.9.5; Buckland, *Textbook*, pp. 504–505.

[30] D. 7.8.4 pr. and 43.16.1.18.

[31] This is supported by the evidence in Crook, *op. cit. supra* note 19, pp. 193–200.

[32] The case of the "apprentice" would suggest this: D. 9.2.5 and 19.2.13.4. (Whether the contract should be classed as *operis faciendi* or *operarum* is irrelevant. The boy's father had an *actio ex locato*; this was the only matter of importance given that the Romans did not distinguish clearly between the three types of *locatio*.) It is explicitly stated that the *conductor*, the *sutor*, had the right of *levis castigatio*. Whether or not the boy is an "apprentice" is irrelevant, and D. 9.2.7 envisaged the father recovering for loss of future earnings from the boy. Anyway, that a master could chastise his *mercennarius* is hardly surprising. The "apprentice" texts are usually discussed within the context of Aquilian liability: J.A.C. Thomas, "The Case of the Apprentice's Eye", 8 *Revue internationale des droits de l'antiquité* (1961), pp. 357–372.

position. Few texts were devoted to *locatio operarum*. These were the skimpy provisions the Roman law bequeathed to the civilian systems.

THE FRENCH LAW OF THE *ANCIEN REGIME*

An adequate account of the reception of the Roman law on *locatio conductio* would be a lengthy work: it is fortunate that such an account need not be given here.[33] In the following discussion, one point should always be recalled: the analysis of *locatio conductio* according to the trichotomy is a modern development. It is contended that two conflicting approaches to servants may be traced in the French juristic writings: one approach deriving from the Roman *locatio conductio*; the other treating the servant as a dependant of his master, not as an abstract contracting individual. The first approach will be demonstrated and exemplified by discussing a treatise of Pothier,[34] the second by discussing the work of Pocquet de Livonière.[35] It will further be shown that under the *ancien régime* wage labour was regulated primarily as a matter of public policy, rather than of private law.

Before codification, little juristic attention seems to have been devoted to *locatio operarum* (to use the term for convenience) in France.[36] Pothier discusses the lease of personal services only in a number of provisions scattered through his discussion of *locatio rei*. He discusses *locatio operis faciendi* separately, as *louage d'ouvrage*. He states that there are two kinds of *louage*: *louage des choses* and *louage des ouvrages*.[37] The lease of personal services, he discusses as an aspect of *louage des choses*. Thus, for Pothier, *locatio operarum* is assimilated to *locatio rei*: he is making a bi-partite division not at all similar to the trichotomy. Further, the rules he enunciates on *louage des services* (*locatio operarum*) are few in number and not clearly worked out.[38] Tucker suggests that Pothier's treatment of *louage des services* (which he refers to as *louage d'ouvrages*) was the result of the fact that "lease of services . . . was not yet important enough to the order of things to warrant careful development. . . . [T]he contract . . . was not economically important enough to merit much more

---

[33] On the reception of *locatio conductio*, much useful material may be garnered from Olivier-Martin, *op. cit. supra* note 18.
[34] Pothier, *T.C.L.*, pp. 1–170.
[35] C. Pocquet de Livonnière, *Règles du droit françois*, 3rd ed., Paris, chez P.G. le Mercier, 1737, pp. 54–58 (bk. 1, tit. 2, s. 4).
[36] See e.g *Œuvres de M. Antoine d'Espeisses, avocat et jurisconsulte de Montpellier où toutes les plus importantes matières du droit romain sont méthodiquement expliquées et accommodées au droit françois. Confirmées par les arrêts des cours souverains, et enrichies des plus utiles doctrines des auteurs anciens et modernes*, ed. by G. du Rousseaud de la Combe, Lyons, frères Bruyset, 1750, vol. 1, p. 87 (part 1, tit. 2, sect. 1), where he defines louage, stating it has two forms: he does not mention the form now called *locatio operarum*, though he was aware of its existence (as is obvious from *ibid.*, vol. 1, p. 92 (part 1, tit. 2, sect. 2 n. 6)). He does not clearly distinguish *locatio operarum* from the other forms.
[37] Pothier, *T.C.L.*, p. 1 (*Préface*).
[38] See *infra*.

than academic notice. . . ."[39] There is undoubtedly some truth in this; but this statement is by no means the whole truth, and requires qualification. First, the existence of regulation of labour by the public authorities would suggest that importance was attached to wage labour (and this will be discussed below). Second, what, above all else, seems to have influenced Pothier's treatment of *louage des services* is the inherited academic tradition of Roman law. Pothier's discussion reflects the Roman attitude of not clearly distinguishing between *locatio rei* and *locatio operarum*. Tucker does not appear to appreciate that the trichotomy was a modern development not followed by Pothier, and that this accounts for the latter's treatment of *louage des services*.[40]

Pothier also follows the Roman law in confining *louage* to lowly services; he excludes the *artes liberales*:

> Observez . . . qu'il n'y a que les services ignobles et appréciables à prix d'argent qui soient susceptibles du contrat de louage, tels que ceux des serviteurs et servantes, des manœuvres, des artisans, etc.
>
> Ceux que leur excellence, ou la dignité de la personne qui les rend, empêché de pouvoir s'apprécier à prix d'argent, n'en sont pas susceptibles.
>
> C'est pourquoi le contrat qui intervient entre un avocat et son client . . . n'est pas un contrat de louage, mais un contrat de mandat.[41]

Neither Cujas nor Bartolus make this distinction between *operae liberales* and other *operae*.[42] In direct contradiction of D. 50.13.1.4 and 5,[43] Cujas states:

> Et juris professor, si ad docendum suas operas exhibeat, ac de mercede paciscatur locator est, discipuli sunt conductores. Quod si juris professor complures in ejus disciplinam se dantes edocendos suscipiat, conductor est, discipuli sunt locatores.[44]

The exemption of the *artes liberales* gained ground, however. Thus, we find Pasquier pouring scorn on the exclusion of advocates from being subject to the contract of *louage* because theirs is a dignified profession. He characterizes this exclusion of advocates as "une hypocrisie de droit inventée par les jurisconsultes, pour auctoriser leur science".[45] Pothier, however, does state what was generally taken to be the law in the eighteenth century.

Pothier provides the example of an author treating *louage des services* from a formal contractual standpoint, using categories inherited from Roman law; but

---

[39] T. W. Tucker, "Sources of Louisiana's Law of Persons: Blackstone, Domat and the French Codes", 44 *Tul. L. Rev.* (1970), pp. 264–295 at p. 273.

[40] *Ibid.* pp. 268–270. Cf. *Pothier's Treatise on the Contract of Letting and Hiring*, trans. by G.A. Mulligan, Durban, Butterworth, 1953, p. 1, translator's note.

[41] Pothier, *T.C.L.*, p. 7 (no. 10).

[42] See Olivier-Martin, *op. cit. supra* note 18, p. 456, n. 3.

[43] See *supra*, text in note 27.

[44] Found quoted in Olivier-Martin, *op. cit. supra* note 18, p. 456, n. 4.

[45] Etienne Pasquier, *L'interprétation des Institutes de Justinien, avec la conférence de chasque paragraphe aux ordonnances royaux, arrestz de parlement et coustumes générales de la France*, Paris, Videcoq aîné, A. Durand, 1847, p. 693 (ch. 56).

his treatment of *serviteurs* as abstract contracting individuals does not fit with the reality of the relationship between master and servant of his period: neither master nor servants would consider each other as equal individuals bound only by the formal tie of contract. What is most obvious in Pothier's account is civilian tradition.[46]

Pocquet de Livonnière treats servants separately from the contract of lease. The fourth section of the first book of his work is entitled "De la puissance des Maîtres": he thus categorizes the relationship between masters and servants as being of the nature of those between fathers and children, and between husbands and wives. His approach is interesting, and radically different from the notions of formal contract found in Pothier and the Roman sources. What seems important to Pocquet about the relationship between master and servant is that *serviteurs* place themselves in the *power* of and under the authority of their *maîtres*. The rules he provides, however, are no more detailed than those scattered through Pothier's discussion; nor, in content, are they radically different from those of the latter. The significance of Pocquet's treatment of the material is his approach: he does not consider the relationship between master and servant as one of formal contract between free, equal and abstract individuals, but rather as one of dependency and power within a definite set of social relations. He may also be influenced by the Roman classification of the first division of the law of persons, and by feudal concepts of service between lord and vassal; but, especially as regards the former, even if existing, such influence is slight. What is worthy of stress is that Pocquet is treating "service" as a *status*, similar to that of being a wife or a child in power. His approach to the tie between master and servant from a perspective other than that of contract would seem to be more in line with the social relations of master and servant than would the approach of Pothier.[47] Traces of the attitude of Pocquet may be found in other works. Thus Merlin acknowledges lease of services as part of *louage*;[48] but he prefers to discuss lease of services under "domestique"[49] and "ouvrière"[50] where an account of the relationship between master and servant will not be hampered by notions and categories inherited from Roman law. His discussion of, for example, "domestique" is far removed from the formal Roman law and, making due allowance for the legal viewpoint, recognizes the real social bond between master and servant described by Ariès.[51]

To state that the law of the *ancien régime* in France on what we have called wage labour is only that found in the juristic writings would be to mislead. Those jurists who discussed the legal aspect of wage labour from a purely Roman perspective would tend, following the Roman tradition, both to give a

---

[46] One obvious reason why Pothier discusses *locatio operarum* with that *rei* is that for both the person who paid was the *conductor*. No doubt sources for this usage could be traced.
[47] See *supra*, text at notes 2–9.
[48] See Merlin, *Répertoire* (4), vol. 7, p. 573 s.v. "Louage".
[49] *Ibid.*, vol. 4, s.v. "Domestique".
[50] *Ibid.*, vol. 8, s.v. "Ouvrière".
[51] See *supra*, text at note 3.

brief account and to show little interest in the topic. Pocquet, on the other hand, because of his stress on the power and authority aspect of master-servant relations, tends to discuss the topic within the confines of domestic service. All this gives an impression of a lack of legal regulation of employment; but such an impression is false. Originally, as in Europe generally, the trade guilds had regulated employment and apprenticeship.[52] The guilds, with their particular rules for admission and apprenticeship, were suppressed by an edict of February, 1776.[53] The position is complex; but one may say that generally industry was regulated and controlled, and that industrial work was regulated corporately by special royal ordinances and the body of industry itself.[54] The regulation of labour was more a matter of policy than of formal law. Hence, the jurists, concerned with the formal law and operating mainly within the inherited Roman tradition, would not be concerned with the regulation of labour; their discussion of service would accordingly be limited to the Roman categories. In this, the redactors of the Louisiana and Quebec codes would be likely to follow the jurists. The C.N. devoted only two articles to *locatio operarum*;[55] they would be a prime source for the redactors in Louisiana and Quebec. The *loi de 22 germinal*, an XI, one year before promulgation of the C.N., regulated industrial work in Napoleonic France, again, as under the *ancien régime*, from a perspective oriented towards policy; the *loi* contained regulations on employment and apprenticeship.[56] This loi, as with the legislation of the *ancien régime*, might not provide a usable source for the two sets of redactors.[57]

THE CASTILIAN LAW

Consideration of the position of wage labourers in Castilian law indicates the same conflict as in the French *ancien droit* between treatment of the labourer according to the categories inherited from Roman law, and recognition of the special relationship between master and servant. The *Siete Partidas* themselves show this conflict of methods of dealing with servants.

On reading through the *Partidas*, the impression one gains is of the servant's place in the family, of his part in the household and of his personal dependency on the head of the household. To demonstrate this, it is sufficient to

---

[52] See Olivier-Martin, *Histoire*, pp. 170–176.

[53] See Merlin, *Répertoire* (4), vol. 3, pp. 226–229 s.v. "Corps des Arts et Métiers", quoting the 1776 edict suppressing the guilds of Paris.

[54] See Olivier-Martin, *Histoire*, pp. 619–632; J. Rivero and J. Savatier, *Droit du Travail*, Paris, Presses Universitaires, 1966, pp. 19–21.

[55] C.N. 1780 and 1781. The *Proj. An. VIII* included rather more; the *Projet*'s articles have been influential on the D.O.

[56] See Merlin, *Répertoire* (4), vol. 1, p. 309 s.v. "apprenti", p. 309; M. Planiol, *Treatise on the Civil Law*, trans. by Louisiana State Law Institute, St. Paul, MN, West Pub. Co., 1959, vol. 2/2, p. 103 (no. 1829).

[57] It is most unlikely that the D.O. redactors would have access to it; perhaps it might also be considered as too dependent on conditions in France.

examine a few texts. Thus, *Part.* 7.33.6 describes those serving (*servientes*) as part of the *familia* under the power of the *señor de la casa*:[58] those serving being both his slaves (*servios*) and other (free) servants (*criados*).[59] The same text defines *domésticos* as domestics, field labourers (*los labradores que labran sus heredades*) and freedmen (*aforrados*), all of whom are also part of the *familia*. *Part.* 7.8.9 states that a master may chastise his servant; although if a master kills his servant, he is subject to the penalty for homicide.[60] *Part.* 3.31.21 states that if a man is given the use (*usus*) of a house, he may live there with his wife, sons and *compaña*, which, in this context, means personal attendants. Under *Part.* 7.14.4, a master may be liable for the crimes of his servants, though only in very limited circumstances. *Part.* 3.2.6 in general forbade servants to sue their masters. All these examples, and especially the last, show that the *Partidas* do not generally envisage the relationship between master and servant as being primarily contractual: in this, the *Partidas* are not following the Roman law on *locatio operarum*. Under the Roman law, one who *locat suas operas* would definitely be able to sue the *conductor* under the *actio locati*. These texts of the *Partidas* consider the servant as a member of the family, a personal dependent of the *señor*, in a position analogous to those of children and slaves. This conception of the relationship is undoubtedly rooted in the social circumstances of the period of compilation of the *Partidas*.

On the other hand, the *Partidas* also contain Roman-inspired versions of the tie between master and servant: and it is instructive in this respect to examine the eighth title of the *Quinta Partida*, a title called "De los Logueros et de los Arrendamientos"; that is, "Of locatio conductio". The treatment of letting and hiring is of a pervasively Roman cast, even to the examples used.[61] The compilers of the *Partidas* paid to *locatio operarum* as little attention as did the Roman jurists: this is instructive. The requirements stated for the contract were the same as in Roman law. There had to be a certain price (*cierto prescio*) which had to be paid in money (*en dineros contados*); if not, there was not *locatio* but instead an innominate contract. There had also to be a thing (*cosa*), the subject of the contract; and this could be work (*obras*).[62] No distinction is made between the various aspects of *locatio conductio*, and, as in Justinian's Digest,

---

[58] See *supra*, chap. 4, where quoted in text at note 166.

[59] Note that in the 1844 Lopez edition, slaves, *servios*, are not mentioned. See *supra*, chap. 4, note 166. The point is not important here.

[60] "Castigar puede . . . el señor á su siervo ó á su home libre. . . . *Home libre* placed here in apposition to *siervo* (slave) must mean servant: literally his free man. It cannot mean freedman, the word for which in the *Partidas* is *aforrado* though no doubt it encompasses such. Sons are also mentioned.

[61] Thus *Part.* 5.8.10 gives as an example the liability of a workman if a precious stone cracks: the same example as used in D. 19.2.13.5. Cf. the barrels in *Part.* 5.8.14 in which oil or wine is put with the wine jars of D. 19.2.18.1. S. Minguijón, *Historia del derecho español*, Barcelona, Editorial Labor, 1927, vol. 1, p. 155, remarks that "Las Partidas se ocupan extensamente de esto contrato [i.e. Arrendamiento] inspirándose en las doctrinas Romanas . . . ." It is unfortunate for us that he does not discuss contracts of service.

[62] *Part.* 5.8.1.

references to what would now be classified as *locatio operarum* are few: *locatio operis faciendi* was obviously of more interest to the compilers.[63] *Locatio operarum* does, however, receive mention. *Part.* 5.8.3 states: "Obras que home faga con sus manos... pueden seer logados ó arrendadas." This would include the contract *operarum*. *Part.* 5.8.9 deals with entitlement to the salary of a deceased ascendant, mentioning, among others, royal officials who appear to have been paid an annual salary: the contract concerned must have been, in modern classification, *locatio operarum*.[64] *Abogados* were mentioned in this text, and though this would (now) be classed as *locatio operis*, it may be concluded that in the *Partidas* not only menial tasks were the subject of *locatio conductio*.

We may conclude this discussion of workers in the *Partidas* with the following remarks. Servants, whether domestic or otherwise, were in a relationship with their masters which was not primarily regarded from a contractual viewpoint. Nevertheless, influenced by the Roman law, there was in the *Partidas* a discussion of *locatio conductio*: a discussion which inevitably touched on contracts of service. The *Partidas*, however, are more concerned with the putting out of work on contract to artisans (i.e. *locatio operis faciendi*).[65] Artisans are also discussed in connection which their apprentices who pay them for training.[66] The stress on individual artisans rather than those who work for wages is an obvious reflection of the perception of the organization of work at the time of the writing of the *Partidas*.

In this discussion, we have been employing the terminology of the modern trichotomy; to do so is, of course, anachronistic. The authors of the *Partidas* are obviously quite unconcerned about the nature of any particular *locatio*: they regard all *locationes* as specific examples of the one contract. This is important. In the *Partidas*, the hiring of workers generally refers to the hiring of artisans to undertake some specific task. In all the *leyes* which refer to the hiring of workers, the reference is fitted in to the general (rather loose) conceptual scheme of the title: thus, *Part.* 5.8.10 and 11 are particular examples of liability for *culpa*; a similar remark may be made on *leyes* 15 and 16. There was no attempt made to differentiate the hiring of work from that, for example, of barrels. One may conclude that the contractual hiring of wage labour was seen by its compilers as relatively unimportant (except for that of artisans for specific tasks) and that service was regarded from a fundamentally different viewpoint: servants were considered part of the family, their bond with their master not being of an abstract contractual nature. Discussion of servants in title eight of the *Quinta Partida* is largely a reflection of the influence of Roman law of academically trained jurists.

---

[63] See *Part.* 5.8.10.11, 12 and 16—all referring to *locatio operis faciendi*.

[64] *Part.* 5.8.15 refers to shepherds—*locatio operarum* or *operis faciendi*? This indicates the problems caused by use of the modern classification.

[65] See *Part.* 5.8.10 and 12.

[66] *Part.* 5.8.11 (influenced by D. 19.2.13.4).

More modern works on Castilian law are also of interest, and show development subsequent to the *Partidas*. Febrero gives a fairly conventional definition of lease and hire (not even making a bipartite division).[67] He remarks:

> Todas las cosas del commercio humano, ya sean muebles, raices, ó semovientes, y las obras de manos pueden ser arrendadas con libre y espontaneo consentimiento del Locador y Conductor. . . .[68]

In the whole of his chapter "De los Arrendamientos" Febrero does not properly deal with *locatio operarum—locatio rei* is what interests him.[69] Asso and Manuel give more consideration to lease of work. They state:

> En tres cosas pues consiste este contrato: en el consentimiento de las partes; en la cosa ó obra que se alquila, ó arrienda; y en el precio.[70]

They point out that only illiberal or mechanical work may be the subject of this contract.[71] Of great interest is the following remark on the price: "el precio ha de ser justo, cierto, y en dinero contado."[72] The notion of lesion has been applied to wages.[73] The *Nueva recopilación* has several relevant *leyes*: but the important point here is that none of the relevant ones are found in its titles on arrendamiento.[74] *Rec. Cast.* 4.15.9 (in the title on prescriptions) states that, in general, those who have been in the service of another have to seek their wages within three years of quitting such service. *Titulo* XI of *Libro Septimo* of the *Recopilación* is entitled "De los oficiales, y jornaleros, y menestrales y mesoneros"; it contains various regulations on menial trades, but makes no allusion to the contract of hire.

Thus, in the Castilian law, as in the *ancien droit* of France, there were two competing traditions for dealing with servants. One tradition, derived from Roman law, treats servants and their masters as parties contracting according to the rules of lease: this approach is best exemplified by Asso and Manuel, who deal with servants only in connection with *arrendamiento*. Even so, there was no developed division of lease into anything similar to the trichotomy in the sources; lease was generally still viewed as a single contract.[75] Only the illiberal, mechanical arts could be the object of lease.[76] Further, by the time of Asso and Manuel, remuneration had to be just. The other tradition treated the servant

---

[67] Febrero, *Contratos*, ch. 6, § 1 no. 1 (vol. 2, p. 306). (For explanation of the citations, see *supra*, chap. 4, note 101. On edition, see abbreviations.)
[68] Febrero, *Contratos*, ch. 6, § 1 no. 4 (vol. 2, p. 307).
[69] *Ibid.* ch. 6 (vol. 2, pp. 304–339).
[70] *Asso y Manuel*, vol. 2, p. 112 (bk.2, tit. 14).
[71] *Ibid.*, vol. 2, p. 112: "Que todas las cosas capaces de uso y las obras iliberales se pueden arrendar."
[72] *Ibid*, vol. 2, p. 112.
[73] *Ibid.*, p. 114 on how disputes over "just" wages were solved. See also *Rec. Cast.* 7.11.3.
[74] See *Rec. Cast.* 9.10, 11, and 12.
[75] Febrero and *Asso y Manuel* show this clearly.
[76] *Asso y Manuel* show the law has changed from the time of the *Partidas*: it should be recalled that Bartolus did not limit the contract to the illiberal arts.

divorced from the Roman contract; the employment of artisans was regulated by the Crown.[77] Relationships between master and servant were based on the dependency of the latter on the former, in a position analogous to that of a child. Servants were not merely wage labourers bound by contractual ties.

THE CODE NAPOLÉON

The C.N. and its 1800 *Projet* were important potential sources for the redactors of the two codes. The C.N. contains only two short articles directly relating to lease of labour, C.N. 1780 and 1781, and it is useful to quote them here for easy reference, along with the more general article 1779:

> Chapitre III.
> *Du louage d'ouvrage et d'industrie.*
> 1779. Il y a trois espèces principales de louage d'ouvrage et d'industrie:
> 1. Le louage des gens de travail qui s'engagent au service de quelqu'un.
> 2. Celui des voituriers, tant par terre que par eau, qui se chargent du transport des personnes ou des marchandises;
> 3. Celui des entrepreneurs d'ouvrages par suite de devis ou marchés.
>
> Section 1re.
> *Du Louage des Domestiques et Ouvriers.*
> 1780. On ne peut engager ses services qu'à temps, ou pour une entreprise déterminé.
> 1781. Le maître est cru sur son affirmation,
> Pour la quotité des gages;
> Pour le paiement du salaire de l'année échue;
> Et pour les à-comptes donnés pour l'année courante.

Other articles relating to lease of labour will be referred to in discussing the C.Q. and D.O.

The C.N. does not draw on the modern civilian trichotomy to analyse *louage*.[78] C.N. 1708 describes it thus:

> Il y a deux sortes de contrats de louage:
> Celui des choses,
> Et celui d'ouvrage.

This might seem to be the same division as that of Pothier;[79] but, as noted, he classed *locatio operarum* as part of *locatio rei*, the other division being only *locatio operis faciendi*. In the C.N., on the other hand, *locatio operarum* and *locatio operis faciendi* are subdivisions of *louage d'ouvrage*. Olivier-Martin suggests that the C.N. redactors were influenced by Domat in their division of

---

[77] As the *Nueva recopilación* shows.
[78] Olivier-Martin, *op. cit. supra* note 18, p. 465.
[79] See *supra*, text at notes 36–46.

louage into two.[80] This may well be so; but the division of *louage* into two forms was common in the eighteenth century.[81]

A further source of provisions on *louage* would be the *Proj. An. VIII.* The Louisiana redactors obviously used this work; the C.Q. redactors must have had access to this *Projet*, though they do not appear to have used it.[82] On *louage d'ouvrages*, in the sense of *locatio operarum*, the *Proj. An. VIII* had four articles not found in the C.N.: *Proj. An. VIII*, 3.13.109 is equivalent to C.N. 1779; *Proj. An. VIII*, 3.13.110 corresponds to C.N. 1781 and 3.13.111 to C.N. 1780. *Proj. An. VIII*, 3.13, 112–116 were excluded from the final redaction of the C.N.; they regulated termination of *louage* and damages.[83] The D.O. redactors used them.

Some Concluding Points

We may conclude this introduction by pointing out that, in general, the two sets of redactors were not provided with any particularly useful set of rules to regulate the employment of wage labour. The traditional Romanist sources provided a minimum of rules; this minimum was not always clearly distinguished from other aspects of the law of lease. In Louisiana, this lack of useful or comprehensive rules might not have been recognized as being important given the organization of manufacturing in the territory and the widespread use of slave labour. In Quebec, on the other hand, since industry was in the process of developing, the nature of the contract for the hire of labour could well have been of acute importance; but it should be pointed out that the redactors might not have considered that there was a need for a more developed regulation of labour, especially when their belief in classic economic liberalism might well have caused them, supporting freedom of contract, to accept the sufficiency of minimal statements embodying formal equality and freedom as found in the traditional civil law.

---

[80] Olivier-Martin, *op. cit. supra* note 18, p. 466. Citing Domat, *Loix civiles*, vol. 1, p. 53 (pt. 1, bk. 1, tit. 4, introd.), he states that "[n]aturellement, [Domat] . . . aussi ignore les trois louages".

[81] For example, G. Noodt, *Opera omnia*, Leiden, Johannes van der Linden, jr, 1724, vol. 2, p. 421: "Ait praetor, *Quod locatum et conductum esse dicetur*. Quid haec verba proprie significant, et quemadmodum distinguantur, non caret difficultate. Mihi sic videtur, quod locatio est duplex: alia rerum, alia operarum. Nonius: *locandi manifesta, significatio est, ut aut operis locandi, aut fundi.*" P.J.J.G. Guyot, *Répertoire universel et raisonné de jurisprudence ...; ouvrage de plusieurs jurisconsultes*, new ed., Paris, Visse, 1784–1785, vol. 11, p. 46, s.v. "Louage", states: "Louage. C'est une sorte de contract dont on distingue deux espèces: l'une est le contrat de Louage des choses; ...l'autre est le contrat de Louage d'ouvrage. . . ." Merlin, *Répertoire* (4), vol. 7, p. 573, s.v. "Louage", still states the same, with the addition of remarks between double square brackets to take account of the C.N.'s wording. An important point is that Guyot (*op. cit.*, vol. 6, p. 162) only discusses *locatio operis faciendi* under louage, for *locatio operarum*, one has to turn to his article on "Domestique".

[82] The *Projet* is printed in vol. 2 of Fenet's *Recueil Complet* (see P.A. Fenet, *Recueil complet des travaux préparatoires du Code civil*, Osnabrück, O. Zeller, 1968 (repr. ed. of 1827)), a work available to the Codification Commission: see Abbreviations, in *The Civil Code of Lower Canada*, ed. T. McCord, Montreal, Dawson Bros., 1867, p. XLVI.

[83] They will be discussed *infra*. Cf. Pothier, *T.C.L.*, pp. 63–64 (nos. 167–177). See also Tucker, *op. cit. supra* note 39, pp. 273–274.

Part One

EMPLOYMENT IN THE 1808 LOUISIANA DIGEST

The contract for hiring labour is part of the general law on contracts in Louisiana, aspects of which will be discussed in a later chapter.[84] Only the special provisions on hire of labour contained in the D.O. will be discussed here. These provisions are found mainly in Title Six of Book One, "Du Maître et du Serviteur", chapter two of which is entitled, "Des Serviteurs Libres", and Title Eight of Book Three, "Du Louage", chapter three of which is called "Du louage d'Ouvrage et de Service", the *Section Première* of this chapter being headed "Du Louage des Domestiques et Ouvriers".

The first article with which we shall deal, however, is from the second title of Book One, "Du Domicile". D.O. 8 (p. 13) states that:

> Les majeurs qui servent ou qui travaillent habituellement chez autrui, ont le même domicile que la personne qu'ils servant ou chez laquelle ils travaillent, *pourvu* qu'ils demeurent avec elle.

This is virtually identical to C.N. 109.[85] The D.L.V. refers to *Part.* 3.2.32, Domat (*Le droit public, suite des loix civiles dans leur ordre naturel*, rather than to his *Loix civiles*),[86] and Febrero.[87] *Part.* 3.2.32 concerns before which judge a plaintiff (*demandador*) ought to bring his action; the connection of this *ley* with D.O. 8 (p. 13) is tenuous. There are two provisions in the *ley* which are slightly related to the D.O. article: first, a wife should answer a summons before the judge having jurisdiction over her husband; and second, a knight (*caballero*) who receives pay or other benefits from a *señor* ("rescibe soldada ó bienfecho de señor") ought to be summoned before the judge of the place where he lives by reason of his service as a knight (*caballeria*). *Part.* 3.2.32 is obviously not a source, nor even an oblique inspiration, for D.O. 8 (p. 13). Domat has a loosely analogous provision. He states: "Il y a des personnes dont les liaisons sont telles, que la domicile de l'une est celui de l'autre."[88] He notes that minor children are normally domiciled with their father; but if they a responsibility or employment that takes them away from their father, and such responsibility or employment is one that a minor can have, their domicile will be where they reside for that responisibility or employment. He also refers to married women, and discusses the domicile of widows. He points out that marriage only changes domicile when accomplished.[89] Febrero has relevant remarks. The passage cited is concerned with deciding who may properly be classed as resident in any

---

[84] See *infra*, chap. 6.

[85] According to Batiza, C.N. 109 is the "almost verbatim" source of the D.O.'s article.

[86] Domat, *Droit public*, p. 90 (bk.1, tit. 16, sect. 3, arts. 10–13).

[87] See Febrero, *Contratos*, chap. 1, § 19 nos. 210–211 (vol. 1, pp. 174–176) for relevant text on domicile. This reference differs very slightly from that in the D.L.V.

[88] Domat, *Droit public*, p. 90 (art. 10).

[89] *Ibid.*, p. 90 (arts. 10–13).

particular domicile: intention to remain is of crucial importance (*ánimo de permanecer*).[90] Sons of a family under the *potestad* of their father, and domestic servants who are unmarried and live and eat in the house (but not those who are married and live outside on the portion given them) are considered to reside with the head of their household. The provision is roughly the same as that of D.O. 8 (p. 13); the mode of expression is, however, very different. It is obvious that the D.O. redactors have followed C.N. 109; the significance of the coincidence of their provision with this statement of Febrero is, however, difficult to assess. The C.N. provision was itself new law settling a disputed point: the prior French law had been uncertain as to the domicile of servants.[91] There were some sources in the Digest of Justinian which could have been used here, and which do seem to have been considered in connection with the C.N. and C.Q.; there is no specific reference to them in the D.L.V. opposite any articles, though there is a general reference for Book One, Title Two to "Digeste liv. 50 tit. 1 ad municipalem et de incolis".[92] Nothing in D. 50.1 has had an influence on the article here discussed, and the title does not deal with servants (unless *liberti* are taken as analogous to servants).[93]

It should be concluded that this article has been adopted from the C.N. The servant appears to have a domicile of dependency, deriving from the authority of his master over him. The suitability of this provision and the extent to which it is compatible with the contractual aspects of service will be considered later.

Title Six of Book One of the D.O. has no equivalent in either the C.N. or C.Q.; indeed (as far as I am aware) there is no similar title in any nineteenth-century code. D.O. 1 (p. 37) states that: "On distingue dans ce Territoire deux espèces de serviteurs, les libres et les esclaves." This article hints at why this title may have been included in the book, "Des Personnes", of the D.O. A slave was a particular kind of juristic person, in law partaking to some extent of the characteristics of both a natural person and an object. In Roman law, the slave was dealt with under the first division of the law of persons: this seems likely to have influenced the redactors in placing the articles on slaves here. This does not explain why master and servant were dealt with here. The redactors must have been influenced by the analogy between a servant and a slave. Chapter Two, on free servants, contains thirteen articles, of which three define the various kinds of *serviteur*— D.O. 2–4 (p. 37). D.O. 5–10 (pp. 37–39), six articles in all, deal exclusively with *engagés* and apprentices. For D.O. 11–14 (p. 39) there appears to be a return to providing regulations for servants generally. *Engagés* and apprentices were bound to their masters in a way rather different from that in which other servants were. A master had more rights over his apprentices and *engagés*: they were in a position more similar to that of a

[90] Febrero, *Contratos*, chap. 1, § 19 nos. 210–211 (vol. 1, pp. 174–176).

[91] *Pan. fran.* vol. 2, p. 427; Merlin, *Répertoire* (4), vol. 4, pp. 10–11, s.v. "domicile". Merlin doubts the wisdom of the C.N.'s provision.

[92] See D.L.V., interleaf facing D.O., p. 12.

[93] These Roman texts will be discussed in connection with the C.Q. Domat in his *Droit public* referred to these Roman texts in his *Droit public*, and was himself cited by the D.L.V.

slave than was that of other free servants. This could have influenced the redactors in their placing of these articles. (In this connection, it may be noted that D.O. 4 (p. 37) refers to the title on *louage* for the regulations on the service of servants other than apprentices and *engagés*, though D.O. 11–14 (p. 37) do apply to the former as well.) As will be shown, Blackstone seems to have had some influence. This whole problem may be pursued more satisfactorily after the discussion of the articles of the code.[94] A further spur to including these particular articles in this part of the code will have been the recent (1806) Act on apprentices and indented servants (*engagés*).[95]

The first article of the chapter "Des Serviteurs Libres", D.O. 2 (p. 37), states that:

> Les serviteurs libres sont en général toutes les personnes qui louent, vendent ou engagent leurs services à quelqu'un dans ce Territoire, pour y être employés à quelque travail, commerce ou occupation quelconque, au profit de celui qui contracte avec eux, moyennant un certain prix ou rétribution, ou à de certaines conditions.

The D.L.V. gives no references. Batiza states the source of the article to be Blackstone's *Commentaries*, classed as a "partial influence".[96] Tucker does not attribute any source to this article;[97] and he must be correct. Batiza must be mistaken in his assertion that Blackstone is the source, as the particular passage he cites does not in any way resemble the Digest article;[98] nor does any other passage from the relevant chapter of Blackstone.[99] The source is unimportant, as the article merely provides a definition of *serviteur libre*: the phrasing and content will be considered *infra*.

D.O. 3 (p. 37) gives the following classification:

> Il y a deux sortes de serviteurs libres dans ce Territoire savoir:
>
> Les serviteurs proprement dits, c'est-à-dire ceux qui se louent ou s'engagent envers un autre pour être employés à un travail ordinaire ou de

---

[94] See *infra*, conclusion to first part of this chapter.

[95] Louisiana Acts, 1806, ch.11 (21 May 1806), "An Act for the Regulation of the Rights and Duties of Apprentices and Indented Servants". In the *1823 Projet* p. 11, the redactors state: "We have been under the necessity of altering this chapter in order to insert in it the principal dispositions of the Act of May 21, 1806, entitled "an act to regulate the rights and duties of apprentices, etc." Though the redactors have recast this part of the D.O., the provisions are not incompatible; they have merely included more of the provisions of the 1806 Act, ch. 11 than did the redactors of the D.O.

[96] W. Blackstone, *Commentaries on the Laws of England*, 9th ed., London, W. Strahan, 1783, vol. 1, p. 427 (ch. 14, § 1, no. 4).

[97] *Persons*, p. 280, note 84.

[98] The passage he cites states: "There is yet a fourth species of servants, if they may be so called, being rather in a superior, a ministerial capacity; such as *stewards*, *factors*, and *bailiffs*: whom however the law considers as servants, *pro tempore*, with regard to such of their acts as affect their master's or employer's property."

[99] This is important, lest the reference have been a misprint. Batiza might not have changed his mind on this attribution: the relevant work was unavailable to me. This, however, would not be important here; the content of the rule is not of interest.

> force; tels que les domestiques de maisons, les ouvriers, manœuvriers et tous ceux qui s'engagent pour travailler aux champs et sur les habitations etc.
>
> Et les apprentifs qui sont ceux qui s'engagent à servir quelqu'un à l'effet d'apprendre quelque art, métier ou profession.

It should be noted that only the D.O. regulates apprenticeship: neither the C.N., *Proj. An. VIII*, nor C.Q. do so.[100] Batiza once again gives passages of Blackstone as the source, classifying them as a "substantial influence".[101] Tucker refers to the 1806 Act, ch. 11, s. l, and Pothier.[102] The section cited of the 1806 Act regulates the indentures of apprentices and *engagés*: it cannot be described as a source, though it may well have to some extent inspired the last paragraph of the article. Pothier's provision cannot be taken as a source either; but his list of the various kinds of work capable of being the object of *louage* has some similarity to the list in the D.O.; but this is hardly surprising given that both the D.O. and Pothier have similar notions of lease of work.[103] Batiza is probably correct in giving Blackstone as the origin of this article, though he ought also to have cited another relevant passage.[104] The wording of the D.O. does not follow Blackstone closely (perhaps it is influenced by Pothier to a slight extent); but what seems to indicate that the redactors were influenced by Blackstone is the similarity of the material covered in his work and in the D.O., and especially the discussion of apprentices, even though apprentices are the subject of the 1806 Act, ch. 11. (It is important to note that Blackstone has a modern discussion of the law on apprenticeship; none of the civilian sources consulted by the redactors seem to have done the same, while the 1806 Act, ch. 11 only regulates certain aspects of the contract of apprenticeship.)

D.O. 4 (p. 37) is of considerable interest:

> Lorsque quelqu'un s'est engagé à en servir un autre pendant un tems fixé, moyennant une certaine somme d'argent une fois payée, cette convention équivalent à une vente, les obligations qui en resultent sont beaucoup plus étroites et plus rigoureuses que celles des personnes qui ne font que louer leurs services journaliers, moyennant de certains gages.
>
> Les obligations de ces derniers et les règles qui en fixent l'étendue et les bornes sont établies au titre *du louage*.

Batiza gives as the source Domat and Pothier, classed as "partial influences".[105] The D.L.V. gives no references; nor does Tucker. Batiza is mistaken in his "sources". Both Pothier and Domat (as cited) are dealing with that *locatio* classed by modern civilians as *operis faciendi*; the D.O. is concerned with

---

[100] This will be considered *infra*.

[101] Blackstone, *op. cit. supra* note 96, vol. 1, p. 426 (ch. 14, § 1, nos. 2 and 3).

[102] See Tucker, *op. cit. supra* note 39, p. 280, n. 84.

[103] See Pothier, *T.C.L.*, p. 7 (no. 10), quoted in relevant part *supra*, text at note 41.

[104] To the reference in note 101 *supra* probably should be added Blackstone, *op. cit. supra* note 96, vol. 1, p. 425 (ch. 14, § 1, no. 1). Note that this article of the D.O. was amended and improved in the *1823 Projet*, pp. 11–12. The *Projet*'s recommendation became C.L. 157.

[105] Domat, *Loix civiles*, p. 60 (pt. 1, bk.1, tit. 4. sect. 7, art. 3, note); Pothier, *T.C.L.*, p. 134 (no. 394).

locatio operarum. The D.O. article deals with *engagés*, or indentured servants, who bind themselves for a fixed time in return for a certain sum of money in a contract regarded as equivalent to or analogous to a sale. It is this reference to sale which seems to have caused confusion for Batiza: the redactors are comparing the contract made by an indentured servant to that of sale (indeed a curious comparison, discussed further below); while Pothier and Domat are discussing whether a contract is one of sale or lease of work. The question posed by Pothier and Domat is one popular with Roman jurists, and it is a question specific to the giving out of work on contract (*locatio operis faciendi*). The nature of this question, and the extent to which it differs from the D.O. article, may most readily be grasped by giving an example. Suppose A contracts with a glover that the latter should make him a pair of gloves. Is the contract lease of the glover's services to make the gloves, with A as *locator* paying and the glover as *conductor* carrying out the work, or is it sale of the gloves by the glover to A? What if A supplies the leather for the gloves, or what if the glover supplies it himself? This is the nature of the debate found in Pothier and Domat, and, as pointed out, it is a debate traditional to civilian jurists.[106]

It is obvious that the provision of D.O. 4 (p. 37) has nothing to do with this debate: in fact, the texts of Pothier and Domat simply cannot be compared to the D.O. article. The only similarity is in the mention of sale. Thus Pothier starts by saying: "Ce contrat a aussi beaucoup d'analogie avec le contrat de vente." Domat makes a similar statement.[107] The Batiza references cannot be to "sources", as the matter being discussed is quite different from that in D.O. 4 (p. 37); nor is there any similarity in the wording of the D.O., Pothier, and Domat such as would entitle one to argue that there has been influence on the language of the code. Batiza is here simply mistaken. If further proof were needed, it should be sufficient to point out that, as regards those who let their services daily, the D.O. here refers to its title on *louge*; no such reference is made for those who let their work for a "tems fixé". *Locatio operis faciendi* is also dealt with in the title on lease, while the service of *engagés* is not, being dealt with in this title of Book One: it is obvious that the D.O. is in this article not dealing with the same subject matter as Pothier and Domat. It may be concluded: first, that D.O. 4 (p. 37) deals with *engagés* and those who lease their services (*locatio operarum*); second, that, following a long tradition, Pothier and Domat (as cited by Batiza) are debating whether certain circumstances amount to sale or lease of labour for a specific task (*locatio operis faciendi*); third, that Batiza is mistaken in his claim that Pothier and Domat are the source of D.O. 4 (p. 37); and fourth, that, Batiza being wrong, and no other source being traced, the redactors must have drawn up this article without borrowing from any single obvious source.

The article, distinguishing clearly between *engagés* and servants who were not indented, was probably prompted by the existence of the 1806 Act, ch. 11:

---

[106] See D. 19.2.2.1 and h.t.22.2. Justinian attempted to solve the problem; see Inst. 3.24.4.

[107] Domat, *Loix civiles*, p. 60 (pt. 1, bk.1, tit. 4. sect. 7, art. 3, note); Pothier, *T.C.L.*, p. 134 (no. 394).

in any case, it provides useful definitions, and refers the reader of the code to the title on *louage*. Indentured servants were very much a part of life in Louisiana: penniless immigrants would bind themselves to serve for a term, and in return would have their passage to the New World paid. A supply of labour and of colonists was thus provided.[108]

D.O. 5 (p. 37) states thus:

> Ceux qui ont vendu ou engagé leurs services pour un certain tems, et moyennant une certaine somme une fois payée, comme aussi les apprentifs qui se sont engagés pour un certain tems, à l'effet d'apprendre un art, métier ou profession, doivent être contraints à l'exécution spécifique de leurs engagemens respectifs, pour le tems qui est marqué dans l'acte à moins qu'ils n'aient une juste cause pour en être dispensés, ainsi qu'il est dit ci-après.

Batiza gives the 1806 Act, ch. 11, s. 1 as a source of "substantial influence" on the D.O. article. D.L.V. also refers to s. 1 of this Act. Tucker states that s. 5 is the "source" of the D.O. article. The first section provides:

> That all and every person or persons who may be bound to serve either as an apprentice in any art, mystery or occupation, or as a servant for the sole purpose of ordinary or hard labor, shall be bound to serve the term of time expressed in their indentures respectively. . . .

The section continues, providing that minors required the consent of their parents, guardians or curators to be bound thus, and that the apprenticeship of minor females should end at or before they reached eighteen years of age while that of minor males should end at or before they reached twenty-one years;[109] if either the male or female were over twenty-one at the time of entering "into indenture of apprenticeship or servitude", they could bind themselves for a period of up to seven years.[110] The fifth section states that absconding apprentices or indentured servants may be forced to serve their masters or mistresses two days for every one day they have been absent without leave, or may be compelled to pay damages. Tucker states thus:

> One wonders why the draftsmen chose the right of specific performance over the already integral English actions for wrongful departure and wrongful retainer. Whatever their motives, the choice must have been a conscious one since the latter are clearly exhibited in Blackstone.[111]

---

[108] See J.H. Deiler, "The System of Redemption in the State of Louisiana", 12 *La. Hist. Quar.* (1929), pp. 426–460; L. Dechêne, *Habitants et marchands de Montréal au XVIIe siècle*, Paris, Plon, 1974, pp. 50–77. Though Dechêne deals with French Canada, her account is best at depicting the system of *engagement* for service in the colonies.

[109] Were there no such parents, guardians or curators in the country where the apprentice or servant resided, the mayor, or judge, or justice of the peace had to consent.

[110] The *1823 Projet*, p. 12 recommended this be changed to five years. C.L. 160 embodied this recommendation.

[111] Tucker, *op. cit. supra* note 39, p. 290, n. 131.

Four points should be made. First, to say that these actions "are clearly exhibited in Blackstone" is to exaggerate.[112] Second, since the redactors are not setting out to codify Blackstone, there can be no reason for surprise at the rejection of the English actions. Third, the "English actions" are "integral" only if one presupposes that the law in this section of the Digest is intended to be, and in fact is, identical to the English law. There is no reason to suppose this was the intention of the redactors. Fourth, the 1806 Act, ch. 11 presupposed that *engagés* and apprentices be forced to the specific implement of their contract. Pothier also points out that servants may be compelled to return to their masters.[113] Thus, in their provision, the D.O. redactors here embodied the existing law on apprentices and *engagés*. As Tucker himself points out, given the existing social and economic conditions in the Territory, to compel apprentices and indentured servants to make specific implement of their contracts was sensible:[114] apprentices and *engagés* traditionally could be compelled to perform their contracts.[115]

D.O. 6 (p. 37) gives a direct reference to the 1806 Act, ch. 11 for the form of the identures of apprentices and *engagés*: as such it need not be considered here.[116]

D.O. 7 (pp. 37–39) states as follows:

> Il est de l'essence de l'engagement formé entre le maître, l'engagé ou apprentif que celui-ci s'oblige à servir le maître pendant tout le tems de l'engagement, et que le maître s'oblige de son côté à le nourrir et entretenir pendant ce tems.
>
> Le maître doit en outre, à l'égard de l'apprentif, l'instruire dans son art, métier ou profession; et il est assez d'usage qu'en raison de cetter dernière obligation, le maître reçoive une certaine somme de l'apprentif, comme prix ou récompense de l'instruction qu'il doit donner.[117]

Batiza describes the 1806 Act, ch. 11, s. 2 as the "substantially influencing" source of this article. The D.L.V. also refers to s. 2 of the Act, as well as to *Part.* 5.8.11 and Febrero.[118] Tucker states the sources to be ss. 1, 2 and 6 of the 1806 Act, and Blackstone.[119] The *ley* of the fifth *Partida* is of relevance. It starts: "Resciben los maestros salario de sus escolares, et otrosi los menestrales de sus

---

[112] There is no discussion of these actions in Blackstone, *op. cit. supra* note 96, vol. 1, ch. 14; Blackstone makes glancing references to causes of departure and servants being retained: see *infra*, passage quoted in note 124 and that quoted in the text between notes 133 and 134.

[113] See Pothier, *T.C.L.*, p. 64 (no. 176).

[114] Tucker, *op. cit. supra* note 39, p. 290, n. 131.

[115] See Blackstone, *op. cit. supra* note 96, vol. 1, p. 426 (ch.14 § 1, no. 2): in some circumstances certain apprentices could be compelled to serve out their time; on the punishments for bound servants who ran away, see Dechêne, *op. cit.supra* note 108, pp. 69–71. She points out (at pp. 66–67) that masters could sell their *engagés*.

[116] 1806 Act, ch. 11, s. 2.

[117] Note that the English version renders: "Il est de l'essence de l'engagement" as: "An implied condition of the contract" and: "nourrir and entretenir" as "to maintain". The significance (if any) of these differences is unclear.

[118] Febrero, *Contratos*, ch. 12, § 4 no. 32, (vol. 3, pp. 284–285).

[119] Blackstone, *op. cit. supra* note 96, vol. 1, p. 426.

aprentices para mostrarles sus menestres"; but then the *ley* goes on to deal with the right of teachers and artisans to chastise their pupils and apprentices, which is the real subject of the text. In so far as the *ley* states that masters may receive payment from their apprentices, it has some relation to the subject matter of D.O. 7 (pp. 37–39); but this is the extent of its relevance. Though this *ley* cannot be said to be the source of D.O. 7 (pp. 37–39), it is quite compatible with the Digest's article. Febrero states that fathers may place their sons as pupils or apprentices with masters who shall teach them some art or trade, to which end, masters may chastise their apprentices as allowed by *Part.* 5.8.11.[120] The passage from Febrero also is obviously compatible with the D.O. article. The Blackstone text is of similar import, stating in relevant part that:

> Another species of servants are called *apprentices* (from *apprendre*, to learn), and are usually bound for a term of years, by deed indented or indentures, to serve their masters, and be maintained and instructed by them. This is usually done to persons of trade, in order to learn their art and mystery; and sometimes very large sums are given with them, as a premium for such their instruction. . . .[121]

(It should be noted that the English version of D.O. 7 uses "premium" for "prix" and "to maintain" for "nourir et entretenir".) The 1806 Act is also relevant. The forms and styles of indentures for apprentices and bound servants found in s. 2 say much the same as D.O. 7, though in considerably more detail. In s. 6 it is said that if there is a school in the place where apprentice or servant are bound, should such apprentice or servant be under twenty-one years of age, a clause must be put in their indentures binding the master or mistress to teach or to cause to be taught the apprentice or servant to read and write, and to be instructed in arithmetic.

The D.O. article is obviously compatible with a whole range of provisions. What is most important, though, is that it gives an abbreviated version of the rules found in the 1806 Act, ch. 11, s. 2: the D.O. here is continuing the law in force. This said, it is obvious that Blackstone has exerted some influence on the wording of the article. The article, however, describes the standard relationship between apprentice and master, the nature of which was identical all over Europe; this is why the D.O. redactors were able to borrow the phrasing of Blackstone, and why the article is compatible with the Castilian texts. This is an important point, and it will be returned to later.

D.O. 8 (p. 39) provides thus:

> Les engagemens faits entre les engagés, les apprentifs et les maîtres peuvent être résolus avant le tems fixé dans le contrat, soit à la réquête desdits engagés ou apprentifs respectivement, soit à celle des maîtres, s'ils ont une juste cause pour demander cette résolution, et dans ce cas, le juge ordonnera la restitution

---

[120] We have already discussed this text of Febrero in connection with *puissance paternelle*; see *supra*, chap. 4, text at notes 587–588.

[121] Blackstone, *op. cit. supra* note 96, vol. 1, p. 426 (ch. XIV, § 1, no. 2).

> d'une partie du prix payé sur l'engagement, proportionné au tems qui reste à courir sur celui qui aurait été fixé, si ce n'est que la résolution ait été causée par la faute de celui qui avait payé ce prix, dans lequel cas il n'y aura lieu à aucune restitution.

The D.L.V. gives no references; Batiza and Tucker both refer to Blackstone,[122] Batiza limiting himself to § 1 no. 2, while Tucker refers to pp. 425 and 426, thus including no. 1 of § 1.[123] Batiza classes Blackstone as a "substantial influence". Batiza must be correct: I cannot see any relevance in no. 1 of § 1, p.425, which deals with menial servants or domestics.[124] The passage of the D.O. does differ from Blackstone, however; Blackstone states: "Apprentices to trades may be discharged on reasonable cause, either at the request of themselves or masters"; he adds that the judges "may . . . if they think it reasonable, direct restitution of a rateable share of the money given with the apprentice. . .".[125] It should be noted, first, that Blackstone appears to describe the judges as having more discretion in the matter of restitution of money, and, second, that he does not mention *engagés*. *Engagés* were included in the article because of the 1806 Act, ch. 11 and their importance in the Territory. Although the 1806 Act, ch. 11 has no section providing specifically as D.O. 8 (p. 39), and although the article has been influenced strongly by Blackstone, the provision is quite compatible with the Act, which, in its s. 3, governed the matter of either party violating the contract: this section states, *inter alia*, that if a master or mistress has not discharged his or her duty towards his or her apprentice or (indentured) servant or if the apprentice or servant has not discharged his or her duty towards his or her master or mistress, the aggrieved party could apply to the judge of the county who could "take such order and direction between the master and mistress, apprentice or servant as the equity and justice of the case may require." This must cover the same circumstances and results as the "just cause" and possible restitution of D.O. 8 (p. 39).[126] Though no Castilian source has been referred to, the law there presumably would have contained similar provisions, as would only have been just (see *Part*. 5.8.11).

D.O. 9 (p. 39) states that:

> Si un maître maltraite son engagé ou son apprentif, ou se conduit cruellement ou ne remplit pas les obligations qu'il avait contractées envers lui; et de même si ledit engagé ou apprentif se sauve ou s'absente de chez son maître, sans permission ou s'il ne remplit pas son devoir ou ses obligations envers lui, chacun

---

[122] Blackstone, *op. cit. supra* note 96, vol. 1, pp. 425–426 (ch. XIV, § 1, nos. 1 and 2).

[123] See Tucker, *op. cit. supra* note 39, p. 280, n. 84.

[124] The only passage from this section of Blackstone that could be taken as having any relevance here is Blackstone, *op. cit. supra* note 96, vol. 1, pp. 425–426 (ch. XIV, § 1, no. 1): "and no master can put away his servant, or servant leave his master, after being so retained, either before or at the end of his term, without a quarter's warning; unless upon reasonable cause to be allowed by a justice of the peace. . .." I am unconvinced that this has any bearing or has had any influence; it has nothing to do with *engagés* or apprentices.

[125] Blackstone, *op. cit. supra* note 96, vol. 1, p. 426 (ch. 14, § 1, no. 2).

[126] The section is quoted *infra*, note 128.

> de ses actes pourra être considéré comme une juste cause pour décharger la partie lésée de ses engagemens, ou pour lui accorder telle autre réparation que l'équité ou la nature du cas pourra exiger, à la discretion du juge.

Tucker and Batiza both give the source of this article as the 1806 Act, ch. 11, s. 3;[127] the latter classifying it as an "almost verbatim, in part" source. The D.L.V. refers to ss. 3 and 5 of the Act, and *Part.* 5.8.11. Tucker and Batiza here are surely correct; s. 3 is the obvious direct source.[128] The fifth section is only concerned with absconding apprentices and bound servants; it states that such may be compelled to serve two days for every day of unauthorized absence, or pay such damages as are decided to be "equitable and just". Thus, though the provision of s. 5 is not specifically covered by D.O. 9 (p. 39), s. 5 is related to the circumstances laid out in the article, and the D.L.V. has referred to a provision which is relevant to the D.O. article, though not a source of same. *Part.* 5.8.11 deals exclusively with masters beating their apprentices pretty severely. There it is said that the apprentice ought to be freed from the apprenticeship, to receive back the payment made (*el daño*), and that the master ought to make amends "como este á bien vista del judgador et de homes bonos". The *Partidas*' text is thus more restricted than the article of the D.O.; it is nonetheless quite compatible with the Louisiana article. The D.O. provision is only reasonable, and is obviously is drawn from the 1806 Act, ch. 11, s. 3. It is likely that any such apprenticeship contract would always be liable to resolution in this way: Blackstone stated that apprenticeships could be dissolved for "reasonable cause";[129] the circumstances narrated in D.O. 9 (p. 39) would undoubtedly have amounted to such "reasonable cause".

D.O. 10 (p. 38) provides:

> A master may correct his indented servant or apprentice for negligence or other misbehaviour, *provided* he does it with moderation; but he cannot exercise such right with those who only let their daily services.[130]

Both Tucker[131] and Batiza claim Blackstone as the source of this article,[132] the latter describing him as the "almost verbatim" source. The D.L.V. cites *Part.* 5.8.11 and Febrero.[133] Blackstone states:

---

[127] Tucker, *op. cit. supra* note 39, p. 280, n. 84.

[128] 1806 Act, ch. 11, s. 3 states: "*And be it further enacted,* That if any master or mistress shall abuse or cruelly or evilly treat or shall not discharge his or her duty towards his or her apprentice or servant, or if said apprentice or servant shall abscond or absent him or herself, from the service of his or her master or mistress, without leave, or shall not do or discharge his or her duty to his or her master or mistress, then said master or mistress, or apprentice or servant, being aggrieved, shall or may apply to the judge of any county where the parties reside for redress, who, after giving due notice to the party against whom the complaint is lodged, and bring said parties (by warrant or otherwise) before him, and take such order and direction between the said master and mistress, apprentice or servant as the equity and justice of the case may require."

[129] Blackstone, *op. cit. supra* note 96, vol. 1, p. 426 (ch.XIV, § 1, no. 2).

[130] The French version, D.O. 10 (p. 39) states thus: "Un maître, peut corriger son engagé ou apprentif, lorsqu'il est négligent ou se conduit mal, *pourvu* qu'il le fasse avec modération, mais il ne peut exercer un pareil droit envers ceux qui ne font que louer leurs services journaliers."

> A master may by law correct his apprentice for negligence or other misbehaviour, so it be done with moderation: though, if the master or master's wife beats any other servant of full age, it is a good cause of departure.

Part. 5.8.11 says, in relevant part:

> [L]os maestros…et otrosi los menestrales… cada uno dellos es tenudo los [sc. escolares et aprentices] enseñar . . . et castigar con mesura . . .; pero este castigamiente debe seer mesuradamiente et con recabdo de manera que ninguno dellos non finque lisiado nin ocasionado por las feridas quel diere su maestro.

It is obvious that *ley* 11 is compatible with the D.O. article; but Tucker and Batiza are correct in giving Blackstone as the source of D.O. 10 (p. 39). *Part.* 7.8.9 deals with the same point in a more general fashion, providing that a *señor* may beat his servants.[134] Febrero states that those instructing apprentices could chastise them, so long as the master "no los lisien en los cuerpos": he cites *Part.* 5.8.11 as authority. If *Part.* 7.8.9 is taken along with 5.8.11, it is possible that D.O. 10 (p. 39) changes the law. Certainly the test of what punishment is permissible (punishment given in moderation) is taken from Blackstone.

It should be noted that implicit in Blackstone's statement is the idea that *any servant not of full age* may be beaten;[135] this is different from the D.O., where it is specifically said that servants who are not apprentices and *engagés* may not be beaten. The reason for the redactors not following Blackstone here is difficult to discover. Given that Louisiana was a slave-owning society, it was probably considered inappropriate for free servants to be chastised, except for those who were indentured, as being rather more at the disposal of their masters. It should be noted that in the *1823 Projet* this article was amended to forbid chastisement of free servants using a whip; it was there stated that: "The reason of this restriction, in a country like ours, needs no explanation."[136] Fear of of the possible consequences of treating free men in the manner of slaves probably led to the restriction of chastisement to apprentices and *engagés* (*engagés*, of course, are mentioned in none of the sources).

D.O. 11 (p. 39) provides:

> Le maître peut intenter une action contre un tiers pour avoir battu ou estropié son serviteur, mais dans ce cas il doit fonder son action sur le tort qu'il a reçu par la privation de son service, et ce tort doit être prouvé lors du jugement de la cause.

---

[131] Tucker, *op. cit. supra* note 39, p. 280, n. 84.
[132] Blackstone, *op. cit. supra* note 96, vol. 1, p. 428 (ch. XIV, § II, 1st part, 2nd para.).
[133] Febrero, *Contratos*, ch. 12, § IV, no. 32 (vol. 3, pp. 245–246).
[134] See *supra*, text at note 60.
[135] The relevant passage states that a master may beat his apprentice, but that if the master or his wife beats "any other servant of full age", it is "good cause for departure": obviously a master may beat any servant not of full age.
[136] See *1823 Projet*, p. 13; C.L. 167.

Batiza claims Blackstone as the "almost verbatim" source;[137] so does Tucker.[138] They are correct.[139] The D.L.V. has no reference; but it is a fair assumption that the Castilian law would have allowed a similar action, though I can trace no exactly equivalent text in the *Partidas*. What is important is that the redactors are following Blackstone here. It may be noted that in this article the redactors have returned to using the generic term "serviteur"; this will be considered later.

D.O. 12 (p. 38) provides:

> A master may justify an assault in defence of his servant and a servant in defence of his master; the master, because he has an interest in his servant, not to be deprived of his service; the servant, because it is part of his duty for which he receives wages, to stand by and defend his master.[140]

Batiza gives Blackstone as the "almost verbatim" source;[141] Tucker does likewise.[142] The D.L.V. refers to *Part.* 7.8.6; this is an obvious mistake for *Part.* 7.8.16. The latter *ley* deals with the duty of slaves and servants to aid their master, mistress and the latter's children, if someone attempts to murder or injure them: "Acorrer deben los servios et los sirvientes de casa al señor ó á la señora ó á los fijos dellos luego que vieren que algunos los quieren matar ó ferir." The *ley* goes on to detail the actions a servant should take in defence of his master, etc.: servants should protect their master by using their hands, or arms, or by putting themselves in the middle of those attempting to commit the murder or by shouting for help. Likewise a servant should prevent his master from murdering himself or his wife or his children in a fit of anger. If any servant failed to do these things, he ought to be killed. The *ley* expands on the penalty and on defences. Nowhere is there mention of the *señor* aiding his servant. The reference of the D.L.V. is to a *ley* with some bearing on the D.O. article; but it is obvious that the Louisiana redactors have copied their provision from Blackstone.

The D.O. states that the master and servant have a reciprocal duty to defend each other, based on their respective rights of service and receiving wages; the *ley* of *Partida Septima* merely states that servants have a duty to defend their masters, without any reference to anything they receive in return, other than

---

[137] Blackstone, *op. cit. supra* note 96, vol. 1, p. 429 (ch. 14, § III, 1st par.).
[138] Tucker, *op. cit. supra* note 39, p. 280, n. 84.
[139] Blackstone states: "A master also may bring an action against any man for beating or maiming his servant: but in such case he must assign, as a special reason, his own damage by the loss of his service; and this loss must be proved upon the trial."
[140] The French version, D.O. 12. (p. 39) states thus: "Le maître peut se justifier d'avoir attaqué quelqu'un, s'il ne l'a fait que pour défendre son serviteur, et le serviteur peut se justifier d'une semblable attaque, lorsqu'il ne l'a faite que pour défendre son maître, parce qu'il est de l'intérêt du maître de n'être point privé de son service, et qu'il est du devoir du serviteur, pour lequel il reçoit des gages, de se tenir près de son maître, et de le defender."
[141] Reference as note 137 *supra*: "A master likewise may justify an assault in defence of his servant, and a servant in defence of his master: the master, because he has an interest in his servant, not to be deprived of his service; the servant, because it is part of his duty, for which he receives his wages, to stand by and defend his master."
[142] Tucker, *op. cit. supra* note 39, p. 280, n. 84.

stating that if they do not defend their masters, they may be executed. The D.O. redactors here must have approved of Blackstone's formulation of a reciprocal duty of protection between master and servant; a duty arising out of their respective rights and duties under the contract. The *Partidas* in this *ley* put forward a very different conception of the relationship between master and servant: one which the Louisiana redactors have not adopted.

D.O. 13 (p. 39) is as follows:

> Le maître est responsable des délits et *quasi* délits commis par son serviteur, suivant les règles établies au titre des *quasi* contrats et *quasi* délits.

Batiza and Tucker[143] purport to find the source of this article in Blackstone[144]: a "substantial influence". The D.L.V. refers to *Part.* 7.13.4. Blackstone merely enunciates a rule of tortious liability:

> As for those things which a servant may do on behalf of his master, they seem all to proceed upon this principle, that the master is answerable for the act of his servant, if done by his command, either expressly given, or implied: *nam, qui facit per alium, facit per se*. Therefore, if the servant commit a trespass by the command or encouragement of his master, the master shall be guilty of it: though the servant is not thereby excused, for he is only to obey his master in matters that are honest and lawful.[145]

This cannot be the "source" of D.O. 13 (p. 39). Given that Blackstone influenced the order of this chapter, it is possible (but only possible) that his work suggested the inclusion of this article. The D.O. article is also referring forward to another title of the code; the rule that a master is liable for the delicts of his servants is stated only as a broad general principle, and to attribute influence to Blackstone is misleading.[146] Delictual liability for servants will be dealt with later, and *Part.* 7.13.4 will be discussed then: it likewise is not a "source" of the article in the D.O.

D.O. 14 (p. 38) provides thus:

> The master is answerable for the damage caused to individuals or to the community in general, by whatever is thrown out of his house into the street or public road, in as much as the master has the superintendance and police of his house, and is responsible for the faults committed therein.[147]

---

[143] *Ibid.*

[144] Blackstone, *op. cit. supra* note 96, vol. 1, p. 429 (ch. 14, § III, 2nd par.).

[145] Blackstone, *op. cit. supra* note 96, vol. 1, pp. 429–430.

[146] Since Batiza founds conclusions on the numerical frequency of sources, the inclusion of a "source" such as this shows that his numerations may be misleading: indeed the rules on the master's liability for servants in the relevant title are in fact of French origin.

[147] The French version, D.O. 14 (p. 39), states thus: "Le maître est responsable pour tout ce qu'on jette de sa maison dans la rue ou dans le grand chemin et qui cause du dommage à quelqu'un en particulier, ou peut être préjudiciable aux habitans du lieu en général, car le maître a la surintendance de la police de sa maison et est responsable de toutesles fautes qui s'y commettent."

Both Tucker[148] and Batiza correctly give Blackstone as the source, classed as "almost verbatim".[149] The D.L.V. cites *Part.* 7.15.25 which deals with objects thrown from the house into the street: it does not mention servants in particular; but it is to be presumed that they would be included in the provisions of the *ley* by implication. Blackstone states that:

> A master is . . . chargeable if any of his family layeth or casteth any thing out of his house into the street or common highway, to the damage of any individual, or the common nuisance of his majesty's liege people; for the master hath the superintendance and charge of all his household. And this also agrees with the civil law; which holds, that the *pater familias*, in this and similar cases, '*ob alterius culpam tenetur, sive servi sive liberi.*'"[150]

Thus, it may be seen that Blackstone states the rule as applying to members of the "family" generally: he obviously classes servants as members of the family. Second, Blackstone notes that the principle he gives is the same as that of the Roman law; by copying the *Commentaries* the D.O. has not adopted a rule of common law. Indeed, the principle of the Roman law is as cited by Blackstone, and is the same as the rule in *Part.* 7.15.25. D.O. 14 (p. 39) differs in specifically applying the rule to servants; but this is merely a particular example of a general rule, and would be comprehended within the Roman provisions.[151]

Blackstone may have prompted the inclusion of this rule here; but the rule has a Roman origin. This article is similar to D.O. 17 (p. 321) (Book 3, title 4), which gives a further refinement of the Roman rule; but this latter article need not be discussed, as its rule is consistent with D.O. 14 (p. 39) and does not have a particular bearing on master and servant.[152]

It is now appropriate to consider Book Three, Title *VIII*, *Du Louage*, and to discuss the provisions it contains relating to master and servant. The first chapter of the title contains some relevant articles. The first is D.O. 1 (p. 373):

> Il y a deux sortes de contrats de louage, savoir:
> Le louage des choses;
> Et le louage d'ouvrage.

---

[148] Tucker, *op. cit. supra* note 39, p. 280, n. 84.

[149] Blackstone, *op. cit. supra* note 96, vol. 1, p. 431 (ch. 14, § III).

[150] Ibid.

[151] See D.9.3.1 pr: Praetor ait de his, qui deiecerint vel effuderint: "Unde in eum locum, quo vulgo iter fiet vel in quo consistetur deiectum vel effusum quid erit, quantum ex ea re damnum datum factumve erit, in eum, qui ibi habitaverit, in duplum iudicium dabo." H.t. 5.1: Si quis gratuitas habitationes dederit libertis et clientibus vel suis vel uxoris, ipsum eorum nomine teneri Trebatius ait: quod verum est." See also Inst. 4.5.1.

[152] It is of interest to note that D.O. 17 (p. 321) is taken verbatim from *Proj. An. VIII*, 3.3.17. This article was excluded from the final redaction of the C.N. D.O. 17 (p. 321) was suppressed by the *1823 Projet* (p. 293) and does not appear in the C.L. of 1825, the relevant chapter of which was recast more to resemble the C.N. The D.L.V. refers to Domat, *Loix civiles*, vol. 1, pp. 175–176 (pt. 1, bk. 2, tit. 8 sect. 1, arts. 1–6) and *Part.* 7.15.20 and 26; all of these give versions of the relevant Roman rules, for which see D.9.3, *De his qui effuderint vel deiecerint*.

(It should be noted that in the English version, "louage d'ouvrage" is rendered "letting out of labour or industry".) Batiza acurately states that *Proj. An. VIII*, 3.13.1 and C.N. 1708 are the equal "almost verbatim" sources of the article. He is correct. The D.L.V. cites *Part.* 5.8.1, Domat,[153] Pothier[154] and Febrero.[155] The *Quinta Partida* contains a definition similar to that in the D.O., but without the clear division found in the latter into lease of work and lease of things:

> Loguero propiamente es quando un home loga á otro, obras que ha de facer por su persona, ó otorgar un home á otro poder de usar su cosa et de servirse della por cierto prescio quel ha de pagar en dineros contados . . . .

Febrero defines *arrendamiento* in a conventional fashion; it lacks the clear division into two found in the French code. Pothier states: "Il y a deux espèces de contrats de louage: le *louage des choses*, et le *louage des ouvrages*." As already noted, he treats *locatio operarum* as part of *louage des choses*:[156] his *louage des ouvrages* deals solely with *locatio operis faciendi* (to use the terminology of the modern trichotomy). Although Pothier's definition appears *ex facie* to be the same as that of the D.O. and C.N., the meaning he attributes to *chose* and *ouvrage* is different from that found in the D.O. and C.N.: he could only have exerted an influence on the *form and wording* of the French code's article. The first sentence of the preamble to Domat's title IV (as cited by the D.L.V.) is compatible with the provisions of the D.O. and C.N.; according to Olivier-Martin, it is the source of the provision of the French code.[157] Domat gives meanings to lease of work and lease of things identical to those found in the C.N., and defines lease as "un contrat par lequel l'un donne à l'autre la joüissance ou l'usage d'une chose, ou de son travail".[158] Thus, in this article the D.O. has followed the French redactors, who themselves have followed Domat. The Castilian sources referred to by the D.L.V. obviously provide similar definitions; but these definitions do not have the developed and clear division of *louage* into two types as found in the French sources, being closer to the unified Roman conception of *locatio conductio*.

The next relevant article in the first chapter, D.O. 3 (p. 373), is as follows:

---

[153] Domat, *Loix civiles*, vol. 1, p. 53 (pt. 1, bk. 1, tit. 4, preamble).
[154] Pothier, *T.C.L.*, p. 1 (Introduction).
[155] Febrero, *Contratos*, ch. 6 § 1 no. 1 (vol. 2, p. 306).
[156] See *supra*, text at notes 37–40.
[157] Olivier-Martin, *op. cit. supra* note 18, p. 466.
[158] Domat, *Loix civiles*, vol. 1, p. 53 (pt. 1, bk. 1, tit. 4, sect. 1, art. 1). At *ibid.* (pt. 1, bk. 1, tit. 4, preamble) he writes: "Ce titre comprend le commerce que font les hommes, en se communiquant l'usage des choses, ou de leur industrie, ou de leur travail, pour un certain prix. . . . Car, comme il n'est pas possible que tous ayent en propre toutes les choses dont ils ont besoin, ni que chacun fasse par soy-même ce qu'on ne peut avoir que par l'industrie, et par le travail, et qu'il ne seroit pas juste que l'usage des choses des autres, ni celuy de leur industrie et de leur travail fut toujours gratuit, il a été necessaire qu'on en fist commerce. . . .[A]insi on fait commerce de l'industrie et du travail ou à prix fait, ou à la journée, ou par des autres marchez."

> Le louage d'ouvrage, est un contrat par lequel l'une des parties s'engage à faire quelque chose pour l'autre, moyennant un prix convenu entre elles.

C.N. 1710 is identical; *Proj. An. VIII*, 3.13.3 is very similar, though phrased to deal with *locatio operis faciendi* alone rather than with it and *locatio operarum*.[159] This explains why the redactors of the D.O. preferred C.N. 1710.[160] The D.L.V. cites *Part.* 5.8.1 and 3, Domat,[161] Pothier,[162] and Febrero.[163] The relevant section of *Part.* 5.8.1 has already been quoted; in relevant part, *ley* 3 of that title states:

> Obras que home faga con sus manos, et bestias [etc.] . . . et todas las otras cosas que home suele alogar, pueden seer logadas ó arrendadas.

The *ley* expands on this, except for giving further details of lease of work. The provision is obviously compatible with D.O. 3 (p. 373), but lacks the clear division of lease, found in the D.O. and C.N., into *louage des choses* and *louage d'ouvrage* (and indeed the same may be said for the whole of this title of the *Partidas*). Febrero, as cited, states:

> Todas las cosas del commercio humano, ya sean muebles, raices, ò semovientes, y las obras de manos pueden ser arrendados con libre, y espontaneo consentimiento del Locador y Conductor por tiempo limitado ò por la vida de alguno de elles, ò de ambos . . . .

Though Febrero distinguishes work from objects of human commerce, he is not making the clear, conceptual distinction of *arrendamiento* into two found in the French sources; indeed, the rest of his chapter does not properly deal with lease of work.[164] In the passage cited, Domat defines lease of things and lease of labour in a way quite compatible with the Digest's article. Pothier deals specifically with *locatio operis faciendi*, not with lease of work as a whole: although D.O. 3 (p. 373) comprehends *locatio operis faciendi*, it also includes *locatio operarum*, which Pothier discusses under *louage des choses*.[165] This article is defitietly copied from the C.N.; but rather than seeing it as contradicting

---

[159] *Proj. An. VIII*, 3.13.3 states: "Le louage d'ouvrage est un contrat par lequel l'une des parties donne quelque chose à faire à l'autre, moyennant un prix convenu entre elles."

[160] Batiza gives C.N. 1710 as the "verbatim" source, with *Proj. An. VIII*, 3.13.3 as a subsidiary.

[161] Domat, *Loix civiles*, vol. 1, p. 53 (pt. 1, bk. 1, tit. 4, sect. 1, art. 1).

[162] Pothier, *T.C.L.*, p. 133 (no. 393).

[163] Febrero, *Contratos*, ch. 6, § 1 no. 4 (vol. 2, p. 307).

[164] *Ibid.* Not everyone agreed with Febrero that one could hire oneself out for life. See *infra*, text and notes at notes 177–178.

[165] The second paragraph of Pothier, *T.C.L.*, p. 133 (no. 393) states: "Dans le louage des choses, c'est le conducteur qui s'oblige de payer le prix du louage au locateur; *contrà*, dans le louage d'ouvrage, c'est le locateur qui s'oblige de payer le prix du louage au conducteur." This explains why Pothier discussed *locatio operarum* with *locatio rei* (as already suggested above in note 46): in the contract *operarum*, the *conductor* paid the *locator*. See *supra*, text at notes 17–18.

the Castilian law, it is best understood as a more developed account, providing a clear analysis of *louage* into two types.[166]

D.O. 5 (p. 373) states that:

> Le louage d'ouvrage, ou service, se subdivise aussi en plusieurs, espèces, ainsi qu'il sera expliqué en son lieu.

This article, noting that lease subdivides into various types, simply refers to subsequent parts of the title. In this position, the C.N. (1711) and the *Proj. An. VIII* (3.13.4) both defined in their respective titles the various forms of *louage*, whether of *choses* or of *ouvrage*, in a single article. The D.O. does this in its articles 4, 5 and 6 (p. 373). This departure from the model of the French redactors holds no significance for us.[167]

The third chapter of this title is headed "Du Louage d'Ouvrage et de Service": this is the chapter equivalent to those entitled by both the C.N. and *Proj. An. VIII* as "Du louage d'ouvrage et d'industrie". It is interesting to note that the English version of the D.O. calls this chapter "Of the Letting out of Labour or Industry" and is thus closer to the C.N. and its *projet*.[168] All three codes start their chapters with a general provision; that of Louisiana, D.O. 55 (p. 383), provides:

> Le louage a trois objets principaux:
>
> 1. Celui des gens de travail, qui se louent au service de quelqu'un;
> 2. Celui des voituriers, tant par terre que par eau, que se chargent du transport des personnes ou marchandises;
> 3. Les devis, ou marchés d'ouvrages.

The first line of the English version reads: "Labour may be let out in three ways," while its third subdivision reads: "Workmen hire out their labour or industry to make buildings or other works." Batiza states that the "almost verbatim" source of this article is *Proj. An. VIII*, 3.13.109, with C.N. 1779 given as a subsidiary source. *Proj. An. VIII*, 3.13.109 is indeed virtually identical to D.O. 55; the only difference of significance being that where D.O. 55 starts "Le louage a . . . ", the *Proj. An. VIII*'s article starts "Ce louage".[169] C.N. 1779 has been quoted already;[170] its first line reads: "Il y a trois espèces principales de louage d'ouvrage et d'industrie", while its third subdivision reads: "Celui des entrepreneurs d'ouvrages par suite de devis ou marches." Thus, it may be seen that *in form* the English version of D.O. 55 is closer to the C.N., while the French version is closer to the *Proj. An. VIII*: in fact, the English version

---

[166] By saying that the French sources are "more developed", I mean only that there has been an attempt to refine the analysis of *louage* to make it more conceptually satisfactory.

[167] Note that in D.O. 4 and 6 (p. 373), there are accounts of the various forms of *louage des choses*, though there are none such for *louage d'ouvrage* in D.O. 5 (p. 373).

[168] It is difficult to see what significance there is in this.

[169] There are two other differences: first, the 1800 Projet has "des" before "marchandises" in its second subdivision; and second, it has no comma after "devis" in its third subdivision.

[170] See *supra*, Introduction to the chapter, section entitled "The Code Napoléon".

resembles a translation of C.N. 1779, rather than a translation of the French version of D.O. 55. In the 1825 C.L., the first line of the French version of D.O. 55 (p. 383), now C.L. 2716, was altered to be identical to the first line of C.N. 1779, though the *1823 Projet* proposed no such change.[171] The significance of all these differences and changes is quite unclear, especially when there is no difference in meaning between the articles. It shows, however, that the redactors were involved in a complex process of borrowing and adaption in compiling the Digest.[172]

The general provisions on lease in the D.O.—setting out the distinction between lease of services (*locatio operarum*) and the other forms of lease—have been explored above, as have the equivalent provisions found in the C.N., the *Proj. An. VIII*, Domat, Pothier, and title *VIII* of the *Partida Quinta*. This enables us to suggest the likely origins of the conceptual scheme of the D.O. on lease (but not that of title VI of Book One, which will be discussed *infra* as raising wider issues).

It is obvious that the D.O. has followed either the C.N. or *Proj. An. VIII* (or both—which is irrelevant) and thus the redactors have adopted the French bipartite division of *louage* that probably originated in the work of Domat. Pothier also has a bipartite division of *louage*; but his is different in substance from that of the D.O. and C.N. The *Partidas* do not contain this division; nor does Febrero: they do distinguish between the various *objects* of lease, but there is no distinction of a *conceptual* nature. In the manner of the Roman sources, neither the *Partidas* nor Febrero classify lease into various types according to the object and form of the contract: in similar fashion, they do not structure their discussion of lease to take account of different types of lease: for them there is one unified contract of lease which may have different objects. Thus, though the references made in the D.L.V. to Castilian sources are to passages related to the subject matter of the articles of the D.O., these passages cannot be said to have been a source of the D.O.'s provisions. The D.L.V. also refers to Domat and Pothier: again, the references are to related passages, though since Domat probably inspired the C.N.'s approach to lease, he is closer to the D.O. than is Pothier. The conceptual scheme and the actual articles on the nature and types of lease found in the D.O. are of French origin, taken from the C.N. and *Proj. An. VIII*, and deriving ultimately from Domat: the reasons for the actions here of the redactors will be canvassed *infra*.

The first section of chapter three of the eighth title of the third book is headed "Du Louage des Domestiques et Ouvriers". It contains five articles. The equivalent sections of both the C.N. and its *Projet* bear the same heading. It will be recalled that the C.N. has only two articles in this section: 1780 and 1781.[173] The D.O. has rejected C.N. 1781 and its 1800 *Projet* equivalent, *Proj. An. VIII*,

[171] The last line of D.O. 55 (p. 383) stayed in its original form.
[172] No satisfactory explanation can be suggested for this article. What of the fact that the English title of the chapter is closer to the C.N. than is the French?
[173] See *supra*, Introduction to this chapter, section "The Code Napoléon".

3.13.110.[174] This article provided that, in certain disputes between master and servant, the master was to be believed on oath. That the oath of the master should be decisory in disputes between master and servant, in the absence of written proof, was the *jurisprudence* of the *ancien droit.*[175] The master's decisory oath cannot have been rejected as being not found in Castilian law, as it is clear that, in such circumstances, the Castilian law would also have permitted proof by oath of the master; the redactors of the Digest presumably knew this.[176] One may only conclude that the redactors considered that disputes between master and servant should not be governed by special rules of proof, and that the master should not be privileged. If this is correct, it could be taken as evidence of the influence of liberal individualism, notions of freedom of contract and belief in the formal equality of contracting parties; but this should probably not be stressed, and the reason for the rejection of this rule should be left undecided, though the rejection does indicate the treatment of relations between master and servant from a more conventional contractual viewpoint.

The first article of this section, D.O. 56 (p. 383) states that "On ne peut engager ses services qu'à tems, ou pour une entreprise déterminée." This is identical to C.N. 1780, and similar to *Proj. An. VIII*, 3.13.111 (the former, according to Batiza, the "verbatim" source, and the latter a subsidiary one). The 1800 *Projet* states: "On ne peut engager ses services qu'à temps, et non pour la vie." The D.L.V. has no citations. A passage from Febrero's work, already quoted, suggests that one may lease oneself out for life.[177] It should be recalled that Febrero makes no distinction between lease of work and lease of things, and is more concerned with the latter than with the former. The issue of whether or not one could do so was much debated in the *ius commune*. Thus, Montalvo, in his gloss on *Fuero real* 4.4.8, also discusses whether or not one could grant a lease of oneself for life (*in perpetum*); he concludes that one could not do so validly, such a lease being unenforceable as *in praeiudicium libertatis.*[178] The *Partidas* say nothing relevant on this. The intention of the redactors of the D.O. is important: would they consider the passage already cited from Febrero to be accurately stating the Castilian law? Since the D.L.V. does not here cite

---

[174] This is identical to C.N. 1781; note that the *Projet*'s equivalent of C.N. 1780 is 3.13.111.

[175] See e.g. Guyot, *op. cit. supra* note 81, vol. 6, p. 102, s.v. "Domestique"; Merlin, *Répertoire* (4), vol. 4, p. 5, s.v. "Domestique".

[176] See *Fuero real*, 4.4.8; *Fuero viejo*, 4.3.5; and the Latin gloss of Montalvo on *Fuero real*, 4.4.8 as found in the 1544 edition. It should be pointed out that in both *Fueros* the provision on oaths is not so dogmatically phrased as in the C.N.: e.g. the *Fuero viejo* states that the *señor* must be "tal ome, que sea sin sospecha a bien vista de judgador, e de omes bonas." Pothier, *T.C.L.*, p. 64 (no. 175) is also less certain than the C.N.: "[L]e juge doit-il s'en rapporter à la déclaration du maître? - Je reponds que la décision doit être laissée à l'arbitrage du juge qui doi déterminer par les circonstances, et par la dignité du maître."

[177] Quoted *supra*, text at notes 163–164.

[178] See 1544 edn., gloss e, Si algun/a soldada. *Inter alia*, Montalvo states: "Si tamen quis operas suas in perpetuum locaret: tali pacto adiecto: ne liceat ei per substitum servire: nec interesse praestando liberari: tunc non valeret talis locatio: quia esset in praeiudicium libertatis [etc.]". But see E.J. Cohn, "Contracts of Service for Life in Comparative Jusrisprudence", 20 *Journal of Compararive Legislation and International Law* 3rd ser. (1938), pp. 45–54.

Febrero, there is nothing to indicate that this aspect of his passage was seriously considered, so the question cannot be answered with certainty. What may be said, however, is that the redactors would have agreed with Maleville, who, after quoting C.N. 1780, stated: "Et non pour toute sa vie, car alors on serait une espèce d'esclave."[179]

D.O. 57 (p. 383) provides:

> Les domestiques attachés à la personne du maître, ou au service des maisons, peuvent être renvoyés en tout tems sans expression de cause, et peuvent de même quitter leurs maîtres.

This is identical to *Proj. An. VIII*, 3.13.112, which is, according to Batiza, the "verbatim" source. There is no equivalent article in the C.N. and the D.L.V. has no references. The reasoning behind this article would best be left undiscussed until the following articles have been taken into consideration.

D.O. 58 (p. 383) states:

> Les personnes qui ont loué leurs services sur les habitations, ou dans toutes autres manufactures pour y être employées aux travaux qui s'y font, ne peuvent, ni quitter le propriétaire auquel ils se sont loués, ni être renvoyées par eux avant le tems convenu, que pour cause grave.

The English version starts: "Labourers who hire themselves out to serve on plantations or to work in manufactures . . . ." There is no equivalent article in the C.N.; *Proj. An. VIII*, however, provides in article 3.13.113:

> Les domestiques attachés à la culture, les servantes de cour, les ouvriers artistes, ne peuvent ni quitter leurs maîtres, ni être renvoyés par eux, avant le temps convenu, que pour cause grave.

Batiza states this is the "almost verbatim last part" source of the Digest's article. The D.L.V. has no citations. That the redactors were directly copying from the 1800 *Projet* is proveded by the curious mistakes in the French of the article: "ils se sont loués" ought to be "elles se sont louées", since the pronoun is referring back to "les personnes", feminine; and "par eux" ought to be "par lui", referring back to "le propriétaire". These mistakes are the result of copying the *Proj. An. VIII* without paying due attention to the *Projet*'s use both of "maîtres", plural, and of the masculine nouns, "domestiques" and "ouvriers".[180] Since the redactors were following the *Projet*, the changes they made were deliberate. Consideration of their reasons is again best left until we have examined the following articles, after which we will consider the other French and Castilian authorities.

D.O. 59 (p. 383) states that:

---

179 Maleville, *Analyse*, vol. 3, p. 401.

180 The 1800 *Projet* has, of course, no equivalent phrase to "ils se sont loués"; but in their composition of the article, the D.O. redactors must have paid too close attention to the *Projet*'s nouns.

> Si hors le cas de cause grave, le propriétaire renvoie la personne qui lui a loué ses services, ainsi qu'il est marqué en l'article précédent, avant l'expiration du tems convenu, il doit lui payer le salaire de l'année ou du tems pour lequel il l'avait loué.

The English version describes the "personne qui. . . a loué ses services" as a "labourer".[181] The *Proj. An. VIII*, 3.13.114 provides thus:

> Si hors le cas de cause grave, le maître renvoie son domestique ou son ouvrier avant le temps convenu, il doit lui payer le salaire entier de l'année, ou du temps pour lequel il l'avait loué, déduction faite de la somme que le domestique ou l'ouvrier pourra vraisemblablement gagner ailleurs, pendant le temps qui reste à courir.

Batiza classes this as the "almost verbatim in part" source. The D.L.V. refers to the *Fuero viejo*, 4.3.5, the *Fuero real*, 4.4.8, and the *Teatro* of Pérez.[182] The provisions of the two *Fueros* are roughly equivalent to that of the D.O. (as are also propositions put forward by Pothier).[183] The page of the *Teatro* cited contains the texts of *Fuero viejo*, 4.3.2–5. They have limited relevance. Why the D.L.V. should cite this when it has already specifically cited one of these *leyes* of the *Fuero* is unclear. This discussion will be pursued later.

The final article of this section is D.O. 60 (p. 383):

> Si c'est au contraire la personne qui a engagé ainsi ses services, qui quitte le propriétaire, sans cause légitime, il perdra le salaire pour le tems qui s'est écoulé jusqu'alors sur son engagement, ou sera obligé de restituer au propriétaire ce qu'il aura reçu de lui d'avance sur l'année courante, ou sur le tems de l'engagement.

The English version once more renders "la personne" as "labourer".[184] *Proj. An. VIII*, 3.13.115 provides thus:

---

[181] The English version, p. 382, states thus: "If, without any just ground of complaint, a man should send away a labourer whose services he has hired for a certain time, before that time has expired, he shall be bound to pay to said labourer, *the whole of the salaries which he would have been entitled to receive had the full term of his services arrived, whether said labourer was hired by the month or by year.*" This could hardly be called an accurate translation; part of the French text is missed out, and the section underlined, were it a correct translation, would read: "the salary for the year or period for which he had been hired." See *La. Leg. Arch.*, vol. 3, part II, p. 1504.

[182] A.X. Pérez y López, *Teatro de legislación universal de España é Indias, por orden cronológico de sus cuerpos y decisiones no recopiladas y alfabético de sus títulos y principales materias*, Madrid, En la Imprenta de Don Antonio Espinosa, 1791–1798, vol. 4, p. 195.

[183] See Pothier, *T.C.L.*, pp. 61–64 (nos. 165–177).

[184] The English version, p. 382, reads thus: "But if, on the other hand, a labourer, after having hired out his services, should leave his employer, before the time of his engagement has expired, without having any just cause of complaint against said employer, the labourer shall then forfeit all the wages which may be due to him and shall moreover be compelled to repay all the money he may have received *either as due for his wages or in advance thereof* on the running year or on the time of his engagement." Note that the italicized section is a mistranslation; were the French version properly translated, this would read merely "in advance". This is a major difference in meaning: the English version severely penalizes a servant who leaves his master. The clause was

> Si c'est le domestique ou ouvrier qui quitte sans cause légitime, il doit être condamné, envers le maître, à une indemnité qui est fixée sur ce qu'il en coûte de plus au maître pour obtenir d'un autre les mêmes services.

Batiza claims this to be the source of the Digest's article, classing it as a "substantial influence". The D.L.V. provides the same references as for D.O. 59 (p. 383); once more they contain provisions roughly equivalent to the terms of the article of the D.O.

In articles 57–60 (p. 383), the Digest appears to divide the servants discussed into two classes: first, *domestiques* attached to the person of a master or in the service of houses (families); and second, those who have hired themselves out to labour on plantations or in manufactures (factories). Following the rubric of this section, the first class will be called *domestiques* (personal servants) and the second *ouvriers* (labourers). The description of the first class is identical to that found in the *Proj. An. VIII*; that of the second class, however, is not: the 1800 *Projet* speaks of farm hands, yard maids and artisans. The redactors of the D.O.may have chosen to describe *ouvriers* as those working on plantations or in factories as more accurately representing agricultural and other production in the territory; it is certain that none of the sources they appear to have drawn on (Pothier, Domat and Blackstone) thus describe *ouvriers* or labourers (the description in *Proj. An. VIII*, 3.13.113 appears to be influenced by, or to be taken from, Pothier).[185] Given that the D.O. distinguishes between *domestiques* and *ouvriers* in this way (and Tucker reaches the same conclusion, if I interpret him correctly),[186] it seems that D.O. 59–60 are intended to apply only to *ouvriers* (and not to *domestiques*), since these articles employ the term *propriétaire*, not *maître*. *Propriétaire* must refer to the owner of the *habitations* and *manufactures*. The *Proj. An. VIII*'s equivalents to D.O. 59 and 60 (3.13.114 and 115) apply to both *domestiques* and *ouvriers*. Here the redactors of the D.O. must be parting deliberately from the *Projet*, since they have changed *maître* to *propriétaire* (as Tucker points out).[187] Against this interpretation of the *Projet*, it could be argued that "domestiques" in the two articles refers to "domestiques attachés à la culture" and not to other *domestiques*. This would seem unlikely, however, for two reasons: first, the normal meaning of *domestique* is that of personal or house servant;[188] and

---

not altered in the 1825 C.L., and still remained in the 1870 Code. See *La. Leg. Arch.*, vol. 3, part II, p. 1504.

[185] See Pothier, *T.C.L.*, p. 64 (no. 176).

[186] Tucker, *op. cit. supra* note 39, pp. 291–292. On other aspects of Tucker's analysis of servants in the D.O., see *infra*, text at notes 222–245.

[187] Tucker, *op. cit. supra* note 39, p. 292.

[188] See Merlin, *Répertoire* (4), vol. 4, p. 2, s.v. "Domestique": "On appelle ainsi quelqu'un qui reçoit des gages et demeure dans le maison de la personne qui le paye. Tels sont les valets, laquais, portiers etc." C.L. 3172 states: "On appelle domestiques ou gens de service, ceux qui reçoivent des gages, et demeurent dans la maison de la personne qui les paye et les emploie à son service personnel ou à celui de sa famille. Tels sont les valets, laquais, cuisiniers, maîtres d'hotel ou autres qui sont à demeure dans la maison." Merlin (or Guyot) is the obvious source of this article. Batiza, "The Actual Sources of the Louisiana *Projet* of 1823: A General Analytical

second, given that two different types of *domestique* have been mentioned in articles 112 and 113, the mention of *domestique* unqualified in 114 and 115 must be, at least, a reference to both, and not to an unusual if possible meaning. Even were it to be accepted that, in 3.13.114 and 115, the *Proj. An. VIII* was referring to *domestiques attachés à la culture* (and it is argued here that it should not be so accepted), the D.O. redactors, in their own articles 59 and 60 (p 383), have departed sufficiently from the *Proj. An. VIII*, for it to be clear that they did not consider they were taking their rule—that D.O. 59 and 60 should not apply to personal servants—from the *Projet*: the Louisiana redactors obviously thought that articles 3.13.114 and 115 of the *Projet* applied to both personal servants and labourers. Thus, the classification of servants into two kinds—*domestiques* and *ouvriers*—found in this section of the D.O., though obviously influenced by the *Proj. An. VIII*, does not exactly correspond to the *Projet*'s classification, in so far as, in the *Projet*, the only distinction between *domestiques* and *ouvriers* is that the former may be dismissed more readily; the other provisions of *Proj. An. VIII* in this section (3.13.114 and 115) apply to both kinds of servants.[189]

The Castilian sources cited by the D.L.V. do not contain this distinction. *Fuero viejo*, 4.3.5 mentions only "mancebo o manceba" and "señor"—general terms meaning "manservant or maidservant" and "master". The *Fuero real* refers only to "mancebo" and "señor". A distinction such as that made here by the D.O. cannot be traced either in the eighth title of the *Partida Quinta* or in Febrero.[190] *Part.* 7.33.6 does recognize a distinction among servants; but this distinction does not appear to have any legal results, as all (apparently) are classed as members of the *familia*. This *ley* accordingly defines *familia* as:

> el señor de la casa . . . et todos los que viven con él sobre que ha mandamiento, asi como los fijos, et los servientes, et los siervos et los otros criados. . . . Otrosi son ilamados domésticos todos estos, et demas los labradores que labran sus heredades et los aforrados.[191]

Thus, although there is recognized to be a distinction between "domésticos" properly so called and "los labradores que labran sus heredades", any servant under the power of the *señor* is part of the *familia*, and no distinction of relevance to the D.O. is made. Further, this *ley* is concerned primarily with definitions, and it defines the relationships in terms of *status*; it does not consider the juridical relationship of *locatio operarum*. The distinction, found in D.O. 57–60 (p. 383), between *domestiques* and *ouvriers* does not originate in the law of Castile.

Survey", 47 *Tul. L. Rev.* (1972–1973), pp. 1–115 at p. 104 gives the source of the identical provision of the *Projet* as Pothier, *T.O.*, p. 391 (no. 710 (5), correctly 709).

[189] There is of course another article in this section of the 1800 *Projet*, 3.13.116, which states thus: "L'ouvrier artiste employé à la journée, n'est pas tenu de la mal-façon de son ouvrage." This article does not relate to the point presently at issue.

[190] See Febrero, *Contratos*, ch. 6 (vol. 2, pp. 304–339).

[191] 1807 Real Academia edition; this varies here slightly from the Lopez edn., but not in a material way. See *supra*, note 59.

The relevant D.O. articles all deal with termination of lease of work (in a wide sense). Domat does not deal with this subject extensively; no precedent may be traced in the relevant sections of his work.[192] Pothier, however, in the few provisions in which he discusses *locatio operarum* (eighteen in total)[193] devotes no fewer than thirteen of them to the ending of the contract.[194] His views would be likely to be of major importance for the redactors of the D.O., the C.N. and the *Proj. An. VIII* (his influence on the *Proj. An. VIII* has been recognized by Tucker).[195] The section of his treatise on hire most relevant for the articles of the D.O. under discussion is that contained in sections 168 to 176.[196] These provisions are in a section of the treatise on remission of rent.[197] No. 168 starts thus: "À l'égard des ouvriers et serviteurs qui louent leurs services pour une année, pour un mois, ou pour quelque autre temps limité . . . [etc.]." The text deals with remission of wages if the *ouvrier* or *serviteur* is ill. In section 169, Pothier discusses remission of wages where a *serviteur* or *ouvrier* of his own accord has left his master's employment; indeed the master can take proceedings to compel the servant to return, and, if he does not, he may be forced to pay damages. In section 170, the case of the servant (*serviteur*) leaving his master for an honourable reason is discussed: though the servant is still due damages, they should be less severe than if he had left for another reason. Pothier deals in section 171 with a servant (*serviteur*) enlisting in the army, either voluntarily or compulsorily. Imprisonment of a servant (*serviteur*) is discussed in section 172. Section 173 concerns a servant (*serviteur*) leaving because of ill-treatment, while 174 deals with a master dismissing the servant. In section 175 Pothier discusses proof of the various complaints. Section 176 is as follows:

> Ces louages de services pour un temps déterminé, sont d'usage à l'égards des serviteurs de campagne, tels que les serviteurs de labour, de vignerons, de meuniers, etc., les servantes de cour. Ils sont aussi d'usage dans les villes à l'égard des ouvriers.
>
> À l'égard des serviteurs qui louent leurs services aux bourgeois des villes, ou même à la campagne aux gentilshommes pour le service de la personne du maître, quoiqu'ils les louent à raison de tant par an, ils sont néanmoins censés ne les louer que pour le temps qu'il plaira au maître de les avoir à son service; c'est pourquoi le maître peut les renvoyer quand bon lui semble, et sans en dire la raison, en leur payant leur service jusqu'au jour qu'il les renvoie.
>
> Mais il ne leur est pas permis de quitter le service de leur maître sans son congé, et ils doivent être condamnés à retourner, ou jusqu'au jour du prochain terme auquel il est d'usage dans le lieu de louer les serviteurs, ou seulement

---

[192] Domat, *Loix civiles*, vol. 1, pp. 53–64 (pt. 1, bk. 1, tit. 4, esp sects. 7–9).
[193] Pothier, *T.C.L.*, pp. 7, 19, 27–28, 29, 61–64 and 127 (nos. 10, 40, 63, 66, 165–177 and 372).
[194] *Ibid.*, pp. 61–64 (nos. 165–177).
[195] Tucker, *op. cit. supra* note 39, p. 274.
[196] Pothier, *T.C.L.*, pp. 62–64 (nos. 168–176). *Ibid.*, pp. 61–62 (nos. 165–167) concerns the hire of labourers for a day. *Ibid.*, p. 64 (no. 177) states that the servants of army officers cannot leave such service until the end of the campaign, on penalty of being treated as deserters.
[197] *Ibid.*, pp. 54–64 (nos. 139–177).

jusqu'à ce que le maître ait le temps de se pourvoir d'un autre serviteur, lequel temps lui est limité par le juge.

On doit, à cet égard, suivre les differents usages des différents lieux.[198]

A first point to make is that Pothier does not use the terms *serviteur* and *ouvrier* to describe certain kinds of servant: *serviteur* is not equivalent to *domestique*, and may describe a farm hand or a *valet de chambre*. *Ouvrier* is used generally in a more restricted meaning, referring to a manual labourer. To indicate that these words are not used in a strict technical sense, it may be pointed out that Pothier talks in one passage of "les serviteurs et servants destinés aux ouvrages de la campagne".[199] Second, Pothier does distinguish, however, between personal and other servants. His nos. 168 to 175 discussed above refer to *serviteurs* and *ouvriers*, and deal with such servants leaving or being dismissed: these provisions apply, as no. 168 states, only to those who let their services for a year, a month or some other limited time. The first sentence of no. 176 states that "[c]es louages de services pour un temps determiné" are customary for rural servants and labourers in towns. The text then points out that the rules for personal servants are different, and then gives details of such rules. Thus Pothier makes the same distinction as the D.O. between personal servants, hired for as long as it pleases their master, though their services be let for a particular amount per year, and other servants, hired for fixed periods.

In applying D.O. 58–60 (p. 382) only to servants who are not personal servants (*ouvriers* as they are called in the rubric) the Louisiana redactors are following Pothier. The fact situations governed by D.O. 59 and 60 (p. 382), though the rules are more generally phrased, are those Pothier deals with in sections 168 to 175 of his *Traité* (though it should be said that other writers of the *ancien régime* make the same distinction as Pothier: see Guyot's *Répertoire*).[200] By doing so, the redactors rejected the application by the *Proj. An. VIII* of its articles 3.13.114 and 115 to both personal servants and *ouvriers*.

---

198 *Ibid.*, p. 64 (no. 176).

199 *Ibid.*, p. 127 (no. 372). Tucker, *op. cit. supra* note 39, p. 274, states that Pothier used the term "serviteurs" interchangeably with "domestique". He is mistaken. Pothier in fact uses *domestique* only once: Pothier, *T.C.L.*, p. 64 (no. 177). *Serviteur* for Pothier clearly meant *one who serves*, no matter in what capacity. See the relevant texts, cited *supra*, note 193. Tucker, *op. cit. supra* note 39, pp. 289–290, n. 129 suggests that Pothier used *serviteur* in the sense of *domestique*. To some extent Pothier contrasts *serviteur* and *ouvrier*; but he generally seems to treat *ouvriers* as a subgroup of *serviteurs*, and often in the phrases "serviteurs ou ouvriers", "serviteurs et ouvriers" he seems to be using a tautology to make his meaning certain. He quite definitely uses *serviteur* to cover *ouvrier*; but he is also not entirely consistent.

200 Pothier, *T.C.L.*, pp. 62–64 (nos. 168–175). Guyot, *op. cit. supra* note 81, vol. 6, p. 102, s.v. "Domestique", states: "Au surplus il faut observer que ce qui vient d'être dit au sujet des louages de service pour un temps déterminé, ne doit s'appliquer qu'à certains Domestiques tels que les valets de labour, les servantes de basse cour, etc. Quant aux Domestiques qui louent leurs services aux bourgeois des villes, ou même à la campagne, aux gentilshommes pour le service de la personne du maître, et quoiqu'il y ait une somme fixée pour les gages d'une année, ces Domestiques ne sont néanmoins censés engagés que pour le temps qu'il plait au maître de les avoir à son service. Ainsi le maître peut les renvoyer lorsqu'il le juge à propos et sans en dire la raison, en leur payant leurs gages jusqu'au jour qu'il les renvoi."

As regards personal servants quitting, in D.O. 57 (p. 383), the redactors have followed *Proj. An. VIII*, 3.13.112 rather than Pothier: why should they have done so? Pothier stated that a master could dismiss a personal servant at will with payment up to the date of dismissal; it may be presumed that this was because he conceived of personal service as based on a personal relationship which went beyond mere contract. A personal servant was his master's dependent—his master could dismiss him at will; but he needed his master's permission (*congé*) to quit. The personal servant was in the power (*puissance*) of his master; were such a servant to quit without permission, he could be made to return to his master until the next term day (or as otherwise provided by local custom). The D.O. redactors apparently recognized this close personal relationship; but, because of the movement towards notions of a more abstract equality in the eighteenth century, they followed the *Proj. An. VIII* in allowing a personal servant to quit with the same freedom as his master could dismiss him.[201] The *Proj. An. VIII* assimilated personal servants to *ouvriers* (doubtless because of recognition of the change in the nature of the relationship between master and servant); the D.O. redactors, however, chose not to follow here, perhaps because of legal conservatism or because they thought there still to be a difference in Louisiana between the personal servant and the labourer or workman: the former still being in a close relationship with his master, to some extent outwith the nexus of abstract contract, the latter being in a relationship fully subsumed within the formal law of contract. Given how closely the D.O. here has followed the 1800 *Projet*, it is quite certain that the maintenance of the distinction between personal and other servants was a deliberate action on the part of the redactors.

The rejection of the Castilian authorities requires explanation. These authorities (as cited in the D.L.V.) did not distinguish between personal and other servants: both were regarded as being in a close personal relationship with the *señor* or *paterfamilias*. The closeness of this personal bond would be inappropriate in Louisiana of the early 1800s, with what has been characterized in the introduction as the "exclusion" of the servant from the family.[202] The understanding of the link between master and servant found in these sources was overly based on the notion of service being a status within the family, for such conception to be appropriate for the social conditions of Louisiana, where there had been a limited development of wage labour. (It should always be remembered that in Castilian law there also was the contractual tradition of lease of services, so that the provisions in the D.O. in general had precedent in the Castilian law.)

One final article concerning servants must be mentioned. The fourth title of the third book of the D.O. is called "Des Engagemens qui se forment sans convention, ou des Quasi-Contrats et Quasi-Délits". Its article 20 (pp. 321–323) states:

---

[201] See *supra*, Introduction, at notes 1–12.

[202] See *supra*, text at notes 2–12.

> On est responsable, non seulement du dommage que l'on cause par son propre fait, mais encore de celui qui est causé par le fait des personnes dont on doit répondre, ou des choses que l'on a sous son garde:
>
> Le père, et la mère après le décès du mari, sont responsables des délits de leurs enfans mineurs;
>
> Les maîtres et les commettans, des délits de leurs domestiques et préposés dans les fonctions auxquelles ils les ont employés;
>
> Les instituteurs et artisans, des délits commis par les écoliers et apprentifs;
>
> La responsabilité ci-dessus, n'a lieu que l'orsque les père et mère, maître, commettans, ont pu empêcher le délit et ne l'ont pas fait. Ils sont censés avoir pu empêcher le délit, lorsqu'il a été commis par suite de leur négligence à surveiller ceux dont ils sont responsables, ou lorsqu'il a été commis en leur presence.
>
> Le propriétaire d'un animal, est responsable du délit ou du dommage que l'animal a causé, soit que l'animal fut sous sa garde, ou qu'il fut égaré ou echappé.

This is virtually identical to *Proj. An. VIII*, 3.3.20 and very similar to C.N. 1384:[203] there can be no doubt that the redactors have copied the former, and in the sections of the article relevant here there are no differences between the D.O. and *Proj. An. VIII.*[204] On this article the D.L.V. cites both the *Partida Septima*, title 13, *ley* 4 and title 15, *leyes* 22, 23 and 24 and Domat.[205] The passage of Domat states:

> Les Maîtres d'École, les Artisans, & autres qui reçoivent dans leurs maisons des Écoliers, des Apprentifs, ou d'autres personnes pour quelque art, quelque manufacture, ou quelque commerce, sont tenus du fait de ces personnes.

This is obviously close to the provision of the D.O.; what is interesting to note is the stress on responsability for those whom *one takes into one's own house* in order to teach them. Domat stresses control over the person under instruction. Another passage of Domat, uncited by the D.L.V., states that:

> Ceux qui pouvait empêcher un dommage, que quelque devoir les engagoit de prevenir, y auront manqué, pourront en être tenus, selon les circonstances. Ainsi, un maître qui voit et souffre le dommage que fait son domestique, pouvant l'empêcher, en est responsible.[206]

This is obviously a relevant text available to the redactors. *Part.* 7.13.4 deals with the liability of a *señor* for a robbery committed by his slaves or by "los otros homes que vivieren con él". If we ignore the question of robbery

---

[203] Batiza gives the farmer as the "almost verbatim" source, and the latter as a subsidiary source.

[204] C.N. 1384 differs in lacking the last paragraph on damage by animals (covered in C.N. 1385), and in that the paragraph in the D.O. and 1800 *Projet* which starts "La responsabilité ci-dessus", has only one sentence: "La responsabilité ci-dessus a lieu, à moins que les père et mère, instituteurs ou artisans, ne prouvent qu'ils n'ont pu empêcher le fait qui donne lieu à cette responsabilité."

[205] Domat, *Loix civiles*, vol. 1, p. 176 (pt. 1, bk. 2, tit. 8, sect. 1, art. 7).

[206] *Ibid.*, vol. 1, p. 181 (pt. 1, bk. 2, tit. 8, sect. 4, art. 8).

committed by a man's slaves, and look at robbery by *homes libres*, we may see that the *señor* with whom such *homes libres* live is not in general liable unless the robbery has been carried out with his approval (*con placer del señor*) or on his orders. *Part.* 7.15.22, 23 and 24 deal with an owner's liability for damage done by animals and are not relevant here. The principle in *Part.* 7.13.4 is similar to that in D.O. 20 (pp. 321–323), though the former deals with that which would now be classed as criminal law.

Though uncited by either the D.L.V. or Batiza, Pothier in his *Traité des Obligations* enunciates a rule similar to that of the C.N. and D.O.: indeed it is probable that the *Proj. An. VIII* and the C.N. drew on Pothier for their rule on *maître* and *domestique*.[207]

The D.O. redactors obviously preferred the provisions of the French code and its *Projet*. These contained a sophisticated rule that dealt with liability for servants acting in the course of their duties. As regards servants, this sophistication was lacking in both Domat and the *Siete Partidas*. It should be noted that the liability for apprentices in the D.O. is greater than that for servants: this is presumably because apprentices, being generally young people, had masters who were more in the position of parents, with greater authority over them. The D.O.'s conception of the master's liability for his servants is more in line with the early-nineteenth-century view of the relationship between master and servant than is that of Domat or the *Siete Partidas*; neither of the latter two sources deal in detail with the question of the master's negligence in supervision nor with the acting of the servant in the course of his duty. The article of Domat cited by the D.L.V. appears to make a master liable for *all* the actions of his apprentices; presumably this is because the apprentices live with him in his household as members of his family, under his authority and control. The other article of Domat quoted above similarly does not mention that for a master to be liable for his servants they should be acting in the course of their duties: it only states that he is liable if he has seen them do damage and has not prevented them.[208] This also presupposes the relationship between master and servant as more than merely one of a contract to work, and as based on the servant's subjection to the authority of his master. There was developing in Louisiana a notion of the tie between master and servant as being essentially contractual in nature: this new notion of the relationship between master and servant would call for a rule more akin to that of the C.N. than to that of Domat.

A final problem in connection with D.O. 20 (pp. 321–323) relates to terms. The French text uses only "domestiques", and does not mention other types of servants (apprentices are mentioned specially). Should this be taken as meaning that masters would not be liable for the actions of their "ouvriers" (or indeed of their "engagés", since they are also not mentioned)? A first point to note is that both *Proj. An. VIII*, 3.3.20 and C.N. 1384 also mention only "domestiques" in this connection; Pothier, however, had stated: "On rend aussi les maîtres

---

[207] Pothier, *T.O.*, p. 58 (no. 121).

[208] See *supra*, text at note 206.

responsables du tort cause par les délits et quasi-délits de leurs serviteurs ou ouvriers."[209] The English version of this article of the D.O. rendered "domestiques" as "servants". A further point is that D.O. 13 (p. 39), which refers forward to this particular article, speaks of masters being liable for the *délits* and *quasi-délits* of his "serviteurs": it thus uses a more general term.[210] D.O. 3 (p. 37) defined "serviteur". It stated there were two kinds of free "serviteurs": first, those who hire or engage themselves to another for ordinary or hard labour, such as "domestiques de maison", "ouvriers", "manœuvriers", and all those who engage themselves to work on the fields or on plantations; and second, apprentices.[211] Thus, D.O. 20 (pp. 321–323) must be read along with D.O. 13 (p. 39); from this we may deduce that the redactors intended all "serviteurs" to be covered ("*serviteurs*" having the meaning attributed to it in D.O. 3 (p. 37)). Tucker would presumably disagree, since he gives a different meaning to "serviteur"; his arguments will be dealt with later.[212] If the above be correct, it is still necessary to explain why the term "domestique" was used in D.O. 20 (pp. 321–323) rather than "serviteur". This is readily done. In D.O. 20 (pp. 321–323) the redactors have copied *Proj. An. VIII* very closely indeed: the only difference is that where the D.O. has "dans les fonctions auxquelles ils les ont employés", the *Proj. An. VIII* has "dans les fonctions auxquelles ils les ont préposés"—the D.O. has here preferred the verb used by C.N. 1384. The D.O. redactors have thus copied the noun used by the C.N. and its 1800 *Projet*, without considering the possible implications of doing so. It must be taken then that the use of "domestiques" in this article does not limit a master's liability for his servants acting in the course of their duty to only the actions of his house and personal servants: the D.O. redactors must have intended the law to be as stated by Pothier.[213] The third paragraph of the article covered liability for the first kind of free "serviteurs" as explained by D.O. 3 (p. 37), while the fourth paragraph (on apprentices) covered the second kind of free "serviteurs". Any other interpretation would be ridiculous: if "domestique" meant only "house" or "personal servant", a master would not be liable if his *ouvrier*, acting in the course of employment, being negligently supervised, and with his master watching, through negligence in his work, injured a third party.

CONCLUSION ON EMPLOYMENT IN THE 1808 DIGEST

The first point to make is that, in all aspects of the law on master and servant discussed above (apart from the provisions in title six of the first book), the influence of the C.N. and its *Projet* of 1800 is pervasive—in the actual

---

[209] Pothier, *T.O.*, pp. 58–59 (no. 121).
[210] See *supra*, text at note 143.
[211] Quoted *supra*, text at notes 99–100.
[212] Tucker, *op. cit. supra* note 39, pp. 289–293, and p. 289, n. 129. See *infra*, text at notes 222–245.
[213] See Pothier, *T.O.*, pp. 58–59 (no. 121), in part quoted, *supra*, text at note 209.

articles, the ordering of the topics, and the matters discussed. The Castilian law has not been followed. The Castilian law is not incompatible with the provisions of the D.O.: this is because of the common foundation of their laws in the Roman contract of *locatio conductio*. Nonetheless, the D.O. redactors have preferred the propositions of law they found in the C.N. and its *Projet*; this must have been because the work of the French redactors provided rules more developed than those of the Castilian sources—rules, moreover, which were in a form easy to borrow. The redactors must also have considered the French sources to be more suitable for the Territory, as is suggested by their alteration of the French articles—presumably to render them more apt for the redactors' view of the needs of Louisiana. Thus, in D.O. 57–60 (p. 383), the redactors have closely followed the *Proj. An. VIII*; but they also make a distinction in these articles (not found in the *Projet*) which seems to originate in Pothier, though they have not followed the latter's view exactly (see further, below).

In Title Six of Book One, the redactors have departed drastically from the C.N. and its *Projet*. Some reasons for the placing of this title have already been canvassed.[214] Blackstone seems to have exerted a strong influence over these articles on servants (though perhaps not as much as Tucker and Batiza believe). Articles 1–4 (p. 37) of this title concern servants in general, and are devoted to defining and describing the various kinds of servants. Articles 5–10 (pp. 37–39) regulate the relationship between masters and their indentured servants (*engagés*) and apprentices. (D.O. 10 (p. 39) mentions other servants as well—but merely to exclude them from the rule propounded.) D.O. 11–14 (p. 39) are devoted to all *serviteurs* and deal with the relationships of master and servant that involve a third party. From the foregoing discussion of the sixth title's articles on servants, it will be seen that there is a possible influence from Blackstone on D.O. 3 (p. 37) and a definite influence on D.O. 8, 10, 11, 12 and 14 (p. 39).[215] It has been argued that all the *rules* in these articles are generally compatible with other sources, though Blackstone has provided the formulation. Thus, the use of Blackstone has not necessarily imported from the common law principles somehow alien to the civil law. Blackstone seems to have exercised influence over the disposition of the relevant articles in the sixth title of the first book, in so far as the treatment of the topics generally follows the order of the treatment of the same topics in chapter fourteen of his first book. Blackstone has obviously been a major source of inspiration for these articles.

There are two issues: first, why include these articles at all; and second, why follow Blackstone? The redactors were faced with a recent act of the territorial legislature, regulating the service of apprentices and *engagés*. They also had to include rules on slavery. It would be obvious to the redactors that, following civilian tradition, slaves should be dealt with in the first book of the code, that on persons. This may have suggested to them the inclusion of some articles not

---

[214] See *supra*, text between notes 93–95.

[215] Tucker and Batiza would attribute influence from Blackstone to other articles. For the reasons for any disagreement, see *supra*, text at notes 94–152.

found in the C.N. to deal with servants—especially with indentured servants and apprentices, for whom there was no place in the scheme of the C.N. If this suggestion is correct, once having decided to discuss *engagés* and apprentices here, it would have been necessary for the redactors to include general articles on the various kinds of servants, in order to make it clear just what was significant about *engagés* and apprentices. After resolving to include these articles, the redactors must have examined their sources to find suitable provisions: the C.N. and *Proj. An. VIII* did not regulate apprenticeship, much less the binding of servants by indentures; neither did Pothier nor the Castilian sources, except for some few provisions in the latter on apprenticeship.[216] The only work readily available to the redactors containing useful and extensive provisions on apprenticeship would be Blackstone. Thus the rules on apprenticeship in the D.O. are an amalgam of Blackstone and the 1806 Act, ch. 11. The use of Blackstone would suggest the inclusion of provisions on other matters with which he deals: hence the redaction of D.O. 11–14 (p. 39). It is not suggested that the redactors necessarily drew up the relevant chapter of the code in the manner here laid out; what is important is that the redactors, influenced by the 1806 Act, ch. 11, decided to regulate apprenticeship and indentured servants, and turned to Blackstone as the only source available to them providing comprehensive rules on apprentices. This said, the inclusion of these rules in Book One of the Digest must indicate that the redactors were willing to contemplate the relationship between master and servant as being more than merely contractual and as being analogous to the ties of dependency between father and son and between husband and wife. As Tucker rightly points out, to some extent to be a servant (according to the sixth title of the first book) is to have a particular status in the ordering of society: a servant is not only an abstract contracting individual but is a legal person.[217] Further, the treatment of master and servant along with husband and wife, parent and child, guardian and ward and even with corporations, could have been influenced by Blackstone.[218]

Tucker (if I understand him correctly) appears to believe that the treatment of servants as a class derives from Blackstone and that the provisions of the D.O. in this matter are somehow alien to the traditions of civilian legal systems.[219] I would suggest that here he is mistaken. Pocquet de Livonnière in his *Regles du droit françois* treated servants as being in the power of their masters in the way a son was in the power of his father.[220] The notion—as *Part.* 7.33.6 shows—was hardly alien to the Castilian law. The law of civilian

---

[216] It should be noted that the Castilian provisions on apprenticeship, e.g. *Part.* 5.8.11, are not part of a complete treatment of the law on apprenticeship, but are mentioned in the discussion of other matters.

[217] Tucker, *op. cit. supra* note 39, p. 286.

[218] The last title (X) of the first book of the D.O. is entitled "Des communautés ou corporations". There is no equivalent in the C.N. or its *Projet*. It is plausible to suggest that the inclusion of this title was suggested by examination of the first volume of Blackstone's *Commentaries*, Book One, "On the Rights of Persons" ,which contains a chapter (18) entitled "Of Corporations".

[219] See Tucker, *op. cit. supra* note 39, p. 275.

[220] See *supra*, text at notes 46–53.

countries in the eighteenth century was well used to legally significant concepts of social status —consider the French *noble*, *roturier* and *bourgeois*. Further, Tucker emphasizes over much the dependency of the rules of the D.O. on the common law: as already argued, the provisions taken from Blackstone are not unique or remarkable, and it is unlikely that the redactors introduced the historical common-law conception of the relation between master and servant as still "colored by the ancient concept of status-estate".[221] The rules taken from Blackstone are perfectly compatible with the traditions of the civilian systems on which the redactors of the Digest drew: there is no necessary connection between the law in the Digest on servants and the concept of tenure, as there would need to be for Tucker's argument to be correct. The rules are perfectly compatible with the traditional civilian treatment of servants as members of the family ()or household or as contracting parties: this is why the rules in title six of the first book of the Digest are compatible with the Castilian sources, and indeed with some French ones. That provisions have been drawn from Blackstone does not really affect the matter. It is clear that the redactors followed a civilian (but not Roman) concept of servant in line with sources describing the social relations between master and servant of the medieval and early modern period; they borrowed from whatever texts they could to provide a coherent statement of their views and Blackstone provided convenient legal propositions and texts. As regards apprenticeship, the rules of Blackstone would be very appropriate, as the incidents of apprenticeship and its form were the same all over Europe: Blackstone would be a convenient source, because of his reasonably extensive discussion of apprenticeship.

The sources from which the redactors borrowed provisions for their articles were the C.N. and its *projet*, Blackstone and Pothier— the last indirectly in D.O. 57–60 (p. 383). They did not adopt rules from any of the Castilian authorities. The rules adopted were not incompatible with the rules in the Castilian authorities; but the authorities the redactors used provided more sophisticated rules than did the Castilian sources: the provision on masters' liability for their servants' actions show this clearly. The rules the redactors borrowed were generally in a form rendering them easy to borrow, and also would be more in line with the redactors' view of the needs of their society.

The D.O. classifies servants into various types. The redactors in D.O. 1–3 (p. 37) use *serviteur* as a general term for one who serves in any capacity, and they divide the class of *serviteurs* into apprentices, *engagés*, and those who lease their services. Those who lease their services are later divided into *ouvriers*, manual labourers on plantations or in manufactures, and *domestiques*. Apprentices and *engagés* are dealt with together in the sixth title of Book One because they are both bound to their masters by indentures; domestics and labourers lease their services.

Before considering the implications of the above, it is necessary to discuss briefly the views of Tucker. He denies that labourers may properly be classed as

---

[221] See Tucker, *op. cit. supra* note 39, pp. 280, 286–288.

serviteurs under the D.O. When the terms of D.O. 11–14 (p. 39) are considered, it may be seen that his views could cause difficulties.[222] He states that:

> Although the Code is not entirely consistent, *serviteur* is apparently a term which gauges the extent of the master's authority (*potestas*) over the particular type of servant. Whether or not the servant is a *serviteur* depends on the degree to which he necessarily becomes part of the master's *familia* as a result of his contract.[223]

It may be pointed out that in D.O. 1–3 (p. 37) the Digest uses *serviteur* to describe *any* kind of servant—even a slave. Furthermore, D.O. 3 (p. 37) purports to define "serviteur" stating that "serviteurs" properly so called are those who lease or engage themselves for ordinary or hard labour, such *serviteurs* being *domestiques de maison*, *ouvriers*, *mainœuvriers*, and all those who engage to work "aux champs et sur les habitations etc.". Thus, the Digest itself is quite clear that a *serviteur* is one who serves *in any capacity*: it does accept in D.O. 3 (p. 37) that an apprentice is not a *serviteur* properly so called, but that is all.[224]

Tucker argues that *serviteurs* are only those servants who may be classed as part of the master's *familia*. There is one relevant article in the Digest, D.O. 78 (p. 127):

> Le mot de famille employé dans cette section, doit s'entendre de la femme, des enfans et des domestiques de celui à qui le droit d'usage ou d'habitation est accordé.

This article refers only to *domestiques* not to *serviteurs*; moreover it refers specifically to the question of use and habitation. Rights of use and habitation were very restricted rights, as Domat, for example, explains:[225] this article is concerned to stress that if one is granted, for example, a right of habitation, one's domestic servants may live with one.[226] In this, the article finds precedent in *Part.* 3.31.21 and in Domat.[227] The D.L.V. refers to *Part.* 7.3.6, here: this is a mistake for 7.33.6, already quoted.[228] *Part.* 3.31.21 and Domat are texts also dealing with

---

[222] These articles use the term *serviteur*.

[223] Tucker, *op. cit. supra* note 39, pp. 289–290.

[224] This no doubt why in D.O. 20 (pp. 321–323) discussed *supra*, text at notes 203–213, there is a separate provision for apprentices, if it is accepted that there *domestiques*, taken with D.O. 13 (p. 39) should be understood as *serviteurs*. Ironically, Tucker, *op. cit. supra* note 39, p. 290 would have to include (by his own logic) apprentices as part of the *familia* and hence as *serviteurs*.

[225] Domat, *Loix civiles*, vol. 1, p. 105 (pt 1, bk. 1, tit. 11, preamble).

[226] See D.O.

[227] Domat, *Loix civiles*, vol. 1, p. 108 (pt 1, bk. 1, tit. 11, sect. 2, art. 8). It seems likely that the term "domestique" in the D.O. is derived from from Domat, who said: "Le droit d'habitation s'étend à toute la famille de celui qui à ce droit. Car il ne peut habiter séparement de sa femme, de ses enfans, de ses domestiques. Et il en est de même si ce droit est acquis à la femme. Ce qui s'entend de l'habitation même qui étoit acquise avant le mariage."

[228] See *supra*, text at notes 58–59 and 191. Batiza on this article of the D.O. wrongly refers to *Part.* 7.23.6, and Tucker wrongly to *Part.* 7.1.6 (Tucker, *op. cit. supra* note 39, p. 285, n. 108). Strange that all three should all give different wrong references.

rights of use and habitation; *Part*. 7.33.6 defines "family". As it stands, this article is quite unexceptional. Tucker only quotes D.O. 78 (p. 127) in a footnote;[229] in his text, however, he quotes article 3522 of the 1825 C.L.:

> *Family*. Family in a limited sense, signifies the father, mother and children. In a more extensive sense, it comprehends all the individuals who live under the authority of another, and includes not only the servants [*les serviteurs*], but also the slaves of the father of family. It is also employed to signify all the relations who descend from a common root.[230]

It seems to be from this article of the C.L. that Tucker has developed the idea that *serviteurs* in the D.O. referred only to servants who lived with their masters. Though Tucker has to recognize that *serviteur* is sometimes used in a broad sense in the D.O., he states that "in a more restricted sense, it is used almost interchangeably with *domestique*. This latter seems to be the sense given it by Pothier."[231] The statement about Pothier is misleading.[232] That the D.O. itself uses *serviteur* interchangeably with *domestique* also seems unlikely: there is no evidence that this is so. It has already been argued that in D.O. 20 (pp. 321–323) *domestique* was used when *serviteur* should have been; but there were obvious reasons why this was so and this usage does not give support to Tucker's statement.[233] The equation of *domestique* and *serviteur* allows Tucker to assimilate C.L. 3522 to D.O. 78 (p. 127). In fact, C.L. 3522 is the only evidence Tucker has for *domestique* having the same meaning as *serviteur*.[234] That this usage of the 1825 C.L. should necessarily be taken to show the intended meaning of the D.O. is questionable: further, it is unrealistic to expect consistency in usage. There can be no gainsaying the redactors' use of serviteur in D.O. 3 (p. 37) to mean *any one who serves in whatever capacity*.[235] Tucker

---

[229] Tucker, *op. cit. supra* note 39, p. 285, n. 107.

[230] C.L. 3522, par. 16; Tucker, *op. cit. supra* note 39, p. 285.

[231] Tucker, *op. cit. supra* note 39, pp. 289–290.

[232] See *supra*, text at note 199 and note 199 itself. At most, Pothier contrasts *serviteur* with *ouvrier*; but he is by no means consistent—he seems to regard *ouvriers* as a sub-class of *serviteurs*.

[233] See *supra*, text at notes 209–213.

[234] It is interesting to note the background to C.L. 3522, paragraph 16. The *1823 Projet* recommended the inclusion of *titre* 23, "De la signification des termes de Droit": pp. 416–424. Paragraph 36 of the one article of this title read thus: "*Famille*. Ce mot appliqué aux personnes dans son sens le plus étendu, signifie toutes celles qui sont soumises à plus puissance d'un autre, et en ce sens il comprend non seulement les domestiques du père de famille, mais même ses esclaves. Strictement on entend par le mot famille, le père, la mère et les enfans. Dans un sens, plus étendu, on entend tous les parens qui dependent d'une souche commune." This became C.L. 3522 (16). Note that *domestiques* is used in the *Projet*, whereas *serviteurs* is used in the C.L.; further, the *Projet* uses *strictement* whereas the C.L. refers to "un sens limité." These changes provoke thought, and could affect Tucker's argument; but we need not consider this here. Batiza, *op. cit. supra* note 188, p. 115 gives as the sources of this provision of the *Projet*: *Part*. 7.33.6 and D. 50.16.195.1–5. (Actually, he gives D. 50.16.1–5; this is an obvious mistake in printing.) D. 50.16 is the famous title, *De verborum significatione*.

[235] Tucker, *op. cit. supra* note 39, p. 289, n 129, does try. He states: "In addition, article 1.6.3 . . . includes among *serviteurs* 'properly speaking', laborers and workmen; this inclusion was

finally looks at D.O. 57–60 (p. 383). D.O. 58–60 deal with *ouvriers*, labourers, and Tucker states:

> It seems certain that this second category, the laborers, is not intended as a class of *serviteurs*. In the first place, the articles refer only to '*propriétaire*' or proprietor throughout, in place of '*maître*' or master; this could hardly be the result of inadvertance, since the articles from the Projet of the Year *VIII*, from which these articles are drawn, refer to the *maître* and *domestique*. In the second place, the service of the laborer is defined in terms of that which is done 'on plantations or... in manufactures'. This is a departure from the service of all other servants, who are bound to serve their masters."[236]

Tucker's first point—the use of *propriétaire*—is quite irrelevant. The D.O. has to use this term because it talks of those who lease their services on plantations or in manufactures: the *propriétaire* is the owner of such plantations or manufactures. In the *Proj. An. VIII*, *maître* and *domestique* are indeed used: in 3.13.113 the term "domestiques" is qualified by the phrase "attachés à la culture";[237] in 3.13.114, *domestique* and *ouvrier* are mentioned[238]; and in 3.13.115 once more both *domestique* and *ouvrier* are mentioned.[239] The difference is that *Proj. An. VIII*, 3.13.114 and 115 apply to all servants, whereas D.O. 59 and 60 (p. 383) apply only to *ouvriers*.[240] Further, the *Projet* has phrased the articles more directly than has the French text of the D.O. (and the French is here the original text):[241] thus the D.O. talks of the person "qui a loué" or "qui a engagé" his services leaving the *propriétaire* of the plantation or manufacture; whereas the *Projet* talks of the *domestique* or *ouvrier* quitting the *maître* or being dismissed by him. The *Projet* could not use the term *propriétaire* because it also talks of domestic servants; the D.O. does not, and follows the usage established in D.O. 58 (p. 383). All that may be said on Tucker's second point is that he is correct, in so far as what differentiated an *ouvrier* from other servants is the nature of the *ouvrier*'s work: that the nature of the employment of an *ouvrier* is different from that of a *domestique* is inevitable and has no bearing on whether or not an *ouvrier*—if this be the correct term for the *personnes* discussed in D.O. 58–60 (p. 383)[242] —classed by the D.O. as a *serviteur*. Thus, these two points of Tucker, though correct in themselves, have no bearing on whether or not an *ouvrier* should be classed as a *serviteur*.

---

suppressed in 1825." This is misleading D.O. 3 (p. 37) was indeed reformed, and became C.L. 157; this new article made no mention of labourers or workmen. This was not because *serviteur* was redefined so as to exclude them; rather, the article was phrased in more general terms, and *ouvriers* (though not mentioned) would still be classed as *serviteurs*. C.L. 157 is quoted *infra*, text at note 257.

[236] Tucker, *op. cit. supra* note 39, pp. 291–292. The elipsis in the passage quoted is Tucker's.

[237] Quoted *supra*, text between notes 179–180.

[238] Quoted *supra*, text between notes 181–182.

[239] Quoted *supra*, text between notes 184–185.

[240] See *supra*, text at notes 185–202, for argument.

[241] The mistakes in the French caused by the copying of the 1800 *Projet* for D.O. 58 (p. 383) show this. See *supra*, text at note 180.

[242] The rubric of course states "Du Louage des Domestiques et Ouvriers".

We may conclude that Tucker has failed to establish that *ouvriers* or labourers should be excluded from the general class of *serviteurs*: thus, contrary to Tucker's opinion, D.O. 11 and 12 (p. 39) would apply to workmen.[243] *Serviteurs* here must be used in the general sense given the term by D.O. 3 (p. 37).[244] What maybe of some significance is that the D.O. nowhere defines *domestique* or *ouvrier*; in D.O. 57 (p. 383) the term "domestique", used in the sense of personal or house servants, is qualified by the phrase "attachés à la personne du maître", while in D.O. 58–60 (p. 383) the French text only refers to those who lease themselves. The D.O. recognizes the different objects of the contracts of lease as having different consequences; but it does not use *domestique* or *ouvrier* as strict technical terms with a particular, defined meaning (though it has been convenient to use them here with such a meaning for purposes of discussion).[245] That is, in the D.O., *domestique* and *ouvrier* (labourer) are essentially used to describe the kind of work, rather than describing a servant in a particular juridical relationship with an employer. An *engagé*, for example, could serve as a *domestique* or as an *ouvrier*.

The division of servants into *engagés* and apprentices, as found in the D.O., and the rules on such *engagés* and apprentices seem reasonable and in line with socio-economic conditions of the Territory, where *engagés* were used extensively and where apprentices to trades would probably play an important part in production—as they did, for example, in Baltimore in the same period.[246] Apprentices were certainly very much a feature of artisan production before industrialization. Domestic servants and manual labourers are distinguished one from the other; this is apparently because the former are in a close personal relationship with their masters, while the latter are not. In the introduction to this chapter, it was pointed out that in the seventeenth century the status of personal servants was lowered towards that of manual workers, though their relationship to their masters still retained a closeness which went beyond a merely contractual connection.[247] In the discussion of the Castilian law, it was shown that in the *Partidas* servants were considered as part of the family of the *señor*: such servants were a fairly wide class, according to *Part*. 7.33.6, going beyond merely personal servants. Such closeness of relationship would be unsuitable for Louisiana as regards manual labourers; but as regards domestic servants, it is difficult to say whether or not they were in a close relationship with their

---

243 Tucker, *op. cit. supra* note 39, pp. 292–293.

244 In *ibid.*, pp. 292–293, Tucker mentions only D.O. 11 and 12 (p. 39): what of D.O. 13 and 14 (p. 39)—surely he should state that *ouvriers* are not covered by these articles, since they too talk of *serviteurs*? In *ibid.*, pp. 289–290, n. 129 at p. 290, he suggests that, in these articles too, *serviteurs* had the meaning of *domestiques*. He does not take account of this, however, in *ibid.*, pp. 290–293. In fact, it cannot be so for D.O. 13 (p. 39), without radically changing the law in a strange fashion: see *supra*, text at notes 143–146 and 209–213.

245 The C.L., of course, in its article 3172, gives a definition of *domestique*; this need not concern us. See *supra*, note 188.

246 See on *engagés*, Deiler, *op. cit. supra* note 108; and on apprentices C.G. Steffens, *op. cit. supra* note 10, p. 107. Also on the latter see *supra*, note 11.

247 See *supra*, text at notes 2–9.

masters—a closeness or dependency going beyond a formal contractual tie. The extent to which the notion of wage labour had developed in Louisiana by this period is unclear, though it is certain that employment in industrial production was negligible. Since industrial employment had not developed, when domestic service is in turn considered, it is tempting to surmise that the notion of service had not become completely subjected to the ideals of contract. Should this be correct, it explains the adoption (and adaption) of the distinction found in Pothier (or Guyot) between domestics and manual labourers.[248] Domestic service was regarded as involving a personal bond or dependency beyond the mere contractual tie. Yet, because of the development of the ideals of liberal individualism and of the exclusion of the servant from the family, the relationship between master and servant was becoming subject to increasing contractual regulation: this explains the tensions in the law and the difference from the law as stated by Pothier or as in Guyot's *Répertoire*.[249]

The more "personal" view of domestic service would explain the rejection of the provisions of the C.N. and its *Projet* which did not distinguish, to any extent, between manual labour and domestic service; indeed, they largely assimilated the latter to the former, rendering personal service much more a division of the rules on contract. The perceived close relationship between the personal servant and his master in Louisiana would explain the adoption of the rule of the C.N. that a servant living with his master acquired his master's domicile.[250] The choice among the sources on the liability of the master for his servants' acts would also seem to reflect the contemporary (more contractual) conceptions of the nature of the bond between master and servant; the master's liability for his apprentices would also seem to reflect the nature of the contract of apprenticeship.[251]

This leads to the conclusion that the redactors of the D.O., while heavily influenced by the civilian tradition, recognized both the personal nature of domestic service, and the very loose tie between a master and his labourers: accordingly, drawing on the sources available to them, they sought to embody this recognition in the propositions of law laid down in their code. Given the terms used by the redactors of the D.O., it is obvious that their focus was on the employment of persons of low status: this probably reflects the outlook of their society, and follows the civilian tradition.

One problem remains: D.O. 2, 4 and 5 (p. 37) all mention "sale" of services. D.O. 2 (p. 37) states: "Les serviteurs libres sont en général toutes les personnes qui louent, vendent ou engagent leurs services [etc.]". D.O. 4 (p. 37) states that the contract by which "quelqu'un s'est engagé à en servir un autre pendant un tems fixé, moyennant une certaine somme d'argent une fois payée" is

---

[248] See *supra*, text at notes 185–202.
[249] See Guyot, *op. cit. supra* note 81, vol. 6, p. 102, s.v. "Domestique", where he makes exactly the same distinction as Pothier between personal and other service; this is quoted in note 200 *supra*.
[250] See *supra*, text at notes 85–93.
[251] See *supra*, text at notes 203–213.

"équivalent à une vente". D.O. 5 (p. 37) states that: "Ceux qui ont vendu ou engagé leurs services pour un certain tems, et moyennent une certaine somme une fois payée, comme aussi les apprentifs qui se sont engagés pour un certain tems [etc.]", may be forced to make specific implement of their contracts. What is the significance of this usage? D.O. 4 and D.O. 5, by stating that it is those undertaking to serve for a specific time for a certain sum of money who "sell" their services, show that it is only indentured servants, *engagés*, who "sell" their services; apprentices are not considered as selling their services, as the wording of these articles indicates.[252] That this is probably the correct interpretation is suggested by the 1825 C.L.: on the recommendation of the 1823 *Projet*,[253] D.O. 3 was reformed and D.O. 4 and 5 suppressed, all to be replaced ultimately by C.L. 157. It provides:

> Il y a trois sortes de serviteurs libres dans cet Etat, savoir:
>
> 1. Ceux qui ne font que louer leurs services à la journee, à la semaine, au mois ou à l'année, moyennant de certains gages;
>
> Les règles qui fixent l'étendue et les bornes de ces contrats, sont établies au titre du louage.
>
> 2. Ceux qui s'engagent à servir pendant un tems fixé, moyennant une certaine somme d'argent, et qui, pour cette raison, sont considérés, non comme ayant loué, mais ayant vendu leurs services;
>
> 3. Les apprentis, c'est-à-dire, ceux qui s'engagent à servir quelqu'un, à l'effet d'apprendre quelque art, métier ou profession.
>
> Ce qui concerne les engagés, dont les services sont vendus pour le payement de leur passage, est réglé par une loi particulière qui n'est point rappelée par ce titre.[254]

Since this article is generally only a reformulation of the material of the D.O., it is, as such, good evidence that only *engagés* were considered by the D.O. redactors as selling their services, apprentices not being considered as doing so. The redactors of the 1825 C.L. have obviously thought this to be the meaning of the D.O. For an apprentice to be considered as "selling" his services is quite illogical anyway. As D.O. 1 (p. 453) states, sale is a contract by which one party gives a thing for a price in money and the other gives the price to have the thing. An apprentice cannot be considered as "selling" his services, for he is getting no money in return; indeed, as D.O. 7 (pp. 37–39) states, often the apprentice paid the master: thus, these articles cannot be referring to an apprentice as "selling" his services. Tucker makes the following remarks on D.O. 4–5 (p. 37):

> The analogy to sale is puzzling and unfortunate. Strictly speaking, the sale of a free man's services in the civil law ought to be a conceptual impossibility. . . .

---

[252] Tucker, *op. cit. supra* note 39, p. 290, states: "Bound servants and apprentices, for example, are considered to have sold their services for the contracts term. . . ." I cannot agree with his view that apprentices—according to the D.O. —sell their services; he must be mistaken.

[253] See *1823 Projet*, pp. 11–12.

[254] The last paragraph was not proposed in the *1823 Projet*, p. 12. The act referred to must be the 1806 Act, ch. 11.

> Even apart from Pothier's later distinction between obligations to do and those to give, a sale of services is problematical; it is difficult to conceive of a man transferring all his interest in his own acts to another, without also selling his body as part of the deal.
>
> There are two possible explanations for this bit of deeming. One is that it lays the theoretical groundwork for the master's right of specific performance (article 1.6.5 (p. 36)). The other is historical. Hire at common law was regarded as sale for a time. Even today, the master at common law hires the *man*, not his services. . . . And in 1808, the incidents of the "hire" more closely resembled those attached to a civil law sale than to lease. In the translation of common law incidents to civil law form, perhaps that form was chosen which most nearly embodied the alien incidents.[255]

It seems unlikely that the intention behind the use of the term "sale" was to ground the master's right of specific performance; such a right of specific performance was integral to the particular contract entered into by *engagés*: further, apprentices could be held to specific implement of their contracts, and they were not considered as having "sold" their services (though Tucker mistakenly thinks they were).[256] The common law influence also suggested by Tucker as perhaps being the reason for the reference to sale in these articles seems unlikely to have been the cause: though it is possible that it was.[257] What seems, however, to have most influenced the redactors was the *nature* of the contract entered into by *engagés*, and their consequent social position: *engagés* were not free men anymore. The 1806 Act, ch 11, s.1 talks of parties "entering into indenture either of apprenticeship or servitude"; rewards were offered for the return of absconding *engagés*.[258] In Quebec, an *engagé* was described as: "un homme tenu d'aller partout et faire ce que son maître lui demande comme un esclave, durant le temps de son engagement."[259] Cargoes of immigrants were advertised as arriving in New Orleans so that they could be bound for a sum of money that they would hand over to the captain of the ship which brought them to pay for their passage.[260] The description of an *engagé* as having sold himself was apt. Tucker states that sale of one's services was conceptually impossible for the civil law; but the D.O. was dealing with circumstances in Louisiana in the early nineteenth century. The D.O. redactors were faced with an institution unknown to the Roman law, but very important in the Territory. They seem likely to have been struck by the obvious analogy of *engagement* to sale; and they used the term "sale" accordingly in their code to enable them to make a distinction between the *indentures* of *engagés* and the contracts of domestics and labourers. The redactors were cautious, however, in their use of the terminology of sale. This is indicated

---

255 Tucker, *op. cit. supra* note 39, p. 290 and n. 130.

256 See *supra*, note 252.

257 Blackstone, *op. cit. supra* note 96, vol. 1, p. 429 (ch. 14, § III), does after all say: "The reason and foundation, upon which all this doctrine is built, seem to be the property that every man has in the service of his domestics; acquired by the contract of hiring, and purchased by giving them wages."

258 See Deiler, *op. cit. supra* note 108, pp. 435–437.

259 So said governor Frontenac in 1681, found quoted in Dechêne, *op. cit. supra* note 108, p. 63.

260 See Deiler, *op. cit. supra* note 108, pp. 433–434 and 440.

by the way in which they couple sale with *engager* in D.O. 2 (p. 37): "vendent ou engagent";[261] they do the same in D.O. 5 (p. 37): "Ceux qui ont vendu ou engagé". D.O. 4 (p. 37) only states that *engagement* is equivalent to sale. The redactors obviously are using the best verb to hand to indicate the nature of *engagement* as an indentured servant—a verb appropriate given the social circumstances. They nonetheless exercise a certain caution in doing so, since they always couple *vendre* with *engager*. There is accordingly no need to posit common-law influence to explain this usage.[262]

In conclusion, it may be said that the redactors, in their articles on servants of all kinds, by selecting among the sources available to them (though with appropriate innovation and adaption), provided a set of rules in line with legal tradition, but which also reflected their views of the socio-economic realities of the Territory. There was adequate account taken of the varying kinds of service in Louisiana, and clear rules were provided. The D.O. conceives of "service" as primarily contractual, but with a residue of older notions of the close personal relationship of dependency of servants on their masters within the "family". It is worth reiterating that though many of the individual provisions in the D.O. on this topic were taken from the work of the French redactors or Blackstone, the redactors were not breaking from the past: they were providing more modern rules taken and adapted from the sources to hand—rules which fitted the tradition within which they worked—and, to a certain extent, the rules in the D.O. (allowing for the colonial institution of *engagement*) could readily be viewed as a development or modernized version of the rules in the *Partidas*. This must be because of the similarity of the notions of service and apprenticeship in Europe before industrialization and because of the Castilian and French laws' common inheritance from Rome.

---

[261] The English version of D.O. 2 renders "louent, vendent ou engagent" as "let, hire or engage".
[262] At a *general* level, comparison of *locatio conductio* to sale was common. See D. 19.2.2; Pothier, *T.C.L.*, p. 2 (no. 2).

Part Two

EMPLOYMENT IN THE 1866 QUEBEC CODE

The only provisions in the C.Q. specifically to deal with employment are found in the seventh title of the third book, "Du Louage", "Of lease and hire". The Codification Commissioners indicate that the English rubric mentioned both "lease and hire" because "lease" alone was not equivalent to the French "louage" or Roman "locatio". They added that translations of both the C.N. and C.L. showed that the extra word was needed.[263] As already pointed out, the C.N. contains, in its article 1708, an analysis of *louage* into two types and it follows this analysis in the scheme of its title on *louage*. By the time of the redaction of the C.Q., many academic Roman lawyers had adopted the trichotomy in their analysis of *locatio conductio*.[264] The trichotomy was known to the redactors of the C.Q., since they cite Ortolan's edition of, and commentary on, Justinian's *Institutes*: Ortolan followed the trichotomy in his treatment of *locatio conductio*.[265] It is of interest to see whether or not the contemporary theory of the trichotomy has had any influence on the redactors' analysis of *louage*: and the implications of the influence, or the lack of influence, of the trichotomy on the Quebec redactors will be studied.

Employment in the modern sense is regulated in the C.Q. by only five articles in Book Three, Title Seven: three more than in the C.N., but considerably fewer than in the 1825 C.L., which generally retained (though modified) the provisions of the sixth title of the first book of the D.O. The provisions in the C.L. on *engagés* might not have been useful, as such indentured servants played no part in the life of mid-nineteenth-century Quebec (at least as far as I can discover), though they had been important at an earlier period.[266] Apprentices, however, were a feature of economic life (indeed, the C.Q. mentions them in some articles)[267] and it would have been of evident utility to regulate their legal existence in the code. This was not done; the example of Louisiana was not followed. Several reasons why may be suggested. First, the method of working adopted by the Codification Commission meant that the ordering of topics in the C.N. was closely followed. There was no title on servants in the first book (Persons) of the C.N. Second, as well as the structure, the Commission closely followed the provision of indidividual articles of the C.N.; but there were none regulating apprenticeship. Both of these aspects of the Commissioners' approach militated against the inclusion of articles on apprenticeship; they are perhaps insufficient in themselves to explain

---

[263] *Fourth Report*, p. 22.

[264] Olivier-Martin, *op. cit. supra* note 18, p. 467: "vers 1830–1840 toute la doctrine allemande et française connaissait les trois louages."

[265] See J.L.E. Ortolan, *Explication historique des instituts de l'empereur Justinien*, 4th ed., Paris, Joubert, 1847, vol. 2, p. 260.

[266] See Dechêne, *op. cit. supra* note 108, pp. 50–77.

[267] See, e.g., C.Q. 1054, 2262 and 720.

completely the choices made here, since the redactors sometimes *did* depart from the structure of the C.N. and the regulation found in its individual provisions. A third reason for the exclusion of regulation of apprenticeship is the reliance the redactors placed on Pothier as a guide to the *ancien droit*—he nowhere discusses apprenticeship (which in his day would have been regulated by guilds).[268] Further, the commentators on the C.N. whom the Quebec redactors consulted likewise contained little or no discussion of the nature and content of the contract of apprenticeship. Finally, not all of title six of the first book of the C.L concerns apprentices; but the nature of this title, with its regulation of slavery, may well have discouraged the redactors from following Louisiana's example in regulating apprenticeship in their code, as the notion of a servant as a particular type of legal person will have been unacceptable to the redactors, working at the high point of liberal individualism, the precepts of which they clearly accepted.[269] The redactors could have placed articles on apprenticeship elsewhere in the code; but there is no evidence that they ever considered doing so. Thus, though the four suggestions as to why the redactors may not have included provisions on apprenticeship cannot be said to have required exclusion of apprenticeship, they do seem likely to have reinforced the redactors' attitude in not regulating the indentures and service of apprentices.

If this is correct, it also explains the neglect of the other articles of the C.L. on servants in its first book.[270] C.L.170 and 171 (formerly D.O. 13 and 14 (p. 39)) would of course be covered adequately elsewhere in the C.Q. The C.L. in its articles 3172 to 3174 both defined domestics and regulated what privileges they had in claims for their wages.[271] The C.Q. regulated such privileges in C.Q. 2006; but the C.L. has not obviously been influential, and the redactors did not take the opportunity to define servants as the C.L. had. Here the redactors were probably guided by the C.N., though their section on privileges, as it relates to servants, does differ from that of the French Code.[272]

Turning to the redactors' general approach to lease of services, they state in the section on mandate in their *Sixth Report* that the distinction between hire of personal services and mandate, when not gratuitous, is insubstantial. They remark that the distinction is not the result of a price being paid or the nature of the service. They point out that the contract is derived from Roman law in all its fundamental rules, and that the distinction in the Roman law was founded upon social differences among the Romans, and upon the fact that arts and professions were exercised by free people (hence "liberal") while other work was left to slaves. Compensation for exercise of the liberal arts was a (voluntary) *honorarium*, while that for the illiberal arts was called *merces* or

---

[268] See *supra*, text at notes 52–57.

[269] See *infra*, chap. 7.

[270] The 1825 C.L. had to some extent reformed the D.O. here. See *supra*, note 95.

[271] On C.L. 3172, see *supra*, note 188.

[272] See C.N. 2101. C.Q. 2006 speaks of domestic servants, hired persons, clerks, apprentices, and journeymen.

pretium. They state that such a distinction, founded only on shifting conditions of social rank, can never become fixed or universal in character.[273] Since this is so—they continue—which contract should be classed as lease of services and which mandate must vary according to the nature of the society: thus, aristocratic societies had regarded mercantile business as disreputable, while it is no longer regarded as such.[274] They point out that inevitably there is great disagreement among jurists as to which professions are properly regulated by mandate and which by lease and hire: thus in Rome painting was subject to lease and hire, while Pothier states that to be a painter in France is to be a member of a liberal profession; Cujas states that advocates and Coquille that attorneys are governed not by mandate but by lease and hire, while others, including Pothier and Merlin, take the opposite view.[275] The redactors comment that, for all practical purposes, mandate and lease and hire of services are identical; yet, only one code in Europe (the Austrian)—they continue—has chosen to treat all services paid for as objects not of mandate but of lease and hire: the distinction was considered "as the offspring and relic of a condition of things which has long since passed away. . . ."[276]

Despite these points, the Quebec redactors did not follow the example of the Austrian Code (article 1163), though they recognized the artificiality of the distinction that some occupations were the object of mandate while others were that of lease and hire. They remark that Marcadé repeats the opinion of Troplong that the dispositions of the Austrian Code were all one would expect from a country that enforces military discipline by blows.[277] (Obviously the redactors did not consult the Austrian code themselves: its provision was only known to them through their use of (probably) Marcadé.)[278] The redactors gave no explanation in their *Sixth Report* of why they kept the traditional distinction; in their *Fourth Report*, however, they stated that lease and hire of work resembles mandate and often the two were so similar as to render it difficult to define wherein the difference lay. The Commissioners added that they were

---

[273] *Sixth Report*, p. 6.

[274] *Ibid.*, pp. 6–8. The statement of the redactors is worth quoting as it holds some interest: "[I]t must vary with the changing estimate which different societies, according to their various constitutions place upon the honour or dishonour of particular employments, either from their imputed excellence, or from the dignity of those who follow them. That occupation which at one time, in an aristocratic state, is regarded as disreputable, at another period, with the diminution of the aristocratic element, may be looked upon as highly honourable; mercantile business affords a familiar illustration of this."

[275] *Ibid.*, p. 8. See *supra*, text at notes 41–45.

[276] *Sixth Report*, p. 8.

[277] See V. Marcadé, *Explication théorique et pratique du Code Napoléon*, 5th ed., Paris, Cotillon, 1859, vol. 6, p. 519 (on C.N. 1779, II, n. 1): "Une telle disposition est sans doute quelque chose de pénible à voir dans le Code d'une nation européenne; mais elle y cadre assez bien, au surplus, comme le fait remarquer M. Troplong, avec la discipline militaire à coups de baton."

[278] I deduce this because the reference to the Austrian code is exceptional. I am sure they gained this knowledge from Marcadé who cites and discusses the Austrian Code. It is significant that they do not cite Troplong's own comment on the code, but rather Marcadé's repeating of Troplong's comment: see *supra*, note 277.

tempted to submit articles connecting the two, but desisted because the contracts had continuously been kept separate, not only in the Roman law, but also in all countries that received Roman law: and—they stated—the distinction was so woven into the doctrine and jurisprudence that to disturb it might lead to unforeseen difficulties and inconvenience. They therefore adhered to the rules which obtained under the *ancien droit* and which were reproduced by the Code Napoléon.[279]

This is a perfectly reasonable explanation for not assimilating mandate and lease and hire of work. Given the reference to Marcadé (and indeed other jurists who discussed the matter), it is tempting to speculate that there may have been other reasons for rejecting the approach of (for example) the Austrian Code. Thus, Marcadé, whose report of Troplong's comment on the Austrian Code the redactors cite (approvingly?), argues against the provision of the Austrian Code using what is fundamentally Romantic language about inspiration and genius, concluding that it would be better for liberal arts and professions to be the subject of a contract *sui generis*.[280] All the evidence however, points to legal tradition as underlying the redactors' rejection of any change. The Austrian Code indicated that change was possible and the Commissioners acknowledged the inadequacies of the traditional civilian distinction between lease of wage labour and mandate, and recognized that this distinction was outmoded; nonethless, because of the influence of tradition, they did not consider that the law should be changed. Cautious legal conservatism led them to maintain tradition, even though they recognized the possibility of change.[281]

Before discussing general divisions of *louage*, and the actual provisions on lease of labour, C.Q. 84, from the third title, "Of Domicile", of the first book, must be examined. It states:

---

[279] *Fourth Report*, pp. 28–30.

[280] Marcadé, *op. cit. supra* note 277, vol. 6, p. 519. The following remarks of Marcadé use the language of Romanticism: "[L]es oeuvres de l'esprit et du coeur ne devraient être, selon nous, ni l'objet d'un mandat ni l'objet d'un louage; car il répugne d'admettre que le zèle de ces missionaires qui vont arracher des peuplades sauvages à la barbarie, que la charité de ces saintes religieuses qui renoncent aux joies de la monde . . . pour soigner dans nos hôpitaux les maladies les plus repoussantes, que le dévouement du médecin, du soldat, de l'avocat et du professeur, que le génie de l'artiste et du savant, avec sa brûlante ardeur, son inspiration et son enthusiasme, que toutes ces saintes et belles choses ne sont que *des choses à louer*, n'est-il pas aussi par trop bizarre et contraires à toutes les idées reçues de voir un mandat, . . . dans tout travail sans prix, de telle sorte que le savetier qui raccammode mes bottes se trouve élevé à la dignité de mandataire le jour ou il veut bien, pour un fois en passant, les raccommoder gratis'. See also *ibid.*, vol. 6, p. 520 where, in respect of *poête*, *artiste*, *savant*, *prêtre*, *soldat*, and *professeur*, he talks of "l'ardent amour du vrai, et du beau, le dévouement à la patrie et à l'humanité, l'enthusiasme du génie, ces nobles et saintes passions des grandes âmes."

[281] Though the titles on mandate and on lease and hire are adjacent in the code, they are the subject of different reports separated by almost a year. Thus, the *Fourth Report* (lease and hire) is dated 20 Feb. 1863, while the *Sixth Report* is dated 1 Jan. 1864. This does not seem significant for us, however. Both titles were originally drafted in English by Commissioner Day. See Brierley, "Codification", p. 538, n. 45; McCord, Preface, pp. viii–ix. Marcadé was studied in connection with the title on lease and hire: his views on the matter and on the Austrian Code must have been familiar.

> The domicile of persons of the age of majority, who serve or work continuously for others, is at the residence of those whom they serve or for whom they work, if they reside in the same house.

This conforms to C.N. 109, from which it is closely copied. The redactors do not note that this article settled a dispute in the old law, though they must have been aware of it, since they refer to both the *Pandectes françaises* and Merlin's *Répertoire*. The authors of the former work comment on C.N. 109: "Cet article décide une question autrefois fort controversée. On doutait si la commoration pour une service ou un travail habituel, attribuait le domicile."[282] The *Pandectes françaises* discuss the two main *arrêts* on the point;[283] Merlin, whom the redactors also cite, does likewise, and gives as his opinion that the C.N. had decided the point wrongly and that a servant ought not necessarily to have the domicile of his master.[284] The redactors also cite provisions of the title *ad municipalem et de incolis* of Justinian's Digest: D. 50.1.6.3 and h.t.22.[285] These Roman texts are only of relevance if servants are equated with freedmen. It is difficult to accept that the Quebec redactors seriously considered these texts; one suspects that they are cited only to give validity to the proposition in the C.Q., by lending it support from the prestige of the *Corpus iuris civilis*.[286] The redactors were seeking workable propositions of law: one may suspect that the solving of the dispute in the *ancien droit* over the domicile of servants was much more important than considering Roman provisions on freedmen, which seem to have been cited as an *ex post facto* justification of the redactors' choice.

The Quebec redactors were here faced with two possibilities: they could give a servant who lived with his master the latter's domicile or they could not. The *ancien droit* was undecided. The C.N. offered one solution (such a servant

---

282 *Pan. fran.*, vol. 2, p. 427.

283 *Ibid.*

284 Merlin, *Répertoire* (4), vol. 4, pp. 10–11, s.v. "domicile", 4 , nos. 1 and 2. The first *arrêt* concerned sieur Nicolas Sautereau, by origin from Burgundy, who was employed as an *Intendant* by the Marquis de Bonnelle between the years 1724 and 1760 with whom he lived and by whom he was fed and lodged. On arbitration, five *avocats* decided Santereau had retained his domicile of origin (Burgundy): the *arrêt* of 13 Aug. 1763 confirmed this. A decision of the Châtelet of 6 May 1768, decided that a domestic was domiciled with his master. *Nouveau Denisart*, vol. 6, pp. 661–662, s.v. "domicile", § II, no. 3 on servants also put the view contrary to that eventually taken by the C.N. The C.Q. redactors do not cite the *Nouveau Denisart*; but they do cite "1 Bour. 90". This is a reference to François Bourjon, *Le droit commun de la France et la coutume de Paris réduits en principes tires des ordonnances, des arrêts, des loix cilies, des auteurs*, Paris, Grangé, Rouy, 1747. This reference is to a section of the title on domicile; in the edition I used, however, that of 1747, there is no allusion to the domicile of servants: and indeed, the work was written before the two *arrêts* already mentioned.

285 D. 50.1.6.3: Libertini originem patronorum vel domicilium sequuntur: item qui ex his nascuntur. I will only quote the proemium of h.t. 22, the subsequent parts not being of particular relevance: Filii libertorum, libertarumque, liberti, paterni et patroni manumissoris domicilium aut originem sequuntur.

286 Maleville, 1 *Analyse*, vol. 1, p. 109 does similarly; on C.N. 109 he only makes the following laconic remark: "Conforme aux lois 8 et 22 ff *ad municip.*" He does not allude to the dispute in the *ancien droit*.

was domiciled with his master); but this solution was the subject of some criticism. The Quebec redactors chose to follow the C.N., which, in article 109, could be understood as suggesting that the relationship between master and servant was not purely contractual. Of course, *ouvriers* working in industrial production would not acquire the domicile of their masters, since they would not live with them.[287] The acquiring of another's domicile is inevitably predicated on some notion of dependency on him: the servant is his master's dependent and hence acquires the latter's domicile. This contradicts the idea that a servant by contract leases his services to his master and in return gains wages: a purely formal arrangement between individuals in which domicile is irrelevant. The redactors believed in the doctrines of freedom and sanctity of contract; but they preferred to follow the C.N. here, though its article could have been interpreted as contrary to current notions of the contractual nature of relations between master and servant. This said, domestic servants living with their masters would indeed be economically and socially dependent on them and could even be seen as having adopted their domicile.

The seventh title of the third book of the C.Q. is entitled "Of lease and hire". Its first article, C.Q. 1600, states:

> The contract of lease or hire has for its object either things or work, or both combined.[288]

This is rather different from its equivalent in the C.N., 1708, which states:

> Il y a deux sortes de contrats de louage:
> Celui des choses,
> Et Celui d'ouvrage.

The Quebec redactors state that the first three articles of this title correspond with the first three of the equivalent (title eight) in the C.N. (1708, 1709, 1710).[289] Indeed, though the organization of this title of the C.Q. follows that of the C.N., and thus follows the latter's analysis of *louage* into two, C.Q. 1600 seems to suggest that there is one contract of *louage*, but with three forms, depending on the object of the contract: further, in their *Report*, the redactors have suggested that the division of *louage* into two found in the C.N. 1708 is inaccurate and that in C.Q. 1600 they have "improved" on C.N. 1708.[290] Before considering further the change from the wording of C.N. 1708 in C.Q. 1600, it is useful to examine the sources referred to by the redactors.

The authorities cited for this article are: C.N. 1708, Justinian's Digest, Cujas, Pothier and Voet. The first of these has already been quoted. The relevant

---

[287] In preindustrial society, workmen and apprentices commonly lived with those artisans whom they served.
[288] In the French version: "Le contrat de louage a pour objet soit les choses, soit l'ouvrage, ou les choses et l'ouvrage tout à la fois."
[289] *Fourth Report*, p. 22.
[290] *Ibid.*

passage of the Digest is D. 19.2.22.1: "Quotiens autem faciendum aliquid datur, locatio est." Cujas, as cited, states:

> Locatio conductio est negotium ἀντίστροφον emptioni et venditioni, quia proximum et simile adeo, ut emptionis venditionis et pretii verbo promiscue utamur etiam in locatione, conductione et mercede. Et est locatio conductio, conventio nuda faciendi fruendive aliquid certa mercede. Locator qui dat aliquid fruendum vel faciendum. Conductor, qui accipit. Et locatori datur actio locati, conductori utraque directa.[291]

Pothier states:

> Ii y a deux espèces de contrats de louage: le *louage des choses, et le louage des ouvrages*.[292]

And:

> Le *contrat de louage* est celui qu'on appelle *bail à loyer*: on l'appelle aussi *bail à ferme*, lorsque ce sont des fonds de terre ou des droits qui en font l'objet.[293]

The citation of Voet is "Voet, ad Inst. 1, 3, t.25, § 1"; this must be a reference to his *Elementa iuris.*[294] In relevant part, it states:

> Locatio conductio est contractus bonae fidei, consensu constans, de usu vel opera cum mercede commutanda. Licet enim in jure nostro occurrat etiam locatio et conductio operis, unde et operam redemtores appellantur, et eius quidem vel per aversionem, vel in pedes mensurasve elocati . . . tamen ipsa conductio seu redemtio operis continet in se locationem operae; dum artifex opus redimens locat operam suam, seu faciendi necessitate. . . .
>
> Nititur haec locatio et conducto lisdem fere regulis iuris, quibus emtio venditio; nam et tria requirit substantialia requisita consensum, et usum vel operam, ac mercedem: et perfecta censetur, quamprimum de usu vel opera et mercede convenit . . . mercesque in ea debet esse certa.[295]

---

[291] J. Cujas, *Paratitla in libros quinquaginta digestorum, seu pandectarum imperatoris Iustiniani, cum notis Alex. Chassanaei et indice obligationem et actionem, et epitome in eundem indicem*, Paris, I. Iost, 1658, pp. 137–138 (19.2, locati conducti). It is interesting to note that Maleville, *Analyse*, vol. 3, p. 372, cites this passage of Cujas, and, on p. 373, cites D. 19.2.22.1: this seems another example of the obvious phenomenon that in the C.Q. redactors' *Reports* less obvious or more obscure writers tend to be cited only if some work that the redactors regularly use (e.g. Maleville, Pothier, *Pan. fran.*) refers the redactors to them. One may conclude that the redactors did not assiduously read all the writings of the numerous authors they cite. If Maleville cited a passage of Cujas, and this passage seemed interesting, the redactors would read it.

[292] Pothier, *T.C.L.*, p. 1 (Introduction). There is in fact no reference to this; but since it is relevant, and known to the redactors, I have included it.

[293] Pothier, *T.C.L*, p. 2 (no. 1). This is the passage to which McCord refers; I have only quoted the relevant section.

[294] J. Voet, *Elementa iuris secundum ordinem Institutionum in usum domesticae exercitationis digesta*, 2nd ed., Leiden, Henricus Teering, 1705. See A.A. Roberts, *A Guide to Voet: Including the Life of Johannes Voet*, Pretoria, The Author, 1933, pp. 15–17.

[295] Voet, *op. cit. supra* note 294, pp. 151–152 (bk. 3, tit. 25) (citations to Roman law omitted).

Voet here apparently makes a fairly conventional division into two types: he would seem to distinguish between lease of the *usus* of an object and of the *opus* or *operae* of a man. He points out that there may also be *locatio et conductio operis* by contractors (*redemtores*), though he adds that such *conductio seu redemtio operis* contains in itself a *locatio operae*: he here echoes D. 19.2.22.2.[296] Olivier-Martin has argued that Voet was the first to develop the modern trichotomy in the analysis of *locatio conductio* in his *Commentarius ad Pandectas*, first published in 1698.[297]

None of the passages cited by the redactors contains a description of *louage* resembling that found in C.Q. 1600, though indeed all the passages are inevitably related to the Quebec code's description of *louage*. The redactors provided in their article that *louage* has three alternative objects, the first two of which are obvious and traditional. The third, however, is problematic: "les choses et l'ouvrage tout à la fois." This cannot be the contemporary theory of the trichotomy, though the trichotomy was known to the redactors:[298] *locatio operis* could not readily be described as a combination of lease of things and work. Where the third aspect of *louage* (lease of things and work combined) in C.Q. 1600 seems to originate is in criticism of the organization of the French code and its treatment of the material. The title of the French code "Du louage" is divided into four chapters. The first of these contains general provisions on *louage*; the second deals with *louage des choses*; the third with *louage d'ouvrage et d'industrie*; and the fourth with *bail à cheptel* (the lease of cattle on shares). The Quebec redactors have followed this scheme exactly. C.N. 1708 said there were two types of *louage*: that of things and that of work. C.N. 1711 said that these two types subdivided into several types, one of which was *bail à cheptel*. Marcadé criticizes the French code. He points out that the code states *bail à cheptel* to be a subdivision of the other two, and he comments thus:

> Or il [i.e. le code] se met ensuite en contradiction avec cette donnée, puisque, au lieu de placer le bail à cheptel dans l'un des deux chapitres précédents, il le range dans un chapitre particulier et en fait un troisième classe indépendante.[299]

He continues, pointing out that of the two approaches the code adopts to *bail à cheptel* (first, treating it as a subdivision of the other two; second, treating it as a third class), the second is the more appropriate, because *bail à cheptel* presents a "nature toute particulière" not only as "tout à la fois louage de choses et louage

---

[296] See note above. D. 19.2.22.2 is quoted *supra* between notes 18 and 19.

[297] J. Voet, *Commentarius ad Pandectas*, 6th ed., The Hague, Petrus de Hondt, 1731, vol. 1, p. 839 (esp. 19.2.33); Olivier-Martin, *op. cit. supra* note 18, pp. 467–468.

[298] Accepting the contemporary view without hesitation, Ortolan, *op. cit. supra* note 265, vol. 2, pp. 260–261 sets out the trichotomy very clearly. The redactors consulted and apparently borrowed from Ortolan for C.Q. 1668: see *infra*, text at notes 331–341.

[299] Marcadé, *op. cit. supra* note 277, vol. 6, p. 418, Comment II on C.N. 1708–1711.

d'ouvrage" but also as closely related to the contract of partnership (*société*).[300] Though the redactors do not specifically cite Marcadé as an authority for C.Q. 1600, they were familiar with his work, and used it extensively: indeed, they cite a passage, next to the one just quoted from, in connection with C.Q. 1602.

It may be concluded that the third aspect of lease adumbrated in C.Q. 1600—"les choses et l'ouvrage tout à la fois"—refers to the fourth chapter of the title, that on *bail à cheptel*. The redactors have improved on C.N. 1708, influenced by comments such as those of Marcadé, though none of the authorities cited specifically in connection with C.Q. 1600 (the Digest, Cujas, Voet, Pothier and C.N. 1708) indicate the origin of the description of *louage* in C.Q. 1600 nor provide a critique of the French code. It is tempting to suggest that Marcadé's phrase "tout à la fois louage des choses et louage d'ouvrage" is the source of C.Q. 1600's "les choses et l'ouvrage tout à la fois"; but this is not necessary for the argument.

The Quebec redactors knew of the trichotomy; nonetheless, they rejected the threefold division of *louage* and followed the scheme of the French code. Some reasons may be suggested as lying behind this. First, had the trichotomy been adopted, the provisions of the C.N., and the model provided by its title, could not have been followed; the redactors would also have had to provide a new title on *bail à cheptel*, even though the latter was of minimal importance in Quebec.[301] Second, the conservative nature of the actions of the Quebec redactors generally would militate against a radical alteration of the ordering of the material on *louage*. A division of *louage* into two was traditional; the Quebec redactors could have seen no real reason for altering that traditional analysis and none of the authorities they cited would have suggested that they should. Thus, the redactors followed the scheme of the Code Napoléon. They altered the general provisions in the first chapter to improve on the descriptions of the various forms of *louage*: this seems to have been prompted by criticism of the Code Napoléon. They maintained the Code Napoléon's treatment of *bail à cheptel* as an aspect of *louage* though this was in some respects unsatisfactory (Pothier, notably, does not treat of *bail à cheptel* in his *Traité* on *louage*).

The first chapter of the title has one further article mentioning *louage* of work, C.Q. 1602. It states:

---

[300] *Ibid.* Marcadé gives as his opinion that *bail à cheptel* should not be treated as an aspect of *louage*, properly so called, because of its connection with partnership.

[301] See *supra* note 298 on the redactors' knowledge of the trichotomy. The redactors, *Fourth Report*, p. 34, point out that there are 32 articles in the C.N. on *bail à cheptel*, but only three in the C.Q. This is because—they say—in certain parts of France the leasing of cattle and sheep on shares was very common. Such provinces as Berry, Brittany, Nivernois and Bourbonnais had abundant and minute provisions on it in their *Coutumes*, and the C.N. has drawn on them. They remark: "In this country, the contract is of little comparative frequency or importance." They rejected the C.N.'s detailed rules as useless and perhaps harmful in Quebec where parties accustomed to make special agreements or conform to local usage in such a *bail*.

> The lease or hire of work is a contract by which one of the parties, called the lessor, obliges himself to do certain work for the other, called the lessee, for a price which the latter obliges himself to pay.

The French text renders "lessor" *locateur* and "lessee" *locataire*. This is similar to C.N. 1710, and the articles of both codes clearly refer to both *locatio operis* and that *operarum* (indeed they combine the two). C.Q. 1602 basically differs from C.N. 1710 only in including the phrases "called the lessor" and "called the lessee." The redactors refer to Cujas and the Digest (both as cited for C.Q. 1600) and to Rousseaud de la Combe and Marcadé.[302] In the relevant passage, Rousseaud de la Combe states that:

> Le locataire appellé en Droit, conductor, est celui *qui dat pecuniam*; le bailleur appellé en Droit, *locator*, *qui eam recipit*. . . .[303]

Rousseaud's account does not consider that in *locatio operis* it was generally the *locator* who paid the money.[304]

The redactors cite two passages from Marcadé's *Explication*. The first gives a lengthy discussion of the various views put forward as to who was *locator* and who *conductor*;[305] the second summarizes Marcadé's opinion and arguments.[306] It states:

> Le louage pur ou parfait est un contrat par lequel une partie qu'on appelle locateur s'oblige à faire jouir, soit d'une chose, soit de son travail ou de son industrie, une partie qu'on nomme locataire et qui s'oblige à lui payer le prix de cette jouissance.

It goes on to summarize further the first passage. A passage, uncited by the C.Q. redactors, may, however, be conveniently quoted as concisely putting Marcadé's views:

> Nous avons prouvé plus haut (art. 1710–III), contre les jurisconsultes romains, et contre Domat, Cujas, Pothier et M. Troplong, que l'idée d'après laquelle le locateur est, dans le louage d'ouvrages, aussi bien que dans le louage des choses, celui qui reçoit le prix, et le locataire celui qui paye, idée qui est consacrée par notre Code, est en effet la seule qui fût vraiment rationelle, la seule qu'une législation logique dût adopter.
>
> Le louage d'ouvrage ou d'industrie est donc un contrat par lequel une partie, qu'on appelle locateur, s'oblige à faire jouir de son travail une autre partie qui s'oblige à le payer et qu'on appelle locataire.[307]

---

302 They refer also to Troplong, whom I have not been able to consult; but see note 308 below.
303 Guy du Rousseaud de la Combe, *Recueil de jurisprudence civile du pays de droit écrit et coutumier par ordre alphabétique*, 4th ed., Paris, Veuve Savoye, 1769, p. 441, s.v. "louage".
304 See *supra*, text at notes 17–18.
305 Marcadé, *op. cit. supra* note 277, vol. 6, pp. 419–424, Comment III on C.N. 1708–1711.
306 *Ibid.*, p. 570, résumé du titre huitième.
307 *Ibid.*, vol. 6, p. 517, Comment I on C.N. 1779.

Marcadé lays great stress on who pays the price as what should distinguish the lessor from the lessee. The C.Q. redactors have adopted Marcadé's view. This means that, no matter the nature of the *ouvrage*, they accept that the person who pays is the lessee or *locataire*. This fudging of one of the distinctions between *locatio operarum* and that *operis* (as developed by the trichotomy) highlights the C.N.'s division of *louage* into two types. The redactors have adopted Marcadé's terminology to avoid the possible confusion over who was *locateur* and who *locataire*: a confusion which the C.N. had apparently given rise to, since Troplong had been of the opinion opposite to that of Marcadé.[308] As is obvious, this adoption of Marcadé's opinion must have caused some problems for the redactors, since it ran contrary to that of many of the writers on the *ancien droit*—notably Pothier[309]—and contradicted the Roman texts. Indeed, it is notable that Marcadé explicitly states that Domat, Pothier, Cujas and the Roman jurists disagreed with him, while citing no jurist of the *ancien droit* in his own support. Marcadé states that only two other writers on the C.N. discussed the point: Duvergier, who agreed with Marcadé, though providing no arguments, and Troplong, who held the contrary view.[310] In following Marcadé, the redactors would be open to the charge of changing the law. The redactors, however, cite a passage from Rousseaud de la Combe to justify their view. This passage agrees with Marcadé's opinion; but Rousseaud's use of the term *bailleur* suggests he only had *louage des choses* in mind, as *bailleur* is a term normally reserved for one who lets out land to another in a contract of *bail à loyer* or *bail à ferme*.[311] The redactors simply remark in their Report is that the proper application of the terms "lessor" and "lessee" is explained to avoid confusion.[312]

The conclusion must be that here the redactors have innovated, following Marcadé. This innovation is probably sensible as avoiding any possible confusion over terms. It amounts, however, to a break with the Roman tradition and with the *ancien droit*, though the citation of Rousseaud suggests that the redactors may have been trying to conceal their change, by or claiming that there was an alternative tradition. Given that the redactors were working at the period when the theory of the trichotomy was becoming influential, such a definite ascription of the terms to the parties would avoid possible confusion (it may be recalled that the trichotomy placed great emphasis on the *conductor operis* being he who was paid while the *conductor operarum* and *conductor rei* were those who paid). The redactors must have considered that not to make he

---

[308] *Ibid.*, vol. 6, pp. 421–424, Comment III on C.N. 1708–1711. The C.Q. redactors cited Troplong (see *supra*, note 302); but the fact Marcadé cites him allows us to know what Troplong said and to know that the C.Q. redactors rejected his views.
[309] See Pothier, *T.C.L.*, p. 133 (no. 392).
[310] Marcadé, *op. cit. supra* note 277, vol. 6, pp. 420–421, Comment III on C.N. 1708–1711.
[311] See Marcadé, *op. cit. supra* note 277, vol. 6, p. 419; and Pothier, *T.C.L.*, p. 2 (no. 1): it could be used also for *bail à cheptel,* but not for *louage d'ouvrage*.
[312] *Fourth Report*, p. 22.

who pays always the *locataire* would be likely to cause confusion, especially given such disagreement over terminology.[313]

C.N. 1711[314] has no equivalent in the C.Q.[315]

The third chapter of this title is that entitled "Of the Lease and Hire of Work" ("Du louage d'ouvrage").[316] Its first section contains a single article, C.Q. 1666:

> The principal kinds of work which may be leased or hired are:
> 1. The personal service of workmen, servants and others;
> 2. The work of carriers, by land and by water, who undertake the conveyance of persons or things;
> 3. That of builders and others, who undertake works by estimate or contract.

In the French text, "workmen" are "ouvriers" and "servants" "domestiques". C.Q. 1666 is similar to C.N. 1779, with one difference significant here: the first type of *louage d'ouvrage* described in the C.N.'s article is "Le louage des gens de travail qui s'engagent au service de quelqu'un". The C.Q. has phrased this form of *louage d'ouvrage* as apparently incorporating a much wider class of workers than does C.N. 1779; this could be the result of a growth in the number of occupations in which one leased one's services. The redactors unfortunately do not say why they here altered the wording of C.N. 1779: all they state is that their proposed article corresponds in character to C.N. 1799.[317] The wider phrasing of C.Q. 1666 must be significant; but the problem is whether "and others" ("et autres") should be interpreted broadly or restrictively. Both Léon Faribault[318] and Pierre-Basile Mignault[319] were of the opinion that this section must comprehend more than domestics, manual labourers, and the like. Mignault points to C.Q. 2260, 2261 and 2262 on prescription, which seem to imply that not only menial tasks are the subject of lease of personal service.[320] If he is correct, the Quebec redactors have widened the scope of *locatio operarum*:

---

[313] Note that Marcadé in disagreeing with Cujas cites a different work of the latter than that cited by the C.Q. The passage of Cujas cited, however, does disagree with the views of Marcadé and C.Q. 1602 in so far as Cujas defines the "locator" as he who hands over something.

[314] See *supra*, text at notes 166 and 167.

[315] The redactors remark, *Fourth Report*, p. 22, that the specification of C.N. 1711 has not been adopted. This, of course, has to do with the new description of *louage* in C.Q. 1600 and with the fact that in C.N. 1711 *bail à cheptel* is stated merely to be a subdivision of lease of things and lease of work. See *supra*, text at notes 297–301.

[316] See *supra*, text at notes 273–281 for general comments of redactors.

[317] *Fourth Report*, p. 30.

[318] *TDCQ*, vol. 12, pp. 289–290.

[319] P.B. Mignault, *Le Droit Civil Canadien*, Montreal, Whiteford & Théoret, 1895, vol. 7 pp. 368–369.

[320] C.Q. 2260 (6) states: "for hire of labour, or for the price of manual, professional or intellectual work and materials furnished." 2261 (3): "For wages of workmen not reputed domestics who are hired for a year or more." 2262(3):
"For wages of domestic or farm servants, merchants' clerks and other employees who are hired by the day, week or month, or for less than a year."

Pothier took a much more restricted view.[321] This broadening of the scope of lease of services must be in response to the growth and complexity of economic life in Quebec; it is also in line with the redactors' wish to assimilate mandate and lease of work.

Section Two of this chapter is entitled "Of the lease and hire of the personal service of workmen, servants and others", "Du louage du service personnel des ouvriers, domestiques et autres". Its first article, C.Q. 1667, states thus:

> The contract of lease or hire of personal service can only be for a limited time, or for a determinate undertaking.
>
> It may be prolonged by tacit renewal.

C.N. 1780 is similar, but without the second paragraph.[322] The wording of C.Q. 1667 is more precise than that of C.N. 1780; but the further significance (if any) of this is unclear. The provision on tacit renewal was found in the *ancien droit*:

> Il paraît que la tacite reconduction doit aussi avoir lieu pour les services des serviteurs, des servants et des ouvriers.[323]

And, of course, tacit renewal would apply under the C.N.[324] The redactors cite D'Espeisses, who stated that "l'homme libre ne peut pas louer ses oeuvres à perpétuité. . ." . He explained:

> Vous avez été achetés par prix; ne devenez point serfs des hommes, . . . parce que ce seroit rendre inutile la liberté, à moins que le louage ne fût fait en faveur de la cause pieuse, comme si on s'étoit loué à servir perpétuellement un Hôpital; car alors ce louage est bon.[325]

As regards the C.N., similar statements are made by Maleville and the *Pandectes Françaises*.[326] The redactors also cite Troplong who was of the opinion that a contract of service for a determinate period, but which would last for the lifetime of the lessor, could be invalid.[327] It is difficult to know what significance to attach to the reference to Troplong.[328] The redactors also cite

---

[321] Pothier, *T.C.L.*, p. 7 (no. 10), quoted *supra*, text at note 41.

[322] See *supra*, quotation between notes 77 and 78.

[323] Pothier, *T.C.L.*, p. 127 (no. 372).

[324] See e.g. Marcadé, *op. cit. supra* note 277, vol. 6, p. 527, Comment III on C.N. 1780–1781.

[325] D'Espeisses, *op. cit. supra* note 36, vol. 1, p. 91, s.v. "Louage" (s. 2 n. 6); Pothier, *T.C.L.*, p. 127 (no. 372).

[326] See Maleville, *Analyse*, vol. 3, p. 401; *Pan. fran*, vol. 13, pp. 190–191. Cl. Serres, *Les institutions du droit françois, suivant l'ordre de celles de Justinien*, Paris, veuve Cavelier & fils, 1753, p. 501 (III.xxv.1), states: "on peut même louer ses oeuvres, son travail et son industrie, pour un certain tems, mais non pas à perpétuité ou à vie: car un tel traité seront nul, comme sentant la servitude et l'esclavage."

[327] Troplong's work was unavailable to me; Marcadé, *op. cit. supra* note 277, vol. 6, pp. 525–527, Comment II on C.N. 1780–1781 discusses him extensively and enables us to know Troplong's opinions.

[328] Supposing that this is the passage the redactors had in mind: see *supra*, note 327.

provisions from Justinian's Digest dealing with attempts to infringe others' liberty of action as regards marriage and domicile.[329]

All that may definitely be said about this provision of the C.Q. is that it follows the *ancien droit* and improves on the wording of the C.N. in making the provisions on tacit renewal express, and in stressing that the term of service was "limited", "limité". (Could this latter be a reaction to Troplong?) All the redactors state in their *Report* is that they have added to C.N. 1780.[330]

C.Q. 1668 provides:

> It is terminated by the death of the party hired or his becoming, without fault, unable to perform the services agreed upon.
>
> It is also terminated by the death of the party hiring, in some cases, according to circumstances.

There is no such article in the equivalent section of the C.N.; the redactors remark that this is a matter which had to be decided and inserted here, the extinction of a contract by the death of one of the parties being an exception to the general rule.[331] There is also no equivalent article in the 1825 C.L. The redactors apparently did consult C.N. 1795, from the next section of the code, which stated:

> Le contrat de louage d'ouvrage est dissous par la mort de l'ouvrier, de l'architecte ou entrepreneur.

Pothier is also referred to—specifically nos. 165–168 and 171–175 of his *Traité*.[332] These concern the effect of *force majeure*. No. 165 enunciates the general principle: "Lorsqu'un ouvrier ou serviteur a loué ses services à un maître, si par une force majeure ces services n'ont pu être rendus, le maître doit être déchargé du prix desdits services." The rest of nos. 165 to 168 explores this point through examples, and deals with the rights and liabilities between master and servant in various circumstances of *force majeure*. Nos. 171 to 175 deal with the difference between *force majeure* and fault in the event of the contract between master and servant coming to an end: should there be fault, the party at fault is liable in damages.[333] Thus, these passages are relevant as regards the contract ending by *force majeure*, or one party *without fault* becoming unable to carry out his bargain. There is no mention of the effect of the death of one of the parties on the contract, and Pothier, indeed, does not discuss the point in the context of the contract for services. On *locatio operis*, Pothier does say that the contract would be dissolved if the obligation depended on the personal work and abilities of the *conducteur*; should it not, the heirs of the *conducteur* had to carry

---

[329] D. 35.1.71.1 and 2, from the title *de condicionibus et demonstrationibus et causis et modis eorum quae in testamento scribuntur*.
[330] *Fourth Report*, p. 30.
[331] *Fourth Report*, p. 30.
[332] Pothier, *T.C.L.*, pp. 61–62 and 63–64 (nos. 165–168 and 171–175).
[333] Further on these passages, see *supra* text at notes 194–199.

out the work.[334] The death of the *locateur*, however, in *locatio operis*, according to Pothier, never ended the contract: this is in line with C.N. 1795 (*supra*), also on the contract *operis*.[335]

The redactors cite no other writers on the *ancien* or *nouveau droit*. They do cite Ortolan's *Explication historique des Instituts de l'empereur Justinien*.[336] Ortolan states thus:

> Pour le louage des services (operarum), le contrat finit par la mort de celui qui a loué son travail, car avec lui périt aussi la chose louée.

This seems to be the direct source of the Quebec rule on death of the parties. It may be pointed out that no such direct rule is made in Justinian's *Institutes*; the only passage the *Institutes* have on this point states that:

> Mortuo conductore intra tempora conductionis, heres eius eodem iure in conductionem succedit.[337]

For the contract *operarum* the *conductor* would be the master or employer; for that *operis*, he would be the person hired.[338]

The redactors' rule must be correct, and for the reason Ortolan gives, even though they produce no authority from the *ancien droit*. Marcadé, for example, states that:

> Le louage des services finit toujours par la mort du domestique ou de l'ouvrier. Le maître ne saurait être contraint d'accepter leurs héritiers à leur place, et ceux–ci réciproquement ne pourraient pas étre contraints par le maître à continuer le travail de leur auteur, le contrat n'ayant été formé de part et de l'autre que pour la personne de cet ouvrier ou de ce domestique. Quant à la mort du maître, son effet ne saurait être indiqué en thèse et d'une manière absolue; car c'est par les circonstances de chaque espèce qu'on verra si le louage n'a été fait qu'en considération du maître, et si la mort des lors doit résoudre le contrat.[339]

This is the rule of C.Q. 1668; indeed any other rule would be unacceptable. The most interesting aspect of this article is not the content of the rule on the effect of death but the fact that the redactors (presumably) could find no source from the *ancien droit* to support their proposition, and ended by citing a textbook on

---

[334] Pothier, *T.C.L.*, pp. 152–154 (nos. 453–456).
[335] *Ibid.* p. 149 (no. 444): "La mort du locateur ne résout pas le contrat de louage d'ouvrage." See on the relation of Pothier's views to C.N. 1795, P.A. Fenet, *Pothier analysé dans ses Rapports avec le Code civil, et mis en ordre sous chacun des articles de ce Code*, 2nd ed., Paris, Au dépot ... et chez Alex-Gobelet, 1829, p. 564.
[336] Ortolan, *op. cit. supra* note 265, vol. 2 p. 269. (The redactors cite p. 271, perhaps the result of use of a different edition.)
[337] Inst. 3.24.6. See also D. 19.2.19.9; Voet, *op. cit. supra* note 297, 19.2.22 and 27.
[338] *Cf.* Pothier's rule, see *supra*, notes 334 and 335.
[339] Marcadé, *op. cit. supra* note 277, vol. 6, pp. 527–528, Comment III on 1780–1781.

Roman law. This may reflect the increased interest in the contract for services in the nineteenth century.

There is one further important point in connection with this article. It will be recalled from the discussion of Louisiana that Pothier and Guyot divided servants into two types: personal servants and *ouvriers*. Masters could dismiss personal servants at will and with impunity; personal servants had not a corresponding right to quit. The rules for *ouvriers* were different; they could neither be dismissed nor held to their contracts in the way in which personal servants could.[340] No trace of such a division between personal and other servants appears in the C.Q., which has here followed the C.N. in not distinguishing between servants according to the nature of their work. In the authorities consulted in connection with C.Q. 1668, it is notable that No. 176 of Pothier's *Traité* is not mentioned: this is the passage that makes explicit the distinction between personal and other servants.[341] The redactors have clearly rejected this distinction found in the *ancien droit*. It is founded on the idea that personal servants are in a close relationship with their master: a relationship outwith the ties of formal contract. The redactors have preferred to place all servants in the position of abstract contracting individuals rather than having personal servants as dependents in the power of their master. C.Q. 1668 thus contains a change in the law not pointed out by the redactors.

The next article in this section, C.Q. 1669, states that:

> In any action for wages by domestics or farm servants, in the absence of written proof, the master may offer his oath, as to the conditions of the engagement and as to the fact of payment, accompanied by a detailed statement.
>
> If the oath be not offered by the master it may be deferred to him, and is of a decisory nature, as regards the subjects to which it is limited.

Though this article is apparently different from C.N. 1781, the principle is the same.[342] The redactors state the provision follows the existing law and is coincident with C.N. 1781.[343] They cite as authority article 127 of the *Coutume de Paris*, Pothier, Guyot's *Répertoire*, and the *Nouveau Denisart*. Article 127 states that there is a prescriptive period of a year for wages; on this Ferrière states:

> [S]i les serviteurs font leur demande dans l'an contre leurs maîtres, ils ne sont pas reçûs à leur serment, au cas que leurs maîtres allegent le payement fait de leurs loyers, mais le serment est déferé aux maîtres. . . .[344]

The *Nouveau Denisart* states that the servant's action against his master prescribes after one year; but a servant may still put his master on oath.[345] Guyot's *Répertoire* states that:

---

[340] See *supra*, text at notes 193–200.

[341] Pothier, *T.C.L.*, p. 64 (no. 176), quoted *supra*, text at note 198.

[342] See *supra*, text at notes 77 to 78.

[343] *Fourth Report*, p. 30.

[344] Ferrière, *Corps et Comp.*, vol. 2, col. 542, no. 16, discussing *Coûtume de Paris*, art. 127.

> Boniface rapporte un arrêt qui a jugé que quand il y a contestation entre le maître et le Domestique sur les conditions de l'engagement et le payement des gages, le serment du maître doit faire foi, à moins qu'il n'y ait un écrit.
>
> Cette Jurisprudence est aussi celle du châtelet de Paris et le parlement l'a confirmée par arrêt du 14 Decembre 1764.[346]

Pothier is cited; but his passage does not repeat an identical rule. He discusses whether, in a dispute between master and servant over the former's dismissal of the latter, a master should produce proof of his allegations of just cause or if the judge should rely on the master's "déclaration". Pothier states: "[L]a decision doit être laissée à l'arbitrage du juge, qui doit se déterminer par les circonstances, et par la dignité du maître."[347] It is obvious that C.Q. 1669 follows the existing law. Pothier's more cautious statement has not been adopted; the redactors presumably preferred the more certain rule of the other authorities.

The reasoning behind the provision is easy to understand. The authors of the *Pandectes françaises* explain:

> En effet, on n'est guère dans l'usage de prendre des quittances des gages que l'on pays à un domestique, et des salaires que l'on donne à un ouvrier. Il est juste, dans ce cas, d'accorder la créance au maître. La règle contraire, ou celle qui exigerait une preuve écrite serait très-embarrassante.[348]

Maleville states as follows:

> On demanda si le domestique ou ouvrier pouvait être reçu à prouver par temoins que le maître avait convenu lui devoir tant, et si malgré l'offre de cette, preuve, l'affirmation devait être déferée au maître.
>
> On répondit que l'offre de preuve ne devait pas être reçue parce que les ouvriers et domestiques se serviraient de témoins entre eux.[349]

The redactors would approve of the class distinctions and attitudes implicit in these statements: servants were presumed to be much more likely to be dishonest than masters. One point of note is that C.Q. 1669 states specifically that it applies only to actions by domestic and farm servants. That this is so specific must mean that other *ouvriers* and employees are not subject to these rules. (It may be recalled that C.Q. 1666 mentions generally "workmen, servants and others".) This means that the provision differs from C.N. 1781, which covers all those who lease their work under the contract of *louage des Domestiques et Ouvriers*. As pointed out, the contract in the C.Q. also seems to be of wider application: more types of work would seem to be covered.[350] Thus,

---

[345] *Nouveau Denisart*, vol. 9, pp. 143–144, s.v. "Gages" no. 3. See also Merlin, *Répertoire* (4), vol. 4, p. 5, s.v. "Domestique", no. IV.

[346] Guyot, *op. cit. supra* note 81, vol. 6, p. 102, s.v. "Domestique".

[347] Pothier, *T.C.L.*, p. 64 (no. 175).

[348] *Pan. fran.*, vol. 13, p. 191; Ferrière, *Corps et Comp.*, vol. 2, col. 542, no. 16, gives the same explanation.

[349] Maleville, *Analyse*, vol. 3, p. 402.

[350] See *supra*, text at notes 316–321.

other wage labourers, such as factory hands, would not seem to be governed by C.Q. 1669. The reasons why are likely to be as follows. The rules of the C.N. and the *ancien droit* presuppose that the master and the servant will be on terms of some familiarity: otherwise the master would not know if the servant, for example, had been paid or not. The Quebec code has broadened the scope of the contract; other classes of workers being parties to lease. Factory production had developed in Quebec—though admittedly to a limited extent. The owners of factories would not know all their workers individually; further, a factory will have accounting procedures to deal with wages, and proof of payment or otherwise would be relatively easy. Also, the broadening of the scope of the contract to include other classes of employees could fudge the class distinction implicit in the rule.

Therefore, it may be concluded that C.Q. 1669 contains a reform of the law in line with changing socio-economic conditions in Quebec. By specifically mentioning only domestics and farm servants, the redactors have deliberately restricted the application of the rule in comparison to C.N. 1781 and the ancien droit; though they do not admit in their *Reports* that they have restricted the rule.

C.Q. 1670 states that the ordinary rules common to all contracts apply to the lease or hire of personal services, which are also regulated in certain respects in the country districts by a special law and in towns and villages by local by-laws. The redactors refer to provincial statute law. C.Q. 1671 refers to provincial and imperial statutes governing the hiring of seamen. We need not consider these articles further.

These are the only articles specifically on *louage* of personal service. There is a relevant article on the master's liability for his servants' acts, and this will be considered below. It is, however, appropriate first to discuss the C.Q.'s rejection of the rules in C.L. 2718–2721 on the dismissal or quitting of servants.[351] In comparison to the C.L. the C.Q. has left this aspect of the termination of lease of services virtually unregulated. The C.N. had also not dealt with this point: this must help explain the attitude taken by the C.Q. redactors, and indeed they make no references at all to the C.L. as regards the *louage* of personal servants. C.Q. 1668 dealt with termination by the death of a party or his becoming— without fault—unable to perform the services agreed upon. The contract would normally end on the date agreed; if the contract became unworkable because of the fault of either party, then C.Q. 1670 would apply, which provided that the rules common to contracts should apply, as well as any special laws and by-laws. Thus, the hire of personal services has been further assimilated to the general law of contract. Mignault remarks: "Le louage des services prend fin pour les mêmes causes que les autres contrats, quand ces causes sont applicable . . . ."[352] By rejecting the example of the C.L., the Quebec redactors have decided against special provisions on the dismissal and quitting

---

[351] These provisions are irtually the same as D.O. 57–60 (p. 383) discussed *supra*, text at notes 179–200.

[352] Mignault, *op. cit. supra* note 319, vol. 7, p. 375.

of servants: this is in line with their rejection of the distinction made by Pothier and the C.L. between personal servants and workmen.[353] The redactors have attempted to rid the law of those provisions that hinted at the relationship between master and servant as being other than purely contractual. The redactors affirmed the formal equality of the parties in a contract of *louage des services*, and rendered the contract itself, as much as possible, part of the general law on contract.

The last article we need consider is C.Q. 1054 in the chapter (the third) of the third title of the third book entitled "Of Offences and Quasi-Offences". The article states as follows:

> He is responsible not only for the damage caused by his own fault, but also for that caused by the fault of persons under his control and by things which he has under his care;
>
> The father, or, after his decease, the mother, is responsible for the damage caused by their minor children;
>
> Tutors are responsible in like manner for their pupils;
>
> Curators or others having the legal custody of insane persons, for the damage done by the latter;
>
> Schoolmasters and artisans, for the damage caused by their pupils or apprentices while under their care.
>
> The responsibility attaches in the above cases only when the person subject to it fails to establish that he was unable to prevent the act which has caused the damage.
>
> Masters and employers are responsible for the damage caused by their servants and workmen in the performance of the work for which they are employed.

In the French text, "masters" is rendered "maîtres", and "employers" "commettants", while "servants" are "domestiques" and "workmen" "ouvriers". C.N. 1384 the equivalent article, is rather different:

> On est responsable, non-seulement du dommage que l'on a causé par son propre fait, mais encore de celui qui est causé par le fait des personnes dont on doit répondre, ou des choses que l'on a sous sa garde.
>
> Le père et la mère, après le décès du mari, sont responsables du dommage causé par leurs enfants mineurs habitant avec eux;
>
> Les maîtres et les commettans, du dommage causé par leurs domestiques et préposés dans les fonctions auxquelles ils les ont employés;
>
> Les instituteurs et les artisans, du dommage causé par leurs élèves et apprentis, pendant le tems qu'ils sont sur leur surveillance.
>
> La responsabilité ci-dessus a lieu, à moins que les père et mère, instituteurs et artisans ne prouvent qu'ils n'ont pu empêcher le fait qui donne lieu à cette responsabilité."

---

[353] See *supra*, text at notes 340–341.

The redactors of the C.Q. cite a number of authorities. They refer: first, to Justinian's Digest (D. 47.6.1.1 and h.t. 5 and 6);[354] second, to Pothier's *Traité des Obligations*;[355] third, to the *Nouveau Denisart*;[356] fourth, to Zachariae's commentary on the French code;[357] and fifth, to Toullier.[358]

Pothier expressed the rule of the *ancien droit*:

> Non-seulement la personne qui a commis le délit ou le quasi-délit, est obligée à la réparation du tort qu'elle a causé, celles qui ont sous leur puissance cette personne, telles que les pères, mères, tuteurs et précepteurs, sont tenues de cette obligation, lorsque le délit ou quasi-délit a été commis en leur présence, et généralement lorsque pouvant l'empêcher, elles ne l'ont pas fait: mais si elles n'ont pu l'empêcher, elles n'en sont point tenues. . . . Quand même le délit aurait été commis à leur vu et su. . . .
>
> On rend aussi les maîtres responsables du tort causé par les délits et quasi-délits de leurs serviteurs ou ouvriers qu'ils emploient à quelque service. Ils le sont même dans le cas auquel il n'aurait pas été en leur pouvoir d'empêcher le délit ou quasi-délit, lorsque les délits ou quasi-délits sont commis par lesdits serviteurs ou ouvriers dans l'exercise des fonctions auxquelles ils sont employés par leurs maîtres, quoique en l'absence de leurs maîtres; ce qui a été établi pour rendre les maîtres attentifs à ne servir que de bons domestiques.
>
> A l'égard des délits ou quasi-délits qu'ils commettent hors de leurs fonctions, les maîtres n'en sont point responsables.[359]

The *Nouveau Denisart* also pointed out that masters were liable for the wrongs done by their servants in the functions for which they were employed, because the master was supposed to have made a bad choice of servant.[360] This stress in the *ancien droit* on the master's responsibility arising out of his failure to choose his servants properly is worth considering. An ordinance of François I of December 1540 had forbidden the taking into service as *domestiques* of people of bad character.[361] In the C.Q. and C.N., the basis of a master's liability has changed to liability for his servants' actions in the course of their employment. Toullier explains the new liability of the master thus:

---

[354] The references given to the texts of Roman law by McCord in his edition of the C.Q. are obviously muddled.

[355] Pothier, *T.O.*, pp. 58–59 (nos. 121–122).

[356] *Nouveau Denisart*, vol. 6, p. 152, s.v. "Délit", § III, no. 5 (concerning parents and children).

[357] K.S. Zachariae, *Le droit civil français, traduit de l'allemand sur la cinquième édition. Annoté et réetabli suivant l'ordre du Code Napoléon par G. Massé ... [et] Ch. Vergé*, Paris, A. Durand, 1854–1860, vol. 4, p. 24, n. 8 (on those who have minors under their care).

[358] C.B.M. Toullier, *Le droit civil français suivant l'ordre du Code… continué et complété par J.B. Duvergier*, 6th ed., Paris, F. Cotillon, 1844–1848, vol. 11, pp. 218–228 and 233–235, nos. 260–278 and 282.

[359] Pothier, *T.O.*, pp. 58–59 (no. 121).

[360] *Nouveau Denisart*, vol. 6, p. 151, s.v. "Délit", § III, no. 2. See also Merlin, *Répertoire* (4), vol. 4, p. 5, s.v. "Domestique", no. VIII.

[361] Guyot, *op. cit. supra* note 81, vol. 6, p. 99, s.v. "Domestique".

> [I]l est considéré comme l'ayant faite lui-même par le ministère de son domestique ou de son préposé, contre lesquels il ne peut par conséquent, avoir de recours. . . .[362]

We may see that the master is now liable because the servant, acting in the course of his employment, is considered as an extension of the master; under the *ancien droit* there was a tendency to render the master liable because of his failure to choose good servants. This change in the reasoning behind the rule (though the rule is the same) must reflect a new conception of the relationship between master and servant: the new reasoning places more stress on the employment, whereas the old emphasized the character of the servants. It is difficult to see what significance this has here; the expression of the rule as regards masters and servants in the C.Q. is derived from the article of the C.N.

The Quebec redactors have replaced the C.N.'s "préposés" with "ouvriers" (workmen). The meaning of the two is rather different. "Commettant" and "préposé" in C.N. 1384 signify a relationship analogous to the English principal and agent. In C.Q. 1054, "commettants" is rendered "employers" in the English text; and this is appropriate given the use of the term "ouvriers" and "workmen". This would seem to be narrowing the applicability of the article. The importance of this alteration is hard to assess; it is obviously an improvement on the wording of C.N. 1384, in so far as the latter only spoke of *domestiques*. The fact that the Quebec redactors felt it important to mention *ouvriers* specifically could indicate the increasing importance of the employment of wage labour in Quebec. Pothier could also have been of influence here in that he also mentions *ouvriers* as well as *domestiques*.[363] A further consideration is that this article comes from a section of the Code almost certainly drafted originally in English by Commissioner Day.[364] It does not seem likely, however, that this has had any particular effect on the article: Day would not have misunderstood *commettants* and *préposés* as meaning "employers" and "workmen". The change must be deliberate It should probably be stressed that difference in meaning between the articles of the C.N. and C.Q. is likely to be effectively minimal: both are intending to signify a relationship of control, where one party carries out the instructions of the other.[365] All that should be understood from this change in the article is that there is more of a concentration on, and recognition of the importance of, the *ouvrier*, workman or wage labourer.

The only comment of the redactors on this article is that the wording has been changed to avoid certain objections to the French article, while there has been the addition to the cases enumerated of paragraphs relating to tutors and the curators of insane persons.[366] For example, the provision on tutors seems to

---

[362] Toullier, *op. cit. supra* note 358, vol. 11, p. 235, no. 282.
[363] See *supra*, text quoted at note 359.
[364] See McCord, Preface, p. ix; and Brierley, "Codification", pp. 546 and 578.
[365] For a slightly different approach on this, see G.V.V. Nicholls, *The Responsibility for Offences and Quasi-Offences under the Law of Quebec*, Toronto, Carswell Co., 1938, p. 65. In interpreting "ouvriers", Nicholls refers to art. 2013a. of the Code, a provision added later.
[366] *First Report*, p. 16.

have been suggested by Zachariae's work.[367] Relevant for us, criticism of C.N. 1308 has resulted in the placing of the paragraph on domestics and workmen at the end of the article; this was because there was some controversy over whether or not the last paragraph of C.N. 1384 referred to *maîtres* and *commettants* though they were not mentioned.[368] Should the last paragraph have been so applied, this could have amounted to a change from the *ancien droit*.[369] The redactors avoided any ambiguity in the Quebec article by altering the sequence of the paragraphs.

CONCLUSION ON EMPLOYMENT IN THE QUEBEC CODE OF 1866

The influence of the French code on this area of the Quebec law has obviously been strong, and before discussing further the changes wrought in the Quebec law, together with the redactors' selection and rejection of sources, it is appropriate to summarize briefly the innovations introduced into the *ancien droit* by the redactors. First, an uncertain point in the *ancien droit* has been decided by following the French code's provision that servants were domiciled with their masters. Second, the scope of *louage de service personnel* seems to have been broadened somewhat. Third, the scope of the master's decisory oath seems to have been reduced. Fourth, the distinction between domestic and other servants has been abolished. Fifth, though the traditional rule on masters' liability for servants' wrongs seems to have been retained, the basis of the rule seems to have been changed. Sixth, and finally, the redactors have followed Marcadé in deciding that the term *locataire* always describes he who pays.

The C.L. of 1825 distinguished between various types of servants. The C.N. did not, apart from with respect to domicile. The C.Q. makes only two tiny distinctions between classes of servants. First, following the C.N., only servants above the age of majority who reside with their master are considered domiciled with him. Second, the master's oath is decisory only in disputes with domestic and farm servants. On the first of these, enough has already been said; on the second, the following remarks may be made. That proof should depend on the master's oath presupposes that receipts will not be given, that records and accounts are not kept and that the relationship between master and servant will be close and informal: as such, the master's oath would seem particularly apt for

---

[367] The note in Zachariae, *op. cit. supra* note 357, vol. 4, p. 24, n. 8 is of course a contribution of the French translators and editors; it is not a point made by Zachariae himself. References not quite relevant for the point considered here have not been discussed. The passages from the Digest, for example, deal in the main with a master's liability for thefts carried out by his slaves; the analogy is indeed obvious.

[368] See e.g. Toullier, *op. cit. supra* note 358, vol. 11, pp. 235–236, no. 283; Maleville, *Analyse*, vol. 3, pp. 162–163. Compare the provision of the 1800 *Projet* and of the D.O.: see *supra*, text at notes 203–204.

[369] See Pothier's statement of the *ancien droit*, quoted *supra* in text at note 359.

deciding matters involving domestic and farm servants, whose service is likely to be supervised directly by the master. The growth of industry, and the development of a class of urban wage labourers would render desirable restriction of the use of the master's decisory oath to domestic and farm servants; the process of factory production would divorce servants (now factory hands) from their masters, while the increased likelihood of proper accounts being kept would provide alternative modes of proof.[370] Factory hands would not be in a relationship with their masters whereby the masters' oath would be a satisfactory means of settling disputes. Thus, the distinction as regards the master's oath between domestic and farm servants and other servants was workable, and the Quebec code's modification of both the *ancien droit* and the Code Napoléon was appropriate given social organization in Quebec. It is obvious that a major distinction is no longer drawn drawn between domestic and other servants: the only one, in fact, is that on domicile. This lack of distinction amounts to a change in the *ancien droit* as expressed by Pothier and Guyot.[371] This distinction had been based on the notion that personal and domestic servants were closely bound to their masters and dependent on them in a manner that transcended the idea that both master and servant were equal contracting individuals. The Quebec redactors, in this respect, have assimilated personal and domestic servants to *ouvriers* (manual labourers): the relationship between a master and his domestic has been reduced to being more within the category of formal contract. The strong social bond described by Ariès as once existing between master and servant has completely disappeared.[372] The law now regards a lease of personal services solely as a formal contract between abstract individuals.

The reduction—in law—of the relationship between master and servant to one in theory between equal individuals undertaking reciprocal obligations has not fully been carried through, however. The rule on domicile shows this: there the redactors followed the French code, though they probably need not have done so. The redactors also adopted the Code Napoléon's division of *louage*, though improving on the expresion of C.N. 1708 and 1711. The only influence traceable in the C.Q. from the contemporary trichotomy of *locatio rei*, *locatio operarum* and *locatio operis faciendi* is in C.Q. 1602's description of *locateur* and *locataire*: the description would seem in part to be a reaction against the trichotomy, prompted by the trichotomy's influence in contemporary academic thought. The redactors were tempted to assimilate lease of services to mandate: this modernization of the law they rejected because of the weight of legal tradition, despite the fact that they thought there was no tenable distinction between mandate which was not gratuitous and lease of personal services.

Traditionally, some kinds of work had been the object of mandate rather than of lease and hire because their nature was not thought suitable for them to

---

[370] See *supra*, text at notes 348–353.
[371] See *supra*, text at notes 340–341 and 195–200.
[372] See *supra*, text at notes 2–3.

be subject to lease and hire, which was identified with menial tasks. Both Pothier and the C.N. clearly limit the application of *louage* to fairly lowly tasks: domestic service and manual labour. In the discussion of the Quebec articles, it has been suggested that the redactors seem to have supposed a wider application for lease of services. It must be stressed that the exact intended width of application of the articles is unclear. Given, however, that the redactors even considered merging mandate and lease of services, it is obvious that they did not see much point in the distinction between the two; they cannot have believed that, since some tasks were supposedly more menial and others more elevated, there should be a distinction between the two. Yet, though widening the scope of lease and hire of services, they do appear to have maintained to some extent the traditional limitation. Legal tradition discouraged the major change recognized as desirable. The extension of the scope of lease and hire of work would probably have been desirable in Quebec at this period: the development of factory production would inevitably have meant the employment of many people other than manual labourers and fairly lowly clerks. Industrial and mercantile enterprises of size could employ people from varied backgrounds in numerous tasks.

From the above discussion, and that of the actual articles, one conclusion, above all, may be drawn: if the historical relationship of master and servant as described in the introduction to this chapter be accurately depicted, the Quebec code represents an increased submission of that relationship to the formal rules of contract. Master and servant are viewed as equal individuals contracting together, though with certain reservations due to specific circumstances and legal tradition. The redectors have modernized the law according to their analysis of Quebec's needs; but the strength of legal tradition prevented them from carrying through all the modernization they considered necessary. The sources consulted by the redactors in their work determined the provisions they made and their solutions to the problems posed were drawn from the civilian tradition. Wage labour was regulated by lease: a worker leased out his services. The provisions on employment were few, and the social nature of the relationship between master and servant was not recognized, except perhaps in C.Q. 84 on domicile and C.Q. 1669 on masters' oaths. The redactors accepted the tenets of nineteenth-century liberalism: they did not reflect on whether or not the employee and employer were on objectively equal levels when it came to bargaining. The mid-nineteenth century was a period of continuous emigration of French Canadians from Quebec to the U.S.A. to find work: there was a shortage of jobs and an abundance of labour. Employers could generally dictate their own terms.[373] Under the *ancien régime*, a whole body of social practice regulated relations between master and servant, and the law was not over concerned with such relations; in France under the C.N. industrial labour was regulated on policy grounds. In Quebec, the few formal statements of law in the code were all the redactors considered necessary. Both the civilian tradition

---

[373] See *supra*, chap. 2, text at notes 88–89.

within which the redactors worked together with their acceptance of economic liberalism and of the doctrine of the maximum possible freedom of contract would support the minimum regulation of master and servant, and the subjection of the relationship to the general law of contract as much as possible (consider C.Q 1670). The Quebec code stresses the contractual nature of relations between master and servant: thus, whereas under the *ancien droit* the master's duty to choose good servants had justified his legal liability for their actions, now, under C.Q. 1054, the liability was justified on the grounds of employment.[374]

GENERAL CONCLUSIONS ON EMPLOYMENT IN THE TWO CODES

In this chapter we have traced the selections made by the two teams of codifiers from the sources available to them. We have attempted to understand the motives for, and reasoning behind, such selections and to discover the relationship of the law and the changes in the law to social life. It remains now to extract some more general information from the preceding discussion of employment in the two codes.

Both Louisiana and Quebec reformed and updated their law. Both did so within the confines of the traditional civilian categories of lease and hire, with the exception of the sixth title of the first book of the D.O. This latter title seems to owe its existence to a combination of influence from Blackstone's *Commentaries* and a desire to take account of recent territorial legislation on apprentices and indentured servants. This title permitted the redactors to include more provisions on the relationship between master and servant; but these provisions—despite borrowing from Blackstone—are generally compatible with the civil law as received and adapted. Bound servants were a particular feature of colonial life. The placing of this title is problematic; but the redactors must have felt that it filled a need not met by the French code, while Blackstone provided provisions suitable for borrowing. The reform of the law in both codes was conservative; the changes still maintained the civilian tradition, and indeed both sets of redactors could have gone further in reform. Thus, the contract for labour was important in Quebec; but the redactors maintained lease of work, though tempted to combine lease of work and mandate.

Social changes were nonetheless reflected in the law. We find in the *Siete Partidas*, the main source of private law in Louisiana under Spain, that the servant was considered primarily as part of the family or household, in a position analogous to that of a son. The same approach to servants may be found in French legal sources; Pocquet de Livonnière notably treats servants as being in the *puissance* of their *maitres*. This treatment by the legal writers broadly reflects social circumstances of preindustrial early modern society.[375] In the

---

[374] See *supra*, text at notes 360–363.
[375] See *supra*, text at notes 1–13.

D.O., personal and domestic servants are distinguished from other servants; the former being in a relationship with their masters of a rather more familial nature in comparison to the latter. This would seem to some extent to reflect Louisiana's society of the period; Louisiana had a mercantile and plantation society involving extensive use of slave labour. In the C.Q., on the other hand, no distinction of significance is drawn between domestic servants and labourers: both are considered as being outwith the family in a relationship with their masters of a primarily contractual nature. One or two anachronistic provisions lingered on (domicile for example); but the change in the social position of servants is obvious.

The relationship of servant to master in the early period had been regulated by norms not dependent on modern notions of contract and correlative obligations. Ariès shows that a servant was dependent on his master in the manner of a child.[376] There did exist, however, a body of civilian texts on lease; texts which were commented on, following the civilian tradition, but which did not adequately distinguish lease of work from lease generally, lease of services seemingly not being of much interest. Ariès tells of the gradual disappearance of the close and strong social bond between master and servant: servants came to be excluded from the family.[377] There seems to have been a corresponding tendency in the legal sources to deal with servants under the formal categories of contract. At the same time, the breakdown of the guild system removed one of the other important methods of regulation of the service of artisans and apprentices;[378] and the guild system had never existed in Louisiana or Quebec as a method of regulating the various trades. The main source of legal provisions to regulate employment was the Roman *locatio conductio*: the civilian sources contained a small body of texts, relating to lease of services, and these texts were used to provide a formal regulation of the contractual relationship between master and servant. The Louisiana redactors used French sources, Blackstone, and a territorial act to provide their law. The texts of these sources were amended to fit with social conditions in Louisiana and with the redactors' conception of the nature of employment: the redactors conceived of personal servants still being to some extent within the family, and they chose their sources accordingly; they considered manual labourers as outwith the family and selected appropriate provisions. The redactors rejected the Castilian provisions available to them, which did not deal with servants in a contractual fashion: the provisions on lease of service were vague and unsystematic and did not differentiate it properly from lease of things. The French sources, however, provided a division of lease of service from lease of things and were conceptually more advanced. In Quebec, servants were considered by the redactors to be in a purely contractual relationship with their masters, and the selection of provisions was made accordingly.

---

[376] See *supra*, text at notes 2–6.
[377] *Ibid.*
[378] On the importance of the guilds in this connection, see *supra*, text at notes 52–54.

There would seem to be two main reasons for the oft-noted fact that there were relatively few provisions on lease of service. First, the civilian sources had never discussed lease of services to any extant. Second, Quebec and Louisiana both codified in the nineteenth century, during the period of the ascendancy of support for economic liberalism and individual contractual freedom. The ideals of freedom of contract would suggest that masters and servants be left as much as possible to be free as equal individuals to bargain for conditions of employment. Thus, the paucity of traditional civilian provisions and the prevailing nineteenth-century ideology would be mutually supportive. The Quebec redactors certainly never seem to have considered the real inequality between the bargaining individuals in this contract. This was crucial, especially in a society where wage labour was of increasing economic importance. In Louisiana in 1808 the economy was based primarily on mercantile activity and slave labour was extensively used; the lack of regulation of the contract of employment would probably not be particularly important. What is most significant is that the provisions embodied in the two codes depended on the redactors' vision of what was necessary and possible; this vision was that of nineteenth-century liberals.

As regards the codes of both Quebec and Louisiana, that contract called *locatio conductio operis faciendi* has not been discussed: both codes devoted rather more articles to this aspect of lease than they did to lease and hire of services. This form of the contract of lease would be of more importance for "artisan production" than would that for the hire of labour. This stress on the contract *operis faciendi* might well have been appropriate in Louisiana; it was not in Quebec where industrialization was supplanting the mercantile economy.

In Louisiana, the D.O. contained a fairly major modernization of the law—a modernization that appears to have provided a system of rules suited to the conditions in the territory. In Quebec, too, the law was modernized; this was not done in a radical fashion, however, and, indeed, not as radically as the redactors themselves would have wished. The Quebec redactors were, and considered themselves to be, constrained by legal tradition. The law in Louisiana before codification was uncertain and outmoded: the redactors used the opportunity provided by codification to borrow wholesale from modern sources and models. The very confusion over the law in force permitted this. The existing law in Quebec was not outmoded and confused in the fashion of that in Louisiana before codification; the sources the Quebec redactors returned to for models and provisions were essentially the same as those used for the Louisiana Digest, fifty years before (though they did indeed make profitable use of commentaries on the French code). In Louisiana, in contrast to Quebec, the law was radically inappropriate, and the redactors had less to tie them to the established rules: the redactors accordingly actively sought to embody in the law what they considered to be the needs of their society, though they worked within the tradition of the civil law. In Quebec, the law was not so outmoded as that of Louisiana; there was less need and less pressure for modernization, while there was also no confusion over the law actually in force: tradition exercised greater restraint over the Quebec redactors; they therefore did not modernise the law as much as they themselves would have wished.

Commission to codify the laws of Lower Canada in civil matters,
Quebec City, QC, about 1865
(*Courtesy of McCord Museum*)

Part III

6

THE 1808 DIGEST OF ORLEANS

Chapter three contained a provisional discussion of the nature of the 1808 Louisiana code—the Digest of the Civil Laws Now in Force in the Territory of Orleans. The study of the law relating to family and employment in chapters four and five now allows us to assess the nature of the 1808 Digest and to suggest solutions to some of the problems identified in the modern scholarly debate over the sources and history of the 1808 code. It also allows evaluation of the importance and significance of the de la Vergne manuscript, which has also been the subject of considerable controversy. Finally, it also makes it possible to draw some conclusions on the working method of Brown and Moreau Lislet and on the reassertion of the "Spanish" (Castilian) law after 1812. This means that we can suggest some solutions to some of the problems posed by Professors Pascal and Batiza in their debate. One problem, however, may be instantly dimissed as being a false problem. It was argued in chapter three that surprise that the redactors copied from French sources, or denial that they did so both resulted from applying inappropriate Austinian notions of legal sovereignty to a Digest whose redactors clearly were influenced by theories of natural law.[1] This will be addressed below.

Except for some articles on the specific contract of *louage*, the 1808 Digest's provisions on obligations have not been examined here. Since the law of obligations is of major importance in the Digest, it is useful to examine some of its key articles on contractual obligations, as this will further help us assess the Digest.[2] This chapter will therefore start with a brief *excursus* on the Digest's approach to contract—an approach derived from the French code.

EXCURSUS

D.O. 34 (p. 267) states:

> Les conventions légalement formées, tiennent lieu de loi à ceux qui les ont faites.

---

[1] See *supra,* chap. 3, text at notes 134–155.

[2] Franklin, "Existential Force", p. 98 would class these articles as "*mobile*" or "*Beweggrund*" or "causa" or "presuppositional" texts.

> Elles ne peuvent êtres revoquées, que de leur consentement mutuel, ou pour les causes que la loi autorise.
>
> Elles doivent êtres exécutées de bonne foi.

This is an exact copy of the famous article 1134 of the Code Napoléon. On it, the D.L.V. cites Domat,[3] who expresses a nearly identical opinion, and Febrero.[4] The two Febrero texts are not directly in point.[5] Domat is in point and could be regarded as a "source" (though secondary to C.N. 1134), while Febrero's texts do not really admit of direct comparison with the Digest's article. D.O. 34 (p. 267) is a fundamental provision expressing classic contractual freedom; as such, however, we cannot be certain that it is uniquely French. Since it is the legal limits to such contractual freedom that are of importance here, we will later explore this point further in relation to sale and lease. To explore the extent of contractual freedom in the Digest, we will also focus on penalty clauses and lesion.

D.O. 126 (p. 285) provides:

> La clause pénale est celle par laquelle une personne, pour assurer l'exécution d'une convention, s'engage à quelque chose, en cas d'inexécution.

This must be read along with D.O. 129 (p. 285):

> La clause pénale, est la compensation des dommages et intérêts que le creancier souffre de l'inexécution de l'obligation principale. . . .

and with D.O. 52 (p. 269):

> Lorsque la convention porte, que celui qui manquera de l'exécuter, payera une certaine somme à titre de dommages intérêts, il ne peut être alloué à l'autre partie, une somme plus forte ni moindre.

These articles are exact copies of C.N. 1226, 1229 (in relevant part) and 1152 respectively.[6] In this, the French code of 1804 differs from the customary law of the *ancien régime*, which allowed penalties to be modified by the judge.[7] Hence, we may say that the French code developed the law on penalty clauses along the

---

[3] Domat, *Loix civiles*, p. 22 (pt. 1, bk. 1, tit. 1, sect. 2, art. 7).

[4] Febrero, *Contratos*, chap. 4, § 5 no. 126, and chap. 7, § 1 no. 26 (vol. 2, pp. 103, 362–364).

[5] Febrero here states that usury is prohibited, before demonstrating a way of avoiding the prohibition.

[6] The second paragraph of D.O. 129 (p. 285) and that of C.N. 1229 are identical; though not quoted in the text, both state that principal and penalty cannot be demanded together, unless the latter is for mere delay.

[7] See Pothier, *T.O.*, p. 179 (no. 345). On the development of penalty clauses, see A. Fliniaux, "L'évolution du concept de clause pénale chez les canonistes du moyen âge", in *Mélanges Paul Fournier*, Paris, Recueil Sirey, 1929, pp. 233–247. See also P. Benjamin, "Penalties, Liquidated Damages and Penal Clauses in Commercial Contracts. A Comparative Study of English and Continental Law", 9 *International and Comparative Law Quarterly* (1960), pp. 600–627 at pp. 606–610. The modern French law has recently reverted to what virtually is the view of Pothier. See the *loi* of 9 July 1975, discussed in S. Sanz, "La consécration du pouvoir judiciaire par la loi du 9 Juillet 1975, ses incidences sur la théorie générale de la clause pénale", 75 *Revue trimestrielle du droit civil* (1977), pp. 268–288.

lines of contractual freedom: "Les conventions . . . tiennent lieu de droit . . . ." The C.N. and D.O. here also avoided problems of proof; but contractual freedom seems of prime importance.

The D.L.V. has no references in connection with D.O. 52 (p. 269): this is significant, especially when it is considered that every reference in its relevant section (IV of chap. 3 of tit. 3 of Book 3) is to Pothier, bar two references to Domat. For D.O. 52 there could be no Pothier reference, as this was a provision contrary to Pothier's view of penalty clauses. For D.O. 126 (p. 285) the D.L.V. refers to *Part.* 5.11.34, Domat,[8] Febrero,[9] and Pothier.[10] For D.O. 129, the D.L.V. cites *Part.* 5.11. 34 and 35, Febrero as above, and Pothier.[11] Indeed, only this one section of Febrero and these two *leyes* of the *Quinta Partida* are cited opposite the articles in the section of the D.L.V. on penalty clauses.[12] Domat, as cited, defines a penalty clause; but he states at article 19 that such a clause's effect is regulated at the discretion of the judge. In essence, what he is saying is in line with D.O. 126 and 129, but possibly not with D.O. 52, when his article 19 (not cited by the D.L.V.) is considered. Pothier as cited is also at one with the D.O. provisions; but again the D.O. provisions must be understood along with D.C. 52, which is contrary to Pothier's conception of *clause pénale*. If we next turn to the Castilian provisions, we find the following. The text of Febrero and the two *leyes* of the *Partidas* cited by the D.L.V. are reasonably similar to the provisions in the D.O.;[13] but we cannot stop here. Once more, the D.L.V. references do not give a true picture of the Castilian law. *Part.* 5.11.40. shows that the law was radically different from that in the D.O. The *Partidas*' provisions also lack the sophistication of those of the C.N. and D.O. *Ley* 40 states, in essence, that usurious penalties are invalid, and lays down how usury in penalty clauses is shown. Usury, of course, much exercised the ingenuity of the canonists of the mediaeval period.[14] This was not a superseded provison of the *Partidas*. The work of Asso and Manuel shows that this method of reducing or forbidding excessive penalties was still operative in the Castilian law just prior to the redaction of the D.O. The 1806 edition of their *Instituciones* states that usurious penalties are not allowed, nor those that comprehend *all* a man's property, nor those that are *double* the amount of the condition or bond.[15] These prohibitions are analogous to Pothier's view that the judge should modify excessive penalties; such prohibitions also limit contractual freedom and prevent

---

[8] Domat, *Loix civiles*, p. 26 (pt. 1, bk. 1, tit. 1, sect. 4, preamble); see also *ibid.* p. 29 (pt. 1, bk. 1, tit. 1, sect. 4, arts. 18 and 19) not cited in the D.L.V.

[9] Febrero, *Contratos*, ch. 10, § 2 no. 29 (vol. 3, p. 200); see also (uncited) *ibid.* ch. 10, § 2 no. 30 (vol. 3, pp. 200–201).

[10] Pothier, *T.O.*, p. 173 (no. 337).

[11] *Ibid.*, pp. 176, 178 (nos. 342 and 343).

[12] On the interleaf opposite D.L.V., p. 276 other sources on penal clauses are referred to: we need not concern ourselves with them.

[13] Thus, the unquoted final paragraph of D.O. 129 (see *supra,* note 6) corresponds to certain statements in the two *leyes*.

[14] See Fliniaux, *op. cit. supra* note 7, *passim.*

[15] See *Asso y Manuel*, vol. 2, p. 40 (bk. 2, tit. 8). Cf. *Fuero Real*, 4.5.10.

the agreement of the parties from making the law between them. Such a restriction is found neither in the D.O., nor in the C.N., which the former is here closely copying. Febrero in his work for notaries did demonstrate how the laws on usury could be circumvented;[16] but this does not affect the point. It would be ridiculous to suggest that the law on penalty clauses in the D.O. is closely copied from the C.N. because the latter represented the Castilian law as avoided by Castilian notaries.[17] The D.O redactors obviously chose to copy the provisions of the C.N., for reasons that will be discussed below, after we have briefly examined two contracts in the D.O. and the Castilian law.

We will here briefly reflect on sale and lease, which in Roman law were *bonae fidei* consensual contracts. (Lease has been discussed already, but only as regards lease of labour:[18] it is still useful to make some remarks here.) It is not proposed in the context of these brief remarks to follow up the D.L.V. references, as this is unnecessary: it is sufficient to examine the approach of Asso and Manuel, which is very different from that found in the D.O.

In their title XIII, *De la Compra y Venta*,[19] Asso and Manuel quote the definition of sale from *Part*. 5.5.1,[20] and then state:

> De esta definicion se sigue: I Que Ia compra, y yenta se perfecciona con el consentimiento de ambas partes. II Que se pueda vender y comprar todo lo que está comercio, ó no se halla prohibido. III Que el precio deba ser cierto, justo, y en dinero contado. IV Que este contrato es oneroso à ambas partes.[21]

This is basically unremarkable and would correspond with the provisions in the D.O., except for the requirement that the *precio* be *justo*. Section 3 of this title is on "lesion enorme" and explains what is meant by *justo precio*:[22] we will return to this after considering lease. Asso and Manuel repeat, in their title on *Arrendamiento* (XIV),[23] that the "precio ha de ser justo, cierto, y en dinero contado".[24] It is also worth noting that the sons of a family had restricted powers of buying and selling appropriate to the extensive *patria potestad* of the Castilian law.[25]

Asso and Manuel state in the third section, on *lesion enorme*, of the thirteenth title of their second book, that because price should be just *any* purchaser or seller can have the contract overturned for enorm lesion, if the object is sold for less than half its value, or for more than one and a half times its value, provided action is taken within four years. A *minor* can rescind for lesion if the price is excessive

---

[16] Febrero, *Contratos*, ch. 7, § 1 no. 26 (vol. 3, pp. 362–364).
[17] Nor—I think—could the D.O. provisions plausible be represented as here abolishing Castilian "legal scaffolding". See Watson, *Society*, pp. 87–96.
[18] See *supra*, chap. 5.
[19] *Asso y Manuel*, vol. 2, pp. 87–111 (bk. 2, tit. 13).
[20] The D.L.V. cites this also at D.O. 1 (p. 453), defining sale.
[21] *Asso y Manuel*, vol. 2, p. 87.
[22] *Ibid*., vol. 2, p. 104.
[23] *Ibid*., vol. 2, pp. 111–119 (bk. 2).
[24] *Ibid*., vol. 2, p, p. 112.
[25] *Ibid*., vol. 2, p. 88; also *supra*, chap. 4, text at notes 137–157.

but under the above limits; if the party is an adult and the price is between half the just price and the just price (or similarly for the upper figure) there can be no rescission, even if there has been deception (*engano*) in the price, provided always there has been no fraud (*dolo*).[26] Similar provisions are found in Castilian legislative sources, such as the *Partidas* and the *Nueva recopilación*.[27] Note that these rules on lesion apply to *any* object sold.

French customary law also had rules on lesion. But these applied only to immoveables—the period for rescission being ten years—and only to sale.[28] There was much debate over whether purchasers could rescind for lesion, though sellers definitely could seek such rescission.[29] These rules on "lesion d'outre moité" (*lesion en mas ó menos de la mitad de justo precio*) were suppressed during the Revolutionary period by the *loi* of 14 *fructidor*, *an* 3. After a prolonged and heated debate, rules on lesion in sale were reintroduced in the *Code civil*, in articles 1674 to 1685.[30] These rules did not reintroduce the *ancien droit in toto*, but in a considerably modified form. Rules on enorm lesion were common in Europe, having developed out of the late Roman *laesio enormis*, the further development of which during the Reception need not be dealt with here. Suffice it to say that the Roman *laesio enormis* applied only to sale of immoveables and only in favour of the seller.[31]

The sixth title of the third book of the D.O. deals with sale. The second section of the fifth chapter of this title is devoted to rescission of sale on the grounds of lesion: D.O. 109 (p. 365) to D.O. 117 (p. 367). This section is an almost exact copy of the corresponding section of the *Proj. An VIII*, 3.9.98–106.[32] It differs in some respects from the corresponding provisions of the C.N. The differences between the *Proj. An VIII* and the D.O. are mainly trivial ones of expression, the exception being D.O. 114 (p. 367), which includes slaves among the class of possessions to which lesion does not apply. Otherwise, for all relevant purposes, we may say the two sets of provisions are the same.

The D.O. and the *Proj. An VIII* both differ from the C.N. in the following respects (*inter alia*). Both provide a four-year period for rescission, the C.N. one of two years.[33] Both state that lesion, to be relevant, has to be "d'outre moitié", the C.N. that it should be more than seven-twelfths.[34] We need not deal neither with other minor differences, nor with the rules relating to minors, who are a

---

[26] *Asso y Manuel*, vol. 2, p. 112.
[27] *Part.* 5.5.56; *Rec. Cast.* 5.11.1.
[28] See, e.g., Pothier, *T.O.*, pp. 20–33 (nos. 33–39); Pothier, *T.V.*, pp. 139–156 (nos. 330–371).
[29] See Maleville, *Analyse*, vol. 3, p. 363. The Roman law had only allowed the seller to recover for *laesio enormis*.
[30] See Maleville, *Analyse*, vol. 3, pp. 354–359.
[31] See C. 4.44.2 and 8; Buckland *Textbook*, p. 486. On the extended application of *laesio enormis* by later civilians, see R.W.M. Dias, "Laesio enormis: The Roman-Dutch Story", in D. Daube (ed.), *Studies in the Roman Law of Sale, Dedicated to the Memory of Francis de Zulueta*, Oxford, Clarendon Press, 1959, pp. 46–63.
[32] Batiza, "Sources", p. 111 (appendix C), p. 111.
[33] D.O. 115 (p. 367); *Proj. An VIII*, 3.9.104; C.N. 1676.
[34] D.O. 109 (pp. 365–367); *Proj. An VIII*, 3.9.98; C.N. 1674.

rather special case. All three codes agree that lesion applies only to *immoveables*,[35] and that the rules operate only in favour of the seller: "La rescission pour d'outre moitié n'a pas lieu en faveur de l'acheteur", state the D.O. and *Proj. An VIII*.[36] The D.O. and *Proj. An VIII* follow the *ancien droit* of northern France except in so far as they reduce the period for rescission from ten to four years and settle the question—previously much debated[37]—as to whether or not a purchaser could rescind for lesion.

The difference between the French laws and the D.O. and the Castilian laws is obvious: the former restrict rescission to the seller and only on sale of an immoveable, the latter's provisions were much wider. It could indeed be stated that the provisions of the *Proj. An VIII* are closer to the Castilian law than are those of the C.N. Despite copious references in the D.L.V., this would not support the argument that the D.O. copied the *Proj. An VIII* because it was closer to Castilian law: the articles of the D.O. and the *Proj. An VIII* are firmly and obviously based on the *ancien droit* of France. The D.O. has adopted that law's restricted notion of enorm lesion and rejected the broad notion of the Castilian law, which had an important concept of *justo precio*:[38] indeed, so important was it that it had been extended to *arrendamiento*,[39] (*laesio enormis* did not apply to Roman *locatio conductio*), while special rules existed as to settling the "just price" of wages.[40] The D.L.V. also cites Domat and Pothier, and indeed the accounts given by these two French authors are much closer to the D.O. provisions than are those of the Castilian sources cited. The fact that this section is copied virtually word for word from the 1800 Projet of the C.N. is, however, incontrovertible.

It is now necessary to complete this rather lengthy *excursus*, and to consider the origins of the approach of the Digest to contract based on the foregoing discussion of certain key articles. It is clear that the provisions of the D.O. are French, and specifically codified French, in origin: whether or not they are closer to the C.N. or *Proj. An VIII* does not really matter, as what is important is that the law in the D.O. is quite different from the Castilian law. The redactors cannot be assumed to have copied these codified French provisions thinking in their ignorance that they represented the Castilian law: what the Castilian law was could have easily been gathered from, say, Febrero.

One must conclude that the French provisions were intentionally copied, and two reasons may be suggested. First, the C.N. and its *Projet* offered a neat concise selection of texts in a form readily borrowed. Second, it was argued in

---

[35] See D.O. 109 (pp. 365–367); *Proj. An VIII*, 3.9.8; C.N. 1674; and the "exclusion" article, D.O. 114 (p. 367); *Proj. An VIII*, 3.9.103; and the less similar C.N. 1684.

[36] D.O. 113 (p. 367); *Proj. An VIII*, 3.9.102; cf. C.N. 1683.

[37] See Maleville, *Analyse*, vol. 3, p. 363.

[38] *Asso y Manuel*, vol. 2, p. 94, state thus: "Del tercer axîoma se sigue: I. Que sera cierto el precio de la cosa, si se dexa a arbitrio de un tercero, y este lo señalese, à cuya decision se debe estar si no que fuse desproporcionado, en cuyo caso se debe enmedar por juicio de hombres buenos."

[39] *Ibid.*, vol. 2, p. 112; see *supra*, text at notes 22–25.

[40] *Asso y Manuel*, vol. 2, p. 114; cf. *Rec. Cast.* 7.11.3.

chapter two that the period up to and past the 1808 codification was one of a movement from a controlled economy to a free market: doctrines of economic liberalism were current and espoused enthusiastically by merchants in the United States. The particular areas of the law of contract studied in this *excursus* were chosen because they highlighted questions of freedom of contract and inviolability of contract (*pacta sunt servanda*). The Castilian provisions on penalty clauses restricted freedom of contract, while the provisions on lesion violated the notion of *pacta sunt servanda*. The C.N. and its Projet's articles on both these areas were much more in favour of contemporary economic liberalism: this must have had some influence in their selection. Thus, D.O. 34 (p. 267) becomes an effective and guiding principle on contracts in the Digest of 1808, because the D.O. has followed the French provisions and approach.[41]

To say that the Louisiana redactors selected these provisions purely because of economic doctrine is, however, too simple; the fact that, in general, they were closely copying the two French codes must have been influential, while the prestige and technical elegance of the French codification also probably influenced them. To determine the historical causes behind these choices of provisions would demand an exhaustive analysis of the law of contract generally, and of the socio-economic background: an analysis outwith the scope of this work. Nonetheless, it can—I think—be confidently asserted that questions of economic liberalism were important, and must be taken to have influenced the D.O. redactors; just as such questions were to influence the redactors of the C.Q. later in the century, when they came to draw up their own provisions on contract.[42]

THE DIGEST OF 1808: "FRENCH" OR "SPANISH"?

It is now possible to assess more fully the theories of Professors Pascal and Batiza on the origins and sources of the Digest of 1808. In some respects, the work of both Professors is—I would argue—unhistorical in approach. Professor Pascal founds his view that the Digest is essentially "Spanish-Roman" simply on an assertion, as he has not provided (as yet) any research to uphold his thesis. Chapters four and five above show that, certainly as regards the law relating to the family and employment, Professor Pascal's thesis cannot be upheld. Professor Batiza has analyzed the individual articles of the code and has concluded that the code is basically of French origin. The work of each Professor will be discussed in turn.

Professor Baade has succinctly explained Professor Pascal's thesis as follows: first, Pascal argues that "Spanish" and not French law was formally in effect in Louisiana when part of the Spanish Empire; second, Pascal states that the redactors of the Digest were instructed to restate the law by which the

---

[41] Quoted *supra*, text at notes 2–3.

[42] *First Report*, p. 12, remark on art. 13.

Territory was then governed; and third, Pascal claims that they did so, so that borrowings were made from the French code of 1804 only because they were a convenient expression of the *substance* of the "Spanish" law that was in effect in the Territory of Orleans.[43]

In chapter three, we discussed the background to the 1808 codification, the instructions to the redactors, and the attitude of civilian systems to transplants or receptions of foreign law. Chapter four showed that the systems of *puissance maritale* and *puissance paternelle* in the Digest did not express the Castilian law: especially as regards *puissance maritale*, the conceptual system and actual provisions of the Digest were contrary to the Castilian law. As regards the labour of servants, apprentices and *engagés* discussed in chapter five, the position is perhaps more complex; but it may be quite categorically stated that these provisions did not amount to an attempt to express the substance of the Castilian law in French (or Blackstonian) terms. This means that Professor Pascal's thesis cannot be accepted. Of course, there was *some* attempt to adopt rules from the Castilian law for the Digest (the "ganancial" community, the division into pupillage and minority); but this does not help Professor Pascal's argument—the conceptual scheme was thoroughly French, as were the bulk of the provisions.[44] The adoption of some rules of Castilian law is hardly suprising.[45] (D.O. 2 to 14 (pp. 37–39) cause problems; but these problems relate to the *form* of the code, which will be discussed below.)

Professor Pascal has claimed that:

> The writer's experience, supplemented by information from some of his colleagues, leads him to affirm that many of the institutions and rules of the Digest of 1808 will prove to be Spanish-Roman, even if often in French dress, or French (especially precodification French) as well as Spanish-Roman. Particularly to be mentioned are the *non-obligations* areas of the law, such as filiation, paternal authority, minority with its divisions into impuberty and puberty and the corresponding tutorship of *impuberes* and curatorship of *puberes*, the rules of lesion applicable to minors, the division of things, riparian rights, and, in general, the law of succession.[46]

In this research, not all of these topics have been covered; but I hope it is clear that as regards paternal authority the thrust of Professor Pascal's somewhat ambiguous (note the "or French (especially precodification French) as well as Spanish-Roman") assertion is simply not borne out. As regards the law on minority, as I have indicated, there is some truth in his observation; but, over all, his basic claim cannot be maintained. The Digest redactors drew freely on many sources; it would have been surprising had some Castilian provisions not been

---

[43] Baade, "Marriage Contracts", p. 83 states: "Professor Pascal does not, however, base his thesis on legal history."

[44] See *supra*, chap. 4, discussion at notes 250–301, where the views expressed in Batiza, "Textual Evidence" are taken into account; Baade, "Marriage Contracts", *passim*.

[45] See *infra*, text at notes 46–47; 56–58; 70–89.

[46] Pascal, "Reply", p. 623, n. 55 (emphasis added).

introduced. Further as emphasized in the quotation, Pascal particularly mentioned "non-obligations". This is significant. There is little point in counting up the articles of the code of 1808 dealing with obligations; but most scholars would agree that in the 1808 Digest obligations constitute a very important and substantial part of the law, as indeed they do in the French code. The provisions on obligations in the code (bar the specific provisions on *louage des services*) have not been subjected to the same investigation as devoted to the articles on *puissance maritale* and *puissance paternelle*; but the *excursus* above shows that certain key articles, adopted in the D.O. from the work of the French redactors, provided a new orientation for the law on obligations away from the Castilian law.

If the above argument be correct, then Professor Pascal's core thesis must be rejected. The 1808 Digest cannot be described as embodying the *substance* of the Castilian law though expressed in the terms of the French code and its *projet*. That some provisions of the D.O. are taken from the Castilian law does not affect the matter: such provisions were not adopted necessarily because the previous law was Castilian, but because the redactors for some reason preferred them to the rules discovered in the other authorities they consulted.[47]

In a vast work, Professor Batiza has attempted to trace all the sources of the provisions of the Digest of 1808. It is appropriate here to form some conclusions on his study.[48] By his own criteria, Professor Batiza has made an occasional mistake; but this is inevitable in a work of such enormous scope and is unimportant here.[49] Though very thorough and painstaking, Professor Batiza's work may nonetheless be misleading. What he has done is as follows. He has taken each provision of the Digest and searched for and located its source. On the basis of these sources he concludes that the Digest is composed, in varying percentages, of provisions drawn from various sources. In so far as he has traced the *individual sources* of *individual* articles, Batiza's work is generally unexceptional. There are, however, some problems connected with this. The Digest is a sophisticated document: Batiza's form of analysis does not explore all the intricacies of its composition.

The most vexed aspect of Professor Batiza's work is the reliance on similarity of wording as indicating the "source" of an article. Such a form of testing has to be used cautiously; but, generally, Batiza must be correct. It is useful to quote an important passage from Professor Batiza's most recently published article on the Digest:

> This writer's position, drawn from the tracing of the sources of the 1808 Code to three different languages, is that clues provided by the wording of a provision are the surest means of identifying a source. Any suggestion that dichotomies exist

---

[47] Such reason could even be that they preferred not to disrupt the *status quo* without this supporting Pascal.

[48] His arguments are now scattered through several journal articles, but have not essentially changed from those set out in Batiza, "Sources".

[49] As Batiza himself has recognized—see Batiza, "Textual Evidence", pp. 82–83, n. 25. Note that the two works Batiza there refers to were unavailable to me. This is unimportant, since I have been able to check all the sources myself.

> between the language and the substance of a provision is untenable since it is clear that, in adopting identical or nearly identical language, the rule or principle therein incorporated is simultaneously received. In fact, it is rather the acceptance of the rule or principle which determines the adoption of the language in the first place.[50]

The first sentence of this passage is correct: given that the redactors have left no indication of the sources from which they adopted or adapted various provisions, comparison of the Digest with various authorities known or likely to have been available to the redactors is an important method of establishing influence. I would suggest, however, that the statement in the second sentence of the passage needs qualification. This is readily demonstrated. D.O. 57–60 (p. 383) copied the wording of the *Proj. An VIII*: the mistakes made in the French of D.O. 58 enable us to be certain of this.[51] Yet the classification of servants contained in these articles is not that of the *Proj. An VIII*, but is instead influenced by (probably) Pothier. The *wording* of the articles is copied to a greater or lesser extent from the 1800 *Projet*, while the *rule* is different. There *can* be a dichotomy between language and substance. Professor Batiza points out that the articles are not identical to those of the *Proj. An VIII*;[52] but the test on the basis of the words is not able to indicate that the rule is derived from the *ancien droit.* Batiza is correct in saying the wording is copied in varying degrees from the *Proj. An VIII*; but, in so far as his work fails to indicate that the rules differ from those of the *Projet*, it could mislead the unwary, while it does not recognize the intellectual complexity of the redaction of the code. As said, Professor Batiza's admirable and exhaustive work is generally correct in indicating the source of the wording (and usually the rule) of an individual article in the Digest; but it must be used cautiously. Thus, the sole test of similarity of wording originally allowed him to cite Gaius' *Institutes* as a source; this is impossible.[53] Similarity of wording as the *sole* criterion is potentially unhistorical, if incautiously used.

Professor Batiza's work is potentially misleading in a further respect. Certain articles are more important than others:[54] thus, Batiza gives an article referring to another area of the Digest the same weight as one laying down an important rule on, for example, contract. To the extent that he may identify the "source" of an article of no significance, Professor Batiza is correct; but in so far as he adds up the individual sources to state that, for example, the French code of 1804 is the source of 709 provisions, he is misleading if it is to be concluded that this represents a necessary correspondence of rules between the two codes. In fairness to Professor Batiza, it must be said that he does *not* draw such a conclusion: he merely claims to be tracing the *individual* sources of *individual*

---

[50] Batiza, "Textual Evidence", p. 84.
[51] See *supra*, chap. 5 at notes 179–200.
[52] He classes D.O. 57 as "v.", 58 as "a.v. (last part)", 59 as "a.v. (in part)" and 60 as "s.i."
[53] Batiza, "Sources", p. 12, p. 34, appendix A, and pp. 37, 38 and 39, appendix B.
[54] Franklin, "Existential Force", p. 98 makes the same point.

articles and does *not* explicitly state that there may be an exact correspondence of rules between the two codes; though such is a tempting inference from his work, especially when he denies that there may be a dichotomy between langaage and substance. Groups of articles cohere to form legal institutions in MacCormick's sense;[55] and these legal concepts (such as that of *puissance maritale*) are of vital importance. Batiza's work does not take this into account. What is *excluded* may also be of vital importance; if all the articles of the C.N. on a particular topic are borrowed for the D.O., bar one, and the exclusion of that article alters the meaning of the articles as a whole, then, although *each individual article* originates in the C.N., it cannot be stated that the *law* in the D.O. is identical to that in the C.N. Batiza's analysis does not recognize this. Again, Batiza does *not* claim that his identification of the sources of individual articles on any particular topic as being drawn from the C.N. means that the law is identical; but the inference is very easy to draw and, unless the exact meaning of Batiza's work and its limitations are recognized, the unwary may be misled.

In conclusion, one may say that Professor Batiza's work, though of very great importance, if used carelessly, has the potential to be ambiguous and to mislead. The form of analysis to which he has subjected the code has its limitations. Comparison of wording to establish sources may misdirect and, without due care, prove unhistorical in result.

The above discussion of the hypotheses of Professor Pascal and the research of Professor Batiza helps focus attention on what Associate Justice Tate has recently called the "splendid mystery of the Civil Code of Louisiana".[56] Though what is at issue in this thesis is not so much the sources of the 1808 redaction as the reasons behind the redactors' choice of concepts and rules, inevitably we have had to take into account the work of Professors Pascal and Batiza, and the above assessment of their work is based on the study of the D.O. in this thesis. Can such study help suggest solutions to the "splendid mystery"? As regards *puissance maritale*, *puissance paternelle*, and employment (to use the term loosely) the question may possibly be answered in the affirmative; but even so, caution is necessary. We may state that the concepts of *puissance maritale* and *puissance paternelle* are essentially founded in the northern French *droit coutumier*, especially as they appear in the French code and its *Projet*, and differ from those of the Castilian law. This cannot be gainsaid; the position is, however, more complex than might at first appear. There has been, on the part of the redactors, a considerable process of selection among sources. It is possible to trace the influence of more than one "source" in some articles of the Digest; and although the over-all conception of one area is, say, northern French in origin, within that area individual rules or articles may be drawn from elsewhere. The redactors quite happily would include articles drawn from any source if they found them suitable. This means that, in any area of law in the

---

[55] N. MacCormick, "Law as Institutional Fact", 90 *Law Quarterly Review* (1974), pp. 102–129.

[56] A. Tate, "The Splendid Mystery of the Civil Code of Louisiana", 25 *Louisiana Bar Journal* (1977), pp. 29–39.

D.O., there may be various layers and lines of influence. Thus, the articles on *louage des services*, and the analysis into two of *louage* in the Digest originate in the *Projet* of 1800 and the Code Napoléon; but Pothier has exercised some influence too. Title VI of Book One of the Digest is rather more problematic. Blackstone has clearly exercised *some* influence, but, as shown in chapter 5, it would be wrong to claim that these articles have a peculiarly English origin, or introduce common-law principles into the Digest. Blackstone provided easily borrowed texts on an area of the law similar all over Europe. The other aspects of the title were concerned with a recent territorial Act and with taking account of particular circumstances in Louisiana (consider *engagés*).

It must be taken as correct that, in the areas of law examined in chapters four and five, and in obligations generally, the Digest owes more to the French Civil Code and its *Projet*, and to the *ancient droit*, than to Castilian law. This, of course, leaves undealt with many of the areas of the Code that, according to Pascal, exhibit signs of Castilian origin.[57] It is worth pointing out, however, that paternal power, which he claims to be "Spanish-Roman", has been demonstrated to be of French origin: and hence caution must be observed before accepting his other claims. There has been no attempt here to examine these other areas of the Digest, as it is indeed not for me to attempt to prove or to refute Professor Pascal's thesis as regards these areas of the law; but I would maintain that the demonstration that important areas of family law and of the law of obligations are not of Castilian or "Spanish Roman" origin allows us to be certain that, over-all, the Digest is not the deliberate or accidental expression of pre-existing Castilian law through French texts.

The debate over whether the Digest is French or Castilian is not of primary importance here, as we are mainly concerned with seeking a pattern among the selection of provisions and concepts that may contribute to an understanding of legal development. Thus, for us, whether or not the law of property is influenced by Castilian law is, in itself, not of great importance;[58] of course, were it in fact to have been influenced by that law, the reasons why would be of great interest. The study of aspects of family law and of the law of employment is sufficient to ground our conclusions. As has been maintained in chapters one and three, the process of codification appears to lend itself to borrowing, selection, and adaption: there is nothing whatsoever inconsistent in the Digest's redactors utilizing both French law *and* Castilian law: they were not legal positivists, but believed in the supremacy of natural law. The use of certain Castilian provisions along with French provisions does not mean that the redactors were consecrating antinomies in the Digest:[59] the provisions would be selected to be

---

[57] See *supra*, text at notes 45–46.

[58] Dargo, *Jefferson's Louisiana*, pp. 161–163; Batiza, "Textual Evidence", p. 92, n. 62, third paragraph.

[59] The terminology is that of Franklin, "Existential Force", p. 75. A reading of Professor Franklin's article would suggest that he categorizes all the "Spanish" law as "mediaeval" or "feudal", in opposition to the "bourgeois" Code Napoléon: this will be discussed further *infra* in connection with the D.L.V.

compatible. (Consider the exclusion of aspects of the French law both pre-code and codified, and of certain aspects of the *Partidas*.)[60] Further, even though some rules may be attributed to the Castilian law, the *exclusion* of other rules is of vital importance. Thus, the statutory community of the Digest may be influenced by the *sociedad de gananciales*; but the whole thrust of the rules on matrimonial property is "French".[61]

We may sum up by saying that rules and concepts in the Digest may be traced to the French *ancien droit*, the C.N., the *Proj. An VIII*, or the *Partidas*; but Moreau Lislet and Brown, while closely following the style of the *Proj. An VIII* and C.N., have produced something new: the Digest is not the product of slavish copying of the C.N. or its *Projet*—it is in many ways unique, built out of varying sources with some original invention. This does not mean that the laws selected were necessarily the most suitable. For example, it would appear that the laws relating to the seashore selected in 1808 were quite unsuitable.[62] (Of course, in 1808, this is indeed unlikely to have been such a great problem as in the present day, as there had, as yet, been no great commercial development of the seashore.) It should be pointed out that these rules are not taken from the C.N., the equivalent provisions of which possibly would have been more suitable, but from Roman law, more specifically from Justinian's *Institutes*.[63]

The relevant articles are D.O. 3, 4 and 5 (p. 95): opposite them, the D.L.V. cites *Part*. 3.28.3 and 4, and Domat.[64] The *Partidas*' rule (3.28.3) is similar to that in the D.O. and the *Institutes*, providing that seashore is one of those things which "pertenescen à todas las criaturas que viven en este mundo . . .". The *Institutes* use the term *res communis*. D.O. 4 (p. 95) states that the seashore is the land covered by the highest tide of the winter season, which is the same as *Institutes* 2.1.3; whereas *Part*. 3.28.4 states: "Et todo aquel logar es llamado ribera de la mar quanto se cubre del agua della quando mas cresce en todo el aňo, quier en tiempo de invierno ó de verano." In Louisiana, the highest tides are during the summer; yet the redactors selected the provision of the Roman law, more suitable for the non-tidal Mediterranean, in preference to the *Partidas* provision, potentially more suitable for Louisiana in allowing the highest tide at any time of the year to be the standard. Why the redactors selected the Roman

---

[60] Consider the significance of the exclusion of C.N. 224 from the D.O., or the fact that the D.O.'s rules on *puissance du mari* are the same as some *individual* rules of the Castilian law but are contradicted by the rules as a whole of the latter.

[61] See *supra*, chap. 4, at notes 250–301, preferring Baade, "Marriage Contracts" over Batiza, "Textual Evidence".

[62] See A. de Castro and A.C. Watson, "Seashore in Louisiana", 8 *Tul. L. Rev.* (1934), pp. 272–277.

[63] Inst. 2.1.1, 3 and 5; M. Franklin, "Some Observations on the Influence of French Law on the Early Civil Codes of Louisiana", in *Le droit civil français: livre-souvenir des journées du droit civil français*, Montreal and Paris, Recueil Sirey, 1936, pp. 833–845 at p. 843 states that these rules were taken from the French law: as regards the *specific* rules he is wrong.

[64] Domat, *Loix civiles*, p. 16 (prel. bk. tit. 3, sect. 1, arts. 1 and 2). The D.L.V. in fact cites bk. 1, prel. tit., 3, sect. 2, loix 1 and 2, which is an obvious error. Domat does not define seashore, though he mentions it: he cites the *Institutes*.

provision can only be a matter of speculation, as with why they rejected the rules of the *Partidas* and the Code Napoléon. It may be said as regards the redactors not following the Code Napoléon here that the first chapter of the first title of the second book of the D.O. has no equivalent in the C.N. The French code's provisions on public domain are somewhat confused and have attracted much criticism:[65] the arrangement of the D.O. is apparently superior, and the problems with the French articles may well have caused the redactors to reject their rules.[66] It should be noted that the D.L.V. does not cite the *Institutes* for any relevant article;[67] but on the interleaf opposite p. 94, the *Institutes* titles 1.1 and 2 are cited, along with Justinian's Digest's title 1.8. For whatever reason the redactors selected the Roman rules here, it was most certainly not because they were most suitable, nor because they expressed the law before codification. To give a definite answer to the question why the Roman rule was adopted here would require an analysis of the whole of the relevant section of the D.O.; but it may be said that the redactors apparently changed the law for no reason other than to obtain a concise rule—a rule which was not advantageous.

In general, the Digest is a mixture of concepts and provisions freely drawn from varying sources: and statements such as that the Digest is predominantly of French origin (or otherwise) are so general as not to have much meaning or significance without some qualification. The Digest is a complex mixture of provisions taken from many and varied sources, though it is obvious that it is most influenced by the work of the French redactors in the C.N. and *Proj. An VIII*. This leads on to a final point. Associate Justice Tate poses another problem. He points out that it is now clear that the redactors used both the French code and its 1800 *Projet* and remarks that "no explanation has been found for the contemporaneous use of the earlier draft along with final code [*sic*] adopted by the French."[68] This is really a false problem. Considering that the 1808 redactors were forming their own code and plundering all the legal materials available to them for borrowable provisions, since both the C.N. and its Projet were available to them, there is no reason why they should not have used both, and many reasons why they should use both. To use both the C.N. and its draft increased the available pool of borrowable provisions. The redactors were not attempting to adopt the C.N. in its entirety. They also seem to have had a preference for the 1800 *Projet* because of their natural-law approach.[69]

---

[65] M. Planiol, *Treatise on the Civil Law*, trans. by Louisiana State Law Institute, St. Paul, MN, West Pub. Co., 1959, vol. 1/2, pp. 809–810 (nos. 3061–3063).

[66] *Ibid.*, vol. 1/2, pp. 808–809 (no. 3060) points out that the old jurists were not interested public domain, but rather in royal domain. (See also *ibid.*, vol. 1/2, pp. 808–823 (nos. 3059–3079) for much useful information.) Pothier, *T.D.P.*, pp. 109–110 (no. 21) mentions the sea and its shore *as res communes*; but that is all he says on the topic.

[67] The citation of Domat opposite the article would serve.

[68] Tate, *op. cit. supra* note 56, p. 37, n. 36.

[69] See following section.

NATURAL LAW INFLUENCE ON THE DIGEST

In many ways, codes would appear to be positive law *par excellence*, and this might well lead to the conclusion that they necessarily were not the product of natural-law thinking. This would be wrong.

An important study here is that of André-Jean Arnaud.[70] He points to an important difference between the Code Napoléon of 1804 and its 1800 *Projet*—the former has not adopted the Preliminary Book of the latter.[71] As noted earlier, this preliminary book was excluded from the final code at least partly because of its didactic nature.[72] Arnaud points out that this opposition given to definition and regulation points to an opposition "qui existe entre science juridique et legislation".[73] He then states that this opposition had various consequences: first, the disappearance of the Preliminary Book of the *Proj. An VIII* with its replacement by a title of six articles; and second, the use of the future tense in the drafting of the code. He comments: "Mais le sens de ces transformations est plus important que le résultat."[74] He states that, under the cover of a change of style and of language, there has taken place a move from a system of *jusnaturalistique moderne* to a system "de conception positiviste". He argues that it should be recognized that the Code Napoléon "dans sa rédaction définitive, s'écarte beaucoup du jusnaturalisme qui inspirait le *Projet de l'An VIII*".[75] The 1804 Code rigorously separated law and morality, and natural law and positive law, thus adopting a form of legal positivism. Arnaud argues that this leads to the suppression of *doctrine* and to the growth of *jurisprudence*, both of these effects being essentially those of legal positivism: he here specially considers the provisions on certainty of rule, the necessity of its promulgation, the subjection of the judge to the *loi*, and the prohibition of interpretation of the law.[76] Arnaud has highlighted a most important matter: the exclusion of the Preliminary Book points to a move from natural-law theories towards positive-law theories. It would seem, for example, that in Austria, in that country's long history of attempts at codification, there was a similar shift from eighteenth-century natural law to a notion of strict law (*strenges Recht*) founded on the Kantian critique of natural law—allowing a disjunction of legal order and moral order—in the 1811 *Allgemeines Bürgerliches Gesetzbuch*.[77]

---

[70] A.-J. Arnaud, *Essai d'analyse structurale du Code civil français*, Paris, Librarie Générale du Droit et Jurisprudence, 1973.
[71] *Ibid.* p. 44.
[72] See *supra*, chap. 3, text at notes 202–204.
[73] Arnaud, *op. cit. supra* note 70, p. 44.
[74] *Ibid.*
[75] *Ibid.*
[76] *Ibid.*
[77] H.E. Strakosch, *State Absolutism and the Rule of Law: The Struggle for Codification of Civil Law in Austria, 1753–1811*, Sydney, Sydney University Press, 1967, pp. 195–215, esp. at pp. 206–215.

How and why this shift from natural law to positive law took place need not concern us; that it took place in the final redaction of the Code Napoléon is what matters here. The redactors of the 1808 Digest possessed copies of both the completed Code Napoléon and its 1800 *Projet*, and they followed either and both in drawing up their code. They included a Preliminary Book based on the 1800 *Projet*, and rejected the C.N.'s brief Preliminary Title; and it is here crucial to discover why.

As indicated in chapter three, this title had a didactic nature, and Franklin has suggested that this would help explain its reception in Louisiana: a territory with no law schools and inadequate legal training.[78] There is probably an element of truth in this. Second, the redactors have an obvious tendency to favour the style and arrangement of the *Projet de l'An VIII* over that of the C.N. Thus, they have adopted the *Projet's* manner of numbering articles by Book, title and article, and rejected the more convenient continuous system of numbering of articles used in the C.N. In the research here, we have come across a number of occasions where Moreau Lislet and Brown favoured the approach of the *Projet*.

First, in the definitions of marriage in chapter one of title IV of Book One (D.O. 1–3 (p. 25)), they copied the arrangement of the *Projet* (there being no C.N. equivalents), although the Act of 1807 provided the legal material.[79] Second, the articles on *louage des services* were closer to those of the *Projet* than those of the C.N.[80] Third, the section on rescission of contract on the grounds of lesion is closer to the *Projet* than the C.N. in both arrangement and actual provisions.[81] Hence it is probably fair to say that there is a recognizable pattern of favouring the *Projet*. (Examples could be multiplied.)

The third possible reason for the adoption of the *Projet*'s preliminary book must be the one suggested by Arnaud: this book embodied notions of natural law as against the (potential) positivism of the C.N.'s short preliminary title. Franklin has rightly stressed the importance of D.O. 21 (p. 7).[82] This article states:

> Dans les matières civiles, le Juge, à défaut de loi précise, est obligé de procéder conformément à l'equité; pour décider suivant l'équité, il faut recourir à la loi naturelle at à la raison, ou aux usages recus, dans le silence de la loi primitive [positive].[83]

Proj. An VIII, Prel. Bk.5.11 provides:

---

[78] Franklin, *op. cit. supra*, note 63, p. 841.
[79] See *supra*, chap. 4.
[80] See *supra*, chap. 5.
[81] See *supra*, text at notes 32–37.
[82] Franklin, "Existential Force", pp. 94 and 99–100; Franklin, *op. cit. supra* note 53, p. 842; M. Franklin. "Equity in Louisiana: The Role of Article 21", 9 *Tul. L. Rev.* (1935), pp. 485–516. See also F.F. Stone, "The So-Called Unprovided-For Case," 53 *Tul. L. Rev.* (1978), pp. 93–104.
[83] "Primitive" is an obvious mistake for "positive". The English text uses "positive".

> Dans les matières civiles, le juge, à défaut de loi précise, est un ministre d'équité. L'équité est le retour à la loi naturelle, ou aux usages reçus, dans le silence de la loi positive.

The D.O.article is based on that of the *Projet.* Indeed the D.O. article strengthens the *Projet's* appeal to natural law by the reference to "reason", the *mot sacré* of the eighteenth-century enlightenment. The D.L.V. here refers to Domat, another natural lawyer, who, as cited, also provides for appeal to universal natural law in the absence of express written law.[84] Undoubtedly, Domat here influenced the *Projet.*

Drawing on Arnaud's analysis of the shift between the *Projet de l'an VIII* and the *Code Civil de l'an XII*, it is fair to conclude that the copying of this title, and of article 21 (p. 7) in particular, evidence the predisposition of the 1808 redactors towards "jusnaturalisme moderne", the secular natural law of the eighteenth century. The Code Napoléon ignored the question of *lacunae*, and merely included a provision (article 4) penalizing the judge who refused to judge by claiming that the law was silent, obscure or insufficient. One can understand why the school of exegesis developed in France. The Code Napoléon, of course, had not completely moved away from natural law: it had a hybrid character.[85] In copying, as noted, the style of *Projet* in giving definitions of marriage, the 1808 redactors again demonstrated their predilection for natural law, where first principles, from which conclusions followed *more geometrico*, were important.[86] Such definitions would be unnecessary in a more positivistic code.

Thus, one can conclude that, over all, the 1808 redactors were heavily influenced by current theories of natural law: they were not legal positivists. This, of course, refers us back to the previous section and to the arguments put forward in chapter three. Some scholars have expressed surprise that, when the law formally in force was Castilian in origin, the Digest should be so strongly based on the French codes.[87] Some have flatly refused to believe that it could be based on the French code of 1804 and its 1800 *Projet.*[88] These attitudes are based on the misconception that the redactors were legal positivists. They were natural lawyers, as one might expect given the period, and as the internal evidence of the Digest confirms. Further, the Louisiana system at the time of redaction was civilian, with the internationalism which that implies. The common base of all civilian systems in Roman law allowed easy transmission of rules, as the basic concepts were nearly always similar. Further, the recognition of Roman law as *ratio scripta* during the period of secular natural law also facilitated reception and transmission. During the nineteenth century, the 1804 French code was itself very influential: it is not too great an exaggeration to

---

[84] Domat, *Loix civiles*, p. 4 (prel. bk. tit. 1, sect.1, art. 23).
[85] Arnaud, *op. cit. supra* note 70, p. 45.
[86] See *supra*, text at note 79.
[87] E.G. Brown "Legal Systems in Conflict: Orleans Territory 1804–1812", 1 *American Journal of Legal History* (1957), pp. 35–75 at pp. 53–59.
[88] Consider Pascal, "Reply", *passim.*

state that it was often received as if it were *ratio scripta*[89]—and this despite the strictures of Savigny and the historical school of jurisprudence.[90] Given the orientation of the redactors towards natural law, given the international outlook of the civil law, given the prestige of the French code, it is surely not a matter of surprise that the redactors should have plundered the French code for material and used it as their model. Further, the acceptance of the doctrines of natural law by the redactors and their international outlook explains why the sources of the Digest are diverse: the redactors did not consider themselves bound by any notion of a "national" law.

THE DE LA VERGNE MANUSCRIPT

In this study, we have paid close attention to the citations of authorities found in the de la Vergne volume. Examination of these authorities permits assessment of the nature of the de la Vergne volume and of its references. From this can be developed some suggestions as to the purpose served by the compilation of the manuscript.

There already is a fairly extensive literature on the de la Vergne manuscript and debate over its importance and significance.[91] We will be able to assess the various arguments put forward as to the nature and purpose of the volume. To aid the following discussion, it is useful to describe the D.L.V. and the other copies of the Digest with similar annotations.

The de la Vergne volume is a copy of the 1808 Digest (of which there was only one edition) bound with interleaves. Opposite the English text, the interleaves contain general manuscript references to Roman, Spanish, and French legal authorities relating to the relevant topics covered by the Digest;

---

[89] The literature on this is voluminous. See, e.g. R. Pound, "The French Civil Code and the Spirit of Nineteenth Century Law", 35 *Boston University Law Review* (1955), pp. 77–95; J. Gaudemet, "Les transferts du droit", 27 *L'année sociologique* (1976), pp. 29–59 at pp. 51–56; A.N. Léger, "De l'influence du Code Napoléon à Haiti et des differences de législation civile entre la France et Haiti", in *Le droit civil français: livre-souvenir supra* note 63, pp. 755–815; C. Baez, "L'Influence du droit français au Paraguay", in *Le droit civil français: livre-souvenir supra* note 63, pp. 829–831; T.R. Tonasce, "Les liberalités en France et en Roumanie", in *Le droit civil français: livre-souvenir supra* note 63, pp. 911–940. See further J. Limpens, "Territorial Expansion of the Code", in B. Schwartz (ed.), *The Code Napoleon and the Common Law World*, New York, New York University Press, 1956, pp. 92–109.

[90] On the German historical school, see now P. Stein, *Legal Evolution: The Story of an Idea*, Cambridge, Cambridge University Press, 1980, pp. 51–68, esp. pp. 56–65 on Savigny.

[91] See e.g. M. Franklin, "An Important Document in the History of American Roman and Civil Law: the de la Vergne Manuscript", 33 *Tul. L. Rev.* (1958), pp. 35–42; J. Dainow, "Moreau Lislet's Notes on Sources of Louisiana Civil Code of 1800", 19 *La. L. Rev.* (1958), pp. 43–51; R.A. Pascal, "A Recent Discovery: A Copy of the "Digest of the Civil Laws" of 1808 with Marginal Source References in Moreau Lislet's Hand", 26 *La. L. Rev.* (1965), pp. 25–27; "Book Note", 30 *La. L. Rev.* (1969–1970) pp. 746–747; R.A. Pascal, "Book Note" 32 *Louisiana Law Review* (1972), pp. 495–496; and L.A. Derby and T.J. McDonald, "A Recent Discovery: Another Copy of Moreau Lislet's Annotations to the Civil Code of 1808", 47 *Tul. L. Rev.* (1973), pp. 1210–1213.

opposite the French text are manuscript references to French, Spanish and Roman law specifically linked to particular articles of the Digest; the latter are the references we studied closely, though the former were also referred to where relevant. The volume is entitled thus:

> Loix de l'Etat de la Louisiane, avec des notes qui réfèrent aux Loix civiles et Espagnoles qui y ont rapport. 1814.

On the leaves following the title is written a long passage entitled "Avant-Propos". The first three paragraphs of the *Avant-Propos* are worth quoting:

> Le but de cet ouvrage est de faire connaitre par des nottes [*sic*] écrites sur des pages en blanc attachees au Digeste des Loix de cet Etat, quels sont les textes des loix civiles et Espagnoles, qui y ont quelque rapport.
>
> À cet effet, on trouvera à coté du texte anglais, une liste générale de tous les titres des loix Romaines et Espagnoles, qui sont relatifs aux matières traitées dans chaque chapitre du Digeste, et à coté du texte français et article par article, la citation des principales loix des divers codes, d'où sont tirées les dispositions de notre statut local.
>
> On ne s'est pas borné en citant les loix qui ont quelque rapport avec les divers articles du Digeste, de marquer seulement celles qui contiennent des dispostions semblables; mais on y a ajouté celles qui, sur la même matière offrent des differences dans ce qu'elles prescrirent ou qui contiennent des exceptions au principe général qui y est énoncé.[92]

The paragraphs following these describe the sources of the "loix Espagnoles" and their order of precedence; they do so accurately.[93] The final paragraph of the *Avant-Propos* states that: "A l'égard des dispositions du droit Romain elles ne peuvent être citées comme Loix en Espagne, mais seulement comme raison écrite."

The Avant-Propos is followed by an "Explication des abbreviations", divided into two sections: one headed "Loix", the other "Auteurs". Among the *auteurs* Pothier is mentioned, though Domat is not. Domat is referred to in the fourth paragraph of the *Avant-Propos*, where it is stated he is used for easy reference to the Roman laws. At the very end of the Digest, the de la Vergne manuscript has a comprehensive alphabetical index.

The outer leather binding of the volume is imprinted "L. Moreau Lislet"; and the tradition of the de la Vergne family ascribes the work to him, though the manuscript is not written in his hand.[94]

Several similar works have been found in Louisiana. The law school of Loyola University possesses two volumes "substantially similar to the de la

---

[92] I have used the 1971 photographic reprint by Claitor: accents, spelling, and use of capital letters as in the original. I shall cite the *Avant-Propos* by paragraph.

[93] Cf. these parapgraphs with *Rec. Ind.* 2.1.2 and see *supra*, chap. 3, text at notes 66–80, where *Rec. Ind.* 2.1.2 is quoted at note 67.

[94] Dainow, *op. cit. supra*, note 91 gives a good physical description.

Vergne",[95] one of which attributes the notes to Moreau Lislet in its manuscript title page:[96] neither is as complete as the D.L.V. itself.[97] Tulane University School of Law also possesses a volume similar to the D.L.V.[98] The Southern Methodist University School of Law possesses a copy of the Digest with marginal annotations: these annotations are apparently unlike those of the D.L.V., and their significance is unknown.[99] The Louisiana State University Library possesses a copy of the Digest, without annotated interleaves, but with marginal annotations.[100] This book bears the name of Moreau Lislet in manuscript on the title page, though it is not his signature.[101] All the marginal references in this volume apparently appear in the D.L.V., though the latter's references are much more numerous.[102] The Louisiana State University copy's marginal annotations contain corrections; they are also in a hand different from that of the D.L.V.[103] Apparently, the hand is that of Moreau Lislet himself.[104] Professor Pascal suggests this copy is earlier than the D.L.V.[105] Another manuscript copy of the annotations has been found in the Tulane University Law School Library.[106] This manuscript belonged to Henry Raphael Denis, a lawyer and contemporary of Moreau Lislet (the "Denis manuscript").[107] The annotations appear to be in Denis' hand.[108] The Denis manuscript can be dated to after 1820, as its pages bear a watermark with that date.[109] It contains an *Avant-Propos*, attributed to Moreau Lislet, identical to that in the D.L.V.[110] The Denis manuscript differs in some important respects from the D.L.V. First, it is not bound with a copy of the 1808 Digest.[111] Second, except for the first five chapters of the first title of the third book, only the annotations opposite the French text of the D.L.V. are found in it: for these five chapters the annotations opposite the English text of the D.L.V. are also found.[112] Third, the manuscript is inscribed thus:

---

[95] I quote Darby and McDonald, *op. cit. supra* note 91, p. 1211: I have not seen these other works.
[96] See preface to Claitor's 1971 reprint of the D.L.V., second page.
[97] *Ibid.*
[98] Darby and McDonald, *op. cit. supra* note 91, p. 1211.
[99] *Ibid.* p. 1211, n. 5.
[100] Pascal, "Recent Discovery", *op. cit. supra* note 91, pp. 25–26.
[101] *Ibid.* p. 25, and n. 3.
[102] *Ibid.* p. 26.
[103] *Ibid.* p. 26.
[104] Professor Pascal and Mr L. de la Vergne compared the L.S.U. manuscript and the D.L.V. with Moreau Lislet's holographic will. See Pascal, "Recent Discovery" *supra* note 91, p. 26.
[105] *Ibid.*, p. 26.
[106] Darby and McDonald, *op. cit. supra* note 91, p. 1211.
[107] *Ibid.*
[108] *Ibid.*
[109] *Ibid.*
[110] *Ibid.* p. 1212.
[111] *Ibid.* p. 1211.
[112] *Ibid.* p. 1213.

> Renvoy aux Principales loix des divers codes d'ou sont tirées les dispositions du digeste de la Loi civile qui est en force dans l'état de Ia Louisiane.[113]

Darby and McDonald surmise that this title is taken from the second paragraph of the *Avant-Propos* (see above).[114] The second paragraph refers to "les dispositions de notre statut local", while the Denis manuscript has rendered this as "digeste de la Loi Civile etc." The interpretation of "notre statut local" has been disputed;[115] Darby and McDonald argue that the title of the Denis manuscript shows which interpretation is correct.

If we turn to consideration of the various views put forward on the D.L.V., we find there are two separate problems. First, there is the nature of the D.L.V. references: are they to "sources" of the articles? Second, what was the *purpose* of compiling the manuscript notes? Professor Pascal claims that the references are to the "sources" of the 1808 Digest, and it is appropriate to consider his views first. The discussion of his views will enable us to come to a conclusion as to the nature of the D.L.V.

Pascal's general thesis on the sources of the Digest has already been discussed.[116] He uses the D.L.V. to support his thesis by arguing: first, that the D.L.V. was compiled by Moreau Lislet; second, that most of the references are to "Spanish" and Roman legal texts; third, that the *Avant-Propos* indicates that the references are to the "sources" of the Digest; and fourth, that there are *no* references to the C.N. or its *Projet*. He concludes that the D.L.V. helps prove his thesis that the Digest of 1808 is the expression of "Spanish-Roman" law in French form. Though the last writing in which he expressed this view was in 1972, it is clear his views are unchanged.[117]

Professor Pascal's first point—that Moreau Lislet compiled the D.L.V. references—should probably be accepted. All versions of the manuscript notes have some association with Moreau Lislet. In the absence of any evidence to suggest who might have been the compiler other than Moreau Lislet, it should be accepted that it was he.

Second, Pascal stresses that most of the references are to Spanish and Roman texts. This ignores Pothier who is cited almost continuously. Of course, Pascal is correct, the citation of Castilian authority is very great; but, as I hope it will now be clear, the Castilian law *as a whole* cited in the D.L.V. as regards *puissance du mari* and *puissance paternelle* differs radically from the law on these matters *as a whole* in the Digest. There is occasional correspondence, but this appears to be generally fortuitous; and only occurs in *isolated articles*. Thus, the D.L.V. quite definitely, as regards the Castilian citations on these matters, does not reveal the *substantive* source of the Digest law. The citations

---

[113] *Ibid.* p. 1212.
[114] *Ibid.*
[115] See *infra*, text at notes 126–136.
[116] See *supra*, text at notes 43–47.
[117] Pascal, "Book Note" *supra* note 91. See T. Hoff, "Error in the Formation of Contracts in Louisiana: A Comparative Analysis", 53 *Tul. L. Rev.* (1979), pp. 329–379 at pp. 331–333, n. 12.

to Pothier are a different matter: he *does* appear to have been influential as regards, for example, aspects of *louage*. The aspects of law examined in chapters four and five are sufficient to show that the D.L.V. references to Castilian law are generally to *analogous* provisions, not to sources. *Locatio operarum* in the Castilian law is similar to that in the C.N. and D.O. This is due to their common Roman inheritance. The bipartite division, and general treatment, of *louage* in the D.O. are, however, derived from the C.N. The important texts on contract we have examined suggest the same. The references to Castilian law in the D.L.V. are *not* to the substantive sources of the Digest. Some of the D.L.V.'s citations are of substantive sources—consider some of the references to Pothier and to Louisiana Acts—but taken as a whole, the D.L.V. does *not* cite the substantive sources of the Digest, as there would have to he references to the C.N. and its *Projet*.

The above also throws light on Professor Pascal's fourth point. There are no references to the C.N. or its *Projet*, not because they were not sources of substantive law in the Digest, but because, whatever else the D.L.V. may be, its references most certainly are generally not to the substantive and conceptual sources of the Digest, though it does refer to some such. As regards matters not touched on in this thesis, they could originate in Castilian law, although this seems improbable; but on the basis of the D.L.V. it cannot be assumed that they do so originate, even should there be correspondence in *some* articles or ideas.

Professor Pascal's third point relates to the *Avant-Propos*. Now the D.L.V. as a work of *sources* must stand and fall on whether the citations are to sources, and it is clear that, in general, the citations are *not* to sources, with some exceptions, such as those to the 1807 Act, ch. 17 and the 1806 Act, ch.11. In other words, the argument of Pascal does not hold up. The Castilian references are *not* to sources, with the exception of certain isolated articles. That some references do reveal sources is irrelevant. The *Avant-Propos*, however, states that the purpose of the manuscript is to make known by notes written on the blank pages attached to the Digest of the laws the texts of civil and Spanish laws that have *quelque rapport* with them.[118] The references opposite the English text are stated to be to the Roman and Spanish laws "qui sont relatifs aux matières" treated of in each chapter of the Digest. The references opposite the French text, article by article, are said to be to the principal laws "des divers codes d'ou sont tirées les dispositions de notre statut local".[119] The third paragraph states that not only these laws that provide similarly to the 1808 Digest have been cited, but also those which have contrary provisions or which contain exceptions to the general principle.[120]

There is no explicit statement that the references are to "sources".[121] The references are stated in the first paragraph to be to laws that have *some relation* to the Digest (and this indeed is true, as appears from chapters four and five

---

[118] First paragraph, quoted *supra*, text at note 92.
[119] Second paragraph, quoted *supra*, text at note 92.
[120] Third paragraph, quoted *supra*, text at note 92.
[121] Sweeny, "Tournament", pp. 596–597, points this out.

above). The general references opposite the English text are again stated to be to laws *relating* to the Digest, and this is indeed correct. The third paragraph cannot be faulted in describing the de la Vergne volume: many citations are to similar laws, to contrary laws, and to works expanding on the topic mentioned in the concise Digest article.

We will leave aside for the moment Professor Pascal's interpretation of the *Avant-Propos*'s statement about the references opposite the French text, and examine his interpretation of the *Avant-Propos*'s statement about the references opposite the English text. He states:

> Those opposite the English text, on the other hand, as the *avant-propos* states clearly, give 'a general list of the Roman and Spanish laws which relate to the matters treated in each chapter of the Digest,' whether 'similar' or 'present[ing] differences or . . . containing exceptions to the general principle.'[122]

Professor Pascal has also said elsewhere that the references opposite the English text are to "corresponding civil laws not used as sources".[123] In the passage I have quoted, he himself quotes passages from an English translation of the *Avant-Propos*; he purports to show that the references opposite the English text are not to "sources" but only to "similar", "different" or "exceptional" rules. Professor Pascal's selection of quotations is, however, very misleading. The description of the references opposite the English text is taken from the second paragraph of the *Avant-Propos* in describing them as these "which relate to the matters treated in each chapter of the Digest". "Similar", "semblable", "differences" and "exceptions" come from the third paragraph of the *Avant-Propos*.[124] There is no reason to apply these comments of the third paragraph only to the references opposite the English text. It is possible that Professor Pascal connects "ont quelque rapport" in the third paragraph with "sont relatifs" in the second (the references opposite the French text being described as to principal laws of the various codes from which *sont tirées* etc.). If this were the reason, it would have been more appropriate to connect the third paragraph with the first: and the first paragraph surely governs all of the second. Further, the third paragraph states "les loix qui ont quelque rapport *avec les divers articles du Digeste*" (emphasis mine), while, in the second paragraph, the provisions cited opposite the English text are said to be "relatifs aux matières traités *dans chaque chapitre du Digeste*" (emphasis mine). Were similarity of expression (i.e. "relate", "some relation") Professor Pascal's reason for construing the third paragraph with only part of the second in this fashion, an argument could be put forward that the third paragraph's statements referred only to that part of the second paragraph dealing with the citations opposite the French text, as both the third paragraph and this part of the second refer to *articles* of the Digest, while the references opposite the English text are stated to refer to *chaque chapitre* of

---

[122] Pascal, "Reply", p. 607.
[123] Pascal, "Book Note", *supra* note 90, p. 496.
[124] *Avant Propos*, quoted *supra*, text at note 92.

the Digest. This last argument is not put forward to indicate the *intended* meaning of the third paragraph of the *Avant-Propos*; it is merely made to indicate that Professor Pascal's interpretation obscures the obvious meaning of this aspect of the *Avant-Propos*.[125]

In the general description in the first paragraph, "ont quelque rapport" is used to describe the significance of *all* the citations for the Digest, both those opposite the English and those opposite the French texts. This general statement must govern the interpretation of the second and third paragraphs that follow, and the third paragraph must refer to *both* sets of citations. This is, in fact, the natural and obvious meaning of the third paragraph. The third paragraph then contains an accurate description of the references in the de la Vergne manuscript: some are to provisions similar to those of the Digest; some are to provisions containing differences from those of the Digest; and some are to provisions containing exceptions to those of the Digest. Pascal's construction of this third paragraph to refer only to the citations opposite the English text of the Digest is quite mistaken.

Pascal argues that the second paragraph of the *Avant-Propos* means that the references opposite the French text are to the sources of the articles. The second paragraph itself states that the citations opposite the French text are to the principal laws of the various codes from which are drawn the dispositions of "notre statut local". The meaning of "notre statut local" has been disputed. In their translations, both Dainow and Franklin suggest "our local statute": that is, it refers to the 1808 Digest.[126] If Darby and McDonald are correct, then the title of the "Denis manuscript" supports this interpretation. [127] Sweeney has argued that, on the contrary, the phrase should be taken as meaning "or local status" or "state of affairs" or something akin to this.[128] In a later work, Franklin argues against this interpretation, and his arguments have considerable force.[129] Nevertheless, why did Moreau write "notre statut local" and not "Digeste", if "Digeste" was intended?

The problems of translation and signification are manifold, and there is probably little point in resolving this dispute. It is fair to say, however, that if Sweeney were correct, and should the *Avant-Propos* be referring to the *previous* state of affairs, the section of the second paragraph at dispute ought to have read "d'où *étaient* tirées les dispositions etc." Instead, the present tense is used: "are drawn" not "were drawn". Hence, if we, for the moment, accept Sweeney's

---

[125] The above discussion of the *Avant-Propos* might seem confusing; see *supra*, quotation at note 92.

[126] Dainow, *op. cit. supra* note 91, p. 45; Franklin, *op. cit. supra* note 91, p. 39.

[127] Darby and McDonald, *op. cit. supra* note 91, p. 1212. Darcy and McDonald argue that the title of the "Denis manuscript" is taken from the last sentence of the second paragraph of the *Avant-Propos*, with the replacement of "notre statut local" by "Digeste de la loi..." For this to be relevant: 1. their statement that the title is taken from that sentence has to be accepted; 2. that Denis meant the title to have the *same* meaning as that sentence; and 3. that Denis correctly understood the meaning of the phrase.

[128] Sweeney, "Tournament", pp. 597–600.

[129] Franklin, "Existential Force", pp. 80–93. Franklin's view will be discussed further *infra*.

suggestion, then the passage *means* something like "from where are drawn the provisions of our local status" *as presently existing.*[130] That present "state of affairs" in 1814 includes the 1808 Digest: in other words, Sweeney's suggestion comes to mean something similar to the meaning attributed to the phrase by his opponents. Sweeney explains and translates the sentence under consideration thus:

> . . . on the blank pages across from the French text, and "article by article" [are] those provisions of civil and Spanish law which *formerly* applied in the Territory, and governed "the local state of affairs". . . .[131]

"Formerly", as italicized, has absolutely no equivalent word or phrase in the *Avant-Propos*, for, as I have pointed out, the sentence is phrased in the present. Hence the two meanings are *not* competing: the variance of views only originates in Sweeney's making the sentence relate to the past, which it does not.[132]

There is further evidence to suggest that "notre statut local" should probably be taken as referring to the Digest. In some early Louisiana cases, the Digest was referred to as a statute.[133] The usage was known and acceptable. If it should be wondered why "our local statute" was used here in the *Avant-Propos* rather than "Digest", it may be suggested that the writer did so for the sake of variety of expression: in the same paragraph, "Digest" and "codes" have already been mentioned.

If the above arguments are correct, then we may go on to consider the meaning attributed to this passage by Pascal. He argues that the passage means that opposite the French text are the "sources" of the articles.[134] From the research detailed in chapters four and five we know that, in some instances, this is true, in some it is not true, and that in general, the references to Castilian law are not to "sources"; rather, they are references to equivalent provisions of the Castilian law. Further, as we saw in chapter four, on occasion, an article in the Digest matched a provision of the *Leyes de Toro*, and thus, the D.L.V. reference might seem to be to a source: however, the provisions of the *Leyes de Toro* on marital authority as a whole were *radically* different from the equivalent provisions in the Digest. Thus the references are occasionally to sources (one thinks of the 1807 Act on celebration of marriages), sometimes are to similar provisions and sometimes to contradictory provisions. How does this fit in with the passage under consideration? The passage states that the references are to the laws of the various codes from which are drawn "notre statut local". Now

---

[130] The italicized phrase has no equivalent in the *Avant-Propos*; but its meaning is implicit.

[131] Sweeney, "Tournament", p. 601. I have inserted "are" to make the passage readable when extracted from context: it does not change the meaning.

[132] Franklin continues too, that both phrases mean the same: see *Existential Force*, pp. 80–93.

[133] See e.g. *Dewes* v. *Morgan* 1 Mart. (O.S.) 1 at 2 (1809); *Sennet* v. *Sennet's Legatees* 3 Mart. (O.S.) 1 at 2 (1809); *Sennet* v. *Sennet's Legatees* 3 Mart. (O.S.) 411 at 416 (1814).

[134] See Pascal, "Reply", pp. 606–607. Note that in his quotation from the *Avant-Propos* he includes "the substance of" while there is no equivalent actually in the *Avant-Propos*: see Batiza, "Rejoinder", pp. 648–649.

this is indeed true, they are. The Digest does contain provisions from the Castilian and civil laws. The passage does not say that the *articles* are drawn from the laws cited opposite them (though sometimes they are), merely that the citations opposite the articles are to the laws of legal systems from which the dispositions of the Digest or "notre statut local" are drawn. (This, of course, leaves unanswered the question of *why* the Code Napoléon and its *projet* are *not* cited, as they also ought to be included as part of the "divers codes". An answer to this is obvious, as will be shown below.) Further, since Professor Pascal's construction of the third paragraph of the *Avant-Propos* must be rejected, the third paragraph applies here and the citations opposite the French articles are allowed to be to exceptional and contradictory provisions. The problem thus resolves itself, and Professor Pascal's construction of the *Avant-Propos* must be dismissed. Hence, the third part of Pascal's thesis can be discounted.

To recap: Professor Pascal's argument on the D.L.V. reduces to four parts. The first—that Moreau Lislet compiled it—is probably correct. The second—that the majority of references are to "Spanish" and Roman sources—is correct but irrelevant. The third—that the *Avant-Propos* states that the references are to the "sources" of the Digest—has been shown to be wrong. The fourth—that there being no references to the French Code or its *projet* shows that they are not sources—can be dismissed, since the D.L.V. apparently is not, in essence, a compilation of references to sources. Thus, his thesis that the D.L.V. proves that the Digest is in essence of Castilian origin does not hold up. The matter of the lack of references to the C.N. or its *projet* will be discussed below.

Professor Pascal is the only scholar who has argued that the citations found in the D.L.V. are in fact to the "sources" of the Digest's articles; though, as will be seen, others have adopted to some extent, aspects of his interpretation of the meaning of the *Avant-Propos*: an interpretation argued against here. For Pascal, the purpose or function of the de la Vergne notes is to make known the "sources" of the Digest. Others, rejecting the contention that the references are to "sources" have to suggest alternative purposes or functions for the compilation of these manuscript citations.

It will be recalled that Dean Sweeney interpreted "notre statut local" as "our local status" or "state of affairs", as existing before the redaction of the Digest.[135] Reasons for rejecting this interpretation have been given.[136] Professor Batiza at one point appears also to have accepted this interpretation;[137] though there is reason to believe that Batiza would no longer agree with Sweeney here.[138] Sweeney has put forward an interesting suggestion as to the purpose of the compilation of the references in the de la Vergne manuscript. He suggests

---

[135] Sweeney, "Tournament", pp. 597–601; *supra*, text at notes 128–132.

[136] See further *supra*, text at notes 128–132.

[137] Batiza, "Rejoinder", p. 648; cf. Batiza "Sources", p. 9, n. 34.

[138] Batiza, "Textual Evidence", p. 81, n. 22, states of the references in the D.L.V. "that their main purpose was to divert attention from the concealed *actual* sources of the 1808 Code—principally, the French *Projet* and Code, and to a lesser degree, Blackstone." This is similar to views of Baade and Franklin: see *infra*.

that the de la Vergne volume was intended to provide a cross-index to the Castilian law, so that lawyers could readily ascertain which provisions of the Castilian law had been superseded.[139] This thesis is attractive; but there are three problems. First, Professor Sweeney's interpretation of "notre statut local" has been shown to be wrong: the references are not the laws *previously* in force. Second, the *style* of the references opposite the French text would militate against the possibility of the use of the D.L.V. as suggested. The lawyer who looked up an isolated provision of Castilian law as cited in connection with a Digest article would not necessarily gain a true impression of that law as a whole. The citation of the *Leyes de Toro* on marital authority shows this clearly: to refer to an isolated *ley* would not give a true idea of the scope and nature of the provisions as a whole. Third, Dean Sweeney's suggestion does not take into account that the period of compilation of the D.L.V. was the period of revival of the Castilian law. Sweeney's hypothesis as to the intended function of the D.L.V. must be rejected.

Professor Franklin puts forward an explanation of the *function* of the D.L.V.: he accepts that as a matter of fact the references are not to "sources".[140] It will be recalled that in 1806 the territorial legislature passed an act, vetoed by Claiborne, to provide for authoritative sources of law.[141] Franklin points out that the de la Vergne manuscript cites the same Castilian works as those vetoed in 1806. He argues that there was a struggle not only between the civil law and the common law, but also between the "mediaeval Spanish Romanist feudal law" and the bourgeois French law. The 1806 Act was intended to secure the victory of the "feudal" forces, while the 1808 Digest won on behalf of the bourgeois French forces, supported by Jefferson. The de la Vergne volume was intended to be a way of transcending the 1808 bourgeois Digest through the importation of the "Spanish feudal" law by means of the doctrine of natural law.[142] That is, the de la Vergne manuscript posits a system of dual contradictory laws one negating each other, unified through the phrase "some relation". Moreau Lislet masked the feudal tendencies of the de la Vergne manuscript through the use of the term "some relation" and by setting up the Spanish feudal law as natural law.

Professor Franklin's discussion is perhaps rather more complex than the above brief exegesis can convey; but the nub of his argument about the purpose of the de la Vergne manuscript is expressed. It must, however, be dismissed. It relies on there being a structural rivalry, expressed in the 1806 Act, between the bourgeois French law and the feudal Spanish law, with the Spanish law supporting the sytem of slavery and the bourgeois French law rejecting it. This

---

[139] Sweeney, "Tournament", p. 601.

[140] See generally Franklin, "Existential Force", *passim*; Franklin, *op. cit. supra* note 91.

[141] See *supra*, chap. 3 *supra*, text at note 147; Franklin, "Existential Force", pp. 69–75.

[142] Franklin, "Existential Force", pp. 73–78; Franklin, *ibid.*, p. 78, states: "the aim of [the de la Vergne manuscript] is to overcome by legal method the bourgeois Digest of 1808 by means of the system of legal materials set out in the manuscript. Thus the defeat of the *projet* of 1806 would be negated."

is unconvincing, as pointed out in chapter two.[143] There is no evidence, in the period leading up to the promulgation of the Digest, of disunity in the civil law camp. There *was* general confusion in Louisiana over the laws in force: hence the passing of the 1806 Act, vetoed not because it was "mediaeval feudalist Spanish", but because it hindered the reception of the common law hoped for by the U.S. administration.[144]

It may be said further that Franklin's use of the term "feudal" is unsatisfactory. To some extent, he equates feudalism with slavery: this is surely incorrect. There is nothing inherently "feudal" about slavery. The feudal mode of production, in the Marxist—or perhaps Hegelian—terminology on which he appears to rely, is not a slave-based mode of production. Slavery *may* exist within feudalism, but this is irrelevant. Similarly, slavery may easily exist in a bourgeois mode of production, if bolstered by a sufficient ideology: and it did so in Louisiana.[145] Further, although some of the Castilian materials (notably, the *Fuero real* and the *Partidas*) were promulgated in a feudal society, once abstracted from that society, they no longer "consecrate" feudal relationships. That is, Louisianian society was not "feudal"; the "feudal" provisions of the *Partidas* could not be applied. Again, not all the Castilian authorities supposed or encapsulated a feudal system of social relations; that they originated in a feudal society is therefore not of importance. The de la Vergne manuscript referred to Domat, Pothier, and territorial Acts of Louisiana. Professor Franklin's view of the D.L.V. does not take adequate account of this. He does allude to Pothier and Domat, pointing out that they influenced the redaction of the French code; but he only comments that they were jurists from before the French Revolution: he thus implies that they too were "feudal".[146] It may also be pointed out that the de la Vergne references are not to "feudal" aspects of the Castilian law. The references to the Castilian law are not to aspects of that law that are in any essential way more feudal than the Digest: they are merely different. It is true that aspects of the Castilian law on contract were based on the "non-bourgeois" concept of "just price", but this does not affect the argument. Because the de la Vergne references have to follow the arrangement and articles of the 1808 Digest, there can only be references to topics covered in the Digest, which thus structures the references to Castilian law.

Professor Franklin claims Jefferson as a supporter of the bourgeois French code and an opponent of the "penchant hispanophile".[147] This is unconvincing. Jefferson favoured the introduction of the common law. He argued in the *Batture* case for the French law as the law in force before adoption of the

---

[143] See *supra*, chap. 2, text at notes 39–45.
[144] Dargo, *Jefferson's Lousiana*, pp. 128–137.
[145] See on these points, O. Patterson, "On Slavery and Slave Formations", 117 *New Left Review* (1979), pp. 31–67.
[146] Franklin, "Existential Force", p. 74. It should be recalled that the fourth paragraph of the *Avant-Propos* stated that Domat was used as a guide to the Roman law.
[147] Franklin, "Existential Force", pp. 80, 95–96.

Digest; but this was not because he supported preservation of the French law, but because in this particular instance it favoured his viewpoint.[148]

It is true that there was from 1812 onwards an attempt to reassert the Castilian law in the courts. This has been discussed in chapter three and will be returned to below. Here it is sufficient to say that this attempted re-assertion need not be interpreted as designed to supplant the Digest and to restore the "feudal Spanish" law because of opposition to the "bourgeois" Digest on the grounds of slavery. It may be more satisfactorily explained in a different manner as will be shown. Further, Moreau Lislet compiled the references in the de Ia Vergne manuscript: he can hardly be associated with an attempt to impose the "feudal Spanish" law as a system of natural law superseding the Digest, especially when his part in the redaction of the 1825 code is considered. (The 1825 Code, it will be recalled, attempted to stop the use of Castilian authorities.)[149]

The final point to be made is that for the de la Vergne manuscript to consecrate an activist legal system introducing "feudal" law to supersede the Digest, the D.L.V. would have needed widespread circulation to be effective. There is no evidence of this. Several copies of its references are known: but this is insufficient evidence. This is a problem with which Professor Franklin does not deal. It could be suggested that the D.L.V. and the 1806 Act are merely outward signifiers of an inward structural rivalry, and thus merely evidence the struggle between "bourgeois" and "feudal" forces. There is, however, no evidence of such an inner structural rivalry apart from the de la Vergne manuscript and the 1806 Act as interpreted by Professor Franklin. All the other evidence suggests that Louisiana was a society safely esconced within bourgeois ideology and social relations. There was no structural rivalry. It may be a truism that any society has contradictory elements; but if there were such in Louisiana, they were hardly of any importance or of relevance here.

Professor Franklin's argument that the function of the D.L.V. was to replace the "bourgeois" Digest with a system of "feudal" Spanish law imported as natural law must be dismissed. There is no evidence to support it.

Professor Baade has suggested that the borrowing of provisions from the French code and *projet* for the 1808 Digest could not publicly be acknowledged: he accordingly suggests that the de la Vergne manuscript was intended to provide through its source notes a "positive law alibi" for the 1808 Digest. He claims that Moreau Lislet prepared the de la Vergne volume for publication in 1814.[150] Professor Batiza has recently seemingly adopted the same or a similar view, when he states that the notes in the de la Vergne volume were intended "to divert attention from the concealed *actual* sources of the 1808 Code—

---

[148] Dargo, *Jefferson's Louisiana*, pp. 74–101, esp. at pp. 86–87; E.G. Brown, "Law and Government in the 'Louisiana Purchase': 1803–1804", 2 *Wayne Law Review* (1956), pp. 169–189 at pp. 182–185.

[149] See *supra*, chap. 3, text at notes 214–220.

[150] Baade, "Marriage Contracts", p. 84.

principally, the French *Projet* and Code, and to a lesser degree, Blackstone".[151] Professor Baade's view is unconvincing. The *Avant-Propos* is indeed equivocal; but it does not specifically state that the citations are to the sources of the articles. Indeed, that the references are generally not to the sources of the articles would have been immediately obvious to any lawyer who examined the passages cited. The de la Vergne volume would not have succeeded in persuading those who examined it that the Digest's provisions were taken from the Castilian law formally applicable in Louisiana before the enactment of the 1808 Digest. Further, Professor Baade's view relies on the citations having been prepared for publication: there is no direct evidence of this other than the appearance of the volume.

Having thus described the de la Vergne volume, and discussed the views put forward on it, and having found them all in some respects wanting, it is now appropriate to consider the nature and purpose of the manuscript. In the passages describing other people's views, a great many comments have been made both on the nature of the references and on the *Avant-Propos*. Several conclusions flow from these, and we will deal with them next.

The *Avant-Propos* is indeed equivocal in its statements; Moreau Lislet has not made his intention in writing it—whatever that may have been—particularly clear. In the critique of Pascal's views offered above, it was emphasized that the *Avant-Propos* can be successfully interpreted to fit the actual nature of the references as being to "sources", similar laws, contradictory laws and exceptions. In the absence of any evidence to the contrary, it is fair to construe the de la Vergne volume as a whole, using the references to illuminate the meaning of the *Avant-Propos*. To avoid doing so, we would need to accept the views either of Franklin or of Baade, and, as argued above, there is insufficient evidence to support the views of either. Thus, if we consider developments in Louisiana law in the early State period, that is, in the period in which the de la Vergne volume's manuscript notes were produced, we may see that knowledge of Castilian law was widespread:[152] any competent lawyer would have known that the D.L.V. did not refer to sources, whether or not it was intended to provide a "positive law alibi".

We are left with the following conclusions. The de la Vergne volume's citations did not provide a guide to the sources used in the redaction of the Digest. Sometimes, of course, the citations do refer to the sources of a provision. In the main, however, the references are to equivalent provisions of the Castilian and pre-codification French laws. These doctrinal (and other) works generally expound the law at greater length than is found in the Digest. There are no references to the *Code Napoléon* or its *Projet*, obvious sources, although the *Avant-Propos* states that the references are to the various codes (in a loose sense) from where the provisions of the Louisiana law are drawn. There are references to territorial Acts, parts of which have formed the "substantive source" of some (and

---

[151] Batiza, "Textual Evidence", p. 81, n. 22.

[152] As an examination of the first series of *Martin's Reports* shows.

indeed a not inconsiderable number) of articles. The volume was composed around 1814, and several copies were made of it. The volume would not serve as a guide to the pre-Digest law. This last point will be expanded on below. All these statements are drawn from the evidence of the volume itself, and leave the *purpose* or *function* (as distinct from the *nature*) of the volume as mysterious as ever. The *Avant-Propos* does state that the purpose (*le but*) of the work was to make known which texts of the Spanish and Roman laws relate (or whatever) to the Digest, but it does not say *why* this should be done. Having shown, if the above arguments are correct, that the views so far put forward must be disregarded, it is now necessary to discover (if possible) why the de la Vergne volume was composed.

But it is first important to point out why the de la Vergne references would not serve as a guide to the pre-Digest Castilian law of Louisiana, as Pascal suggests they would, and Sweeney comes near to suggesting they would (if, in this respect, I understand both correctly).[153] The reason for this is simple, and will have become obvious in the examination of substantive law in chapters four and five. The de la Vergne references follow the order of the 1808 Digest. Thus, any particular reference (as distinct from the general chapter-by-chapter references) must be opposite and linked to a Digest article. As will have been seen, as regards the treatment of *puissance maritale*, the sections of the Digest follow the treatment in the French codes. This treatment is based on the northern French concept of *puissance maritale*. Now, this concept is quite different from any Castilian concept of *puissance maritale* (to use the term loosely). This has the result that, because of the different approach and concept, the Digest deals with this aspect of husband and wife relationships in a way very different from the Castilian law, and, indeed, provides rules that have *no* equivalent in the Castilian law. Hence the references in the Digest, because they are based around the French legal approach, give references to the Castilian law that are misleading, if these references are all that is examined. There are some Digest articles for which there are *no* Castilian provisions, and there are some aspects of the Castilian law that *cannot* appear in the de la Vergne volume *because* there are no French and Digest equivalents. Further, the Castilian law cannot be understood merely through the "statutory" provisions of the *Nueva recopilación* or the *Siete Partidas*. The Castilian juristic writings are of great importance. The *Leyes de Toro* have very important provisions on the capacity of married women: the only Castilian writer cited as providing an explanation and exposition of the relevant *leyes* is Febrero, who was a notary rather than a learned jurist, and wrote his *Librería* as a guide for notaries. His book was much used in Mexico and Spanish North America, however, presumably because it was both convenient and practical in its orientation; but one looks in vain in the D.L.V. for the citation of important jurists such as Gomez or Llamas y Molina

---

[153] Pascal, "Reply", pp. 625–626; Sweeney, "Tournament", p. 601.

who authoritatively commented on the *Leyes*.[154] Thus, the de la Vergne references, unless supplemented, do not necessarily give an accurate picture of the Castilian law. The citations opposite the French text, since they are only to *specific* Castilian provisions, most certainly do not give an adequate account. This is, as pointed out, inevitable given certain important conceptual differences between the Castilian law and the law in the Digest. The areas of *séparation de biens* and *séparation de corps* show this clearly, as do the articles on *puissance maritale*.

If we now return to the *purpose* behind the compilation of the de la Vergne volume, a number of hypotheses may be put forward. The de la Vergne volume itself being enigmatic, it is necessary to examine its historical context. It will be recalled that, in the early State period, there was a series of Louisiana court decisions, conventionally regarded as starting with *Hayes v. Berwick*,[155] which re-asserted the "Spanish" law to some extent to the detriment of the 1808 Digest, and which culminated in the famous case of *Cottin v. Cottin*.[156] We have already looked briefly at these cases in another connection;[157] we will return to them again later.[158] These cases tell us something important about the matter on hand: namely, that over the period during which the de la Vergne manuscript was written, the Castilian law came into prominence once more. For matters outwith the areas covered in the Digest, there had always been a tendency to rely on the Castilian law (although one will find other laws cited); but during the period 1812–1817, and thereafter, the Digest came to be interpreted in the light of the Castilian law. The reasons why need not concern us at the moment.[159] During the same period, we also find the de la Vergne manuscript notes appearing, and their various copies. Though speculative, it is plausible to infer that there is some connection.

If this is correct, the reason for the compilation of the manuscript notes by Moreau Lislet becomes obvious: Castilian provisions equivalent to the Digest articles were of a practical interest to Louisiana lawyers. It became of practical importance to see if there was a way of winning a case for one's client through the citation of Castilian authority in point. By arguing that a particular provision should be interpreted in the light of a Castilian authority, a lawyer could win an otherwise potentially hopeless case: this appears to have been the position in *Cottin*. Why the Louisiana courts accepted this will be considered below.[160] The utility of a series of cross-references to the Castilian law would be obvious, and Moreau Lislet was an able enough lawyer both to realize this and to carry out

---

[154] In the citations on husband and wife opposite the English text, the only Castilian writer cited is Febrero. In the *Avant-Propos*, Gomez is cited, but only his *Variae resolutiones*, not his *Commentarius ad leges Tauri*.

[155] 2 Mart. (O.S.) 138 (1812).

[156] 5 Mart. (O.S.) 93 (1817).

[157] See *supra*, chap. 3, text at notes 208–227.

[158] See *infra*, "Reaction of the Courts to the 1808 Digest", text at notes 173–238.

[159] *Ibid.*

[160] *Ibid.*

the task. One may surmise that his colleagues would also appreciate the benefits of a series of cross references such as those in the D.L.V., and have copies made for themselves or indeed copy the references themselves, as Denis seems to have done. Further, a code such as the Digest requires interpretation, and included among the de la Vergne references are references to Domat and Pothier, both of whom discussed, at great length, legal provisions very similar to those in the Digest. The passages of Domat and Pothier would suggest arguments and help interpret the Digest. The references to the territorial Acts had a similar function. Not all the provisions of the 1807 Act on the celebration of marriages, nor all the provisions of the 1806 Act on apprentices and *engagés* were included in the Digest.[161] The de la Vergne volume's references conveniently directed the lawyer's attention to these important Acts. Hence, it seems plausible to suggest that the *function* of the manuscript notes in the de la Vergne volume was to aid the practising lawyer in interpreting the Digest, by providing authority for arguments in court. Moreau Lislet was a busy advocate, and such a compilation would be invaluable to him. (It will be recalled that it was he who, along with another, translated parts of the *Siete Partidas.*)[162]

This explains the *nature* of the references: to Castilian, French and Roman law, and to territorial Acts. If the purpose of the volume had been to reveal the "actual Castilian sources", some of the references would be irrelevant: other references would be irrelevant if the purpose were to pretend that the sources were Castilian and to provide a "positive law alibi"—likewise were the purpose to introduce the Castilian law as natural law. This explains the content of the *Avant-Propos*. It should be said that the *Avant-Propos* is, to some extent, still mysterious; but the explanation offered does not contradict what is said in the *Avant-Propos*, does not pervert its meaning, and is in line with what it states. This also explains why the *Avant-Propos* discusses at length the sources of the Castilian law: it allows the lawyer to sort out the precedence of the varying authorities. Further, we can now explain why there are no references to the Code Napoléon and its *projet*. Such references were unnecessary, as the articles of the French code and its *projet* would not help *interpret* the Digest. The *absence* of references to the C.N. and its *projet* is only mysterious if it is thought that the purpose of the notes was to reveal "sources"; once it is accepted that the purpose is to provide references to provisions to *interpret* the law, the mystery disappears. It must have been obvious to any Louisiana lawyer that the Digest was to a very considerable extent copied from the work of the French redactors: the two texts needed merely to be put side by side. There were copies of the French code in Louisiana; there can have been no mystery as to the origins of much of the Digest. If we consider that the *Avant-Propos* states that opposite the French text are references to the "divers codes d'où sont tirées les dispositions de notre statut local", the reason why references to the C.N. were not included must be that no one doubted that the French code was a source. This is of course

[161] Louisiana Acts, 1807, ch. 17, (6 Apr. 1807); Louisiana Acts, 1806, ch. 11 (21 May 1806).
[162] See *supra*, chap. 3, text at notes 221–222. The other translator was Henry Carleton.

an argument *e silentio*, but nonetheless valid for that. If it is accepted, as argued here, that the de la Vergne volume provides references to aid interpretation, references to the French redaction would be unnecessary, as all that would be found would be articles which were identical, or nearly so, to the Digest; this would hardly aid interpretation. Further, it must be recalled, that Jeremiah Brown wrote in 1806:

> It is a matter of public notoriety that our St. Domingo Lycurgus is avowedly copying his new code from that of Bonaparte, to the infinite delight of the whole party by whom he is employed.[163]

The St. Domingo Lycurgus is, of course, Moreau Lislet. This suggests many must have known of the provenance of the Digest's articles. Indeed, if he were correct in stating that it was a matter of public knowledge that Moreau Lislet was copying the French code for the Digest because Moreau Lislet made no secret of the fact that this was what he was doing, we can be certain that the Louisiana legal profession knew the origin of the bulk of the articles of the Digest. The suggestion that the D.L.V. was intended to conceal the origins of the articles of the Digest is therefore beyond probabilty.

A further point arises. It is clear that Blackstone has had some influence, as regards both parent and child and apprenticeship. Why is he not mentioned? That the de la Vergne volume is intended to aid interpretation must be the answer. It was pointed out in chapter five that the provisions on apprentices influenced by Blackstone were fairly universal; in other respects his wording was used but the real foundation of the law was the 1806 Act.[164] To have referred to Blackstone would not really have aided interpretation of the law: to refer to the 1806 Act would, and hence it is referred to. As regards the provisions on parent and child, Blackstone's texts were grafted onto a thoroughly French conception of paternal power. To have referred to Blackstone would not have aided interpretation or understanding of that power. Further, even were Blackstone regarded as a "source", the de la Vergne volume does not refer to sources, but to provisions aiding interpretation and argument in court. The Castilian law was referred to because of its importance in the courts; Blackstone would, in these circumstances, have no importance.

In conclusion, we can state that the de la Vergne volume provided lawyers with cross-references to Castilian and French law, and to relevant territorial Acts; these references had the practical function of aiding interpretation of the law. This conclusion is satisfactory in terms of the legal history of the period of compilation of the D.L.V.; it describes the nature of the references; and it is in line with the *Avant-Propos*. It explains why there are no references to the Code Napoléon and its *projet.* It does not force us to believe that Moreau Lislet lied in the *Avant-Propos*, as would the suggestion that the D.L.V. was intended to

---

[163] J. Brown, *A Short Letter to a Member of Congress Concerning the Territory of Orleans*, Washington, D.C., 1806, p. 21, found quoted in Dargo, *Jefferson's Louisiana*, p. 231.
[164] Louisiana Acts, 1806, ch. 11 (21 May 1806).

conceal the origins of the Digest's articles; nor does it make him the unconscious agent of hidden structural forces. Were Moreau Lislet deliberately attempting to conceal the origins of the Digest, he would have appeared ridiculous to his contemporaries, who, as the law reports show, had a good knowledge of the Castilian law; we also have evidence that originally the copying of the French code for the Digest was well known and that Moreau Lislet openly admitted that much of the Digest was taken from the French code.[165] Moreau Lislet would be well able to construct such a series of cross references as he must have been aware of the provisions of the Castilian law and the *droit coutumier* in order to have used them in the redaction of the Digest, which he had undertaken with James Brown. Should the above be accepted, it provides a solution to the problems of the purpose and nature of the notes in the de la Vergne manuscript.

THE WORKING METHOD OF THE REDACTORS

The following hypothesis on the working method of James Brown and Louis Moreau Lislet in their redaction of the Digest was put forward in chapter three: it was suggested that either the 1800 *Projet* or the 1804 Code Napoléon was adopted and served for the Digest as a model from which exclusions were made or to which inclusions were made as the redactors thought fit; indeed both together might have been used. In so far as this hypothesis is capable of verification, it must be accepted as correct; and—I am sure—few would disagree with it.[166] Pascal's thesis that the French code was adopted as a model because of its resemblance to the "Spanish Roman" law must now be rejected.[167] Can any more specific conclusions be drawn?

First, it must be accepted that the adoption of the French code or its *projet* as a model was a deliberate action taken because of the excellence of the French code and its usefulness as a model: the French code was not adopted as a model because it was thought largely to follow the Castilian law. This can readily be deduced from the fact that the redactors obviously compared the C.N.'s provisions with those of the Castilian law. Thus, the redactors sometimes departed from their model to follow some Castilian provision (such as the division of nonage into pupillage and minority); for them to do this, they must have compared critically the French code with the Castilian law and must have been aware of the differences. The acceptance of the C.N. and/or its *projet* was deliberate; they were not followed unthinkingly. This is not to deny that the C.N. was used as a model because it allowed the preservation of the civil law by facilitating a quick redaction of a code, without causing too great a rupture with the past.

---

[165] See *supra*, text at note 163.
[166] See *supra*, chap. 3, text at notes 266–281.
[167] See Pascal, "Reply", pp. 605–607.

Second, the redactors, while following either the C.N. or its *projet*, examined along with each French article corresponding provisions in other sources available to them. Hence, they appear to have systematically collated the French articles with provisions found in territorial Acts, various treatises of Pothier, Domat's *Droit Civil* and *Droit Public*, Febrero's *Librería de escribanos*, the *Nueva recopilación*, in the *Leyes de Toro*, the *Siete Partidas* and even Blackstone. This may be deduced from the fact that the French codes have been departed from or have subtly been altered in favour of provisions taken from these sources. Thus, it is again fair to posit that the redactors carefully selected provisions they thought suitable, for whatever reason and by whatever criteria they set themselves. As has frequently been pointed out, the adoption of the French redactions as a model did impose a certain dynamic or structure on the code, which necessarily affected the provisions chosen. Nevertheless, within that structure, the redactors were free to depart from the provisions of the French law; they merely had to include provisions on certain topics that the logic of the French codes required to be covered.

Third, from this use of many sources, we may deduce there was a selection among them, and it is thus possible and correct to suppose there were reasons behind each particular selection: reasons which may be deduced from comparison of competing potential provisions. This is, of course, what has been done in chapters four and five.

The above three points are of course closely related, and this separation of them is perhaps artificial; but it is, however, justifiable for the purpose of exposition. The above deductions were, of course, the hypothesis behind the present study, and the arguments behind their adoption as a hypothesis were put in Chapter One. It perhaps could be argued then that this study has been self-fulfilling or circular, in that the method here necessarily dictated the result; but this would be wrong. First, the results justify the method: it has been fruitful in shedding light on the reasons behind the adoption of certain provisions and the process of legal development in general. Second, the method was deduced from certain principles related to the task on hand: it was not based in a self-fulfilling way entirely on what was known of the Digest. Third, the hypothesis on the method of working of the redactors, when shown to be plausible and confirmed by what can be gathered from the internal evidence of the Digest, may be supported by outside evidence from other codes. That is, although it would have been wrong to suppose that the redactors of the Digest would have worked in the same way as the redactors of another civil code, if we can establish that the Digest redactors appear to have worked in a certain way, and if we can then point to another set of redactors of a civil code who worked in a similar way or the same way, then we have particularly strong evidence to support our hypothesis and our interpretation of the evidence. In the Reports of the Quebec codifiers we have such support. In chapter three,[168] drawing on the excellent

[168] See *supra*, chap. 3, text at notes 416–435.

study of Brierley,[169] the Preface of McCord[170] and the Reports of the Commissioners for Codification in Lower Canada,[171] we described the working method adopted in the redaction of the Quebec Code. That working method was based round the French code, with a critical examination of the French code in the light of other potential sources. This working method is indeed similar to that here suggested as having been used in the redaction of the 1808 Digest. Since this is so, based on examination of the evidence, we can conclude that the suggestion put forward here is probably correct. The 1808 redactors drew up their code on the basis of a critical examination of the French code in comparison with other sources and with an alteration of the French codal articles where thought necessary because of preference for provisions discovered in other sources. Conversely, where articles from the work of codification in France were left unaltered, we may assume this was because they were preferred to provisions found in other potential sources. Thus, the assumptions on the working method of the redactors—assumptions necessary for this study— must be taken to be correct. This working method would be speedy, while also permitting a critical assessment of the law, within the general framework of the French code.[172]

REACTION OF THE COURTS TO THE 1808 DIGEST

In chapter three there was a discussion of the attitude of the courts to the 1808 Digest in connection with the dispute between Pascal and Batiza over whether the 1808 redaction was a "digest" or a "code".[173] It is now appropriate to expand on this topic and to assess the use made of the Digest in the courts. This does not purport to be an exhaustive study of the courts' attitudes to the Digest;[174] but the study here is sufficient to raise some important points.

Elizabeth Brown has explored the attitudes of the Louisiana courts;[175] so has George Dargo.[176] His examination has been discussed earlier, but it is useful to repeat that he argues from certain cases that the courts treated the Digest as a compilation of the previous law, and that this is evidence both for the sources of the Digest and for the Digest not being an amendment of or derogation from the Castilian law. The accuracy of his facts, and the nature of his arguments from a

---

[169] Brierley, "Codification", pp. 542–573; *supra*, chap. 3, note 416.
[170] McCord, Preface, pp. v–ix.
[171] See *supra*, chap. 3, quotations in text at notes 423 and 424.
[172] Batiza, "Textual Evidence", pp. 105–106 must be correct about drafting technique. Baade, "Marriage Contracts", pp. 83–84 stresses the speed of the technique; I would disagree with his arguments as to why the French code was followed: see *infra*, "Conclusions on the 1808 Digest".
[173] See *supra*, chap. 3, text at notes 208–227.
[174] Of immeasurable help in elucidating Louisiana's legal history would be an exhaustive study of the courts' methods of reasoning, of the authorities relied on, and of the treatment of the Digest and law.
[175] Brown, *op. cit. supra* note 87, pp. 59–75.
[176] See *supra*, chap. 3, text at notes 208–227.

historical point of view have already been considered; but it is important to note that Dargo bases his arguments on only two cases: *Hayes v. Berwick*[177] and *Cottin v. Cottin.*[178] In discussing the relationship of the Digest to the Spanish laws, Brown likewise discusses only these two.[179] As a sample of the *general* treatment of the Digest by the judges this is insufficient. *Cottin* especially was an exceptional case, changing the law to such an extent that it encouraged the legislature to appoint Moreau Lislet and Carleton to translate the *Partidas.*[180] For a proper *historical* picture of the courts' attitudes, as distinct from tracing the mere growth of *one* legal principle, it is necessary to examine other cases, ones which, unlike *Cottin*, were not introducing new law in a significant way. In his LL.M. thesis on the interpretation of the Louisiana codes, T.W. Tucker has devoted rather more attention to the courts' attitudes to the Digest.[181] Tucker's discussion is of rather a different nature from the one following; it is also fairly brief.[182] He makes some important points that will be acknowledged where relevant. He does not appear, however, to argue the major point on the courts' treatment of the Digest as an ordinary statute, though he does recognize that they did so.[183] Further, he does not examine a sufficient number of cases to trace the development and changes of patterns of treatment of the Digest by the courts: he is more concerned to trace the courts' development of the *Cottin* doctrine and does not point out the contradictory tendencies.

The following matters need to be discussed: first, the courts' construction of the Digest and whether or not that construction varied or changed over the years; second, the nature of the authorities cited; third, whether or not there was an assertion of "Spanish" law from the earliest cases or only from later; and fourth, should there have been such a reassertion of "Spanish" law, the reasons for such a happening. It is convenient to discuss these matters by discussing the cases, and pointing out what may be gleaned from them before reaching conclusions. Again, it should be stressed that this study is not exhaustive;[184] but it is sufficient to assess the traditional views on *Hayes* and *Cottin* and the courts' attitude to the Digest.

The first case to be considered is *Dewes* v. *Morgan* of 1809.[185] It concerned the recovery of the price of a slave who died, and the plaintiff's action was based on D.O. 80 (p. 359). Brown, for the plaintiff, stated that "[i]n this instance, the statute follows the law of this country as it stood before its

---

177 2 Mart. (O.S.) 138 (1812).

178 5 Mart. (O.S.) 93 (1817); Dargo, *Jefferson's Louisiana*, p. 158.

179 Brown, *op. cit. supra* note 87, pp. 61–63.

180 See *supra*, chap. 3, text at notes 221–223; Dargo, *Jefferson's Louisiana*, pp. 159–160; T.W. Tucker, "Interpretation of the Louisiana Civil Codes, 1808–1840: The Failure of the Preliminary Title", unpublished LL.M. thesis, University of Glasgow, unpublished LL.M. thesis, 1972, pp. 115–117.

181 Tucker, *op. cit. supra* note 180, pp. 109–115.

182 *Ibid.*

183 *Ibid.* pp. 109, 112–113.

184 Though it is the most exhaustive known to me.

185 1 Mart. (O.S.) 1 (1809). This is the first case reported in Louisiana.

passage";[186] he goes on to cite copiously from the *Partidas*, the *Curia philippica* and Justinian's Digest.[187] (Brown's statement acknowledges that the Digest (statute) was conceived of as, in many other "instances", not following the previous law.) Hennen, counsel for the defendant, quoted Domat, Justinian, the *Partidas*, and Gregorio Lopez.[188] The judge, Lewis J., found for the plaintiff; but what is significant here is that he construed D.O. 80 (p. 359) in the light of D.O. 71 (p. 359), operating the Digest as a coherent system of rules in typical civilian fashion for construing a civil code.

In *Caisergues* v. *Dujarreau*, 1809, D.O. 32 (p. 409) was interpreted in the light of Castilian authority, cited by both counsel.[189] This, it should be pointed out, is a traditional method of interpretation, and *in no sense* was the rule of the article displaced or circumvented.

An interesting case is *Miner* v. *The Bank of Louisiana*, which concerned the honouring of a bill drawn on a bank.[190] The case dealt with the law in 1805, when the note was issued. Moreau, for the defendant, made the following interesting statement:

> The principles of the civil and Spanish laws which regulated this territory in the year 1805, when the note was issued, are in unison with those of the common law of England.[191]

He nonetheless went on to cite *Part*. 3.18.114 and Pothier,[192] and the other defence counsel, Mazureau, cited the *Curia philippica*,[193] which was also cited by Duncan for the plaintiff, who nevertheless also cited Pothier and a range of English cases.[194]

What is notable about commercial litigation is that a large number of English cases are often cited, although civilian learning is adduced too, and, indeed, civilian authority often governed the court's decision. Such a case is *Stackhouse et al.* v. *Foley's Syndics*, where, although many English cases were cited, the court stated: "The ordinance of *Bilbao* must determine this case."[195] However, as with *Miner* (*supra*), it was sometimes (and often enough to be worth pointing out) remarked in commercial matters that the English law follows the civilian (in matters such as law merchant).[196] Commercial cases such

---

[186] *Ibid*., p. 2.
[187] *Ibid*., p. 3.
[188] *Ibid*., p. 4.
[189] 1 Mart. (O.S.) 7 (1809). This is the second case reported.
[190] 1 Mart. (O.S.) 12 (1809). This is the third case reported.
[191] *Ibid*., p. 14.
[192] *Ibid*., pp. 14 and 15 respectively.
[193] *Ibid*., p. 18.
[194] *Ibid*., p. 19.
[195] 1 Mart. (O.S.) 228 (1811).
[196] See, e.g., *Peretz* v. *Peretz et al.* 1 Mart. (O.S.) 219 at 220: "The Spanish authority cited by the plaintiff's counsel, fully supports him. The rule is the same in the courts of equity in the United States and in the court of Chancaery in England, in which the practice is according to the rules of the civil law."

as *Stackhouse* and *Miner* are not really relevant here, as the Digest did not cover commercial law: nonetheless, what these cases tell us is that all kinds of authorities were used. In no sense could the common law be said to be in force in Louisiana; but in these lawsuits judges and counsel were willing to attempt to assimilate the civil law to the common, the latter law being the one in which many of them, especially the judges, were trained. Courts and counsel were eclectic in citation of authority. Tucker states that in commercial law "the Ordinance of *Bilbao* controlled"; he does not point out that in commercial cases English authority was frequently cited, nor that commercial law did not come within the orbit of the Digest. It should in fairness be pointed out that he is merely attempting to demonstrate the regularity and frequency of the citation of Spanish authority.[197] He later does point out that "even English treatises and cases" were cited;[198] though he does not expressly indicate just how extensive the use of English authority was.

The attitude of the court in *Territory* v. *Nugent*, 1810, which concerned libel, is intriguing.[199] This case was at first argued and decided purely on the basis of English common law. The same case came later before Martin, J., who, in his opinion, discussed the English and U.S. authorities.[200] He then stated that the absence of any case overruling the principle in England or the U.S.A. would be conclusive, especially when it was considered that the French and Spanish laws conformed to the common law of England.[201] He then merely cited some French and Spanish authorities. The reference to the civil law appears here as an afterthought.

In 1812 came the case of *Hayes* v. *Berwick*, [202] of which no more need be said than to remark that the court used the Digest as an explanation of the law in 1805, before its adoption. The court included the French law with the Spanish as the law in force in 1805.[203]

Le Breton v. *Nouchet* followed in 1813.[204] Livingston, counsel for the appellant, stated that Louisiana is "still peculiarly governed" by the laws of Spain.[205] He argued that a particular Castilian *ley* should be applied. He was opposed by Moreau as counsel for the other side. Livingston lost the appeal.

An important case is *Morse* v. *Williamson and Patton's Syndics*, decided in 1814.[206] Here the court recognized that the provisions of the Digest under

---

[197] Tucker, *op. cit. supra* note 180, p. 111.
[198] *Ibid.*
[199] 1 Mart. (O.S.) 102 (1810).
[200] 1 Mart. (O.S.) 108 (1810).
[201] He said: "If any doubt remained, the absence of any case, in which it was overruled in England, or such of the United States, in which no legal provision exists, would be conclusive, especially when it is considered that the French and Spanish laws, which were heretofore in force here, are comformable in this respect to the common law of England."
[202] 2 Mart. (O.S.) 138 (1812).
[203] Tucker, *op. cit. supra* note 180, p. 113; Brown, *op. cit. supra* note 87, pp. 61–62.
[204] 3 Mart. (O.S.) 59 (1813).
[205] *Ibid.*, pp. 62–63.
[206] 3 Mart (O.S.) 282 (1814).

consideration conflicted with the Castilian authorities. After mentioning these authorities, the court stated:

> But all these laws we conceive to be virtually repealed and abrogated, in all cases where the same things have been provided for in a different manner, by the legislature of the late territory, or of the state.
>
> The case must, then, be determined principally on that clause of the Civil Code which gives . . . [etc.].[207]

Here is a position similar to *Cottin*; yet the court decided differently, applying the code, and regarding the "Spanish" law as superseded.

Sennet v *Sennet's Legatees*, 1814, is another significant case.[208] It concerned the inheritance rights of natural children. Porter, counsel for the plaintiff, argued on the basis of the Digest. Counsel for the defendant, Brent, put forward the following interesting argument:

> Upon another ground: suppose the statute [i.e. the Digest] to be absurd, inexplicable and contradictory, the previous law of the land, the Spanish law, clearly gave this power to the testator; its books breathe no other principle: and if the statute should be considered by the court as contradictory, or not sufficiently plain or explanatory, it is the previous existing law of the state, like the common law of England, unaltered by statute, which must govern and direct, and this in favour of the appellees.[209]

What is remarkable about this is that he argues: first, the Digest being apparently contradictory, Spanish law should apply, and second, that this is so because the Digest should be interpreted in the manner in which the English common law would interpret a statute. That is, Brent argues for common-law canons of statutory interpretation for the Digest. The court rejected Brent's argument and, applying the Digest, found for the plaintiff.[210]

The next case we should consider is *Rogers* v. *Beiller*, 1815.[211] It turned in part on the interpretation of the Digest in the light of an ordinance. The judgment of Martin, J. is instructive about his attitude to the Digest; a lengthy quotation is therefore justified:

> In 1808, the Civil Code was published. This act purports to be a digest of the law, theretofore in force; a declaratory act. The person, who, according to it, is to attend to the estate of an intestate, in the absence of the next of kin is called a curator, the expression of the civil law corresponding to that of the English or Amercian law, *administrator*.
>
> We conclude that neither the act of the legislative council, nor the Civil Code have repealed the ordinance under consideration.
>
> A general provision does not repeal a particular one by *implication*. If a particular thing be given or limited in the preceding part of a statute, this shall

---

207 *Ibid.*, pp. 283–284.
208 3 Mart. (O.S.) 411 (1814).
209 *Ibid.*, p. 416.
210 *Ibid*, pp. 417–418.
211 3 Mart. (O.S.) 665 (1815).

> not be altered or taken away by subsequent general words of the same statute 6 *Bacon's Abr.*, 231 *verbo Statute*; *Stanton* vs. *Univ. of Oxford*, 1 *Jones*, 26. In this case, the provision was not in the same statute, but it was in one *in pari materia*, and all such are to be taken as if they were *one. Douglas*, 30.
>
> Unless the ordinance cannot exist with the Civil Code, it must be holden repealed. Now, the duties it imposes are not more at war with the provisions of the Civil Code, than with the act of the legislative council. We conclude it is not repealed.[212]

More quotations could be taken from the judgement; but this is sufficient for our purposes. Analysis of Martin's statement has the following results. First, he takes it as certain that the 1808 redaction is a digest, in a restrictive sense, of the previous law: a mere declaratory act. Second, since this is so, it proves that the ordinance is unrepealed. It will be recalled that the Digest purports *to amend* the law, as well as stating some of the previous law. Third, Martin equates the Digest with an English statute. Fourth, relying on English authority, he argues that it should be interpreted in the manner of an English statute, and concludes that the ordinance should be construed *along with* the Digest, as, both being statutes and *in pari materia*, they should be regarded as *one statute.* This approach is much more linked with a typical common-law methodology than with that of the civil law. Indeed, Martin's manner of reasoning seems inappropriate given the nature of the Digest and of colonial royal ordinances. He has adopted restrictive common-law canons of statutory interpretation that allowed him to sidestep the Digest's provisions.

Cottin v. *Cottin* is itself the next relevant case. Its arguments of which are well known.[213] The Digest is stated to be a declaration of the laws previously in force, so that these laws are untouched, wherever the alterations or amendments in the Digest do not reach them, and are only repealed if contrary to or incompatible with the Digest.

Can any pattern be seen in these cases that would allow reflection on the four matters under consideration? Because this study has not been exhaustive, the results are not definitive; but I would suggest that there is enough evidence to warrant the drawing of the following tentative conclusions.

First, the early case of *Dewes* would suggest that originally the courts were prepared to interpret the Digest as a sufficient statement of the law, one which could be construed by reference to its provisions as a totality: and the case of *Caisergues* does not contradict this, because interpretation, using previous law, of a brief article is justified, as it is still the article which governs the law, not the prior law governing the article, there being no attempt to displace the Digest's provisions.

Second, if the above is correct, the case of *Hayes* perhaps marks a change; but this is uncertain. In *Hayes*, it will be recalled, the Digest was used as giving a statement of the law in 1805: in effect the Digest was used in place of the pre-

---

[212] *Ibid.*, pp. 671–672.

[213] 5 Mart. (O.S.) 93 (1817).

Digest law and not *vice versa*. *Hayes*' importance for historians is the statement that the Digest did *not* amend the law and was evidence of the older law. Nonetheless, by this argument on the *origins and nature* of the Digest, the court started to give scope for its displacement by the earlier law.

Third, if, in retrospect, *Hayes* did presage a change, it was far from certain that suh a change would take place. This is clearly shown by the case of *Morse*, in which the court rejected an interpretation of the Digest through the medium of the Castilian law. The arguments were virtually identical to those in the later case of *Cottin*; but the court rejected the interpretation later accepted in *Cottin*, and decided that the previous law had been abrogated. The important case of *Morse* does not appear in this respect to have attracted the notice of Louisiana's legal historians.[214] This is unfortunate because this case clearly demonstrates that the *jurisprudence* of the Louisiana courts, in the period from 1812 to 1817, was not tending exclusively towards the *Cottin* view—there was also contradictory precedent. The approach taken in *Cottin* was not as inevitable as it has been suggested in the past.[215]

Sennet is important; in it counsel argued for the Digest to be interpreted as *an English statute*—a method of interpretation that would permit the revival of the Castilian law. The court rejected this argument; but, in the fourth phase, in the case of *Rogers*, we find the court, in the person of Martin J., following this line of reasoning. The Digest is construed as an English statute, the principle being that statutes are interpreted as restrictively as possible; it is construed along with an ordinance, looked upon as a statute of equal value to the Digest. Now, if the Digest is construed in the manner of a statute in English law, then the necessary corollary is that the pre-Digest law is of a nature equivalent to the English common law. Thus, the position is reached that the Castilian law is in force except in so far as it is inconsistent with the Digest—the latter being now interpreted as restrictively as possible. This attitude culminated in *Cottin*, despite the protest of Livingston.[216]

Should the above analysis be correct, we may now discern a pattern of change in interpretation of the Digest and in the courts' attitude to the Digest. At first, the courts applied the Digest as if it were a whole, entire in itself; so, understandably, they interpreted its brief statements by using other texts: a common method of interpreting new civil codes.[217] The case of *Hayes* shows that it next became possible to argue that the Digest was merely a statement of the law before codification: this case, however, did not displace the Digest by

---

[214] Cf. Tucker, *op. cit. supra* note 180, pp. 109–117; Brown, *op. cit. supra* note 87, pp. 61–63. Both ignore this important case, jumping straight from *Hayes* to *Cottin*. Louisiana legal historians seem to have concentrated over much on the interpretation that came to predominate.

[215] Consider the views, e.g., of Pascal and Dargo.

[216] See *supra*, chap. 3, text at note 211.

[217] As the commentaries on the C.N. show. A neat example is P.A. Fenet, *Pothier analysé dans ses rapports avec le Code civil, et mis en ordre sous chacun des articles de ce Code*, 2nd edn., Paris, l'auteur, 1829, where Pothier's texts were placed under the C.N. articles by Fenet to aid interpretation of the code: see *ibid.*, pp. i–iii. Batiza, "Textual Evidence", p. 79, note 14 seems to believe Fenet wished to indicate sources.

the law prior to its promulgation. *Morse* shows that in 1814 the court could still recognize that the Digest was something new and different from the Castilian law, which was stated to have been abrogated by the Digest provisions; counsel's argument in *Sennet* and Martin's judgment in *Rogers* show that the Digest could next be recognized as statute in English fashion, and the Castilian law as an immutable common law. *Cottin* shows that now the Castilian law could be revived to supersede the Digest where possible. It would appear then, that, in the period from 1812 to 1817, the Castilian law was reasserted by the argument that the Digest was a statute in the English style and that the Castilian law was a common law in the English style. The Act of 1808 promulgating the code had repealed, by s. 2, all laws contrary to or irreconcilable with the Digest.[218] This provided a "loophole" that the lawyers and courts could utilize to reassert the Castilian law, especially through their restrictive interpretation of the Digest by common-law methods.

If the above be accepted, we may then provide a solution to the first and third of the problems posed towards the beginning of this subsection. The construction of the Digest varied over the years, and the change in method of construction permitted the later reassertion of the Castilian law as a common law in force where not specifically abrogated by the Digest.

Before we consider the fourth problem—that of why this was done, as distinct from how—it is appropriate to deal with the second, on the nature of the legal authorities cited. There is little point in giving any kind of arithmetical count of citations; for our purposes the following impressionistic survey is sufficient. There is no need to mention specific instances of the extensive citation of Castilian authority: it pervades all the early court reports, so that citations of Febrero, the *Nueva recopilación*, Gomez, the *Curia philippica*, and the *Partidas* are commonplace. As indicated, early English cases are often cited. Both bench and bar often cite Pothier,[219] as well as Denisart,[220] Pigeau's *Procédure du Châtelet*,[221] Domat,[222] the *Coutume de Paris*,[223] and Ferrière.[224] Of the *droit nouveau* in France, the Code Napoléon itself is cited,[225] as are Maleville's *Analyse*[226] and the *Pandectes francaises*.[227] The *Corpus iuris civilis* is also cited.[228] Wider ranging references are those to Voet's *Commentarius ad*

---

[218] See *supra*, chap. 3, text at notes 184, 204–207.

[219] See, e.g., *Minor* v. *Bank of Louisiana* 1 Mart. (O.S.) 12 (1809); *D'Argy* v. *Godefroi* 1 Mart. (O.S.) 76 (1809); and *Beauregard, Exectuor* v. *Piernas and Wife* 1 Mart. (O.S.) 280 (1811).

[220] See, e.g., judgement of Martin J., in *Denis* v. *Leclerc* 1 Mart. (O.S.) 297 at 310–311 and 313 (1811); *Hayes* v. *Berwick* 2 Mart. (O.S.) 138 (1812).

[221] See Martin J. in *Denis* v. *Leclerc* 1 Mart. (O.S.) 297 at 309–310 (1811); and *Hayes* v. *Barwick* 2 Mart. (O.S.) 138 (1812).

[222] See e.g., *Dewes* v. *Morgan* 1 Mart. (O.S.) 1 at 3 (1809); *Marr* v. *Lartigue* 2 Mart. (O.S.) 88 (1811).

[223] See e.g., *Marr* v. *Lartigue* 2 Mart. (O.S.) 88 (1811).

[224] See *Ibid.*; *Hayes* v. *Berwick* 2 Mart. (O.S.) 138 (1812).

[225] *Smith* v. *Kemper* 4 Mart. (O.S.) 409 (1816).

[226] *Ibid.*

[227] *Chretien* v. *Tuerd* 2 Mart. (N.S.) 299 (1824)

[228] See *Dewes* v. *Morgan* 1 Mart. (O.S.) 1 (1809); and *Marr* v. *Lartigue* 2 Mart. (O.S.) 88 (1811).

pandectas,[229] and the works of Bartolus,[230] Ulric Huber,[231] Struvius,[232] and Gothofredus.[233] Lord Kames's wor *Principles of Equity* is found cited once.[234] These examples show the breadth of learning adduced in cases as authority for the arguing of points. When counsel such as Moreau Lislet and Edward Livingston appeared opposing each other, the authority cited would be extensive and varied in origin, as both could obviously draw on a vast range of civilian and other learning.[235] Tucker also points to the enormous range of the authority cited.[236] The above brief account does not do justice to the extent of the civilian learning displayed by some counsel in court; but it is sufficient to indicate how wide the citation of authority was: it also supports the statement made by the redactors of the 1825 Code in their 1823 *Projet* about the problems caused by wading through a mass of obscure civilian learning.[237]

Why did the Louisiana bench and bar thus reassert the Castilian law by interpreting the Digest in the fashion of an English statute? An answer to this question is inevitably speculative, but four factors seem to have brought about this result. First, many lawyers, both at the bar and on the bench, were trained in the common law. They would be accustomed to common-law methods of statutory interpretation, and this could well have influenced their treatment of the Digest. Second, the procedure in court was based on counsel arguing the points between them, with the judge acting as referee and coming to a decision based on the arguments. Given the attraction of common-law methods of interpretation, this form of procedure made the citation of legal authority of paramount importance where points of law were at issue. Third, given this stress on authority, and the common-law-influenced interpretation of the Digest, Castilian law became an attractive source of legal authority, and thus tended to be revived. Fourth, the procedure being contentious, and lawyers wishing to win for their clients, the revival of the Castilian law permitted the search of many varied sources for authority. The circumvention of the Digest permitted the examination of the Castilian law itself and of the civil law more generally, both in the *Corpus iuris* and its modern commentators. Thus, we find even commentators on the French *droit coutumier* and on the French code being cited in court as authority. Lawyers had great scope in searching for authority—a scope that they seem to have utilized to the full. If one considers the amount of legal sources that the circumvention of the Digest permitted lawyers to use, it is

---

229 See *Seguin* v. *Debon*, 3 Mart. (O.S.) 5 (1813).
230 *Denis* v. *Leclerc* 1 Mart. (O.S.) 297 at 300 (1811).
231 *Marr* v. *Lartigue* 2 Mart. (O.S.) 88 (1811); *Le Breton* v. *Nouchet* 3 Mart (O.S.) 59 (1813).
232 *Marr* v. *Lartigue* 2 Mart. (O.S.) 88 (1811).
233 *Duplantier* v. *Pigman* 3 Mart. (O.S.) 236 (1814) at 238.
234 *Clark's Executors* v. *Cochran* 3 Mart. (O.S.) 353 (1814) at 354.
235 See e.g. *Marr* v. *Lartigue* 2 Mart. (O.S.) 88 (1811); *Denis* v. *Leclerc* 1 Mart. (O.S.) 297; and *Orleans Navigation Co.* v. *Mayor etc. of New Orleans* 2 Mart. (O.S.) 9 (1811) and 2 Mart. (O. S.) 214 (1812).
236 Tucker, *op. cit. supra* note 180, pp. 111–112.
237 "Preliminary Report of the Code Commissioners, Dated February 13, 1823", in *La. Leg. Arch.*, vol. 1, pp. LXXXV–XCV at p. XCII, quoted *supra*, chap. 3 text at note 151.

obvious that, with diligent research, a lawyer could come up with authority for virtually any propositon of law, while working within the Castilian framework. That is, the revival of Castilian law and the downgrading of the Digest, influenced by conceptions drawn from the common law, permitted lawyers to act in an opportunist fashion in finding and quoting authority. Professor Franklin has stated that:

> As there was tremendous land speculation in Louisiana in the period under consideration certain Anglo-American common lawyers supported the *penchant hispanophile* because of the incognoscibility of the feudal Spanish Romanist materials. [238]

Although I obviously would not agree with the terminology, Professor Franklin has raised an important point, relevant to the present discussion, and in line with the arguments above. The revival of Castilian law, and all that it brought in its train, allowed opportunistic lawyers access to a vast pool of diverse and varying Castilian and other civilian anthority which could be cited in court before a bench whose occupants were often not familiar with civilian legal systems and their methodology.

Thus, it may be concluded that the revival of Castilian law in the period from 1812 to 1817 was due to opportunist lawyers exploiting a loophole in the 1808 Act promulgating the Digest, and was facilitated by the habituation of the legal profession to the common law's methods of statutory interpretation—thus permitting the downgrading of the Digest. As already indicated, this point is speculative; but the important aspect is that arguments based on *Hayes* and *Cottin* as to the *nature* of the Digest and its sources are untenable, if their full historical context is examined. The apparent downgrading of the Digest and revival of the Castilian law evidenced by *Cottin* was a *real* downgrading and a *real* revival: it is no evidence as to the *nature* of the Digest nor as to its source origins. What actually was happening in the Louisiana courts and why is a subject deserving of greater study—a study outwith the scope of this work—but the brief sketch above indicates roughly what was happening and the conclusions (although speculative) are reasonable given the present state of knowledge.

CONCLUSIONS ON THE 1808 DIGEST

The historical background of the 1808 Digest is now familiar. The work of Dargo explains and sets out the political and legal motives for codification: preservation of the civil law from the threat of the importation of common law and settling confusion over the authorities relevant, while reducing the law to an easily used, comprehensive code.[239] The pressure of these two motives acting

---

[238] Franklin, "Existential Force", p. 96.
[239] Dargo, *Jefferson's Louisiana*, chaps. 5–7.

together resulted in the redaction of the 1808 Digest. The law was overhauled, reformed, and rendered into more readily accessible languages. It must be remembered that the confusion over the laws in force had been a real confusion producing much uncertainty.[240] Thus, we must conclude that the 1808 redaction of the Digest was, first, the result of a desire to end this confusion over the laws and to reduce the laws to an accessible and easily consulted form, by abolishing the necessity for reference to a mass of juristic material and, second, of a desire to preserve the civil law from common-law encroachments. It should be noted that commercial law was not codified, and there was no equivalent to the French *Code de commerce.* This is a point that will be considered *infra* after discussion of the Quebec codification.

The two codifiers, Moreau Lislet and Brown, based the Digest on either the French *Code civil* of 1804 or its 1800 *Projet*, or both. Which was used and why need not concern us here.[241] Their acceptance of either or both of these two redactions was a critical one. They modified the codes in the light of each other and in the light of other material available to them. The redactors appear to have carefully selected provisions from either the *Code civil* or its *projet* or from the *Partidas*, Febrero, Pothier, and other similar material. This thesis has been concerned to explore the reasons why; but the complexity of the work of selection indicates the care put into the selection of provisions and justifies the assumption that the selection was based on reasons, rather than arbitrary whim, even if the two redactors have left us no accoimt of why they chose the provisions they did. Suffice it to say that they borrowed extensively from many varied and competing potential sources, and for the reasons explored in chapters four and five *supra*.

The 1808 Digest is not a codification of the Castilian law which through the authority of the *Recopilación de las Indias* was technically in force prior to its redaction. The redactors clearly did not interpret their instructions to mean that they should codify the Castilian law. The reasons why have been explored to some extent in chapter three; but it is worthwhile to devote some brief attention to the matter. First, the relevant Act stated that the civil law presently in force should form the basis of the code.[242] This could be ambiguous, but clearly for the redactors, influenced by natural law, the civil law referred to the modern usage of Romanist legal systems. In their task of modernizing the law they clearly preferred to use the French code, a very modern statement of law both accessible and amenable to borrowing. In the course of the nineteenth century the *Code Civil* was received in many countries both in Europe and South America—and it even had some influence in Japan.[243] In using the French *Code civil* as a basic source, the redactors were acting within both their mandate and

---

[240] See *supra*, chap. 3, text at notes 130–170.
[241] See *supra*, text at notes 69–89.
[242] See *supra*, chap. 3, text at notes 240–241.
[243] For references, see *supra*, note 88; N. Sugiyama "Les transformations du droit civil Japonais et l'influence du droit civil francais", in *Le droit civil français: livre-souvenir supra* note 63, pp. 673–689.

the civilian tradition. They went on to use Pothier, Domat, the *Corpus iuris*, and Castilian laws and juristic commentaries—all to compile their own modern civil code according to the criteria they set themselves. And this they did admirably. The Digest of 1808, although the vast bulk of its provisions are borrowed from elsewhere, is unique. The transplanted law has been put together to form a law that, though based on other laws, forms together a new system of laws. Professor Hans Baade has recently put forward a new theory as to the reasons for the copying of the French code.[244] He suggests that the "living law" of the territory was French and that this explains the close copying from the French code.[245] The particular research on which this conclusion has been based has already been discussed in this thesis in connection with matrimonial property.[246] There it was accepted that he must be correct in that the revival of French legal folkways after 1803 would certainly facilitate the adoption of a matrimonial property law of a French "contractual" type. Certainly, it has been pointed out in chapter three that there does generally seem to have been a revival of French law after 1803; but this would seem to be part of the initial general confusion over the laws in force in the early Territorial period.[247] Professor Baade's thesis, however, must be rejected in so far as it attempts to provide a *general* explanation for the copying of the French code and its *projet*. He suggests that the "French *Code Civil* of 1804 had to serve as the basic text and was generally acceptable to the extent it reflected or harmoniously advanced the 'living law' of the Territory, the Custom of Paris".[248] As pointed out, to claim that the Custom of Paris was the "living law" of the Territory is to exaggerate: there had been a revival of French law, but only as part of the general confusion over the laws in force in the Territory. There seems no evidence to suggest that the redactors generally were attempting to embody in their code the "living law". Blackstone was copied for provisions on the concept of *puissance paternelle*; his *Commentaries* cannot really be described as "living law" for the Territory. The redactors were concerned to provide a civil code in a short period, and used the French code as a model. But they used the French code in a critical fashion: they did not copy it unthinkingly. They changed some of its articles, and introduced provisions taken from other sources they consulted for various reasons. They do not seem generally to have been concerned with embodying the "living law". As regards Professor Baade's theory, it must be correct in so far as the fact that the "living law" of marriage contracts was French may well have encouraged the redactors to copy French provisions; but there is no evidence that the redactors generally were concerned to embody the "living law" in their code.[249]

---

244 Baade, "Marriage Contracts", pp. 83–84.

245 *Ibid.*

246 See *supra*, chap. 4, text at notes 256–301.

247 See *supra*, chap. 3, text at notes 156–171.

248 Baade, "Marriage Contracts", p. 84.

249 Professor Baade's thesis is most attractive and ingenious, and as said here, does help explain why the readactors adopted the French "contractual" model of matrimonial property. Generally,

The period of 1812 to 1817 saw a movement for revival of the Castilian law and circumvention of the Digest. This movement resulted in the compilation of the de la Vergne manuscript notes and the translation of the *Partidas* into English. The movement for the re-assertion of the Castilian law does not reflect on the nature of the Digest, but rather on the activities of the Louisiana bar and the inability of many of its members to grasp how the code could have been used. Further, the movement reflects on the opportunist nature of attorneys in their task of winning cases for their clients by exploiting the loophole in the Act promulgating the Digest thus restricting the application of the Digest as far as they could. The Castilian law would still have governed civil matters outwith the scope of the Digest: commercial law for example, in which the courts often applied the Ordinance of Bilbao. It was this revival that led to the 1808 Digest being replaced in 1825 by a new code, in which many of the Digest's articles were included.

The 1808 Digest is thus the result of confusion over the laws and fears of the introduction of Anglo-American common law and is a modern civil code introducing innovations and updating the law; it drew on many sources, but essentially is based on the French code or its *projet*. The disharmony of the conflicting sources was resolved into one coherent whole, rejuvenating and modernizing the Louisiana law. This was achieved through extensive transplantation within the civilian tradition.

---

the redactors may indeed have wished to follow the law they knew to be being applied; but this would require proof. It is difficult to accept that, as regards seashore, Justinian's *Institutes* were the "living law". It seems much more likely that the redactors deliberately updated and modernized the law: knowing that the Castilian laws were formally in force, the redactors used the materials at hand to provide a civil code relatively quickly in order to prevent reception of the common law. The common civilian foundation in Roman law would make the change relatively easy.

7

The Civil Code of Lower Canada

It was pointed out in chapter three that the Codification Commission in Quebec was instructed to draw up the code on the basis of the law actually in force; it was apparently no easy task to discover what that law in fact was.[1] Arising out of the argument in chapters four and five, some aspects of the actions of the codifiers merit the further discussion to which this chapter is accordingly devoted. Fortunately, in comparison to the 1808 Digest, the matters of controversy are relatively few; this chapter will accordingly be appreciably shorter than the preceding, being merely devoted to the actions and task of the codifiers.

Walton summed up the work of redaction thus:

> Our civil code, then, codifies the old French law of Quebec, as modified by statutes, and also codifies, but only as to its broad principles, the commercial law of the province, which is derived from English as well as from French sources.[2]

Brierley states that the bulk of the code is derived from the host of French legal writings of the *ancien régime*.[3] Both these opinions are correct; but both have the potential to mislead, since they tend to diminish the importance of the codifiers as innovators. The redactors were indeed conservative in their work; they did not boldly innovate—but, nonetheless, their very actions in selecting among provisions, given the considerable uncertainty in some areas of the law, held the potential to reform the law. The rationalizing of the law into a code also had a necessary modernizing effect.[4] Furthermore, the redactors also suggested amendments and improvements; these were, in themselves, hardly negligible, as will be shown below.

One author who has not adopted the common view of the 1866 Code as being of an essentially conservative nature is Munro, given he expressed the opinion that "it is probably well within the bounds of truth to suggest that more Roman Law found its way into the contemporary legal system by way of the

---

[1] See *supra*, chap. 3, text at notes 423–424; Brierley, "Codification", pp. 547–554.

[2] F.P. Walton, *The Scope and Interpretation of the Civil Code of Lower Canada*, Montreal, Wilson and Lafleur, 1907, p. 23.

[3] See Brierley, "Codification", p. 553, found quoted *supra*, chap. 3, note 421.

[4] See *supra*, chap. 1, text at notes 50–53.

Code Napoléon than through any other single channel, or, possibly, through all other channels combined."[5] By this he means that it was through *copying* the Code Napoléon that the redactors of the Quebec Code introduced Roman law.[6] The accuracy of his view has already been contested in chapter three, and there is no need to repeat the arguments here.[7] Despite Munro's strictures, most authors would obviously agree with the traditional view of the extreme conservatism of the Quebec codification. This view enabled a judge of the supreme court, in contrasting the Quebec Code with the French, to state:

> Au contraire, ici, nous n'avons pas subi cette influence de 1789, et c'est aux véritables sources du droit national français que nous avons un droit civil français plus historique que les Français eux-mêmes.[8]

This is misleading. There may well have been no Revolution in 1789 in Quebec; but the ideals of the Revolution and of the new society based upon it were not without impact in the distant *quelques arpents de neige*. Limpens also stresses that the Quebec code resembles the *ancien droit* of the northern France rather than the C.N.:

> The Quebec Code of 1866 is certainly not a direct offspring of the Code Napoleon; it is above all—and the fact is worthy of attention—a codification founded on the Custom of Paris. Nevertheless one is bound to note, in addition to certain striking borrowings, a great similarity of drafting in the matters common to both codes.[9]

Even with the major qualification in the last sentence, this cannot be accepted. The codified law of Quebec has a radically different appearance from that of France under the *ancien régime*, as it bears the unmistakeable stamp of influence from the French code. Thus, the law of obligations in the Quebec code may bear a closer relationship to Pothier than to the Code Napoléon as regards many individual provisions and the divisions in the law;[10] it is undoubtedly the case, however, that the whole thrust of the law of contractual obligations is towards promoting freedom and security of contract to facilitate the easy and secure

---

[5] W.B. Munro, "The Custom of Paris in the New World", in F. Berolzheimer (ed.), *Rechtswissenschaftliche Beiträge: Juristische Festgabe des Auslandes zu Josef Kohlers 60. Geburstag 9. März 1909*, Stuttgart, F. Enke, 1909, pp. 132–148 at p. 148.

[6] C.P. Sherman, "Roman Law in the Quebec Civil Code", 25 *Boston University Law Review* (1945), pp. 196–228 simply compares the C.Q.'s articles with Roman texts to discover where they correspond; as legal history it is unsatisfactory.

[7] See *supra*, chap. 3, text at notes 327–334.

[8] See R. Taschereau, "Le siècle de la renaissance et son influence sur le droit civil de Québec," in 12 *Revue juridique Thémis* (1962), pp. 7–17 at p. 16.

[9] J. Limpens, "Territorial Expansion of the Code", in B. Schwartz (ed.), *The Code Napoleon and the Common-Law World*, New York, New York University Press, 1956, pp. 92–109 at p. 99.

[10] See *First Report*, pp. 6–8.

transfer of moveable and immoveable property. In this, it is closer to the "modern law" of the French code than to the *ancien droit* found in Pothier.

The work of the codifiers in Quebec is best approached by examining two matters: first, what the codifiers declared they were doing and how they saw their task; and, second, what they actually did. The first encompasses examining the statements they made as to *why* they selected certain topics and how they saw their selections in relation to their society, while the second necessitates an examination of the sources the redactors used and the selection they made. Both of these are, of course, the subjects of chapters four and five; but here it will be possible both to draw on the experience of those two chapters, and to develop more clearly the work of the redactors by using the *Reports* in which they made many statements of policy.

HOW THE CODIFICATION COMMISSION SAW ITS TASK

The members of the Codification Commission started their *Second Report* with a long comment on the task confronting them.[11] The instructions of the legislature have been discussed in chapter three, as has the working method of the redactors; there is little point in discussing them again here. The Commission's comment does have some relevance for us, however, because in it they point out that "on an infinity of points there is uncertainty and difference of opinion". They go on to state that this is because authors disagree, while there is no legislation, and the courts do not concur. This shows the extent to which the Commission recognized that it had to *choose* between conflicting views and select among sources in order to determine the law, much less suggest amendments to the law. The redactors have left a number of statements about how they selected the law in force and why they suggested amendments; we shall reflect on these here.

A statement of great importance comes at the end of the *First Report* of the Codification Commission: though phrased to refer only to that *Report*, there should be no doubt that this statement may be generalized to refer to the entire work of the Commission.[12] It has already been quoted;[13] it justifies the general approach adopted here towards the Quebec codification, since it indicates that the redactors were well aware that they were involved in a continual process of choosing between alternative provisions. They had to choose not only between competing statements of law in force, but also between competing potential reforms. The codifiers did not, however, say by what criteria they judged which provision was "the most convenient and beneficial".[14] McCord does tell us that

---

[11] *Second Report*, pp. 139–143.
[12] *First Report*, p. 32.
[13] See *supra*, chap. 3, text at note 424.
[14] *First Report*, p. 32, found quoted *supra*, chap. 3, text at note 424 *supra*.

the Commissioners chose amendments that would harmonize the law with their society and adapt the law to the changes society has undergone.[15]

This matter may be pursued further by examining statements made by the codifiers in the *Reports* where they mentioned they were exercising a choice. Second, it may be explored by drawing inferences from the choices made when all the potential provisions examined by the codifiers are analysed. The two approaches should really be combined, as we have combined them in the earlier analysis of the code's provisions on family and employment. Nonetheless, it is useful here to broaden the scope of our understanding by examining some of the codifiers' policy statements as to why they chose a certain provision.

We may first to direct our attention to the codifiers' treatment of contract. It will be recalled that it was argued in chapter two that codification took place in Quebec in the period of greatest influence of nineteenth-century economic liberalism. If we look briefly at the codifiers' actions in the area of contract law, we find that they accepted the doctrines of economic liberalism and tried to introduce them into the law.

C.N. 1134 has no direct equivalent in the Quebec code. C.Q. 1022 is indeed analogous, but lacks the fine imperative statement found in the French code;[16] as pointed out, however, in discussing Louisiana, the *content* of the law of contract should be examined to give meaning to such declarations of principle.

As was done in discussing Louisiana, it is helpful to examine the codifiers' attitude to penalties and stipulated damages. It will be recalled that C.N. 1229 (D.O.129 (p. 285)) assimilated penalty clauses to stipulated damages. The Quebec redactors decided not to do this, and in their *Report* on this section of the code, they said:

> The articles . . . embrace the subject of obligations with a penal clause. They make no departure from the rules established in the articles of the French code, numbered from 1226 to 1233, except in the omission of the article 1229, declaring the penalty to be compensation for damages suffered from the inexecution of the obligation. The Commissioners think this declaration by which stipulated damages and penalties are assimilated without qualification, is a confounding of things which are in many respects different, and governed by different rules, and they have therefore rejected it.[17]

This is a reasonable analysis. If we examine the relevant articles on stipulated damages in the Quebec code, we find that the Quebec codifiers have adopted the rule of the Code Napoléon that stipulated damages cannot be reduced by the courts.[18] The redactors argue that the French code having removed the right of

---

[15] McCord, Synopsis, p. II; found quoted *supra*, chap. 3, text at notes 428–429.
[16] See *supra*, chap. 6, text between notes 2 and 3.
[17] *First Report*, p. 24.
[18] C.Q. 1070–1078.

the courts to diminish stipulated damages, it is desirable to alter the law of Quebec to the same as that in France. They explain:

> The evils which arise from regarding certain clauses in contracts as merely comminatory, and therefore not to be enforced, are obvious, and of daily occurrence. Under the jurisprudence which had grown up in France, the courts constantly modified or disregarded clear stipulations in contracts, for the purpose of substituting to the declared will of the parties, an uncertain equity in the settlement of their rights. In this country perhaps the interference has not been carried to the same length; but it is equally objectionable in principle; and although sustained by the authority of Dumoulin and Pothier, does not seem to have been derived from the Justinian code, or to have been justified by any positive legislation in France.[19]

The law was therefore changed so that the court could not vary stipulated damages. Morin was not in favour of this change in the law; but the majority view was accepted for the code. From the quotation above, it may be seen that notions of both freedom and sanctity of contract were what motivated the two redactors in favour of change. Perhaps ease of proof was also influential; but this is not mentioned in their *Report*. There is unfortunately no indication of why Commissioner Morin objected to the proposed change: his reasons would have been of great interest. If we return to penalty clauses proper (C.Q. 1131 to 1137), we find that the Commissioners, Morin once more dissenting, had recommended the prohibition of the reduction of such clauses by the courts—and for the same reason as they had recommended the prohibition of the reduction of stipulated daniages. The recommended new article became C.Q. 1135.

The *ancien droit*'s rules on lesion had been restricted by the French code.[20] The Commissioners followed the Code Napoléon in restricting the rescission of contracts on the ground of lesion, and even extended this restriction. Thus, the Commissioners recommended that minors should not be restored for lesion if all the relevant solemnities provided by law for the alienation of their property had been carried out:[21] in this, the rule of C.N. 13114 was adopted. As regards adults, the Commissioners recommended that they never be able to rescind contracts on the grounds of lesion: this amendment was adopted and became C.Q. 1012. This went beyond article 1313 of the French code. The Commissioners made the following revealing remarks. Their action, they said, "may be easily shewn to be more consistent with the circumstances and the state of society in this country than the old rule".[22] They state:

---

[19] *First Report*, p. 18.

[20] See Pothier, *T.O.*, pp. 20–22 (nos. 33–39); Pothier, *T.V.*, pp. 139–156 (nos. 330–371); C.N. 1304–1314. See C.N. 1313 referring to C.N. 1674–1675. See *supra*, chap. 6, discussion at notes 6–17.

[21] *First Report*, p. 12.

[22] *Ibid.*

> [T]here seems to be no sound reason upon which in this country, where real property is transferred so easily and made an object of daily speculation, a person in the full exercise of his rights should be relieved from imprudence in this description of contract more than in any other. *The rule violates that integrity of contracts upon which the Commissioners throughout the title have been anxious to insist and they have no hesitation in recommending the adoption of the article suggested by them in amendment of the present law.*[23]

Here the Commissioners have provided rules embodying the notion of *pacta sunt servanda* because of their belief in economic liberalism. Thus, in the section on rescission of sale for lesion, the C.N. has articles 1674 to 1685 inclusive, whereas the C.Q. has only one article, 1561, which merely refers to the section of the D.O. presently under discussion.

The Quebec redactors obviously sought to change the law to favour economic liberalism by imposing rules that favoured freedom and sanctity of contract. They thought this was necessary given the nature of economic life in Quebec. Hence, the redactors' statement on contract shows that in this area of the law the redactors strived to shape the law to fit socio-economic "reality". They recognized that land was now as marketable a commodity as any moveable and that there could be no longer a "just price". (This change possibly also reflects the fact that for the merchant classes of Quebec, but not of course for the peasant farmers, land no longer necessarily represented wealth: it might be a means to acquire wealth through speculation, but in the developing industrial economy of North America wealth was measured in money rather than land, and money did not depend on land.) Further, the redactors were also adopting the economic and legal theories of their time.[24]

A similar emphasis on the free and easy disposal of property, and certainty of rights and claims may be found in the reforms in the law of prescription, registration and in the transfer of property. In the last, the old rule, *traditionibus non nudis pactis dominia rerum transferuntur*, was abolished in favour of the

---

[23] *Ibid.* (emphasis added).

[24] See *ibid.*, p. 18: "it is certain that the doctrine of judicial interference with the plain meaning of contracts is regarded with disfavor by modern jurists." It is interesting to note that reversal of the Quebec law here recommended by the new Draft Civil Code. Book 5, title 1, chapter one contains an article (37) reintroducing a broad notion of lesion: "Lesion vitiates consent when it results from the exploitation of one of the parties by the other, and brings about a serious disproportion between the prestations of the contract. Serious disproportion creates a presumption of exploitation." Civil Code Revision Office, *Report on The Québec Civil Code*, Quebec, Editeur Officiel, 1977, vol. 1, p. 337; vol. 2/2, pp. 604–605 discusses this article, stating (p. 605): "Recognition of lesion is part of the tendency in modern legislation to protect one party against explointation by another." See also *ibid.*, vol. 2/2, pp. 551–553, where (at p. 551) it states: "From an economic standpoint, and on the basis of juridical morality, it was the State's duty to intervene in order to maintain equity in the juridicial relations between its citizens, or even to re-establish equity."

French code's rule that consent suffices to transfer property.[25] Reforms in the law of testamentary succession also encouraged the easy disposal of property. In all these reforms, as in the reforms on obligations, the redactors were attempting to fit the law to society and to render the law on these matters appropriate to a modern commercial country. What must be emphasized is that the codifiers stressed the integrity of contracts, and limited in so far as possible judicial interference with bargains;[26] and, further, the redactors stressed that immoveable property changed hands frequently in Quebec, and accordingly considered the law should facilitate such transfers.[27]

The above examples relate to obvious commercial matters, where the redactors were seeking to adapt the law to the economic ideology of their period. In some other articles, one can trace a similar attempt to fit the law to the circumstances of Quebec.[28] Thus, in the law on usufruct, there had always been a prohibition on the falling of trees in a usufruct of land, apart from in certain clearly specified exceptions. One of the rights of a usufructuary was to use for firewood wood from trees accidentally uprooted or broken down. The Codification Commissioners extended this rule so that the last section of C.Q. 456 now states that the usufructury "may even fell trees for fuel if there be any of the kind generally used in the locality for that purpose". Fuel would of course be of prime importance in a country with the fierce North American winter; and the Commissioners comment:

> The addition, which is not found in the Code [Napoléon], has been considered as necessary in a country where, as in this, fuel is of so great importance, at the same time that, in certain places it is found in great abundance, whilst in others it is scarce and difficult to be obtained.[29]

The Commissioners did not present this as an amendment of the existing law, since they considered that it accorded with the usage and jurisprudence of the country. What is important here is that the redactors attempted to fit the law to the physical conditions of Quebec.

Another interesting example of the attempt to fit the law to the circumstances of the country appears in C.Q. 503 in relation to running water. In C.N. 644, the equivalent article, a proprietor of land is said to be able to use

---

[25] C.Q. 1025: see C.N. 1583 and C.L. 1903. The redactors pointed out that the same rule applied in England.

[26] See *Fourth Report*, p. 16 where a provision is stated to be "consistent with the principle of maintaining the integrity of contracts, observed throughout by Commissioners . . ."; and also p. 18: "These articles . . . harmonize with the system of adhering to contracts and preventing the modification and enlargement of them by the courts."

[27] *Fourth Report*, p. 16: "The inconvenience of such a rule [as to title where price unpaid] especially where immoveable property changes hands so frequently as in this country, is obvious."

[28] E.F. Surveyor, "La province de Québec et le Code civil français", 12 *La Revue Légale* (new series) (1906), pp. 12–17 at pp. 14–15 lists major changes.

[29] *Third Report*, p. 377.

running water crossing his land *only for the purpose of irrigation*. The Quebec codifiers did not follow this, arguing that *any* use of the water for the benefit of the land should be allowed, provided that such use were not to interfere with the rights of other proprietors to use the water. The new article "appeared to the Commissioners to be more, than that of the Code [Napoléon], applicable to the circumstances of this country, where what is called in France irrigation is very little or not at all practiced."[30]

Further examples of the codifiers' attempts to fit the law to the circumstances of life in Quebec could be supplied;[31] but these few are sufficient to demonstrate the point. It has, however, been pointed out in chapter four that many of the provisions relating to family embodied in the Code could have been amended by using sources available to the redactors, such amendments being more in tune with family life in the province. Detailed reasons for the rejection of such potentially useful reforms have been set out in chapter four, and we need not repeat them here, bar to remark that the Quebec codification was in some ways conservative in nature, while the existing rules on the family were supported by an ideology of supremacy of husbands and fathers and by a strong conservative family tradition. On the other hand, the rules restricting easy transfer of property and interfering with contractual liberty were antithetical to actual commerce and to the dominant ideology of economic liberalism. The laws on employment were also modernized, but modernized on the basis of existing sources. This is also an important point: all the reforms in contract, and transference of property were "borrowed" from source materials to hand. The codifiers attempted, using the materials they had, to modernize their law; but these materials, while suggesting amendments, could also limit modernization, since amendments generally could only be suggested by the source materials consulted: the codifiers did not attempt, to any appreciable extent, to make up their own new provisions.

THE SOURCES USED

As will have been seen from chapters four and five, the redactors used a great variety of sources. The 1804 Code Napoléon, the 1825 Civil Code of Louisiana,[32] writers on the *droit coutumier* and *droit écrit*, the *Corpus iuris civilis*, civilian writers such as Voet, humanists such as Cujas, *jurisprudence*, *ordonnances*, statutes, the Code of the Swiss Canton Le Vaud, commentators on the French code, Scots, English and American writers (especially on

---

[30] See *ibid.*, p. 387, and also *ibid.*, p. 385.

[31] See McCord, Synopsis, *passim*.

[32] See J.P. Richert and E.S. Richert, "The Impact of the Civil Code of Louisiana upon the Civil Code of Quebec of 1866," 8 *Revue juridque Thémis* (1973), pp. 501–520.

commercial matters), Quebec cases: all these were consulted and referred to and could suggest what the law was or ought to be.[33]

Brierley has shown that the redactors constructed their code round a critique of the Code Napoléon, working from that code as a basic text.[34] Is it possible to tell how they sifted the mass of material available to them? We can, first of all, rely on the sources referred to with each article, since we know that these sources were those consulted in drawing up that article. From the frequency with which certain sources are cited, we can deduce that a standard procedure must have been to take each article of the Code Napoléon, and then, on its provision, consult certain works, such as those of Maleville and Toullier, the *Pandectes françaises*, and, above all, Pothier's treatises. The modern French commentators gave a critique of the Code Napoléon in operation: a critique that the redactors often accepted and drew up their own article accordingly.[35] Pothier was obviously not the only author on the *ancien droit* automatically consulted; but he was the most important. The next step, one may suggest, was that the redactors would follow any apparently interesting references in the works consulted. Thus, if, say, Maleville referred to Cujas, the redactors might examine Cujas. This is how some fairly unexpected authors come to be referred to. These authors were consulted only when works more regularly used referred to them. That this is what the redactors did is obvious if the sources cited are examined carefully. Similarly, often a text of the *Corpus iuris civilis* seems to have been cited only when an author consulted cited it. There is little point in attempting to demonstrate this further, although some instances have been pointed out in chapters four and five.[36]

---

[33] A. Morel, "L'apparition de la succession testamentaire", 26 *R.duB.* (1966), pp. 499–521 at p. 501 estimates more than 300 titles consulted; Brierley, "Codification", pp. 552–553.

[34] Brierley, "Codification", pp. 563–565; see *supra*, chap. 3, text at notes 321–435.

[35] Instances of this will have been noted, *supra*, in chaps. 4 and 5; but the following examples will serve as illustrations. The form of C.Q. 1600 seems to be the result of Marcadé's criticism of the C.N.: see *supra*, chap. 5, text at notes 288–301. C.Q. 1602's definition of *locateur* and *locataire* comes from the same source: see *supra*, chap. 5, text at notes 302–313. The rubric of the title on marriage covenants arises out of criticism of that of the C.N.: see *supra*, chap. 4, text at notes 792–793. The C.N. restricted a husband's power to donate community property; the C.Q. redactors rejected this innovation; the criticisms of Toullier were probably influential: see *supra*, chap. 4, text at notes 803–805. See the redactors' remarks on C.N. 1429 (husbands granting leases of their wives property), *supra*, chap. 4, text at notes 824–825, referring to commentators on the C.N. On the problems over the wording of C.N. 127, see *supra*, chap. 4, text at notes 907–913. For further examples, see *First Report*, p. 22: C.Q. 1118's improvement on C.N. 1214; and C.Q. 1121–1130's improvement on C.N. 1215–1217. The redactors say they adopted Marcadé's views. *Second Report*, p. 197: new rubric result of criticism of C.N.

[36] See *supra*, chap. 4, text at notes 954–955, where the redactors were apparently referred to Rousseaud de la Combe by Maleville, and also at notes 936–938 where their references to Pothier seem to have been suggested by *Fenet sur Pothier*. Further, see *supra*, chap. 5, note 291, where it is pointed out that Maleville referred the redactors to Cujas.

Some surprizing works seem to have influenced the redactors. For example, a nineteenth-century textbook on Roman law seems to have suggested one of the articles on *louage des services*.[37] The redactors did not consult only writers on the *droit coutumier*; thus, they used, for example, the work of Claude Serres, a writer on the *droit écrit*. He is referred to, for example, in respect of *tutelle*.[38]

All the above demonstrates that the redactors consulted works not only to find the existing law, but also to find possible provisions which could be useful for their elegance of expression or analysis and for potential reforms. In some areas of the law, notably obligations, there was no strong independent customary law tradition, and in these areas, generally derived from Roman law, the codifiers obviously felt free to research within the modern civilian tradition more generally, as well as examine the Roman texts themselves. This would explain why the redactors examined Voet's *Elementa iuris* and Ortolan's *Instituts* in considering *louage*. *Louage* was a contract derived from Roman law; Voet was one of the most distinguished of the modern civilians, while Ortolan's book was a modern textbook on the Roman law itself.[39]

There are many references to texts of the *Corpus iuris civilis*; it would be of interest to study them to find out if there is any particular reason why the redactors sometimes cited Roman texts. For example the Codification Commission had an obvious tendency in its *Reports* to bolster a view with a reference to Roman law. Thus, in adopting what became C.Q. 1043, and rejecting the possible amendment suggested by C.N. 1372, the redactors said: "The old rule is conformable to the principles of Roman law and ought to be preserved."[40] On article 1062, the redactors state that it is "not in the French code, but is taken from Pothier, as derived from the Roman law."[41] On the question of judicial reduction of damages, discussed above, one of the points against the *ancien droit* made by the redactors was that it "does not seem to have been derived from the Justinian code."[42] Although, this does not seem to have been the main reason for following the C.N., the fact that Roman law was mentioned at all is significant. Again, in preferring their own proposed article 1087, third paragraph, to C.N. 1182, the redactors stated: "The old rule is founded on Roman law and is unquestionably preferable to the modern one."[43] As regards the interdiction of prodigals, the redactors thought it important to remark that the old law, which they are following, is conformable to Roman

---

[37] See *supra*, chap. 5, text at notes 331–341, discussing C.Q. 1668.
[38] Cl. Serres, *Les institutions du droit françois, suivant l'ordre de celles de Justinien*, Paris, veuve Cavelier & fils, 1753; C.Q. 284 and 293. *Tutelle* in C.Q. followed the *droit coutumier*; that of the *droit écrit* was rather different.
[39] See *supra*, chap. 5, text at notes 288–301 and 331–341.
[40] *First Report*, p. 16.
[41] *Ibid.*
[42] *Ibid.*, p. 18.
[43] *Ibid.*, p. 20.

law, whereas the C.N. provision is not.[44] At the beginning of their discussion of their title on usufruct, the redactors stated: "The rules of usufruct, adopted by the Code Napoléon, and, in great measure, reproduced in the following articles, are, with a few exceptions, derived from Roman law and conformable to the old French jurisprudence"'[45] We also find the codifiers stating: "All the articles of this chapter [i.e. that on use and habitation] . . . are conformable to the Roman and to the new law, as also to the old French jurisprudence . . .."[46] We find article 560 described as conformable to the Roman law and the old jurisprudence, though differing from C.N. 704.[47] The French code had no provisions on emphyteusis, whereas Quebec has, and these provisions were described as "conformable to our jurisprudence, and almost exclusively taken from the Roman law".[48]

Roman texts have been cited in regard to some of the articles of the Quebec code studied in chapters four and five. In C.Q. 1418, 1419 and 1425, the redactors departed from the terms of the *ancien droit*: they appear to cite Roman texts and to stress the conformity of their articles to Roman law in order to support their copying of the C.N.[49] In respect of C.Q. 188, the redactors again seem to cite Roman provisions to support their departure from the *ancien droit*.[50] The redactors cite a Roman text in respect of C.Q. 84 on the domicile of servants: this citation was perhaps to support the redactors' following of the criticized provision of the French code, when the *ancient droit* was uncertain.[51]

More examples of the redactors' references to Roman law could be given; but this is unnecessary. One point to be noted is that when the redactors specifically refer to Roman law,[52] they always describe the Roman law as being the same or "conformable" to the old law or the C.N.: nowhere do they state that they are introducing a rule of Roman law purely because it is the Roman law. A second point is that the references to Roman law are generally unnecessary: since the redactors are codifying the *ancien droit* with amendments, to refer to a proposition as being derived from the *ancien droit* is sufficient, the references to Roman law are in a sense redundant. It is different, of course, when the mention that they are copying an article of the C.N. that differs from the *ancient droit*, and then cite a Roman text in its support: though they obviously are copying the French code, the Roman text is adduced to give extra authority. Were more time available, it would be interesting to explore this further to assess the accuracy of

---

[44] *Second Report*, p. 223.
[45] *Third Report*, p. 375.
[46] *Ibid.*, p. 383.
[47] *Ibid.*, p. 407.
[48] *Third Report*, p. 407.
[49] See *supra*, chap. 4, note 863.
[50] See *supra*, chap. 4, text at notes 1017–1020.
[51] See *supra*, chap. 5, text at notes 284–286.
[52] As distinct from merely citing a text under an article without comment.

the redactors' remarks and to examine all the articles under which Roman law is cited. What can be said is that the references show an attempt to bolster propositions of law with the prestige and authority of Roman law. One could also quote examples where the redactors stated that the law they were reducing to articles was contrary to Roman law.[53] This shows that the redactors felt it necessary to explain why they did not follow it: its prestige still counted.

The overall impact of texts of Justinian's Digest on the Quebec code is unclear, and no attempt has been made here to trace it. It may be stated that the references to Justinian's *Corpus iuris* examined in chapters four and five show that the texts have had no positive influence on the law in the code:[54] the redactors have not adopted any provisions from Roman law contrary to the *ancien droit* or the French code.[55] (This does not mean that other references not examined have not had an effect on the law—though I cannot spot any.) Any "Roman" provisions embodied in the code as here studied, have always come from other works: in adopting a "Roman" proposition of law, the redactors were following, for example, the *ancien droit*, and the fact that the proposition is ultimately of Roman origin is irrelevant. The knowledge that much of the law in force was of Roman origin combined with frequent references to Roman law in the authors the redactors studied, must have led the redactors to examine the Roman law, and to cite its texts from time to time; but it would appear that the Roman law proper has had little *direct* influence on the Quebec code.

One other potential source of provisions in the Code were the decisions of the Quebec courts. Surprizingly little use, however, was made of them. (It will have been noted that none were referred to in chapters four and five.) Professor Morel states that:

> Si l'on néglige le quatrième livre du Code, consacré en réalité aux lois commerciales, on ne peut retenir que 64 articles sur un total de 2277 qui compose les trois premiers livres où soient invoquées des decisions de nos tribunaux. Rarement, d'ailleurs, trouve-t-on plus d'un arrêt sous un même article: toute la jurisprudence canadienne que nous laissent connaître nos codifications se ramène á decisions, dont quelques-unes sont reprises à deux occasions differentes.[56]

Indeed, court decisions were not used to any great extent even in the fourth book, that on commercial law, since Brierley informs us that only 95 decisions are cited in *all* the *Reports*.[57]

Since in chapters four and five we have not met with any refernces to Quebec cases, nothing will be said here as to their use by the redactors. We

---

[53] *First Report*, p. 16; *Second Report*, p. 203; *Third Report*, p. 403. More examples could be given.
[54] See as well as *supra*, notes 48–50; *supra*, chap. 4 notes 1099 and1104.
[55] Cf. Louisiana: see *supra*, chap. 6, text at notes 62–66.
[56] Morel, *op. cit. supra* note 33, p. 502. See also *infra*, note 58.
[57] Brierley, "Codification", p. 551 n. 87.

may, however, comment generally on the lack of citations. By the time of codification, relatively few volumes of reports had yet been published;[58] this undoubtedly would depress the potential importance of court decisions as a source. Further, the method adopted for codifying the law, as discussed above, would tend to emphasize doctinal writings at the expense of court decisions. Doctrinal writings tend to give a complete synthesis of the law grouped in convenient classifications; court decisions, on the other hand, tend to turn on one or two points, do not give convenient syntheses of the law, and, being scattered through volumes collected generally by year, would not be convenient to use. Indeed the redactors make this very point.[59] The Codification Commission referred to several French *recueils* and *répertoires* of *jurisprudence*, such as those of Denisart, Merlin, and Guyot: in contrast, these would be convenient to use, purely by reason of their organization of the material. These are, of course, only suggestions, a thorough examination and analysis of cited court decisions and their relationship to the articles though instructive is outwith the scope of this work. Morel examined the influence of court decisions on testamentary succession in the Code;[60] it is perhaps significant that decisions were important in this area of the law, introduced by statute and somewhat different from the *ancien droit.* Cases *had* to be used, since the writers on the *ancien droit* did not deal with the matter in a relevant fashion.

It has been pointed out that the redactors also used English, American, and Scots writers. These authors were mainly relied on in the book on commercial law;[61] accordingly, they have not featured in the discussion in chapters four and five. That these authors should have been used in these areas of law and not in others is worthy of comment. In the "traditional" areas of private law—property, obligations, family—the redactors did not consider that Erskine, Bell, Kent, or Blackstone had anything useful to tell them, or could suggest new insights or useful wording. (Compare with this the use of Blackstone in the 1808 Louisiana Digest.) In a sense, the action of the redactors is hardly surprizing: they had been instructed to codify the law in force, and it would have been difficult to argue that these Anglo-American and Scots authors stated the private law in force in Lower Canada; similarly, these authors would not provide useful models, the French code being pre-eminent in this respect. The nature of commercial law in the province encouraged the use of these Anglo-American and Scots authors.

To show some of the reasons for the use of the Anglo-American and Scots authorities, it is necessary first to set out briefly the nature of the Fourth Book of the Quebec Code. The redactors recognized that many of the provisions on

---

[58] At *ibid.*, Brierley states that 32 volumes were available by 1865.

[59] See *Seventh Report*, p. 216 where, on commercial law, the redactors state that they refer to jurists and textwriters as more covenient than to the cases on which their opinions were based.

[60] See Morel, *op. cit. supra* note 33, *passim.*

[61] Walton, *op. cit. supra* note 2, pp. 139–147 shows where these authors were used.

contracts in the third book affected trade no less than private transactions.[62] Descending from the Roman law, these contracts were part of the traditional law on obligations of the civil law of Europe. Nonetheless, these traditional contracts did not fully cover the complexity of the legal transactions necessary in a modern commercial society. In France, the *Code de commerce* provided for the purely commercial aspects of the law (such as shipping and bills of exchange). The 1808 Louisiana Digest provided no regulation of purely mercantile affairs, and the Louisiana courts had initially tended to utilize the Castilian law in this respect. The Quebec redactors provided a fourth book to cover commercial law, and in this departed from the scheme of the Code Napoléon. They were, however, following the instructions of the legislature.[63] After recounting that the contracts in Book Three also *could* pertain to commercial law, the Codification Commission stated:

> [T]here remains a class of subjects which so exclusively belong to the law merchant that it has been necessary to collect the rules concerning them under a distinct general heading, and for that purpose add another to the three great divisions of the French code.[64]

It is telling that the codifiers followed this with the comment that this is a class of subjects on which the law is less fixed than on others in the code.[65]

The redactors stated that some rules of commercial law may be found in statutes or the French *Ordonnances*; but that much is to be sought only in usage and jurisprudence, and that the Quebec system ("if system it may be called") has been borrowed indiscriminately partly from France and partly from England.[66] They stressed that there is no orderly design and regular practices are the result of tacit usage. They therefore concluded that the system of usage should be left as such to be developed by interpretation and modification when necessary. They declared:

> This course is consistent with the history and character of commercial law in all countries. It has always begun in usage, and positive legislation has done little more than to follow, and to declare the general and fundamental rules which such usages has originated.[67]

They stated that such caution is even more necessary in Quebec than in an "older and more developed" country.

From the above, we can see that the redactors felt that there should be the minimum of regulation in commercial law: business practices should be allowed

---

[62] *Seventh Report*, p. 214.
[63] C.S.L.C., ch. 2, s. 4: see *supra*, chap. 3, note 385 for reference.
[64] *Seventh Report*, p. 214.
[65] *Ibid.*
[66] *Ibid.*
[67] *Ibid.*, p. 216.

to develop on their own as much as possible, with legislation only on certain key or core points. They further stated that established usages in Quebec were drawn from both French and English practice. The redactors commented later that they cited not only the old and modern law of France and the law of England but also Scots and American jurists and continental law. They stated that no difficulty arises from doing so, because "the laws of commerce are of universal application".[68]

It becomes obvious why the redactors consulted these non-French sources in Book Four. They felt it better to leave the law fairly general. The law merchant was universal. English law already influenced current commercial usages. These three considerations allowed the redactors freedom in selection of sources for consultation. Nonetheless, they limited this freedom, in that they considered they had to try, as best they could, to state the existing law. Thus, we find them stating that a treatise of Pothier cannot be used because it was based on a 1673 ordinance that most people regarded as not having been received in Lower Canada.[69] (This dispute over the legal status of Royal ordinances will be recalled.)[70] The new French *Code de commerce* ought to have been ignored for the same reason as Pothier's treatise was ignored: its provisions could never have been regarded as the law of Lower Canada. Yet an important consideration supported the redactors in their use of the modern French law—its *modern* nature. This suggests that had the redactors had a use for this treatise of Pothier, they would have used it anyway.

There is another reson why the argument for ignoring Pothier's treatise is not totally convincing. If we turn to that section of the *Report* dealing with maritime law, we find a brief history of maritime law from the *lex Rhodia de iactu* onwards. The 1681 *Code de la marine* is praised highly, and the redactors state that it gave maritime law to a large portion of the continent and to England.[71] They go on to say that it cannot have had force in Quebec, first, because of the problematic nature of the validity of such Royal legislation in Quebec, and second, because the change in sovereignty would have done away with the old admiralty law anyway. Nonetheless, the redactors use this French legislation to a very considerable extent because they regarded it as written reason of universal sanction and authority, even though the *Code de la marine* was not registered in Quebec.[72] We can accordingly see that the redactors could easily have defined any of the French ordinances as written reason and used them in the code, had they so wished.

Thus, though the redactors were willing to reject some sources as not being in force in Quebec, they were willing to classify other sources as written reason

---

[68] *Ibid.*, p. 216.
[69] *Ibid.*
[70] See *supra*, chap. 3, text at notes 324–325.
[71] *Seventh Report*, p. 224.
[72] *Ibid.*, p. 226. Cf. Walton, *op. cit. supra* note 2, p. 139.

and draw on them for their code. The argument could be turned to favour the Anglo-American and Scots sources: they, if required, could be defined as written reason expressing the universal law merchant. What was obviously of importance was the *modernity* and utility of the source: thus the use of the *Code de commerce*. This stress on modernity would influence the redactors in their use of contemporary English, American and Scots law. Indeed, the Commissioners explicitly state that the courts refer more to modern French law and the English law (in commercial cases) rather than the *ancien droit*,

> from the want of completeness and full adaption [of the *ancien droit*] which an extended commerce and enlarged jurisprudence have given to the law of the present day, and not less from absence of treatises of a character to fix as a system the law of that earlier period.[73]

In Bell, Story, and the like, the Commissioners found a modern comprehensive statement of commercial law; a *necessary* modern statement, as the *ancien droit* dealt with a society where commerce was not so highly developed as in mid-nineteenth-century Quebec.

The reasons why the Anglo-American and Scots textbooks were used so extensively in the Fourth Book are now obvious, as are the reasons why they were only used in the Fourth Book. The *nature* of commercial law demanded this use; the modernity of these sources facilitated their use, while equitable principles of the universal law merchant could be relied on to validate any references. We also find that the Commissioners regarded the Scots law as being often analogous to that of Quebec; they accordingly frequently referred to Bell's *Commentaries*.[74] These reasons for the use of these sources would not be applicable when other areas of the code were considered. In other areas there was a strong French tradition: the laws were certain and fixed except in so far as the French sources themselves gave differing views. There could be no possible argument for reference to the Anglo-American law by reason of its modernity; the French code was far more modern in its provisions and exposition of the law.

We can conclude this general section on how the redactors used the sources available to them by commenting that by far and away the bulk of the code was culled by the redactors from the writings of French jurists of the *ancien* régime, writings which the redactors synthesized using the French code; the French code itself, as commented on by the modern jurists, suggested provisions. Much of the Code Napoléon could be taken (and was so taken by the redactors in Quebec) as the expression of the *ancien droit* in a modern synthesis. This synthesis the redactors compared with the *ancien droit* and the criticisms of the

---

[73] *Seventh Report*, p. 216.

[74] *Ibid.*, p. 230: "The Scotch law, which is exposed by Bell with his usual precision and clearness, has been consulted as analogous to our own." See also Walton, *op. cit. supra* note 2, pp. 140–146, for an account of the use of Bell.

modern commentators; they drew up their own code on the basis of this sustained critical evaluation of the French code, selecting their provisions as they saw fit, whether the reasons behind the selection were legal conservatism, a support for economic liberalism, or whatever. (Chapters four and five will have shown to some extent the reasons behind selections; these reasons will be discussed further *infra*.)[75]

PROMULGATION OF THE CIVIL CODE OF LOWER CANADA

Prominent in the discussion of the Louisiana Digest of 1808 has been the vexed question of the Digest's relationship to the pre-existing law. This question arose because of disputes over the nature of the Digest as a "code". No such dispute exists over the Quebec code; no one doubts its nature as an authentic code in the modern civilian tradition, and we thus need not discuss the interpretation of the code by the courts. The Quebec redactors, in a passage concluding their *Seventh Report*, urging caution in legislative amendment of the code, put forward their own view of the code. It concisely expresses the nature of a modern civilian code:

> The Code is intended to cover, either by express terms or by legal implication, all questions belonging to the wide range of subjects with which it deals. It constitutes a system, with careful adaption of its different parts to each other, and any fragmentary legislation, with a view to particular changes, may seriously affect parts of the work not intended to he touched, and lead to great and unforeseen derangement and confusions.[76]

The codifiers thought that their code was a unified whole composed of interrelating and interpenetrating legal propositions, capable of extension by reasoning to cover circumstances for which there were no express provisions.

Nonetheless, the redactors did consider the question of the relationship of the Code to the old law; and to explain this relationship, they inserted at the end a general article, 2613, applicable to the whole Code.[77] It provided:

> The laws in force at the time of coming into force of this code are abrogated in all cases:
>
> In which there is a provision herein having expressly or impliedly that effect;
>
> In which such laws are contrary to or inconsistent with any provisions herein contained;
>
> In which express provision is herein made upon the particular matter to which such laws relate . . ..[78]

---

[75] See *infra*, chap. 8.

[76] *Seventh Report*, p. 262.

[77] *Supplementary Report*, p. 369.

It should be read along with article 2615:

> If in any article of this code founded on the laws existing at the time of its promulgation, there be a difference between the English and French texts, that version shall prevail which is most consistent with the provisions of the existing laws on which the article is founded; and if there be any such difference in an article changing the existing laws, that version shall prevail which is most consistent with the intention of the article, and the ordinary rules of legal interpretation shall apply in determining such intention.

From these two articles, it can be clearly seen that the redactors still considered the pre-codification law as applicable in interpreting the code: the old law was not totally abrogated, and had potential utility.[79] As Brierley points out, this means that the Quebec code was not to be the exclusive source of Quebec private law: it is only the primary source in a hierarchy of sources.[80] The former law still had a secondary role to play: the use of the pre-codification authority to interpret the code is known even for the Code Napoléon, though for that code, use of such authority is more *imperio rationis* than *ratione imperii*, while the pre-codification law in Quebec still has some formal force.[81] In effect, the position of the Quebec code vis-à-vis the old law is not so radically different from the position of the 1808 Digest, and shows that those scholars who deny the Digest the status of "code" are blinded by the almost complete abrogation of the *ancient droit* in the promulgation of the French code: they thus do not see that each codification may be unique in its effect on the previous law.[82] However this may be, the important point is that the Quebec redactors did not envisage their codification as a point of rupture from the old law, except in so far as its provisions amended or abolished that law; but rather, they viewed it as a continuation and restatement of the old law. They nonetheless did innovate and consciously select among provisions; and their code is in some essential sense—even if only in that of providing a synthesis—new law. As was stressed at the beginning of this chapter, the Civil Code of Lower Canada resembles the Code Napoléon far more than it does the *ancien droit*. To argue that it has remained truer to the pure spirit of the *ancien droit* would be pointless. The Quebec code is a true nineteenth-century code, and the genuine offspring of the French code.

---

[78] The code concludes with a short general section of three articles: 2613–2615. For our purposes, C.Q. 2614 is irrelevant.

[79] Brierley, "Codification", pp. 556–558; P.B. Mignault, *Le Droit Civil Canadien*, Montreal, Whiteford & Théoret, 1895, vol. 1, pp. 51–55. Mignault, *ibid.*, vol. 1, p. 52, remarks: "[I]l n'y a pas, à proprement parler, de droit ancien ni de droit noveau en cette province." See also Walton, *op. cit. supra* note 2, pp. 80–131; P.B. Mignault, "Le Code civil de la province de Québec et son interprétation", 1 *University of Toronto Law Journal* (1935), pp. 104–136.

[80] *Codification*, pp. 557–578.

[81] One thinks of Fenet on Pothier. Maleville, the *Pandectes françaises* and other early commentators also referred to the *ancien droit* in their explication of the C.N.

[82] See *supra,* chaps. 1, 3 and 6, *passim.*

CONCLUSIONS ON THE CIVIL CODE OF LOWER CANADA

As discussed in chapter three, the Quebec code was the product of the need felt for a useful synthesis of the law in both of the languages of the Province. The existing sources of private law were numerous and confused; and the whole was in need of rationalization. It is unnecessary to explore this in any greater detail because of Brierley's work.[83] It is just possibile that a fear of the introduction of common law was instrumental in supporting the idea of codification; but the evidence for this is slight. It would seem that, at the time of codification, the French Canadian laws were secure and unlikely to be abrogated; and all the available evidence suggests that the "legal or technical factors", in Brierley's phrase, were what primarily brought about codification. It cannot be doubted, however, that the protection of their laws was dear to French Canadian hearts.

Brierley highlights the point that it is quite remarkable that, in the early period, there had been no advocacy of codification "simply as a measure of intelligent reform".[84] In the next chapter, we will consider the respective timings of the Quebec and Louisiana codifications; but it is important to point out here that Brierley's statement that codification was not publicly advocated until 1846 is not quite accurate. I have discovered two other references to codification before this date, and they will be considered in the next chapter. It is appropriate to say here, however, that for various reasons codification was not seriously considered until the period of union of the two Canadas.

We have seen that the redactors of the code considered their task to be as much as possible to codify the existing law, using the French code as a model, while drawing inspiration also from the 1825 code of Louisiana. They carried out their work by means of a critique of the French code, as already explained, and, because of their method of working, were always able to consider many possible amendments of the law. Further, as they themselves realized, even deciding what was the law actually in force involved them in a process of selection, a selection which they tried to fit, according to their own account, to the state of the Province.[85] It will have been seen that, as regards the law of obligations, the redactors innovated in a very important way to promote security and freedom of contract. Freedom of contract was in line with the dominant contemporary ideology of economic liberalism. Similar influences seem to have affected their choice of provisions on the transfer of property, registration of title, and the like. These innovations were of immense importance and give the 1866 code an obvious nineteenth-century appearance. If we consider the material covered in detail in chapters four and five, a rather different picture

---

[83] Brierley, "Codification", pp. 526–542; see *supra*, chap. 3, text at notes 386–399.
[84] Brierley, "Codification", pp. 529–30.
[85] See *supra*, text at notes 12–31; and *supra*, chap 3, text at notes 423–429.

emerges, however. The laws on family were very traditional and not obviously fitted to the state of the province: the redactors, with the material available to them, could have selected provisions more suitable to Provincial life. They preserved the old law; this preservation of the old law was—certainly as regards *puissance maritale*—supported by current ideology. Similarly, the provisions on employment, while in line with the ideas of classic contractual freedom current in the Province, were obviously inadequate for an industrializing society.

One important point is that virtually all the provisions considered above were drawn from other sources. The innovations promoting freedom and security of contract were largely taken from the French code (though amended in transplantation); the conservative provisions on family were taken from the *ancien droit*. Very little was made up by the redactors. For example, the improved definition of *louage* to take account of *bail à cheptel* was suggested by Marcadé. The codifiers might have researched widely for what they considered suitable law; but their research was restricted by the materials available to them, and by the fact that they themselves deliberately excluded certain materials from their research. For example, the redactors did not consider that Blackstone might have had provisions on family law that they might usefully have borrowed. It should be remembered that although the redactors were instructed to codify the laws in force, their conservatism in family law was not imposed. The fact that they felt free to innovate in contract means that they could have proposed (in theory at least) a substantial reform of family law; that they obviously *never* even considered such a reform is significant. The redactors' indebtedness to other legal systems for innovation is all-pervasive. Thus it is doubtful if they would have considered the amalgamation of mandate and lease and hire of services had not Marcadé pointed out that the Austrian code, the *Allgemeines bürgerliches Gesetzbuch*, had chosen to treat all services paid for as objects, never of mandate, but *always* of lease and hire.[86]

We may conclude that the Quebec code of 1866 provided the Province with a rationalized and modernized system of private law. The code is in many ways something completely new and unique, although this uniqueness is the result of a redaction drawing on many different sources. The Commissioners for Codification in Quebec borrowed extensively to draw up their own new code. There are few articles that cannot be traced to some definite source. The Quebec code is original in that it is a new assemblage of old provisions garnered from many sources, through a process of selection by the codifiers.

---

[86] *Sixth Report*, p. 8; see *supra*, chap. 5, text at notes 272–280.

8

CONCLUSION

Codification, Lawmaking and Legal Change

Codification

Both the Civil Code of Lower Canada of 1866 and the Digest of Orleans of 1808 are transplanted or borrowed codes.[1] The codifiers utilized a foreign code both as a model and as a quarry of accessible and readily borrowable provisions. Both codes are obvious offspring of the 1804 Code Napoléon. Indeed, very many codes either are borrowed from other countries or are heavily influenced by foreign codes.[2] The form of a code seems to facilitate borrowing. That is, the arrangement of the law into concise propositions forming a coherent whole of relatively short length is easy to borrow wholesale and is attractive because of its rational, logical structure. For most of the nineteenth century, the Code Napoléon was the archetypal code, the paradigm copied by countries as diverse as Italy (1865) and Haiti (1825).[3]

We can say that the Quebec and Louisiana codes are both borrowed codes; but this does not mean they are necessarily slavish, unthinking copies. In fact, as will have been seen, both codes deviate in certain areas from the French code: this is as regards both substantive provisions and topics chosen or arrangement. From this we can deduce that any copying was deliberate: the redactors appear always to have considered alternatives and to have assessed the "suitability" (by their own criteria) of the Code Napoléon. There is sufficient evidence for us to assume that radical changes in the law made by codification were in fact quite deliberate.

The lack of originality in codification is worth stressing. Very many codes have been adopted from other countries, or if not, have been influenced as regards individual provisions or institutions by the law of other countries. Lack of originality is also betrayed by the use of existing material for the confection

---

[1] Watson, *Society*, p. 136.

[2] *Ibid.*; A. Watson, *The Nature of Law*, Edinburgh, Edinburgh University Press, 1977, pp. 107–108.

[3] A.-N. Léger, "De l'influence du Code Napoléon à Haiti, et des differences de legislation civile entre la France et Haiti", in *Le droit civil français: livre-souvenir des journées du droit civil français*, Montreal and Paris, Recueil Sirey, 1936, pp. 755–815. See also *supra*, chap. 6, text at notes 88–90.

of codes. *As a code*, the Code Napoléon is new; but much of it is composed of old material.[4] The old material is combined to make something new (i.e. a code); but there is no necessity for a code to introduce sweeping changes in the law, although it may well do so.

In many respects both the 1866 Quebec code and the 1808 Digest are different from their model(s). These differences do not indicate originality in composing provisions by redactors, as the provisions are generally drawn from other sources, but rather originality in putting old sources together in a new way. (Similarly, of course, much of the Code Napoléon is composed of old provisions combined in a new way.) What is most relevant here is why the redactors selected the provisions they did.

This brings us to an important consideration: that of sources. We have noted that the redactors of the 1808 Digest were willing to rely on Blackstone in traditional areas of private law, while, in these traditional areas, the Quebec codifiers used only French and civilian sources. How can we account for this difference? The reason why the Quebec redactors did not utilize common law sources in these areas must have been their consciousness that their task was to codify the law in force. Blackstone, for example, would be understood as unlikely to suggest any useful, borrowable, improvements or provisions. From our examination of the areas of the Louisiana law in which Blackstone was used, we can state, as a general rule, that the provisions taken from Blackstone were not such as to modify the system of the modern civil law, but, rather, such as would harmonize with it and cover a situation which the redactors felt required a legal provision. If, for example, we look at the use of Blackstone's texts in the section of the Digest dealing with apprentices, we find that Blackstone provided a series of propositions of law which were useful and could be borrowed without difficulty and without doing violence to the system of the civilian code. It should also be recalled that the Digest redactors were more adventurous than their Quebec equivalents and innovated more freely (perhaps because of their natural-law philosophy and approach). Another point to be considered is that, for the redactors of the Digest, Justinian's compilation was still a living source of law, whereas for Quebec, despite references to the Roman laws, it does not appear that the *Corpus iuris* was a living source. This could be because of the more adventurous spirit of the Louisiana redactors and because the Castilian law authorized the Roman law to be used as a source *imperio rationis*. (Although the Roman provisions selected for governing the seashore as pointed out above are not particularly sensible.) The Quebec redactors appear to have used the Roman law in their *Reports* to bolster decisions already made, whereas the Louisiana redactors used it as a quarry for potential provisions. (It was of course feasible for the Quebec redactors to have incorporated Roman provisions; but they do not appear to have done so.)

Three points arise out of the foregoing brief discussion of sources. First, redactors may use sources that are not part of their traditional law, but which

---

[4] As its compilers recognized.

may be fitted into its structure. The Digest redactors used Blackstone because he provided inspiration and also wording that could usefully be incorporated into their system of law, not because they wished to introduce English law. They could regard Blackstone's propositions as general statements of universally valid law. Second, redactors may reject sources for ideological reasons. The Quebec codifiers did not consider Blackstone as a source in the law of persons *because* he was a common lawyer. They would fear the introduction of common law—and the preservation of the civil law was an emotive topic in French Canada. (Their anxieties were reasonable: consider the problems caused by the use of the term "consideration" in the code.)[5] Third, the prestige of a legal system may influence redactors: thus, the prestige of the Code Napoléon influenced both the Quebec and Louisiana redactors, while, similarly, the Quebec redactors used Roman law to support their decisions, although it does not appear to have been an effective cause of those decisions.

Both the 1808 Digest and the 1866 Quebec code are offspring of the French code, yet nearly 60 years separate them. Why did Quebec codify only in 1866, while Louisiana codified in 1808? The reasons for this difference must be sought in the histories of the two jurisdictions.

In Louisiana, the purchase of the Territory by the U.S. brought legal confusion. The early period of the U.S. administration seems to have seen a revival of the French law alongside the Castilian.[6] An 1805 court decision had decided that the French, Roman, and Spanish laws were the laws in force.[7] At the same time, the U.S. administration hoped for a reception of the common law in the newly acquired Territory.[8] Both to settle the confusion over which were the authoritative sources of law, and to help forestall the possible introduction of the common law, the territorial legislature passed a bill stating which sources of law were authoritative.[9] Governor Claiborne vetoed it. In the same year the legislature appointed Brown and Moreau Lislet to prepare a code.[10] For various reasons, investigated by Dargo, Claiborne allowed the redaction of the Digest.[11] Thus, a desire both to settle the laws in force and to prevent reception of the common law seems to have motivated the redaction of the Digest in 1808 and influenced the codifiers.

Brierley expresses surprise at the lateness of codification in Quebec and at the fact no one seems to have considered codifying the Quebec laws until the 1840s.[12] This may be explained though examination of the history of the Province in the first half of the nineteenth century.

---

[5] See C.Q. 984 and 989. It seems likely that Day only intended to use an alternative form of expression for *cause*; he did not intend to introduce the English doctrine of consideration. See *First Report*, p. 10; Brierley, "Codification", p. 564.
[6] See *supra*, chap. 3, text at notes 156–170.
[7] See *supra*, chap. 3, text at notes 168–169.
[8] See above all, Dargo, *Jefferson's Louisiana*, *passim*, esp. at pp. 105–153.
[9] *Ibid.*, pp. 136, 146.
[10] *Ibid.*, p. 141.
[11] *Ibid.*, pp. 141–153 and 154–160.
[12] Brierley, "Codification", pp. 529–30.

The period leading up to the unification of the two Canadas in 1840 had been one of great political strife, culminating in the rebellions of 1837 and 1838. One point at issue was the Quebec civil law. It is undoubtedly the case that many of the anglophone inhabitants of Lower Canada wished for the introduction of the English common law. As pointed out in chapter three, the Canada Tenures Act, s. 8, appeared to mean that some areas of English law were applicable in Quebec, causing the law to seem confused. The French Canadians in the 1820s feared for the preservation of their law, while the anglophones apparently wished its abolition. The question of codification appears briefly in the evidence given by John Neilson before the Parliamentary Select Committee on the Civil Government of Canada. Neilson remarked that in Louisiana "they have adopted a code very much like the Code Civile [*sic*]; and if there were a code drawn up, there would be no objection to the laws in Lower Canada, for the objections arise more from ignorance than any thing else."[13] Neilson's remark is in the nature of an aside: codification does not seem to have been seriously considered.

First, given the confused state of the law, the partial introduction of aspects of English law, and the fact that the judges were in general common-law trained, it is conceivable that any attempt to codify would have been construed by French-Canadians as an attempt to introduce the common law or to preserve those aspects of the common law already introduced. Papineau forcibly expressed this anxiety in 1832. In a speech devoted to the legal system and laws, and reported *in La Minerve*, he said:

> La rédaction d'un code de nos lois ne peut dans ce moment-ci offrir de grands bienfaits parce que nous avons des juges politiques qui maîtrisent les déliberations des conseils. . . .
>
> L'état de la Louisiane . . . nous offre quelqu' analogie par rapport aux systèmes de lois qui y ont prévalu. On a senti la nécessité d'un refaite et dans le travail on a taché de se rapprocher autant que possible du Code-Napoléon, monument de législation le plus vaste, le plus judicieux qui ait été donné à l'humanité. Tandis que l'on poursuivant ce grand travail qui devait entraîner de si grands avantages, ici on a voulu introduire la masse de la jurisprudence anglaises que les Anglais eux-mêmes malgré leur partialité national qui leur a fait admirer l'exagération tout ce qu'ils ont de bon, reconnaissent pour être le code civil le plus imparfait d'Europe.[14]

Given the applicability of some aspects of English law in some areas of Quebec, given what was seen as the ignorance of the judges and their partiality for common law, it is hardly surprising that no moves were made to

[13] G.B. Parliament, Select Committee on the Civil Government of Canada, *Report, 22 July, 1828*, p. 97 [in Parliamentary Papers 1828, vol. 7: pp. 3–13 (*Report*), pp. 14–321 (*Minutes of Evidence*), pp. 322–359 (*Appendix*)].

[14] L.J. Papineau, *Papineau: textes choisis et présentés par F. Ouellet*, Quebec, presses de l'université Laval, 1970, p. 41.

sort the legal confusion through codification, lest the English law be introduced in the process of codifying.[15]

Second, the 1820s and 1830s were periods of political and constitutional upheaval in Lower Canada, with constant conflict between the elected Assembly and the Government of the Province. For much of this time the Assembly was prorogued, because of its refusal to pass Appropriation Acts. Undoubtedly, the state of affairs in the legislature was not such that a comprehensive programme of legislative reform such as codification could be embarked on and successfully carried through.[16] Codification would hardly be considered during the power struggle between the Governor and Assembly.[17]

Third, the nature of the laws militated against codification. The laws were confused and unsatisfactory. The feudal system of land tenure was still in force and the object of major dispute, while apparently retarding the commercial development of the province;[18] it would have been unthinkable to have codified the feudal law, but not to do so would have required a comprehensive but complex programme of reform in the process of codification. Political circumstances conspired against this, as did fears that such a reform might result in the introduction of the English laws.

Hence, we can see that although codification might have been a sensible solution to problems over the law, the situation of the country rendered it impossible. In the 1840s, the situation had changed. The country was politically stable. Important and necessary reforms were undertaken relating to hypothecs, unifying the law and abolishing feudal tenure. The necessary political stability allowed the comprehensive reform required for codification to take place.[19] In Louisiana, circumstances were very different. There was indeed antagonism between the governor and the elected legislature, with a variety of political and social tensions; but the Territory was generally stable and unlikely to break into revolt against the central government. Further, preservation of the civil law was a greater issue than in Quebec, whose laws were more secure: similarly, there seems to have been greater confusion over the laws in force in Louisiana.

The above discussion illustrates that codification can be a political issue or depend on political considerations. In a country where there is a great political dispute, as in Lower Canada in the 1820s and 1830s, a programme of codification—rationalizing, consolidating and reforming the law—is not considered, with matters

---

[15] See *supra*, chap. 3, text at notes 337–370.

[16] Consider the difficulties encountered in codifying in France under the National Assembly, Legislative Assembly, Convention and Directorate. See [various authors], *A General Survey of Events Sources Persons and Movements in Continental Legal History*, ed. by J.H. Wigmore, Continental Legal History Series, vol. 1, London, John Murray, 1912, p. 280.

[17] See, e.g. H.T. Manning, *The Revolt of French Canada, 1800–1835: A Chapter in the History of the British Commonwealth*, London, MacMillan, 1962; H. Wade, *The French Canadians*, rev. ed., Toronto, Macmillan, 1968, vol. 1, pp. 152–219; J.M.S. Careless, *The Union of the Canadas: The Growth of Canadian Institutions, 1844–1857*, Toronto, McClelland and Stewart, 1968.

[18] See *supra*, chap. 2, text at notes 101–106 and *supra*, chap. 3, text at notes 337–370.

[19] See *supra*, chap. 3, text at notes 371–399.

other than reforms of the law of a largely technical nature. Basic politics are of more immediate importance. Politics promoted a code in Louisiana; in contrast, the lack of a movement for codification in Quebec is to be attributed to powerful political tensions. The legal-technical need for codification, even with obvious models available, is not sufficient to promote a code. There must be both a desire for codification and sufficient stability to allow such a comprehensive, lengthy task to be carried out.

A point related to the above should be considered: codification required a necessary ideological consensus or stability and certainty of ideas. A few examples will illustrate this. Codification as a process demands reflection on the laws and on the general principles underlying them: if there is no general agreement as to what these principles should be, the codification process is likely to be frustrated. This meant that, prior to the redaction of the *Projet de l'An VIII*, the various governmental organs in France from the Revolution onwards failed to promulgate a code. Although political instability hampered their actions, a major difficulty was lack of agreement on the nature of the code: how general it should be, how detailed, how "philosophical".[20] If codification had been considered in Lower Canada in the 1820s and 1830s, whether or not feudal tenure should have been retained, and whether or not the Canada Tenures Act, s. 8, should have been preserved, would have caused probably insuperable problems.[21]

Similar problems confronted the 1945 French Civil Code Reform Commision. Léon Julliot de la Morandière remarked thus in this 1953 Preliminary Report:

> [T]he revison of the Civil Code . . . poses more problems than mere juridical technique. The moral, philosophical, economic and political bases of its rules have to be examined.[22]

This posed particular problems in the law of property and obligations; and in France after 1945 there was a conflict between socialist and liberal principles: was private property still an inalienable right? Should freedom of contract prevail rather than there being a controlled economy? These conflicts and doubts hampered the work of the Commission.[23] Codification was not taking place in a period of ideological certainty, which meant it was very difficult to decide on basic principles. On the

---

[20] See *General Survey supra* note 16, p. 280.

[21] On this section, see *supra*, chap. 3, text at notes 364–366. It was the section which decided English law governed land held on socage.

[22] L. J. de la Morandière, "Preliminary Report of the Civil Code Reform Commission of France", trans. J. Dainow, 16 *Louisiana Law Review* (1955), pp. 1–56 at p. 17.

[23] *Ibid.*, pp. 17–19; B. Audit, "Recent Revisions of the French Civil Code", 38 *Louisiana Law Review* (1978), pp.747–804 at pp. 755–756. Audit (*ibid.*, p. 755) states: "[T]he formulation of a code with as wide a scope as the Code Napoleon requires strong political support for both its ideological foundations and the effort necessary for its realization. . . . [T]he Commission of 1945 pursued its task in the midst of a political and economic crisis." Audit still foresaw problems in revising the law on property and contract. See *ibid.*, pp. 803–804.

contrary, the period of codification in Quebec and Louisiana was a period of ideological certainty: no one doubted that freedom of contract should prevail. In both countries the laws were reformed to support these principles, the relevant articles being culled from the Code Napoléon, which itself reformed the law of France in this way. The redactors of the Code Napoléon similarly had no doubts as to the principles their code should embody. Codification in general, because of its emphasis on law as a logical system, requires reliance on first principles, whether these principles are stated in the code or merely implicit in it. Periods of great instability in ideas do not readily permit codification, because of the lack of a firm ideological consensus to underpin the basic principles supporting a code.[24]

One further difference between the codes of Quebec and Louisiana is of interest. Quebec included in its code a fourth book dealing with commercial law: in doing so, Quebec innovated, as the Code Napoléon did not deal with commercial law, which was served by its own separate code. Nevertheless, the Quebec Code, in codifying a body of commercial law distinct from the civil law, was, in a general sense, following the French pattern, and indeed a traditional civilian distinction between *droit civil* and *droit commercial*. Louisiana did not codify its commercial law. In the territorial and early state period, its courts continued to apply in general the commercial law of Spain.[25] When the Louisiana legislature proposed codification in 1806, the French *Code de commerce* did not exist. It seems likely that the idea of codification in Louisiana was suggested by the obvious advantages of the French code that was closely followed as a model, the 1808 redaction being highly derivative and confined within boundaries set by the 1804 French *Code civil*.[26] It is probable, then, that no one in 1806 in Louisiana conceived of codifying commercial law, since the *Code de commerce* had not yet appeared to prompt such a codification and to serve as a model. The *Code de commerce* was not finished until the end of August 1807, and came into effect only on 1st January, 1808. It apparently did not occur to anyone in Louisiana to codify laws other than those traditionally designated "civil" laws, that is, those embodied in the French code. The Resolution appointing Brown and Moreau Lislet to carry out the codification talked only of "Civil Code" and "Civil Laws".[27]

The lack of such a Code of Commercial law has one curious effect on the 1808 Digest. In chapter four it was shown that the 1808 Digest, the 1866 C.Q. and the 1804 C.N., all have provisions on the authorization of married women by their

---

[24] It is interesting to read the Report on the new Draft Civil Code, which seems to reveal a new form of consensus about the nature and objects of the law: a consensus involving fairness in contracts and recognition for unions other than marriage (to give two examples). See the foreword by P.A. Crepau, in Civil Code Revision Office, *Report on The Québec Civil Code*, Quebec, Editeur Officiel, 1977, vol. 1, pp. XXIII–XXXVI.

[25] See *supra*, chap. 6, text at notes 193–200; R. Batiza, "The Unity of Private Law in Louisiana under the Spanish Rule", 4 *Inter-American Law Review* (1962), pp. 139–156 at pp. 151–156.

[26] There is no direct evidence that the appearance of the C.N. prompted codification in Louisiana; but this is a natural inference—the C.N. showed what could be done, and served as a model.

[27] Found quoted in J.H. Tucker, "Source Books of Louisiana Law", in *La. Leg. Arch.*, vol. 1, pp. XV–LXXIV at p. XVIII.

husbands.[28] There is no necessity for such authorization if the wife is a public trader acting in course of her trade. Article 4 of the French *Code de commerce* provides that a wife may not be a public trader without the consent of her husband. This provision appears in the C.Q. in the section on authorization of married women, being taken from the French commercial code.[29] There is no equivalent in the Digest. Hence, because the 1808 Digest in this respect followed the C.N., which was to some extent relying on the future existence of the *Code de commerce*, the Digest lacks a provision on a rule of some importance.

In the 1820s, when the Commission of Livingston, Derbigny and Moreau Lislet was at work, drawing up the new code of civil law, a Code of Commerce was drawn up;[30] but it was not adopted. The reasons for the rejection of this Code are unknown. This unenacted commercial code followed the French *Code de commerce*, although with some variation.[31] Thus, we find in the projected commercial code a provision stating that married women must have the consent of their husbands to their being public traders.[32]

Conclusions as to why the projected commercial code was rejected would be entirely speculative, and with one exception below, we need not concern ourselves with them here.[33] However, that the French commercial code was followed in the redaction of the *projet* in Louisiana must be of significance, in that it supports the argument that no-one in 1806 conceived of codifying the commercial law, because there was no model either to suggest such a codification or available to be followed.

This difference between the 1866 Quebec code and 1808 Louisiana Digest can be assigned to the fact that the two countries codified at different times. Louisiana codified before the French *Code de commerce* could serve as a model, while Quebec codified long after the promulgation of the *Code de commerce*. In Quebec, because the pre-code commercial law was an amalgam of French and English principles, the *Code de commerce* could hardly be copied as readily as the Code Napoléon had been copied. Further, the inclusion of the commercial law as a separate book in the civil code was one of obvious convenience, and one that did

---

[28] See *supra*, chap. 4, text at notes 380–464 and 876–981.

[29] C.Q. 179: see *supra*, chap. 4, text at notes 914–919.

[30] M. Nathan, "In Search of a Missing Link: Edward Livingston and the Proposed Code of Commerce for Louisiana", 48 *Tul. L. Rev.* (1973), pp. 43–54; H.R. Sachse, "Report to the Louisiana Law Institute on Article Nine of the Uniform Commerical Code" 41 *Tul. L. Rev.* (1967), pp. 505–554 at pp. 526–527. Nathan, *op. cit. supra*, p. 47 suggests that Livingston drafted the Code.

[31] Nathan, *op. cit. supra* note 30, p. 48, describes the projected Commerical Code thus: "Indisputably the Code followed the French *Code de Commerce* as a model, but the French code was more a springboard than a matrix. Although the formats are similar, and many of the articles identical, the Louisiana Code added many provisions of its own and omitted many of the French provisions." Book two, on maritime commerce, was almost identical to that of the French commercial code. Other books varied to a greater or lesser extent. Unfortunately I have been unable to see a copy of Louisiana's projected Commercial Code.

[32] Proposed Code of Commerce, art. 5.

[33] See Nathan, *op.cit. supra* note 30, p. 53.

not detract from the traditional separation of "civil" and "commerical" law. The failure to codifiy commercial law in Louisiana in 1808 may be taken to suggest just how important models may be in codification, as both a quarry and a stimulus.

Nathan suggests that the *projet* of the 1820s was rejected in part because the socio-economic state of Louisiana did not warrant a separate code for merchants, Louisiana being an agrarian society.[34] Should he be correct for the 1820s, his arguments would apply *a fortiori* to Louisiana in the territorial period. This speculation of Nathan's is questionable, for, as shown in chapter two, there was a fairly strong mercantile community in Louisiana based in New Orleans: the territory was not merely composed of plantations. Further, there are a significant number of early Louisiana cases which deal with commercial matters outwith the scope of the 1808 Digest, and in which the courts relied on Spanish sources of commercial law. This would surely indicate that a Code of Commerce would have been useful in the early period.[35]

One must conclude that, whatever contributory factors there may have been, it is most probable that there was no codification of commercial law in Louisiana because there was no foreign model to copy and from which to borrow. The importance of a model for many codes cannot be stressed enough: there was no commercial code not because there was no need, but because there was no model. Had the *Code civil des français* of 1804 had a fourth book on commercial law after the pattern of its descendant in Quebec, we can be confident that, in 1808, Louisiana would have adopted a code of four books with the last book devoted to commercial law.

The complexity of the circumstances surrounding the genesis of a civil code should be stressed. Legal-technical reasons for codification, though a factor in promoting codification, on their own are not necessarily sufficient to bring about codification: Quebec shows this clearly. Political circumstances may promote or prevent codification, as both Louisiana and Quebec show. The general political state of a country must be such as to facilitate codification. The actual *form* the code takes may be influenced by a variety of factors, such as the existence of foreign models, contemporary philosophy or legal science. *The content* of the code may be influenced by similar factors. But it is possible to suggest a distinction. The *form* of the code seems to have been most influenced by existing models and current philosophy; the *content* seems most to have been most influenced by provisions in the laws both of the codifying country and of foreign countries. Codes are at the same time both new and deeply rooted in the past. For a country to codify is to give a dramatic new form to the law; while the process of codification aids and prompts reflection on the law and the need for its modernization. The provisions tend to have definite historical sources: codifiers do not appear to attempt often to work out a code

---

[34] *Ibid.*

[35] See *supra*, chap. 2, text at notes 6–38 on mercantile community. On Spanish commercial law in the courts, see *supra*, chap. 6, text at notes 192–200.

of law from first principles. Codification, because it promotes reflection on, and reform of, the law tends to result in borrowing of provisions. Conversely, the form of a code and its manner of expression are easy to borrow: codes are readily transplanted.

In sum, the form and content of any civil code appear to depend on a series of complex historical contingencies: from the sources available to the codifiers to their views on what the law ought to be. It would serve little purpose here—even were it possible—to describe all such contingencies: suffice it to say that they are legion.

CODIFIERS AS LAWMAKERS

This study has stressed the actions of the redactors in reforming or preserving the law in their task of selection among competing potential provisions. Technically, of course, any reforms were made by the legislature who enacted the two codes: it cannot be doubted, however, that the real innovators were the two respective sets of redactors as codifiers. It was they who sifted the source material; they who selected provisions; they who drew up the code for the legislature basically to accept or to reject. It is true that in Quebec the legislature did not accept all the proposed reforms of the Codification Commission, but this does not really affect matters. Essentially, the task of the two legislatures was to accept or reject *in toto*; but, even if the legislatures scrutinized the texts closely, even if they modified parts, the task of reforming (or preserving) through codification was essentially that of the redactors: it was they who were the "lawmakers". Brierley points out that the Quebec Codification Commission "enjoyed the most complete freedom and responsibility in all of its work".[36] As all codes are indeed bound to be, the Quebec codification especially was "a work for full time legal experts".[37]

This being so, the motives we have to concentrate on to discover the reasons for change or stasis are those of the redactors. Hence, presupposing that the redactors were acting purposively and reasonably, their motives should be discoverable, if they have not stated them explicitly, and it should be possible to ascertain the criteria they used in making or rejecting changes. This much has already been explained in chapter one, and the results obtained support the view.

Problems potentially flow from this. This emphasis on the motives and actions of the codifiers as lawmakers could eventually reduce itself to a concern with the psychology of the redactors and their particular views of the world; it would be wrong, however, to become so caught up in the subjectivism of the redactors' views. The reason for this is the objectification of law: its existence as a body of theory outwith and separate from the redactors allowed them to view it as separate from them and to act upon it in a manner divorced from

---

[36] Brierley, "Codification", p. 572.
[37] *Ibid.*, p. 573.

subjective social considerations.[38] That is, questions of the redactors' subjective opinions of the world do not arise. The redactors viewed themselves as actors in an objective world existing separate from them, and which they could manage through the mechanism of law. Consequently, the nature of the economy, the family or whatever was, for them, a fact objectively existing.

It is, of ocurse, also a mistake to oppose "society" to "law": law is one aspect of society and effective within social life. The manner in which legal regulations may have, or are intended to have, an effect on social life may be obvious;[39] but it is not easy to grasp how social phenomena may have an effect on law. Often, "society" and "law" are opposed to one another with a vague relationship of mutual influence supposed. This approach is generally unsatisfactory and does not readily permit analysis of the relationship between "law" and "society" in causal terms. If it is accepted that lawmkers construct the law, examination of the actions and motives of lawmakers permits an understanding of the causes of legal development or stasis by other social phenomena.[40] This involves treating legislators (in a wide sense) as mediators between "society" and "law"; mediators as conscious agents, acting deliberately for various reasons.[41] By studying the social context, and by studying the codifiers' actions in the face of the various choices presented to them, it is possible to show how the redactors have attempted to shape the law according to the various criteria they have set themselves. The redactors need not have consciously thought out such criteria; their society, and their position within that society, may result in their making assumptions as to what is desirable. Legislators bring about legal development or legal stasis by acting as mediators between "society" and "law".[42] The relationship of causality between all the factors potentially influencing law and the law itself is dependent on those who make the law: it is they who make these various factors effective on the law in their construction of the law. The recovery of all factors influencing legislators or lawmakers is undoubtedly impossible; but I would hope that this thesis has

---

[38] The following remark of P.L. Berger and T. Luckmann in *The Social Construction of Reality*, London, Penguin, 1971, pp. 103–104, is instructive: "Especially on the theoretical level it is quite possible for knowledge to attain a great deal of detachment from the biographical and social interests of the knower."

[39] This is not to say that any law may have only an intended result; not all of any law's effects may be intended.

[40] Cf. some of the approaches outlined *supra*, chap. 1, text at notes 2–33.

[41] Cf. the following remarks of Z. Bauman, *Hermeneutics and Social Science*, London, Hutchinson, 1978, p. 12: "Men and women do what they do on purpose. Social phenomena, since they are ultimately acts of men and women, demand to be understood in a differenct way than by mere explaining. Understanding them must contain an element missing from the explaining of natural phenomena: the retrieval of purpose, of intention, of the unique configuration of thoughts and feelings which preceded a social phenomenon and found its only manifestation, imperfect and complete, in the observable consequences of action."

[42] Using "society" in a very wide sense: see *supra*, chap. 1, text after note 33. It should not be forgotten that *geography* may have an impact on law.

shown that it is possible to recover enough of these factors, and to delineate them in sufficient detail, to allow the reconstruction of the historical causes of legal development or legal stasis in such a way as to permit the making of suggestions aiding a move towards a more general theory of legal development. And this will be done in the following section.

To state that law is a human construct is to repeat an obvious truism; but it is a truism worth stressing. Law is a human construct, and it is in human actions and their underlying causes that the reasons for legal change or stasis should be sought. A change in economic organization or ideology (in itself a human construction) does not in itself cause a change in the law: a lawmaker has to see the change and then act to change the law because of the change in the economy. (Law is not a self-perpetuating living body: it only exists through human actions.) Indeed in the hypothetical example of change in the economy, the lawmaker may see the change, may realize that it requires (or might require) a change in the law; but yet for other reasons the lawmaker may not bring about such a change (reasons of ideology and the like) and legal stasis might result. The method we have adopted here is only valid for investigating the effect of factors other than law on law: for the effect of law on other social phenomena, another method would be required, as a change in the law may have effects on society quite different from those intended.[43]

THE HISTORICAL CAUSES OF LEGAL DEVELOPMENT AND LEGAL STASIS

In this study we have examined in detail two areas of two codes, and have briefly glanced at other aspects of the same codes. It is appropriate now to assess the more general implications of these investigations. We shall here be concerned with drawing out what is of more general import in the conclusions already drawn on family, employment and the brief investigation of contract as they appear in the law of both codes: from this investigation of the changes—or lack of changes—in the law, we shall assess the influence on, and causes of, legal development and legal stasis, so as to help depict the effect of social circumstances on law.

To this end, it is useful to consider in outline the main argument of the thesis.

It was argued that there is considerable dispute over the nature of the relationship between law and other social phenomena, and that this was a topic worthy of investigation. What was chosen for investigation was the effect on law of the social and other circumstances in which it is located (rather than, for example, the effect of law on the conduct of social relationships); and it was

---

[43] For example the *intention* of legislation to raise taxes is usually to raise revenue for the government (it may of course be to discourage imports and the like); a major effect is often the employment of the tax lawyers to avoid payment of such taxes.

argued that the proper method to study this effect was to examine the changes made in the law at a period of rapid and increasing social change.

Reliance was placed on the fact that law has generally developed through borrowing, and that legislators generally choose between particular and potential rules to revise the law. Hence, a study of the rules examined in considering reform would suggest why the enacted rule was chosen. (And indeed, in both Louisiana and Quebec, redactors, in codifying their laws, obviously confined themselves to the examination of certain legal works and codes.) Furthermore, since codification focused attention on the state of the law, and provided an unrivalled opportunity for modernization of the legal provisions, it was convenient to study codification. Louisiana and Quebec were most attractive for study because of their rich juridical culture and the transformations their societies were undergoing at the period of their respective codifications.

This being so, it was possible, by investigation of contemporary social trends in Louisiana and Quebec, and comparison of such trends with the trends in development or stasis of the law, to ascertain why the redactors of both codes selected the provisions they did. Of course, this places great stress on the actions of the redactors; but this is—I would argue[44]—necessary, as the connection in the social structure between abstract legal formulations—such as codes—and other social phenomena is made by those whose task it is to create law. In this case, the redactors mediate between the wider society and its formulated law. Evidence is lacking for the 1808 Digest; but the redactors of the 1866 Quebec code obviously acted in the manner suggested here: they consciously selected provisions to fit in with their views of how the law should be.

In order to carry out this plan, it was necessary to build up a picture of the societies of Louisiana and Quebec at the relevant periods; and this was done: special attention was paid to the legal culture of both societies to emphasize the likely influences on the redsctors. The general picture of both societies was sufficient to allow us to develop a broad understanding of trends within those societies: however, when we came to discuss the chosen topics of family and employment, it was necessary to be more careful in analysing what is meant by family and employment and in describing their development. This was done, paying some attention to recent developments and controversy in the historiography of the family.

The family was analysed through two fundamental relationships: between parent and child and husband and wife. The change and stasis in the law referring to these two fundamental relationships in the Digest of 1808 and Code of 1866 were depicted and analysed: and the conclusions deduced therefrom laid out as to the factors (historical causes) influencing the redactors' actions. Employment was analysed in a similar fashion, describing the move from the

---

[44] See *supra*, text at notes 35–42.

servant as part of the family to the servant as employee or wage-labourer in a formal contract with his employer that was devoid of any personal associations. Some general provisions on contract were also examined; from them it was obvious that both sets of redactors were concerned to embody the ideals of liberal individualism in their codes.

All the above raised many questions about the codification of the law in both jurisdictions. The Louisiana codification is the subject of major controversy among scholars; we were able to suggest solutions to some of the problems concerning the relationship of the Digest to the previous law, the nature of the Digest and the significance of the de la Vergne manuscript. The research further elucidated the process of codification and the activities of the codifiers as lawmakers.

From our investigations, we can state that, in the most general of terms, the Quebec codification of 1866 was highly conservative (with one exception) in comparison to the 1808 Louisiana Digest. Of course, this statement is so general that it could be regarded as a major distortion of the activities of the Quebec redactors; but, nonetheless, it is probably fair to say that in the law on husband and wife and parent and child, the Quebec redactors rejected many potentially useful reforms. Further, their provisions on employment would rapidly become anachronistic in an industrializing society; and the redactors' general conservatism prevented them from following the lead of the Austrian code in amalgamating lease of work and mandate—an amalgamation they themselves considered desirable. The one exception to this conservative trend in the 1866 Quebec code is the law of contract: it will be recalled that the redactors gave the law of contract a new orientation along the lines indicated by the 1804 French code, but surpassing the latter in strict adherence to freedom and sanctity of contract. That the 1866 codification should be generally conservative in results is understandable given the conservative instructions of the legislature and the strong commitment of the members of the Codification Commission to the preservation of the French Canadian law. It was pointed out in chapter three that these two factors were likely to inhibit massive legal change, in that the restrictive nature of the instructions and the desire to protect the law would cause the redactors to be over-cautious lest they in some way subvert the integrity of the Quebec legal tradition.[45] This said, it must be recalled that the conservatism of the redactors and of the codification in general did not inhibit them from giving law of contract a new orientation. This is a very significant point; it will be returned to later.

The 1808 Digest of Orleans presents a rather different picture. The redactors introduced and consolidated major reforms in the law relating to husband and wife. These reforms had been fore-shadowed by the earlier Act on the

---

[45] See *supra*, chap. 3 at notes 436–437

celebration of marriages;[46] but this Act merely indicated a new direction for the law: the redactors consolidated the trend set by the Act, and enthusiastically gave a new direction to this whole area of the law. Thus, the law on the relationship of husband and wife became northern French in style and provisions—a complete change from the previous Castilian law. As regards parent and child, investigated through the notion of *puissance paternelle*, it is clear that there has been a similar radical change: the law from being Castilian has changed to French, and the broad Castilian *patriapotestad* has given way to a narrow northern French model of *puissance paternelle*—this despite the preservation of the Castilian division of nonage into minority and pupillage. The Digest redactors also provided a modern law on the traditional civilian *locatio operarum* on the contract for wage labour; they drew especially on the *projet* of the French code of 1804, though other sources, notably Pothier, were influential. Other rules on employment, especially those relating to apprentices and *engagés*, were drawn from Blackstone and a recent territorial Act.[47] These provisions were such as to harmonize with the civil law. All these provisions on employment were compatible with the old Castilian law; but they were more modern and more suited to Louisiana society of the period. The law of contract also was radically modernized, following the French code. Here again there was a major shift away from the Castilian law on the topic. Lest it be thought that these changes were unconscious, due to ignorant reliance on the French codification rather than due to a desire to change the law to be similar to the French, it should be recalled that the redactors in many instances departed from the French code: consider minority, seashore, and the like.[48] We can be sure that the Digest redactors consciously rejected the Castilian provisions in favour of those deriving from the French code and its *projet*.

That this is so is not surprising. As was shown in chapter three, the civilian legal systems were amenable to the easy transmissability of legal provisions, and indeed, the Code Napoléon, during the course of the nineteenth century, was borrowed by many jurisdictions.[49] Further, the redactors' identifiable natural-law bias, and their rational, systematic outlook would tend to lead them to favour the superior French code, especially when there seems to have been a return to French legal ways in Louisiana just prior to the promulgation of the Digest.[50]

---

[46] Louisiana Acts, 1807, ch. 17 (6 Apr. 1807). See *supra*, chap. 4, text at notes 370–371 and 451–464.
[47] Louisiana Acts, 1806, ch. 11 (21 May 1806).
[48] See *supra*, chap. 6, text at notes 62–66.
[49] See *supra*, chap. 3, text at notes 136–170; *supra*, chap. 6, text at note 88.
[50] As Baade, "Marriage Contracts" shows. On the revival of French law, see also *supra*, chap. 3, text at notes 156–170. As argued *supra*, chap. 6, text at notes 247–250, I accept Baade's argument in so far as the revival of French law—to a limited extent—as a "living law" (in so far as it took place) would facilitate the adoption of French law in the Digest. I do not accept that the redactors were attempting to codify the "living law" as the law in force, that "living law" being French.

If we analyse the choices made by the redactors, we get the following results. We noted that in Quebec there were many opportunities for the redactors to update the law: in codifying; but that, in general, these opportunities were not taken. Thus, the wife still suffered many traditional contractual incapacities and required authorization by her husband. Broadly, this follows the C.N.; but, unlike in the latter, lack of authorization, under the Quebec code, rendered the wife's actions null. Again, following the C.N., the wife can only separate from the husband on the ground of his adultery if he has kept his concubine in the marital home. With certain exceptions (for our purposes here unimportant), the Quebec code has kept very close to the *ancien droit* under the Coutume de Paris as regards *puissance du mari*, much closer than has the Code Napoléon. Many of the possible reforms found in the C.N. or in *coutumes* other than that of Paris, or in the 1825 Louisiana Code, would have rendered the law more appropriate and convenient economically, making for greater certainty and ease in transactions by women. However, the ideology of nineteenth-century Quebec supported subjection of the wife to the husband, regarded as undisputed head of the household. The redactors were doubtless quite content to preserve the old law on this point, as it fitted their notions of what was proper. They merely updated the law to make it easier to operate: witness the reform of the manner of authorization. It is surely significant in this respect that the redactors never even considered whether or not married women should be incapacitated: further, virtually all the sources they consulted would support the notion of *puissance du mari*, and indeed, the position of the wife under the Quebec law as regards her property was perhaps somewhat better than that of women under English law before the Married Women's Property Acts of the late-nineteenth century.[51] We should also consider that the inconveniences of marital authorization would probably be slight in practice, and that the ideology of the supremacy of the husband, for which the old law was eminently suited, would cause the retention of the *status quo*. The stasis in the law was not caused by the use of the Code Napoléon or the lack of foreign models: the redactors did not follow the C.N. completely, and models for provisions improving the lot of the wife were not lacking for the redactors. The redactors obviously preferred the almost complete superiority of the husband, and their choice of provisions must have been dictated by the ideology of the period: not by any vision of the material needs of society. The C.N. to some extent expressed better, in its rules on *puissance maritale*, nineteenth-century ideology of the affective family; but there being no *necessity* for such a change, the Quebec redactors preserved in this respect the old law.[52] We can see that the ideology of the

---

[51] A.H. Manchester, *A Modern Legal History of England and Wales*, London, Butterworths, 1980, pp. 368–373. A direct comparison of the position of wives in both the laws would be rather hazardous.

[52] This orientation of the French Code towards expressing the ideals of the affective family relates to its apparent conception of the reason for the *puissance du mari* because of C.N. 224 on

authority of the husband and general legal conservatism must have worked together, in the face of no necessity for change, to preserve the existing law with only some technical improvements.

The Quebec provisions on paternal power are also highly conservative. Aspects of them (for example, the rejection of the Napoleonic provisions enhancing the role of grandparents) are directly contrary to the reality of Quebec family life of the period. Further, the denial to fathers of the automatic right to the tutorship of their children and to administration of their children's property also runs contrary to the ideology of the era. On the other hand, the provisions are all workable and reasonably consonant with the needs of the period, while some updating of the law has indeed been undertaken. We may conclude that stasis here has resulted from traditionalism or conservatism among the lawyers, facilitated by the rough suitability of the law and the powerful traditions of control over children.

If we look at the Louisiana provisions on husband and wife of 1808, we may note that there has been a major change from the Castilian law. Under the Castilian law, there was a very loose requirement of marital autborization, and the law was in many respects quite contrary to the French. Yet, we find that the redactors of the Digest adopted the French conception of *puissance du mari*, and as a result, the actions of wives became much more restricted in law. To modern eyes, the liberal Castilian provisions seem much more suitable for early nineteenth-century Louisiana, and the adoption of the French provisions a puzzling retrograde step. The explanation, however, is not difficult to find. In chapter four, we pointed out that the redactors were heavily influenced by the general excellence of the Code Napoléon: its modernity, its conciseness, its coherence. Further, the facts surrounding codification such as the drawing up of the code in French, the 1807 Act on the celebration of marriages, and the limited revival of French legal ideas suported adoption of these articles from the Code Napoléon. However, we know that although the Code Napoléon may be classed as the *causa causans* of the choice, the choice would not have been exercised had the rules not been consonant with the general family ideology of early nineteenth-century Louisiana: quite simply, the redactors, and their society, believed that wives should be subject to their husbands. Here the reasons for the selection of the particular rules were the *prestige* of the French code, its comprehensiveness in comparison to the fragmentary Castilian treatment, and the ideology of supremacy of the hushand. Thus, what might seem a retrogade step, when viewed from perspective of economic efficacy, is explicable in terms of legal culture and social values.

---

authorization by minors: see *supra*, chap. 4, text at notes 947–962; this does not affect the comments made in the text above on rejection of potential reforms—consider the nullity of wives' unauthorized acts—because of the ideology of the supremacy of the husband. The ideal of the affective family is different from that of the supremacy of the husband: also, it is not so obvious that C.N. 224 has this effect, as the other provisions of the C.N. derogate from the *puissance du mari*.

The Digest redactors also radically changed the law on parent and child, rejecting the Castilian extended, almost Roman, *patria potestad* in favour of a more liberal version of the Code Napoléon's limited *puissance paternelle*. To modern eyes, this change appears an obvious one of great utility. The motives of the redactors can be more precisely pinpointed in that the Code Napoléon provided them here with modern texts more suitable to conditions in Louisiana. There can be little doubt that the prime motive for reform here was the desire to update the law (the old law must surely have been virtually unworkable) and that the codifiers' selection of the Napoleonic texts was motivated by a desire to modernize, and the French code provided the most suitable modern provisions. That the desire to modernize was the main motive is evidenced by the Digest's departures from the French code and, indeed, by the Digest's more liberal provisions.

Hence, from the provisions on family law in both codes, we see that reform can be the result of the prestige of a particular system from which borrowings are made,[53] the desire to reinforce some social value or ideology not directly related to material conditions, and the desire to render the law more consonant with material conditions and ideology. The social origins of the reform may be many and varied.

As regards stasis, we can see that it also can result from various causes. Ideology in Quebec, combined with a conservative legal tradition, prevented useful development of the law on *puissance paternelle* and *puissance maritale*, though some reforms were undertaken. Conversely, C.N. 224 suggested a new interpretation of *puissance maritale* in line with the current ideology of the affective family, as did the C.N.'s provisions on parental rights of tutorship and administration: legal conservatism combined with the lack of need for such a change to prevent such a developnent taking place.

Before going on to assess the significance of these origins of stasis and development, it is useful to look at some other results.

In both codes, we noted that the law of contract was given a new orientation around the ideals of freedom of contract and sanctity of contract. This is, out of the areas of law we looked at, one of the most important changes. This was an updating of the law due to a change in ideology, and a change in the economic system: in short, it would appear that here there is a development resulting from changed material social conditions and changed ways of regarding those social conditions. The timing of the change in both countries is significant. Louisiana moved towards the classic nineteenth-century view of contract both earlier than Quebec and before Louisiana had reached an equivalent level of industrial and economic development. The reasons why Louisiana adopted these provisions are obvious, such as current economic theory, ideology of liberalism, and the

---

[53] Cf. A. Watson, "Comparative Law and Legal Change", 37 *Cambridge Law Journal* (1978), pp. 313–336 at p. 326 on "Transplant Bias".

attraction of modernity. Much more interesting is the lateness of Quebec. The difference is entirely attributable to the fact that codification in Quebec took place sixty years after that in Louisiana. The reasons for the differences in the times of codification have been canvassed above, and need not be repeated here.[54] It cannot reasonably be doubted that, had the opportunity presented itself earlier, the Quebec law on contract would have been revised along the lines on which it was to be revised in 1866: nonetheless, what was necessary was *opportunity* for lawmakers to act. This example of reform shows neatly that, although the reform may be supported by ideology of the society and by material circumstances, the actual reform may depend on the contingencies of politics; here the fact that codification, for various reasons, was sixty years earlier in Louisiana than Quebec: the important point being that change in law does not mechanistically, in a necessary fashion, follow on change in society.

If we look at the rules on employment adopted in both codes, we find that they were dictated by legal tradition and the ideology of contractual liberalism. Effectively, in Louisiana, we can say that the rules were probably a fair reflection of the requirements of the relationship between employer and employee at the period: as regards Quebec, however, it is doubtful if this was so. The rules were insufficient to meet the needs of the contract for wage labour in mid-to-late nineteenth century Quebec. The rules were, however, supported by the ideology of contractual liberalism.

If we draw all the above discussion together, we find that the following pattern emerges. First, there is little in either of the two codes that is new. Reforms were generally borrowed; even potential reforms that were rejected would have been borrowed. This is an obvious point and does not need to be stressed. Second, we find that reform or stasis may be caused by varying factors. That is, the immediate cause of any reform or lack thereof can be one or a combination of an infinite variety of individual factors. The process of reform (here codification) may affect the reform: the need for a coherent statement of law inherent in codification imposes a certain dynamic on the reform or restatement of the law resulting in certain changes.[55] Similarly, the prestige of a foreign system may be an important factor in reform. Ideology rather than "practical" needs or utilitarian considerations may be of importance in either reform or stasis. Examples of factors promoting or hindering legal change could be multiplied; but tit is unecssary to do so. We can summarize the broad changes in the law thus: in Louisiana the prestige of the Code Napoléon (legal-cultural factor) aided by the ideology of the period, resulted in the reform of the law on husband and wife; in Louisiana, the grossly inappropriate nature of the

---

[54] See *supra*, text at notes 12–18.

[55] M. Weber, *Max Weber on Law in Economy and Society*, ed. by M. Rheinstein, trans. by E. Shils, Cambridge, MA, Harvard University Press, 1954, p. 205: "The force of the purely logical legal doctrines let loose, and a legal practice dominated by it, can considerably reduce the role played by considerations of practical needs in the formation of the law . . .."

Castilian *patria potestad* (material factor) coupled with the ideology of the period resulted in reform of the law on parent and child: in Louisiana, the ideology of liberalism and the nature of economic activity led to the reform of the law on contract. In Quebec the same factors also led to the reform of the law on contract. Employment in Louisiana was reformed to fit material conditions and liberal ideology, whereas employment in Quebec was reformed to fit liberal ideology but not material conditions. The *lack* of reform in Quebec in the law on husband and wife and parent and child may be attributed to the ideology of the period and the conservative nature of the Quebec codification.

We may note that there was always a *reason* for the selection of any provision, but the reason may be other than that of practical needs. In both countries, the drastic reforms, or lack of reform, in the provisions of family law studied generally owe nothing to material conditions or practical considerations (in so far as the latter are ascertainable). The ideology of the society and legal-cultural factors were what determined the choice of the redactors. With the law relating to employment, again the ideology of the society played a role; but in Louisiana material conditions were probably reflected, whereas in Quebec they were probably not, for the reasons canvassed above. The law on contract in both codes was fairly radically re-oriented in order to fit in with the current notions of freedom and sancity of contract. In making this change, the redactors recognized both the reality of business affairs in their period and the current ideology of liberal capitalism.

It may be seen that generally the redactors were not guided by the material and economic circumstances of the two countries; but, rather, other considerations promoted the selection of particular rules. For example, family life in Quebec would stress the grandparent to grandchild relationship; but the redactors, following the *ancien droit*, gave this relationship no importance when dealing with the condition of the parentless child. Here the redactors valued legal tradition above change: the existing conception of *puissance paternelle* was extended logically, the legal culture's stress on coherence and tradition outweighing consideration of the nature of family life in Quebec.

The preceding summary of the findings of this thesis shows that law develops or stands still as a result of many and differing influences, and that these influences can be located in the legal culture itself as well as in the wider society. It is important to stress, however, that there is no immediate connection between a change in any particular state of affairs and a corresponding change in the relevant law. The effect of social circumstances on law is always and inevitably mediated through lawmakers. Because lawmakers act as mediators between society and law, the immediate causes of change or stasis will always tend to be found in the intellectual climate or ideology of their society as familiar to the lawmakers. Hence we may see, as we have seen here, that in their reforms the lawmakers are concerned with embodying in the law the ideals of their legal and social culture, confident in the notion that the legal provisions will have an effect in society. (Whether or not these changes or lack of changes have the intended effect is a rather different point.)[56] It is thus relevant to consider the particular social background of the lawmakers in ascertaining the reasons for any change or stasis; although; as pointed out above, we can expect a reasonable detachment on the part of the lawmakers from their own particular circumstances.[57] We may state there is an immediate cause for every example of stasis and change, and also indeed for the whole thrust of any area of the law or a whole code: these causes are many and cannot be reduced in any obvious way to a simple proposition. The positive law in any given legal system cannot in any way be taken to be inevitable.

This said, it must be conceded that the above begs many important questions. We have succeeded in attributing aspects of legal change and stasis to a plurality of causes within society, without in any way discussing, how that society itself is determined, or how the law relates to other aspects of society, that is, the effect of law on other social phenomena. These are important points, but ones outwith the scope of this study and we need not discuss them. What we have established is that no narrow mechanistic model of legal change or stasis and their relationship to social phenomena is sufficient. Legal development or non-development is a complex process, involving the interplay of many factors. What we have found in this study above all else is that legal change is likely to reflect the ideology of society as endorsed by the lawmakers. We can make no necessary connections between material circumstances, objectively viewed, and law. Law existing as a human construct in the realm of ideas is, when opportunity for reform arises, more likely to reflect those ideas than any other social phenomenon. This is shown most obviously by the change in the law on husband and wife in Louisiana: the change was caused by legal ideology (the superiority of the French code) and social ideology (the supremacy of the husband) not by any functional consideration of the family structure. Similarly with employment and contract: the ideology of the period is more important than any consideration of the "needs" of industry and commerce in a functional sense.

We have thus indicated the range of factors likely to be the immediate causes of legal change or stasis: as pointed out above, this enterprise leaves untouched the whole question of total shifts in the structure of society and their effect on law. It should here be stressed once more that, viewed from a "macro-structural" position, the law is itself part of the total structure. We have viewed the societies of Louisiana and Quebec in a period of transition, the period of the move towards industrialization, of the development of the liberal economy, and of the growth of the affective family. We have, for the reasons indicated in chapter one, distinguished between law and society to permit the examination of the influence of "non-law" on law; but it should be recalled that this is primarily

---

[56] Cf. S. Herman, "Legislative Management of History: Notes on the Philosophical Foundations of the Civil Code", 53 *Tul. L. Rev.* (1979), pp. 380–397.
[57] See *supra*, text at notes 35–42.

a device to allow us to focus our attention on the relationship of law to other social phenomena. Conceiving of society as a totality, the transformation of the law is one aspect of the continuing transformation of that society. This study, however, has drawn attention to the actions of lawmakers, and has shown that the proper method of study of legal stasis or legal development is to examine the actions of lawmakers as social actors: that is, as members of, and influenced by, their society and of a particular grouping or class of that society, they are involved in an activity (law making) which is both conscious and purposive. They cannot be said to be acting as mere reflections of a class grouping, nor as unconscious agents of some hidden deeper structure (whether of the unconscious mind or of society is irrelevant). Nor are these lawmakers as redactors actors in some functionalist sense: the law we find in the 1808 Digest or 1866 Code is not a mere expression of the aims of bourgeois society, nor an attempt to embody the most efficient way of carrying out some aim in either an economic or utilitarian sense. Influenced by any number of factors drawn from their social grouping and the legal culture, redactors clearly act consciously to embody in their codes their beliefs as to what the law should be. That is, they act consciously, but not subjectively: their position as lawmakers gives distance to their actions, and they conceive of themselves as acting in an objective sense. Lawmakers mediate between law and other social phenomena: they regulate the effect the latter has on the former.

The mediation carried out by lawmakers is a complex process, subject to many influences. Opportunity for reform is necessary, and this can be affected by many circumstances. General political circumstances and the institutions regulating the legal system may enable or prevent reform.[58] When the causes of legal development or legal stasis are what is at issue this process of mediation is the proper object of study. What are necessary to futher knowledge of causes of legal change are studies of this process of mediation in its wider social context. What this study has shown is that explanations of legal change based on some mechanistic social principle are inadequate, as indeed are all explanations that do not take adequate account of the purposive activity of lawmakers and legislators and their intervention and mediation between law and the wider society.

---

[58] Cf. P. Hirst, *On Law and Ideology*, London, Macmillan, 1979, p.113: "Law and legislation must be conceived as processes . . . . The process of legislation has attached to it conditions of access and operation, and through these conditions many and varying influence and circumstances express themselves. The conditions and influence acting upon the process are effective and are given form through its procedures. Conditions and influences are not themselves legal forms or effects: it is only through and as legislation and legal practice that are effective." See also Watson, *op. cit. supra* note 53.

BIBLIOGRAPHY

PRIMARY SOURCES

An Account of Louisiana, Being an Abstract of Documents, in the Offices of the Departments of State, & of the Treasury, Philadelphia, William Duane, 1803

Argentré, Bertrand d'. *Commentarii in patrias Britonum leges, seu consuetudines generales antiquiss. Ducatus Britanniae*, Brussels, Apud Franciscum Foppens, 1664

——. *Coustumes generales du pays et duché de Bretagne reformées en l'an mil cinq cents quatre-vingts*, Amsterdam, J. Stammius, 1664

Argou, Gabriel. *Institution du droit françois*, ed. by B.J. Bretonnier & E.J. Barbier, Paris, P. Emery, 1719

Asso y del Rio, I.J. de and Miguel de Manuel y Rodriguez, *Instituciones del derecho Civil de Castilla*, 7th ed. by Joaquin María Palacios, Madrid, Tomás Alban, 1806

Austin, John. *The Province of Jurisprudence Determined*, ed. by H.L.A. Hart, London, Weidenfeld & Nicolson, 1954

——. *Lectures on Jurisprudence*, 5th ed. by R. Campbell. London, J. Murray, 1911

Basnage, Henri, *Œuvres de Maître Henri Basnage*, 4th ed., Rouen, Knapen, 1778

——. *La coutume reformée du pais et duché de Normandie, commentée par Me Henry Basnage [etc]*, 2nd ed., Rouen, veuve Maurry etc., 1694

Baudry des Lozières, L. N. *Voyage à la Louisiane, et sur le continent de l'Amerique septentrionale, fait dans les années 1794 à 1798*, Paris, Dentu, an XI [1802]

Berquin-Duvallon, P.L. *Travels in Louisiana & the Floridas in the year 1802, Giving a Correct Picture of those Countries*, trans. by J. Davis, New York, I. Riley, 1806

Blackstone, William. *Commentaries on the Laws of England*, 9th ed., London, W. Strahan, 1783

Blackstone, William. *Commentaries on the Laws of England*, Chicago, University of Chicago Press, 1979

Bourjon, François. *Le droit commun de la France et la coutume de Paris réduits en principes tires des ordonnances, des arrêts, des loix civiles, des auteurs*, Paris, Grangé, Rouy, 1747

Brown, James. Padgett, J.A. "Some Letters of James Brown of Louisiana to Presidents of the United States", 20 *La. Hist. Quar.* (1937), pp. 58–136

——. Padgett, J.A. "Letters of James Brown to Henry Clay, 1804–1835", 24 *La. Hist. Quar.* (1941), pp. 921–1177

Burge, William. *Commentaries on Colonial and Foreign Laws Generally: And in Their Conflict with Each Other and with the Law of England*, London, Saunders & Benning, 1838

Cujas, Jacques. *Paratitla in libros quinquaginta digestorum, seu pandectarum imperatoris Iustiniani, cum notis Alex. Chassanaei et indice obligationem et actionem, et epitome in eundem indicem*, Paris, I. Iost, 1658

Delaporte, J.B. and P.N. Riffé-Caubray, *Les pandectes françaises: ou, recueil complet de toutes les lois en vigueur, contenant les codes etc.*, Paris, Perlet, 1803–1806

Demolombe, Charles. *Cours de code Napoléon*, Paris, A. Durand, L. Hachette [imprint varies], 1854–1878

Denisart, J.B. *Collection de décisions nouvelles et de notions relatives à la jurisprudence actuelle*, 7th ed., Paris, veuve Desaint, 1771

——. *Collection de décisions nouvelles et de notions relatives à la jurisprudence actuelle*, 8th ed. by J.B.F. Bayard and A.G. Camus, continued by L. Calenge, Paris, veuve Desaint, Lamy [imprint varies], 1783–1807

Documents Relating to the Seigniorial Tenure in Canada: With a Historical Introduction and Explanatory Notes, ed. by W.B. Munro, Toronto, Champlain Society, 1908

Domat, Jean. *Les loix civiles dans leur ordre naturel; le droit public, et legum delectus*, new ed., Paris, Michel Brunet, 1735

——. *Les loix civiles dans leur ordre naturel; le droit public, et legum delectus*, new ed., Paris, veuve Cavelier, 1766

Durham, J.G. Lambton, Earl of, *Lord Durham's Report on the Affairs of British North America*, ed. by C.P. Lucas, Oxford, Clarendon Press, 1912

Espeisses, Antoine, d'. *Œuvres de M. Antoine d'Espeisses, avocat et jurisconsulte de Montpellier où toutes les plus importantes matières du droit romain sont méthodiquement expliquées et accommodées au droit françois. Confirmées par les arrêts des cours souverains, et enrichies des plus utiles doctrines des auteurs anciens et modernes*, ed. by G. du Rousseaud de la Combe, Lyons, frères Bruyset, 1750

Febrero, José. *Librería de escribanos, é instrucción juridical theórico práctica de principantes. Parte Primera divida en tres tomos. Trata de testamentos y contratos*, Madrid, Impr. de P. Marin, 1789

——. *Librería de escribanos, é instrucción juridíca theórico práctica de principiantes. Parte Segunda divida en tres tomos. Trata de los juicios de inventario, y partición de bienes de difunto, ordinario, executive, y de concurso, y prelación de acreedores*, Madrid, Impr. de P. Marin, 1790

——. *Febrero adicionado ó librería de escribanos: instrucción teórico práctica de principantes.* Madrid, Impr. de Alban, 1806–1808

Fenet, P.A. *Pothier analysé dans ses rapports avec le Code civil, et mis en ordre sous chacun des articles de ce Code*, 2nd ed., Paris, Au dépot ... et chez Alex-Gobelet, 1829

——. *Recueil complet des travaux préparatoires du Code civil*, Paris, Au depot, 1827, repr. Osnabrück, Otto Zeller, 1968

Ferrière, Claude de. *Corps et compilation de tous les commentateurs anciens et modernes sur la coutume de Paris*, 2nd ed., Paris, Henri Charpentier, 1714

Ferrière, C.J. de. *Dictionnaire de droit et de pratique*, 3rd ed., Paris, Theodore le Gras, 1749

France. Laws. *Code civil des français: edition originale et seule officielle* [*Code Napoléon*], Paris, Imprimerie de la République, 1804

——. *Code de commerce*, Paris, Imprimerie impériale, 1807

French Regime, The, Canadian Historical Documents Series vol. 1, ed. by Cameron Nish, Scarborough, Ont., Prentice-Hall of Canada, 1965

Gomez, Antonio. *Ad leges Tauri commentarius, cui accesserunt Doctoris Diegi Gomezij, ... annotationes utilissimae, & pernecessariae*, Antwerp, Petrus et Joannes Belleri, 1624

Guyot, P.J.J.G. *Répertoire universel et raisonné de jurisprudence ...; ouvrage de plusieurs jurisconsultes*, new ed., Paris, Visse, 1784–1785

Henrys, Claude. *Œuvres de M. Claude Henrys conseiller du roi; ... contenant son recueïl d'arrêts, ses plaidoiers et harangues, et vingt-deux questions postumes tirées des écrits de l'auteur trouvés après son decès. Avec des observations sur les changemens de la jurisprudence arrivés depuis la mort de l'auteur. Une conference de la jurisprudence de tous les païs du droit écrit du Roiaume. Et des moiens faciles et sures pour la rendre certaine & uniforme dans tous les tribunaux*, ed. by B.J. Bretonnier, Paris, Michel Brunet, 1708

Hobbes, Thomas. *Leviathan: Or, the Matter, Forme and Power of a Commonwealth Ecclesiasticall and Civil*, ed. by Michael Oakeshott, Oxford, Basil Blackwell, 1946

Justinian I, Emperor of the East, *Corpus iuris civilis*: vol. 1, *Institutiones*, ed. by Paul Krüger, *Digesta*, ed. by Theodor Mommsen; vol. 2, *Codex Iustinianus*, ed. by Paul Krüger; vol. 3, *Novellae constitutions*, ed. by Rudolf Schöll, various editions, Berlin, Weidmann, 1902–1906

Lebrun, Denis. *Traité des successions, divisé en quatre livres*, 3rd ed., Paris, Michel Guignard & Claude Robustel, 1714

Llamas y Molina, Sancho de. *Comentario critico-juridico-literal á las ochenta y tres leyes de Toro*, Madrid, Repullés, 1827

Loisel, Antoine. *Institutes coustumieres ou manuel de plusieurs et diverses reigles . . . du droit coustumier et plus ordinaire de la France*, ed. by M. Reulos, based on 3rd ed. of 1611, Paris, Sirey, 1935

Lousiana. Laws. *Acts Passed at the First Session of the First Legislature of the Territory of Orleans*, New Orleans, Published by Authority, Printed by Bradford & Anderson, Printers to the Territory, 1807

——. *Acts Passed at the Second Session of the First Legislature of the Territory of Orleans*, New Orleans, Printed by Bradford & Anderson, Printers to the Territory, 1807

——. *A Digest of the Civil Laws Now in Force in the Territory of Orleans with Alterations and Amendments Adapted to its Present System of Government*, New Orleans, Published by Authority, printed by Bradford & Anderson, 1808

——. *Civil Code of the Stae of Louisiana*, New Orleans, Printed by J.C. de St Romes, 1825

——. *Louisiana Legal Archives*, New Orleans and Baton Rouge, T.J. Moran's Sons & State of Louisiana, 1937–1942

——. *A Reprint of Moreau-Lislet's Copy of A Digest of the Civil Laws now in force in the Territory of Orleans (1808) Containing Manuscript References to its Sources and Other Civil Laws on the Same Subjects*, Baton Rouge, Claitor's Publishing Division, 1971

Lower Canada Reports: décisions des tribunaux du Bas-Canada, Quebec, Impr. de E.R. Fréchette [imprint varies], 1851-1888

Maleville, Jacques de. *Analyse raisonnée de la discussion du Code civil au Conseil d'État: contenant le texte des lois: le précis des observations faites sur chaque article, et les motifs de la décision du Conseil: l'indication de la conformité et de l'opposition de ces articles aux lois anciennes : les arrêts rendus par la Cour de cassation, pour en fixer le sens : et les observations particulières de l'auteur*, 2nd ed., Paris, Garnery, 1807

Marcadé, Victor. *Explication théorique et pratique du Code Napoléon*, 5th ed., Paris, Cotillon, 1859

Martin's Reports of Cases Argued and Determined in the Superior Court of the Territory of Orleans and in the Supreme Court of the State of Louisiana, by F.-X. Martin, New Orleans, Samuel M. Stewart, 1846–1853

Marx, Karl. *Economy, Class.and Social Revolution*, ed. by Z.A. Jordan, London, Nelson, 1971

——. *Early Writings*, London, Penguin, 1975

—— and Friedrich Engels, *Manifesto of the Communist Party* (1848), Peking, Foreign Languages Press, 1972

Maynard, Gerard. *Illustres controversiae forenses, secundum iuris civilis Romanorum normas in amplissimo Senatu Tholosano decisae, quas collegit . . . Dn. Gerardus de Maynard, I.C. consiliarum regius et Suprema Curiae Tholosano senator, atque e Gallico sermone in Latinum transtullit . . . Hieronymus Bruckner*, Cologne, Alexander Pernet, 1611

Merlin, P.A. *Répertoire universel et raisonné de jurisprudence*, 4th ed., Paris, Garnery, 1812–1815

——. *Répertoire universel et raisonné de jurisprudence*, 5th ed., Paris, Garnery, 1827–1828

Montesquieu, Charles de Secondat de. *The Spirit of the Laws*, trans. by Thomas Nugent, New York, Hafner, 1949

——. *The Spirit of the Laws: A Compendium*, ed. by D.W. Carrithers, Berkeley, University of California Press, 1977

Noodt, Gerhard. *Opera omnia*, Leiden, Johannes van der Linden, jr, 1724

Normandy. Laws. *Le grand coustumier du pays et duché de Normendie* [*sic*], Rouen, N. Le Roux pour F. Regnault ... J. Wallard ... & pour G. Anger, 1539

——. *La coutume reformée du pais et duché de Normandie, commentée par Me Henry Basnage* [*etc*], 2nd ed., Rouen, veuve Maurry etc., 1694

——. *Coutumes du pays et duché de Normandie*, Rouen, J.B. Besonge, 1732

Papineau, L.J., *Papineau: textes choisis et présentés par F. Ouellet*, Quebec, presses de l'université Laval, 1970

Paris. Laws. *Coutume de Paris*. See Ferrière, Claude de

Pasquier, Etienne. *L'interprétation des Institutes de Justinien, avec la conférence de chasque paragraphe aux ordonnances royaux, arrestz de parlement et coustumes générales de la France*, Paris, Videcoq aîné, A. Durand, 1847

Pigeau, E.N. *Notions élémentaires du nouveau droit civil, ou, exposé méthodique des dispositions du Code civil pour en faciliter l'intelligence*, Paris, Chez Rondonneau, 1803–1805

Pocquet de Livonnière, Claude. *Règles du droit françois*, 3rd ed., Paris, chez P.G. le Mercier, 1737

Pothier, R.J. *Œuvres de Pothier, annotées et mises en correlation avec le Code civil et la législation actuelle*, ed. by Jean-Joseph Bugnet, Paris, Cosse et Marchal, Henri Plon, 1861

——. *Pothier's Treatise on the Contract of Letting and Hiring*, trans. by G.A. Mulligan, Durban, Butterworth, 1953

Public Archives of Canada, *Documents Relating to the Constitutional History of Canada, 1791–1819*, ed. by A.G. Doughty and D.A. MacArthur, Ottawa, C.H. Parmalee, 1914

——. *Documents Relating to the History of Canada, 1759–1791*, ed. by A. Shortt and A.G. Doughty, 2nd ed., Ottawa, J. de L. Taché, 1918

Quebec/Lower Canada. Laws. *An Abstract of those Parts of the Custom of the Viscounty and Provostship of Paris, which were received and practised in the Province of Quebec, in the Time of the French Government. Drawn up by a Select Committee of Canadian Gentlemen, well skilled in the Laws of France and of that Province. By the Desire of Guy Carleton, Esquire, Governor in Chief of the said Province*, London, Charles Eyre & William Strahan, 1772

——. *The Sequel to the Abstract of Those Parts of the Custom of the Viscounty and Provostship of Paris, Which Were Received and Practised in the Province of Quebec, in the Time of the French Government: Containing the Thirteen Latter Titles of the Said Abstract*, London, Charles Eyre & William Strahan, 1773

——. *Consolidated Statutes for Lower Canada*, Quebec, S. Derbishire & G. Desbarats, 1861

——. *Reports of the Commissioners Appointed to Codify the Laws of Lower Canada in Civil Matters*, 2nd ed., Quebec, G. Desbarats, 1865

——. *Code civil du Bas Canada: Civil Code of Lower Canada*, Ottawa, Printed by Malcolm Cameron, Law Printer to the Queen, 1866

——. *The Civil Code of Lower Canada*, ed. by Thomas McCord, Montreal, Dawson Bros., 1867

——. Civil Code Revision Office, *Report on The Québec Civil Code*, Quebec, Editeur Officiel, 1977

Rousseaud de la Combe, Guy de. *Recueil de jurisprudence civile du pays de droit écrit et coutumier par ordre alphabétique*, 4th ed., Paris, Veuve Savoye, 1769

Russell, W.O. *A Treatise on Crimes and Misdemeanors*, 2nd ed., London, J. Butterworth, 1826–1828

——. *A Treatise on Crimes and Misdemeanors*, 3rd ed., by C.S. Greaves, London, Saunders & Benning, 1843

Selkirk, Thomas Douglas, Earl of. *Lord Selkirk's Diary, 1803–1804: A Journal of his Travels in British North America and the Northeastern United States*, ed. by P. White, Toronto, Champlain Society, 1958

Serres, Claude. *Les institutions du droit françois, suivant l'ordre de celles de Justinien*, Paris, veuve Cavelier & fils, 1753

Smith, William. *The Diary and Selected Papers of Chief Justice William Smith 1784–1793*, ed. by L.F.S. Upton, Toronto, Champlain Society, 1963–1965

Spain/Castile. Laws. *Fuero real de España: diligentemente hecho por el noble Rey Don Alonso IX*, glossed by A.D. de Montalvo, Medina del Campo, printed by Pedro de Castro for Guillermo de Miles, 1544

——. *[Nueva] recopilación de las leyes destos reynos, hecha por mandad del Rey Don Felipe Segundo*, Madrid, C. de Barrio y Angulo y D. Diaz de la Carrera, 1640-1641

——. *Fuero viejo*, ed. by I.J. de Asso y del Rio and M. de Manuel y Rodriguez, Madrid, J. Ibarra, 1771

——. *Recopliación de leyes de los reynos de las Indias*, 4th Imp., Madrid, viuda de D. Joaquin Ibarra, 1791

——. *Novísima recopilación de las leyes de España*, Madrid, s.n., 1805-1807

——. *Las siete partidas del rey don Alfonso el sabio: cotejados con varios códices antiguos*, Madrid, Real Academia de la Historia, 1807

——. *Las siete partidas de las leyes del sabio rey Don Alfonso el nono, glosadas ... por Gregorio López*, Madrid, s.n., 1843-1844

Statutes, Treaties and Documents of the Canadian Constitution, ed. by W.P.M. Kennedy, 2nd ed., London, Oxford University Press, 1930

Stephen, H.J. *New Commentaries on the Law of England*, 3rd ed., London, Butterworths, 1853

Tocqueville, Alexis de. *Journey to America*, trans. by George Lawrence, ed. by J.P. Mayer, London, Faber & Faber, 1959

Toullier, C.B.M. *Le droit civil français suivant l'ordre du Code... continué et complété par J.B. Duvergier*, 6th ed., Paris, F. Cotillon, 1844–1848

Voet, Johannes. *Elementa iuris secundum ordinem Institutionum in usum domesticae exercitationis digesta*, 2nd ed., Leiden, Henricus Teering, 1705

——. *Commentarius ad Pandectas*, 6th ed., The Hague, Petrus de Hondt, 1731

Weber, Max. *Max Weber on Law in Economy and Society*, ed. by Max Rheinstein, trans. by Edward Shils, Cambridge, MA, Harvard University Press, 1954

Zachariae, K.S. *Le droit civil français, traduit de l'allemand sur la cinquième édition. Annoté et réetabli suivant l'ordre du Code Napoléon par G. Massé ... [et] Ch. Vergé*, Paris, A. Durand, 1854–1860

WORKS OF REFERENCE

Dictionary of American Biography: Under the Auspices of the American Council of Learned Societies, ed. by Allen Johnson, London, Oxford University Press 1928–1958

Dictionary of Canadian Biography, ed. by G.W. Brown, Toronto, University of Toronto Press, 1966–

Encyclopédie, on dictionnaire raisonné des sciences et des arts et des métiers par une société de gens de lettres, ed. by Denis Diderot and Jean Le Rond d'Alembert (eds.), Paris and Neufchastel, Briasson et al. [imprint varies], 1751–1765

Jowitt, W.A. Jowitt, Earl. *Jowitt's Dictionary of English Law*, 2nd ed. by John Burke, London, Sweet & Maxwell, 1977

The MacMillan Dictionary of Canadian Biography, 3rd ed. by W.S.Wallace, London, MacMillan, 1963

Walker, D.M. *The Oxford Companion to Law*, Oxford, Clarendon Press, 1980

Williams, Raymond. *Keywords*, London, Fontana, 1976

SECONDARY SOURCES

Aiton, A.S. "The Diplomacy of the Lousiana Cession", 36 *American Historical Review* (1931), pp. 701–720

Arena, C.R. "Landholding and Political Power in Spanish Louisiana", 38 *La. Hist. Quart.* (1955), pp. 23–39

——. "Philadelphia-Spanish New Orleans Trade in the 1790's", 2 *Louisiana History* (1961), pp. 429–445

——. "Land Settlement Policies and Practices in Spanish Louisiana", in J.F. McDermott (ed.), *The Spanish in the Mississippi Valley*, Urbana, University of Illinois Press, 1974, pp. 51–60

Ariès, Philippe. *Centuries of Childhood*, trans. R. Baldwick, London, Jonathan Cape, 1962
Arnaud, A.-J. *Essai d'analyse structurale du Code civil français*, Paris, Librarie Générale du Droit et Jurisprudence, 1973

Audit, Bernard. "Recent Revisions of the French Civil Code", 38 *La. L. Rev.* (1978), pp. 747–804

Baade, H.W. "The Form of Marriage in Spanish North America", 61 *Cornell Law Review* (1975), pp. 1–89

——. "Marriage Contracts in French and Spanish Louisiana", 53 *Tul. L. Rev.* (1978), pp. 1–92

——. "The Formalities of Private Real Estate Transactions in Spanish North America", 38 *La. L. Rev.* (1978), pp. 655–745

Baez, C. "L'Influence du droit français au Paraguay", in *Le droit civil français: livre-souvenir des journées du droit civil (Montréal, 31 août-2 Septembre 1934)*, Paris, Sirey, 1936, pp. 829–831

Batiza, Rodolfo. "The Unity of Private Law in Louisiana under the Spanish Rule" 4 *Inter-American Law Review* (1962), pp. 139–56

——. "The Louisiana Civil Code of 1808: Its Actual Sources and Present Relevance", 46 *Tul. L. Rev.* (1971), pp. 4–165

——. "The Actual Sources of the Louisiana *Projet* of 1823: A General Analytical Survey", 47 *Tul. L. Rev.* (1972), pp. 1–115

——. "Sources of the Civil Code of 1808, Facts and Speculation: A Rejoinder", 46 *Tul. L. Rev.* (1972), pp. 628–652

——. "The Actual Sources of the Marriage Contract Provisions of the Louisiana Civil Code of 1808: The Textual Evidence", 54 *Tul. L. Rev.* (1979), pp. 77–116

Baudouin, Louis. *Le droit civil de la province de Québec*, Montreal, Wilson & Lafleur, 1953

Bauman, Zygmunt. *Hermeneutics and Social Science: Approaches to Understanding*, London, Hutchinson, 1978

Bendix, Reinhard. *Max Weber: An Intellectual Portrait*, London, Methuen, 1966

Benjamin, Peter. "Penalties, Liquidated Damages and Penal Clauses in Commercial Contracts: A Comparative Study of English and Continental Law", 9 *International and Comparative Law Quarterly* (1960), pp. 600–627

Berger P.L. and Thomas Luckman, *The Social Construction of Reality*, London, Penguin, 1971

Berkner, L.K. "Inheritance, Land Tenure and Peasant Family Structure: A German Regional Comparison", in Jack Goody, Joan Thirsk and E.P. Thomson (eds.), *Family and Inheritance: Rural Society in Western Europe, 1200–1800*, Cambridge, Cambridge University Press, 1976, pp. 71–95

Besnier, Robert. "Le régime des tenures en droit canadien français" 14 (4th ser.) *R.H.D.F.E.* (1935), pp. 734–747

Bieys, Pierre. "Southern Quebec", in J. Warkentin (ed.), *Canada: A Geographical Interpretation*, Toronto, Methuen, 1970, pp. 281–333

Blanchard, Raoul. *Le centre du Canada français: "province de Québec"*, Montreal, Beauchemin, 1947

Boule, P.H. "French Reactions to the Louisiana Revolution of 1768", in J.F. McDermott (ed.), *Frenchmen and French Ways in the Mississippi Valley*, Urbana, University of Illinois Press, 1975, pp. 143–157

Boyé, A.J. "Les destinées de la Novelle 61 chez les romanistes et les canonistes du moyen âge", 3 (4th ser.) *R.H.D.F.E.* (1924), pp. 473–514

Braverman, Harry. *Labor and Monopoly Capital: The Degradation of Work in the Twentieth Century*, New York, Monthly Review Press, 1974

Brierley, J.E.C. "Quebec's Civil Law Codification", 14 *McGill Law Journal* (1968), pp. 521–589

——. "Husband and Wife in the Law of Quebec: A 1970 Conspectus", in Derek Mendes da Costa (ed.), *Studies in Canadian Family Law*, Toronto, Butterworths, 1972, vol. 2, pp. 795–844

Brissaud, Jean. *A History of French Private Law*, trans. by Rapelje Howell, Continental Legal History Series, vol. 3, London, John Murray, 1912

Brown, E.G. "Law and Government in the 'Louisiana Purchase': 1803–1804", 2 *Wayne Law Review* (1956), pp. 169–189

——. "Legal Systems in Conflict: Orleans Territory 1804–1812", 1 *American Journal of Legal History* (1957), pp. 35–75

Buckland, W.W. *A Textbook of Roman Law*, 3rd ed. by P.G. Stein, London, Cambridge University Press, 1963

Burns, F.P. "The Spanish Land Laws of Louisiana", 11 *La. Hist. Quar.* (1928), pp. 557–580

C., J. "De la publicité des hypothèques dans le Bas-Canada", 3 *Revue de Legislation et de Jurisprudence* (1847), pp. 24–33

Cahall, Raymond du B. *The Sovereign Council of New France: A Study in Canadian Constitutional Hisory*, New York, Columbia University Press, 1915

Cain, Maureen and Alan Hunt. *Marx and Engels on Law*, London, Academic Press, 1979

Calasso, Francesco. *Introduzione al diritto comune*, Milan, Giuffrè, 1951
——. *Medio evo del diritto*, Milan, Giuffrè, 1954

Calhoun, A.W. *A Social History of the American Family*, New York, Barnes & Noble, 1945

Careless, J.M.S. *The Union of the Canadas, 1844–1857*, Toronto, McClelland & Stewart, 1968

Castel, J.G. *The Civil Law System of the Province of Quebec*, Toronto, Butterworths, 1962

Castro, Alfredo de and A.C. Watson. Comment, "Seashore in Louisiana", 8 *Tul. L. Rev.* (1934), pp. 272–277

Cauchon, J.E. *L'union des provinces de l'Amérique britannique du Nord*, Quebec, Imprimerie de A. Coté et Cie., 1865; reprint East Ardsley, Yorks., S.R. Publishers, 1968

Chénon, Émile. "Le droit romain à la Curia Regis de Philippe-Auguste à Philippe-Le Bel", in Edmond Meynial (ed.), *Mélanges Fitting*, Montpellier, Imprimerie générale du Midi, 1907–1908, repr., Aalen, Scientia, 1969, vol. 1, pp. 195-212

——. *Histoire générale du droit français public et privé: des origines à 1815*, Paris, Sirey, 1926 & 1929

Clark, J.G. *New Orleans 1718–1812. An Economic History*, Baton Rouge, Louisiana State University Press, 1970

——. "The Role of the City Government in the Economic Development of New Orleans: Cabildo and City Council 1783–1812", in J.F. McDermott (ed.), *The Spanish in the Mississippi Valley*, Urbana, University of Illinois Press, 1974, pp. 138–148

Cohn, E.J. "Contracts of Service for Life in Comparative Jurisprudence", 20 (3rd ser.) *Journal of Comparative Legislation and International Law* (1938), pp. 45-54

Coing, Helmut. "The Roman Law as *Ius Commune* on the Continent", 89 *Law Quarterly Review* (1973), pp. 505–517

Coles, H.L. "The Confirmation of Foreign Land Titles in Louisiana", 38 *La. Hist. Quar.* (1955), pp. 1–22

Colin, Ambroise and Henri Capitant. *Traité de droit civil*, revised by L.F. Julliot de la Morandière, Paris, Dalloz, 1957

Corbett, P.E. *The Roman Law of Marriage*, Oxford, Clarendon Press, 1930

Crook, J.A. *Law and Life of Rome*, London, Thames & Hudson, 1967

Dainow, Joseph. "Moreau Lislet's Notes on Sources of Louisiana Civil Code of 1808", 19 *La. L.Rev.* (1958), pp. 43–51

Darby, L.A. and T.J. McDonald, "A Recent Discovery: Another Copy of Moreau Lislet's Annotations to the Code of 1808", 47 *Tul. L. Rev.* (1973), pp. 1210–1213

Dargo, George. *Jefferson's Louisiana: Politics and the Clash of Legal Traditions*, Cambridge, Harvard University Press, 1975

Dart, A.L. Comment, "Adultery as a Defense to a Divorce Action in Louisiana", 11 *Tul. L. Rev.* (1936), pp. 95–112

Dart, H.P. "Legal Institutions in Louisiana", 2 *La. Hist. Quar.* (1919), pp. 72–103

——. "Courts and Law in Colonial Louisiana", 22 *Louisiana Bar Association Reports* (1921), pp. 17–63

——. "Law Library of a Louisiana Lawyer in the Eighteenth Century", 25 *Louisiana Bar Association Reports* (1924), pp. 12–19

Daube, David. *Roman Law: Linguistic, Social and Philosophical Aspects*, Edinburgh, Edinburgh University Press, 1969

——. *Civil Disobedience in Antiquity*, Edinburgh, Edinburgh University Press, 1972

David, René. "The Civil Code in France Today", 34 *La. L. Rev.* (1975), pp. 907–919

Dawson, J.P. "Codification of the French Customs", 38 *Mich. L. Rev.* (1940), pp. 765–800

Dechêne, Louise. *Habitants et marchands de Montréal au XVIIe siècle*, Paris, Plon, 1974

Deconde, Alexander. *This Affair of Louisiana*, New York, Scribner, 1976

Deiler, J.H. "The System of Redemption in the State of Louisiana", 12 *La. Hist. Quar.* (1929), pp. 426–460

Deleury, Edith, Michèle Rivet and J.-M. Neault, "De la puissance paternelle à l'autorité parentelle: une institution en voie de trouver sa vraie finalité", 15 *Les Cahiers de Droit* (1974), pp. 779–870

Dias, R.W.M. "*Laesio Enormis*: The Roman-Dutch Story", in David Daube (ed.), *Studies in the Roman Law of Sale, Dedicated to the Memory of Francis de Zuleuta*, Oxford, Clarendon Press, 1959, pp. 46–63

Doutre, Gonzalve and Edmond Lareau, *Le droit civil canadien suivant l'ordre étable par les codes, précédé d'une histoire générale du droit canadien*, Montreal, A. Lareau, 1872

Dubuisson, Edward. "The Codes of Louisiana (Originals Written in French; Errors of Translation)", 25 *Louisiana Bar Association Reports* (1924), pp. 143–157

Dunbar-Nelson, Alice. "People of Color in Louisiana", 2 *Journal of Negro History* (1917), pp. 51–78

Eccles, W.J. *Canadian Society During the French Regime*, Montreal, Harvest House, 1968

——. "The Social, Economic and Political Significance of the Military Establishment in New France", 52 *Can. Hist. Rev.* (1971), pp. 1–22

——. *France in America*, New York, Harper & Row, 1972

Edelman, Bernard. *Ownership of the Image: Elements for a Marxist Theory of Law*, trans. by Elizabeth Kingdom, London, Routledge & Kegan Paul, 1979

Elder, G. "Family History and the Life Course", in T.K. Hareven (ed.), *Transitions: The Family and Life Course in Historical Perspective*, New York, Academic Press, 1978, pp. 17–56

Esmein, André. *Le mariage en droit canonique*, Paris, Larose et Forcel, 1891

Everett, D.E. "Emigres and Militiamen: Free Persons of Color in New Orleans 1803–1815", 38 *Journal of Negro History* (1953), pp. 377–402

——. "Free Persons of Color in Colonial Louisiana", 7 *Louisiana History* (1966), pp. 21–50

Faucher, Albert. *Québec en Amérique au XIXe siècle: essai sur les caractères économiques de la Laurentie*, Montreal, Fides, 1973

Feenstra, Robert and C.J.D. Waal, *Seventeenth Century Leyden Law Professors and their Influence on the Development of the Civil Law: A Study of Bronchorst, Vinnius and Voet*, Amsterdam, North Holland, 1975

Feyerabend, Paul. *Against Method: Outline of an Anarchistic Theory of Knowledge*, London, Verso, 1978

Flandrin, J.-L. *Families in Former Times: Kinship, Household, and Sexuality*, Cambridge, Cambridge University Press, 1979

Fliniaux, André. "L'évolution du concept de clause pénale chez les canonistes du moyen âge", in *Mélanges Paul Fournier*, Paris, Recueil Sirey, 1929, pp. 233–247

Franklin, Mitchell. "Equity in Louisiana: The Role of Article 21", 9 *Tul. L. Rev.* (1935), pp. 485–516

——. "Some Observations on the Influence of French Law and the Early Civil Codes of Louisiana", in *Le droit civil français: livre-souvenir des journées du droit civil (Montréal, 31 août-2 Septembre 1934)*, Paris, Sirey, 1936, pp. 833–845

——. "Libraries of Edward Livingstone and of Moreau Lislet", 15 *Tul. L. Rev.* (1941) pp. 401–414

——. "The Place of Thomas Jefferson in the Explusion of Spanish Medieval Law from Louisiana", 16 *Tul. L. Rev.* (1942), pp. 319–338

——. "The Eighteenth 'Brumaire' in Louisiana: Talleyrand and the Spanish Medieval Legal System of 1806", 16 *Tul. L. Rev.* (1942), pp. 514–561

——. "An Important Document in the History of American Roman and Civil Law: The de la Vergue Manuscript", 33 *Tul. L. Rev.* (1958), pp. 35–42

——. "Some Considerations on the Existential Force of Roman Law in the Early History of the United States", 22 *Buffalo Law Review* (1972), pp. 69–105

Friedman, L.M. *A History of American Law*, New York, Simon & Schuster, 1973

——. *The Legal System: A Social Science Perspective*, New York, Russell Sage Foundation, 1975

Funiak, W.Q. de. *Principles of Community Property*, Chicago, Callaghan, 1943

Gacto Fernández, Enrique. *La filiación no legítima en el derecho histórico español*, Seville, publicaciones de la Universidad de Sevilla, 1969

Galpin, W.F. "The Grain Trade of New Orleans, 1804–1814", 14 *Miss. Vall. Hist. Rev.* (1928), pp. 496–507

García Gallo, Alfonso. *Manual de historia del derecho español*, 2nd ed., Madrid, Artes Gráficas y Ediciones, 1964

Garigue, Philippe. *La vie familiale des Canadiens français: précédée d'une critique*, Montreal, Presses de l'université de Montréal, 1970

Gaudemet, Jean. "Les transferts du droit", 27 *L'année sociologique* (1976), pp. 29–51

General Survey of Events, Sources, Persons and Movements in Continental Legal History, ed. by J.H. Wigmore, Continental Legal History Series, vol. 1, London, John Murray, 1912

Génestal, M.R. "La formation et le développement de la Coutume de Normandie", in *Travaux de la Semaine d'histoire du droit tenue à Guernsey du 26 au 30 mai 1927*, Caën, A. Olivier, 1928, pp. 37–55

Gény, François. *Méthode d'interprétation et sources en droit privé positif*, trans. J. Mayda, 2nd ed., [St Paul, West Pub. Co.], for the Louisiana State Law Institute, 1954 [1963]

Gérin-Lajoie, A. "Introduction de la Coutume de Paris au Canada", 1 *R.duB.* (1941), pp. 61–65

Gilmore, M.P. *Humanists and Jurists: Six Studies in the Renaissance*, Cambridge MA, Belknap Press, 1963

Giraud, M. "France and Louisiana in the Early Eighteenth Century", 36 *Miss, Vall. Hist. Rev.* (1950), pp. 657–674

——. *Histoire de la Louisiane française*, Paris, Presses universitaires de France, 1953–1974

Gorla, Gino. "A decision of the *Rota Fiorentina* of 1780 on Liability for Damages Caused by the 'Ball Game'", 49 *Tul. L. Rev.* (1975), pp. 346–357

Groulx, Lionel. *Histoire du Canada français*, 4th ed., Montreal, Fides, 1968

Hahlo, H.R. "Here lies the Common Law: Rest in Peace", 30 *Modern Law Review* (1967), pp. 241–259

Hahlo, H.R. and Ellison Kahn, *The South African Legal System and its Background*, Cape Town, Juta, 1968

Hamelin, Jean. *Économie et société en Nouvelle France*, Quebec, Presses universitaires Laval, 1960

Hamelin, Jean and Yves Roby, *Histoire économique du Québec, 1851–1896*, Montreal, Fides, 1971

Hardy, J.G. "The Superior Council in Colonial Louisiana", in J.F. McDermott (ed.), *Frenchman and French Ways in the Mississippi Valley*, Urbana, University of Illinois Press, 1965, pp. 87–101

Hareven, T.K. "Introduction", in T.K. Harven (ed.), *Transitions: The Family and Life Course in Historical Perspective*, New York, Academic Press, 1978, pp. 1–15

Hareven, T.K. "The History of the Family as an Interdisciplinary Field", in T.K. Rabb and R.I. Rotberg (eds.), *The Family in History: Interdisciplinary Essays*, New York, Harper & Row, 1973, pp. 211–226

Harlow, V.T. *The Founding of the Second British Empire*, London, Longmans, 1952–1964

Harris, R.C. *The Seigneurial System in Early Canada: A Geographical Study*, Madison, University of Wisconsin Press, 1966

H.L.A. Hart, "Positivism and the Separation of Law and Morals", 71 *Harvard Law Review* (1958), pp. 606–612

——. *The Concept of Law*, Oxford, Clarendon Press, 1961

Haskins, G.L. "The Legal Heritage of Plymouth Colony", in D.H. Flaherty (ed.), *Essays in the History of Early American Law*, Chapel Hill, University of North Carolina Press, 1969, pp. 121–134

Herman, Shael. "Legislative Management of History: Notes on the Philosophical Foundations of the Civil Code", 53 *Tul. L. Rev.* (1979), pp. 380–397

Hindess, Barry and Paul Hirst. *Mode of Production and Social Formation: An Autocritique of Pre-Capitalist Modes of Production*, London, Macmillan, 1977

Hinjosa, Eduardo de. "La Réception du Droit Romain en Catalogne", in Edmond Meynial (ed.), *Mélanges Fitting*, Montpellier, Imprimerie générale du Midi, 1907–1908, repr., Aalen, Scientia, 1969, pp. vol. 2, pp. 39–408

Hirst, Paul. *On Law and Ideology*, London, Macmillan, 1979

Hoff, Timothy. "Error in the Formation of Contracts in Louisiana: A Comparative Analysis", 53 *Tul. L. Rev.* (1979), pp. 329–379

Hood, J.J. "The History and Development of the Louisiana Civil Code", 19 *La. L. Rev.* (1958), pp. 18–33

Huussen, A.H. Jr. "Le droit du mariage au cours de la Révolution Française", 47 *Tijdschrift Voor Rechtsgeschiedenis* (1979), pp. 9–51, 99–127

Jackson, B.S. *Essays in Jewish and Comparative Legal History*, Leiden, Brill, 1975

Jolowicz, H.F. *Roman Foundations of Modern Law*, Oxford, Clarendon Press, 1957

Jones, Kelvin, Book Review, 8 *International Journal of the Sociology of Law*, 1980, pp. 83–90

Kagan, R.L. *Students and Society in Early Modern Spain*, Baltimore, Johns Hopkins University Press, 1974

Kahle, L.G. "The Spanish Colonial Judiciary", 32 *Southwestern Social Science Quarterly* (1951), pp. 26–37

Kaser, Max. *Roman Private Law*, trans. by Rolf Dannenberg, Durban, Butterworths, 1965

Keat, Russell and John Urry, *Social Theory as Science*, London, Routledge & Kegan Paul, 1975

Kendall, J.S. "New Orleans' 'Peculiar Institution'", 23 *La. Hist. Quar.* (1940), pp. 864–886

Knaup, Kathianne. "The Transition from Spanish Civil Law to English Common Law in Missouri", 16 *St. Louis University Law Journal* (1971), pp. 218–231

Kniffen, F.B. *Louisiana: Its Land and People*, Baton Rouge, Louisiana State University Press, 1968

Kondert, Reinhart. "Les Allemands en Louisiane de 1721 à 1732", 33 *R.H.A.F.* (1979), pp. 51–65

Koschaker, Paul. *L'Europa e il diritto romano*, trans. by Arnaldo Biscardi, Florence, Sansoni, 1962

Kuhn, Thomas. *The Structure of Scientific Revolutions*, Chicago, University of Chicago Press, 1962

Kunkel, Wolfgang. *An Introduction to Roman and Legal Constitutional History* 2nd ed., trans. by J.M. Kelly, Oxford, Clarendon Press, 1973

Lamarche, P.E. "French Civil Law under British Rule", 31 *Canadian Law Times* (1911), pp. 420–441

Lanctôt, Gustave. *A History of Canada*, trans. by J. Hambleton and M.M. Cameron, Cambridge MA, Harvard University Press, 1963–1965

Laslett, Peter. *The World We Have Lost*, 2nd ed., London, Methuen, 1971

——. "Preface to the First Impression", in Peter Laslett assisted by Richard Wall (eds.), *Household and Family in Past Time*, Cambridge, Cambridge University Press, 1972, pp. ix–xi

——. "Introduction: The History of the Family", in Peter Laslett assisted by Richard Wall (eds.), *Household and Family in Past Time*, Cambridge, Cambridge University Press, 1972, pp. 1–90

——. "Mean Household Size in England since the Sixteenth Century", in Peter Laslett assisted by Richard Wall (eds.), *Household and Family in Past Time*, Cambridge, Cambridge University Press, 1972, pp. 125–158

——. *Family Life and Illicit Love in Earlier Generations: Essays in Historical Sociology*, Cambridge, Cambridge University Press, 1977

Le Conte, René. "The Germans in Louisiana in the Eighteenth Century", 8 *Louisiana History* (1967), pp. 67–84

Lefebvre, Charles. *Le droit des gens mariés aux pays de droit écrit et de Normandie*, Paris, Sirey, 1912

Léger, A.N. "De l'influence du Code Napoléon à Haiti et des differences de législation civile entre la France et Haiti", in *Le droit civil français: livre-souvenir des journées du droit civil (Montréal, 31 août-2 Septembre 1934)*, Paris, Sirey, 1936, pp. 755–815

Lemesurier, Charles. "The Marriage Law of Quebec", in *Le droit civil français: livre-souvenir des journées du droit civil (Montréal, 31 août-2 Septembre 1934)*, Paris, Sirey, 1936, pp. 135–154

Lepointe, Gabriel and Raymond Monier. *Les obligations en droit romain et dans l'ancien droit français*, Paris, Sirey, 1954

Levy, Ernst. "Vulgarisation of Roman Law in the Early Middle Ages", in E. Levy, *Gesammelte Schriften*, Cologne, Böhlau, 1963, vol. 1, pp. 220–247

Limpens, Jean. "Territorial Expansion of the Code", in Bernard Schwartz (ed.), *The Code of Napoleon and the Common-Law World*, New York, New York University Press, 1956

Lloyd of Hampstead, Dennis Lloyd, Baron. *Introduction to Jurisprudence*, 3rd ed., London, Stevens, 1972

Lortie, Léon. "The Early Teaching of Law in French Canada", 2 *Dalhousie Law Journal* (1975), pp. 521–532

Lucas, J.R. "The Phenomenon of Law", in P.M.S. Hacker and Joseph Raz (eds.), *Law Morality and Society: Essays in Honour of H.L.A. Hart*, Oxford, Clarendon Press, 1977, pp. 85–98

Luig, Klaus. "The Institutes of National Law in the Seventeenth and Eighteenth Centuries" 17 (new ser.) *Juridical Review* (1972), pp. 193–226

MacCormick, D.N. "Law as Institutional Fact", 90 *Law Quarterly Review* (1974), pp. 102–129

MacKay, Angus. *Spain in the Middle Ages: From Frontier to Empire, 1000–1500*, London, Macmillan, 1977

McCutcheon, R.P. "Libraries in New Orleans, 1771–1833", 20 *La Hist. Quar.* (1937), pp. 152–158

——. "Books and Booksellers in New Orleans, 1730–1830", 20 *La. Hist. Quar.* (1937), pp. 606–618

Maher, Gerard. "Analytical Philosophy and Austin's Philosophy of Law", 64 *Archiv für Rechts-und Sozialphilosophie* (1978), pp. 401–416

Maine, H.S. *Ancient Law: Its Connection with the Early History of Society and its Relation to Modern Ideas*, London, J. Murray, 1930

Manchester, A.H. *A Modern Legal History of England and Wales*, London, Butterworths, 1980

Manning, H.T. *The Revolt of French Canada, 1800–1835: A Chapter in the History of the British Commonwealth*, London, Macmillan, 1962

Margadant, G.P. "The Hallowing and the Hollowing of Roman Law", in *Festschrift für Pan. J. Zepos*, Cologne, Ch. Katsikalis Verlag, 1973, vol. 3, pp. 595–614

Marty, Gabriel and Pierre Raynaud, *Droit civil, tome 1: Introduction générale à l'étude du droit*, Paris, Sirey, 1972

Masters, D.C. *The Reciprocity Treaty of 1854: Its History, Its Relation to British Colonial and Foreign Policy and to the Development of Canadian Fiscal Autonomy*, Toronto, McClelland & Stewart, 1963

Mayrand, Albert. *Les successions ab Intestat*, Montreal, Presses de l'université de Montréal, 1971

Middleton, Christopher. "The Sexual Division of Labour in Feudal England", 113–114 *New Left Review* (1979), pp. 147–168

Mignault, P.B. *Le droit civil canadien*, Montreal, Whiteford & Théoret, 1895-1916

——. "Le code civil de la province de Québec et son interpretation", 1 *University of Toronto Law Journal* (1935), pp. 1–136

Minguijón, Salvador. *Historia del derecho español*, Barcelona, Editorial Labor, 1927

Moore, J.P. *Revolt in Louisiana: The Spanish Occupation, 1766–1770*, Baton Rouge, Louisiana State University Press, 1976

Morandière, L.J. de la. "Preliminary Report of the Civil Code Reform Commission of France", 16 *La. L. Rev.* (1955), pp. 1–56

Morel, André. "La réaction des Canadiens devant l'administration de la justice de 1764 à 1774", 20 *R.duB.* (1960), pp. 53–63

——. "L'apparition de la succession testamentaire", 26 *R.duB.* (1966), pp. 499–511

Morison, W.L. "Some Myths about Positivism", 68 *Yale Law Journal* (1958), pp. 212–233

Morrow, C.J. "An Approach to the Revision of the Louisiana Civil Code", 10 *La. L. Rev.* (1949), pp. 59–72

Munro, W.B. *The Seigniorial System in Canada: A Study of French Colonial Policy*, New York, Longmans, Green & Co., 1907

——. "The Custom of Paris in the New World", in F. Berolzheimer (ed.), *Rechtswissenschaftliche Beiträge: Juristische Festgabe des Auslandes zu Josef Kohlers 60. Geburstag 9. März 1909*, Stuttgart, F. Enke, 1909, pp. 132–148

Nathan, Max. "In Search of a Missing Link: Edward Livingston and the proposed Code of Commerce for Louisiana", 48 *Tul. L. Rev.* (1973), pp. 43–54

Neatby, H.M. *Quebec, Quebec: The Revolutionary Age, 1760–1791*, Toronto, McClelland & Stewart, 1968

——. *The Administration of Justice under the Quebec Act*, London, H. Milford, Oxford University Press, 1937

Newton, L.W. "Creoles and Anglo-Americans in Old Louisiana: A Study in Cultural Conflicts", 14 *Southwestern Social Science Quarterly* (1933), pp. 31–48

Nicholls, G.V.V. *The Responsibility for Offences and Quasi-Offences under the Law of Quebec*, Toronto, Carswell Co., 1938

Olivier-Martin, François. "Des divisions du louage en droit romain", 15 (4th ser.) *R.H.D.F.E.* (1936), pp. 419–475

——. *Histoire du droit français des origines à la Révolution*, Paris, Domat Montchrestien, 1948

Ortolan, J.L.E. *Explication historique des instituts de l'empereur Justinien*, 4th ed., Paris, Joubert, 1847

Ouellet, François. "L'abolition du régime seigeurial et l'idée de propriété, 14 *Hermès* (1954), pp. 21–36

——. *Histoire économique et sociale du Québec, 1760–1850*, Montreal, Fides, 1966

——. *Elements d'histoire sociale du Bas-Canada*, Montreal, Hurtubise HMH, 1972

Parizeau, Gérard. *La société canadienne française au XIXe siècle: essais sur le milieu*, Montreal, Fides, 1975

Pascal, Robert. "A Recent Discovery: A Copy of the 'Digest of the Civil Laws' of 1808 with Marginal Source References in Moreau Lislet's Hand", 26 *La. L. Rev.* (1965), pp. 25–27

——. "Book Note", 30 *La. L. Rev.* (1970), pp. 746–747

——. "Book Note", 32 *La. L. Rev.* (1972), pp. 495–496

——. "Sources of the Digest of 1808: A Reply to Professor Batiza", 46 *Tul. L. Rev.* (1972), pp. 603–627

——. "The Work of the Louisiana Appellate Courts for the 1974–75 Term: Matrimonial Regimes", 36 *La. L. Rev.* (1976), pp. 409–416

Paton, G.W. *A Textbook of Jurisprudence*, 4th ed., Oxford, Clarendon Press, 1972

Patterson, Orlando. "On Slavery and Slave Formations", 117 *New Left Review* (1979), pp. 31–67

Perrault, Antonio. "Le conseil spécial, 1838–1841" 3 *R.duB.* (1943), pp. 139–144, 213–230, 265–274, and 299–307

Pierson, G.W. *Tocqueville and Beaumont in America*, New York, Oxford University Press, 1938

Pineau, Jean. *Mariage, séparation, divorce: l'état du droit au Québec*, Montreal, presses de l'université de Montréal, 1978

Planiol, M.F. *Treatise on the Civil Law*, trans. by Louisiana State Law Institute, St. Paul, MN, West Pub. Co., 1959

Poster, Mark. *Existential Marxism in Postwar France: From Sartre to Althusser*, Princeton, Princeton University Press, 1975

——. *Critical Theory of the Family*, London, Pluto Press, 1978

Pound, Roscoe. *Interpretations of Legal History*, Cambridge, Cambridge University Press, 1923

——. "The French Civil Code and the Spirit of Nineteenth Century Law", 35 *Boston University Law Review* (1955), pp. 77–95

——. "Codification in Anglo-American Law", in Bernard Schwartz (ed.), *The Code Napoleon and the Common-Law World*, New York, New York University Press, 1956, pp. 267–297

Pred, Allan. "Manufacturing in the American Mercantile City, 1800–1840", in K.J. Jackson and S.K. Schultz (eds.), *Cities in American History*, New York, Knopf, 1972, pp. 111–142

Progress of Continental Law in the Nineteenth Century, Continental Legal History Series, vol. 11, London, John Murray, 1918

Pugh, N.N. "The Spanish Community of Gains in 1803: *Sociedad de Ganaciales*", 30 *La. L. Rev.* (1969), pp. 1–43

Renaud, Louise. "La Cour d'appel à l'aube de l'Union (1839–1849)", 8 (new ser.) *La revue juridique Thémis* (1973), pp. 465–499

Renner, Karl. *Institutions of Private Law and their Social Functions*, ed. by Otto Kahn-Freund, trans. by Agnes Schwarzschild, London, Routledge & Kegan Paul, 1949

Reulos, Michel. *Étude sur l'esprit, les sources et la méthode des Institutes coutumières d'Antoine Loisel*, Paris, Sirey, 1935

Richert J.P. and E.S. Richert, "The Impact of the Civil Code of Quebec of 1866", 8 (new ser.) *La revue juridique Thémis* (1973), pp. 501–520

Rivero, Jean and Jean Savatier, *Droit du travail*, 4th ed., Paris, Presses universitaires, 1966

Roberts, A.A. *A Guide to Voet: Including the Life of Johannes Voet*, Pretoria, The Author, 1933

Ruben, Eira. "John Austin's Political Pamphlets, 1824–1859", in Elspeth Attwool (ed.), *Perspectives in Jurisprudence*, Glasgow, University of Glasgow Press, 1977, pp. 20–41

Ryerson, S.B. *Unequal Union: Roots of the Crisis in the Canadas, 1815–1873*, 2nd ed., Toronto, Progress Books, 1973

Sacco, Rodolfo. "Definitions savantes et droit appliqué dans les systèmes Romanistes", 17 *R.I.D.C.* (1965), pp. 827–837

Sachse, H.R. "Report to the Louisiana Law Institute on Article Nine of the Uniform Commercial Code", 41 *Tul. L. Rev.* (1967), pp. 505–554

Saint-Laurent, Louis. "Majeurs et mineurs: quelques particularités du droit de Québec à cet égard", in *Le droit civil français: livre-souvenir des journées du droit civil (Montréal, 31 août-2 Septembre 1934)*, Paris, Sirey, 1936, pp. 155-162

Sanz, Sylviane. "La consécration du pouvoir judiciaire par la loi du 9 Juillet 1975, et ses incidences sur la théorie générale de la clause pénale", 75 *Revue trimestrielle du droit civil* (1977), pp. 268–288

Schulz, Fritz. *Classical Roman Law*, Oxford, Clarendon Press, 1951

Schuyler, R.L. *The Fall of the Old Colonial System: A Study in British Free Trade, 1770–1870*, London, Oxford University Press, 1945

Séguin, Maurice. "Le régime seigneurial au pays de Québec, 1760–1844", 1 *R.H.A.F.* (1947–1948), pp. 382–402 and 519–532

Sherman, C.P. "Roman Law in the Quebec Civil Code", 25 *Boston University Law Review* (1945), pp. 196–228

Shorter, Edwin. *The Making of the Modern Family*, London, Collins, 1976

Sinclair, André. "L'avocat au Québec: 209 ans d'histoire", 16 *Les Cahiers du Droit* (1975), pp. 689–702

Smith, T.B. *A Short Commentary on the Law of Scotland*, Edinburgh, W. Green, 1962

Smith, William. "The Struggle over the Laws of Canada, 1763–1783", 1 *Can. Hist. Rev.* (1920), pp. 166–186

Sohn-Rethel, Alfred. *Intellectual and Manual Labour: A Critique of Epistemology*, London, Macmillan, 1978

Stanley, F.G. *New France, The Last Phase, 1744–1760*, Toronto, McClelland & Stewart, 1968

Stannard, D.E. *The Puritan Way of Death. A Study in Religion, Culture and Social Change*, New York, Oxford University Press, 1979

Steffens, C.G. "Changes in the Organisation of Artisan Production in Baltimore, 1790–1820" 36 (3rd ser.) *The William and Mary Quarterly* (1979), pp. 101–117

Stein, Peter. "Adam Smith's Jurisprudence-Between Morality and Economics", 64 *Cornell Law Review* (1979), pp. 621–638

——. *Legal Evolution: The Story of an Idea*, Cambridge, Cambridge University Press, 1980

Stone, F.F. "A Primer on Codification", 29 *Tul. L. Rev.* (1955), pp. 303–310

——. "The Civil Code of 1808 for the Territory of Orleans", 33 *Tul. L. Rev.* (1958), pp. 1–6

——. "The So-Called Unprovided-For Case", 53 *Tul. L. Rev.* (1978), pp. 93–104

Stone, Lawrence. *The Family, Sex and Marriage in England, 1500 – 1800*, London, Wiedenfeld & Nicholson, 1977

Strakosch, H.E. *State Absolutism and the Rule of Law: The Struggle for Codification of Civil Law in Austria, 1753–1811*, Sydney, Sydney University Press, 1967

Sugiyama, Naojira. "Les transformations du droit civil japonais et l'influence du droit civil français", in *Le droit civil français: livre-souvenir des journées du droit civil (Montréal, 31 août-2 Septembre 1934)*, Paris, Sirey, 1936, pp. 673–689

Sumner, Colin. *Reading Ideologies: An Investigation into the Marxist Theory of Ideology and Law*, London, Academic Press, 1979

Surveyer, E.F. "La province de Québec et le Code civil français", 12 (new ser.) *La Revue légale* (1906), pp. 12–17

Sweeney, J.M. "Tournament of Scholars over the Sources of the Civil Code of 1808", 46 *Tul. L. Rev.* (1972), pp. 585–602

Taschereau, Robert. "La codification de nos los civiles", in *Le droit civil français: livre-souvenir des journées du droit civil (Montréal, 31 août-2 Septembre 1934)*, Paris, Sirey, 1936, pp. 657–671

——. "Le siècle de la Renaissance et son influence sur le droit civil du Québec", 12 (old ser.) *La revue juridique Thémis* (1962), pp. 7–17

Tate, Albert. "The Splendid Mystery of the Civil Code of Louisiana", 25 *Louisiana Bar Journal* (1977), pp. 29–39

Taylor, J.G. "The Foreign Slave Trade in Louisiana after 1808", 1 *Louisiana History* (1960), pp. 36– 43

Thomas, J.A.C. "Locatio and Operae", 3 (3rd ser.) *Bullettino dell'Istituto di Diritto Romano "Vittoria Scialoja"*, (1961), pp. 231–247

——. "The Case of the Apprentice's Eye", 8 *Revue internationale des droits de l'antiquité* (1961), pp. 357–372

Tonasce, T.R. "Les liberalités en France et en Roumanie", in *Le droit civil français: livre-souvenir des journées du droit civil (Montréal, 31 août-2 Septembre 1934)*, Paris, Sirey, 1936, pp. 911–940

Tregle, J.G. "Early New Orleans Society: A Re-Appraisal", 18 *Journal of Southern History* (1952), pp. 20–36

Tremblay, Robert. "La formation matérielle de la classe ouvrière à Montréal entre 1790 et 1830", 33 *R.H.A.F.* (1979), pp. 39–50

Trudel, Gérard et al. *Traité de droit civil du Québec*, Montreal, Wilson & Lafleur, [1942]–1958

Trudel, Marcel. *The Beginnings of New France, 1524–1663*, trans. by P. Claxton, Toronto, McClelland & Stewart, 1973

——. *La population du Canada en 1663*, Montreal, Fides, 1973

Tucker, J.H. "Source Books of Louisiana Law", in *La. Leg. Arch.*, vol. 1, pp. xvii–lxxxiv

Tucker, G.N. *The Canadian Commercial Revolution, 1845–1851*, ed. by H.C.J. Aitken, Toronto, McClelland & Stewart, 1964

Tucker, T.W. "Sources of Louisiana's Law of Persons: Blackstone, Domat, and the French Codes", 44 *Tul. L. Rev.* (1970), pp. 264–295

——. "Interpretation of the Louisiana Civil Codes, 1808–1840: The Failure of the Preliminary Title", unpublished LL.M. thesis, University of Glasgow, 1972

Ullmann, Walter. "The Prohibition of Roman Law in Paris", 60 *Juridical Review* (1948), pp. 177–186

——. *Law and Politics in the Middle Ages: An Introduction to the Sources of Medieval Political Ideas*, London, Sources of History Ltd., 1975

Van Alstyne, R.N. "The Significance of the Mississippi Valley in American Diplomatic History, 1686–1801", 36 *Miss. Vall. Hist. Rev.* (1949), pp. 215–238

Vance, J.T. *The Background of Hispanic-American Law*, New York, Central Book Co., 1943

Vanderlinden, Jacques. "Code et codification dans la pensée de Jeremy Bentham", 32 *Tijdschrift voor Rechtsgeschiedenis* (1964), pp. 45–78

——. *Le concept de code en Europe occidentale du XIIe au XIXe siècle: essai de définition*, Brussels, Éditions de l'Institut de sociologie de l'Université libre de Bruxelles, 1967

Van Kleffens, E.N. *Hispanic Law Until the End of the Middle Ages*, Edinburgh, Edinburgh University Press, 1968

Van Wetter, Paul. "Le droit romain et Beaumanoir", Edmond Meynial (ed.), *Mélanges Fitting*, Montpellier, Imprimerie générale du Midi, 1907-1908, repr., Aalen, Scientia, 1969, vol. 2, pp. 533–582

Verdon, Michel. "The Stem Family: Towards a General Theory" 10 *Journal of Interdisciplinary History* (1979), pp. 87–105

Vinogradoff, Paul. *Roman Law in Medieval Europe*, 2nd ed., Oxford, Clarendon Press, 1929

Wade, Mason. *The French Canadians*, rev. ed., Toronto, Macmillan, 1968

Wallas, Graham. "Notes on Jeremy Bentham's attitude to word Creation", in Logan Pearsall Smith et al., *Needed Words etc.*, Society for Pure English, Tract no. XXXI, Oxford, Clarendon Press, 1928

Walton, F.P. *The Scope and Interpretation of the Civil Code of Lower Canada*, Montreal, Wilson & Lafleur, 1907

——. "The Historical School of Jurisprudence & Transplantation of Law", 7 (3rd ser.) *Journal of Comparative Legislation* (1927), pp. 183–192

Watson, Alan. *The Law of Obligations in the Later Roman Republic*, Oxford, Clarendon Press, 1965

——. *Legal Transplants: An Approach to Comparative Law*, Edinburgh, Scottish Academic Press, 1974

——. *The Nature of Law*, Edinburgh, Edinburgh University Press, 1977

——. *Society & Legal Change*, Edinburgh, Scottish Academic Press, 1977

——. "Comparative Law & Legal Change", 37 *Cambridge Law Journal* (1978), pp. 313–336

Whitaker, A.B. *The Mississippi Question, 1795–1803: A Study in Trade, Politics & Diplomacy*, American Historical Association, New York, D. Appleton-Century Co., 1934

White, A.R. "Austin as a Philosophical Analyst", 64 *Archiv für Rechts-und Sozialphilosophie* (1978), pp. 379–399

Winch, Donald. *Adam Smith's Politics. An Essay in Historiographic Revision*, Cambridge, Cambridge Univeristy Press, 1978

Winston, J.E. "The Free Negro in New Orleans, 1803–1860", 21 *La. Hist. Quar.* (1938), pp. 1075–1085

Yver, Jean. "Les caractères originaux du groupe de coutumes de l'ouest de la France", 29 *R.H.D.F.E.* (1952), pp. 18–79

——. *Égalité entre héritiers et exclusion des enfants dotés*, Paris, Sirey, 1966

Zajtay, Imre. "La permanence des concepts du droit romain dans les systèmes juridiques continentaux", 18 *R.I.D.C.* (1966), pp. 353–363

Zoltvany, Y.F. "Esquisse de la Coutume de Paris", 25 *R.H.A.F.* (1971), pp. 365–384

Index

www.ingramcontent.com/pod-product-compliance
Lightning Source LLC
LaVergne TN
LVHW080645210926
848485LV00003B/328